CRISES OF EMPIRE

DECOLONIZATION AND EUROPE'S IMPERIAL STATES

Second Edition

Martin Thomas, Bob Moore, and L. J. Butler

Bloomsbury Academic
An imprint of Bloomsbury Publishing Plc

B L O O M S B U R Y
LONDON · NEW DELHI · NEW YORK · SYDNEY

Bloomsbury Academic

An imprint of Bloomsbury Publishing Plc

50 Bedford Square	1385 Broadway
London	New York
WC1B 3DP	NY 10018
UK	USA

www.bloomsbury.com

BLOOMSBURY and the Diana logo are trademarks of Bloomsbury Publishing Plc

First published 2015

© Martin Thomas, Bob Moore and L. J. Butler, 2015

Martin Thomas, Bob Moore and L. J. Butler have asserted their right under the Copyright, Designs and Patents Act, 1988, to be identified as Authors of this work.

British Library Cataloguing-in-Publication Data
A catalogue record for this book is available from the British Library.

ISBN: HB: 978-1-4725-2642-7
PB: 978-1-4725-3025-7
ePDF: 978-1-4725-3018-9
ePub: 978-1-4725-3121-6

Library of Congress Cataloging-in-Publication Data
A catalog record for this book is available from the Library of Congress.

Typeset by Deanta Global Publishing Services, Chennai, India
Printed and bound in Great Britain

CONTENTS

Preface   vii
List of Maps   viii
List of Abbreviations   ix

Introduction: Constructions of Decolonization   1

Part I British Decolonization _Larry Butler_   **13**

    Introduction to Part I: The British Empire   15
1 The British Empire, 1918–45: Interwar Change and Wartime Pressures   19
2 The First Wave of British Decolonization: Commonwealth Territories,
    the Indian Subcontinent, and the Gold Coast, 1945–51   43
3 British Decolonization, Insurgency, and Strategic Reverse: The Middle
    East, Africa, and Malaya, 1951–7   64
4 Winds of Change: The Final Waves of Decolonization in Africa
    and Asia after 1957   84

Part II French Decolonization _Martin Thomas_   **111**

    Introduction to Part II: The French Empire   113
5 The Roots of French Decolonization: Ideas, Economics,
    and Reform, 1900–46   117
6 Decolonizing the French African Federations after 1945   136
7 People's War and the Collapse of French Indochina, 1945–54   158
8 From French North Africa to Maghreb Independence: Decolonization
    in Morocco, Tunisia, and Algeria, 1945–56   178
9 Algeria's Violent Struggle for Independence   193
10 Territories Apart: Madagascar, the Togo Trusteeship, and French
    Island Territories   210

Part III Dutch Decolonization _Bob Moore_   **223**

    Introduction to Part III: The Dutch Empire   225
11 An 'Ethical Imperialism'? The Dutch Colonial Empire before 1945   229
12 Indonesia: The Politics of Delusion, 1940–7   244
13 Indonesia: Conflict and Diplomacy   262
14 Unfinished Business: New Guinea as a Last Outpost of Empire   279
15 Decolonization by Default: Dutch Disengagement in Suriname   293

Contents

Part IV Contrasting Patterns of Decolonization *Martin Thomas*   **305**

    Introduction to Part IV: The Belgian and Portuguese Empires   307

16   Contrasting Patterns of Decolonization: Belgian and Portuguese Africa   309

Conclusion: Changing Attitudes to the End of Empire   333

Notes   347

Select Bibliography   429

Index   443

PREFACE

The second edition of this book, like the first, stems from a desire to match the voluminous literature on the decolonization of the British Empire with a comparative volume, which synthesizes the parallel experiences of the continental European imperial states. Alongside the British experience, we have focused primarily on the two largest European empires; namely those of France and the Netherlands. To that end, we have endeavoured to provide detailed case studies of British, French, and Dutch decolonization. We also investigate the collapse of Portuguese and Belgian colonial rule in Africa, drawing out the parallels between their paths to decolonization and those of their European neighbours. While the book's case studies are intended to guide the reader through the major events leading to colonial withdrawal, they are also designed to elucidate deeper, conceptual issues surrounding the end of European empires.

No book of this nature could be written without the help of numerous individuals and institutions. In this connection, we would like to thank Robert Aldrich, Alice Conklin, Daho Djerbal, Ruth Ginio, Chris Goscha, Bill Hoisington, Talbot Imlay, Peter Jackson, Simon Kitson, Sebastien Laurent, Mark Lawrence, Jim Le Sueur, Fred Logevall, Patricia Lorcin, Bart Luttikhuis, Martin Shipway, Sylvie Thénault, the late Dick van Galen Last, Mathilde von Bülow, Nicholas White, colleagues at the Universities of Exeter, Sheffield, and East Anglia, the Leverhulme Trust, the British Academy, the Arts and Humanities Research Council, the Nuffield Foundation, the National Archives, Kew, the School of Oriental and African Studies, University of London, the Centre des Archives d'Outre-Mer, Aix-en-Provence, the Service Historique des Armées at Vincennes, the Nederlands Instituut voor Oorlogsdocumentatie, Amsterdam, the University of Sydney, and the National Europe Centre, ANU, Canberra. We are very grateful to Claire Lipscomb, Emma Goode and Anita Singh at Bloomsbury for their help in producing the second edition.

Our final word of thanks goes to our friend and colleague, Kent Fedorowich, whose ideas and critiques were central to the writing of this book.

Martin Thomas, Exeter
Bob Moore, Sheffield
Larry Butler, Norwich

LIST OF MAPS

Map 1 Indian partition, 1947 48
Map 2 Britain's interests in Africa and the Middle East 105
Map 3 French West Africa after the First World War 139
Map 4 French Equatorial Africa and Madagascar after the First World War 141
Map 5 French Indochina Federation 162
Map 6 The Indochina War, 1946–54 172
Map 7 French North African territories 184
Map 8 The colony of Algeria with department boundaries 202
Map 9 Dutch Indonesia 260
Map 10 Netherlands West Indies 302
Map 11 The Belgian Congo, 1960 315
Map 12 Portuguese Africa 326

LIST OF ABBREVIATIONS

Territories, parties, and organizations

ABAKO   *Assocation des Bakongo*: Bakongo [Cultural] Association.

AEF   *Afrique Equatoriale Française*: the federation of French Equatorial Africa, comprised of French Congo, Oubangui-Chari, Gabon and Chad. The former mandate of French Cameroon, declared a UN trust territory in 1945, retained close economic links with AEF.

AFPFL   Anti-Fascist People's Freedom League (Burma).

ALN   *Armée de Libération Nationale*: armed wing of the Algerian FLN.

ANZUS   Australia-New Zealand-US defence treaty, 1951.

AOF   *Afrique Occidentale Française*: the federation of French West Africa, comprised of Senegal, Mauritania, French Soudan, Niger, Ivory Coast (Côte d'Ivoire), Guinea, Dahomey and, from 1948, Upper Volta (Haute Volta). Federal authorities in Dakar also retained links with Togo, another former mandate made a UN trust territory in 1945.

ARP   *Anti-Revolutionaire Partij*: Anti-Revolutionary Party, Netherlands.

CEFA   *Comités d'Études Franco-Africaines*: Franco-African study groups.

CFOA   *Compagnie Française d'Afrique Occidentale*: major West African trading company, founded in 1906.

CFTC   *Confédération Française des Travailleurs Chrétiens*: French Catholic trade union confederation.

CGO   Committee of Good Offices, Indonesia.

CGT   *Confédération Générale du Travail*: French trade union confederation.

CGTT   *Confédération Générale du Travailleurs Tunisiens*: Tunisian trade union confederation

CHU   *Christelijk Historische Unie*: Christian Historical Union, Netherlands.

CMAG   Chinese Military Advisory Group (in Vietnam after 1950).

COMININDO   Interministerial committee on Indochina.

CPP   Convention People's Party: founded in the Gold Coast, 1949.

DOMs   *Départements d'outre-mer*: French overseas departments, post-1946.

DRV   Democratic Republic of Vietnam: established in Hanoi in 1945.

ECA   European Cooperation Administration.

EFO   *Établissements Français d'Océanie*: French Oceania

EFTA   European Free Trade Area.

ENA   *Etoile Nord-Africaine*: The North African Star: first Algerian nationalist party led by Messali Hadj, founded in 1926.

EOKA   *Ethniki Organosis Kyprion Agoniston*: National Organization of Cypriot Fighters.

FIDES	*Fonds d'Investissement pour le Développement Economique et Social*: Economic and Social Development Fund: set up in 1946.
FIDESTOM	*Fonds d'Investissement pour de Développement Économique et Social des Territoires d'Outre-Mer*: Overseas Territories' Economic and Social Development Fund, created in 1947.
FLN	*Front de Libération Nationale*: Algerian National Liberation Front founded in 1954.
FNLA	*Frente Nacional de Libertaåo de Angola*: Angolan National Liberation Front.
FRELIMO	*Frente de Libertação de Moçambique*: Mozambique Liberation Front.
GONG	*Groupe d'Organisation Nationale de la Guadeloupe*: Guadeloupe National Organisation Group.
HBMs	*Habitations à bon marché*, cheap multi-storey worker-housing blocks
ICP	Indochinese Communist Party: formed in 1930.
INA	Indian National Army
IOM	*Indépendants d'Outre-Mer*: West African parliamentary bloc created in 1948.
KADU	Kenya African Democratic Union.
KANU	Kenya African National Union.
KTPI	*Kaum Tani Persatuan Indonesia*: Indonesian Farmer's Party (Suriname).
KVP	*Katholieke Volkspartij*: Catholic People's Party, Netherlands.
MDP	Masai Development Plan, 1951.
MDRM	*Mouvement démocratique de la rénovation malgache*: Madagascar nationalist party, founded in 1946.
MFA	*Movimento das Forças Armadas*: [Portuguese] Armed Forces Movement.
MNA	*Mouvement National Algérien*: rival to the FLN, led by Messali Hadj.
MNC	*Mouvement National Congolais*: Congolese National Movement.
MPLA	*Movemento Popular de Libertação de Angola*: Popular Movement for Angolan Independence.
MRP	*Mouvement Républicain Populaire*: Christian Democrat Party, founded in 1944.
MTLD	*Mouvement pour la Triomphe des Libertés démocratiques*: Algerian nationalist forerunner to the FLN.
NATO	North Atlantic Treaty Organization: set up in April 1949.
NBS	*Nationalistische Beweging Suriname*: founded in Suriname, 1959.
NICA	Netherlands Indies Civil Administration.
NKG	New Kenya Group.
NLM	National Liberation Movement (Gold Coast/Ghana).
NPS	*Nationale Partij Suriname*: Suriname National Party.
OAS	*Organisation de l'Armée Secrète*: reactionary counterterror group.
OS	*Organisation Spéciale*: pre-FLN paramilitary group linked to the MTLD.
PADESM	*Parti des déshérités de Madagascar*: Party of the Disinherited of Madagascar.'
PAIGC	*Partido Africano para a Independência da Guiné e Cabo Verde*: African Party for the Independence of [Portuguese] Guinea and Cape Verde.
PA.NA.MA	*Parti nationaliste malgache*: nationalist party strongest in southern Madagascar.

PCF	*Parti Communiste Français*: French Communist Party, established in 1920.
PDCI	*Parti Démocratique de la Côte d'Ivoire*: established in 1946.
PDI	*Parti Démocratique de l'Indépendance*: Moroccan party rival to the Istiqlal.
PETA	*Pembela Tanah Air*: Volunteer Army of Defenders of the [Indonesian] Homeland.
PNP	*Progressieve Nationale Partij*: Progressive National Party, Suriname.
PNR	*Partij van de Nationalistische Republiek*: Party for a National Republic (Suriname).
PPA	*Parti Populaire Algérien*: Algerian Popular Party: Messalist Algerian nationalist party, founded in 1937.
PPM	*Parti Progressiste Martiniquais*: Martiniquan Progressive Party.
PRA	Parti du Regroupement Africain: pro-federalist West African political party.
PSD	*Parti social démocrate*: [Malagasy] Social Democratic Party.
PSV	*Progressieve Surinaamse Volkspartij*: Progressive People's Party (Suriname).
PUTERA	*Pusat Tenaga Rakjat*: Centre of People's Power, Indonesia.
PvdA	*Partij van de Arbeid*: Netherlands Labour Party.
RAPWI	Recovery of Allied Prisoners of War and Internees.
RDA	*Rassemblement Démocratique Africain*: established in 1946.
RDPT	*Rassemblement Démocratique des Peuples Tahitiens*: Tahitian Peoples' Democratic Union.
RENAMO	*Resistência Nacional Moçambicana*: Mozambiquan National Resistance.
RF	Rhodesian Front.
RPF	*Rassemblement du Peuple Français*: Gaullist movement, launched in 1947.
RUSI	Republic of the United States of Indonesia.
SAA	*Syndicat Agricole Africain*: West African planters' association.
SAS	*Sections Administratives Spécialisées*: army civil affairs specialists in Algeria.
SAWO	*Surinaamsche Arbeiders en Werknemers Organisatie* Suriname trade union formed in 1932.
SCOA	*Société Commerciale de l'Ouest Africain*: West African trading company, founded in 1887.
SEAC	South East Asia Command.
SEATO	South East Asia Treaty Organisation: established 1955.
SFIO	*Section Française de l'Internationale Ouvrière*: unified French Socialist Party, founded in 1905.
TANU	Tanganyika African National Union.
TKR	*Tentara Keamanan Rakjat*: [Indonesian] People's Security Army.
TOMs	*Territoires d'outre-mer*: French overseas territories, post-1946.
UC	*Union Calédonienne*: [New] Caledonian Union.
UDI	Unilateral Declaration of Independence (by Southern Rhodesia).
UDMA	*Union démocratique de Manifeste algérien*: Algerian proto-nationalist group led by Ferhat Abbas.
UGSCM	*Union Générale des Syndicats Confédérés du Maroc*: legalized Moroccan trade union.
UGTAN	*Union générale des travailleurs d'Afrique noire*: African trade union confederation.

UDSR	*Union Démocratique et Sociale de la Résistance*: French centre-left party.
UGCC	United Gold Coast Convention: founded in 1947.
UMNO	United Malays National Organization.
UNCI	United Nations Commission for Indonesia.
UNIP	United National Independence Party (Northern Rhodesia).
UNITA	*União Nacional para a Independência Total de Angola*: National Union for the Total Independence of Angola.
UNSCOP	UN Special Committee on Palestine.
UPC	*Union des Populations du Cameroun*: Cameroon party linked to the RDA.
UPLG	*Union Populaire pour la Guadeloupe*: Guadeloupe Popular Union.
VHP	*Verenigde Hindostaanse Partij*: United Hindu Party (Suriname).
VNQDD	*Viet Nam Quoc Dan Dong*: Vietnam National Party, founded in 1927.
VOC	*Verenigde Oostindische Compagnie*: United Dutch East India Company.
VVD	*Volkspartij voor Vrijheid en Democratie*: Netherlands.
VWP	*Dang Lao Dong Viet Nam*: Vietnamese Workers' Party, designation for the Vietnamese Communists from 1951.
WIC	*Westindische Compagnie*: United Dutch West Indies Company.
ZANU	Zimbabwe African National Union.
ZAPU	Zimbabwe African People's Union

Archives

AN	Archives Nationales, Paris
ARA	Algemeen Rijksarchief, The Hague
CADN	Centre des Archives Diplomatiques, Nantes
CAOM	Centre des Archives d'Outre-Mer Aix-en-Provence
MAE	Ministère des Affaires Etrangères, Paris
SHA	Service Historique de l'Armée, Vincennes
TNA	The National Archives, UK
USNA	United States National Archives, College Park

Journals

JAH	*Journal of African History*
JICH	*Journal of Imperial and Commonwealth History*
MAS	*Modern Asian Studies*

INTRODUCTION
CONSTRUCTIONS OF DECOLONIZATION

This book has been written to help students understand the major conceptual arguments about the origins, the nature, and the supposed finality of decolonization for the European colonial powers. We have revised and updated the second edition to take account of the wealth of excellent work on the collapse of European colonialism published since 2008. This edition also includes an extended introduction, additional commentary in the chapters, and summaries that introduce each of the book's main sections.

Our aim is to offer suggestions about how we might interpret decolonization, whether as process or event. This, in turn, leads us to challenge the validity of such commonly used terms as 'transfer of power' and 'end of empire', among others. Most treatments of decolonization in the English language concentrate primarily on the British Empire, the largest of the colonial empires. We have sought to redress this imbalance. In addition to the British Empire, the authors consider the French and Dutch examples, while drawing some comparisons with the Belgian and Portuguese experiences. We do not study other large and contiguous empires that formed a single, linked territorial agglomeration, such as the Ottoman, Austro-Hungarian, or Tsarist/Soviet cases. This is partly because the clashes between them in the early twentieth century ensured their demise, and partly because their decolonization either destroyed them as political entities or reconfigured their geography as single empire-states.[1] We do, though, acknowledge the influence both of these regions and of these differing imperial experiences on the overseas colonial empires on which we focus.

What, then, do we mean by colonial empire? Political scientist Ronald Suny provides useful guidance. He defines empire in terms of an unequal, hierarchical relationship created between a 'metropole' (imperial historians' shorthand for a 'mother country' or dominant state) and a 'periphery' (in other words, dependent territory, or colonies, beyond that metropole). In putting the needs of the metropole above those of the periphery, the relationship thus established may be termed 'colonial' insofar as the extraction of resources, the determination of ethnic identity and cultural attributes, and the concentration of political power serve the metropolitan interest above all. Empire, then, necessarily implies inequality because it involves the subordination of certain societies or groups to the advantage of others. Particular cultural constructions of difference relating to ethnicity, gender, intellect, and organizational capacity typically provide the ideological rationale for imperial control. The need for stronger discursive justifications for the rule of one community by another was amplified during the late nineteenth and twentieth centuries by two external, transnational pressures. One was ethnocentric nationalism, an organizing principle whose global influence did not stop at the colonial frontier. The other was the democratization that accompanied industrial modernization, a force whose attractiveness proved equally compelling. Colonial empires, which ultimately precluded the realization of either outcome – national sovereignty or participatory democracy – were thereby confronted with unprecedented risks of delegitimization or overthrow.[2] Michael Reynolds gets to the essence of the dilemma: 'The normative contradiction between the national idea and their own colonial empires was too obvious to suppress indefinitely. … Doubts about the legitimacy of empire gnawed at imperial administrators and fuelled fears, often imaginary, of uprisings by imperial subjects.'[3] Decolonization, in other words, became an imminent threat, not a distant spectre.

Two further points bear emphasis. One is that the underlying inequality between metropole and colony does not mean that the two elements should be treated separately. The interplay between the mother country and its dependencies and, in particular, the movement of people, ideas, and cultural practices between them was profound indeed. These connections, which were built up over decades, sometimes over centuries, refashioned the 'imperial nations' as surely as they did the societies over which these imperial states claimed dominion.[4] Empire, then, was globally transformative.[5] The second point is that the domination integral to colonialism should not blind us to the fact that empire remained popular, not just in metropolitan societies, but also among discrete communities, groups, and individuals within dependent territories as well. Imperialism cannot, in other words, be reduced to exploitation and unremitting, binary opposition between colonizers and colonized. Colonial rule, did not always close down the political and cultural space of those living under it. As we shall see, it was more complex and, for many, more benevolent than this implies.

Returning to the structure of the book, our approach is broadly chronological. We examine the British, French, and the Dutch cases in turn, focusing first on long-term developments in imperial governance before investigating individual instances of colonial disengagement from the late 1940s onwards. The British section concentrates on Africa, India, South East Asia, and the Middle East. The French section discusses Indochina, Algeria, francophone sub-Saharan Africa, and French island territories, while the Dutch section investigates Indonesia, New Guinea, and Suriname. A further chapter considers Belgian and Portuguese decolonization from Africa, bringing matters into the mid-1970s and beyond.

What is decolonization?

As historians, to identify the phenomenon of decolonization we need to locate it in a temporal setting. When does decolonization begin, and when does it end? On the eve of Algeria's independence from French colonial rule in July 1962, the American State Department's Bureau of Intelligence and Research was in no doubt. All that was left worldwide were 'remnants of the colonial system'.[6] Even if this analysis held some geographical validity – the main European colonial federations and most populous dependent territories were no more – colonial rule persisted in three continents. A deeper question is whether we should consider the withdrawal of the colonial rulers and decolonization as exactly contiguous anyway? Apparently a neutral term, decolonization takes on a loaded political meaning as soon as one tries to define it using shorthand terms: the process of colonial collapse, the progress of imperial withdrawal, the end of empire, and so on. Each of these labels is informed by a number of underlying assumptions: that the end of European colonial empires amounted to a clear process of socio-economic change; or that imperial powers recognized the need to end their colonial control and deliberately set about withdrawal; or, more fundamentally, that colonialism and formal empire ('formal' meaning sovereign power directly exercised by a foreign state over another society) can be chronologically compartmentalized.

Some of these approaches deny any agency to local actors, writing colonial populations out of the script of their own transitions to national independence. Some make the clamour for decolonization an arid exercise in constitutional history – a story of electoral reforms granted, government changes enacted, treaties signed; in short, nothing more than what some scholars dismiss as 'flag independence'. Some create a false dichotomy between formal imperial rule and the more informal but no less iniquitous ties of neocolonial control through which the industrialized world still determines the terms of trade, economic organization, currency values, and regional security in the supposedly postcolonial international system.[7] And some imply that the consolidation and growth of colonial domination can be easily distinguished from the decline and disintegration of colonial empire, thus denying that the violence and racial exclusion inherent in colonialism was self-destructive from the start.[8] These interpretations are problematic when applied singly to individual colonies, let alone when set in the comparative perspective of European colonialism. Yet they still set the agenda for academic discussion and policymakers' reviews of how and why European decolonization occurred in the twentieth century. Moreover, an equally two-dimensional portrayal of unthinking colonial oppression has been central to national myth-making and identity formation in numerous postcolonial nation states.[9] The historian of empire must be wary of the fact that those with a political stake in decolonization tended to paint it in stark colours.

Perhaps the extreme incarnation of the metropolitan-focused, 'flag independence' view of decolonization has been the British contention, still not entirely eradicated, that independence for its colonies had always been Britain's goal: the post-1945 years of colonial rule, in effect, marked the final preparations for this outcome. Arguably, this suggestion was intended more to reassure domestic opinion at a time of rapid imperial contraction than to convince rightly sceptical colonial populations of British benevolence. It cannot be argued plausibly that the British political elite foresaw the two intense phases of British colonial withdrawal – those immediately after 1945 and again after 1957. If anything, the speed of the pull out mirrored British anxieties that any other course risked inviting catastrophic crises of local control.[10] Furthermore, as Britain's imperial historians have increasingly recognized, a satisfactory interpretation of decolonization must allow for the phenomenon of 'informal empire', where an external power exerted effective influence over a territory without imposing full political control or imperial sovereignty. Egypt, for example, offers a case where a nominally independent state remained under close foreign (British) management long after 'flag independence' had been achieved. Like many such states, it sits uncomfortably with the traditional British model of decolonization culminating in a clear-cut 'transfer of power'.[11]

Clearly, then, the term decolonization is problematic. It is, after all, a construction of historians and political scientists rather than a word in common usage among the policymakers, nationalists, and anti-colonial protesters who acted out the dramas that brought down the curtain on European empires. Translated from English, the Gallicized word *décolonisation* was not cited in French until 1952.[12] In August of that year, leading French economic historian Alfred Sauvy also coined the phrase *tiers monde* (third world), a deliberate evocation of the Third Estate of the French Revolution. As Odd Arne Westad points out, Sauvy's expectation that the new states of Africa, Asia, and Latin America would break the bipolar pattern of Cold War politics proved over-optimistic.[13] If anything, the reverse applied. Cold War rivalries in the new nation states born out of colonial collapse were often so intense that they sustained proxy wars, as in Vietnam, Angola, and Mozambique.[14] In these examples, violent imposition of a communist-style system in imitation of a Cold War patron caused long-term societal upheaval. Conversely, in other newly independent states, the attempt to 'westernize' societies still numerically dominated by peasant farmers and sharecroppers often favoured the political dominance of urban oligarchies. These new rulers, often having deep connections with the government and the armed forces, usually favoured modernization programmes which were, in practice, just as destructive as the leftist dictatorships they abhorred. In such cases, the construction of administrative structures, functioning legal and fiscal systems, police services, public utilities, and international commercial connections became bound up with the sectarian interests of a governing elite.[15]

The question we have to ask is obvious: was 'independence' real? The analytical problem the question raises is harder: how do we measure the reality or otherwise of decolonization? As historian Martin Shipway puts it, decolonization cannot be reduced to 'an incidental by-product of a "bigger" process of imperial decline and fall'.[16] For one thing, that is to misunderstand transformations in European colonial methods of rule that, broadly, occurred in the decades either side of the Second World War. Their objective was less to prepare for the end of empire than to make governance more effective through reconstruction and reform. The resultant shift towards distinct 'late colonial states' that were more bureaucratized, more inclusive, and more forward-thinking was, in many instances, a case of too little, too late. The point, though, is that those most intimately involved, whether as policymakers and officials or as their local opponents, saw neither decolonization nor 'imperial decline and fall' as inevitable but simply as highly likely in due course. Time and again, formal transfers of power were accompanied by international recognition, even material aid, to newly independent states that had yet to assemble the fundamental building blocks of state sovereignty and functioning administrative apparatus. The result was the proliferation throughout the developing world in the 1960s and 1970s of what the political scientist Robert H. Jackson terms 'quasi-states' – states that were legally recognized, but that barely functioned as ordered governments.[17] Westad reaches an equally stark conclusion:

> With decolonization, within two decades more than one hundred new states emerged, each with elites that had their own ideological agendas, often connected up to the ideals constituted by the superpowers. Instead of reducing tensions in society, decolonization – for the formerly colonized – often increased them, and gave rise to state administrations that were, for the peasants, *more* intrusive and *more* exploitative than the colonial authorities had been.[18]

Decolonization, then, was no panacea, nor did it signify the end of a historical process. 'Process' is far too orderly a word to reflect the violence that often accompanied the end of colonial rule and the precipitous removal of civil–military authority and metropolitan funds. Conversely, the idea of 'process' suggests an underlying logic to other, less traumatic, decolonizations, particularly, it must be said, British ones, where the withdrawal of the governor's retinue raised little enthusiasm locally and scarcely a whimper in the 'mother country'. Sometimes the lights of formal colonial control were not abruptly switched off; they just gradually faded from view.[19] If applied generically, discussion of a decolonization process may resolve itself into an analysis of high politics, privileging government policies devised in response to the actions of westernized elites that demanded, contested, or negotiated final independence agreements. This is much too narrow an approach. But, for some, it has the advantage of focusing attention on a central problem: why was it that so many newly independent former colonies came to be dominated by elites of Western-educated, predominantly bourgeois, leaders who either acquiesced in the continuation of Western economic hegemony or proved powerless to prevent it? Some analysts have interpreted this phenomenon as the direct consequence of colonial modernization.[20] Others have stressed the importance of elite education as a means of acculturation to foreign values.[21] There are two aspects to this viewpoint. The first relates to what might be dubbed the suicidal tendency of late colonial states. In their pursuit of development programmes that flattened the differences between rulers and ruled by extending economic activity, improving living standards and access to education, colonial governments pressed their own self-destruct button. Achievements in development ultimately nullified the colonial rulers' rationale for their oversight of 'backward' societies. At this stage, the second aspect comes into view: it was the introduction of Western languages, educational structures, industrial infrastructure, and economic organization that led to the emergence of a self-consciously 'modern' westernized indigenous elite.[22] And this elite accrued power during the process of decolonization, often replacing the erstwhile imperial ruler, whether by consent or force. Ironically, once in positions of authority after independence, postcolonial elites were every bit as determined to continue the process of economic modernization as their colonial forebears.[23]

In this reading of events, to borrow Partha Chatterjee's phrase, anti-colonialism was 'a derivative discourse' that accepted the very premises of 'modernity' on which colonial domination was based.[24] Or, to borrow the phraseology of French sociologist Bertrand Badie, the sociopolitical complexion of former colonies was so marked by erstwhile colonial practices and bureaucratic structures that the result was 'an imported state'.[25] In practice, this meant a continued reliance on foreign economic aid and technical expertise in what would come to be characterized as a 'neo-colonial' relationship. Just as the indigenous westernized elites are pivotal to arguments over modernization, so, too, they are identified as the primary culprits in a related theory: dependency. At root, the concept of dependency insists that formal transfers of political power were an elaborate deceit designed to conceal the persistence of Western economic imperialism. Worse, the supposedly nationalist elites that typically took office after independence were often complicit in allowing foreign states and corporate interests to retain their hold over the economic destiny of former colonial territories.[26]

If modernization theory and the concept of dependency retain some appeal in respect of decolonization in British and French West Africa, for example, each becomes more tenuous when applied to those locales where decolonization was synonymous with political violence and armed insurgencies. It may be a truism to note that political changes in state authority and in public office holders were rarely matched by an equivalent shift in economic and financial control from the metropolitan power to its former colony. But the idea that political control and sovereign authority were transferred in orderly fashion from colonial ruler to independent nation state, the better to preserve underlying Western economic domination, makes even less sense in territories where violence, or international intervention catalysed the end of empire.

As Crawford Young points out, 'states pursue the goal of maximum feasible autonomy'. They require internal authority and international legitimization, and must have control of a revenue base (in other words, tax-raising powers or some other income stream) to function effectively.

These prerequisites render the idea of an overnight transition to full independence unsustainable. At best, some measure of economic and military reliance on client states, outside agencies, or even the former colonial power was bound to follow the formal grant of independence. At worst, newly sovereign states entered a new era of neocolonialism in which rival superpowers and former colonial rulers sought to impose regional dominance and privileged access to trade and investment. Inevitably, the very phrase, 'transfer of power', misleadingly devised by the British to label their withdrawal from India, is politically charged.[27]

Indeed, in the Indian case, nominally one in which decolonization did not trigger open warfare, at least until after the colonial occupiers went home, civil resistance and mass protests determined imperial responses to questions of reform.[28] At a more global level, transnational hostility to colonialism and racial discrimination generated greater support among publics, media outlets, and international agencies worldwide as the twentieth century wore on. Anti-colonialists, American civil rights campaigners, and those living behind the Iron Curtain began to identify shared objectives, drawing parallels between their local situations which made the governments that ruled them squirm with embarrassment.[29] How could the United States profess colonial freedom when much of its African American population lived under varying degrees of segregation? Could Soviet anti-colonialism be reconciled with Russia's domination of Eastern Europe and Central Asia? Surely those living under the Soviet yoke in this 'Second World' would acquire distinct – potentially subversive – views of the 'Third World' and the triumph of decolonization within it.[30] Most obvious of all: how could Britain, France, or the Netherlands practice democracy at home while denying majority rule to their colonial subjects?

What did decolonization signify?

Historian Frederick Cooper has stressed that the fact that we know the end point of formal colonial rule makes it harder to clarify the processes at work in decolonization. It is all too easy to ascribe undue influence to abstract forces of nationalism, Cold War pressures, or a collapse of will to govern among the colonial powers. Such simplistic generalizations may ignore decisive initiatives by Africans themselves and treat both rulers and ruled as essentially homogenous. Furthermore, they begin from the dubious presumption that decolonization was both clearly discerned and either firmly resisted or consciously sought. The label 'anti-colonial nationalism' is also too neat, too reductive to explain the multiple perspectives of those driven to challenge colonial authority. In many cases, local opponents of empire are better described as members of social movements. Their grievances often concerned the most basic elements of life – the availability of land, employment, even food or access to education, healthcare, and other critical resources. These protests might be harnessed to nationalist causes, but they were, first and foremost, expressions of popular activism that neither fitted a precise chronology of decolonization, nor ended with the departure of colonial rulers.[31] Taking local activism seriously, we discover a vast middle ground of alternative possibilities lying somewhere between uncompromising anti-colonial nationalism and more hard-nosed, pragmatic efforts to secure improvements in living standards and basic rights.[32]

Cooper's analysis of trade unionism in British and French Africa shows us what this could mean. French African politicians, labour leaders, journalists, and writers were profoundly split over what the end of French control would signify – and whether such a complete rupture was desirable anyway. For some West African leaders, a rush to independence risked the entrenchment of poverty, the reification of artificial borders between the region's states, and the loss of valuable French aid, investment, and cultural patronage for a wider grouping of francophone African states.[33] Others disagreed. A French pull out would enable independent African nation states to aspire to living standards and democratic freedoms akin to those enjoyed by their former rulers. Not surprisingly, this model appealed primarily to those among their fellow Africans with a foot on an economic, educational, or administrative ladder, whether as industrial workers, junior bureaucrats, or school-educated *commerçants*. For its more radical grass-roots supporters, notably in French Guinea, decolonization would free Africans to chart a distinct and more revolutionary political course, certainly not one defined in relation to Western values or capitalist organization.[34]

Raymond Betts captures the mood of the anti-colonialist writers in the French Empire for whom decolonization amounted to a cultural renaissance:

> To decolonize was to cleanse as well as to reject. Almost all authors writing of the situation in the French possession in which they resided saw the withdrawal of the French as the opportunity for cultural renewal, for the creation of a new sort of community, one distinguished by solidarity, co-operation and unity, one in which Western competitive individualism and class distinctions would not exist.[35]

For Frantz Fanon, undoubtedly the most persuasive literary supporter of this viewpoint, political violence was not only justifiable, it was essential. Its high political objective of bringing colonial rule to an end was only part of the deeper cleansing of all aspects of colonialist culture and subservience from the minds of former subject peoples.[36] Why fight against colonial domination if those called upon to resist it were destined to live in an ersatz replica of the Western-style socioeconomic systems against which they had rebelled? This would be the ultimate paradox: postcolonial states would have accepted the original justifications advanced for nineteenth-century colonialism; namely, that European rule would bring social and material progress to backward indigenous societies. As Cooper has shown, this tension between demands for the same freedoms and economic opportunities as the colonial power and the outright rejection of any form of social organization identifiable with France was clearly apparent in the development of African trade unionism across French West Africa in the years 1945–58.[37]

Postcolonialists, who stress colonialism's power as a discourse of domination, a way of representing and crystallizing cultural difference, have also been outspoken critics of the concept of decolonization. Theorists of postcolonialism have objected to the state-centred approaches implicit in the study of empires' end, which, after all, has often been analysed as the replacement of one central state authority by another. They question the equivalence of colonialism and colonial rule. From the ways in which academic 'knowledge' about colonial societies was constructed to the depiction of African, Asian, or Caribbean cultural traits as somehow primitive, fetishistic, or otherwise inferior, the language of colonialism did not disappear overnight with the advent of sovereign independence in former colonies. Aspects of colonialism such as racialism and economic dependency, they would argue, outlasted the formal end of empire.[38] And, as mentioned earlier, aspects of the colonial condition still endure for once colonized peoples who are denied the same access to markets, emigration, or even basic human rights as their erstwhile European masters. Critics of postcolonial theory have turned the arguments of the postcolonialists against them, stressing that the very term 'post-colonialism' privileges the era of European control within the study of Third World societies. Postcolonialism challenges conventional narratives of imperial history through its study of cultural discourse. It thus questions the validity of a straightforward periodization of colonial rule. But the terminology used in postcolonial theory to describe cultural practices in former imperial states and formerly colonized societies needs to set itself apart from the features of the postcolonial condition being described. Here, one necessarily returns to the problematic nature of decolonization. How should one distinguish between states that were once under European control? Are they all equally postcolonial? Are some under a neocolonial yoke of Western economic influence and others not? And how far does their previous colonial history hold the key to understanding their current social, economic, and political condition? Surely the impact of colonization differed immensely between territories. Algeria, Angola, and Rhodesia, for example, underwent what Anne McLintock terms 'deep settler colonization'. Their near neighbours, respectively Tunisia, Namibia (former German South West Africa), and Botswana (Bechuanaland), were altogether less touched by a large European presence. A key limitation of postcolonial theory perhaps lies in its failure to make sufficient allowance for regional variation.[39] Too often, it seems, postcolonialists just do not know their colonial history.

As the editors of a key work on colonial cultures remind us, 'Any effort to compare different imperial systems – or even parts of a single empire – raises questions about what it is that we should be comparing: similar chronologies across different colonial contexts, or disparate chronologies but similar patterns and rhythms of rule?'[40] The disharmonies that emerge in comparing rhythms of rule underscore a central point: imperial elites may have *viewed* their domains from a metropolitan centre, but their actions, let alone their consequences, were not necessarily *determined* there. Since empires were in competition as well as in contact, the question of conjunctures still arises. How far should we link specific contests within colonies to concurrent trends of European history and global conflict?

This tension between the singularity of history in each and every colony and the unifying effects of extraneous pressures on the imperial powers themselves is an inescapable feature of any comparative study of European decolonization. Putting aside Marxist-Leninist theories of the inevitability of capitalist imperial decline, it remains tempting to view empires as almost organic, their initial growth and eventual decline part of a finite lifecycle. This, however, is little more than Whiggish teleology. It is easily debunked and is of little use as an analytical tool. Imperialist expansion and the clashes between Europeans and indigenous colonized peoples that followed cannot be reduced to an economic imperative realized in practice thanks to the triumph of modern technologies over tribal traditionalism. Alice L. Conklin makes the point succinctly:

> Imperialism is, of course, an economic system; but it also engendered new administrative elites, vast new bodies of knowledge, networks of petty traders and poor missionaries, sexualized and racialized representations of the other, discursive as well as physical forms of violence, and a global culture of consumption.[41]

In large, multi-ethnic colonial territories, such as the Belgian Congo, the culture wars between competing metropolitan and indigenous ways of life, language usage, and religious practice were more critical in the long-term social history of colonized peoples than their often brief armed resistance against imperial invaders.[42]

It does, however, seem fair to state that the precise circumstances of early imperial consolidation usually set the agenda for modes of governance in particular colonies. This, in turn, helped determine the degree of stability achieved by a colonial regime. In Portuguese Africa, the dictatorship of Dr António de Oliveira Salazar struggled to reconcile imperialist theories that identified the entire population as part of a single 'Lusotropical' community with harsh, authoritarian methods of rule that coerced African labour to serve the interests of Portuguese trading companies and the colonial state.[43] The early emphasis in French colonial doctrine on imparting French cultural and political values to their dependent peoples rarely translated into any sustained effort to make colonized peoples 'French'.[44] This doctrine, which came to be known as 'assimilationism', was always reserved for a select few. Assimilation, or making colonial subjects into model French citizens, was necessarily exclusive and elitist. It embraced a privileged minority while rejecting the overwhelming majority, usually on grounds of language, culture, or economic status. As one author puts it, 'Frenchness in the colonial world represented a zero-sum game in which the assimilationist gains of a few signified a loss for others.'[45]

If anything, the contrasts often drawn between highly interventionist French-style colonial rule and the British preference for forms of 'Indirect Rule', of governing through indigenous elites where possible without, in the process, disrupting local cultures the better to maintain political stability seem to be exaggerated. In both cases, the colonial impact was initially constrained by practical, especially financial, limitations on the fledgling colonial state's scope for action.[46] That said, the French tendency to view their own society as objectively superior informed the determination among colonial officials after 1945 to ensure that *la présence française* outlasted the formal end of colonial rule, an objective shared, if less explicitly articulated, by the British.[47] Furthermore, the greater degree of anthropological training and functional specialization among post-war colonial officials imbued with ethnographical concepts of indigenous societies and how best to modernize them was used to justify French tutelage before an increasingly sceptical international audience at the UN and elsewhere. After 1945, adherence to this 'scientific colonialism', characterized by intellectual concern for the welfare of subject peoples, became a stock justification for continued imperial rule.[48]

To its advocates, then, the French Empire was unique precisely because it was more a cultural project than a set of exploitative economic relationships. Its foremost goal was the transformation of subjects through cultural contact rather than anything as crudely mercantilist as the extraction of wealth or as nakedly expansionist as the extension of global strategic advantage. France's tools of empire were language, legal codes, and republican values. Engineers, missionaries, educators, generals, and trading companies might serve the project, but their individual interests in construction projects, religious observance, schools, conquest, and commerce were ultimately subordinate to the overarching purpose of cultural elevation. Framed in this light, decolonization was regarded, not as a rupture between motherland and colony, but as a shift towards equitable interdependence rather than colonial domination. Such attitudes found a more receptive audience in black Africa, where the benefits of French economic and military aid were most apparent. But in North Africa and Vietnam, interdependence was seen for what it was: neocolonialism.[49]

The emphasis on fundamental continuities – in political relations, strategic interests, economic ties, and cultural connection – is certainly evident in the ways in which successive British governments thought about decolonization. Policymakers with a private aversion to the term 'independence' anticipated continuing, strong links between the metropolitan power and its former overseas territories. Diplomatic and even military connections would be reinforced by trade and shared cultural interests. They would be further cemented by the promise of development aid. Symbolizing these links was the British Commonwealth, a multiracial, international body composed of former dependencies, whose significance in British eyes echoed that attached by France to the French Union. Just as Paris was, theoretically at least, to remain epicentre of the French Union, so London's place at the heart of the Commonwealth would help amplify Britain's voice in world affairs.[50] At its grandest, this interpretation sees British decolonization as an elaborate attempt to substitute new networks of informal influence and control for the costly, inconvenient, and ethically dubious system of colonial rule, a piece of 'fancy footwork' reflecting a conjuncture of irresistible pressures: metropolitan economic weakness, increased resistance among colonial populations, and (perhaps decisively) fears that the colonial territories were fertile ground for Soviet and Communist Chinese penetration. The first two factors were not new in the two decades after 1945. Nor were the ideological shifts in global politics, which could be traced at least back to the impact of the First World War. Even so, the intensification of Cold War anxieties by the late 1950s may (partially) account for the *timing* of so many of Britain's retreats from Empire during the early 1960s.[51]

Central to recent British analyses of decolonization has been a revival of the long-familiar concept of 'collaboration' as the means by which Britain's imperial interests – material, strategic, and cultural – were secured. Faced with mounting internal and external constraints and unable to use coercion to maintain colonial rule *in the long term*, the colonial powers had to identify elite groups willing to collaborate with them. If such collaboration formed the basis of colonialism, then decolonization could be interpreted as the attempt to renegotiate collaborative arrangements when the original framework proved unable to meet the challenges of modernization, war, and rapid social change in the colonies. Further incentive derived from metropolitan attempts to extract greater economic benefits from the colonies or, more simply, to calculate whether colonial commitments were financially remunerative, both features characteristic of the years after 1945.[52]

The logic behind such an interpretation of decolonization might be summarized in the following question: could it be, ironically, that the colonial powers unwittingly engineered their own expulsion by the increasingly intrusive nature of their colonial presence? In Britain's case, as will be suggested, a 'reformed' style of colonialism introduced after 1945 ran counter to pre-war attempts to minimize the disruptive effects of social and economic 'modernization' (always, it might be argued, a doomed aspiration). Finding their local dominance and elite status increasingly challenged, traditional collaborating groups found their position undermined by new coalitions of anti-colonial forces, often ascribed the general epithet of 'nationalists'. In these circumstances, the colonial power faced the choice between preserving its interests by force, an option increasingly unacceptable for political and practical reasons, or, alternatively, trying to construct a new 'collaborative bargain', in which it might yet choose its successors.[53]

What, then, of the finality of decolonization? Contemporary relationships between the former colonizers and their colonial subjects have inevitably been shaped by the nature of decolonization itself, nowhere more so than in debates over immigration and social integration.[54] In matters of overseas policy, since the 1960s French governments have jettisoned the colonial vocabulary of *la plus grande France*. France's continuing role in black Africa – witness the recent interventions in the Ivory Coast and, more recently, Mali – is more usually justified on humanitarian grounds as a restoration of order, and on cultural grounds as a defence of *la francophonie*, literally, the global community of French-speaking peoples. The economic and security benefits that France accrues from its privileged financial and trade links with West Africa and its military bases in Equatorial Africa are less readily admitted.[55] Aside from this, the assumption of shared cultural interests between a former colonial power and states previously compelled to adopt the colonizer's language is questionable. In much of supposedly francophone Africa, only a minority speak Western languages. And usage of French, English, or Portuguese inevitably recalls the colonial period in which the imposition of a common language was a prerequisite to control over the means of cultural reproduction within societies. In an equation where culture denotes the human construction of meaning, language is power. Its chief weapons were schools, the religious hierarchy, the local bureaucracy, and judicial systems.[56] And the after-effects of this discursive domination can be long indeed. Postcolonialism may be right after all.

The Dutch case differs markedly from that of the French. The destruction wrought on Dutch political, social, and cultural institutions by the Japanese on the Indonesian archipelago during the Second World War, coupled with the violent break from the European motherland in the years after 1945, meant that the colonial legacy in Indonesia was limited. The Indonesian language, developed to provide linguistic uniformity after independence, borrowed something from Dutch but was nonetheless deliberately separate. Dutch military intervention, whether invited or uninvited, would have been unthinkable after 1950. The Dutch had neither the will nor the resources to police their former territories and the wider world would not have stood by in such circumstances. Memory of an imperial past remained strong in the metropole and Indonesian affairs continued to loom large in the Dutch national press for many years but, save for protests by the irredentist Moluccans, these were no more than memories and attention soon turned to the practical issues of economic survival in the regenerated European economy. Empire persisted in the Caribbean primarily because there was no pressure for change, and the independence of Suriname was more a result of a specific and peculiar set of political circumstances than a product of sustained campaigning by a majority of the population. For that reason, the Antilles have remained as a relic of the Netherlands' imperial past, but culturally and economically all these territories came under the influence of an increasingly dominant American Anglophone world.

It is, above all, over the violence connected with colonial collapse that a British tendency towards 'exceptionalism' has, perhaps, been particularly evident in the historiography of decolonization. Unlike the French, the Dutch, and the Portuguese, it has sometimes been implied, the British 'disengaged' from their Empire in a relatively painless, blood-free manner. The self-congratulation embodied in this perspective is clear. It may be true that the British were fortunate in having some important precedents from which to learn, and that British policymakers sought to avoid elsewhere the spiral of conflict into which the French descended in Algeria. As our discussion will suggest, however, closer examination of Britain's experience reveals patterns of violence at least matching, and sometimes even exceeding, those of the continental colonial powers.[57]

For Belgium and Portugal, too, troubled memories of decolonization are bound up with the violence that accompanied it and the diasporas that it created. Similarly, the territories of former Belgian and Portuguese Africa had mountains to climb to overcome their colonial legacies of war and inter-communal hostility, bureaucratic underdevelopment and chronic poverty.[58] It is perhaps fitting that the last chapter of this book addresses the roots of these problems, which stand as perhaps the most tragic examples of what could occur when decolonization was either unprepared or fiercely resisted. Our first task, however, is to consider conditions in Europe's other colonial Empires – the British, the French, and the Dutch – before the first winds of decolonization turned into a whirlwind in the aftermath of the Second World War.

PART I
BRITISH DECOLONIZATION
Larry Butler

INTRODUCTION TO PART I
THE BRITISH EMPIRE

Because it was the largest of the European overseas empires, the British Empire arguably holds a special place in the history of decolonization. What is particularly striking is that for most of its history the Empire lacked any clear sense of purpose. The Empire fulfilled numerous roles, benefiting a variety of groups, both in Britain and within the individual territories. But the British did not have an avowed 'mission', or notion of what the outcome of imperial rule was expected to be. Given the economic, military, and other constraints facing Britain, constraints which intensified as the twentieth century developed, it seemed clear that a global imperial system could only be run if it made minimal demands on the metropole. This meant that, as far as possible, coercion was to be avoided: it was expensive and increasingly likely to attract criticism, both within Britain and in the international arena. The aim of securing cheap, non-controversial rule in the dependent empire involved a search for groups willing to collaborate with the British, groups normally drawn from indigenous elites. In theory, the relationship would be mutually beneficial, with Britain safeguarding the political and social status of such elites in return for guarantees of the protection of its own commercial and strategic interests.

Beyond these simple guidelines, it is often difficult to discern any coherent British 'policy' for empire. Pragmatic improvisation, rather than detailed and principled planning, seemed to characterize the British approach. After the First World War, this began to change. Firmer commitments were made to ultimate self-government for India, the symbolic heart of the Empire, and its most valued component. And the white Dominions asserted their individuality with increasing assurance, not just culturally, but politically and economically too. For the rest of the dependent empire, it was not until the Second World War that the first serious steps were taken towards planning a controlled process of political reform, designed to lead to self-government for most (though not all) of the colonial territories within a refashioned British Commonwealth.

Trying to anticipate political change in the colonies, Britain hoped to 'manage' nationalism, or anti-colonialism, channelling its energy into new, constructive partnerships that would allow London to retain control over the pace and outcomes of decolonization. In practice, for much of this period, British policymakers often found themselves overtaken by events on the ground, forced to respond to local developments and changing circumstances. Repeatedly, the vague timetables for innovation in the colonies drawn up in London had to be reassessed and dramatically foreshortened. The entire process of imperial retreat was far swifter than anything imagined by policymakers even as recently as the 1940s. As the pace of decolonization accelerated, nationalist politicians, previously dismissed as unrepresentative and without legitimate popular mandate, were reappraised and designated suitable inheritors of political power.

Dismantling the Empire revealed a number of important contradictions in Britain's attitudes towards imperial management. Most apparent was the ongoing tension between reform and repression as instruments of colonial rule. A long-cherished national myth contends that, unlike other European powers, Britain succeeded in disengaging from empire in a relatively peaceful manner, its emphasis being on political reform and material development in order to prepare colonial territories for self-government. This image sits uncomfortably with the reality of sustained attempts to repress challenges to British rule. Such repression, often involving aerial bombardment, military force, and martial law, began soon after the First World War. It continued during the interwar period and into the Second World War (most notably in India and Palestine), and reached its zenith with protracted and bloody counter-insurgency campaigns in the post-war decades in Palestine, Malaya, Kenya, and Cyprus, to name only the most prominent instances.

Accumulating evidence is forcing historians to reconsider the use of violence to protect British interests. So, too, the implications of authoritarian colonial rule for the nature and stability of the postcolonial order in many countries are attracting greater interest. Such reassessments also render it necessary to interrogate British assumptions about ethnicity; in particular, the way in which, despite talk of 'multiracialism' as an ideal, the privileging of certain ethnic groups continued to be a feature of British policy. Perhaps most apparent in the treatment of white settler aspirations in Africa, this tendency can also be seen in the identification of particular indigenous groups, in Kenya, Nigeria, Malaya, and elsewhere as desirable and compliant 'partners', judgements often grounded in lingering racial stereotypes.

The two world wars convinced many key policymakers of the value in imperial connections, while simultaneously releasing forces that would, ultimately, cast doubt on the Empire's long-term viability. More immediately, the Empire's wartime contribution reinforced the presumption that supervision of a global system of influence underpinned Britain's continuing pretensions to world power status. The Cold War, a core ingredient in analyses of Britain's handling of decolonization, solidified the connections between sustained imperial bonds and Western strategic dominance. In the transition from political control to anticipated postcolonial political influence, a central British concern, endorsed by Britain's influential American ally, was to ensure that regimes friendly (or at least not hostile) to the West inherited power, blocking the ascendancy of politicians sympathetic towards the Communist Bloc.

The interwar Depression, the Second World War, the need to appease its American ally, and the pressure to meet mounting demands from colonial populations in the context of Cold War rivalries persuaded British planners of the need to buttress the imperial system by espousing a new commitment to raising colonial living standards through a process of economic and social development. This, it was hoped, would not only give British territories stronger foundations to support new, representative, political structures, but would also confer benefits on a British economy struggling to cope with recurrent financial crises. Paradoxically, the British found that mobilizing the very assets which made the dependent empire so attractive in wartime (and during post-war metropolitan reconstruction) risked antagonizing the populations of individual territories, fuelling local resentments and making more likely the coalescence of multiple grievances into coherent movements of anti-colonial protest. Ironically, 'development', the touchstone of British colonial policy after 1940, failed either to raise living standards as quickly as colonial populations had been encouraged to expect, or to lay down the material and other foundations on which political reform could be securely built.

As for Britain itself, decolonization would be accompanied by important domestic developments with lasting consequences. Among these, arguably the most important was the post-1945 phenomenon of immigration from the 'New' Commonwealth, which brought unprecedented diversity to the metropolitan population, exposing it to a wide range of new cultural influences. Immigration, along with a growing awareness of political and other developments within the dependent empire, affected British attitudes towards the populations of soon-to-be ex-dependencies. An important factor here may have been experience of the military repression of anti-colonial challenges, which placed many British people into a direct, conscious relationship with the colonial world for the first time. While generating a spectrum of racial stereotypes about the 'other', and giving new resonances to some old prejudices, Britain's counter-insurgency campaigns also stimulated new debates about the moral basis of empire, triggering unease in some quarters, especially, perhaps, among the young, who were unconvinced of the Empire's relevance to a Britain undergoing fundamental economic and cultural change. Successive British governments, unlike the ruling elites of France and Portugal, for example, were fortunate that their retreat from empire never became a destabilizing political issue in Britain itself. But this may not have been accidental: arguably, the painful precedents of France's experiences in Indochina and Algeria were a potent warning to policymakers in London of the need to make timely concessions to cooperative Third World elites in anticipation of mutually beneficial relations in a new, postcolonial framework. If this could be done successfully, the extent of Britain's changing world position could be concealed from a metropolitan population traditionally unaware of the realities of life under imperial rule.

CHAPTER 1
THE BRITISH EMPIRE, 1918–45: INTERWAR CHANGE AND WARTIME PRESSURES

It would be misleading to suggest that, before the Second World War, Britain's 'imperial system' comprised a coherent bloc. Between the wars, Britain's formal Empire consisted of a highly varied collection of territories demonstrating marked differences in political, economic, and social development and comprising unique local cultures. The British connection was often all that linked them, but this, too, differed between territories. The most senior members of the Empire, the 'Dominions' or 'settlement colonies', were legally autonomous, but bound to Britain by economic and defence arrangements, and by ties of language, culture, and kinship. India, long considered the most valuable 'possession', was so important in the imperial system that it technically constituted an 'empire' in itself. The remainder of the 'dependent' Empire comprised around sixty colonies, protectorates, and 'mandates'.[1] Beyond these three broad categories was a more subtle grouping, representing Britain's 'informal' Empire, consisting of countries, for example in the Middle East, which, while not formally components of the British Empire, were under varying degrees of British financial, economic, or strategic control. Their economic and strategic value to Britain often exceeded that of the dependent territories, particularly because informal ties avoided the expense of direct administration and were thought, not always correctly, to be more acceptable to local populations than formal rule.

Given the Empire's size and diversity, it is not surprising that, as John Darwin has stressed, it was never subject to any single, overarching 'project' or purpose. The limitations on British resources, and the constant need to improvise policy in response to developments on the ground, precluded this. What has struck commentators, however, is the Empire's adaptability in the face of changing circumstances. A major unifying theme in policy, visible throughout the period discussed here (and before) was Britain's need to recruit local collaborators, or 'partners', without whose consent and assistance, imperial rule would have been untenable.[2]

Recent scholarship has demonstrated that the British public was exposed to a bewildering variety of images, literature, and other artefacts connected with, or designed to promote, the concept of empire. Much less easy to establish, however, is the impact that media coverage, advertisements, exhibitions, and, increasingly, film and radio, had on popular attitudes towards the Empire. Crucial here was the need to distinguish between the intention which lay behind the creation of this material, and the way in which it was received by mass audiences.[3] A similar problem arises when assessing the influence of metropolitan groups, generally on the left, and hostile in varying degrees to the very idea of empire. Although they existed and were active throughout the period being discussed, it is notoriously difficult to gauge the extent of the impact they made.[4] After the First World War, there was a tendency for various liberal and left-orientated groups to blend traditional humanitarian concern about colonial issues with awareness of a wider, global, 'race' question, fuelled not only by developments within the Empire, but also by the presence in Britain of a small but vocal population of black intellectuals, students, and others, increasingly organized into groups such as the West African Students Union and the League of Coloured Peoples. The engagement of metropolitan critics of empire with the black community in Britain was one element feeding into what would become a radical black consciousness, which would eventually contribute to a climate of opinion which saw the weakening of British imperial resolve, especially when potentiated by the combined effects of the Second World War and post-war political developments within the colonial territories.[5]

Important figures to emerge from this process of intellectual exchange included C. L. R. James, the distinguished West Indian intellectual and ardent enthusiast for cricket (itself an important intra-imperial bond), who lived in Britain for most of the 1930s. Putting aside the imperial values he acquired during his early socialization, James would exchange his liberal humanism for Trotskyist socialism and pan-Africanism, in the process doing much to deepen understanding of the African diaspora within Britain and beyond. Equally influential, perhaps, was James's collaborator and fellow West Indian, George Padmore, whose communist and Pan-Africanist leanings led him to examine rigorously the racism and violence which he saw as fundamental to the British imperial system, forcing sympathizers in Britain to re-evaluate the paternalism which had long been a hallmark of the metropolitan anti-imperial tradition.[6]

James and Padmore were just two of the leading figures in a process of transcultural exchange which gathered momentum in Britain between the wars, and would continue to resonate throughout the era of decolonization. This process raised metropolitan awareness of the Empire and its problems, especially among sections of society already predisposed to be critical of imperialism. Perhaps more importantly, such exchanges were critical to the emergence of new strains of anti-colonialism within dependent territories.[7] Intellectuals such as James and Padmore offered their readers searing critiques of empire whose lasting power derived from their basis in *personal* experience.

Turning to metropolitan anti-imperialists, it is worth recalling that some were driven by abhorrence towards the exercise of power over other peoples (an ethical stance of long vintage), while others were animated by concerns about the damaging consequences the imperial role might have for Britain, in the form of a reflexive authoritarian tendency, the militarization of metropolitan institutions and attitudes, and the skewing of the British economy with an attendant drag on long overdue modernization.[8] The two positions were not incompatible. A British trade unionist might, for instance, be opposed to empire on ideological grounds while combining this outlook with fears of unemployment resulting from industrial competition within the Empire and the presumed unfair advantage of 'sweated labour'. Yet another strand of thinking among critics of the imperial status quo came from those, particularly the Fabian socialists, who felt that Britain was not being active enough in 'developing' its colonial territories. For this lobby, a reformist social and economic agenda was the prerequisite to eventual political reform. Advocates of this view, which increasingly chimed with official thinking in London, would coalesce in 1940 to form the Fabian Colonial Bureau, a hub of communications linking activists in many territories with their British counterparts, and the body from which the Labour Party would draw most of its ideas on colonial policy.[9]

Rethinking the Empire after the First World War

For British governments after 1919, it was impossible to conceive of a world without the Empire: its absence or disintegration was unimaginable. Managing the Empire therefore rested on unspoken assumptions about Britain's overseas interests and status. Certainly before the Second World War, policymakers were usually free from the unwelcome attentions of a British public preoccupied with domestic issues or with more immediate European threats. Like its French counterpart, the British Empire not only survived the First World War intact, but greatly increased its territorial extent. The peace settlement ushered in a new age of mandates, under which responsibility for administering former German and Ottoman territory was delegated by the League of Nations to the victor powers. As a result, the British Empire extended to almost a quarter of the world's land area. Yet, as the interwar years were to illustrate, a larger empire posed unprecedented problems of imperial defence within a highly unstable international system. Nevertheless, in August 1919, the Cabinet informed the armed services that they should assume that 'the British Empire will not be engaged in any great war during the next ten years'. This 'Ten Year Rule' became the keystone of British defence thinking and was renewed for a further ten years in 1928, arguably with fatal consequences.

After 1918, Britain needed to economize. The scale of war debts demanded wholesale cuts in government spending. Britain thus abandoned any thought of further imperial expansion, trimmed some of its responsibilities, introduced new techniques of imperial management, and explored means of conciliating indigenous nationalism. In the Middle East, this would involve a search for amenable local collaborators and attempts to substitute informal control for direct rule. In India, it would involve limited constitutional reform, drawing a growing number of Indians into the political process. In Ireland, it hastened signature of the Anglo-Irish Treaty of 1921 and partition. For the remainder of the 1920s, while the other leading powers were absorbed primarily in their own domestic concerns, the British Empire could plausibly be regarded as the world's sole 'superpower'.[10] Yet this situation could continue only in the absence of a hostile power, and provided that no major war threatened Britain's global interests. At the same time Britain had to accept that it could no longer assume common interests in foreign affairs between itself and the Dominions, nor were the Dominions themselves united by a common outlook, as was shown by their indifferent response to the Chanak Crisis of 1922 when Britain came close to war with Turkey over enforcement of the peace settlement.[11] The peacemaking process revealed that Australia, New Zealand, and South Africa had developed their own 'sub-imperial' ambitions, seen in their bids to acquire former German colonial territory in the Pacific and southern Africa respectively. The Chanak Crisis toppled Lloyd George's Coalition and led his Conservative successor, Andrew Bonar Law, to declare that Britain's role was not to be 'the policeman of the world'. At the Imperial Conference in 1923, Australia and New Zealand advocated a genuinely 'imperial' foreign policy which would reflect the views of the Dominions.[12] Dominion hostility to involvement in European affairs persisted in the later 1920s. This position reflected the thinking of British military chiefs, who, throughout the 1920s, took a global and imperial view of defence planning. The British Army, for example, saw its major role as being to protect the frontiers of the Empire, especially in Asia, where the traditional fear of Russian/Soviet aggression lingered, leading Britain to station a third of its army in India and in the Middle East, in order to defend the Suez Canal and Britain's new regional interests. Beyond this, the army's role was to sustain imperial garrisons and to perform policing duties in the colonial empire. Yet this also led to complications, with the Government of India warning that the use of Indian troops in the Middle East at Indian taxpayers' expense might provoke 'a complete breakdown in the political situation', inflaming nationalist hostility.[13]

Cost was a decisive consideration in imperial defence planning in the 1920s.[14] Where possible, economies were made by introducing new technologies to perform old functions. Thus Britain exploited the possibilities of air power to subdue restless populations, in the Middle East. Air bombing of insurgents, practised in Iraq and elsewhere, saved imperial manpower and was less visible to metropolitan and international critics of colonial repression.[15] At the Washington Naval Conference of 1921–2, Britain formally accepted naval parity in capital ships with the United States, which in effect meant pursuing a policy of disarmament. But it was the associated decision to forego the alliance with Japan which marked a critical turning point in British defence policy, one which would have enormous implications for the future.[16]

Under the Statute of Westminster (1931), the independent status of the Dominions, defined at the Imperial Conference of 1926, was formally recognized. The position of the Irish Free State remained anomalous: questions were already being asked whether a republic (which Ireland appeared set to become) could remain a member of the Commonwealth. This puzzle would assume major practical significance after the Second World War. It was the flexibility and ambiguity of 'Dominion status' that made the concept so appealing to some Dominion politicians. It enabled them to maintain an official position of support for the Empire, through the common bond of loyalty to the Crown, while also allowing them to assert their political maturity and autonomous interests. This was particularly important in the more 'volatile' Dominions, South Africa and the Irish Free State.[17] In reality, between the wars, the Dominions all appreciated the important advantages of their links with Britain, especially in the areas of economics and defence. Dependence on emigration from Britain was another cohesive influence, even when it threatened local labour or, in the case of South Africa, aroused Afrikaner suspicion of an unwelcome reinforcement of 'British' influence.[18] Harder to measure, but arguably equally significant, were the binding effects of 'race sentiment', founded chiefly on assumptions of racial superiority, on that part of the Dominions' population descended from British migrants. For Britain, too, the cultivation of a distinctive 'Imperial' culture was an important aim in the interwar period. The potential of wireless broadcasting to reinforce intra-imperial ties was soon recognized. Despite the general mood of retrenchment, funding was provided for the BBC to launch its Empire Service in 1932.[19] Empire-related matters were prominent in the pre-war BBC's domestic programming, too, emphasizing imperial values in order to reinforce British national identity during a period of mounting uncertainty. This trend would develop further after the war's outbreak when government exploited the cohesive power of radio more fully. The extent to which the BBC counteracted popular metropolitan ignorance of the Empire nevertheless remains debatable. Even more elusive is the question of whether broadcasting forged a purposeful sense of identification with imperial concerns.[20]

During the interwar years, Britain entered an important phase of economic readjustment witnessing unprecedented attempts to integrate the imperial economic system as a global economic bloc. Crucial to this was the introduction of discriminatory tariff protection, designed to promote increased trade within the Empire at a time when the volume of world trade was shrinking. 'Imperial Preference' had been introduced in 1919 and was taken much further after the onset of the Depression in 1929. The National Government introduced import tariffs in 1931 as a 'temporary' device pending the construction of more durable arrangements, which followed during 1932. Various reciprocal trade agreements were negotiated at the Imperial Economic Conference held that year in Ottawa.[21] However, for the British government, the Ottawa Conference had a political significance almost as great as its economic importance. Neville Chamberlain, then Chancellor of the Exchequer, believed that the conference had done much to reinforce the Commonwealth connection.[22]

Yet Ottawa also revealed the Dominions' ability to extract concessions from Britain. They were simply unwilling to play the role of permanent sources of food and raw materials to the mother country and sought to develop their own secondary industries so as to diversify their economies.[23] For its part, Britain, concerned about the likely effects on its own farming industry, was reluctant to give the Dominions exclusive privileged access to the metropolitan agricultural sector.[24] In the colonies, Britain had greater leeway to shape economic activity in its own interests. The Ottawa agreements were applied to the colonial Empire, and the colonies received preferential access to British and Dominion markets, and were obliged to provide preferences in return. An important consequence of Imperial Preference for the colonies was to spur the development of manufacturing industry in some territories, particularly in the Far East.[25] Other measures in the early 1930s included the creation of the Sterling Bloc, which served Britain's principal aim of regaining financial influence and stability.[26] During the 1930s the Empire became increasingly attractive to British investors. This was partly because the Dominions and colonies had good records of paying interest and sinking fund liabilities, unlike numerous foreign governments.[27] The Empire therefore attracted a growing proportion of Britain's overseas investments. In turn, the Empire relied increasingly on the London money markets when raising loans. Britain's political elite viewed the Sterling Bloc, even more than the system of Imperial Preference, as the expression of Britain's global power, offering the means to reclaim at least some of the financial leverage lost to the United States during the First World War.[28]

The interwar period also saw a transport revolution which had enormous implications for the cohesion of the Empire, shrinking what were still formidably long, and potentially vulnerable, maritime arteries. A combination of concern about stubbornly high domestic unemployment levels after the First World War, and a broader dream of strengthening Britain's imperial ties, led the British government to encourage emigration to the Empire. The 1922 Empire Settlement Act offered financial help to those emigrating to the Dominions. With what proved to be unjustified optimism, the British government continued, until the onset of the Depression, to see emigration as a panacea to metropolitan difficulties.[29] Although the 1922 Act was renewed in 1937, the government's emigration policy was a disappointment: during the worst years of the Depression, migrants entering Britain outnumbered those leaving it. Nevertheless, historians have increasingly recognized the significance of the human interactions made possible by migration. The opportunities created for people from a variety of backgrounds – and driven by a complex blend of motives – to gain direct experience of life in the Empire enriched metropolitan perceptions of an otherwise bewildering patchwork of territories. Such opportunities expanded further in the years after 1945, partly in reaction to social and labour market constraints within austerity Britain, and partly in response to the demands created by major shifts in colonial policy, especially in relation to development.[30]

Increasing imperial security threats

During the early 1930s, a new set of international circumstances emerged to challenge Britain's ability to preserve its global system. Growing intimations of the aggressive intentions of Japan, Germany, and Italy exposed new pressure points, and the different strategic priorities formulated in London and the Dominion capitals reminded policymakers that defence was the Empire's Achilles' heel.[31] Evidence of a clear threat first appeared in the Far East where the decision to allow the Anglo-Japanese alliance of 1902 to lapse left Britain dangerously exposed, inspiring the Admiralty to propose the construction of a major new naval base at Singapore. Metropolitan aversion to high defence spending meant, however, that work on the base was often interrupted, and it took the Japanese invasion of Manchuria in 1931 and the attack on Shanghai in 1932 to convince London to speed up construction. Even then, the base's importance was predicated on the assumption that Britain could reinforce it in time of emergency by sending a fleet to the Far East. This, in turn, presupposed that the Royal Navy would not be facing a simultaneous threat closer to home in European waters. It was German rearmament and the growing appreciation of Italy's Mediterranean expansionism which called the whole plan into question. Looming over the 1930s were doubts about whether Britain was in any condition to contemplate another war, and what the economic and financial effects of such a war might be. For Chamberlain, policy towards Nazi Germany was partly a reflection of apparent British popular reluctance to face war over the fate of Eastern or Central Europe, but also of the strong strategic argument that a European war might jeopardize the Empire's security.[32] Meanwhile, Mussolini's invasion of Ethiopia in October 1935 threatened British imperial communications through the Mediterranean and exposed the fragility of Britain's Middle Eastern position.[33] In February 1937 the Chiefs of Staff listed in order of priority the Commonwealth's strategic commitments. These were: the security of the global imperial communications system; Britain's own defences against German aggression; the security of imperial interests in the Far East against Japanese incursions; the security of the Mediterranean and the Middle East; and finally, safeguarding India against possible Soviet aggression.[34]

Britain sought both to reassure the Dominions and to clarify Dominion attitudes towards the developing international climate. The British government promised its partners that if war came, the twin pillars of imperial security would be the defence of Britain and of the Singapore base. In turn, the Dominions asked for firm commitments that regardless of developments in the Mediterranean, a fleet would, if necessary, be sent to the Far East.[35] Although there were growing strains and anxieties, the Commonwealth relationship appeared to be holding firm. Previously, at the end of 1937, the Cabinet endorsed the recommendations of Sir Thomas Inskip, Minister for the Co-ordination of Defence, in whose new schema preparing an Expeditionary Force for despatch to the continent in the event of war became the lowest priority, precedence being given first to the defence of Britain itself and second to the defence of the Empire and overseas trade. Yet as Inskip himself warned the Cabinet only two months later, Britain could not realistically plan the defence of the Empire simultaneously against three major aggressors.[36]

The coming of the Second World War

The Second World War tested every aspect of the British imperial system.[37] The European war forced Britain to seek US support. During the so-called 'ABC' talks, held early in 1941, the initiative rested with the still neutral United States, which, largely for domestic political reasons, still avoided firm commitments to Britain. At the talks, to which Canada, Australia, and New Zealand sent observers, Britain and the United States agreed that the defeat of Germany and Italy was the priority, and that they needed to deter Japanese aggression. Less congenial were Anglo-US exchanges on the priority Britain attached to the Middle Eastern and Mediterranean theatres and especially its Far Eastern strategy.[38]

As in the First World War, Britain looked to the Dominions and the dependent empire to provide military and economic assistance to the war effort. As it did in the earlier conflict, the Empire provided forces that played a key role in all the major theatres of war.[39] Dominion governments were closely consulted by London throughout the war, and the volume of communication between London and the Indian and colonial governments also expanded dramatically. One important innovation was the attempt to coordinate the imperial war effort on a regional basis, for example through the East African Governors' Conference, the West African War Council, and the Eastern Group Supply Council, established under the umbrella of the Government of India with satellites in East Africa and the Middle East. However, the process of mobilizing imperial resources ultimately weakened the entire system. The colonial territories in particular felt the effects of government regulation to an extent never seen in peacetime.[40] At the outbreak of war, the Colonial Office had introduced a panoply of emergency controls, similar to those imposed in wartime Britain. With the end of the 'Phoney War', the colonies faced a new phase of marked austerity. As Britain's limited dollar reserves evaporated, Indian and colonial production assumed growing significance for the war effort.

One of the most important results of wartime imperial economic mobilization was the consolidation of the Sterling Area, building on the arrangements introduced after the financial crisis of 1931. A further financial shift arising directly from the war was the widespread introduction of more progressive taxation regimes, including income tax. This important departure, in part resulting from the need to curb inflation arising from import shortages, offered the long-term promise of freeing cash-strapped colonial governments from some of their dangerous dependence on revenue from imports and exports. This encouraged some optimism during the war that future colonial economic development could be financed to an increased extent from local resources.

The most important economic change affecting many colonies was direct government intervention in the purchase and marketing of their major products. Political considerations, above all the need to avoid colonial unrest in wartime, and fears about the effects disrupted exports might have on colonial government revenues, led Britain to introduce bulk-purchasing schemes for many colonial commodities. Improvised in 1939 to meet the immediate problem of West African cocoa, this involved crops being bought at fixed prices on behalf of the Ministry of Food in London. State marketing in West Africa proved so lucrative to Britain that in 1944, London published plans to extend the system into the post-war period. However, the wartime need for collaboration between big business and the colonial state fuelled African suspicions that the interests of local entrepreneurs were being subordinated to those of powerful British firms, intensifying the colonial hostility to the latter which would become increasingly evident after the war, eventually contributing to the alarming unrest which erupted in the Gold Coast in 1948.[41]

Growing wartime intervention gave the colonial state considerable experience in economic management, which accordingly lost some of the terrors that had haunted administrators during the Depression, and laid the foundations for a more 'managerial' post-war style of colonialism. But their new responsibilities, especially in the economic sphere, frequently drove administrators to introduce unpopular measures that threatened to erode the delicate political balance maintained in many parts of the dependent empire between the wars. Nevertheless, the growth in the colonial state's range of activities during the war would set an important precedent for more centralized, *dirigiste* post-war colonial policies.[42]

The war's social consequences for the colonies were often disruptive and unsettling. Increased opportunities for employment and inclusion in the cash economy were accompanied by urbanization and greater awareness of the colonial state's growing intrusiveness, creating conditions receptive to the development of anti-colonial sentiment. India's military contribution was enormous: some two and a half million Indians performed military service, while the civilian contribution, in maintaining economic production, was vital.[43] At the war's peak, possibly one million Africans were in uniform. Around 15,000 black soldiers from Anglophone Africa died on active service. Although the British generally sought to avoid conscription, they could rely on cooperative African chiefs to produce 'volunteers' by employing varying degrees of coercion.[44] Long-standing beliefs about the inherently militaristic nature of certain African societies persisted: in Kenya, for instance, officials identified the Kikuyu and Kamba peoples as examples of 'martial races'.[45] The effects of wartime military service for colonial populations are less easy to establish. While these could lead to colonial troops acquiring new technical skills, broader horizons, and heightened political expectations, it seems that for many returning Africans the priority was to resume their pre-war lives as quickly as possible, prioritizing individual rather than collective interests, and that those who had stayed at home during the war were more likely to be active in post-war politics. However, in some cases, such as the Gold Coast, the post-war frustration of demobilized soldiers' demands certainly catalysed local unrest.[46]

The region within the Empire most directly affected by the war was South East Asia. The Japanese attack on Malaya and the fall of Singapore on 15 February 1942 led to the loss of around 138,000 British and Commonwealth troops, in Churchill's words the 'worst disaster and largest capitulation in British history', an event which exploded any remaining myth of white 'supremacy', and fatally eroded the prestige essential to European colonialism.[47] This appalling military reversal triggered outrage in Britain, along with painful questions about the failings of imperial rule that had apparently made such a defeat possible. The fall of Malaya deprived the Allies of access to around half the world's supplies of strategically vital rubber and tin, while making easier Japan's entry into the Dutch East Indies and Burma. With Australia and India now exposed to the threat of Japanese invasion, the Empire appeared more vulnerable than ever before. Some Indian nationalists took heart from this British reversal. Australia and New Zealand, meanwhile, were obliged to seek US protection, emphasizing the empty nature of Britain's pre-war guarantees to them, and weakening Britain's bonds with its

Pacific Dominions. Moreover, the failure of the population in Malaya to respond energetically to the invasion was also a source of deep embarrassment, signifying a lack of empathy with colonial ambitions.

Meanwhile, the implications of Japanese occupation for the territories affected included a massive dislocation of civilian populations, a huge refugee problem, slave labour (for example on the infamous Burma Railway), and the exploitation of tens of thousands of 'comfort women', many brought to the region from Korea, for the benefit of the Japanese military. Singled out for especially severe treatment was the region's Chinese population. The so-called 'purification' of Singapore involved the massacre by the Japanese of between 50,000 and 100,000 Chinese. It is not surprising, therefore, that some of the most sustained resistance to the Japanese occupiers would come from the Chinese community.[48]

Ironically, this nadir in imperial fortunes also signalled the beginning of sustained attempts to resurrect a metropolitan sense of the Empire's purpose. Awareness that Malaya's civilian population had initially offered relatively little resistance to the invasion suggested that pre-war colonial propaganda had failed to inculcate much identification with British aims: new messages were required, stressing the 'partnership' between Britain and its colonial subjects. The Japanese occupation of Malaya involved important changes for the territory which Britain would find it difficult to undo: there was no question that recovery of the South East Asian territories was a priority for Churchill's wartime government, but this called for both a major military campaign and a revision of pre-war colonial assumptions.

The interruption of European rule by fellow Asians inevitably stimulated nationalist aspirations in the region. Japan's emphasis on the creation of a 'Greater East Asian Co-Prosperity Sphere', excluding European influence, was at least partially successful in disguising the expansionism of General Tojo's regime. With British colonial rule swept away under Japanese occupation, the local political implications were complex. Opportunities arose for collaboration, seen in Japan's installation of a puppet dictator in Burma, Ba Maw. In Malaya, the local sultans generally retained their positions and Malay administrators kept their posts. Meanwhile, only the largely Chinese communists under Chin Peng mounted meaningful resistance. Paradoxically, the British found themselves supporting anti-colonial groups because these offered the most effective resistance. For example, Britain's Special Operations Executive trained Malayan Chinese communists in sabotage against the Japanese, but these skills would prove equally effective against the British after 1948 during the communist insurgency. Shifting wartime alignments could also generate ideological confusion: South East Asian communists sometimes proved immune to Comintern blandishments about the need to cooperate with European imperialists in their struggle with 'fascists'. Occasionally, occupation provided scope for alternating strategies of resistance and collaboration, exemplified by Aung San in Burma. Economically, Malaya suffered from the disruption of traditional trade networks, though physical damage arose chiefly because of the 'scorched earth' policy adopted by the retreating British following the Japanese invasion.[49]

India and the challenge of nationalism

During 1917 the Montagu Declaration had set out the goal of responsible government for India within the British Empire in order to maintain Indian loyalty to the war effort and to pre-empt the growth of hostile nationalism at a time when British military resources were preoccupied. The 1919 Government of India Act introduced the principle of 'dyarchy'. Indians acquired a considerable role in provincial government, leaving Britain responsible for central administration, especially for those areas such as security and finance, which underpinned the Raj. Central to these reforms was the British belief that local, Indian affairs could safely be separated from larger, imperial issues, and that dyarchy would largely satisfy Indian political ambitions, enabling Britain to concentrate on those matters which emphasized India's value to the imperial system.[50] Introduced at a time when nationalist sentiment was intensifying, stoked by episodes of repression, particularly the Amritsar Massacre of April 1919, this constitutional reform was partly an attempt to conciliate Indian opinion, as it became clearer that continued reliance on force to maintain colonial rule in India was untenable.[51]

The 1919 reforms had important consequences for the character of Indian politics. An ever-widening range of groups quickly grasped that participation in the new political structures created at provincial level would advance their broader interests. The first tentative steps towards creating a democratic system were, arguably, being taken, with approximately one tenth of the adult male population being enfranchised. Winning elections became a major concern for the enfranchised elite, and this, in turn, impacted on the nature of Indian political organizations. Most impressive of all was the reorganization after 1920 of Congress as a genuinely nationwide, mass-based party, with a structure mirroring that of the Raj at provincial, district, and village levels.[52] Under Gandhi's influence, Indian nationalism acquired a moral ascendancy over the Raj that perplexed the British, now firmly cast in the role of oppressors without legitimacy. By renouncing violence, at least in theory, and by deploying weapons such as strikes, demonstrations, and commercial boycotts, Congress won international sympathy.[53]

Yet these tactics also fostered tensions between Congress and its anti-colonial supporters on the British left, reducing the prospects for concerted action by the two groups, an outcome which both the British government and its representatives in India dreaded. Earlier in Congress's history, its British supporters enjoyed cordial relations with the movement, but, on the British side, this reflected a paternalistic view wedded to racist assumptions. Given its own history, the mainstream British Labour movement, thoroughly committed to the parliamentary road to change, was inclined to see its development as a model which Congress should imitate. Provided that Congress kept to the path of legalism and moderation, it was acceptable, but when, under Gandhi, it began to adopt extra-parliamentary and indigenous political tactics and non-violent direct action, a gulf opened between Congress and its British friends. The two sides, it seemed, had never entirely understood one another.[54] When Gandhi visited Britain in 1931, partly to examine the impact of the Indian nationalist boycott of British goods, he bemused some metropolitan supporters of self-rule, partly because of his unfamiliar, morally inflected rhetoric and religious references.[55] It took a follow-up visit in 1935 by Gandhi's more urbane and emollient lieutenant, Nehru, speaking the language of development and reform, to reassure progressive British opinion. By the late 1930s, the metropolitan campaign for Indian independence was enjoying renewed vigour.[56]

Although Indian nationalism endured its own interwar setbacks and crises, it obliged the British to revise their basic assumptions about India's future. Nevertheless, long-held prejudices about the essentially fractured nature of Indian society persisted, reinforcing a

British belief that Congress was an 'artificial', unrepresentative, entity, and that communal and status divisions precluded the development of an authentic nationalist movement.[57] Although keen to avoid politically controversial, and potentially expensive, confrontations with Indian nationalism, British governments were deeply reluctant to make political concessions under duress. Much to Britain's dismay, instead of encouraging the growth of a class of 'responsible' elected Indian politicians, dyarchy fostered greater interest among nationalists in exploiting the new electoral machinery. Meanwhile, in an attempt to pre-empt a potentially dangerous conflict with Congress, the Viceroy, Lord Irwin, declared in 1929 that Britain's aim for India was Dominion status. This announcement seemed to reflect a strengthening bipartisan consensus on India's future in Britain.[58]

Britain's last major initiative in Indian policy before the outbreak of war was the Government of India Act of 1935. Building on the Montagu-Chelmsford reforms, this extended 'dyarchy' to full provincial self-government.[59] In proposing a federal legislature which included not only greater communal representation but also representatives of the Indian princes, the British hoped to prevent Congress securing control of central government, while encouraging conservative-leaning groups as a corrective to what was seen as the radicalism of Congress.[60] Although it is possible to interpret the 1935 Act as part of a long-term process of British disengagement, it can also be seen as an attempt to reassert British interests by reinforcing India's role within the imperial system, especially in the diplomatic and military spheres. Consolidation, rather than retreat, seemed to be Britain's fundamental aim. If nationalism could be emasculated in this way, it seemed possible that India's dependence on Britain for capital, security, and administrative expertise, along with the less easily defined bonds inevitably arising from nearly two centuries of interaction, would allow Britain at some stage in the future to guide India towards Dominion status without jeopardizing fundamental British interests. Meanwhile, the transfer of responsibility for many day-to-day issues to Indian politicians would, it was thought, free the Raj from nationalist criticism.[61]

Deeper structural changes in the Anglo-Indian relationship were also under way. The development of indigenous Indian industry created vigorous competition for British exporters, particularly of cotton textile goods, for which India had been the most important single market before 1914. The 1935 Act included various safeguards designed to protect British economic interests in India from possible discriminatory action by a future Congress-controlled central government.[62] Similarly, it became evident from the 1920s onwards that India could no longer provide Britain with a large and cheap army for deployment wherever imperial interests dictated. The 1930s saw the long-awaited modernization of the Indian army, but at British government expense in order to forestall nationalist objections to the cost. Nevertheless, during the 1930s, ultimate British control over the Government of India's financial policies ensured that the military and administrative expenses of the Government of India in Britain continued to be paid from Indian taxes, and that the Indian economy helped keep sterling stable and supported Britain's balance of payments.[63] A central aim of future British planning for India would be to ensure that even if India's constitutional status changed, as many of the benefits of imperial rule (to Britain) as possible would be protected. This, perhaps, explains Britain's vigorous attitude towards Indian nationalism on the eve of the Second World War.[64]

Although the federal system envisaged in 1935 was not implemented, provincial autonomy did proceed.[65] The elections of 1937 initially gave Congress control of seven provinces. The

Muslim League only won a quarter of the seats allocated to Muslims, although experience of life under Congress provincial ministries helped crystallize Muslim fears about a Hindu-dominated central government.[66] Here, as in so many fields, it would be the Second World War that created opportunities for decisive change.

The onset of war led London into a crucial error of judgement that had lasting significance. Without any prior consultation, Indians were simply informed by the reactionary Viceroy, Lord Linlithgow, in September 1939 that they were at war. Struck by this proof that, for all the pre-war suggestions of near-Dominion status, India was still seen by Britain to be firmly within the dependent empire, Congress demanded a role in central government. When this was refused, the Congress provincial ministries resigned in protest. While effective power therefore reverted to British administrators, perhaps convenient in wartime, lasting mistrust was sown between them and Indian nationalists.

Partly to appease Washington (increasingly sympathetic to Indian ambitions), to guarantee India's uninterrupted contribution to the war effort, and also to mollify Labour members of the War Coalition, Churchill decided in March 1942 to send Sir Stafford Cripps, a senior figure in the British government (and a possible rival to Churchill) on a mission to India to negotiate a way through the political impasse in relations with nationalist leaders.[67] The 'Cripps Mission' could only repeat proposals already made in 1940, to offer India full Dominion status after the war (or the option to secede from the Empire-Commonwealth), in return for wartime Indian cooperation and the suspension of further political advance for the duration of the war. An important caveat to the offer was the stipulation that no part of India could be forced to accept membership of the post-war state, whatever form this might take.[68] The Cripps initiative had several consequences. It won admiration in the United States, where the complexities of the subcontinent's political situation became better understood. But Congress was unimpressed and held out for immediate inclusion in India's central government. When this was not forthcoming, Gandhi launched the nationwide 'Quit India' campaign. This triggered a tough British response: some 2,500 Indians were shot and many thousands were detained. In political terms, the campaign led to a ban on Congress and a permanent souring of relations between its leaders and the British. Seen in this light, 'Quit India' backfired: the absence of figures such as Gandhi and Nehru until their release in the spring of 1945 left a dangerous political vacuum, creating opportunities for groups willing to collaborate with the Raj.[69]

Of these, the most important was the Muslim League. Skilfully led by Mohammed Ali Jinnah, the League won British recognition of its claim to represent all India's Muslims, giving it a crucial position in India's wartime government and future.[70] Because of the all-important caveat to the Cripps Offer, the Muslim League had been awarded an effective veto on the precise form a self-governing India would take. The League was committed to achieving 'Pakistan', a separate homeland for India's Muslims. Jinnah's key achievement was to redefine what had been an internal, 'communal' problem as an international one. Exploiting the wartime shift in international sympathies, he argued that India's Muslims constituted a nation in their own right entitled to self-determination, and meanwhile to equal representation in India's government.[71] The specific character of a future Pakistan remained unclear, even to its chief advocate, Jinnah. It might, for instance, take the form of a Muslim homeland within a loose federal structure. Nevertheless, the idea's appeal to India's Muslims grew rapidly, providing the League with a powerful political weapon in its dealings with the British.[72]

There were practical reasons for Britain to court the League during the war, as around half of the Indian Army was Muslim. However, the apparently privileged position that this gave Muslims encouraged nationalist claims that Britain was cynically following a 'divide and rule' strategy, with fateful consequences for India's post-war integrity. The heightened Asian consciousness inspired by Japan's military successes also created new opportunities for those in India who opposed British rule. For the greater part, this took the form of support for Congress, but a small minority opted for the Japanese-contrived Indian National Army (INA) led by renegade Congress leader Subhas Chandra Bose. The INA had some 11,000 members by 1943, with a further 20,000 in training. Militarily insignificant, its importance lay in demonstrating that Indian loyalty to the Allied war effort could not be taken for granted.[73]

By the end of the war, around two and a quarter million men were serving in the Indian armed forces, and the subcontinent had developed into an enormous supply base for Allied operations in Asia and the Middle East. The demands of recruitment and supplying the armed forces, along with general economic mobilization, prompted unprecedented intervention in everyday life by the British authorities.[74] Until 1943, when rationing and price control schemes were imposed, ordinary consumer goods prices rose sharply. The subcontinent experienced particularly serious food shortages, aggravated by hoarding and distribution difficulties. This led to one of the war's most appalling civilian catastrophes, the Bengal famine of 1943, in which an estimated three million Indians died. The loss of Burma (the source of around 15 per cent of Bengal's rice imports), cyclones, flooding, and transport shortages, aggravated by the British 'scorched earth' policy, designed to deny boats to the advancing Japanese, all helped to accentuate a deepening crisis. Despite warnings from British officials since early 1942, the government in London was unwilling to meet Viceroy Wavell's pleas for help by diverting shipping from the immediate war effort to send food aid to Bengal. This may have reflected resentment in London towards 'disloyal' Indians. Certainly, the disaster exposed the sham of British claims to be administering India efficiently; arguably, the British authorities' reputation never recovered.[75] Overall, the effect of the war was to upset the precarious pre-war stability on which British policy and planning for India had been based. Crucially, Britain lost control over the timing of India's independence. By 1945, the question facing London was no longer *whether*, but *when* India would achieve Dominion status. The full implications of this would provide the post war British Labour government with one of its most urgent problems.[76]

The Middle East

Britain's expanded Middle East empire after 1918 also brought with it onerous and unforeseen burdens. The mandates distributed by the League of Nations, against the wishes of the Arab populations affected, reawakened the nineteenth-century British vision of a continuous swathe of Empire stretching from Suez to Singapore, yet policymakers were preoccupied by questions of cost, the security of imperial communications and oil supplies.[77] Immediately after the war, they tended to assume that challenges to regional security could best be contained through military force ('War Imperialism'). This view, however, was based on the mistaken assumption that wartime patterns of imperial cooperation would continue, and that defending the newly enlarged Empire would be a shared imperial enterprise. In the view of the post-war Foreign

Secretary, Lord Curzon, since territory in the Middle East had been acquired above all to strengthen India's defences, therefore logically the Government of India should contribute financially to its upkeep.[78] However, this argument was difficult to maintain while Britain was attempting to conciliate moderate nationalist opinion in India by unveiling limited constitutional reform. The Dominions were even less enthusiastic than the Government of India about contributing more to imperial defence, and the British public, wearied by total war, seemed equally reluctant to continue supporting artificially inflated defence budgets.[79] The dangers inherent in trying to impose the kind of highly centralized administration the British had developed in India were made abundantly clear by the Kurdish and Shi'ite rebellions that gripped northern and southern Iraq in 1919–21.[80] These were eventually brought under control, but they highlighted the fallacy of 'War Imperialism'.

A more sensible course seemed to be reversion to earlier, indirect styles of imperial control, predicated on alliances with local rulers, which reduced British administrative costs to a minimum. This led to deals with the Hashemite princes Feisal and Abdullah, and their installation as the rulers of Iraq and Transjordan respectively. Palestine, prized by Britain as a protective buffer for the Suez Canal Zone, in addition to being a key element in the overland route to India, was an important exception to the new trend towards indirect control. Commitments made in the Balfour Declaration (1917), promising British support for the Zionist goal of a Jewish National Home, precluded government through an Arab ruler, and a 'colonial' style administration was created, answerable to the Colonial Office in London. This more conventional form of direct administration was soon tested as Jewish immigration increased and communal tensions escalated.[81] Nevertheless, during the 1920s, in its extensive new sphere of 'informal' empire, Britain was broadly successful in finding local rulers enthusiastic to collaborate, ranging from the monarchies of Egypt and Iraq to the tribal leaders of the Arabian Peninsula. Ruling 'indirectly' through them, Britain was able to run its Middle Eastern empire relatively economically.[82] Moreover, an important contrast emerged between British and French styles of mandatory rule in the Middle East: whereas in Syria, French officials ran all government departments, in British-controlled Iraq, for example, Iraqi ministers were notionally in charge of their departments.[83]

In 1930, Britain conceded that Iraq would become 'independent' in 1932. This enabled Britain to reduce its military presence in the country in exchange for an alliance and a new military base. London had no intention of allowing Iraq's changed status to have any substantive effect on British interests and it was expected that considerable informal influence over the country would remain. Effective power lay in the hands of a small group of 'notables', with Britain itself retaining the dominant role, even after Iraq achieved nominal independence in 1932.[84] In the short term, such arrangements suited British needs, but the elites through whom Britain operated would inevitably become increasingly detached from the mass of the population, and from the mood of nationalism developing across the Middle East between the wars. British policymakers also had to be aware of the growth of Pan-Islamic ideas in the region in this period. Their response was to demonstrate a moderate sympathy for Arab nationalism, on the assumption that it need not necessarily conflict with wider imperial interests.[85]

The core of Britain's Middle Eastern empire was Egypt, whose Suez Canal was vital to British trade. Moreover, British policymakers believed that control of the region between the Nile and the Persian Gulf ensured the security of the western approaches to India. British power in Egypt derived from military occupation, and from the presence of British personnel in the civil service, army, and police. In April 1919, however, local resentment at increased wartime British interference, together with fears that Egypt might be subjected to full colonial rule, sparked an uprising in Cairo, suppression of which intensified nationalist feeling, symbolized by the growth of the mass Wafd movement. The veteran empire builder Lord Milner, sent to Egypt to investigate, recommended measures to reconcile British interests with Egyptian nationalism.[86] In 1922, under the 'Allenby Declaration', Egypt became technically independent, but this was diluted by the so-called 'reserved points', issues which Britain insisted were non-negotiable. Among these were foreign policy, defence, and control of the Suez area.[87] However, the Wafd, a democratic party enjoying broadly based support, sought complete independence. Eventually holding the majority of seats in parliament, it formed Egypt's government, and represented a clear threat to British interests. Among the issues which strained relations between Britain and the Egyptian nationalists was the question of the Sudan's future. After the First World War, Egyptian politicians stepped up their demands for the incorporation of the Sudan into Egypt, which Britain opposed. Anti-British violence among Egyptian units based in the Sudan escalated, and in 1924, Sir Lee Stack, commander of the Egyptian Army and governor general of Sudan, was assassinated in Cairo.[88] This provided Allenby with the pretext to destroy the Wafd: he insisted that Egypt pay an indemnity and withdraw its troops from the Sudan, triggering the Egyptian Prime Minister's resignation.

During the interwar years, the character of Egyptian nationalism underwent some important shifts, which would have major long-term consequences. During the 1920s, Egyptian nationalism had a 'western' style, based on the earlier European model of nationalism, emphasizing Egypt's unique and long history. It typically stressed Egypt as an entity distinct from the wider Arab world, even involving a certain hostility towards Egypt's Arab neighbours. To some extent, this reflected the Arab role in the British-inspired revolt against Ottoman rule during the First World War. Increasingly, however, Egyptian nationalism took on a broader, less exclusive form, seeing Egypt as part of a larger Arab, Muslim and anti-colonial community. As in other parts of the world, political attitudes during the 1930s reflected the impact of the Depression. Egypt did not escape the declining living standards often characteristic of these years. These coincided with urbanization and the spread of education among the middle classes. The resulting strains on the young parliamentary system, and the political repression which followed, undermined the pro-Western elites and stimulated the growth of radical political movements, such as the nationalist Muslim Brotherhood, which emphasized Islam as the most important determinant of Egypt's identity. Yet another strand of nationalism was chauvinistic, even militaristic, with an expansionist view of Egypt's regional role. This would subsequently feed into the country's wider ambitions, especially in the 1950s and 1960s under the regime of Gamal Abdel Nasser.[89]

By the mid-1930s, the threat from Italy in both Libya and East Africa led to the Anglo-Egyptian Treaty of 1936, which tied Egypt into Britain's regional security system through an alliance. In return for withdrawing its political 'advisers', replacing its High Commissioner with an ambassador and promising to withdraw its armed forces from Cairo and Alexandria once new facilities in the enormous Canal Zone were ready, Britain secured a twenty-year military pact with the Egyptian government.[90]

The deteriorating international climate of the later 1930s had major implications for Britain's position in the Middle East. So, too, did increasing Jewish immigration into

Palestine, which aggravated already tense Anglo-Jewish relations in the mandate.[91] The British had sought to maintain an uneasy balance by fostering distinct communal authorities in Palestine, the Jewish Agency and the Supreme Muslim Council. These arrangements could not survive the strains imposed by a twelve-fold increase in Jewish immigration as Nazi persecution in Germany intensified. Growing Arab frustration with British rule led to increasing political radicalization, erupting in 1936 into open rebellion. A national strike was organized, aimed at stemming the flow of Jewish immigration, ending the sale of land to Jews and the creation of an Arab national government. This not only paralysed the Arab economy, but degenerated into violence, especially attacks on 'collaborators', in which some 5,000 Arabs died and around 5,600 were imprisoned. The British security clampdown also involved the suspension of the Arab Higher Committee, a loose coalition of political parties, and the deportation of many Arab leaders, including the Mufti of Jerusalem, who had been a leading advocate of political violence.[92] Because Palestine ranked second in importance only to Egypt in British calculations, the Arab Rising, which continued until 1939, was profoundly dangerous to Britain's wider regional interests.[93] At its height, the revolt tied down eighteen British battalions and threatened to increase hostility to British imperialism throughout the Muslim world. One consequence of this episode was that neighbouring Arab states increasingly saw themselves as the champions of Palestine's Arabs. As the Second World War loomed, this 'pan-Arab' dimension could not be ignored by Britain. London responded to the Arab rebellion by limiting Jewish immigration and appointing a Royal Commission. However, plans for partition into autonomous Arab and Jewish regions were quickly eclipsed by Britain's 1939 White Paper on Palestine, which unashamedly courted the Arab majority by explicitly rejecting a Jewish state in Palestine.

The Second World War underlined both the Suez Canal's vital importance to imperial communications and the crucial contribution of Middle Eastern oil supplies. These two factors explain Britain's uncompromising attitude to political developments in the region, and its willingness to coerce Arab populations when challenged.[94] However, crude force, even in wartime, offered no secure basis for projecting British influence, and strong-arm tactics were still tempered with conciliation. For example, Foreign Secretary Sir Anthony Eden tried to soothe Arab sentiment in 1941 by promising Britain's 'full support for any scheme of Arab unity which commands general approval', though in practice little support was forthcoming.[95] By 1943, following the decisive second battle of El Alamein, Britain's position seemed more secure, and the Middle East stabilized as a supply zone for other theatres in the war. Although by the end of the war, Britain's dominance in the Middle East appeared impressive, especially in its possession of a greatly expanded informal empire, this was threatened both by the impact of the war itself, and by Britain's own wartime actions. Intervention by the British authorities had generated local friction whose effects would become manifest after the war. At an international level, Britain's position was complicated by the growing interest being shown in the Middle East by the United States and the Soviet Union. The former assiduously cultivated its influence in oil-rich Saudi Arabia, while the latter, with a foothold in Iran already established, hoped to extend its influence into Turkey, and even to secure trusteeship over Italy's ex-colony, Libya, which had been under British military rule since 1943.[96]

The continuing importance of the Middle East to Britain was confirmed in a series of government discussions during the last phase of the war. One viewpoint, championed by Eden, held that Britain's strategic and political interests dictated that it must remain the predominant power in the region, and that it should become permanently responsible for defending the Suez Canal. In the event, the War Coalition took no firm decisions on Britain's presence in the region, bequeathing this problem to Attlee's incoming Labour government.[97]

The Colonial Empire: 'Trusteeship' and 'development'

During the 1920s, a British colonial 'policy' barely existed: moreover, London seemed in no hurry to formulate one.[98] The fundamental assumption shaping British policymakers' attitudes was that the evolution of colonial rule would be measured and controlled, principally because in most colonies, unlike India, there was no force of nationalism yet offering a serious challenge to British rule. In British Africa, this certainly appeared to be the case. Although policymakers were increasingly preoccupied by the problems posed by settler communities in East and Central Africa, an embryonic discussion on African political development was already beginning.

In contrast to the pre-1914 period, when British rule was in many cases largely notional, the interwar period saw a greater degree of effective colonial control. In theory, each British colony remained a distinct constitutional and financial entity. Although the colonial state's activities were inevitably circumscribed by a lack of finance and personnel between the wars, local populations increasingly felt its presence. Tax-collecting and maintaining 'law and order' constituted the bulk of most administrators' work. According to the concept of the 'dual mandate', Britain, like the other colonial powers, had two major responsibilities arising from colonial rule. First, it had an obligation to protect the interests of the colonial populations; secondly, it had a duty to the rest of the world to ensure that colonial economic resources were exploited for the world's benefit.[99] But at odds with the comfortable vision of colonial rule encouraged by trusteeship rhetoric was evidence between the wars of mounting dissatisfaction among colonial populations. Often this related to specific issues, such as industrial relations on the Northern Rhodesian Copperbelt, or the marketing of cocoa in West Africa. Cumulatively, it pointed to Africans' mounting capacity and greater propensity to act collectively in defence of their interests.[100]

Before the Second World War, there was a growing recognition among colonial administrators that many of the problems confronting particular colonies were broadly similar and might be tackled in a coordinated way. One practical outcome of this was the creation of 'subject' departments within the Colonial Office, handling broad themes such as economic policy, and the appointment of specialist advisers on problems such as education, labour, and health. One of the central concepts of interwar British colonial government, as it affected Africa, was 'Indirect Rule'.[101] This was based on the idea of administering colonial populations through indigenous agencies ('chiefs' and 'Native Authorities'), enjoying legal and financial power. Not only did this obviate large, costly complements of expatriate administrators (fewer than 8,000 officials staffed the mainstream apparatus of British colonial Africa in the late 1930s), it also had a respectable imperial ancestry, having been employed in the Indian 'princely' states and elsewhere.[102] This approach reflected a belief, reinforced by much contemporary anthropological opinion, in Britain's self-appointed role as the 'trustee' of the 'less developed' peoples until they achieved a 'higher' stage of development. At a time when most African populations were still seen as being 'primitive', caution appeared far preferable to an artificial acceleration of social and political development.[103] One practical reflection of racial assumptions between the wars was the absence of Africans in senior posts in colonial civil services.[104] A fundamental assumption in the system of Indirect Rule, not always justified, was that traditional 'chiefs' existed through whom the British could rule. This view tended to ignore the tradition of collective leadership characteristic of some African societies, and risked handing to collaborating chiefs an undue degree of authority, enabling them to consolidate, and sometimes abuse, their political power.[105] For much of the 1920s, when financial conditions dictated conservatism in colonial policy, buttressing the authority of traditional local elites seemed both expedient and sensible. It did, however, make even more unlikely the notion of introducing far-reaching social and economic reforms despite growing evidence that such changes were needed.[106]

The weaknesses of Indirect Rule were underlined in the landmark *African Survey*, published by the experienced Indian administrator, Lord Hailey, in 1938. He argued that the static conception of administration conflicted with a growing recognition of the need to improve colonial living standards by promoting welfare services and economic development. Conservative-inclined Native Authorities could hardly be expected to implement the kind of interventionist policies increasingly judged necessary to the survival of colonial rule. Nor did such sedate bodies offer many openings for the growing number of Western-educated Africans. Hailey identified the need to give this group a greater role in the technical branches of colonial government. More fundamental still was the question of how Indirect Rule could be reconciled with the development of parliamentary institutions. Hailey, while stressing the importance of this issue, could offer no clear solutions.[107]

In the interwar period, London assumed an increasing responsibility for colonial economic development. An important justification for such measures was the colonies' potential value in creating or preserving jobs within Depression-stricken Britain itself.[108] Severe unrest in Jamaica and Trinidad from 1935 to 1938, triggered by the collapse of the sugar industry and strikes in Trinidad's oil industry, made the need for colonial development appear more urgent. For the Colonial Office, these episodes underlined the need to redefine development priorities, placing the colonies' welfare needs above short-term British economic interest. As war approached, it also seemed vital to introduce reform in the West Indies in order to disarm American anti-colonial sentiment.[109] Official discussions on colonial welfare inevitably raised more fundamental questions about the wider purpose of colonial rule, exposing the philosophy of 'trusteeship' to more searching scrutiny. One victim of the new direction taken by official discussions was the cosy assumption, reinforced by the impact of the Depression, that in times of difficulty, the burden of embarrassing problems such as colonial unemployment could be transferred to the rural heartlands and kept away from the more politically and socially volatile cities.[110] Already shown to be a fiction, this presumption would collapse entirely once wartime mobilization transformed social conditions in many colonies, bringing with it a dramatic surge in urban growth.

Despite the financial problems obstructing a greater metropolitan commitment to raised colonial living standards, by the end of the interwar period, the Colonial Office had become convinced of the need to present the colonial Empire in favourable terms to opinion both in Britain and abroad. Partly responding to growing international interest in colonial affairs, officials recognized that policy had to be depicted as being energetic and purposeful, with

London and the colonial governments collaborating productively in the interests of local populations' welfare.[111] As in other areas of policy, war would test this new commitment.

Wartime change and post-war planning

As they had done in the First World War, the components of the Empire made a very significant contribution to Britain's overall war effort. The Dominions, for example, were important providers of manpower as well as money and raw materials. Only Ireland remained technically neutral, but large numbers of Irish men nevertheless served in the British armed forces.[112] Especially important to Britain was the fact that the Dominions agreed at the start of the war that they would meet the costs of deploying their own forces. They also asserted greater independence during the war, and became more ambitious in developing diplomatic ties to suit their own needs. The most dramatic expression of this shifting relationship was the Dominions' response to the series of military reversals suffered by Britain between 1940 and 1942, and their attempts to develop new ties with the United States, amounting to a 'strategic revolution' that Britain could not reverse after the war.[113] The fall of France, similarly, revealed the fragility of Britain's pre-war defence pledges to Australia and New Zealand, specifically the promise that any Japanese aggression would be met with the despatch of naval contingents to the Far East. Once the full implications of Britain's Far Eastern disaster became clear by February 1942, Australia understandably felt abandoned, its confidence in British protection shattered. The relationship between Britain and Australia never entirely recovered from this episode, which resulted in much closer defence links between Australia, New Zealand, and the United States after the war, culminating in the ANZUS Pact of 1951.

Britain's relations with South Africa were a source of increasing concern to London during the war. The traditions of anti-British sentiment among the Afrikaner community resurfaced and the continuation of imperial bonds seemed to hinge on the fate of the pro-imperial Prime Minister, General Jan Smuts. Yet South Africa also seemed determined to expand its own influence in Africa, bringing it potentially into conflict with British interests. For example, in 1943 the Southern Rhodesian parliament voted for cooperation with South Africa in arranging a pan-African conference to map out the coordinated development of central-southern Africa. A further British concern was that South African anti-imperial attitudes might migrate northwards, infecting white settler communities in East and Central Africa.[114]

On a wider perspective, one of Britain's most difficult problems during the war was the fact that its key ally, the United States, had a long anti-colonial tradition, and there was a strong American aversion to help Britain prop up its Empire. Ideological distaste was reinforced by a practical desire to prize open the lucrative markets currently shielded by Imperial Preference, creating opportunities for US exporters. In August 1941, even before the United States entered the war, President Roosevelt had persuaded Churchill to endorse the 'Atlantic Charter', apparently committing Britain to accept the right of all peoples to choose how they were governed. The Americans also showed a sustained interest in bringing all the European colonial empires under some form of international control, something which Britain naturally sought to resist. The collapse of British rule in South East Asia, and continuing problems in India, helped strengthen US hostility to British colonialism. Dependent on its ally's aid, Britain could not refuse to discuss the future of the colonial Empire, though it stalled at every opportunity.[115]

Prolonged attempts failed to produce a satisfactory joint Anglo-American statement on colonial issues, but this cleared the path for the Colonial Office to clarify its own thoughts and promote a unilateral declaration on British policy. After late 1942, with the prospect of eventual victory now more realistic, officials propounded a modernized, progressive approach to colonial rule, characterized by a distinctive sense of long-term mission. By mid-1943, the momentum and direction first achieved by the Colonial Office before the war was recovered, leading to the most important wartime statement of British colonial policy, delivered in the Commons by Colonial Secretary Oliver Stanley in July 1943, which was in effect a declaration of Britain's independence from Washington in the formulation of colonial policy.[116] The novelty of Stanley's proposals lay in their gathering together in a forceful and confident declaration of Britain's long-term intentions. What had previously been implicit or neglected in colonial policy now appeared to coalesce in a coherent agenda for liberal imperialism. Britain's stated aim was to guide the colonial territories towards 'self-government within the framework of the British Empire'. No timetables for colonial political advance were offered but particular emphasis was placed on the need for adequate economic and social development to create the foundations for constitutional progress.[117] The unspoken assumption was that this preparatory process would take place over decades, if not longer.[118]

A further important characteristic of British colonial policy by 1943 was that it seemed to reflect a broad consensus between the two major parties, a feature that served to smooth the transition between the War Coalition and Attlee's government in 1945. Armed with its declaration of policy aims, the Colonial Office could embark on planning the colonies' post-war reconstruction.[119] One obvious priority was the acceleration of colonial development in its widest sense: only substantial economic growth in the colonies could provide secure foundations for the spectrum of social improvements, and ultimately political progress, to which London was now committed.[120] The Colonial Office also oversaw a fundamental reappraisal of Colonial Service organization and training. Few officials in London pretended that the machinery established in 1940 to promote colonial development was really adequate: the dismal experience of colonial governments' preliminary attempts at 'planning' had only reinforced this view. This strengthened a growing tendency for the initiative in colonial policy formation to be assumed by the Colonial Office, introducing a degree of centralization and control from London quite alien to the relatively relaxed interwar pattern of devolved colonial administration. One consequence of wartime discussions was to raise expectations in the colonies that the cessation of hostilities would soon be followed by improved living standards, but it remained to be seen at the end of the war whether Britain would be in any position to implement its ambitious development policy, or whether wartime commitments had been rhetorical, delivered primarily for propaganda and diplomatic reasons.

Apart from Jamaica, which became internally self-governing in 1944, and adjustments to the constitutions of the Gold Coast, Nigeria, and British Guiana, little actual constitutional reform took place in the colonial Empire during the war.[121] Political development was effectively suspended, and in some colonies, for example in Kenya, the authorities clamped down on local political organizations and detained potentially troublesome activists. Crucially, wartime discussions on political development took place with little overt guidance from ministers, or an informed sense of the aspirations of colonial populations. Inevitably, given the sheer diversity of the dependent empire, there could be no single, comprehensive plan. India's future had arguably been mapped out before the war, but some lessons were learnt and the Colonial Office was keen that 'errors' made in India should not be repeated in the colonies: specifically, hasty concessions should not be made to vocal, but possibly unrepresentative and even irresponsible intellectual elites, and in Africa, for example, greater care would be needed to forge more durable alliances with traditional elites.

One colony where wartime developments proved crucial, and which in some ways resembled India, was Ceylon. By the outbreak of war, there was general agreement within the British government on Ceylon's future trajectory. In 1939, the colony was awarded a quasi-cabinet system of government, and it seemed that continuing progress towards full cabinet government would arise from the cooperative partnership between local ministers, representing the Sinhalese majority, and British officials. With the outbreak of war, however, the Colonial Office placed a moratorium on further change, but officials chose not to inform their Sri Lankan collaborators until August 1941. Meanwhile, in marked contrast to India's nationalists, local politicians cooperated in the war effort, and Ceylon became the source of two-thirds of the Allies' rubber after the loss of Malaya.[122]

Although often regarded as a 'model colony', Ceylon experienced a vigorous and at times bitter anti-colonial campaign producing demands in 1942 for independence by the Sinhalese political leader, D. S. Senanayake. Associated with this heightened politicization was growing tension between the Sinhalese majority and the Tamil minority, which raised the question whether wartime loyalty would lead to political concessions from Britain.[123] In 1943, Senanayake's persistence resulted in a British commitment to full responsible self-government, and in 1944 the Soulbury Commission was appointed to advise on Ceylon's future. Its report, published in 1945 as the war drew to a close, provided the framework for the colony's independence in 1948.

In Africa, official thinking on future political development entered a new phase, in which the fundamentals of policy were examined in an increasingly systematic manner. At the start of the war, the reforming Colonial Secretary, Malcolm MacDonald, recognized that the war might awaken African political aspirations, and he believed that Britain needed to clarify the purposes of colonial policy, and their likely result. In particular, he raised the most difficult question – what would be the outcome of Indirect Rule? How could reliance on the native administrations, for example in West Africa, be reconciled with the development, however gradual, of genuinely representative legislatures? What were Britain's long-term intentions in African territories with mixed ethnic populations, such as Kenya, and what would the implications be for closer association of the territories in East and Central Africa? As the war progressed, these questions arose in relation to an overarching problem: how could nascent nationalism be co-opted and persuaded to collaborate in the work of reform now planned by the Colonial Office? Once again, Lord Hailey was sent to Africa, to undertake a comprehensive review of the political situation.[124]

Hailey's report became a key text in British official thinking on Africa. He concluded that British policy could not continue along its pre-war lines and even though he did not yet detect any significant force of nationalism, he believed that economic and social development would enlarge the number of Western-educated Africans with political aspirations for whom a 'safe' outlet must be found. A fundamental problem was that as the development initiative gathered pace, colonial governments would become more interventionist, making them the focal point of local grievances, which might undermine the colonial state. Asking the awkward question how far Britain could assume colonial acceptance of its rule, Hailey emphasized the importance of being able to argue (especially to Washington) that the logical outcome of London's policy was eventual colonial self-government. One of Hailey's most important conclusions was that the existing native authorities of rural Africa could not deliver political advance, and that the participation of more educated Africans was needed, both in regional councils and in the administration.[125]

During the war, there was also a parallel attempt to identify potential sources of political opposition in Africa, and to create a new set of workable alliances with likely future leaders of African nationalism. In May 1943, for example, Stanley invited the African editors of leading West African newspapers to Britain, a strategy that has been described as 'managing nationalism'. Among these was the Nigerian, Nnamdi Azikiwe, who submitted a plan ('The Atlantic Charter and British West Africa') that showed that the thinking of West African nationalists was not significantly different to that of the Colonial Office. In other parts of British Africa, especially where there were sizeable white settler populations, there seemed little scope for constitutional speculation on the West African model. Britain's wartime dependence on the commodities produced in East and Central Africa, especially after the loss of South East Asia, had not only enabled the settlers to entrench themselves among the colonial state's levers of power and attempt to seek compensation for their pre-war economic difficulties, but had also highlighted the gulf between settler aspirations for self-government and territorial amalgamation, and long-standing metropolitan pledges to protect the interests of the African majority.[126]

To forestall this, the Colonial Office produced tentative proposals for a federal structure for East Africa, composed of five provinces, one of which, the White Highlands of Kenya, would become a largely autonomous settler enclave.[127] Harold Macmillan, then Parliamentary Under-Secretary at the Colonial Office, rejected this scheme and, in suggestions that reinforced his reputation as an unorthodox Tory, called for the large-scale nationalization of land in Kenya and its dedication to African collective farming. Only after the appointment of Sir Philip Mitchell as governor of Kenya at the end of 1944 was a way found out of this impasse. An East African High Commission was unveiled in 1945, designed to foster closer *economic* but not *political* links through the development of common services, but this did not eradicate concern in London about settler ambitions for the region.

Meanwhile, in Central Africa, the Bledisloe Commission had recommended in 1939 that Britain should work towards the long-term goal of drawing Northern and Southern Rhodesia, and their impoverished neighbour Nyasaland, closer together, with the proviso that African interests must be safeguarded. The Commission provided no concrete plans, partly because of the variety of 'native' policies currently in operation. This did not deter Central Africa's settlers, especially those in Southern Rhodesia, who, under the leadership of their premier, Sir Godfey Huggins, dreamed of creating a new dominion under effective Rhodesian control.[128] The settlers' long-standing desire for full amalgamation of the three territories evoked some sympathy from members of the War Coalition, but the Colonial Office sought to devise arrangements that would protect the Africans of the two northern territories, while securing a better deal for those in the 'self-governing colony', Southern Rhodesia. In doing so, it hoped to pre-empt domestic and international criticism of British colonial rule and to neutralize the threat of South African northward expansion. British officials doubted whether the 85,000 settlers had the capacity to administer a new state containing a majority of five million Africans. If trouble erupted, direct British intervention might drive the settlers into South Africa's orbit.[129]

The question of integrating colonial territories into larger, more viable groupings was relevant beyond Africa. In the West Indies, for example, the possibility of some sort of federation had been discussed fitfully for many years before being addressed squarely in the report of the Moyne Commission in 1940 in the context of promoting regional economic and social development. However, following a visit to the West Indies in 1942–3, the Permanent Under-Secretary at the Colonial Office, Sir Cosmo Parkinson, had concluded that outside Jamaica, where a new constitution had already been agreed, there was no great desire for such change. Instead, Parkinson advised that the views of the various colonial governors in the region should be sought on the question of federation.[130] London was aware of the need to tread carefully, as Washington took a particular interest in developments affecting what it saw as its own 'backyard' and it was questionable if the smaller islands could stand alone as self-governing states.[131] This problem would continue to exercise officials in London in the post-war period, merging with their wider ongoing discussions on the future of smaller colonial territories.

Given the depth of the humiliation experienced by Britain in South East Asia, it is hardly surprising that planning for this region's post-war future should have been a major preoccupation for London during the war. For Churchill, stung by American criticism of colonialism's record, recovering Britain's territories in the region was an absolute priority. To some extent, it was convenient that the US preoccupation with defeating Japan freed British Far Eastern forces to concentrate on this overriding strategic goal. The broad moral of the collapse of Malaya and Singapore was that there could be no return to the ramshackle political arrangements of the pre-war years. Officials already convinced of the need for reform used the disaster as an opportunity to propose ambitious new schemes, basing renewed British claims to colonial legitimacy on the complementary ideas of 'nation-building' and 'partnership', while the region's likely post-war strategic importance and economic value to Britain provided a convincing rationale for wholesale change.[132]

The Colonial Office and the War Office secretly conducted wartime planning for South East Asia on the grounds that the region would initially come under British military administration. The Colonial Office was keen to explore the benefits of closer territorial association, but its plans for South East Asia were particularly bold and ambitious. At the end of May 1944, the War Cabinet approved a plan for a new Malayan Union to incorporate the previously diverse collection of Malay states under varying degrees of British rule. The creation of a modern, centralized colonial state in Malaya had two major justifications. First, stemming from the lessons of 1942 was the hope that integration would produce a territory easier to defend and more amenable to rapid economic development, which would be very much in impoverished Britain's post-war interests. Secondly, planners sought to give all Malaya's ethnic communities a stake in a new multiracial system, and proposed to extend citizenship privileges to the territory's Chinese and Indian populations. This would not only create a state which could eventually become self-governing, perhaps as part of a larger South East Asian dominion, but it would also give the non-Malay population, especially Chinese entrepreneurs, a vested interest in cooperating in future economic development, and in participating fully in the life of the territory. Furthermore, this new Malayan Union would be under direct British control, Sarawak and North Borneo were also to be brought under Crown Colony government, and a governor general appointed to coordinate government policy throughout the region.[133] Singapore would remain a separate colonial territory.

What was supposed ultimately to be a step towards regional devolution therefore involved a striking interim reassertion of imperialism by Britain, representing a fundamental shift in relations between the British authorities and the traditionally privileged Malay elite. In effect, the Malayan Union scheme called for the renegotiation of existing treaties between Britain and the Malay rulers under which the latter would keep their social status but lose their sovereignty and be induced to share political power with their Indian and Chinese neighbours. Such a radical change would inevitably provoke Malay opposition, but Britain's enforced absence from the peninsula during the war precluded local consultation and the full assessment of grass-roots opinion. Of course, London's wartime inability to embark on any meaningful consultation with the Malay sultans strengthened the hand of officials eager to push through more radical alternatives, though it also meant that dangerous political sentiments would be unleashed after the war when the Union scheme was finally revealed.

A final theme to surface during the war embraced both political development and 'development' in its broader, contemporary sense. In the colonial context, the first indications of local political mobilization were often associated with the emergence of labour movements. Early in the war, the Colonial Office had grasped the potential challenge that colonial trade unions posed to phased reform. It therefore aimed to prevent these unions from becoming too radical. To do so, it enlisted the aid of the Trades Union Congress, which before long was sending out advisers, while colonial officials continued the work of gathering information on labour conditions in several regions.[134]

By the end of the war, London could look approvingly at an imperial system which was, apparently, not merely intact but had also survived the strains and rigours imposed by the conflict, and seemed to have acquired a new sense of purpose and direction. Much play had been made of the reformed style of colonial rule to which Britain seemed committed. Economic and social development would, it was thought, be the precursors to planned political development leading ultimately to self-government within the British Commonwealth. These commitments had been the necessary price of securing the full mobilization of imperial resources and of appeasing a sometimes troublesome American ally. Yet these commitments inevitably encouraged expectations in the colonial Empire that Britain was neither willing nor able to satisfy. Given Britain's own impoverished circumstances after 1945, there seemed little prospect of accomplishing the wide-ranging social and other reforms which were central to the outlook nurtured within the Colonial Office since the days of MacDonald. Moreover, the impact of the war itself had let loose uncontrollable pressure for change in both the 'Dependent Empire' and the 'informal' empire. Shifts had occurred which would prove irreversible. As one historian has commented: 'Paradoxically, the ultimate cost of defending the British Empire during the Second World War was the Empire itself.'[135]

CHAPTER 2
THE FIRST WAVE OF BRITISH DECOLONIZATION: COMMONWEALTH TERRITORIES, THE INDIAN SUBCONTINENT, AND THE GOLD COAST, 1945–51

For Clement Attlee's Labour government, which took office in July 1945, maintaining Britain's position as a global power was an absolute priority. The task would not be easy. Exhausted by the demands of war, the British economy faced difficult readjustments. Extended overseas commitments had, somehow, to be financed alongside the government's ambitious social reforms at home. Internationally, the onset of the Cold War brought with it heightened and hostile Soviet interest in the British Empire, a problem matched by the unwelcome focus on colonial affairs evident in the discussions of the new United Nations. Yet financial problems and the developing Cold War further convinced Attlee's Cabinet of the Empire's economic and strategic value, a view reinforced by their recent wartime experiences.[1]

As John Darwin has argued, the decisions taken by Attlee's government from 1945 to 1948 marked a watershed in Britain's development as an international power: these decisions, the retreat from South Asia and Palestine, the search for a new *modus vivendi* in the Middle East, the cultivation of the US 'special relationship', the redefinition of the nature of the British Commonwealth, and the adoption of new policies towards the political evolution of the dependent empire, especially in Africa, would shape Britain's external policies for a generation.[2]

The economic context of external policy

A major, perhaps decisive, determinant in policy during this period was Britain's economic position. Attlee's ministers were unfortunate in having to confront three major crises during their time in office: in 1947, in relation to sterling and the dollar shortage; in 1949, over the devaluation of sterling; and in 1950–1, the financial implications of massive rearmament. These would all have important repercussions for Britain's imperial policies. Obliged to liquidate more than a billion pounds worth of overseas assets during the war, Britain was now the world's largest debtor, to the tune of around £4.7 billion. Washington's abrupt termination of Lend-Lease in August 1945 made matters worse. A subsequent American loan of $3.75 billion (at 2 per cent interest), and the writing off of Lend-Lease debts of $21 billion for $650 million, came with unwelcome 'strings' attached. Especially problematic for Britain was the promise to ratify the 1944 Bretton Woods Agreement, by making the pound fully convertible into dollars by the middle of July 1947. It is generally agreed that the time was not right in summer 1947 to launch the convertibility operation, which involved removing the controls on exchanging sterling into dollars.[3]

During summer 1947 the drain on Britain's meagre exchange reserves accelerated as the date of convertibility drew near. The crisis was eventually eased by the suspension of convertibility in August. Subsequently, a mammoth export drive was launched to try to restore the balance of payments position. This, combined with the promise of $2.7 billion in Marshall Aid funding, which became effective in spring 1948, gave Attlee's government a brief respite.[4] Yet the events of summer 1947 strengthened a metropolitan tendency to see the Sterling Area as the key to Britain's economic salvation. Continuing the wartime pattern, the Sterling Area became a mechanism for the 'pooling' and rationing of the dollar resources of the Empire and Commonwealth. Put simply, an increasing proportion of Britain's trade was conducted within the Empire, reaching its zenith in the early 1950s. Not surprisingly, Britain's growing financial problems led to calls within the government for major reductions in Britain's overseas commitments, especially its military spending. Not only would this save dollar expenditure, but it could also free scarce labour for deployment in the vital export drive.

All of this coincided with a deteriorating situation in India and Palestine. Evidently, cuts had to be made. The result was a series of decisions in February 1947, which had far-reaching consequences for Britain's world role. Chief among these was Foreign Secretary Ernest Bevin's declaration that the question of Palestine's future would be referred to the United Nations and that Britain would withdraw from India by June 1948. These decisions were taken under duress, in an atmosphere of crisis, but they did not signal any surrender of Britain's overall global role. There was no question, for instance, of withdrawing from the Middle East, or of abandoning plans to consolidate British influence in South East Asia or Africa.[5]

As a result of the failure of convertibility, and in order to assist its export programme, the government decided, in September 1949, to devalue the pound by over 30 per cent, to a new value of $2.80. Significantly, the Sterling Area's members were not consulted over devaluation. Initial results seemed promising and, after all, sterling remained a major international currency, the vehicle for about half of all international trade. This hopeful trend was interrupted by the outbreak of the Korean War in June 1950, and by the accompanying rearmament programme, encouraged by Washington, on a scale unprecedented in peacetime, but justified by fears of a wider campaign of communist aggression. Nevertheless, the devaluation of 1949 can be seen as the point at which US pressure to dismantle the Sterling Area evaporated, with Washington accepting Britain's distinctive, extra-European position in the world economy.[6]

Labour and the Commonwealth

For Attlee and his ministers, securing the Commonwealth's cooperation in defence, diplomacy, and economic policy was the key to Britain's continuing great power status. The government's vision was of an expanding and multiracial grouping, closely bound to Britain politically, strategically, and economically. It was essential to consolidate ties with the 'old' Commonwealth members, the Dominions, but beyond this, the Commonwealth must be able to absorb former dependencies as they became independent. It was a source of enormous satisfaction to Britain that most former colonies did join the Commonwealth in this period. The major exceptions, Palestine and Burma were, given their special circumstances, perhaps understandable. The inclusion of India and Pakistan was a watershed, making multiracialism a reality. Equally important was the Commonwealth's ability to retain India as a member, even when it later opted for a republican constitution.[7] In April 1949, the conference of Commonwealth prime ministers (the successor to the pre-war Imperial Conferences) agreed a new formula under which the King was recognized as 'Head of the Commonwealth', although this was a development hardly likely to convince the Irish Free State to continue its membership after it formally became a republic in 1949.[8]

The Commonwealth remained a body whose members had remarkably little in common, beyond their British connection.[9] Indeed, friction between them sometimes threatened to destabilize the entire structure. In the 1940s, the most dangerous case of this was the dispute between India and Pakistan over Kashmir, an unresolved legacy of independence. A further, deepening difficulty, which would haunt successive British governments, was how to reconcile the inclusion of South Africa, committed after 1948 to racist policies of apartheid, within a multiracial community.[10] Anticipating difficulties that would resurface later in the course of decolonization, South African Prime Minister Malan argued in 1951 that existing members should hold a veto over the entry of a newly independent country into the Commonwealth, a clear signal of Pretoria's hostility to the development of a multiracial Commonwealth.[11] Unofficially, an 'inner club' of senior Commonwealth members coalesced, with Britain and the 'old' Dominions maintaining much of their long-accustomed intimacy in everything from intelligence liaison to sporting links.[12] Suspicion within the British intelligence community about the reliability of newer Commonwealth members had particularly important consequences for relations with India, whose High Commissioner to Britain, Krishna Menon (subsequently a Cabinet Minister), was rumoured to be a communist 'stooge'.[13]

An important measure of the Attlee government's Commonwealth commitment was its promotion of emigration from Britain to the Dominions and Southern Rhodesia, surprising at a time when Britain was facing a persistent labour shortage. London's initiatives, including the offer of free passages overseas to demobilized servicemen, were justified in terms of safeguarding the interests of settler societies and bolstering the Commonwealth. Significantly, practical counterarguments to this policy, especially the fear that emigration would promote the development of overseas economic rivals, were eclipsed by racially based assumptions, namely the notion that the British 'race', however dispersed globally, would retain its distinctive identity, and, by strengthening Commonwealth links, reinforce Britain's global influence.[14]

In practice, there were limits to an expanded Commonwealth role. While India and Pakistan made plain their non-aligned preference, disappointing the Chiefs of Staff's hopes for continuing post-independence military cooperation, the older Dominions were already looking beyond their immediate links with Britain to safeguard their security. Canada's premier, Mackenzie King, stood firm against centralized Commonwealth policymaking, preferring instead to increase cooperation with the United States through NATO. Australia, preoccupied with the deepening Cold War in Asia, was reluctant to contribute to Middle Eastern defence, as was South Africa, whose primary interests lay south of the Sahara.[15] Meanwhile, the growing strategic alignment between the United States, Australia, and New Zealand led in 1951 to the conclusion of the ANZUS Pact, from which Britain was pointedly excluded, thus avoiding any 'colonialist stigma'.[16]

Elsewhere, British plans to develop a major strategic base in East Africa were eventually abandoned, in the face of intractable problems of transport infrastructure and force deployment. Other attempts to achieve greater Commonwealth defence coordination were equally disappointing. Following the Communist takeover of China in October 1949, Attlee's government, although eventually willing to recognize Mao Zedong's new regime, sought Commonwealth assistance to reinforce vulnerable Hong Kong. Anti-colonial India was explicitly hostile, while other Commonwealth governments proved indifferent, or willing to make only token contributions.[17]

A further pressure arising from post-war changes within the Commonwealth was the perceived need to clarify the meaning of British nationality. Partly in recognition of the colonial contribution to the war effort, the British Nationality Act (1948) created a form of 'second-tier' Commonwealth citizenship, which extended to the colonial populations the right to enter Britain.[18] In turn, this development prompted more searching explorations of the connections between nationality and ethnicity, an issue that would assume growing importance with the onset of large-scale migration to Britain from the 1950s. In effect, while all those who belonged to the Commonwealth or to colonial territories would continue to be regarded as 'British subjects', their citizenship would be determined according to whether they originated in one of the self-governing countries of the Commonwealth (now including India and Pakistan), or in one of the colonial territories. In practice, the distinction made little difference: all enjoyed the right to enter Britain and take up residence there. Not until 1962, and the passage of the Commonwealth Immigration Act, did restrictions on immigration, long discussed but previously avoided by successive British governments, come into effect, highlighting explicitly the racial dimension to the immigration issue.[19]

South Asia

The Labour government's most pressing imperial problem in 1945 was the future of India. Here, the manner in which decolonization unfolded suggests that a loss of control, caused by a worsening local situation, rather than considered planning, shaped London's eventual decision to withdraw in 1947.[20] While sympathetic to Indian demands for self-determination, Attlee harboured doubts about the integrity of Indian nationalism, a view reinforced by recollection of the wartime 'Quit India' movement, whose suppression he had endorsed. More immediately, the Labour government needed to pre-empt accusations of a policy of 'scuttle' in India, liable to damage Britain's prestige and trigger political protest at home.[21]

Yet, by summer 1945, Britain's grip on India was rapidly loosening. Gandhi's Congress had been alienated during the war, during which independence had been promised and then withheld. The Muslim League feared losing face with its supporters if it appeared too accommodating to British efforts to resurrect the constitutional framework set out in 1935, which envisaged Dominion Status for an Indian Federation. A Cabinet Mission dispatched in spring 1946 in an attempt to preserve Indian unity, proposed a three-tier Federation, with a central government retaining control of foreign affairs and defence.[22] It was a dead letter: the Viceroy, Lord Wavell, and the Mission negotiators failed to persuade either Congress or the League. Seen from London, neither Congress domination, nor a partition of the country, was acceptable. Both threatened to exacerbate inter-communal tensions, leaving British plans for post-independence cooperation in tatters.[23] A friendly India, associated with Britain by Commonwealth membership and prepared to serve militarily as an anti-communist bulwark, seemed essential.[24] Central to British thinking at the highest levels of government was the notion that strong political and military links with India would underscore Britain's continuing status as a global power.[25]

Meanwhile, Congress stepped up its demands for immediate independence, inadvertently heightening Muslim support for Jinnah as it became clear that Britain might jettison the communal safeguards enshrined in the 1935 Government of India Act in the interests of rapid withdrawal. Muslim alarm at the prospect of a Congress-dominated India was partly inspired by the fact that Congress, nominally a secular body, exploited popular Hindu symbolism and idioms, identifying with religious concerns over issues such as cow-killing. As communal tensions increased after the war, Congress drew closer to Hindu groups at a local level, blurring the boundaries between them and stoking Muslim fears of a post-independence 'Hindu Raj'.[26] Having failed to secure for Muslims half the seats in Nehru's new interim government, during August 1946 Jinnah launched the 'Direct Action' campaign, which triggered rioting across northern India. Thousands died in the ensuing violence, which the security forces could not contain. By the end of the year, Viceroy Wavell favoured a phased withdrawal of British personnel, a viewpoint that cost him his position and cleared the way for a decisive metropolitan initiative.[27] Ironically, the British authorities, too, realized that their coercive power was spent: there was insufficient military manpower available and it was questionable whether the local administration (more than half of which was Indian) would cooperate in any colonial repression. The desire for continuing ties after independence also precluded the use of force. After nearly two centuries of relying upon the ultimate sanction of coercive power in India, Britain was obliged to abandon it as an adjunct to political manoeuvring.[28] It was vital, nonetheless, to portray Britain's departure from India as pre-planned and deliberate and not the chaotic prelude to wider imperial collapse.[29]

On 13 February 1947 the Cabinet confirmed that Britain would leave India by June 1948, an announcement that Lord Louis Mountbatten, chosen as Wavell's successor, had made a precondition to his appointment.[30] Once in office, Mountbatten quickly recognized that, if Britain were to avoid becoming entangled in a civil war, there was no alternative to partition and a rapid exit from India. Under his 'June Plan', power was to be transferred to separate states, India and a 'moth-eaten' Pakistan, physically divided by Indian territory, which left millions of Muslims in India. Congress achieved its goal of an independent, secular state, but at a high price.

Forever referred to in British accounts as a negotiated 'transfer of power', South Asian decolonization was appallingly violent and calamitously anarchic, accompanied by an unprecedented migration of millions of panic-stricken refugees seeking sanctuary with their co-religionists.[31] Indian independence was a quintessentially pragmatic manoeuvre by London. Although trumpeted by Attlee as one of his government's greatest achievements, it could not credibly be claimed as a triumph for the anti-colonial British left: it resulted more from a cool reappraisal of British interests, prompted by Indian resistance and disintegrating conditions in the subcontinent.[32] Britain had not wanted partition: it came because Congress and the Muslim League rejected anything less. Among the incidental victims were those collaborating Indian princes who had long been a mainstay of British rule, but who were now abandoned. However, a more pressing problem for Mountbatten was to prevent India's departure from the Commonwealth. This was resolved by Attlee's announcement in June 1947 that the two post-partition successor states would be free to determine this question for themselves.[33] For their part, Congress and the League accepted partition in order to avoid even greater chaos.

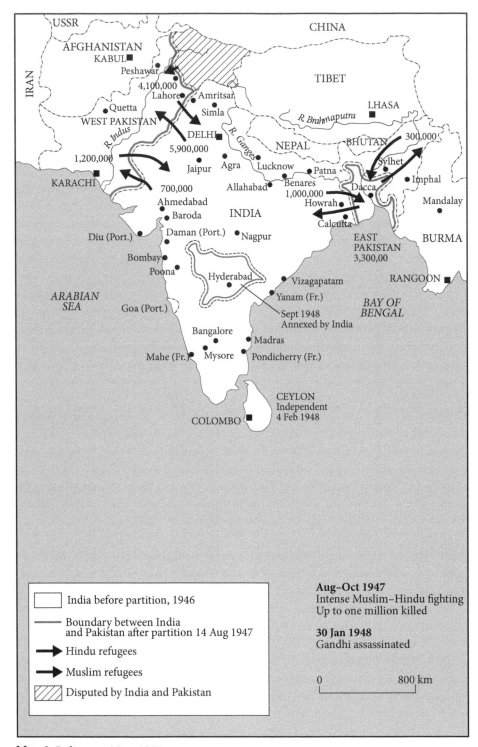

Map 1 Indian partition, 1947.

Britain escaped from India remarkably unscathed, something that, according to some historians, prevented the fundamental reassessment of Britain's overseas commitments that Indian independence should, logically, have encouraged.[34] India's independence raised a wider question: if Britain was unwilling or unable to keep its most valued colonial possession, what did this suggest for the future of the rest of the dependent empire? As the British found in India (and the Dutch would find in Indonesia), once a colonial power lost its most prized overseas territory, the 'normality' of empire could no longer be taken for granted, and this fundamental geopolitical shift was not lost on an emerging generation of politicians in the global South.[35]

Once India and Pakistan had become independent, it was difficult to withhold similar concessions from Ceylon. In February 1948 it became the first Colonial Office territory to achieve independence. The Second World War had demonstrated Ceylon's strategic value, leading Britain in 1943 to promise the island limited self-government, with the British controlling foreign, defence, and currency questions.[36] Things were not that simple. As in India, there was an important ethnic/communal dimension to Ceylon's decolonization. Sinhalese politicians sought responsible government, and Dominion Status, in order to pre-empt British introduction of a constitution designed to secure the political rights of the Tamil minority. The Soulbury Committee, which examined the Ceylon question late in the war, had concluded that it was better to make generous concessions than to grant 'too little, too late', an approach which would become a recurring theme in the history of British decolonization. Colonial Secretary Arthur Creech Jones hoped that this would demonstrate to colonial populations that Britain's commitment to eventual colonial self-government was genuine.[37]

British negotiators played on the conservatism of the Sinhalese political elite, knowing that they were alarmed by the possibility of mass anti-colonial protests. As elsewhere in Asia, the war had encouraged the growth of the radical left, which after successes in the 1946 elections, joined forces with other opposition groups in demanding full independence outside the Commonwealth. If the conservative elite were to contain the growth of radical nationalism, it was essential to speed up the process of negotiated withdrawal. This, and the background of rapid change in India, prompted the Sinhalese nationalist leader Don Stephen Senanayake to escalate his demands for immediate independence. Instinctively sympathetic to this 'moderate' elite, London accepted the Sinhalese case, once assurances of future diplomatic and defence cooperation were secured.[38] In what would become the defining *leitmotif* in subsequent episodes of decolonization, Britain identified an indigenous political class to which power could safely be transferred with no apparent threat to fundamental British interests, albeit not without substantial international criticism, particularly at the United Nations.[39]

Burma's fate was also partly shaped by developments elsewhere in South Asia. Unlike Ceylon, Burma's wartime experience was profoundly disruptive, and eroded Britain's ability to maintain a collaborative relationship. Conquered by the Japanese in 1942, the country enjoyed brief 'independence' until being reclaimed by the British in 1945.[40] Like Ceylon, Burma had been promised self-government by Britain as soon as was practicable, but Aung San, the Burmese leader whose Independence Army had briefly aligned with the Japanese, was viewed by some in London as a traitor. Others, including Attlee, sought to include Aung San's Anti-Fascist People's Freedom League (AFPFL) in plans for a Burmese national assembly. There was effectively no alternative. Britain had neither the resources nor the will to mount operations against Burmese nationalist insurgents. Furthermore, only the AFPFL, it seemed, could hold ethnically diverse Burma together. When Britain's wartime promise was finally implemented in January 1948, Burma became a republic. Reluctant to reopen the door to British and Indian business interests, Burma's leaders rejected Commonwealth links with Britain.[41] This was viewed from London with unusual equanimity, largely because the bulk of Burma's exports were bought by India, and so earned no dollars for the Sterling Area. The position would be very different in relation to major dollar-earning territories, such as Malaya and the Gold Coast.[42]

The Middle East

Even as India's future was being debated in London, Attlee's government was increasingly preoccupied with Britain's delicate position in the Middle East. Anxious to reinforce Britain's informal influence in the region in the face of growing Arab nationalism, Foreign Secretary Ernest Bevin proposed a more constructive partnership with the Arab world, predicated on British aid to help raise living standards dispensed through a new British Middle East Office. Again, there was no real alternative: coercive tactics were no longer feasible in view of the mounting constraints on British military spending. As would be the case with Britain's other overseas aid initiatives, what proved to be unrealistic initial expectations gave way to a more modest, but relatively successful development programme. Bevin's ambition to secure the support of a younger generation of politicians and technocrats was, however, ultimately obstructed by the Treasury's refusal to fund it. Most revealing, perhaps, was the fact that, rather than forge new bonds with the Middle Eastern masses, the underlying intention of British policy was to lend greater legitimacy to existing systems of government in the region, thereby pre-empting more revolutionary measures of redistribution such as land reform, which Iraq, for instance, seemed so badly to need. Ironically, those local elites that London sought to woo often concluded that their interests were better served by the adoption of anti-British, nationalist postures.[43] Meanwhile, in Iraq for instance, instead of a 'trickle down' of wealth generated by development, the resulting gains were substantially confined to a privileged few, fuelling further discontent. Even the limited efforts at land redistribution were largely manipulated in the interests of the existing elite, foreshadowing problems later encountered in Britain's most ambitious attempts at colonial land reform – in Kenya in the 1950s.[44]

The Foreign Office also hoped that British promotion of regional partnership would bear fruit in a new cluster of treaties with Arab states, especially with Egypt, cornerstone of Britain's Middle Eastern position. Here, too, success was limited. An agreement with Transjordan in 1946 (the year Britain's mandate ended), amended two years later, safeguarded British base rights, but a similar agreement with Iraq in 1948 collapsed amid local protests.[45]

In contrast to the common assumptions that informed British imperial policy in other theatres, the diversity of post-war government opinion on the Middle East is striking. In 1946, Attlee was willing to 'think the unthinkable', questioning the rationale for a British presence in the Arab world. His thinking was shaped in part by eagerness to avoid provoking the Soviet Union, in part by the apparent strategic revolution arising from airborne atomic weapons, and in part by India's imminent independence. Bevin and the Chiefs of Staff viewed matters very differently, emphasizing the need for Middle East airbases within striking distance of Soviet targets.[46] Central to the chiefs' case was the argument that British withdrawal would leave an eastern Mediterranean vacuum that the Soviets would surely fill.[47]

The Middle East, of course, was much more than a strategic nexus and a protective shield to non-communist Africa. It was a region in which Britain had substantial economic and commercial interests. Middle Eastern oil was vital for Britain's own needs. It was by far Britain's single most important raw material asset (and, crucially, could be paid for with sterling). Moreover, it was a valuable revenue earner. In 1947, some 60 per cent of British oil needs were met by Middle Eastern supplies. This figure was expected to exceed 80 per cent by 1951, reinforcing British anxiety about rival US oil interests and complicating an increasingly touchy Anglo-American relationship in the Middle East.[48] British companies were heavily involved in the region's oil industry, especially in Iran and Iraq. This economic interest lent added weight to the strategic argument for maintaining a large British military presence.[49] Whether Britain actually had the resources to defend the Middle East, however, remained debatable. Its biggest concentration of military power, and the largest military base in the world, was in the Suez Canal Zone in Egypt, a vast complex of facilities, the size of Wales, which by 1951 sheltered around 40,000 troops. This made Egypt by far Britain's most important Middle Eastern foothold.[50] The British post-war goal was to place the Suez Canal base on a more secure footing, through friendly cooperation with Egypt, rather than relying on a military occupation bound to poison Britain's relations with the Arab world. The government accepted the principle of force withdrawal in May 1946, on condition that Britain retained the right to re-enter Egypt in an emergency. Attempts to devise a new Anglo-Egyptian Treaty, however, were unsuccessful. For one thing, Egypt linked the question to its claims to sovereignty over the Sudan, theoretically an Anglo-Egyptian Condominium, which Britain was unwilling to concede. For another, the Egyptian government, conscious of local nationalist sentiment, was determined to minimize the British presence. Negotiations foundered early in 1947. In the short term, Britain invoked the original 1936 Anglo-Egyptian Treaty to sustain its Suez occupation in the face of mounting Egyptian protests. A more modest attempt to involve Egypt in Middle Eastern defence did not bear fruit until 1954.[51]

Britain's position elsewhere in the Middle East proved even more fragile as popular pressure against it increased, above all in the Palestine Mandate. Here, the Labour government acquired a bitter inheritance: the irreconcilable promises made to the Arab and Jewish communities during and after the First World War, a huge influx of Jewish settlers from the early 1930s onwards, and endemic inter-communal violence on the ground. The British objective in 1945 remained the creation of a binational state, with guaranteed rights for a population comprising approximately two-thirds Arabs and one-third Jews. The plan was soon derailed. In the immediate post-war period, as in India, communal hatred escalated beyond British control. Intense international interest in the fate of the Mandate, stirred by widespread sympathy for Holocaust survivors and for the Zionist cause, further complicated the situation. President Harry Truman, aware of America's sizeable Jewish constituency, endorsed the case for a Jewish state. As a first step, the US administration urged Britain in October 1946 to implement a liberal immigration policy to replace the tougher restrictions imposed in 1939. Britain, still involved in negotiating the terms of the enormous US loan, could not afford to antagonize Washington on this question, but feared that increased Jewish immigration would arouse Arab hostility.

As in India, the British authorities simply lost control of events. British forces became the target for attacks by Jewish terrorist groups, most notoriously the bombing in July 1946 of the King David Hotel in Jerusalem, headquarters of the Mandate administration.[52] Humiliating though this was, the Palestine problem's adverse impact on Anglo-Arab and US-British relations dominated British governmental thinking. Once again, hopes of a solution to bridge the communal divide, this time by introducing provincial autonomy for Arab and Jewish areas as the prelude to later independence, soon foundered on Britain's inability to impose any kind of solution on Palestine.[53] In February 1947 Bevin announced the referral of the entire Palestine problem to the United Nations, which retained ultimate responsibility for the Mandate, hoping that the pro-Arab majority of UN members would engineer a settlement favourable to British interests.[54] Yet by abdicating responsibility for this question, and failing to make any recommendations to the United Nations, Britain conceded the bankruptcy of its Palestine policy.

In September 1947, the UN Special Committee on Palestine (UNSCOP) recommended partition, a suggestion approved by the General Assembly in November. Britain, unwilling to shoulder responsibility for implementing a solution that neither local community accepted, and one that threatened to provoke Arab rebellion, chose to evacuate Palestine by August 1948.[55] A continued presence was incompatible with wider efforts to conciliate pro-Western Arab rulers, but the circumstances of withdrawal offered compelling evidence of declining British imperial power in the changed post-war international system.[56] Acting contrary to the accepted definition of successful decolonization, Britain withdrew from Palestine in 1948 without 'transferring power' to any effective administration. As predicted, the declaration of the state of Israel triggered an immediate invasion by neighbouring Arab states. This first Arab-Israeli war soon demonstrated the emptiness of Britain's previous security guarantees to its Arab partners. British refusal to become involved antagonized both warring parties.[57] The embittered atmosphere generated by Britain's role in the creation of Israel rendered Bevin's earlier promotion of Middle Eastern development redundant, although efforts to rebuild relations with the Arab world continued. Meanwhile, the debacle in Palestine, and continuing uncertainty over the Suez Base, reinforced Britain's interest in developing a strategic presence in Libya, where a unified client state under King Idris was eventually created.[58]

Late in the Labour government's life, a fresh nationalist challenge erupted, this time in Iran. In 1951, the Iranian government of Dr Mohammad Mossadegh nationalized the country's predominantly British-owned oil refineries, valued at around £120 million. This manifestation of Iranian nationalism was stimulated by the conclusion, in December 1950, of an unprecedented deal between US oil conglomerate Aramco and the Saudi Arabian government, under which Saudi oil revenues were divided equally between the two, an arrangement held up as a model in the industry. The British government's tame reaction to the 'Abadan crisis' not only confirmed Britain's inability to withstand nationalist pressure, but also its dependency on the United States. Washington, hostile to what it saw as London's imperialist and paternalist attitude, opposed military intervention, and US opinion could not be flouted.[59] However, events in Egypt only five years later would suggest that this lesson was not fully grasped in British governing circles.[60] Meanwhile, the loss of oil production resulting from the Abadan crisis was comfortably compensated for by increased output from the oilfields of the British-protected states of the Persian Gulf, especially Kuwait. This, in turn, lent added significance to defending the region from any Soviet or other encroachment.[61]

Policy towards the colonial territories

For the extremely diverse group of dependencies for which the Colonial Office was responsible, Attlee's government saw itself as pioneering an unprecedented worldwide experiment in 'nation-building', preparing the colonies for self-government along the lines set out in Oliver Stanley's watershed Commons speech in July 1943.[62] For the majority, Britain's aim was to create stable states, with democratic systems, to which power could safely be transferred after what was expected to be a lengthy process of political, economic, and social development.[63] Policymakers hoped to avoid confrontations with nationalist groups, where they existed or were emerging; rather, the aim was to manipulate nationalism instead of being manipulated by it. Within the colonial territories, ideas on long-term political trajectories could still be remarkably hazy. As part of recent revisionist reassessments, intended to loosen the grip of officially endorsed 'nationalist' historiographies, often entrenched after independence in the 1960s, historians have pointed out that the Western-style centralized nation state was not the only option available to emerging colonial politicians. At the Pan-African Congress, held in Manchester in October 1945, for example, those attending were yet to construct a clearly defined alternative to colonial rule.[64] There was, theoretically, a growing reluctance to retain colonies by the use of force, but, equally, there was no desire to impose independence on communities which were not considered 'ready' for it, as this might leave a 'dangerous vacuum' liable to be filled by less cooperative strains of nationalism.[65] In practice, Britain's willingness to employ force to bolster its colonial interests would soon become apparent, revealing a pattern that persisted throughout the process of decolonization.[66]

International pressures and peripheral realities soon undermined metropolitan calculations. For one thing, the United Nations became a forum for colonialism's international critics. For another, the intrusion of Cold War rivalries and rising fear of communist subversion distorted metropolitan readings of popular anti-colonialism.[67] The result was a policy of carrot and stick. Colonial policy sought to neutralize the appeal of radical leftism (in particular, the threat posed by growing labour unrest) by raising colonial living standards, while intelligence gathering, political policing, and broadcast propaganda all intensified. Efforts were also made to co-opt colonial civil society through support for compliant trade unions, cooperatives, and other institutions.[68] Building on its wartime expansion, radio assumed a great importance, offering a cheap means of reaching large, still predominantly illiterate audiences. While intended to propagate London's version of developments in the colonies, the spread of broadcasting ironically brought the Empire's components closer to each other allowing political activists in one territory to follow shifts elsewhere. A more transnational exchange of powerfully disruptive ideas was thereby facilitated.[69]

In the immediate post-war period, colonial economic policy was dictated by two major factors: world shortages of many basic requirements, especially food, and problems of transition from wartime to peacetime production. Colonies were warned that Britain could not meet their demands for exports, requiring them to produce more goods for themselves. Global commodity shortages at least offered opportunities for colonial producers to increase primary product exports such as cocoa and minerals. Herein lay the seeds of British governmental hopes that the combined resources of Western Europe and the British and French colonies in Africa could be fused into a new economic bloc, 'Eurafrica', the core of a 'Third Force' on a par with the two 'superpowers'.[70]

Britain's acute dollar shortage also shaped colonial economic policy, which, as David Fieldhouse remarks, became characterized by blatant 'neo-mercantilism'. Colonial resources were exploited either to earn precious dollars, to be pooled in the Bank of England, or to supply Britain with dollar-saving imports. Malaya, for example, became particularly valuable, its tin and rubber exports earning $170 million during 1948 alone.[71] The major colonial dollar earners, Malaya and the Gold Coast, were prevented from using the dollars they earned to buy the goods they needed from outside the Sterling Area, even though Britain was at this time in no position to supply substitute goods. Forced to accumulate ever-growing sterling balances in London, the colonies were in effect supplying Britain with compulsory 'loans' at very low rates of interest.

After the 1947 convertibility crisis, British officials also sought to integrate metropolitan and colonial planning more effectively than hitherto.[72] A Colonial Primary Products Committee was created in May 1947 to examine the scope for expanded colonial production to ease Britain's balance of payments position. Similarly, an interdepartmental Colonial Development Working Party was established in Whitehall to investigate the allocation of the capital goods required for colonial development. In their wake, a Cabinet Committee on Colonial Development was formed. The aim of all this activity was less to benefit colonial populations directly than to restore Britain's economic independence. It is widely accepted, by historians of widely varying outlooks, that colonial economic policy during the later 1940s was exploitative. The interests of colonial populations were subordinated to those of Britain, a situation described by one historian as 'social imperialism'.[73] These policy initiatives were also poorly thought out. Typical in this respect was the Colonial Development Corporation, operative from 1948, supposedly a vehicle for development and economic diversification. The vehicle soon stalled, representing a Colonial Office failure only eclipsed by the Ministry of Food's ill-fated East African Groundnut Scheme, a misguided and untested attempt to promote the mechanized production of peanuts in Tanganyika, intended to help ease the persistent fats shortage.[74] This was only the most infamous example of a general post-war enthusiasm for mechanized agriculture, inspired by earlier US and Soviet experiments, and thought to offer the key to rapid increases in production. Most colonies in the 1950s underwent attempts at mechanization with varying degrees of success.[75]

Ironically, the colonial state's commitment to development left it vulnerable to more criticism than in the interwar period, when its role had been negligible. As the state became increasingly interventionist in promoting 'development', extending the reach of bureaucratic power into the rural hinterland of many colonial territories, its actions could be interpreted as those of an intrusive, even oppressive, external power, operating in a manner never previously experienced.[76] The 'Second Colonial Occupation' of the post-war years brought with it new personnel ('experts') and new methods (especially in conservation measures designed to enhance agricultural efficiency) liable to antagonize colonial opinion, resentful at interference and the degree of compulsion associated with production drives.[77] Even relatively generous funding initiatives such as the Colombo Plan, a six-year programme launched in 1950 to stimulate economic and social development in South East Asia, were derided as being driven by strategic interest rather than economic altruism.[78] At the same time, policymakers quietly shelved earlier, tentative discussions about nationalizing key colonial industries, such as copper mining in Northern Rhodesia, in the interests of maximizing production. Thus, despite an apparent turn towards greater state intervention, the post-war climate continued to privilege expatriate private enterprise.[79]

Central to the development initiative was a dominant faith in 'modernization', the ubiquitous catchphrase of the decolonization years and after.[80] Ironically, policymakers in Britain (and France) viewed development as the key to re-establishing the legitimacy of colonial rule, in the process allowing them to secure the cooperation of emerging Westernized elites enthusiastic to pursue 'modernization'. Yet it quickly became a set of commitments, not only to increased material standards, but also to the promotion of social welfare against which the supposed 'benefits' of the colonial rule to local populations could be measured.[81] Unwittingly, officials had constructed an arena in which they found themselves competing with colonial politicians who claimed with growing stridency that they could deliver the fruits of development more effectively than any colonial regime. The concept of development was thus remobilized in the service of anti-colonial movements.[82] Moreover, the growing intrusiveness of the colonial state embodied in the development initiative – and its insistence on orderly, uniform production to unbending, centrally determined schedules – intensified discontent among colonial populations, accelerating the growth of anti-colonial resistance. Links between urban-based political movements and the large rural hinterlands increased, greatly expanding the potential anti-colonial constituency.

Not surprisingly tensions within the imperial state and within individual colonial bureaucracies also grew, with bitter arguments over the impact of maximized production on the maintenance of 'stability'.[83] Complicating this process was the scope for greater dispute *within* colonial societies – as well as between rival colonial political movements – over competition for slender development resources and over the prioritization of specific projects.[84] The fact that development as a goal could be so hotly contested by different actors undermines traditional claims that development embodied a coherent and consistent vision.[85] In the longer term, as Corinna Unger and others have made clear, in relation to the philanthropic funding of education in Africa after 1945, the transfer of knowledge came to occupy a central place in the deepening global Cold War. For US officials concerned about the future political orientation of colonies it made sense to invest in colleges, universities, and other educational institutions (and to encourage African and other students to visit the United States) to nurture pro-Western sentiment among newly educated elites.[86] For all that, as Frederick Cooper has stressed in relation to Africa, the late 1930s and 1940s represent a genuine watershed in the continent's history, witnessing the start of a period in which attempts at state-led development became the almost universally accepted goal.[87]

The tensions which development could reveal are captured in the ambitious Masai Development Plan (MDP), unveiled by the Tanganyikan government in 1951, intended to improve water supplies and grazing practices, and to eradicate disease vectors. Whereas before the war, concern to reinforce Indirect Rule led the colonial state to idealize the ethnic distinctions on which it depended, in the new political climate, the pastoralist Masai population was depicted as an obstacle to 'modernization', triggering new interventions in their lives from a colonial state increasingly disdainful of their traditionalism. This was ironic, given the previous enthusiasm shown by the Masai for some forms of development, such as education, which they had been willing to support from their own funds. The MDP helped provoke new frictions, and ultimately anti-colonial mobilization, deriving from the Masai's fear that their land would be alienated to others, especially the more economically 'productive' community of white settlers. These fears would subsequently be aggravated by growing Masai anger at their expulsion from the Ngorongoro Crater and the Serengeti National Park in the name of wildlife conservation, another theme increasingly prominent in late colonial policies. Previously conservative Masai elders migrated towards support for political change as a consequence of the MDP, surrendering power in local institutions to the younger, educated groups who would form the nationalist movement, which, like most such movements, had its own vision of 'development'.[88]

Malaya

Despite the cataclysms of war, British imperialism in South East Asia was far from dead after 1945. Although the old colonial structures had been swept aside by the occupying Japanese, new ones were devised by the British in an attempt to rebuild and maintain Britain's stake in the region. Malaya, especially, was valued more by Britain after 1945 than it had ever been (this territory alone would generate up to one-third of the dollar earnings of the entire Sterling Area in the immediate post-war years). Reclaiming Britain's control of its South East Asian colonies, including the reoccupation of Malaya in 1945, was a source of great satisfaction for London. Fortunately, the British did not have to reconquer the colony, and physical damage to the local economy was minimal. The two most important industries, rubber and tin production, were untouched by the retreating Japanese Army, and could resume production, relatively quickly.[89] British planners had devised new policies for Malaya during their enforced wartime absence. The aims were threefold: economic modernization, consolidation of a stable, centralized, pro-Western administration, and political reforms resulting eventually in self-government. Here, as elsewhere in the colonial Empire, Britain hoped to retain the initiative, controlling a process of orderly evolution, and forestalling the growth of nationalism before it became unmanageable. Fortunately for Britain, Malay nationalism was markedly conservative in character, closer in spirit to that of Ceylon than of India. Initially, the British adopted a relatively liberal course in Malaya, in relation to politics and trade union activity. Yet the British failed to allow for the serious economic and social problems afflicting the territory in the wake of wartime occupation.[90]

The Malayan Union scheme, introduced in January 1946, was based on treaties negotiated by Sir Harold MacMichael, Britain's special representative, with the Malay Sultans late in 1945.[91] The Sultans ceded much of their traditional authority to a governor, who would replace the pre-war High Commissioner under the new arrangements. Meant to prepare Malaya for eventual self-government, the Union also involved unprecedented centralization: in effect, Malaya was to be run as a 'typical' colony. Its citizenship proposals were especially controversial, stimulating Malay fears of eventual Chinese ascendancy. By extending citizenship rights to the non-Malay majority, Britain hoped to steer local Chinese attention away from communism while enhancing opportunities for Chinese entrepreneurial participation in the territory's economic development. The policy reflected an entrenched British tendency to see the Malays as *bumiputera* (sons of the land), best suited to farming and civil administration, echoing similar stereotypes applied by the British in India and Africa.[92]

The Union encountered immediate resistance from traditional Malay rulers, and their supporters in Britain, principally former administrators. By May 1946, the Sultans, who boycotted Sir Edward Gent's installation as governor in April, had formed the United Malays National Organization (UMNO) led by Dato Onn.[93] Although UMNO defended Malay interests vigorously, it was not inherently anti-British. Shocked by the Sultans' unexpectedly forceful resistance, anxious to appease UMNO, and unnerved by the deteriorating situations in India and nearby Indonesia in summer 1947, London reversed its policy and abandoned the Union. In its place came the Federation of Malaya, inaugurated in February 1948, a heavily modified version of the Union, which restored most of the Sultans' powers, and most Malay political privileges, though within a much more simple political structure than had existed before 1939. The office of colonial governor reverted to that of high commissioner. Attlee's government also retreated from the multiracial citizenship code (although this remained, in theory, a goal of British policy): for the time being, only a small proportion of the non-Malay community gained political rights.[94]

The new system may have preserved the autonomy of the Malay states, but it also fulfilled the core objective of the original Union plan, a strong and financially stable central government.[95] British officials viewed the Federation as the basis of Malaya's future self-government, but this was not expected to be imminent. Before the outbreak of the Emergency, even UMNO's leader considered Malaya unready for independence.[96] But the reversal of British policy created a new dilemma. By reaffirming the foundations of Anglo-Malay collaboration, the British only deepened communal tensions by alienating important sections of the Chinese population. This was only aggravated by British attempts to reassert control over land settlement and to confront the problem of 'squatting' in forest reserves.[97]

The eruption of a serious, and largely unforeseen, communist insurrection in June 1948 led to the declaration of a state of emergency and threatened Britain's goals for the gradual development of South East Asia. The insurrection, beginning with the murder of three European planters and their Chinese assistants, was depicted as being Moscow- or Beijing-inspired, although there was little evidence to support this claim. Nor, in retrospect, should the insurrection have come as a surprise, given the extent of violence and labour unrest in the territory since 1945, triggered by rampant inflation (touching 800 per cent during 1945–6) and the authorities' efforts to curb wage rises.[98] But Malaya's strategic importance as a 'front-line' state in the Asian Cold War, together with its indispensability as a dollar-earner for the Sterling Area, hardened Britain's resolve to suppress the Emergency. The Malayan Communist Party was banned as a large-scale counter-insurgency effort began.[99] By April 1950, when Lieutenant-General Sir Harold Briggs took over as Director of Operations, Britain had committed 40,000 soldiers and 80,000 auxiliaries. Initially, however, the authorities were reluctant to employ tough anti-guerrilla tactics, both to avoid accusations of harsh repression and prevent the insurgents from going underground. Meanwhile, although temporarily suspended, Britain's commitment to Malayan 'nation-building' remained in place.

The Malayan case undermines the argument that Britain capitulated before the onslaught of Asian nationalism after 1945; retreat, planned or otherwise, was ruled out. Ironically, the communist challenge eased Britain's task of promoting political evolution. The Sultans, and the Malay population generally, shared Britain's concern to tackle the Malayan Communist Party in the interests of Malay nationalism. Defeating the insurrection certainly required the cooperation or, at least, the compliance of the bulk of the population.[100] After the arrival of a new high commissioner, Sir Henry Gurney, late in 1949, the authorities focused on two major goals: isolating the insurgents from disaffected communities which might give them aid, especially Malaya's thousands of landless squatters, and forming an association to compete with the communists for the political allegiance of the ethnic Chinese.[101] British methods could be inventive, even risky. Allies were sought across the ideological spectrum. For instance, during the Emergency, the British authorities sought to recruit Christian missionaries, including some recently expelled from communist China, to help immunize the Chinese community against the appeal of communism even though this risked antagonizing the largely Muslim Malay population.[102]

Experience of the Emergency, not unlike the earlier lessons of India, underlined the risks involved in obstructing, rather than promoting, political reform. Britain's regional Commissioner-General, Malcolm MacDonald told South East Asian governors in June 1950 that the original British target of full self-government for Malaya in twenty-five years had been superseded. Accelerated reforms and social welfare initiatives became an essential complement to armed counter-insurgency.[103] These approaches were meshed together in the 'Briggs Plan', launched in early 1950. Under the impetus of the Director of Operations, squatters were forcibly relocated in 'New Villages' to isolate them from the insurgents. To sweeten the pill, measures to win 'hearts and minds' were introduced.[104] While the efficacy of the plan is hotly disputed, it bears emphasis that British 'success' in Malaya was only achievable because a privileged ethnic group, the Malays, needed British help to resist the emergence of the predominantly Chinese challenge to their own political supremacy.[105] Nevertheless, Britain's successful Malayan counter-insurgency established a paradigm for the handling of similar colonial crises in the future. Crucially, the British approach had combined concessions to nationalism with a tough response to communism. It was a policy that London urged both the French and the Dutch to imitate.[106]

Britain's African empire

With the days of the Indian Raj numbered, the centre of gravity in Britain's colonial policy shifted westwards, not only to the Middle East but also to Africa. Here, with the exception of the Gold Coast, and despite evidence of the local antagonisms, seen especially in the wave of labour unrest which gripped much of the continent in the years immediately after 1945, organized anti-colonial nationalism during the late 1940s remained in its infancy.[107] However, an important symbolic indicator of African political aspirations came in October 1945, when 90 delegates from Africa, the West Indies, and the United States met in Manchester as the fifth Pan-African Congress. The delegates, including a strong West African contingent and future African nationalist leaders such as Kwame Nkrumah of the Gold Coast and the Kenyan Jomo Kenyatta, demanded an end to colonial rule and racial discrimination. Inspired by the Atlantic Charter and the Charter of the new United Nations, the congress saw new forms of international cooperation emerging from the war. Nevertheless, no specific suggestions on how to achieve its aims were put forward, although it was critical of the reformist talk of the colonial powers. The Colonial Office declined an invitation to attend the congress, but Special Branch officers were there. They reported that the proceedings did not threaten Britain's immediate colonial interests.[108] Although British officials remained confident that they could regulate the pace of African colonial change, the Colonial Office, conscious that the interwar years had been characterized by 'aimlessness and drift', still sought coherent policy objectives.[109] Indirect rule had outlived its usefulness. Meaningful African participation in government was now unavoidable, not least because African cooperation was needed to make economic development a reality. This involved seeking a broader base of support for colonial rule than had ever obtained in India, with the encouragement of an educated middle class as adjuncts, to replace Britain's traditional allies, the chiefs. The new elite was to be given practical experience of democratic practices by participating in a revitalized system of local government, as Colonial Secretary, Arthur Creech Jones, outlined in February 1947.[110] This emphasis on local government demonstrated British officials' concern to distract the politically 'immature' African elite away from ideological engagement and national political organization. Implicit in the new policy was London's recognition that progress on these lines might have to be faster than local populations had been led to expect.[111] The goal was not only to demonstrate that colonial rule could be progressive, but also to prepare for an orderly transfer of power to stable, pro-British governments. Britain's innovations were not, therefore, merely a response to a perceived nationalist challenge; rather, they signified an attempt to *pre-empt* the growth of nationalism and create the foundations of a future 'informal' empire.[112] Meanwhile, by promoting the concept of *participatory* government, the post-war colonial state attempted to bolster its own legitimacy.[113] But, as the British would soon discover, the consequences of such political adjustments were difficult to control. Encouraging participatory politics stimulated the emergence of new political parties, many with larger, national aspirations.[114]

During spring 1947, preparations for a conference of African governors revealed key officials' thinking about the thrust of Britain's African policies. Within a generation, it seemed, several large colonies would become self-governing within the Commonwealth (the term 'independent' was scrupulously avoided). A basic assumption in the Colonial Office was that African populations would be content with management of their own internal affairs, rather than a more fundamental breach with Britain.[115] Such thinking underscored a crucial report prepared in May 1947 by Andrew Cohen, one of the Colonial Office's most influential policymakers, preparatory to the African Governors' Conference. Written for internal consumption, the report proposed the staged evolution of the African colonies towards eventual self-government. Taking the earlier development of the Dominions as a model, Cohen suggested that the existing colonial state could evolve into a Westminster-type political system. This would begin when each colonial legislature had an elected majority of 'unofficial' members, and the colonial government had devolved its administrative powers to individual departments, each headed by a British civil servant. Next, unofficial members of the Legislative Council might be appointed to the Executive Council, some of them having responsibility for minor government departments. On particular issues, the governor could follow the advice of the majority of Executive Council members. Gradually, the Executive Council would develop into a cabinet, accountable to a wholly elected legislature, with the governor retaining the powers of a prime minister. The final stage in this process would be reached when the governor was able to transfer full power to a prime minister heading a cabinet responsible for all areas of internal government, and accountable to a fully elected legislature. At this stage, full independence would be the logical outcome.[116]

In Cohen's view, the final two phases in this evolutionary model would take a long time to be achieved, because they would require essentially artificial colonial territories to develop authentic identities and functioning civil societies with national leaders serving communities familiar with democratic principles. The regional diversity within Britain's African empire also had to be considered. Territories in East and Central Africa, for example, with their entrenched (and growing) settler populations, would require different treatment to a relatively advanced, and predominantly African, colony like the Gold Coast. Unmistakable in Cohen's approach was a deeply paternalistic outlook, an infantilization of African populations, and an unswerving belief in the supremacy of Western social democracy.[117] With hindsight, it is tempting to add a lack of realism to this list. In less than three years, Cohen's prescriptions were cast aside. The pace of sociopolitical change in Africa made plain that the days of constitution-mongering in a cool, detached environment had passed.

The Gold Coast

Social and economic ferment in the post-war Gold Coast had multiple causes. Shortages of key imports, inflation, unemployment among demobilized soldiers, resentment at the low prices farmers received from state marketing boards, and at the measures taken by the colonial state to deal with a serious outbreak of swollen shoot disease which affected the territory's main export crop, cocoa, all helped to create a mood of frustrated expectation. Attempting to sustain the reformist momentum built up by the colony's liberal governor, Sir Alan Burns, since 1941, Attlee's government approved a new Gold Coast constitution in 1946. Like the Malayan Union scheme, this was intended to achieve a more centralized, integrated state, while extending popular political representation. Driven by the same modernizing impulse, the 'Burns Constitution' convinced the Gold Coast's politically active urban elite that if their interests were to be defended in the country's developing organs of government, especially the expanded Legislative Council, and if they were not to be overshadowed by the more conservative elites of the rural hinterland, they had to participate in the new central institutions, and to organize themselves politically to make that participation effective. These were the conditions in which the United Gold Coast Convention (UGCC) came into existence in 1947 as mouthpiece of the colony's numerically small professional class. The UGCC seemed intent on exploiting the political machinery approved by Britain rather than subverting colonial rule entirely.

However, the apparent political calm of the Gold Coast was shattered in February 1948 by rioting in the capital, Accra, provoked when police fired on a demonstration by aggrieved ex-servicemen. Attacks on European-owned shops underlined the rioters' economic grievances. Against the background of an intensifying Cold War, the newly installed colonial governor, Sir Gerald Creasy, saw in this unrest a communist guiding hand. As we shall see, compared to the military campaigns then being waged by the French in Indochina, and by the Dutch in Indonesia, the Accra Riots were a relatively minor affair. Their importance lay in the disproportionate state response they elicited. The colonial authorities declared a state of emergency and detained the leaders of the UGCC. A battalion was put in readiness to fly out to the Gold Coast from Gibraltar, and two ships were sent from the Cape. Although initial reactions to the Accra Riots assumed a communist plot, in reality there was none, only pervasive practical discontent.[118]

Showing an impressive independence of mind, the Colonial Secretary, Creech Jones, was sceptical about the alleged communist threat in the Gold Coast. He replaced the ailing Creasy with a new governor, Sir Charles Arden-Clarke (who had recent experience of combating insurgency in South East Asia), and set up a commission of inquiry under Aiken Watson KC. The Watson Commission reached the embarrassing conclusion that the 1946 Constitution, held up as the most enlightened in British Africa, had been 'outmoded at birth'. The Commission recommended accelerated self-government for the Gold Coast, with an enlarged Legislative Council elected under a wider franchise and the inclusion of Africans in government.[119] Although the Watson Commission's findings were not at odds with progressive Colonial

Office thinking, the timescale envisaged for the introduction of fundamental changes was far in advance of what London had previously contemplated.

To its credit, the British government accepted the Watson Commission's advice and established an all-African committee under Sir Henley Coussey to make detailed recommendations on constitutional change. But this step was not all it seemed. The Coussey Committee was selected carefully, excluding 'unreliable' African opinion while favouring 'moderate' views. Meanwhile, Arden-Clarke began reorganizing the colony's intelligence and security structures. In October 1949, the Coussey Committee proposed the creation of an entirely elected legislature, chosen indirectly by manhood suffrage, to which the Executive Council, including African ministers, would be answerable. Simultaneously, checks and balances were to be introduced to discourage local 'radicals'. For instance, age restrictions would curb the threat from younger election candidates, and a system of indirect voting in the rural areas was intended to favour conservative groups.

Events on the ground, however, were taking a different turn. During 1949, the young UGCC organizer, Kwame Nkrumah, impatient with his party's moderate leadership, seceded to form the more radical Convention People's Party (CPP). Nkrumah mobilized the collective resentments of the so-called 'verandah boys', drawn from the Gold Coast's swelling population of educated, underemployed, and consequently frustrated youth. Adopting the techniques of earlier Indian nationalists, and displaying some of their charismatic qualities, in early 1950 Nkrumah embarked on a campaign of 'Positive Action', demanding 'Self-Government Now'. Having opened the Pandora's box of contested national elections, the colonial authorities supported their favoured candidates, the UGCC, at Nkrumah's expense. Officials were inclined to believe UGCC claims that Nkrumah lacked broad support, and depicted the colony's rural heartland as politically quiescent. This was far from the case. Nkrumah's achievement was to bring together disaffected Ashanti farmers and the Western-educated coastal, urban elite, together with the unemployed and dispossessed, in an effective, if transient, political alliance. Taken by surprise once again, the colonial authorities took a tough line against the CPP's Positive Action campaign. Nkrumah and his senior colleagues were arrested and another state of emergency was declared.

Another new constitution unveiled at the end of 1950 included features designed to favour the moderate UGCC and penalize Nkrumah's 'radical' CPP. Ministerial responsibility was only partly entrusted to African politicians, and among the members of the Executive Council, three would be nominated officials, and eight would be elected 'unofficials'). CPP organizers initially condemned the new constitution, but, once preparations for the Gold Coast's first general election got under way, they worked assiduously to see that the party's supporters registered to vote and asserted their political rights. Thus, the CPP turned the colonial government's declared support for grass-roots democratic inclusion against it. The result was a resounding victory for Nkrumah, even though he had conducted his election campaign from his prison cell. He was released in February 1951 to take up his new duties as Leader of Government Business.[120]

Leaving aside his necessarily inflammatory rhetoric, Nkrumah before long showed that he could play the game of constitutional development according to British rules, and that he was willing, implicitly, to admit Britain's continuing control over that process. Arden-Clarke, who still retained considerable powers over justice and security, soon reassessed Nkrumah and his ministers, who seemed surprisingly 'competent and reasonable'. It was the governor who, aware of the political pressures on Nkrumah from his own supporters, urged London to maintain the momentum of constitutional progress. In summer 1951, Britain accepted that Nkrumah would soon be granted the coveted title of 'prime minister'.

Developments in the Gold Coast made a nonsense of Cohen's devolution timetable. Responsible cabinet government had arrived within two years, not the twenty or more that Cohen had envisaged. Moreover, it was difficult to confine change to the Gold Coast. Labour ministers accepted that similar political concessions would have to be granted to Nigeria, and here, a new constitution approved in 1950 gave African politicians an increased role both in central and in regional government, the latter acquiring greater autonomy to reflect the colony's ethnic diversity.[121] Nigeria, too, was speeding towards eventual independence.

East and Central Africa were a different proposition. Here, although the broad goal of colonial policy theoretically mirrored that of West Africa, namely self-government within the Commonwealth, British policymakers faced additional communal problems: the presence of a white settler population, and, in East Africa's case, a South Asian minority. London's response was to promote limited African political involvement, leading eventually to rough equality in the political status of the various ethnic groups, or a multiracial 'partnership'. The key to stability, in Colonial Office eyes, was interracial cooperation, but on terms decided by the whites. It was tacitly assumed that the settlers would continue to enjoy a privileged position, lending their entrepreneurial flair to the region's economic 'development'. In contrast to the Gold Coast, there was no attraction in promoting 'nationalism', whether settler or African.[122] If there was little respect for Kenya's privileged settlers among Whitehall officials, few had the stomach to confront them, for a confrontation might trigger a political crisis just when Britain's economic circumstances required the uninterrupted production of East (and Central) African commodities, for which settler cooperation was deemed essential.[123]

The reappraisal of long-term colonial policy towards Central Africa was more fundamental. The region's settlers had long sought to amalgamate Northern and Southern Rhodesia and Nyasaland, a scheme resisted by the British government since the three territories were neither politically nor economically comparable. However, concern at the possible northward expansion of South African influence, and a desire to promote faster regional economic development, based especially on Northern Rhodesia's booming copper industry, led Attlee's government to consider linking the three territories in a new federal structure strong enough to resist any encroachment from the south, but still under London's ultimate control.[124] Even otherwise 'liberal' policymakers, such as Andrew Cohen, stifled their misgivings about the fate of the African majority under a federal system dominated by white settlers. Shortly before the Labour government's fall from power in 1951, a conference was held at Victoria Falls at which representatives of the several governments involved adopted the principle of federation. The problem of safeguarding African interests in such an arrangement was bequeathed to the returning Conservatives.

The problem of South Africa

Plans for a Central African Federation hinted at Britain's increasingly fraught relationship with South Africa, where a hostile nationalist government under Dr Malan took office in 1948, committed to the racist policy of 'apartheid', or 'separate development'. Although it took time for the full implications of apartheid to become clear, British ministers privately recoiled from its early symptoms and the international criticism it attracted. For its part, South Africa became increasingly alarmed at British colonial reformism in black Africa, fearing that the constitutional changes initiated in West Africa might be applied to territories with settler populations.[125]

Yet economics and Cold War strategy kept Britain and South Africa aligned. A member of the Sterling Area with a booming mining sector, South Africa had provided Britain with an £80 million gold loan in 1948.[126] Strategically, too, South Africa was considered an essential partner with a vital naval base at Simonstown and invaluable uranium supplies for Britain's atomic programme. Britain even offered to sell scarce military supplies to secure a South African commitment in 1950 to share the burden of Middle Eastern defence.[127] Attlee's government also acquiesced in Pretoria's long-standing claim to the UN Trust Territory of South West Africa (Namibia) as the necessary price for South African cooperation in other fields. Nevertheless, Britain was uncomfortably aware of the need to reconcile its eagerness, on Cold War grounds, to keep South Africa within the Commonwealth, with its overriding concern, also fuelled by Cold War considerations, to develop a genuinely multiracial Commonwealth. Because the loss of South Africa, a 'founding member', might reduce the Commonwealth's stature, Attlee's government opted to work with Malan's regime as closely as it could.[128] This did not stop London from trying to limit the spread of South African influence further north, and this was the prime motive for creating the ill-fated Central African Federation in 1953.[129] Similarly, Britain continued to refuse to surrender the neighbouring High Commission Territories, coveted by Pretoria, to South Africa, in view of their populations' reluctance to be absorbed. Yet, concern to appease the South African government did influence Britain's own policy towards these territories. Most famously, in 1949, when the heir to the largest kingdom in Bechuanaland, Seretse Khama, married his English secretary, deference to horrified white South African sentiment led Britain to banish both Seretse and his uncle, an episode which concluded only in 1956 when Seretse surrendered his claims to the throne.[130]

The years between 1945 and 1951 witnessed a fundamental reorientation in Britain's management of its Empire. The government's experiences, perhaps especially in the Middle East and South Asia, underlined Britain's declining ability to project its colonial power effectively. The experiences of Attlee's government reinforced London's commitment to the broad policy of promoting political development in the colonial Empire, but developments in India, Egypt and, latterly, West Africa, had shown that nationalist pressure for change could be contained only by accommodation, if necessary by making timely concessions in order to maintain ultimate control over the pace of political change. This concern to strengthen British control over the processes subsequently termed 'decolonization' would also be expressed in one of the hallmarks of British policy over the next decade, the drive to identify 'moderate' nationalist leaders, who could block more threatening challenges from 'extremists' (as defined by London and its agents). If this succeeded, then the greatest prize of all might be secured: the maintenance of a close, cordial relationship with former dependencies, expressed in the expansion of the Commonwealth to include newly independent countries, and their pro-Western orientation in the all-important global ideological struggle.

CHAPTER 3
BRITISH DECOLONIZATION, INSURGENCY, AND STRATEGIC REVERSE: THE MIDDLE EAST, AFRICA, AND MALAYA, 1951–7

When the Conservatives returned to power in October 1951, Prime Minister Winston Churchill spoke of a three-pronged strategy to maintain Britain's widespread overseas commitments. The first objective was to hold together the Empire-Commonwealth, which still formed the core of Britain's claims to great power status. The second was to consolidate relations with the English-speaking world, in some respects, shorthand for cementing the special relationship with the United States. Finally, the new British government aimed to encourage greater Western European integration, without becoming directly involved in that process. By the time the Conservatives eventually fell from office in 1964, decolonization was largely an accomplished fact and the US global reach even greater.[1]

For Anthony Eden, Churchill's second-time Foreign Secretary and eventual successor, there were compelling reasons to uphold Britain's major commitments, but at the same time he was caught in a dilemma whether to prevent Soviet incursion, to safeguard Britain's trading interests, or to burnish Britain's image in Washington as a valued ally. One means to tackle this situation was to share as many of these burdens as possible with other countries, particularly the United States and other members of the Commonwealth. If this strategy succeeded, Britain could devote more resources to defending its position in the Middle East, Asia, and Africa. Yet in the early 1950s Britain was already chronically overstretched, spending huge sums on rearmament, and deploying troops on a large scale in Korea, Europe, and the Middle East, while simultaneously tackling major insurgencies in Malaya, Kenya, and, soon, Cyprus. A key policy review document, the 1952 'Global Strategy Paper', identified the core problem: the tension between the objectives of reducing Britain's overseas obligations on financial grounds, and maintaining them for reasons of strategic projection or international standing.[2]

Given these considerations, Britain's ambitions to remain a major world player would have to be based increasingly on its guardianship of the Sterling Area (since half the world's trade was still conducted in sterling) and on its possession of nuclear weapons. Nevertheless, the current thrust of policies was untenable: Britain's post-war economy simply could not support the greatly enlarged responsibilities the country had taken on, and so priorities would have to be redefined. Of these, defending sterling took precedence. It was recognized that since the war, Britain had been gambling dangerously in managing its currency without adequate reserves. Correcting this situation would require a trimming of consumption at home, including cuts in social expenditure, and a reappraisal of responsibilities abroad. Britain's salvation, it was hoped, might lie in thermonuclear weapons: the nuclear deterrent would enable Britain to cut its conventional defence spending in favour of subtler, more economical, methods of fighting the Cold War, including political persuasion and propaganda.[3]

The British Commonwealth

The Commonwealth remained a key to Britain's global system of power and influence. The overall goal of colonial policy remained self-government *within the Commonwealth*. Some senior 'imperially-minded' Conservatives, including Churchill and Lords Salisbury and Swinton, feared that the addition of new members would inevitably alter the Commonwealth's character, a view strengthened by India's embarrassing shift since independence towards non-alignment and republicanism.[4] These sentiments were echoed among some older Commonwealth members. Australian Prime Minister, Robert Menzies, privately doubted whether the new Asian members would remain within the fold. From Pretoria, too, came warnings that Malan's nationalist government would resist any proposal to admit a black African state to the Commonwealth.[5] Faced with what they interpreted as a danger of disintegration and a loss of British leadership, some ministers became interested in the idea of creating different gradations of Commonwealth membership.[6] Discussions on the possibility of a 'two-tier' Commonwealth, designed to preserve the special bonds between the distinctively 'British' members, eventually concluded that the idea was unworkable: junior status would inevitably be resented by states to whom it was offered, and might provoke their complete withdrawal. This did not, however, prevent Britain from maintaining especially close relations, particularly in the defence sphere, with certain members, as was already the case in practice. Since 1948, when London and Washington had agreed to share military intelligence, sensitive information had been passed to older Commonwealth members, but seldom to the newer South Asian members.[7]

Meanwhile, the immediate concern of achieving greater Commonwealth cohesion in the defence field remained a British priority, as it had been under Attlee. Until the mid-1950s, a common assumption among the governments of Britain, Australia, and New Zealand was that in the event of another world war, Australian and New Zealand contingents would reinforce the defence of the crucial Middle Eastern zone, as had happened after 1939. This assumption had, however, to be revised in the face of the deteriorating Far Eastern situation, with war still raging in Korea, the Malayan Emergency at its height, and the French position crumbling in Indochina. In 1953, Britain urged Australia to add ground forces to the air support already being provided in Malaya.[8] By 1955, however, London had accepted that Australian and New Zealand priorities must inevitably focus on their own local interests. In practical terms, this gave rise to the formation of the Commonwealth Strategic Reserve, based in Malaya, with British, Australian, and New Zealand forces serving together.

Migration was another increasingly central issue in Commonwealth relations. Churchill called for a report on the question of UK immigration from the colonies in 1952. The issue divided Conservative Ministers. Some stressed the economic advantages of immigration, at a time when some sectors of the economy still faced labour shortages. Others gloomily predicted dissent among an unprepared host community. Integration of immigrants, successful or otherwise, would impact upon the wider 'multiracialism' espoused in colonial policy. As some observers commented, in most colonies and Commonwealth countries opinion was broadly hostile to the free flow of migrants. There had long been antipathy, for example, in West Africa, towards the entry of Lebanese traders, giving rise after the war to a restrictive immigration code. During the lifetime of the Churchill and Eden governments, ministers refrained from introducing legislation based on explicitly racial criteria. But they struggled to find a formula which, while limiting the entry of immigrants from the West Indies, India, and Pakistan, would not disadvantage those from older Commonwealth members. For the most part, these difficult political questions were sidestepped.[9]

Economics and Empire

In the early 1950s, London still expected the colonial economies to perform the function of supplying Britain with raw materials, and of being earners of valuable dollars to be pooled within the Sterling Area, at a time when the latter as a whole was in deficit with dollar countries. By the mid-1950s, colonial markets accounted for about 13 per cent of British exports, while Britain took about 10 per cent of its imports from the colonies.[10] Around a quarter of colonial trade was conducted with Britain, making the colonies more dependent on Britain than the latter was on them. Like Attlee's government, the Conservatives were initially optimistic about the prospects for increasing colonial productivity, and so of easing Britain's own economic difficulties further. The realities of colonial economic conditions, especially the continuing scarcity of money and equipment, soon intervened, blocking any dramatic increase in the colonies' output. The colonies' inability to draw on their accumulated sterling balances to purchase development goods compounded the problem as did the metropolitan government's general preference to direct exports to more desirable markets.[11]

The Conservative government was committed, perhaps on emotional as much as financial grounds, to imperial preference as a trading system valuable to Britain. But the system, a response to the world depression and reinforced by the effects of the Second World War, was beginning to unravel. Independent members of the Commonwealth looked beyond their traditional trading networks and, as the Korean War commodity boom dissipated after 1952, Commonwealth primary producers were keen, if possible, to diversify their economies, reducing their vulnerability to fluctuations in world commodity prices.[12] By the mid-1950s, the independent members of the Sterling Area pursued their own economic development needs, no longer subordinating these to the needs of the Area as a whole.[13] It also became increasingly clear in the 1950s that Britain's major exports needed wealthy, technologically advanced markets, which few members of the imperial economic system could offer. Equally, Sterling Area members were unwilling to consolidate their commercial ties with Britain (and with one another) at the expense of more profitable relationships with North America and Western Europe.[14] British efforts to conserve the benefits of its existing system of imperial preference, while simultaneously expanding the scope for trade with wealthier European countries resulted in plans for a European Free Trade Area (EFTA). This was intended to give Britain access to lucrative European markets *in addition to* traditional Commonwealth ones.[15] Underlying this 1955 proposal was a deeper transition, signalled by the Conservative Party Conference of 1954, which acknowledged Britain's commitment to a free-trading system.[16]

Colonial development

A central strand in British colonial policy remained preparing the colonies for self-government through sustained economic and social development. However, many of the difficulties in promoting development, seen most clearly in the ill-fated East African Groundnuts Scheme, had not been overcome. The Conservatives did not share their predecessors' enthusiasm for state-driven development. Stressing the importance of private enterprise, the government finally disbanded the Overseas Food Corporation in 1954, and made the Colonial Development Corporation subject to more stringent regulation. Development embodied a wide range of economic and social activities, from prestige initiatives like the Gold Coast Volta River hydroelectric project to basic research into tropical agriculture. As the 1950s progressed, it became more apparent that development was inherently slow and difficult, and that funding it adequately was a major long-term commitment.[17] Sensing growing pessimism in Treasury circles, the Colonial Office, under Oliver Lyttelton, seized the initiative in 1953, seeking an extension of existing Colonial Development and Welfare (CD & W) provision, due to expire in 1955. Lyttelton secured a further £115 million from the Treasury to cover the period 1955–60, arguing that the cost involved had to be measured against the potential long-term benefits to Britain. Nevertheless, under the chancellorship of Harold Macmillan after 1955, Treasury criticism of spending on the colonies would resume.

The post-war trend towards large-scale, centralized, and *planned* development schemes continued unabated into the 1950s. Enshrining the role of the Western 'expert', these programmes were strongly hierarchical, stressing the role of the developers, not of those being 'developed'. They often involved the resettlement of populations on a huge scale. Such schemes called for a range of technical and other services, and scientists and other specialists came to enjoy enhanced status and influence within a colonial state firmly committed to developmentalism. The concept of planning which underpinned the development strategy was itself the product of assumptions about the need for state intervention to undertake large-scale, unprecedented development in complex societies, which, in turn, required the presence of such 'experts'.[18]

Typical of the entire development initiative were attempts to corral peasants into stable, more productive, and hence larger units. By the mid-1950s, over seventy such schemes were operating in British African territories – the East African Groundnuts Scheme and the Swynnerton Plan being only two of the best known. What is so striking about these schemes is the degree to which they involved government intervention in almost every aspect of peasant life, and the fact that they would fundamentally shape the course of post-independence development programmes.[19]

Yet 'development' was an inherently ambiguous term, and, ominously, a highly contested concept, one that was interpreted in different ways by colonial officials and African politicians (and their supporters).[20] Crucially, development dramatically altered expectations, not least among colonial populations. The development equation was no longer dominated by 'benevolent outsiders' dispensing charity: increasingly, it revolved around colonial citizens claiming what was their due.[21] This was particularly relevant for the urbanized youth of Africa, a volatile ingredient in the post-war social mix. Young city dwellers exposed to Western education in the newly developing secondary schools stood to benefit from the rapid expansion of government recruitment.[22] Meanwhile, colonial politicians became experienced in manipulating development goals and promising new services and patronage to their supporters.[23]

The problem of South Africa

Britain's relationship with South Africa in the early 1950s demonstrated the major role played by the Union in British policy calculations. The northward migration of Afrikaner racial philosophy was considered especially dangerous, threatening to destabilize Britain's African interests, by fomenting racial unrest. Nor could Britain's claims to be an 'enlightened' colonial power be taken seriously if it were closely allied to an overtly racist state. London needed, therefore, to follow a course which balanced cooperation with South Africa with containment of the latter's disruptive potential.[24] In their common concern to prevent South Africa complicating Britain's colonial policies north of the Limpopo, Attlee's and Churchill's governments had basically similar, if unstated, objectives. The Conservatives adopted and developed Labour's scheme for a federation of the three Central African territories, to form a physical barrier to the spread of South African influence, benefiting the region's white settler minority with disproportionate political power at the expense of the African majority. Similarly, London remained adamant that the High Commission Territories (Bechuanaland, Basutoland, and Swaziland) should not be absorbed into the Union, despite the latter's long-standing ambitions in that direction.

The Middle East

In the early 1950s Britain was determined to remain the major foreign power in the Middle East. As well as operating the Suez Base, it had airfields in Iraq, a major naval base at Aden, and ran the Arab Legion in Jordan. A treaty concluded in 1953 with nominally independent Libya enabled Britain to maintain bases there. Middle Eastern defence requirements also explained Britain's continuing military interest in Malta and Cyprus. However, Britain's position infuriated Arab nationalists, who resented this intrusive physical presence and recalled Britain's *de facto* role in the creation of Israel.

The Suez Base was a case in point. Enormously expensive to maintain, the Base had itself become a major irritant in Anglo-Egyptian relations. A situation already strained by the Second World War had steadily become worse, and in October 1951, the Cairo government abrogated the 1936 Treaty that entitled Britain to maintain the Suez Base for another twenty years. In January 1952, the situation deteriorated sharply, when British forces tried to disarm local auxiliary police, resulting in extensive anti-Western riots in Cairo, and contributing to the military coup of July, among whose key players was Colonel Gamal Abdel Nasser. The militarization of Egyptian politics was itself in part a consequence of defeat in the 1948 war with Israel, a microcosm of the wider shock which that episode had triggered throughout the Arab world.[25] Nasser, from that generation of Egyptian nationalists for whom imperialist occupation was a simple but ever-present humiliation, was determined to evict the British.[26]

Foreign Office efforts to defuse the situation prompted Eden to seek a deal with Cairo under which control of the Suez Canal would be internationalized, Egypt would enter a regional defence pact, and Britain would evacuate the Suez Base, preserving the right of return in an emergency. As part of the wider process of normalizing relations with Egypt, Britain resolved in 1953 to withdraw from the Sudan by 1956, in return for Cairo's abandonment of its claim to suzerainty over the entire Nile Valley. Thus, it was the Sudan that was the pioneer of British decolonization in sub-Saharan Africa.[27]

Eventually, in October 1954, Britain and Egypt reached agreement on the evacuation of the Suez Base, a move intended by Eden to demonstrate London's sensitivity towards Egyptian aspirations.[28] Britain failed, however, to persuade Egypt to join a regional defence organization. Under the terms of the agreement, British forces would be withdrawn within twenty months, but the Suez Base would be maintained, and Britain secured the right of return for a seven-year period. With hindsight, this episode can be seen as the first tangible acknowledgement by the new British government that a reconfiguration of Britain's overseas presence had become inevitable, although Churchill personally preferred to rationalize it not as a retreat but as a reorganization of military forces intended to bolster Britain's Middle Eastern role.[29]

Having apparently resolved the Suez Base question satisfactorily, Britain turned next to questions of regional defence, and in 1955 created the Baghdad Pact, centred on Turkey and Britain's most important ally in the region, Iraq. Pakistan and Iran subsequently signed up as members. London hoped that the promise of Western capital for the prestigious Aswan High Dam project might persuade Egypt to join the Pact. Ironically, the Baghdad Pact, a poor substitute in British eyes for the Middle East Defence Organization which it had sought, proved counterproductive. Aggravating tensions in the Middle East rather than ensuring stability, it involved promises of military assistance to its members which Britain was in no position to fulfil. Nasser, who had by now ousted his senior, Neguib, saw the Pact as an attempt to divide the Arab world, and this, together with continuing Israeli incursions, led Egypt to seek military aid from the Soviet bloc, radically altering the regional balance of power. Britain and Egypt became locked in a struggle for regional influence.[30]

When Britain promoted Jordan as the next Baghdad Pact signatory, Nasser's government orchestrated demonstrations in the Jordanian capital that led King Hussein to dismiss the British Commander of the Arab Legion, General Glubb ('Glubb Pasha'), in March 1956. Eden, who increasingly identified Nasser with dictators such as Mussolini and regarded any compromise with him as unacceptable (evoking painful memories of 1930s-style 'appeasement'), briefly contemplated reoccupying Suez. Meanwhile, London and Washington plotted a coup in Syria to prevent its merger with Egypt. Despite Foreign Office misgivings, the British government resolved that Nasser must be removed from power; Egypt's July 1956 nationalization of the Suez Canal offered the perfect pretext.[31] The methods used by Britain to try to reassert its regional sway during the ensuing Suez Crisis owed much to the temperament, and shortcomings, of the ailing Eden, although it might be argued that his Cabinet colleagues should share some of the responsibility for the fiasco.

The shape of colonial policy

The Churchill government was perhaps the last in which old-style enthusiasts for Empire held sway. Foremost among them, perhaps, was the Prime Minister who, as late as 1954, talked of giving the Colonial Office an impressive new home at the heart of Westminster. His first Colonial Secretary, Oliver Lyttelton, often regarded as a right-winger on colonial issues, was a keen supporter of the settler cause in Central Africa, and took a tough line in confronting colonial dissent. His successor at the Colonial Office, Alan Lennox-Boyd, has acquired a similarly conservative reputation. Even more uncompromising was Lord Salisbury, Lord President of the Council between 1952 and 1957, who, having urged his colleagues to strengthen the powers of colonial governments to quell unrest, resigned over the proposed release from gaol of the Greek Cypriot leader, Archbishop Makarios, and thereafter offered increasingly bitter criticism of government policy from the sidelines.[32]

The Conservative government's handling of colonial policy has aptly been described as attempting to keep change 'within bounds'. In practice, this required Britain to remain in control of developments in the colonies, limiting change where it could rather than actively promoting it.[33] Increasingly, however, London would appreciate that blocking reform might be the more dangerous option. In the revealing words of Sir Charles Jeffries, a senior Colonial Office official, writing in 1956:

> I think there is too much tendency to consider whether these places are 'ready' for Statehood. Of course they are not, any more than the Gold Coast is 'ready' for independence, or than one's teenage daughter is 'ready' for the proverbial latch-key.[34]

Before this, the British government believed that, although colonial policy was constrained by economic circumstances, by international opinion, and, increasingly by the resistance of the colonial populations themselves, there was little sense in Whitehall of any imminent policy reappraisal, nor was there yet any serious attempt to calculate systematically just what benefits (or disadvantages) accrued to Britain from its possession of colonies.[35] Support for devolutionary constitutional development and 'moderate' colonial elites continued, and political challenges were sometimes followed by decisive intervention, as in British Guiana in 1953, where an elected government under Cheddi Jagan was suspended because of its unacceptable radicalism and its plans to reduce the powers of foreign-owned enterprise.[36] Nevertheless, as the 1950s unfolded, there was a growing metropolitan distaste for confrontation in the colonial sphere. This was probably less a reflection of shifting moral perspectives than a pragmatic recognition that tough measures might be counterproductive, fomenting political opposition. Conciliation, on the other hand, might buy time and greater freedom to manoeuvre in defence of British interests.[37]

Meanwhile, residual public support for empire appeared to be cooling, a shift encouraged by activist groups such as the Movement for Colonial Freedom (chaired by veteran leftist campaigner Fenner Brockway).[38] As always, hard evidence of such attitudinal changes is tantalizingly elusive. But a perceptible willingness to disengage from imperial commitments may have reflected a variety of influences. Among these was the unpalatable reality of colonial counter-insurgency campaigns (although their ferocity was often carefully concealed from the public's gaze). Less altruistic were developing fears that the longer Britain devoted increasing resources to the Empire, the greater the risk of being overtaken by economic competitors untrammelled by imperial responsibilities. It appeared to some that the Empire might, after all, be delaying Britain's own much-needed modernization – a recurring complaint since the late nineteenth century.[39]

Another feature of the 1950s was the growing involvement of Christian denominations both in resisting racism and helping to develop indigenous churches in colonial territories. Missionary organizations sometimes sought to distance themselves from the heritage of colonialism. Many became active on secular, humanitarian issues, moderating their emphasis on religious belief in favour of a more generally acceptable stress on charitable work.[40] But it was particularly in relation to those African colonies with a significant white settler population that British missionaries became embroiled in the politics of decolonization, embarrassing the British government through their identification with African interests and consequent criticism of official policy.[41]

An important area of continuity between the Labour and Conservative governments was concern about the future of territories which, by themselves, might not form viable nation states. The preferred solution was to group such neighbouring territories together in order to enhance their political and economic prospects. This policy, which produced a number of 'federations', was pursued with enthusiasm, even when local populations were obviously hostile to the idea, as was the case in the most important example, the Central African Federation (Federation of Rhodesia and Nyasaland), itself an indication of London's confidence in its ability to shape the development of colonial polities. Other regions considered suitable for this federal treatment were East Africa and South East Asia, while the Caribbean and South Arabia were other possible candidates. The federal option was no novelty in imperial policy: Canada, Australia and, more painfully, South Africa, had all been earlier products of this integrative impulse. It was striking that while federal solutions were highly acceptable to Britain within the Empire, they were shunned in the European context.

In keeping with its emphasis on maintaining control, the Conservative government was willing to employ force in response to threats to British authority. The Conservatives took a firm line in Malaya, sending General Sir Gerald Templer to devise a new counter-insurgency campaign. In Kenya, the Mau Mau Emergency soon absorbed eleven British infantry battalions in addition to many thousands of locally recruited 'auxiliaries'. In Uganda, the troublesome Kabaka of Buganda was sent into exile. In Cyprus, a vigorous antiterrorist drive was mounted by Field Marshal Harding. Colonial 'emergencies' could be a useful means of gaining the time needed to cultivate 'moderates' and undermine the influence of 'extremists'.[42] Viewed in these limited terms, British counter-insurgency, often accompanied by aggressive intelligence gathering and black propaganda campaigns aimed at neutralizing political opponents, could even be considered a success.[43] But its human costs were terribly high, and such 'successes' could generate misleading expectations about the future stability of territories still tied to Britain. As the 1950s progressed, British colonial policy seemed beset by a paradox: in its determination to uphold what it liked to regard as a distinctively liberal form of imperialism, Britain was relying to a growing extent on *illiberal* methods.[44]

Nationalism

The greatest single challenge to British colonial rule in this period was likely to come from the opposition of local colonial populations, a factor increasingly, though often inaccurately, described as 'nationalism'. Colonial demands to share the fruits of development promised during the war were strengthened by a new language of colonial rule, which recognized basic democratic principles: with citizenship, it was argued, came rights.[45] A growing body of research has revealed how complex anti-colonial movements could be, and how much scope there was for this developing political force to involve conflicts and rivalries within colonial societies, both before and *after* independence.[46] The image of colonial populations giving unwavering support to all-embracing, monolithic resistance movements and nationalist parties does not bear close scrutiny: internal political cleavages apparent in the postcolonial years were sometimes evident long before independence.[47] Similarly, there is growing awareness that nationalist politicians in Africa, for instance, drew, not just on sympathetic international opinion and the specific precedent provided by Indian independence, but also on the experiences of fellow nationalists in other African colonies.[48] The continuation of British colonial rule depended heavily on the ability of the colonial state to channel this pressure into a peaceful, pro-Western political orientation. Ministers were not always quick to grasp that they were increasingly being forced to respond to changes unfolding in the colonies, and that apparent control of colonial political environments might be diminishing. Within Whitehall, meanwhile, nationalism could evoke contrasting responses. The Foreign Office, for example, drawing on its Middle East experience, tended to view nationalism as a destructive, inherently threatening force, which required firm handling. As Foreign Secretary, Anthony Eden thought that the pace of change in West Africa, for example, had been incautious. The Colonial Office, meanwhile, was more willing to view nationalism indulgently as a dynamic force, which, with care, could be moulded into a progressive and even cooperative movement.

Whitehall was also divided over the cost of maintaining colonial rule. The Colonial Office, for which metropolitan expenditure on Colonial Development and Welfare remained essential, inevitably favoured increased British subventions. Departments involved in limiting colonial unrest, however, sought greater expenditure on security, while the Treasury, long sceptical about 'subsidising' colonial living standards, was anxious to limit its financial commitments to development aid. Whatever misgivings individual ministers may have nursed, the Cabinet, accepting that it could not set aside established policy, usually acquiesced in measures of devolution advocated by the Colonial Office. Nevertheless, the government was equally determined to avoid giving the impression that it was in retreat from its colonial responsibilities, or that Britain had lost the will to be a colonial power. Remarkably, even as late as 1954, when London attempted to predict which colonies would become independent during the next twenty years, its list of candidates was confined to the Gold Coast and Nigeria, the Central African Federation, a Malayan Federation, and an as yet unformed West Indian Federation. Up to twenty colonies were judged unsuitable for full independence, and were thought to be candidates only for internal self-government. In 1954, the Colonial Office minister Henry Hopkinson was famously wrong-footed in the House of Commons, admitting that some colonies were so important to Britain that their independence was inconceivable. He was referring in particular to the then still relatively tranquil island of Cyprus, where British forces, eventually numbering 25,000, would soon become embroiled in a bitter counter-insurgency campaign, confronting Greek Cypriot fighters (EOKA) who sought not only independence from Britain, but *Enosis*, or union, with mainland Greece. Although Britain found itself involved in a three-year long struggle to contain terrorism, prompting growing qualms at home about the acceptability of preserving colonial rule by force, ministers were reluctant to make concessions to Greek Cypriot demands: no longer having access to the Egyptian base, they considered a stronghold in Cyprus even more necessary. Moreover, it was deemed vital not to alienate Turkey, on whom Britain's calculations for Eastern Mediterranean defence largely hinged; and, perhaps most importantly, Eden needed to appear resolute over this question, especially as the 1954 Suez agreement had exposed dissatisfaction among imperial 'die-hards' in his own party. As Holland has commented, the early 1950s suggest a process of 'realistic adjustment' in British colonial policymaking. This involved acceptance that control of sizeable territorial units was not in itself essential to British interests: in the age of air power and nuclear weapons, a much smaller number of critically important territories, an 'empire of points', springboards for the rapid projection of British power, seemed more relevant to changing British requirements.[49]

The reservations voiced by some in Whitehall about the rate of colonial constitutional change were shared by a growing number of colonial government officials charged with implementing policy, in other words by those administrators whose function was increasingly to introduce changes which would ultimately make most of them (literally) redundant. Successive colonial secretaries in the 1950s, especially Alan Lennox-Boyd, found themselves preoccupied with the fate of colonial civil servants whose long-term career prospects were being undermined by political devolution and the indigenization of local administrations.

Ironically, the size of the Colonial Service had grown dramatically since the war. In 1950, a total of 1,510 appointments were made, compared with 551 in 1920, the best interwar year, before depression and retrenchment had taken their toll.[50] Although recruitment increased by 50 per cent in the decade after 1947, the number of resignations by disillusioned staff also grew, especially in those African territories where British officials found themselves increasingly answerable to local politicians. This prompted the Colonial Office to pilot the creation in 1954 of an 'Overseas Civil Service', which could hire out experienced personnel to newly independent countries in addition to administering the remaining colonies.[51]

Malaya

At the core of Britain's vital interests in the Far East was South East Asia, incorporating Singapore, a crucial business and communications hub and naval base, and Malaya, important both strategically and economically as a supplier of key strategic commodities such as rubber and tin, whose value had increased because of the Korean War and the Cold War background. By 1955 the Malayan Emergency was estimated to be costing the British and Malayan governments up to £100 million a year.[52] The Churchill government dispatched General Templer to coordinate counter-insurgency operations, giving him combined oversight of civil and military affairs. Templer's appointment and early success in the areas of policing, intelligence, and 'psychological warfare' are generally seen as marking a critical stage in Britain's handling of Malaya, representing a determination to achieve both a military and a political solution to the territory's problems. During 1953 Malacca was declared the first area free of insurgent activity. Templer, however, built on foundations laid before his arrival, the Briggs Plan foremost among them.[53]

Meanwhile, the continuing violence in the territory served to confirm the broad outline of British policy, highlighting the need for collaboration between the British and the Malays, and the importance of securing Chinese cooperation both in the counter-insurgency campaign and in the policy of 'nation-building', leading eventually to the calling of local elections. The British had made it clear that before there could be major changes in Malaya's constitutional status, the territory would have to prove that it could produce a convincingly multiracial political party. To cooperate in campaigning for local elections in 1952, UMNO and the Malay Chinese Association accordingly established an alliance, formalized early in 1953, which the Malayan Indian Congress joined in the following year. The fact that within the alliance,

Malaya's different ethnic communities remained distinct made the organization less than perfect in British eyes, and their tendency to dismiss it as an 'artificial' group, given cohesion chiefly by the influence of its leader, Tunku Abdul Rahman, in some ways echoed British attitudes towards the Indian National Congress in the 1930s. By September 1953, however, military success gave Templer the confidence to invite alliance politicians into his Executive Council to begin preparations for elections at the state and federal levels.

From 1954 onwards, Abdul Rahman intensified his demands for independence for various reasons. Not only did the improved security situation make political campaigning feasible, but the Tunku was also coming under pressure from more radical elements within the alliance. Malay leaders, in particular, were anxious to achieve self-government *before* the Chinese community became more politically organized. Britain, meanwhile, was itself operating within an increasingly pressured environment. Circumstances in Malaya, and in Britain's other South East Asian territories (Singapore, Sarawak, Brunei, and North Borneo) could not realistically be isolated from broader developments in the region as a whole. Instability in Indochina was of particular concern to Britain, but sympathy for France fell short of a willingness to provide military assistance, despite US encouragement. In contrast, Britain's continuing ambition to construct a regional defence grouping centred on Malaya reflected not only the latter's growing strategic importance to Britain as independence loomed, but also London's concern to reinforce Britain's voice within the Western Alliance by constructing an Asian defence bloc outside Washington's immediate sphere of influence.[54]

Britain's South East Asian concerns were not confined to the defence sphere. There was also enthusiasm for the potentially cheaper option of promoting economic and social development as a practical counterweight to the spread of communist influence. For Britain, the most important example of this approach had been the Colombo Plan, begun under Attlee, but continued under Churchill.[55] This, however, succumbed to Treasury demands for retrenchment, and like Britain's other Third World development initiatives, never received the level of funding it required to have much effect. Tension persisted between two strands of British policy: first, to lay the foundations for ultimate Malayan self-government; secondly, to safeguard Britain's key interests in the territory, particularly its desire to use Malaya as the core of its regional defence plans, in partnership with other Commonwealth members.

In July 1955, the alliance won a landslide election victory, taking fifty-one out of fifty-two elected seats on the Federal Council, and Tunku Abdul Rahman became the territory's chief minister. Unprepared for this development, the British had no alternative but to accept Abdul Rahman as the leader of a multiracial movement held together by its support for independence. Early in 1956 a conference in London set out the framework for Malaya's independence in August 1957, two years earlier than the alliance's own target. The Colonial Office assured the Malayan delegates that the transfer of power would neither be obstructed nor delayed by Britain. It is important to point out that Malaya's independence was reached *before* Britain's principal goals had been achieved: the emergency was not yet over (fighting would continue for another three years); the multiracial national identity which the British sought had not yet been created; and Britain's ambition to weld Malaya into a larger political unit with Singapore and Borneo was yet to be realized. Furthermore, pressing British concern to secure Malay cooperation in the continuing counter-insurgency campaign made the authorities reluctant to address the delicate issue of converting the Malay sultans into genuine constitutional rulers.[56]

Nevertheless, London took comfort from the fact that a broadly pro-Western, independent Malaya would continue to supply rubber and bank its earnings within the Sterling Area (even though natural rubber's importance was being challenged by the use of synthetic alternatives, particularly in the United States). Also, through a defence treaty, Malaya would still provide Britain with a major strategic foothold in South East Asia.[57] The fact remains that it was the alliance's unstoppable political momentum that compelled Britain to concede self-government. Few in Whitehall would have predicted such an outcome when Malaya fell in 1942.[58] The introduction of electoral politics in the colonial context, had, once again, caught the British government off guard.

The Gold Coast

The Gold Coast set the precedent for the Conservative government's approach to decolonization.[59] The Colonial Office, which saw few helpful guides in the British retreat from South Asia or Palestine, was determined that political change here should be carefully 'managed'.[60] After 1951, responsibility for government was shared by British officials and African politicians, an arrangement reminiscent of the 'dyarchy' operating in India between the wars. Both the Colonial Office and Nkrumah's CPP assumed that this would be a brief, transitional phase, leading to internal self-government, and ultimately to full independence within the Commonwealth. Of great symbolic importance was the award of the title of prime minister to Nkrumah in 1952.

From Accra, Governor Arden-Clarke suggested that the momentum of devolution must continue in order to ensure that the Gold Coast was 'governed by consent'. This would involve surrendering responsibility for financial, and possibly judicial, matters to African ministers. It is clear, however, that London still sought to avoid a fundamental reorganization of the balance of power in the territory. Lyttelton, who visited the territory in 1952, described the system being created in the Gold Coast as a 'stucco façade' and sought to keep sensitive topics such as intelligence and security in British hands. Control of the police was a particularly delicate area, revealing British government fears that after independence, the police might be vulnerable to political interference.[61] Lyttelton was also adamant that before further major revision of the Gold Coast constitution, there should be 'proper consultation' with the population and the chiefs, followed by a general election. The Governor of Nigeria, Sir John Macpherson, was meanwhile voicing concerns about the impact of Gold Coast devolution in Nigeria as he knew, fundamental reforms in any one colonial territory were bound to reverberate in neighbouring dependencies. Nevertheless, in September 1953, it was agreed that the Gold Coast should, as the Accra government proposed, advance towards a single legislative chamber, with a cabinet appointed on the Prime Minister's advice, and reserve powers entrusted to the Governor.[62]

Beneath the surface, however, political tensions were crystallizing in the territory, challenging the claims of Nkrumah and the CPP to be fully representative of the population. Ironically, it was economic growth, especially in the south, which exposed fissures within Gold Coast politics. Once in power, Nkrumah decided to maintain the state commodity marketing schemes which were a hallmark of late British colonialism, giving the CPP government considerable powers of patronage. In the Ashanti region, there was deepening resentment that profits accruing to the Cocoa Marketing Board, derived from Ashanti cocoa production, were directed into development projects elsewhere, particularly in the south of the territory. Vocal elements of the northern population resented the low prices being paid for their cocoa. Many chiefs, too, felt excluded from the country's increasingly centralized political system, and called for a second chamber.[63] In its pursuit of 'nation-building' and centralization, Britain came to neglect local government, which had, ironically, been so prominent in British thinking immediately before the Accra Riots. This, in turn, would have serious long-term implications for democracy and the bulk of the territory's population.[64] Although the CPP won another election in 1954, in Ashanti the National Liberation Movement (NLM) rose to represent disgruntled cocoa farmers and chiefs in particular, and gained some sympathy among the expatriate business community and the Conservative Party in Britain.[65] The NLM was committed to a federal system, intended to pre-empt CPP dominance over the whole territory, but this posed a major challenge both to Nkrumah's ambitions and to London's plans, and brought the Gold Coast close to civil war.[66] In July 1955, a constitutional committee, appointed by Nkrumah but boycotted by the NLM, rejected the federal option and instead proposed the creation of regional councils. At the end of the year, a constitutional adviser appointed by the new Colonial Secretary, Alan Lennox-Boyd, recommended the establishment of regional assemblies, enjoying powers devolved by the central government. Lennox-Boyd insisted that before a date for the Gold Coast's independence could be finalized, the CPP would have to demonstrate its popular support at the polls, and in July 1956, Nkrumah led his party to yet another election victory, the prelude to full independence in March 1957. The private reactions of British officials were muted. The Commonwealth Relations Office, responsible for post-independence relations with what became Ghana (named after an ancient African empire, though not one contiguous with the Gold Coast), feared that Britain might be obliged to provide substantial development aid to the new nation, if only to prevent it becoming an embarrassing critic of colonialism. Even more fundamentally, there were grave, if private, misgivings about the alleged corruption and undemocratic tendencies of African ministers, raising concern in London about the prospects for Ghana's post-independence stability. The Commonwealth Relations Secretary, Lord Home, observed at the beginning of 1957 that he was 'full of foreboding about the whole Gold Coast experiment', feelings shared by the new Prime Minister, Harold Macmillan.[67] It was highly significant that one of Nkrumah's first acts after independence was to ban all political parties organized regionally, including the NLM.

East and Central Africa: Settler complications

If the Conservative government resigned itself to the ultimate goal of self-government under majority rule in the West African colonies, there seemed little prospect in the early 1950s of applying the same formula to the ethnically diverse territories of East and Central Africa. Here, the existence of small, but vocal, settler populations, along with Asian communities, persuaded London to opt for a policy of multiracialism, based on shared power between the ethnic groups. While this might have appeared to be relatively liberal in the 1950s, the racial assumptions that underpinned it were far from progressive. The policy bestowed on minority groups a strikingly disproportionate influence in political life, specifically preserving the privileged status of the vastly outnumbered Europeans. The logic of this policy was that these territories' long-term economic development depended primarily upon white settler enterprise, supplemented in some cases by the business skills of the Asian community. Gradually, it was hoped, a new African entrepreneurial class would be formed, identifying more with the existing economic and social structure than with the aspirations either of the growing urban working class or the landless rural poor.

Pursuit of the multiracial goal reassured policymakers in London that they could still control events on the ground. Towards the end of 1955, Lennox-Boyd proposed 'systems of qualitative democracy' for these settler colonies. The idea of universal suffrage was to be replaced by elaborate structures in which African political participation would depend upon economic and educational qualifications. Different ethnic groups – European, Asian, and African – would be given separate electoral rolls, a long-established colonial device which had fateful consequences in British India.

In the case of Kenya, the colonial edifice was shaken to its foundations by the Mau Mau uprising, which originated in violence among the Kikuyu community during the later 1940s, and led to the declaration of a state of emergency in 1952. It quickly became obvious that the Kenyan authorities could not deal with the situation and needed outside assistance. This not only required expensive metropolitan military intervention, but revealed the degree of self-delusion among settlers who aspired to inherit unrivalled authority over the territory. Indeed, Mau Mau was itself substantially the result of growing settler influence within the colonial state. The causes and course of Kenya's emergency proved difficult for European contemporaries to interpret. Rather than being merely an outburst of anti-colonial energy, Mau Mau was predominantly a phenomenon which affected Africans: by far the majority of the victims of violence were Kikuyu who were seen to be collaborating with, or benefiting from, colonial rule. Social disintegration under a variety of external pressures, rather than a spirit of nationalism, seemed to be its core. Often depicted by the British as a 'primitive', barbaric movement, a rejection of the modernizing thrust of the late colonial state, Mau Mau appeared to involve resistance to the idea of 'development', currently central to British colonial policy.[68] Specifically, it seemed to be inspired by anger among the rural Kikuyu population at the implications of the post-war development initiative. Conservation policies, originating in the pre-war ecological disaster of soil erosion, involved forced (African) labour on projects which did not themselves produce higher yields. The impact was felt particularly by the substantial population of Kikuyu squatters, who had migrated from overcrowded African land to white settler farming areas. As the settlers embarked increasingly on intensive farming, encouraged by the post-war commodity boom, the squatters found themselves being expelled, to be replaced by wage labour. Ironically, squatters returning to their ancestral lands were not welcomed by the Kikuyu elite which, under state encouragement, was keen to expand its own production of cash crops. Put simply, the squatters were effectively squeezed between settler agriculture and emerging African capitalism. Compounding these tensions was a growing reaction, especially among younger Kikuyu, to prolonged government efforts to eradicate traditional practices. In some sense a generational conflict, Mau Mau witnessed violence against conservative chiefs, urban disorder, which soon spread to the rural areas, and raids on settler farms and government buildings by forest-dwelling guerrilla fighters bound by oaths which seemed unfathomable to whites.[69]

A closer examination of the situation in Kenya also exposes an important gender dimension to tensions within the Kikuyu community. As pressure on available land intensified during and after the Second World War, struggles developed between men and women. Men sought to redefine customary law in order to deprive women of their claims to land, transferring the burden of producing food to women and appropriating the profits of women's crop production. Given their already considerable responsibilities, it is not surprising that women were at the forefront of protests at the colonial state's attempts to extract compulsory labour for land improvement initiatives, notably hill-terracing schemes.[70] Similarly, the bitter disputes over government efforts during the 1950s to eradicate 'female circumcision' (clitoridectomy) were less a reflection of African resistance to colonial rule than of deep cleavages within African society along generational, gender, and class lines.[71]

This point, in turn, raises a larger issue: the excision from the collective memory of women's role in anti-colonial movements. Traditional narratives of nationalism typically attribute most significance to Westernized, male elites in directing resistance movements. Such was far from the case. Tanganyika offers one example in which, virtually from its inception, the nationalist movement was not merely supported by women, but reliant on them. Large numbers of self-employed, urbanized, and often independent women took leading roles in the organization of the movement, helping to define its ideology. Ironically, the colonial state, which so frequently depicted women as 'objects for improvement', would be confronted by highly politicized women who were often impelled by their expectations of what a postcolonial order might mean for them.[72]

Mau Mau is associated above all with extreme violence, but it was not primarily a conflict between Africans and the British, but rather one among Africans themselves. In other words, the conflict resembled a civil war in which the Africans were the principal victims. An estimated 1,800 Africans died at the hands of the Mau Mau, compared with thirty-two white settlers. As many as 20,000 Mau Mau fighters may have perished in the conflict. In addition, 'state executions' totalled over a thousand – paradoxically at a time when the movement within Britain to abolish capital punishment was gaining momentum. Britain's experiences of counter-insurgency in Malaya inevitably influenced its response to the Kenyan crisis, and similar tactics were employed to deprive the Mau Mau fighters of grass-roots support.

As is now recognized (and confirmed by a High Court ruling in London in 2011), the British campaign descended into criminality that included the manipulation of trials and the use of torture.[73] Many thousands of fighters were detained in 're-education' camps in which brutal treatment and poor conditions claimed yet more lives. Detention was used much more extensively in Kenya than in Malaya, where the authorities had the option of deporting suspects to China. Moreover, Mau Mau detainees lacked an influential champion within the international community capable of drawing attention to their plight. Damning accounts of the treatment meted out to detainees began to circulate even so, providing ammunition for metropolitan and other critics of British practices in Kenya. This process would eventually culminate in 1959 in the horrifying revelations of brutality practised at the Hola detention camp, which would have major implications for the government's attitude to colonial policy.[74]

Meanwhile, the military operation was generally judged a success in official circles, even though its director, General Sir George Erskine – whose contempt for the settlers was notorious – was removed in 1955, possibly as a gesture to soothe white feelings.[75] Explanations of the scale of violence used to counter Mau Mau hinge on the fact that Kenya was not merely a colonial state, but a 'settler' state. The particularly harsh treatment of Mau Mau detainees, compared with practices elsewhere in British Africa also mirrored long-standing settler fears about the breakdown of law and order.[76] Recent re-examinations of the Mau Mau evidence have served as a powerful reminder of the *systematic*, not *random*, violence with which British decolonization was associated, a point sometimes dismissed a little too readily by earlier generations of historians. No longer is it possible to treat the British case as exceptional, a liberal oasis in a sea of brutal late colonial policies, as practised by powers such as France or Portugal.[77] Also exposed have been the measures taken by successive British governments to conceal the historical records needed to contextualize late British colonial policy adequately. A good deal of further revisionist research can be expected.

At the political level then, Britain's espousal of multiracialism was accompanied by a tough attitude towards African political restlessness, and a determination to stifle the development of nationalism. The leading Kikuyu activist and President of the Kenya African Union, Jomo Kenyatta, accused by the British of being a key instigator of Mau Mau violence, was given a seven years' prison sentence after what is now widely thought to have been a rigged trial. Political parties beyond the district level remained outlawed in Kenya long after the insurgency was contained.[78] But the coercive aspect of suppressing unrest, involving the detention of some 80,000 alleged Mau Mau fighters by 1954, had, London understood, to be balanced with attempts to construct stable foundations for future development. This involved measures to expand representative government, in which Britain's aim was to encourage the settlers, in return for an expanded role in the colonial state, to accept a measure of power-sharing with Kenya's Asian and African communities. Although multiracialism, not majority rule, remained the goal, Britain planned to award constitutional concessions to those Africans not associated with 'extremism'. As African participation gathered momentum, especially after the general election of 1957, so, too, did calls for increased representation for the majority population. Once again, the logic of introducing electoral politics catalysed political processes that proved impossible for Britain to predict, still less to control.[79]

Recent research has also refocused attention on those sections of Kenya's African population that chose to remain loyal to the British during the Mau Mau episode. As with so much else associated with decolonization, the situation was dynamic. Members of the same social class might adopt quite different positions, and allegiances could shift, reflecting an opportunism perhaps encouraged by conditions of civil war. Those loyal to Britain, and willing to cooperate with the counter-insurgency operation, could expect a variety of rewards, such as an accelerated political franchise, redistributed land, even a role in government.[80]

The most important grievance fuelling Mau Mau had been the chronic land hunger of the Kikuyu, a problem accentuated by African resentment that much of the colony's best farming land, the 'White Highlands', was reserved for settlers.[81] In 1953, Kenya's Governor, Sir Philip Mitchell, engineered the appointment of the East Africa Royal Commission to investigate the related questions of land and population, with a view to promoting higher African living standards. In its report, published in 1955, the Commission proposed steps to encourage market-orientated farming rooted in security of tenure for African farmers. This involved ending the settlers' traditional monopoly of Kenya's prime land. Significantly, these broad conclusions had been anticipated by the Kenyan government, which had presented its ambitious Swynnerton Plan, a bid to create a class of African peasant entrepreneurs, which would have a vested interest in political stability. Recognizing the importance of practical conciliatory gestures to complement the continuing counter-insurgency campaign, London provided an initial grant of £5 million.[82] Preferential treatment in the allocation of development funding was also a means employed by Britain to discourage ethnic groups, such as the Kamba, from taking part in Mau Mau.[83]

Meanwhile, long-term British plans to federate its East African territories also began to have a tangible impact on the political temperature across the region. In Uganda, the new Governor, Sir Andrew Cohen, appointed in 1952, set about democratizing the previously autocratic government of the kingdom of Buganda. This coincided with renewed talk of regional federation sparking African fears that the region might come under effective white settler domination. When the ruler of Buganda refused to cooperate until he received assurances that federation was not planned, Cohen exiled him. For the remainder of the decade, Britain's principal aim in Uganda was to find a means of integrating Buganda into the larger territory.

The ambitious attempt to foster multiracialism in Central Africa had even more serious consequences. Here, London had eventually opted not for the amalgamation of Northern and Southern Rhodesia, which local settlers had sought, but a federal structure to which impoverished Nyasaland was added.[84] From the outset, the majority African population remained implacably opposed to the Federation. London's attitude was that Africans had failed to understand what constituted the common good. As John Darwin has put it: 'With its telescope clapped firmly to its ear, London declared that opposition could be neither seen nor heard.'[85] African concern was not assuaged by the inclusion of mechanisms to safeguard majority rights, but intensified as growing numbers of white immigrants arrived in the Federation, often bringing with them sharper racial attitudes than those of old Rhodesia hands. The Federation undeniably enjoyed economic growth, fuelled by the wealth generated by its minerals and other commodities, and expressed in the building boom in its capital, Salisbury (Harare). But its immediate benefits accrued disproportionately to the settlers, not to the majority population. Reinforcing settler privilege was the 'colour bar' in the work place, which served to counteract the challenge of cheap African labour.

The feasibility of the federal idea hinged, ultimately, on the willingness of the settlers to share power with the African majority, a proposition which exposed the tensions between policymakers in Britain and white politicians in the Federation. To complicate matters, key figures such as Lord Malvern and his successor as federal Prime Minister, the bullish Roy Welensky, cultivated close links with the Conservative Party's hard right. To the settlers, conscious of the pace of political reform elsewhere in British Africa (and impressed by the achievement of South Africa's whites), the Federation's obvious goal was Dominion status, free of British meddling. Concerned that any delay might permit organized African nationalism to develop, and convinced of their own qualifications to supervise the region's affairs (prejudices broadly shared in London), the settlers sought full self-government as rapidly as possible.

An additional settler aim was to secure independence while the Conservatives were still in office; a future Labour administration might, it was thought, be less sympathetic to settler ambitions. These hopes were disappointed. In 1956 the British government insisted that federal independence under white rule was impermissible, although a cosmetic adjustment of the federation's status was contemplated. London's reservations were informed less by sensitivity to African concerns than by a desire to avoid political complications in Britain or moves liable to discredit the federal experiment then being canvassed for East Africa, and under active consideration for other groups of dependent territories. The entire Central African situation was to be reviewed in 1960, but long before then, some British officials foresaw the possibility that settler politicians denied independence on their terms might resort to illegal methods to achieve their aims.

The international background to colonialism

Because the momentum of British decolonization appeared to stall after 1948, a fact seemingly confirmed by the eruption of widespread anti-colonial violence in the early 1950s, many observers felt that British claims to colonial liberality were hollow, even duplicitous. India was among the most ardent critics of colonial rule, especially at the United Nations. Some African nationalists, notably Kwame Nkrumah, looked to the example of Gandhi as a guide to achieving independence, while others acknowledged the Mahatma's influence on their thinking. Certainly, India's stance on colonialism would continue to embarrass Britain. Prime Minister Nehru even used the 1953 anniversary of the Amritsar Day massacre to pledge India's support to Kenya's Mau Mau fighters, causing muffled outrage in London. In 1955, as a key actor at the Bandung Conference, and thus a highly visible champion of Third World independence, India further enhanced its reputation in Africa.[86] Yet by the time many African states had won their independence, African enthusiasm towards India was cooling, prompted by shifts in international relations, not least the Sino-Indian conflict (1962), and doubts about India's value as a developmental model.[87] Not surprisingly, Britain was consistently anxious to evade accountability to the United Nations for its colonial actions. In practice, however, British tactics were pragmatic, accepting that the United Nations had an interest in colonial issues, and providing information to the UN's Trusteeship Council, while setting clear limits to British cooperation.[88] These tactics were broadly successful in the early to mid-1950s, although, as the ranks of the anti-colonial lobby grew, it became harder to prevent unwelcome General Assembly scrutiny, a fact brought home first by the escalation of the Cyprus disorders from 1954 onwards.[89] Abiding fears over Washington's traditionally anti-colonial stance occasioned far greater concern. By 1956 Washington was convinced that the development of colonial nationalism, and deepening international hostility to European colonialism meant that the age of colonial empires was drawing to a close. In these circumstances it made sense for Britain to demonstrate its willingness to make concessions to 'friendly' pro-Western, nationalists, rather than risk unnecessary conflicts by prolonging its imperial connections. The force of UN criticism and, even more, of decisive US disapproval of British imperial actions was brought home as never before during the Suez Crisis in late 1956.

Suez

It is hard to resist the widespread conclusion that Suez was a 'turning point' along the road to British decolonization. In July 1956, shortly after the last British troops had evacuated the Suez Base, Nasser nationalized the Suez Canal, in retaliation for British and American refusal to provide funding for his prestigious Aswan High Dam project. In public, the British government emphasized this event's economic implications, particularly the threat it posed to Britain's oil supplies. Privately, however, it was clear that London's objectives were, admittedly, to ensure long-term international control of the Canal, but meanwhile, to use this opportunity to remove

Nasser, an aim rooted in the morbid obsession with fading British international prestige and its consequences for the wider empire.[90] Early in the crisis, the government apparently resolved to use military force, if necessary alone. Most extraordinary was Eden's presumption that Britain could act independently of the Eisenhower administration, fatally misjudging the wider context of international policy and misreading the signals from Washington.[91]

The United States wanted a diplomatic settlement of the crisis, and between August and October, Britain, the United States, and the Western powers ostensibly worked together to find one. Meanwhile, Washington warned London not to try to coerce Egypt, although it had previously colluded with Britain in 'Plan Omega', which envisaged covert political and economic pressure to topple Nasser's regime. In September, President Eisenhower told Eden that he feared that military action against Egypt would lead the peoples of the Middle East to look to Moscow for support, possibly bringing with them the Afro-Asian bloc of nations.[92]

On 24 October, Britain, France, and Israel concluded a remarkable secret accord, the cold arrogance of which – not to mention the duplicity – is stunning. An Israeli invasion of Egypt would be followed by intervention by Britain and France to 'separate the combatants', occupy the Canal Zone and, it was hoped, remove Nasser. As David Reynolds has commented, this collusion with Israel in particular conflicted 'spectacularly' with Britain's long-standing quest for more secure relations with the Arab world, and underlines the extent to which the Foreign Office was temporarily marginalized in Eden's Whitehall. Military operations began on 29 October with the pre-arranged Israeli attack. British and French air raids on Egyptian airfields soon followed. Despite US, Soviet, and UN calls for an immediate ceasefire, the invasion went ahead, provoking widespread international condemnation. Opinion in Britain divided rancorously. Washington's adverse reaction, however, was decisive. Secretary of State John Foster Dulles, certainly no Anglophile, publicly attacked British 'colonialism', sentiments echoed by Eisenhower. But the rift in the special relationship had more practical and immediate consequences: on 6 November, the United States warned London that if a ceasefire did not follow immediately, Washington would withdraw support for an International Monetary Fund loan to Britain. This money was essential to Britain's financial stability as the invasion had triggered a run on the pound, draining Britain's precarious reserves of more than $300 million. Britain's position was particularly vulnerable: unlike France, and despite the advice of Treasury officials and the Bank of England, the British government had failed to take out adequate loans from the IMF *before* the invasion began.[93] With the very existence of the Sterling Area under threat, Britain had little option but to comply with US demands, and the withdrawal of its forces was completed by 22 December. Shortly afterwards, Eden, his health broken and his reputation shattered, resigned from office.

The ethics of the Suez collusion aside, the invasion was profoundly counterproductive. It cemented Nasser's position as champion of the Arab world, and gave encouragement to anti-colonial movements around the world. Commonwealth nations had split and, albeit as expected, Nehru condemned Britain openly and sided with Egypt.[94] On pragmatic as well as ethical grounds, the Canadian government, an active UN supporter that had assiduously developed ties with the non-aligned countries, was appalled at Britain's behaviour.[95] Although no country actually left the Commonwealth over Suez, the crisis inevitably damaged the delicate Commonwealth relationship, and even raised fresh questions about the association's future.[96]

Suez represented an unambiguous failure to recover a lost position by a show of strength: the underpinnings of that strength were exposed as illusory. Nevertheless, the crisis and its aftermath did not mark the abdication by Britain of its Middle Eastern role. The British military presence in Jordan, Iraq, and Aden remained intact and seemed, for the time being, secure. The Baghdad Pact, engineered by Britain, was still in place, and British influence in the Persian Gulf remained. Admittedly, anti-Western nationalism in the region was galvanized, as would soon be demonstrated by the revolution in Iraq, the lynchpin in Britain's Middle Eastern system. Yet the extent of Britain's continuing confidence would soon be revealed when plans were unveiled for an ambitious, if ultimately unworkable, South Arabian Federation, based on Aden. Further afield, Britain's East of Suez role was unaffected, and was even enhanced early in 1957 by the conclusion of a defence treaty with newly independent Malaya. Even the strained special relationship would be restored with remarkable speed, thanks to the efforts of Eden's successor, Harold Macmillan, and the fact that Washington had no wish to undermine Britain's position any further, particularly its still valued role in defending the oil sheikhdoms of the Persian Gulf.[97]

If Suez intensified local pressure for decolonization, there is little to suggest that the Suez Crisis *in itself* caused Britain to accelerate plans for colonial withdrawal.[98] Ironically, one practical consequence of the crisis was to highlight the military value of Cyprus (which became home to Britain's Middle Eastern headquarters following the evacuation of the Suez Base), redoubling British resolve to retain control of the island.[99] However, the most important lesson arising from the Suez debacle was that never again could Britain allow itself to become so isolated and vulnerable as a result of its external policies. If the broad aims of Britain's global policy remained unchanged, the methods used to secure them would require caution, flexibility, and greater sensitivity to international, and especially, American opinion.

CHAPTER 4
WINDS OF CHANGE: THE FINAL WAVES
OF DECOLONIZATION IN AFRICA AND
ASIA AFTER 1957

During the years 1957–64 the vast majority of Britain's remaining colonial possessions became independent. Meanwhile, Britain's traditional reluctance to become more involved in Europe dissipated as evidence gathered of the success of the new European Economic Community, culminating in Britain's unsuccessful bid for entry in 1961. Any attempt to achieve greater involvement in Europe in turn inevitably raised questions about the Commonwealth's future. These were among the problems faced by a new Conservative government. Harold Macmillan, described by Harold Wilson as 'first in, first out' during Suez, succeeded Eden as Prime Minister in January 1957. Macmillan inherited Churchill's belief in Britain's unique world role as the point of intersection of the three great circles: the Commonwealth, the Atlantic alliance, and Europe.[1] Yet there was plenty to suggest that the new Prime Minister's sympathies lay more with colonial populations than with the pursuit of imperial interests as traditionally perceived. During the war, he had made radical suggestions on Kenya's future, for instance, proposing that white settler landowners should be bought out by the state and their lands redistributed among the African population, in order to ease popular hunger for land. But he tended to become involved directly in colonial policy only when it impacted upon wider international relations or the government's standing in the country.

Initially, at least, Macmillan's handling of colonial policy was cautious, and involved no startling initiatives. Both Ghana and Malaya became independent in 1957, in accordance with plans made before Suez. In accordance with his emphasis on restoring the special relationship, Macmillan met President Eisenhower twice during his first year in office, first in Bermuda in March 1957, and then in Washington in October. At these meetings, close ties were re-established, and the two leaders committed themselves to coordinated policies in world affairs, for example in Asia and Africa, on the implicit assumption that Britain would never again attempt to mount a major overseas military operation without prior US approval. The Americans, like the British, were unconvinced that most of colonial Africa was 'ready' for independence, but saw no realistic alternative strategy. These exchanges prepared the ground for an attempt by London and Washington to examine the closer coordination of their policies towards Africa. The fundamental aim of both governments has been described as the creation of a new 'informal' empire in Africa, under joint Anglo-American auspices.[2]

Although his immediate priority after Suez was to rebuild close ties with Washington, Macmillan also needed to heal differences with members of the Commonwealth. Macmillan seems to have developed a high regard for the Commonwealth and its potential as a multiracial organization with a common heritage and outlook. This view, shown in hindsight to have been exaggerated, was reinforced by the highly successful (and reassuring) Commonwealth tour Macmillan made in 1957–8, the first by a serving British Prime Minister. Macmillan subsequently became far more pessimistic. Developments in the South African apartheid state, in particular, threatened to destroy the Commonwealth. Here, the Sharpeville Massacre (March 1960), in which sixty-seven African demonstrators were killed, sparked international outrage. This highlighted not only the difficulties for Britain in defending its significant investments in the country, but also the problems inherent in holding the Commonwealth together.[3]

Although not in itself a consequence of Suez, the government's reassessment of Britain's defence requirements, expressed in the 1957 Defence White Paper, also shaped a revised global outlook. This fundamental review, driven above all by financial considerations and the need to economize, transferred resources from conventional to nuclear capability. The armed forces were to be cut from 690,000 to 375,000 by the end of 1962. This made possible the ending of conscription in 1960, but potentially circumscribed Britain's ability to fight large-scale counter-insurgency campaigns in the colonies.[4]

It was also in the years after 1957 that several looming economic problems of the early 1950s finally became inescapable. Hopes for a significant increase in export earnings gave way to the reality of a large deficit in 1960, and in the following year a sterling crisis threatened. A pattern was developing characterized by 'stop-go' economic activity, in which economic expansion tended to encourage a higher level of imports than of exports, which in turn put pressure on the value of sterling. The government's customary response was to raise interest rates, thereby cutting consumer demand in order to reduce imports, but this strategy could trigger symptoms of recession such as heightened unemployment after mid-1961.

Officially, at least, Britain still retained its faith in the Commonwealth as an important and valuable trading bloc. In practice, however, British trade with the Commonwealth continued to decline. Whereas in 1950, over 47 per cent of Britain's exports went to Commonwealth destinations, by 1960 the figure was a little over 40 per cent. Imports from the Commonwealth shrank by a similar proportion in the same period. By the early 1960s, moreover, there were growing misgivings in Britain about whether the country should be exporting so many talented people to Commonwealth countries, robbing the British economy of skilled personnel while strengthening the competitive potential of its trading partners.[5] British policymakers remained convinced that London was, and should remain, a major international financial centre, the heart of a complex network of commercial and political relationships.[6] But the success of Britain's competitors, and the arguments for increased metropolitan – not imperial – investment, raised questions about Britain's ability to continue as a world banker. By the late 1950s sterling had declined in status to being a 'negotiated' currency, one which Britain had to *persuade* other countries to use in their transactions.[7]

Although they intensified after the Second World War, the economic shifts which were a component of decolonization were not new. The Lancashire cotton industry, for instance, had famously long felt the effects of competition within the Empire, especially from India, inspiring a protracted, ultimately unsuccessful, campaign for measures to protect Commonwealth markets. After 1945 economic changes that were in some way associated with the Empire were not felt evenly in Britain; on the contrary, their impacts varied by region. Thus, while London prepared to take advantage of the new opportunities for the shipping industry created by expanding trade with the EEC, Liverpool, whose earlier development as a major port hinged, in part, on its imperial links, continued to decline.[8]

The background of gloomy economic prospects, and a continuing desire to obtain the best returns from the expenditure of dwindling resources, prompted an important initiative soon after Macmillan became Prime Minister. In January 1957, Macmillan called on the Cabinet Colonial Policy Committee to establish which colonies might soon become self-governing, which ones would become eligible to join the Commonwealth, and what the fate of those ineligible for entry should be.[9] There has been much speculation about the extent to which this represented a determination to shed Britain's colonial responsibilities. In the event, the results of this 'audit' of the colonial Empire were inconclusive. The report of the Colonial Policy Committee suggested that Malaya, Nigeria, a West Indies Federation, and the Central African Federation were the territories most ready for independence. Accelerated political change was also predicted for both East and West Africa. More than a dozen territories appeared to be candidates for self-government during the forthcoming decade.[10]

However, any impression of a post-Suez retreat from empire must recognize Britain's distinctive role 'East of Suez', which, if anything, expanded after 1956. It was typified by Britain's continuing presence in Malaya after independence in 1957. In exchange for Malaya's continued membership of the Sterling Area, Britain provided Malaya's new indigenous rulers with the military aid they needed to suppress the country's continuing internal guerrilla threat. Similarly, although Singapore achieved self-governing status in 1957, London retained responsibility for its defence and external relations, highlighting Britain's determination to preserve the island as a major strategic base.

The East of Suez commitment was more than a symbol of the hubris of a power in decline: there were practical reasons for Britain's preoccupation with this region. Britain, whose coal industry appeared to be facing extinction, was heavily dependent on imported energy resources, and almost half its oil came from the Persian Gulf. Moreover, around a quarter of Britain's exports were sold to countries bounded by the Indian Ocean and the Western Pacific.[11] Britain's military planners also emphasized the region's importance to them. All three services were struggling to establish niches for their expertise in the wake of the uncertainties introduced not only by pressure to economize, but also by the ongoing strategic reappraisal of the mid-1950s. Late in 1957, it was concluded that an effective East of Suez role required the establishment of a strategic reserve in Kenya. Soon, an enormous, and expensive, military base there was being planned.[12] As Kenyan independence loomed into view in 1960–1, planners switched their attention instead to Aden, where Britain's military presence had already increased four-fold between 1957 and 1959, with the colony becoming home to Britain's Middle East Command. Here too, however, London would find its calculations upset during the 1960s by escalating resistance to British rule.[13]

The Middle East

In his first Cabinet meeting as Prime Minister, Macmillan insisted that Britain should not give any impression of retreat from its remaining Middle Eastern footholds.[14] Policymakers' attitudes seemed unaltered: the belief that Nasser was the most serious threat to Britain's Middle Eastern interests was not diluted, but rather strengthened by the events of autumn 1956: containing this threat remained a basic policy aim. Ironically, while the 'three circles' model of Britain's global system was influential in Whitehall, Nasser borrowed the concept, plausibly defining

Egypt as being at the intersection of the Arab, Islamic, and African circles. The most important external challenge came from another quarter entirely. The unveiling of the 'Eisenhower Doctrine' in January 1957 extended US activities unambiguously into the Arab world, offering military assistance and economic aid to countries threatened with communist aggression or subversion. Its implication was that American muscle and money would gradually supplant British influence in the region. Or perhaps not: subtler methods, a shift in strategic focus to Aden and the Persian Gulf, and amicable cooperation with the United States were the tenets of Britain's revised Middle East policy.[15] The American administration, for its part, recoiled from deeper engagements liable to antagonize its existing regional partners, Israel and Saudi Arabia.

The fly in the ointment was Iraq, whose economy was still dominated by the Iraq Petroleum Company, in which Britain was the major shareholder. In February 1958, Egypt and Syria announced their merger in the United Arab Republic. The pro-Western governments of Iraq and Jordan, alarmed by this demonstration of Nasserite radicalism, responded by creating the Arab Federation, and Iraq looked to Washington and London for economic help. Macmillan's government promised aid in the event of Iraq's oil pipeline being disrupted by hostilities with Syria, but it was unnerved by Iraqi Prime Minister Nuri Said's eagerness for Britain to relinquish its protectorate over oil-rich Kuwait so that the latter could join the Arab Federation. Ever since Iraq's own independence, it had seen itself as the legitimate heir to Ottoman suzerainty over Kuwait, regarded as a hotbed of Nasserite and communist propaganda.[16] Far greater concerns soon took priority. The pro-Nasserite Iraqi revolution of 14 July 1958, which brought down both the Hashemite monarchy and Nuri Said, precipitated a crisis with regional ramifications even greater than Suez.[17] The July Revolution exposed the dangers in Britain's dependence on an unpopular elite to uphold imperial interests and safeguard metropolitan oil supplies. Reliance on a self-interested ruling class challenged by rapid demographic growth, profound socio-economic change, and emergent 'middling' interest groups hastened the collapse of Britain's neocolonial influence. Britain's failure to promote economic modernization, combined with the fact that its development strategy tended, if anything, to benefit the privileged, only sharpened anti-British feelings. London's key collaborator, Nuri Said, had thus found himself increasingly isolated as his domestic opponents circled around him.[18]

Alarmed by the Baghdad coup, the pro-Western regimes in Lebanon and Jordan quickly turned to Britain and the United States for assistance against the pan-Arabist military threat from Egypt, Syria, or Iraq. Jordan's request posed the most immediate dilemma for Britain, still the major external influence on the former. Domestic hostility to links with Britain influenced the elections held in October 1956, which produced a government ready to cultivate ties with Egypt and the communist world. In March 1957 the authorities in Amman abrogated the Anglo-Jordanian Treaty. Unnerved by the growth of Nasserite influence, domestically and externally, Jordan's King Hussein successfully defused a military coup in the same month, but turned to Washington for assistance. The United States would soon become Jordan's senior patron, displacing Britain. Facing renewed threats of internal upheaval, two days after the Iraqi revolution, Hussein formally requested Anglo-American assistance. Macmillan's government, aware of Nasserite support among Palestinian refugees in Jordan, however, only authorized limited intervention, airlifting 4,000 troops from Cyprus to secure the airfield in Amman and the royal palace. Washington, this time fully consulted about British intentions, was itself preoccupied with fulfilling a similar request for help from the Lebanese government.

Putting economic interest above former clients, Britain and the United States opted to recognize Brigadier Qassem's new Iraqi regime as regional tensions eased during the autumn of 1958.[19] British and US troops quietly withdrew from Jordan and Lebanon during October and November. Although Britain's intervention threatened to erode the residual legitimacy of the Amman regime by underlining its status as a Western client, growing rivalry between Iraq and Egypt for regional influence would eventually work in Jordan's (and Britain's) favour. Even Nasser saw the wisdom of playing down his anti-Hussein rhetoric.[20]

The Jordanian crisis added weight to the basic moral of the Suez debacle, namely, that Britain, now clearly a secondary power, could no longer act independently in the region without prior American assent. But the episode also revealed London's continuing determination to safeguard its regional interests. As the immediate crisis of July 1958 receded, Britain sought to consolidate relations with the new Baghdad regime. Diplomats hoped to exploit the potential for fractures in Arab nationalism, thereby isolating Egypt while at the same time dissipating the Iraqi challenge to British interests in Kuwait, whose rapid development as an oil producer had helped to compensate for the loss of Iranian oil after the nationalization of the Abadan refinery in 1951.[21] Revised plans for British military intervention were made, nonetheless.[22] The practical consequences of the Iraq coup for Britain were considerable. The federation between Iraq and Jordan soon disintegrated, and Iraq eventually withdrew from the Baghdad Pact, the centrepiece of Britain's regional planning, in March 1959. More ominously, Qassem's government soon established relations with the Soviet Union and China, a sign of its intention to pursue an independent foreign policy, despite the fact that the new regime drew 70 per cent of its revenue from Iraq Petroleum Company operations.[23]

In June 1961 the Iraqi regime once again claimed sovereignty over Kuwait, fuelling fears of an imminent invasion. Kuwait was, by then, the region's largest oil producer, supplying around 40 per cent of Britain's requirements. It also invested substantially in the British economy and was therefore an overseas economic asset of prime importance to Britain. In the months preceding Iraq's claim, Kuwait's ruler had urged London to grant the emirate independence.[24] An agreement terminating the protectorate also made provision for British military assistance if required. Indeed, it bears emphasis that it was Kuwait's imminent independence that triggered the renewed Iraqi claim. Fearful that Iraqi forces, once entrenched, could not easily be dislodged, and worried about a loss of credibility with the other Gulf emirates, Britain deployed some 10,000 troops in Kuwait in late June 1961 to deter an Iraqi invasion.[25] Initially supportive, at the United Nations and elsewhere, John F. Kennedy's new US administration soon questioned the assumptions behind what was the largest British operational deployment since Suez, especially as the threatened Iraqi attack never came.[26]

The Kuwait episode forced a rethink about Britain's interests in the Persian Gulf, and on how to defend them. Judged a success, the operation was thought to have laid the ghost of Suez to rest. However, British military resources had been severely stretched, and it had been shown that Britain was unable to contain two simultaneous crises, a fact which would have implications for London's subsequent response to deteriorating conditions in Central Africa. In September 1961 the Cabinet Secretary, Sir Norman Brook (echoing uncannily the thrust of Bevin's post-1945 philosophy), urged Macmillan to reconsider the traditional policy of trying to meet Britain's oil requirements through deals with essentially undemocratic rulers, underpinned by the promise of British military protection. The number of places in the world where foreign troops were tolerated was shrinking, yet Britain's current policy took 'no account of the rising tide of nationalism in these countries, and, so long as it forces us to support the Sheikhs and Rulers, we are bound to find ourselves, in the end, on the losing side'.[27] Significantly, other Arab states did most to change the region's strategic position anyway. Albeit for different reasons, Saudi Arabia and Egypt were equally determined to prevent Iraq's absorption of Kuwait. During the summer of 1961, international support grew for a local solution to a local problem, one that would make UN intervention unnecessary. In July, Kuwait was admitted to the Arab League, which permitted the replacement of British forces by an Arab League security force.

In Southern Arabia and Aden, meanwhile, Britain's efforts to retain influence were reinforced by the belief, central to the East of Suez policy, that a secure Middle Eastern foothold, beyond the reach of Egyptian pan-Arabism, was essential. Southern Arabia seemed to meet this requirement, as its traditional society was judged inimical to the rapid growth of secular, modernist nationalism. The local rulers of the protectorates neighbouring Aden, alarmed by the threat of incursions from Yemen, accepted the logic of closer association. Accordingly, in 1959 the British inaugurated the Federation of South Arabia, to which Aden was subsequently added.[28] Theoretically under British protection, the Federation was soon destabilized by a combination of revolutionary fervour in South Yemen and labour unrest in Aden, which erupted into nationalist protest and violence. Again, British assumptions about the strength of popular nationalism proved to be wrong.[29]

Cyprus and the West Indies

British forces had been engaged in a bitter struggle with Greek Cypriot insurgents since 1955. The options of partition into separate Greek and Turkish zones, or independence for the island in return for continued British military base rights were initially ruled out in London. Increasingly, however, the Cyprus problem attracted international interest. In early 1957 the UN General Assembly debated the issue, despite British objections. But the resulting proposal for NATO mediation between three of its members – Greece, Turkey, and Britain – seemed constructive. To enhance prospects for dialogue, and at US prompting, the Greek Cypriot leader Archbishop Makarios was released from detention by Britain, a move that infuriated Tory 'diehards' such as Lord Salisbury. Makarios abandoned the aim of *enosis* with Greece, accepting the principle of independence on British terms, which, in turn, alienated Georgios Grivas, the leader of EOKA, the Greek Cypriot paramilitary organization committed to ending British rule.

Communal violence on the island continued unabated in 1958, just as the Iraqi coup shattered the Baghdad Pact, making Cyprus more crucial as a British military outpost in the eastern Mediterranean, a point the Eisenhower administration appreciated. Meanwhile, international pressure mounted on both Greece and Turkey to accept a compromise. In February 1959, an agreement was concluded between Makarios and the governments of Britain, Greece, and Turkey, under which Cyprus would become an independent republic in 1960. Britain would retain bases at Akrotiri and Dhekelia. Makarios, it seems, accepted independence to avert the possibility of the island's partition into ethnic enclaves.

At independence, Cyprus, despite its small population (half a million) and size, joined the Commonwealth. This set a precedent for the future treatment of the West Indian islands, the two most economically important of which, Jamaica and Trinidad, achieved independence in 1962, thereby sealing the fate of the short-lived Federation of the West Indies created in 1958.[30] British officials had assumed that the ten territories comprising the Federation would become independent as a single unit, viable politically and financially self-sufficient. Although a 1947 conference at Montego Bay explored the possibility of a West Indian Federation, it had been thought sensible to allow time for the idea to generate support in the region. Once again, events ran a course at variance with metropolitan predictions. The unexpectedly rapid advance of individual West Indian colonies towards self-government during the 1950s, as well as the rapidity of economic development in Jamaica and Trinidad and Tobago, made their separate independence harder to resist. Nor were local rivalries and wrangling over the Federation's financial arrangements ever overcome. In January 1960 Colonial Secretary Iain Macleod made clear that he would not oppose Jamaica's independence and a Jamaican referendum in September of the following year endorsed independence and departure from the Federation. London accepted this verdict, soon to be followed by that of oil-producing Trinidad, where there was widespread fear that the island would be left with financial responsibility for the rest of the Federation. Now utterly undermined, the Federation was wound up in May 1962, paving the way for the separate independence of its components.[31]

The wind of change

The year 1959 was pivotal in British decolonization, a year of flux that paved the way for accelerated imperial retreat between 1960 and 1964, during which a total of seventeen colonies, mostly in Africa, became independent. Amounting to a 'revolution' in policymaking, the telescoping of constitutional change reflected London's growing belief that the alternative might be to risk an imperial collapse similar to that experienced in South Asia after 1945.[32] With a British general election due in autumn 1959, the declaration of an emergency in Nyasaland followed by the revelation in June of atrocities at Kenya's Hola detention camp placed colonial embarrassments under intense media scrutiny, threatening to damage the Conservatives' public standing.[33] Domestic questioning of the government's record certainly intensified during the later 1950s. For a Labour Party constrained by broad agreement on the outlines of government domestic policy, and riven by disputes over defence policy, colonial affairs was one realm in which Labour politicians could safely attack their Conservative opponents freely. There were limits, even so: electoral considerations made sympathy towards colonial nationalists potentially risky. Further to the left, most active was the Movement for Colonial Freedom, although this could hardly hope to rival the success of similar campaigning bodies like the Campaign for Nuclear Disarmament.[34] The Conservative Party was itself divided, former Colonial Secretary Lennox-Boyd and Macmillan's close ally, Lord Home, both being hostile to rapid colonial withdrawal.[35] Macmillan therefore shied away from any 'hasty shift' in policy.[36] He did, however, initiate an interdepartmental review on 'Africa: the next ten years', both to clarify Whitehall's own thinking and to satisfy US pressure for action.[37] For at least one historian, this report marked the 'real' beginning of the 'wind of change'.[38]

The resulting report by the Africa Official Committee concluded that the only means to curb Soviet encroachment in Africa would be to install pro-Western, independent regimes composed of cooperative nationalists. The greatest menace to this delicate operation, as officials realized, was the risk of ethnic conflict, and here the Central African Federation presented the prime threat. White settlers, responding to political change in West Africa and Nkrumah's championing of pan-Africanism, sought to establish an independent federation to pre-empt black majority rule. There were already fears in London that Southern Rhodesia, where the settlers were most entrenched, might seize independence unilaterally, wrecking British relations with the rest of Africa in the process. The Colonial Office recognized that failure in Central Africa could cost Britain its amicable postcolonial relationships with other African states. Somehow, Britain had to prove that it was not committed to propping up white supremacy.[39]

Some of these concerns had already been evident in Britain's handling of Nigeria, an example of decolonization which bridged the official assumptions of the later 1950s and early 1960s.[40] Nigeria, which came into existence after the amalgamation of the protectorates of Southern and Northern Nigeria in 1914, received a federal constitution in 1951 which gave each of the territory's three regions its own assembly, suggesting that Nigerian politics would continue to evolve on basically ethnic lines. The settlement allowed the colonial government to capitalize on mutual suspicions between the Muslim north and Christian south, and so delay discussions on full self-government.[41] Lennox-Boyd, temperamentally more sympathetic to the conservative Muslim elites of the north than to the 'westernized' population of the south, feared that rapid political change might lead to chaos, perhaps provoking northern secession. Obstructionism, however, might unite Nigerian opposition to any continued British presence, whether political or commercial. In October 1958, the British government finally agreed that 1960 should be the target date for the territory's independence, an about-turn in policy made in reaction to the gathering strength of international anti-colonialism and the chance to conciliate a moderate nationalist elite seen as a potential counterweight to the growing radicalism of Ghana's Kwame Nkrumah.[42]

Nigeria pointed a way forward after the Conservatives won the October 1959 election. Macmillan's new government, now equipped with a cabinet-level Africa Committee, devoted far greater attention to accelerated African decolonization, hoping to create an enlarged Commonwealth capable of playing a major role in the Cold War.[43] The new Colonial Secretary, Iain Macleod, was committed to greater African political representation and abandoned his department's painstaking gradualism.[44] During his two-year ministerial tenure, five colonies gained independence and preparations were made to establish majority rule in another six, prompting the initially sympathetic Macmillan to conclude that Macleod had moved too fast, too soon.[45] Set against the background of the Algerian War, the Congo crisis, worsening racial tension in South Africa, and the recent Central African emergency, Macleod's urgency stemmed from an underlying fear of bloody confrontation in Africa.[46] Practical, as well as moral, considerations informed this position: Britain lacked the resources to fight protracted colonial wars. The use of force to tackle nationalist resistance, even if it were practicable, would bring international condemnation, and might even trigger intervention by the United Nations. Nor could it be assumed that British public opinion would acquiesce in a coercive colonial policy. For Macleod, as for Macmillan, the purpose of decolonization was to preserve as much of Britain's overseas influence as possible, through arrangements acceptable to political elites in the colonies, designed to create successor states friendly to the West, not the Soviet bloc.[47]

By November 1959, Macmillan had decided to visit Africa. Eager to gauge the strength of African nationalism, the Prime Minister nonetheless recognized that white settlers, not the African majority, were the principal impediment to British colonial policy, a fact confirmed by Lord Devlin's damning inquiry into the authorities' handling of unrest in Nyasaland during the 1959 Emergency.[48] Macmillan toured Ghana, Nigeria, the Central African Federation, and South Africa during January and February 1960. He assured West African leaders of Britain's sympathy with African aspirations.[49] Better known, however, was his attempt while in the Federation, and especially in South Africa, to persuade white settlers to come to terms with the force of African nationalism. Most famously, in February 1960 he distanced the British government from apartheid, telling the South African parliament in Cape Town that British, and, by implication, South African, policies must respond to the force of African nationalism – the 'wind of change' blowing through the continent.[50] Arguably, he had little to lose: later in 1960, South Africa would vote to become a republic and would soon leave the Commonwealth, much to the relief of many of its existing and future members. To the government's right-wing Tory critics, however, Macmillan's speech was a capitulation, and was the immediate cause of the formation of the Conservative Party's Monday Club.[51]

Unlike Macmillan, such reactionary opinion took little account of wider international trends such as the precedents in African decolonization set by France and Belgium, the increasing assertiveness of the Afro-Asian nations at the United Nations, and the liberal drift in US governmental opinion under President Kennedy.[52] Prior to Suez, Britain had generally succeeded in containing UN interference in its colonial policies. Increasingly after 1956, however, Britain found itself dangerously exposed in the General Assembly, the target of mounting international criticism.[53] Domestically, not all criticism came from the hard right. Sir Andrew Cohen, by then British representative on the UN Trusteeship Council, noted ruefully in 1961 that the emphasis on preventing the spread of communism into Africa conflicted with the Colonial Office's long-declared aim of preparing colonies for long-term viability after independence.[54]

East and Central Africa

It was in East and Central Africa that the post-1959 shift in British colonial policy was most dramatic. Here, settler populations made the kind of policies already pursued in relation to West Africa seem unrealistic. The region also illustrated the fundamental problem confronting policymakers in London, that the colonial territories could rarely be treated individually, in isolation: on the contrary, developments in one territory or country shaped expectations in its neighbours.

Early in 1959, a governors' conference met at Chequers to discuss East Africa's prospects, the first attempt to delineate a tentative timetable for independence for the region's three territories. The conclusions were cautious. Although Uganda and Tanganyika were candidates for eventual African majority rule, perhaps by the late 1960s, the same could not be said of Kenya where, according to Lennox-Boyd, more time was needed to encourage the development of a 'moderate', non-racial political grouping. In terms of London's outlook, Macleod's arrival was decisive. By early 1960, the timetables for East African political advance confidently drawn up in mid-1959 were already redundant.[55]

Tanganyika led the way. A UN Trust territory with only a small settler population, since 1955, the United Nations had called for African majority rule in its legislature. Following Britain's introduction of a revised constitution in April 1957, Julius Nyerere's Tanganyika

African National Union (TANU) won a resounding victory in subsequent national elections. Formed in 1954, TANU in many respects embodied an 'ideal-type' nationalist organization. Under the charismatic leadership of Dr Julius Nyerere the party harnessed both rural and urban support, tapping into widespread popular grievances provoked by development projects (such as the Sukumaland development scheme). By offering much-needed services, such as basic schooling, TANU also highlighted the evident shortcomings of a colonial state supposedly committed to 'development'.[56] TANU's electoral success appeared to represent a convincing rejection of the colonial government's aim of cultivating multiracialism. Governor Sir Richard Turnbull responded in March 1959 by proposing a new Council of Ministers, still with an official majority, and the appointment of a committee to investigate further constitutional changes. But the balance of colonial power had already shifted decisively. By May, Turnbull was warning London that the elected members were demonstrating solidarity in calling for constitutional reform, and (ironically) of TANU's cross-ethnic appeal. In this respect, Macleod's appointment in October 1959 helped to clear the policy impasse. Macleod, who visited East Africa late in 1959, was impressed by Nyerere, and resolved to press ahead with reforms in Tanganyika, combining these with new initiatives in Kenya. He conceded fresh elections and a wider franchise, enabling Nyerere to become chief minister in 1960, and to follow a relatively unobstructed path to full independence late in 1961.[57]

Although Uganda had few settlers, its situation was complicated by the strength of regionalism, in particular the Kingdom of Buganda's distinctive and privileged position within the territory. When democratic elections to the legislature were proposed in 1959 the Baganda elite refused to cooperate. Macleod was undeterred, announcing elections for 1961, to be followed by a constitutional conference to decide Uganda's future. Uganda's political elites faced the choice either of extending their appeal nationally, or becoming identified with narrower regional interests. While the Uganda People's Congress, led by Milton Obote, emerged as the focus for nationalism, the conservative Baganda marked their disapproval of political centralization by boycotting the elections held in March 1961, setting a dangerous precedent for the future. Again, Macleod strode on, and in September 1961 a Baganda delegation attended the constitutional conference, hoping to achieve some sort of federal solution. In 1962, after full internal self-government had been achieved, fresh elections saw Milton Obote emerge as the political leader who, later that year, took Uganda to full independence with Buganda being accorded semi-autonomous status.

The Ugandan episode captured a problem which, in the excited mood of the late 1950s and early 1960s, was prone to be overlooked: that the unitary national state, as traditionally conceived in the West, was not the *only* possible outcome of decolonization. Given the ethnic and linguistic diversity of many former colonies, postcolonial regimes could not assume the identification of the mass of the population with the new dispensation. As experiences in Africa, above all the disastrous Nigerian civil war and the horrific dictatorship of Idi Amin in Uganda would show, regionalism remained an entrenched problem. It was aggravated by the privileging of certain ethnic groups under colonial rule, particularly the British tendency to attribute 'martial' qualities to such groups.[58]

In Kenya, Britain's encouragement of multiracial politics, along with the economic reforms embodied in the Swynnerton Plan, was in reality intended to obstruct 'extreme' African elements from seeking African majority rule on the basis of 'One Man One Vote' (OMOV).[59] Unlike Tanganyika and Uganda, constitutional innovations in Kenya, while superficially democratic, were intended to conserve European privileges. In response, from November 1958 the African members of the colony's legislature boycotted its sittings in support of their demand for majority rule. They had little alternative. If they were not to lose credibility, Kenyan African politicians could only cooperate in the multiracial experiment if it were a transitional step to eventual majority rule.[60]

Early in 1959 Kenya was still technically under emergency rule, and the territory's future leader Jomo Kenyatta was still in detention. Since the declaration of the emergency, attempts had been made to 'rehabilitate' Mau Mau detainees. Events at the Hola detention camp on 3 March 1959 made clear what this meant. Faced with a growing number of unrepentant fighters, Britain, in an effort to speed up the rehabilitation process, developed an 'unofficial policy' under which psychological pressure on detainees frequently degenerated into physical violence. Eleven inmates were beaten to death by their guards at Hola. According to Macleod, it was this incident more than anything else which required the government's fundamental reappraisal of policy towards Kenya, and Africa more generally.[61] Especially embarrassing for the government was the condemnation of the Hola affair by the Conservative ex-minister, Enoch Powell, particularly his damaging claim that standards of public conduct expected in Britain were being disregarded in the African colonies.[62] Earlier in 1959, while Lennox-Boyd was pondering the wisdom of publicly endorsing the goal of eventual majority rule, a 'moderate' settler leader, Michael Blundell, formed a new political party, the New Kenya Group (NKG), committed to multiracialism, and backed by sections of the business community. From the colonial government's point of view, this made the NKG the preferred candidate for power, and it seemed vital to do nothing to obstruct the development of this valuable potential counterweight to African nationalism. Meanwhile, a conference on Kenya's future was planned for 1960. It was in preparation for this conference that, late in 1959, the African members of the legislature temporarily shelved their differences to demand majority rule and Kenyatta's release. For the Colonial Office, which had hoped that divisions among African nationalists would create opportunities for the NKG, this came as another unpleasant surprise. Once again, London had underestimated the organizational sophistication of African nationalist groups.

Yet still Britain retained leverage over Kenya. For one thing, the immediate Mau Mau threat had been neutralized. For another, the settler community had trebled since 1945, with an influx of officials and businessmen without the strong sense of identification with the Kenyan soil characteristic of their aristocratic and upper-middle class predecessors. The new arrivals were quicker to learn the central lesson that Mau Mau had finally exploded settler aspirations to control the colonial state. At the Lancaster House Conference in January 1960, Macleod called for the creation of an African-elected majority in the Legislative Council, together with equal representation for Africans and non-Africans in the Executive Council. Meanwhile, the Colonial Office reiterated the 1923 Devonshire formula that Kenya was, after all, a predominantly African country, sending a clear message to the territory's nationalist politicians: those who were willing to operate the new political system could, in time, expect eventually to achieve majority rule. State of emergency restrictions were also lifted and there was talk of political amnesties, partly, it seems, to forestall further embarrassing revelations of brutality towards detainees.[63]

In addition to these elaborate political manoeuvres, measures were introduced to consolidate Kenyan political stability through fresh economic reforms designed to remove some of the more obvious sources of African (particularly Kikuyu) grievance, which had originally helped to trigger Mau Mau. The British government funded the purchase of around 186,000 acres of land in the prized White Highlands, for redistribution among African farmers, the aim being to help foster a vigorous class of capitalist smallholders. Settler farmers who could not adapt to political change in the territory were also given the opportunity to sell up. Nevertheless, British policymakers still clung tenaciously to their hopes for a multiracial Kenya. A new constitution, introduced in 1961, was intended to assist the growth of Blundell's New Kenya Group. Two major African parties emerged, the Kenya African National Union (KANU), composed chiefly of the Kikuyu and Luo and looking to early independence, and the Kenya African Democratic Union (KADU), representing many of Kenya's other African communities, which subsequently merged with the NKG. KADU advocated '*majimboism*', or regionalism. Essentially, it was hoped that a decentralized political system, consisting of several states of roughly equal status, would shield smaller communities from domination by larger groups, such as the Kikuyu. Unsurprisingly, this view was ridiculed by KANU as 'tribalism', recidivist and out of step with the party's nationalist, centralizing vision.[64]

In the 1961 elections, KANU received twice as many votes as KADU, but used the issue of Kenyatta's continuing detention to demonstrate its nationalist credentials, refusing to take office until he had been released. This remained a deeply sensitive issue, Kenyatta having been described by the Governor, Sir Patrick Renison, as recently as 1960 as a 'leader unto darkness and death'. Even Macleod, conscious of mounting right-wing criticism, initially refused to release him.[65] KADU managed to form an interim coalition government with the support of the NKG, but having no wish to be outdone by KANU in its championing of nationalist demands, it, too, campaigned for Kenyatta's release. This time Macleod reacted differently. His threat of resignation helped secure Kenyatta's release in August 1961, cooling a tense Kenyan political climate.

The pace of change in Kenya did not slacken after Reginald Maudling replaced Macleod in October 1961. New constitutional changes were introduced in January 1962, which, by creating regional assemblies, were intended to benefit KADU, and prevent KANU securing an unchallengeable political position. In April, encouraged by Britain, which sought to reduce possibly destabilizing tribal tensions, KANU and KADU formed a coalition, in which Kenyatta became Minister for Constitutional Affairs and Economic Planning. The new grouping oversaw the final stages of devolution. As in previous episodes of decolonization, the British found that once they had unleashed electoral politics, its outcome was difficult to predict, still less to control. Kenyatta and KANU proved to be simply more effective than their rivals in exploiting the new constitutional framework. Following another election in 1963, in which KANU achieved a convincing majority, Kenyatta became Prime Minister and Kenya won full internal self-government, the prelude to independence in December. This was a radically different outcome to the one London still believed practicable only four years previously.[66]

To all appearances, decolonization in Kenya had successfully resolved what had been seen as a difficult colonial problem, yet the 'safeguards' negotiated by Britain in its retreat proved flimsy. The attempt to avoid a strongly centralized, Kikuyu-dominated state, did not long survive independence, and KANU emerged as not only the dominant, but eventually Kenya's only party. Furthermore, the policy of land redistribution, although initially successful, soon gave way to the resale of land to wealthier farmers, leaving many agricultural labourers and landless squatters no better off than they had been before Mau Mau. Finally the Asian community, the third projected component of London's planned multiracial Kenya, was left exposed to post-independence pressure for the 'Africanization' of their interests, although those Kenyan Asians who at independence had opted to retain British citizenship theoretically had, at least, the right of entry into Britain.

After years of neglect, the contribution made by Indians to Kenyan nationalism, especially in financial terms, is at last being recognized by historians. A picture is emerging that contradicts post-independence claims that South Asians stood aloof from the independence struggle (claims which would be used to help justify discriminatory postcolonial measures against an ethnic group labelled economic 'exploiters').[67] For a number of postcolonial regimes in Africa, Africanization was a tempting option, though its significance varied from one country to another. Initially, its impact was greatest in Kenya, where, in a series of populist measures, Indian access to government positions and to trading licences was formally restricted. Along with the prospect of achieving rapid results (and a redistribution of economic assets in Africans' favour), targeting the Indian minority was also a portent. The Kenyan government soon moved to dissolve its major party rival, KADU, edging closer to entrenching a one-party state, a course which numerous ex-colonies would imitate. The Kenyan leader, Jomo Kenyatta, confirmed his authority by becoming president. The multiculturalism he had espoused during the liberation struggle was made to seem hollow and expedient.[68]

The Central African Federation

Central Africa was the most intractable of British decolonizations. African opposition to the Federation of Rhodesia and Nyasaland had been gathering pace ever since the latter's inception. It gained fresh impetus in 1957 when Macmillan's government endorsed constitutional changes intended to reinforce settler political privileges over the African majority. This not only called the sincerity of the multiracial ideal into question, but inevitably fuelled African fears of indefinite subjugation in a white-ruled, self-governing nation. These anxieties were expressed in increasingly effective political mobilization, which drew on Africans' experience of trade unionism, especially among mineworkers. The anti-Federation campaign gathered pace in the late 1950s, attracting support from some surprising quarters. For instance, while the Roman Catholic, Anglican, and Dutch Reformed churches tended to distance themselves from active political involvement, the Church of Central Africa Presbyterian (CCAP), which had a well-established position in Nyasaland and elsewhere, embraced the cause with enthusiasm, bringing it to a wider metropolitan audience.[69]

An alarming signal of hardening settler attitudes came early in 1958 when the reform-minded Prime Minister of Southern Rhodesia, Garfield Todd, was ousted by his own United Federal Party. Meanwhile, the Federal Prime Minister, Roy Welensky, denounced proposals for modest increases in African representation in Northern Rhodesia, arguing that this would generate support for the (racist) Dominion Party. Later in 1958, the Commonwealth Relations Secretary, Lord Home, attributed the dilemma facing Britain to its irreconcilable commitments over the Federation. On the one hand, in the wake of the Gold Coast's independence in 1957, Britain led the federal administration in Salisbury to believe that it would achieve independence by 1960. On the other hand, Churchill's government had promised in 1953 that the protected status of Northern Rhodesia and Nyasaland would not be abrogated without their populations' assent. It was this second pledge that Home believed might have to be re-examined, in favour of the Federation.[70]

Through it all, London clung to the fiction of multiracial 'partnership', supposedly inculcated in the Federation, a 'middle way' between the unacceptable extremes of African and settler nationalism. British policymakers continued to hope that a gradual extension of political rights to Africans who satisfied educational and property qualifications would eventually modify the settlers' political dominance. It was a pipedream. Even the Federation's most prestigious development project, the Kariba Dam, designed to harness the enormous hydroelectric potential of the Zambesi River, betrayed a fundamental ambiguity, typical of the entire federal experiment. Ostensibly of benefit to *all* ethnic groups, Kariba demonstrated that at the heart of the modernizing project of late colonialism, there lay an inherent ambivalence between empowerment and domination.[71]

Evidence of deep-seated African discontent surfaced before the end of 1958. Earlier that year, Dr Hastings Banda, who had lived in Ghana since 1953, returned to Nyasaland to assume the leadership of the Nyasaland African Congress and its anti-federal campaign. Combined with this was resentment against the restrictive soil conservation policies introduced by government since the early 1950s, which had hit peasant farmers hard (especially women, who took a major role in food production).[72] Disturbances gripped the territory in October, prompting demands from local settlers for tighter security measures. When fresh unrest broke out in January 1959, the federal authorities devised a scheme to evict Banda from Nyasaland. Intelligence gathered by the Federal Special Branch supposedly uncovered an insurrectionary plot by Banda's Congress, targeting Nyasaland's small European community. Accordingly, when violence broke out once more, the Southern Rhodesian government declared an emergency. Soon afterwards, Governor Armitage of Nyasaland, a veteran of the Cyprus conflict, initiated 'Operation Sunrise', under which over 1,000 nationalist organizers, including Banda, were rounded up.[73] Similarly tough measures were taken against African nationalists in Northern Rhodesia. There, the disturbances which had erupted early in 1956 prompted fears among sections of the nationalist leadership that violence would give the colonial authorities an excuse to embark on large-scale repression.[74]

Declaring a state of emergency, however, brought with it the official requirement for an investigation. The resulting Devlin Report, with its embarrassing references to the 'police state' in Nyasaland during the emergency, threatened to bring down Macmillan's government. Leaving settlers (or their sympathizers) in charge – whether of detention camps in Kenya or of administration in Central Africa – involved an unacceptable political risk. Typically, the British governmental response was another review commission, this time chaired by a senior Conservative politician, Sir Walter Monckton.

Welensky remained confident that the impending review of the Federation's constitution would facilitate progress towards self-government. Settlers' electoral privileges could be conserved and secession by any of the three Federation territories could be ruled out. He dismissed mounting evidence of African opposition as the treasonous rejection of a pioneering, and economically successful, federal project. Certainly, one of the most powerful, if often discreet actors in federal affairs was expatriate big business, which was caught between two rival strands of nationalism (white settler and black African) within the Federation. In the critically important copper mining industry, for instance, the two major groups of companies adopted different approaches, one 'progressive', the other more conservative. Their different choices, in turn, reflected the contrasting outlooks of their respective US and South African controlling interests.[75]

With the British Labour Party bitterly critical of the Federation, and investor confidence declining, Macleod and Macmillan concluded that the Federation's survival hinged on constitutional reform in Nyasaland.[76] More popular than ever, Banda would have to be freed to give evidence to the Monckton Commission, which had arrived at Victoria Falls in February 1960. Banda's subsequent release was politically and symbolically decisive. It highlighted British governmental recognition that, in the wake of the Devlin Report, coercion against nationalists in Nyasaland was no longer an option. Arguably a true 'turning point' in the history of decolonization, this has been seen as the moment at which the Central African Federation's fate was decided.[77]

The Monckton Commission reported in September 1960. Most Commission members recognized the Federation's economic rationale, but considered it politically unsustainable in the face of such clear African nationalist opposition. Set against this realism, the Commission reiterated a familiar multiracialist line, proposing measures to win African approval for the Federation, including equal representation in the Federal Assembly and reforms in the component territories expected to produce African legislative majorities. The Monckton report also made clear that Britain retained the power to consider individual territories' secession requests, and called on the government to state that it would do so. Although the Commission gave Macleod and Macmillan the justification they needed to introduce constitutional reforms, its comments on secession had been overtaken by events. A Nyasaland constitutional conference, which met in London in July 1960, accorded the territory's legislature an African majority. Given Banda's commitment to secession, and his excellent prospects in the upcoming elections scheduled for 1961, the Federation looked set to disintegrate. The burning question was how the other two federal territories would react.

As predicted, in 1961 Banda was elected to power on a secessionist platform. British recognition of Nyasaland's right to self-government followed in November 1962. Its secession from the Federation seemed only a matter of time, a view strengthened by Banda's renewed victory in fresh elections in 1963. Whereas for Federal Prime Minister Welensky, loss of Nyasaland was unfortunate, secession by copper-rich Northern Rhodesia, the Federation's economic dynamo, was inconceivable. It was the future of this northern territory, and the review of its constitution announced by Macleod in October 1960, that set the federal authorities on a collision course with their imperial masters. Welensky suspected that the British government was willing to contemplate the break-up of the Federation as a means to appease African nationalism.[78]

An abortive Federal Review Conference, which opened in London in December 1960, did nothing to dispel these fears. With no overall agreement reached, only separate constitutional reform proposals for Northern and Southern Rhodesia remained. At talks on the Northern Rhodesian constitution in January 1961, another stalemate ensued when settler leaders walked out, unable to accept British plans for concessions which could 'safely' be offered to African nationalists. Macleod was, by now, committed to black majority rule for Northern Rhodesia and (like Washington) saw Kenneth Kaunda's United National Independence Party (UNIP) as the most promising partner in achieving it.[79] In February 1961 the Colonial Secretary therefore proposed equal representation for Africans in the Northern Rhodesian legislature.

Welensky reacted furiously. The federal administration mobilized troops, supposedly to deal with 'eventualities' but, it was rumoured, actually to stage a coup to safeguard settler dominance. The British responded in turn by readying forces in Kenya, although doubts surfaced over whether some British officers would fire on their Rhodesian 'kith and kin'. The British Cabinet was no less divided, prompting another resignation threat from Macleod, while settler groups successfully exploited their contacts with Conservative Party right-wingers such as Lord Salisbury and the Beaverbrook press, putting pressure on the government to reconsider. Over one hundred Westminster MPs urged the government to abandon its plans for majority rule. In the entire process of decolonization, it was the issue of Northern Rhodesian constitutional reform that brought the Conservative Party closest to splitting apart.[80] The government backed down, producing revised constitutional proposals in June 1961, which would ensure a small settler majority. Perhaps predictably, violence erupted and further talk of reform was postponed.[81]

Meanwhile, in self-governing Southern Rhodesia, where violence late in 1960 had demonstrated African hostility to the Federation, Prime Minister Sir Edgar Whitehead was persuaded to introduce a marginally more liberal constitution, giving Africans greater, though still unequal, representation. Whitehead had already asked London to remove its remaining restrictions on full Southern Rhodesian self-government. With the Monckton Commission's Report then still pending, the issue was especially delicate. If Britain renounced its remaining powers to intervene in Southern Rhodesia's affairs, the African population would surely deduce that they were being left to the mercies of the white minority, and that this was London's intention for the entire Federation.[82]

Whitehead had introduced tough security measures in response to earlier unrest, but he hoped that a package of relatively liberal social policy measures would win him enough African support to negotiate independence from Britain. These reforms, including the prohibition of some forms of racial discrimination and the repeal of the Land Apportionment Act, were designed to woo middle class Africans away from nationalism and towards collaboration with 'liberal' settler elements. In the event, Whitehead's comparative liberalism was woefully outdated. Few enfranchised Africans, most of whom boycotted the October 1962 elections, were prepared to listen. By contrast, Whitehead's reformism infuriated white settlers, driving many of them into the arms of the hard-line Rhodesian Front, led by Winston Field.

Meanwhile, in February 1962, London unveiled a new constitution for Northern Rhodesia, this time composed along lines similar to those already established for Nyasaland, with the prospect of an African legislative majority following elections in October. With the precedent of the two northern territories before them, settlers in Southern Rhodesia insisted that their independence, too, should be based upon the constitutional foundations devised early in 1961, even though these stood in the way of speedy progress towards African majority rule. This remained the stumbling block in discussions between London and the territorial government in Salisbury.

Wearying of Central Africa and the domestic, African, and international problems to which it exposed his government, Macmillan persuaded his deputy, R. A. Butler, to accept the unenviable task of overseeing the Federation during what seemed likely to be its terminal phase. Butler's initial premise was that, while continuing political association between the Federation's components was unrealistic, some form of economic relationship might be preserved. In the event, elections in both the Rhodesias in October 1962 brought to power governments opposed to continued membership of the Federation. There was little further point in withholding the right of individual territories to secede, although it might be argued that Banda's release in 1960 had made this outcome inevitable all along. Nyasaland's right to secede was finally confirmed in December 1962. In March 1963, as expected, the new nationalist coalition government in Northern Rhodesia followed suit. Given that Southern Rhodesia was, by then, governed by politicians intent on their own separate independence, there seemed little choice but to give the Federation as decent a burial as possible. A conference, held at Victoria Falls in summer 1963, distributed the Federation's assets among its three constituent territories.

Some observers noted anxiously that the lion's share of the Federation's considerable military resources went to Southern Rhodesia, equipping its government to take a more intransigent line in its dealings with London. By late 1963 the Federation, created with such hopes a decade earlier, was dead, marking yet another reversal for British policy. Northern Rhodesia and Nyasaland achieved independence in 1964, but, given the extent of Southern Rhodesia's African opposition, there could be no question of this territory receiving independence on the terms of its 1961 constitution. The Rhodesian problem was far from being resolved when the Conservative government fell from power in 1964.

Losing an empire, finding a role?

Meanwhile, deciding what Britain's world role was to be remained a sensitive issue for Macmillan's government. Late in 1962, the former US Secretary of State, Dean Acheson, commented that 'Great Britain has lost an Empire and has not yet found a role'. Significantly, this remark irritated members of the Conservative Party, some of whom had already been unsettled by the pace of decolonization and Britain's apparent shift towards a closer relationship with Europe. Macmillan was lucky that he had not had to face simultaneous crises arising from decolonization. He was also fortunate that right-wing dissent within his own party was blunted by the fact that Lord Salisbury, the obvious focus of dissent, had left the Cabinet in 1957 in protest at the government's handling of the Cyprus question, robbing right-wingers in the government of a natural leader. Equally, the 'die-hard' vision of a white-run Commonwealth had been dealt a fatal blow in 1961 when South Africa was excluded, despite Macmillan's efforts to secure a compromise. This foreshadowed the Commonwealth's increasingly independent position on the problem of apartheid, a development which would in future years leave Britain isolated and condemned by its former friends. By the mid-1960s, British government assessments of the Commonwealth, on which so many of Britain's aspirations to maintain a world role had been built since 1945, were increasingly pessimistic.[83]

Paradoxically, within Britain itself, the ideal of multiracialism, considered central to the Commonwealth's prospects for success, was being threatened by the question of immigration. During the 1950s, specific sectors in Britain, including the National Health Service and London Transport, actively recruited workers from the West Indies. The resulting immigration was helped by the relatively low cost of sea passages, and, in the 1960s, by the falling cost of air travel.[84] Not all immigrants saw their relocation as being permanent: for many, the intention was to return home after a period of employment in Britain. In 1962, after considerable hesitation, the British government adopted measures to control immigration from the Commonwealth into Britain. At the time, non-white immigrants were arriving at the rate of more than 130,000 per year, whereas in the early 1950s the annual figure had been less than 10,000. Racial tensions had been rising, fuelled by the violence of the Notting Hill Riots in 1958 (for which immigrants were blamed).[85] Ironically, given his previously liberal stance on this issue, legislative changes were associated especially with the Home Secretary, Rab Butler. Since 1959 right-wing Conservative opinion at grass-roots level had been hardening on this question, against a background of an ailing domestic economy, growing interest in the possibilities of the European Economic Community, and a corresponding decline in enthusiasm for the Commonwealth's potential. By May 1961, Macmillan was becoming increasingly concerned about this, and the fissures among his ministers it provoked. Under the 1962 Commonwealth Immigrants Act, a controversial new 'voucher' system was introduced for immigrants, those from Ireland being exempted. Skilled applicants and those assured of employment received preference, since the act was intended to limit the entry of unskilled workers with no job waiting for them.[86] Inevitably, the impact on would-be migrants in South Asia and the West Indies was considerable, intensifying anxieties that families would be prevented from joining relatives who had already settled in Britain.[87] As subsequent British governments would discover, these questions would grow in significance, tapping into popular sentiments which many in the political establishment found repugnant.

As expected, the 1962 Act led to a sharp drop in immigration from the 'New Commonwealth'. Many West Indian migrants began to look to Canada as an alternative destination. Further restrictions introduced in 1965, including the abolition of vouchers for unskilled workers, made immigration even more difficult. In 1968, following the influx of South Asian migrants expelled from recently independent Kenya, Asian UK passport holders lost their right of entry. In 1971, the Immigration Act abolished vouchers and restricted automatic entry to 'patrials', those who could demonstrate that they (or their parents or grandparents) had been born in the United Kingdom. In effect, the 'Open Door' principle was swept away, and with it the notion that *all* citizens of the Commonwealth enjoyed access to the British labour market. Britain's growing integration into Europe after 1973 served only to confirm this trend. By 1981, of a total British population of 53,697,000, some 1,472,000 were immigrants from the New Commonwealth. They were still outnumbered by immigrants from the Commonwealth's older white settler societies, and from other countries, including the Republic of Ireland.[88]

The experiences of these newcomers varied widely. Some found the jobs and other opportunities they craved. Many others encountered hostility from their host community and faced effective social exclusion, most evident in access to housing and employment. The fact that this has been the experience of nearly all incoming groups has led some to propose that xenophobia has long been an entrenched feature of British social attitudes. Discrimination, often expressed in casually repeated negative stereotypes, had long been experienced by migrants from Ireland, and by Jews.[89] In other words, British racism was not *exclusively* a product of empire (although imperial rule may have sharpened it).

Alongside intensified restrictions on immigration went attempts to tackle racial discrimination. Beginning with legislation in 1965, efforts were made to create a legal framework to permit this. Applying only to public places, and overseen by a weak Race Relations Board, the 1965 Act could have only a limited impact. In 1966, under the reformist Home Secretary, Roy Jenkins, government policy switched from 'assimilation' to multicultural integration. Subsequently, discrimination in employment was outlawed and, in 1976, the Commission for Racial Equality was established, empowered to help the victims of discrimination. Meanwhile, the immigrants themselves dealt stoically with the problems they encountered, often preferring not to confront discrimination directly. Many sought solace, and a reinforcement of their shared identity, through social activities and religious observance.[90]

Superficially, Britain's experience of immigration during the decolonization era appeared to be relatively painless. There was nothing, for example, to compare with the orgy of anti-Algerian violence witnessed in Paris in 1961.[91] Nevertheless, problems could persist in a lower register, and yet be equally insidious. Especially, though not exclusively, among the community of West Indian descent, persistent allegations arose of disproportionate and discriminatory policing, targeted particularly at young black men. Moreover, despite growing evidence of racially motivated attacks on them, immigrants and their children seemed to be denied the police protection they needed. Questions about policing methods escalated after disturbances at the annual Notting Hill Carnival in the mid-1970s, and especially following serious rioting in Brixton, south London, in 1981. Most embarrassing was the official verdict that, in its bungled investigation of the murder of a black student, Stephen Lawrence, in London in 1993, the Metropolitan Police had shown itself to be 'institutionally racist'. In the wake of so damning a judgement, police forces throughout Britain were compelled to re-examine their attitudes and policies towards race.[92] Meanwhile, the education system, initially poorly equipped to cater for the needs of a new immigrant community, explored ways both of promoting multiculturalism, for instance by heightening the host community's awareness of other cultures, and by addressing a perceived need to improve educational achievement among ethnic minorities.[93]

Less apparent in the literature, yet arguably of great significance, was the fact that decolonization involved *reverse* migration: the return to Britain of people among the many, disparate groups for whom the Empire had been a home. Especially for those raised overseas, the encounter with a mother country visibly in straitened circumstances could be perplexing. It shattered long-held perceptions about metropolitan power, along with social and political attitudes that were already being superseded. For some, the experience was too much, and prompted a continuing search for a new home which might offer the opportunities (and privileges) once enjoyed by settlers and other 'orphans of empire'.[94]

The Wilson government and East of Suez

By the time the Labour Party returned to power under Harold Wilson in 1964, the greater part of British decolonization was over. In opposition, the Labour Party had shown considerable sympathy for African nationalism, suggesting that the new government could cultivate friendly relations with many postcolonial regimes. However, Wilson's administration was also committed to uphold British commitments East of Suez, arguing that a strong military presence was needed to safeguard Britain's commercial interests and investments, and its supplies of oil and other raw materials.[95] As US involvement in Vietnam escalated, Washington policymakers also attached greater value to Britain's East of Suez role. Wilson's government steered clear of participating in Vietnam but did accede to the creation of a British Indian Ocean Territory in 1965 to permit the development of joint British-US military bases on the island of Diego Garcia, whose 2,000 residents were abruptly relocated to Mauritius, only winning the right to return over forty years later.

The depth of Britain's commitment to an East of Suez role was clearly illustrated by London's response to deteriorating relations between Malaysia and its expansionist neighbour, Indonesia.[96] As previously discussed, Malayan independence in 1957 did not see the abandonment by Britain of attempts to pursue closer integration in South East Asia. It had long hoped to bring Malaya, Singapore, and the Borneo territories into closer association, but Malayan independence and Singapore's achievement of 'statehood' in 1959 seemed to contradict this policy. Nevertheless, among Singapore's own anti-communist political elite, a merger with Malaya soon came to be viewed as a safeguard of the new state's survival as a major commercial centre. Independence within a larger federation seemed to offer protection against communist encroachment. When the Malayan ruler, Tunku Abdul Rahman, formally proposed a merger of Malaya, Singapore, Sarawak, North Borneo (Sabah), and Brunei in 1961, London's response was enthusiastic: here, it seemed, was a means of promoting greater regional cohesion and settling the issue of the fate of Britain's remaining possessions in the region.[97] The creation of 'Malaysia' in 1963, from which Brunei decided to opt out (finally becoming independent in 1983), and Singapore seceded in 1965, was backed by British promises to defend the new association. Soon, however, tensions escalated between Malaysia and Sukarno's Indonesia, which had its own territorial ambitions towards Borneo. Between 1963 and 1966, British troops, numbering 50,000 at the conflict's height, along with Malaysian and New Zealand detachments, defended the new federation from Indonesian aggression.[98]

In practical terms, the weakness of the East of Suez concept was that it depended on British access to a secure base somewhere on the Indian Ocean rim from which military operations could be mounted. In the late 1950s, it had been thought that Kenya might fulfil this role, but that colony's rapid progress to decolonization had invalidated these assumptions, leading the planners to switch their attention to Aden, where large investments were made in developing adequate military facilities. However, mounting unrest here, as a civil war spread from the interior to the coast, steadily made this foothold unreliable.

Much of Labour's domestic appeal had rested with Wilson's image as a 'modernizer', committed to a revived Britain 'forged in the white heat' of a 'technological revolution'.[99] Yet the economic realities were more prosaic. Labour inherited from Macmillan's government a balance of payments deficit of some £800 million, and for the next three years Wilson struggled to redress this problem without devaluing sterling. By the time the government unveiled its hastily improvised 'National Plan' late in 1965, designed to achieve sustained growth, economic optimism was already turning to doubt and renewed perceptions of relative national decline.

Eventually, expenditure cuts appeared to be inescapable, particularly to curb the escalating costs of Britain's defence and overseas commitments, but also affecting development aid, a central plank in any serious attempt to maintain 'informal' influence in former colonial territories. Wilson was keen to expand Britain's aid programme, creating a new Ministry of Overseas Development to coordinate these efforts. Assistance, nevertheless, was not given unconditionally: by the late 1960s, over 40 per cent of Britain's bilateral aid was contractually tied to the purchase of British goods and services.[100] Furthermore, after 1965, British overseas investment effectively came to a 'shuddering halt', due both to voluntary agreements and exchange controls. Although government overseas spending stabilized, the days of sterling's role as a reserve currency were henceforth numbered.[101] By the time the decision was taken to devalue the pound, in November 1967, the British government's foreign debts were proportionately greater than those of any other country. Fundamental to Britain's difficulties in maintaining its cherished world role was uncertainty about the country's ability to maintain its existing defence capacity in the light of these worsening financial problems.

In the midst of this economic dilemma, Wilson's government nonetheless restated its belief in the East of Suez role, even though this was becoming more difficult to fulfil, given the prolonged, and costly, 'Confrontation' with Indonesia and the intensification of anti-British terrorism in Aden.[102] The manner of Britain's withdrawal from Aden, announced by London in November 1967, combined speed with embarrassment, and offers a clear instance where local nationalism proved decisive in decolonization. Britain found itself unable to protect the emirs, through whom it ruled, against the National Liberation Front which, crucially, had secured the support of Nasser's Egypt. With alarming ease, Britain's ramshackle federal solution was swept aside by the (Marxist) People's Democratic Republic of Yemen.[103] A White Paper issued in February 1967 had declared that when Southern Arabia became independent, British forces would be withdrawn entirely. Six months later the government went further still, acknowledging that the East of Suez commitment was unsustainable. By 1971, British forces in Malaysia and Singapore were to be halved, and withdrawn completely by the mid-1970s. Aden was to be evacuated immediately, although a presence in the Persian Gulf would be maintained.

Given the importance attached to the region by Britain for so long, it was ironic that events in the Middle East should have encouraged a long-delayed realization of Britain's diminished power. The Six Day War of June 1967 between Israel and most of its Arab neighbours was accompanied not only by unrestrained financial speculation but also by the closure of the Suez Canal, which forced Britain to buy more expensive oil from outside the Middle East, draining the country's dollar reserves.[104] These developments also precipitated the November 1967 devaluation of sterling from $2.80 to $2.40, reducing Britain's reserves by around £1 billion. In its wake came a radical reappraisal of Britain's ability to maintain ambitious overseas commitments. The Treasury's urgent need to cut social expenditure proved decisive. The announcement of a parallel cut in the defence budget was intended to soften the political impact of reduced welfare spending.[105] In short, it was devaluation more than anything else that revealed the emptiness of Britain's pretensions to a world role.

The decision to withdraw, described by the former Foreign Secretary Patrick Gordon Walker as 'the most momentous shift in our foreign policy for a century and a half', shocked Persian Gulf rulers, some of whom, concerned about the regional ambitions of their much larger neighbours, Iran and Saudi Arabia, offered to underwrite continuing British protection.[106] Significantly, however, when the Conservatives returned to power in 1970, they did not reverse their predecessors' decision to withdraw from the Gulf, even though attacks on Labour's policy of retreat had featured in their general election campaign. In 1971 it was announced that Britain's treaties with the Gulf states would be wound up by the end of the year.[107] It was perhaps no coincidence that Kuwait, until recently so vital to Britain, had shown its readiness to align more closely with the Arab world by joining the Arab states' embargo on oil supplies to the West, following the Arab defeat in the Six Day War.[108]

Rhodesia and 'UDI'

The most taxing legacy of British Empire in the 1960s was Rhodesia. For many white settlers, it seemed that the dissolution of the Central African Federation offered the opportunity for

Southern Rhodesia to achieve independence on the same terms as its northern neighbours. As settler restlessness intensified, the Rhodesian Front, led from April 1964 by Ian Smith, suppressed African opposition, banning both ZAPU and ZANU and imposing controls on the media, measures designed to convince London that White Rule was there to stay. Once it became clear that the Labour government disagreed, Smith's Rhodesian Front, emboldened by an election victory, issued a unilateral declaration of independence (UDI) in November 1965, in effect a rebellion against British authority in Southern Africa as the map below indicates.[109]

'UDI' did not come as a surprise, but it was difficult to counter. British military intervention, which Wilson had already publicly ruled out, would have been intensely divisive and

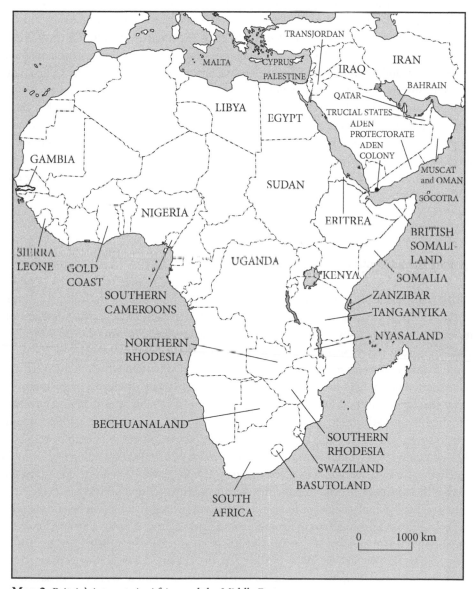

Map 2 Britain's interests in Africa and the Middle East.

prohibitively expensive.[110] Nor did London respond enthusiastically to Canadian initiatives to prevent UDI, an episode which further exposed cleavages among 'Old' Commonwealth members.[111] Nevertheless, Britain remained adamant that Rhodesian independence was not negotiable until African political representation was increased and racial discrimination outlawed. Meanwhile, London imposed economic sanctions on Rhodesia, which, thanks largely to South African contravention, were rapidly undermined.

In an effort to break the deadlock and prevent a loss of domestic support, Wilson twice met with Smith, in 1966 aboard HMS *Tiger*, and again in 1968 on HMS *Fearless*. The meetings proved fruitless. Far more significant in the long term, African guerrilla units, belonging to the rival factions ZANU and ZAPU, supported respectively by the Soviet Union and China, began raids into Rhodesian territory from 1966 onwards. By 1972 these incursions were escalating into a civil war that would last for fifteen years. Ultimately, external factors, above all the regional implications for southern Africa of the Portuguese Revolution of 1974 (after which newly independent Angola and Mozambique became vital bases for guerrilla incursions into Rhodesia), and mounting pressure on Salisbury from South Africa and the United States, forced Ian Smith's regime to seek a political compromise. In 1978, the so-called 'Internal Settlement' was concluded between Smith and one wing of the African nationalist movement, under which Bishop Abel Muzorewa became Prime Minister in 1979. Rejecting this outcome, the rival nationalist coalition, the Patriotic Front, fought on. In late 1979 a settlement was finally negotiated at Lancaster House, scene of so many previous 'transfers of power'. Under this agreement, Britain briefly resumed authority over Rhodesia while preparations were made for elections, won by Robert Mugabe's Patriotic Front. Zimbabwean independence followed in April 1980.

Last outposts of Empire

Once the last sizeable territories were gone, the residue included some of those imperial 'points' once thought likely to comprise a residual global network. In a few of these, wider international complications impeded any rapid transition to independence. Gibraltar, for example, could not easily be restored to Spanish sovereignty (vigorously claimed by Madrid) in the face of resolute hostility from its small but fiercely Anglophile population, whose views were made clear in a referendum held in 1967. The Falkland Islands, largely unknown in the metropole, became the occasion of an extraordinary outpouring of post-imperial British sentiment in 1982 when Argentina's military junta occupied the Islands in support of its long-standing claims to sovereignty. Few writers on imperial decline, accustomed to the muffled transitions of the 1960s and 1970s, could have anticipated that much of Britain's remaining navy would be dispatched to reclaim the islands by force. In retrospect, the episode underlined the dangers of assuming that the old imperial impulse had been extinguished, and served as a corrective to historiographical complacency, the tendency to stress the 'exceptionalism' in Britain's handling of imperial retreat, apparently so much more foresighted than that of the luckless continental colonial powers. If the Falklands crisis harked back to an earlier era, British retrocession of Hong Kong to the People's Republic of China in 1997 seemed a definitive confirmation of the passing of British Empire, if not of Commonwealth ties and a host of imperial cultural connections.

The legacies of Empire

While few would dispute the significance of the end of the period of formal British colonial rule, the impact this process had on Britain itself remains less clear.[112] Despite the loss of its Empire, Britain did not appear to have abandoned a belief in its own role as a global power, although its 'special' relationship with the United States was arguably of greater practical significance to Britain than the Empire had been.[113] Equally, while the appeal of traditional economic links with parts of the Empire still resonated with some sections of British political opinion, trade with rapidly recovering Western Europe, and with North America, was proving increasingly attractive to British business. In time, they would be joined by other trading partners, notably in the Middle East and Asia.[114]

In political terms, it could be said with some confidence that decolonization had not become a major issue within Britain – on the contrary, the process seemed to be associated with a good deal of voter indifference (raising questions about the effectiveness of previous campaigns of imperial propaganda). This did not mean, however, that British politicians could relax in their efforts to present decolonization as a controlled process that posed no fundamental threat to British interests, and which (it was claimed) represented no diminution in Britain's global stature.[115] Popular attitudes towards empire are notoriously difficult to evaluate, and this is especially true when considering a period on which so much research remains to be done. While it seems reasonable to assume that among the working classes, awareness of the Empire had grown – in many cases reinforced by personal experience such as military service – this does not necessarily imply any *endorsement* of empire.[116] It is harder still to generalize about opinions within Britain's expanding middle class. For a wide variety of professionals, especially those with a technical or scientific background, the post-war empire, with its stress on development, appeared to offer boundless opportunities for career progression. Equally, the expanding role of the state, first in India, and later in the colonial territories, called for greatly enlarged bureaucracies, although the process of 'indigenization', expedient on political grounds as decolonization progressed, would place some limits on the opportunities for British recruits.[117]

There is plenty of scope to consider the possible impacts possession of an empire had on the development of politics within Britain. For instance, while managing a global system created many opportunities for self-advancement among the United Kingdom's Celtic populations, especially the Scots, it seemed in retrospect that one consequence of nation-forming and empire-building had been a loss of certainty about what a distinctively 'English' identity might mean. Only in the early twenty-first century would this question resurface with much urgency.

One interpretation of this phenomenon stresses the importance of non-white immigration, and the racism it was liable to reveal, as a perceived 'threat' to English identity. Reinforcing such attitudes, it has been claimed, were the generally negative representations of colonial territories such as Malaya and Kenya in films dealing with counter-insurgency operations in the 1950s.[118] It has even been suggested that the hostility towards non-white immigration visible from the 1950s onwards not only ignored the common British citizenship of Commonwealth migrants to Britain, but discussed their presence using language resembling the 'siege' narratives which typically accompanied colonial insurgencies of the period.[119] A central political issue – the role of the state in regulating society and managing the economy – would dominate metropolitan discussions in the post-war decades, at least until the 1980s. It was ironic that the habit of intervention had first been acquired in the heyday of the British Raj in India: only subsequently would its domestic potential be appreciated.[120]

For former colonial territories, similarly fundamental questions emerge concerning their inheritance from the years of colonial rule. Although contemporaries were inclined to view independence as marking a definitive break with the past, an opportunity to make a fresh start, with ex-colonies enjoying the sovereignty they needed to pursue their own development as they wished, historians have detected important continuities between the colonial and postcolonial periods.[121] In the first flush of independence, it was tempting to overlook the fact that postcolonial regimes inherited the structures and trappings (and sometimes the attitudes) of the late colonial state. During the anti-colonial struggle, political leaders, not least in Africa, effectively promised a redefinition of the state, not as something imposed by external agents, but as a structure desired and constructed by the people, and serving their needs.[122] This underscored the sometimes extravagant promises made before independence about the fruits of modernization after it: having berated the colonial state for its lethargic approach to development, new regimes were under pressure to make good their promises.[123]

Once in office many of these politicians followed a different path, coveting the coercive power and political capital of the colonial administrative legacy. A major claim has therefore been that postcolonial regimes often inherited the authoritarian apparatus and outlook of their predecessors, who had themselves, by prioritizing the maintenance of order and economic production, helped to undermine any scope for democratization.[124] Even before independence was achieved, some nationalist parties affirmed that the power of the state must be preserved. Certainly, expectations that living standards would rise seemed to imply a continuing, even enlarged, role for the state.[125] Crucially, given their desire to achieve rapid development, not least to reward their supporters, postcolonial politicians continued many of the governmental practices of colonial rule, including its more repressive aspects.[126]

While this interpretation has been popular among those disappointed by the practical outcomes of independence, an alternative view suggests that postcolonial states were fragile and prone to political instability.[127] In that sense, weak colonial states, hampered by financial and other constraints, carried over into the postcolonial era.[128] Close examination of the nationalist movements that inherited power at independence suggests that in several cases both their legitimacy and their hegemony have been exaggerated. In practice, the promised redistribution of wealth eagerly awaited by anti-colonial activists was a hostage to fortune. Sometimes the failure of incumbent leaders to live up to their promises hardened popular opposition to them.[129]

Ironically, given its central importance in late British colonial policy, development in a postcolonial context would become an arena in which Britain's contribution was steadily eclipsed. Newly independent countries found that they could exploit international rivalries accentuated by the Cold War, playing potential aid donors off against others until the best 'deal' was secured. There was little prospect of Britain sustaining a challenge to donors such as the United States and the Soviet Union, or even West Germany. Similarly, postcolonial regimes, no longer restricted to following the British path, could choose from a number of developmental models. On the other hand, former colonial powers were no longer obliged to provide development aid, though they often did so for a variety of reasons. This, in turn, converted the former colonies' position from one of 'entitlement' into one of 'supplication'. Meanwhile, as 'gatekeepers' of development aid, the new postcolonial governing elites enjoyed considerable patronage with which to reward their friends and supporters, not least the young militants who had provided the anti-colonial movements with physical clout.[130] At the same time, not only did the postcolonial state inherit numerous presumptions about development, especially the pursuit of modernization, but many former colonial bureaucrats from Britain were seconded to independent countries. Some degree of intellectual continuity and even external influence was thereby assured.

Often embedded in elite attitudes was an authoritarian approach to achieving rapid economic and social change, expressed in a renewed enthusiasm for technocratic solutions.[131] While nationalist political rhetoric had stressed popular, democratic participation in such schemes, centralization and bureaucratic control were often more apparent.[132] The intrusions caused by development initiatives could therefore be resented after independence as much as they had been under colonial rule.[133] Yet some contemporary African leaders cannot resist rehearsing the powerful slogans of the independence era, the familiar mantras of nation-building, liberation, and development. It might be argued that this kind of rhetoric is both a deliberate attempt to identify the political parties of today with the heroes of the past and a means to distract audiences from the very real problems of the present.[134]

As the post-independence decades were soon to demonstrate, the seeds of representative politics sown during late colonialism sometimes produced delicate roots. Democratic institutions faced an uncertain future, mirroring the fragility of many new nation states. Despite the problems facing it, India, Britain's most treasured overseas possession, and the territory which pioneered the dissolution of the British Empire, managed to preserve its democracy, with a brief interlude of 'emergency' rule during the mid-1970s. But the long years of Congress hegemony, and the charismatic leadership of Jawaharlal Nehru, stoked criticism of the development path Congress adopted, of the state economic controls it employed, and of its failure to reduce some of the inequalities so pronounced in Indian society. Most tragically, Congress, the self-proclaimed party of secularism and social inclusion, failed to prevent the resurgence of communalism, which continues to menace one of the world's major emerging powers, a complex and dynamic society still reconciling itself to its colonial inheritance.[135]

PART II
FRENCH DECOLONIZATION
Martin Thomas

INTRODUCTION TO PART II
THE FRENCH EMPIRE

To study the French Empire's unravelling is to study apparent contradictions. France was, for most of the late nineteenth and twentieth centuries, a republican state committed to ideals of civic nationalism and citizens' rights enshrined in law. Over the same period it first built and then lost an overseas empire in which the cultural distinctions, legal discriminations, and social segregation between whites and non-whites were, for the most part, just as pronounced as within the other European empires. Yet, if the rhetoric of French imperialists, politicians, ethnographers, and empire traders was to be believed, French colonialism was different. For one thing, its declared mission, reformulated by multiple governments in multiple constitutional regimes from the 1830s onwards, was educative and convergent. As millions of new colonial subjects came under French imperium, so the global reach of French cultural practices, social standards, and political values would spread. The French language was the basic vector of transmission in this socialization to the French standards of the day, a process which, at its most colonially ambitious, was framed as 'assimilation'.

The contradictions here might seem obvious in hindsight. Judging civilizational advancement in terms of French language skills and other, more intangible attributes of 'Frenchness' precluded the vast majority of colonial peoples for whom formal schooling was a remote unaffordable privilege. Catholic evangelism helped close this gap in some places, Southern Vietnam for instance. But successive governments of what from 1905 was an avowedly secular French Republic were loath to admit their tolerance of – still less, any reliance on – missionary activity. Settler colonization could also accelerate acculturation. In practice, though, the presence of significantly large white populations in the French Empire, as in others, tended to heighten social segregation as well. Less densely populated than Britain or the Netherlands, mainland France also produced fewer emigrants to its colonies. Settlers were numerous in some territories, the former slaving settlements of the French Caribbean, the cities of Northern Morocco and Tunisia, and, above all, the pre-eminent French imperial prize: Algeria. But mobilizing empire migration to create a 'French world' akin to its British rival was never seriously entertained by the government or the people of France. With the critical exception of Algeria, it was for colonial peoples to adopt the mannerisms of France rather than for French men and women to remake colonial societies through migration and settlement.

Of course, this imperial project was never – could never be – so vertically controlled. Treating empire as a process of emulation ignored the innumerable cultural interactions and resultant hybridity of behaviour that made French colonialism – like any other – a two-way street. Consider, for a moment, the experience of French women in the early twentieth century. Some, unable to find local employment in male-dominated professions, took up colonial positions, notably in education, in healthcare, and in public administration. Others whose family obligations took them to the colonies faced strong social pressure to conform to bourgeois norms as mothers, homemakers, and supporters of local charities.[1] Most returned to France profoundly affected by their colonial experiences. France, in other words, was just as reshaped by its Empire as vice versa. And, while the underlying imperialist objective might be ever-closer union, the persistent inequalities of colonial rule nourished the local grievances that would eventually split the Empire apart.

These disintegrative processes began to manifest themselves in the early decades of the twentieth century. And so another contradiction: the same post-First World War years that saw the French Empire reach its largest geographical extent were also a point from which incipient national movements, colonial intellectuals, and other civil society groups disparaged France's 'republican imperialism' as a sham. The protracted economic crisis of the 1930s catalysed further dissent. Barely were economic conditions improving when renewed global conflict brought severe colonial deprivation. It was not long before this Second World War divided the French Empire along new fault lines. Some were opened by France's 1940 defeat and the establishment of the reactionary, ultra-authoritarian Vichy regime. Others were carved by external actors such as imperial Japan, which marauded South East Asia; by Germany and Italy, which depredated North Africa; and by the United States and Britain, which made demands on the material resources of francophone Africa to feed insatiable, global 'war efforts'.[2] But the sharpest fault line of all was between rulers and ruled. The Empire's administrative elites, still overwhelmingly French in composition, were caught up in a Franco-French civil war between Vichy and its opponents. Their perspective on the primacy of metropolitan politics – of France's destiny after Nazi occupation – was not shared by wider colonial populations. For them the Second World War was experienced in more visceral terms: as martial law, harsher exactions, and shortages of food so chronic that epidemic and famine became widespread.

Little wonder, perhaps, that for the French Empire, as for the British, the immediate post-war saw the conjunction of two opposing forces – rebellion and reform. A May 1945 uprising in and around Sétif, eastern Algeria, elicited French repression so severe that it radicalized an entire generation of young men and women caught up in it. The bitter war of independence to come was foretold in the demands made by the May 1945 protesters, in their resort to violence, and, most of all, in the ways in which their actions were greeted by the colonial authorities. Meanwhile, at much the same time, the French administration in Mandate Syria was finally compelled to leave, not just at Syrian, but at British behest. Elsewhere, Franco-British imperial rivalry was less conspicuous. In September 1945 Britain's South East Asia Command helped transport a French expeditionary force to Southern Vietnam. Its contested return unfolded against a backcloth of a devastating northern famine and the establishment of a Vietnamese communist-nationalist regime in Hanoi determined to resist any restoration of colonial authority. The subsequent descent into war in Indochina and a year of domestic political turmoil in France obscured the severity of the imperial crackdown in Madagascar, the vast island territory where a brief spring 1947 revolt was mercilessly put down over subsequent weeks and months.

Organized, state-sanctioned colonial violence was certainly more pervasive after the Second World War than before it. Even so, such disorder was not apparent everywhere. If insurgency, the clamour of protest and war would come to dominate the final years of French imperial rule in North Africa and Indochina, the picture in sub-Saharan Africa, the Caribbean, and other Ocean territories was much different. The new reformism that saw the Empire reconfigured as the French Union in October 1946 registered its deepest impact on France's two black African federations as well as the clutch of island dependencies reassigned as 'overseas territories' and 'overseas departments' of France. Alongside these constitutional changes, other changes to law and legal rights were perhaps more imminent to colonial communities. Forced labour would go. The scope for arbitrary arrest narrowed. Rights to citizenship widened, albeit not wholly equalized between French and non-French. Franchises expanded. Perhaps most important, basic employment protections and welfare provision became integral to the process of colonial governance as never before. So much so, indeed, that discreet voices in colonial societies – unionized workers, students, women's groups, even some avowedly 'national' political parties – were prepared to work with France rather than against it. Widening political space, greater cultural respect, and the prospect of rising living standards promoted lasting dialogue over how best to secure enhanced rights and entitlements inside a French imperial system. For those involved, this was not decolonization deferred. Quite the reverse: to analyse the post-war political cultures of French West African territories in anticipation of the end of empire risks missing the point that for much of the post-1945 decade, empire politics was predicated on a lasting French connection.

We return, then, to the contradictions we have to grapple with if the processes of French colonial collapse are to be understood. The chapters that follow suggest that alongside instances of discrimination or violence, attempts were made to improve colonial lives, whether those efforts originated within colonial communities, among local administrations, or at the epicentre of imperial power in Paris. To be sure, certain aspects of French imperial rule were systemically unfair, economically exploitative, and culturally destructive. Merely identifying empire as unequal, extractive, and homogenizing does not take us very far towards explaining its dynamics, however. This section tries to unravel causes and consequences of French decolonization rather differently: by working through the many contradictions of France's republican imperialism.

CHAPTER 5
THE ROOTS OF FRENCH DECOLONIZATION: IDEAS, ECONOMICS, AND REFORM, 1900-46

The French Third Republic was a hybrid. It claimed to be a liberal parliamentary democracy at home, yet throughout its existence, ardent republicans denied voting rights to women and withheld legal equality from them. This liberal Republic was also the supreme authority of an empire largely secured by violent conquest and sustained by authoritarian rule.[3] Contrary to the state's gender discrimination in France, in theory, within the overseas empire the conferment of political and legal rights depended first and foremost on the supposed cultural 'evolution' of the indigenous subject.[4] In practice, after 1918 French constructions of colonial culture and indigenous capacities for self-rule were still employed to justify the restriction of individual freedoms. As Gary Wilder puts it,

> If after World War I, the stereotype of Africans as big children partly superseded that of dangerous savages, this did not indicate a softening of colonial racism. Rather, it expressed an institutional process that racialized them in a specific way: as different but improving; destined to become autonomous individuals but currently too immature to exercise political rights responsibly.[5]

As this quote suggests, a common thread linked contending theories of French colonial rule in the early twentieth century. This was the attempt to reconcile the universalist values of French republicanism with the racial hierarchy and social inequalities embedded in the colonial order.[6] The belief that the French Empire was more than a racially ordered hierarchy enabled interwar imperialists to argue that colonialism could be a progressive force, capable of nurturing indigenous civil society and supporting individual advancement while maintaining overall French supremacy.[7] During the 1920s and 1930s, distinct constituencies of otherwise liberal opinion, such as the schoolteachers' union, feminist groups, and pacifist organizations, increasingly criticized acts of colonial repression and blatant instances of racial discrimination, especially the marginalization of children born to French fathers and non-white mothers; but most stopped short of condemning the Empire itself.[8] As French historians Nicolas Bancel, Pascal Blanchard, and Françoise Vergès point out, the problem faced by such republican imperialists was that in trying to square the circle between democratic values and republican egalitarianism on the one hand, and colonial hierarchy and racial stratification on the other, they would merely open a Pandora's Box of popular demands for political and legal rights. The verdict of Bancel, Blanchard, and Vergès is harsh. Republican imperialism was at once a utopia and a fast track to decolonization. Its protagonists were chasing shadows. Their cultural arrogance blinded them to the racism at the core of the colonial project.[9] Eric Savarese is similarly critical. He argues that republican imperialists reduced colonized peoples to stereotypes made to fit a grand design of supposedly benevolent French rule.[10]

Furthermore, the emerging community of educated and predominantly urban young Africans, those who could most plausibly claim to be acculturated to French values, found themselves deliberately frozen out of local government and public service for much of the interwar period.[11] Some found common cause with their Caribbean counterparts from the French Antilles, many of whom were linked to one of the oldest colonial community networks in Paris. The consequent alienation of these *évolués* (literally, 'the [culturally] evolved') in French Africa was pivotal to the emergence of two distinct strands of opposition to colonialism. The first, and more moderate of the two, was the Negritude movement, developed by a select group of black African and Antillean students, writers and political activists in interwar Paris. Theirs was a predominantly literary opposition that stressed the distinctiveness and intrinsic value of African cultures, but which also acknowledged the utility of a continued relationship with France.[12] The second strand of opposition was more radical: a genuinely anti-colonial nationalism defined by its articulation of an alternative vision of African society based on modernization and merit rather than conservatism, ruralism, and tradition. These black anti-colonialists were sometimes less than united. They disagreed over ideology (communism in particular) and over tactics (should anti-colonial writing concede a place for direct action or worker protest?). Even nomenclature could divide them (did *noir* or the more loaded *nègre* better express the way in which French society constructed their identity?) But the degrees of separation – in education, the workplace, in arts and leisure – that made discrimination a lived reality animated them all.[13]

Thus, at the very moment that colonial governments across francophone black Africa were championing a less intrusive style of governance, dubbed associationism, which claimed to respect traditional hierarchies, local customs, and cultures, those *évolués* previously deemed capable of 'assimilation' to French citizenship were excluded once more.[14] In Mahmood Mamdani's analysis, after the First World War, French colonial rule amounted to a 'bifurcated state', meaning that it brought two distinct centres of power – the French administrative system and the tribal hierarchies it privileged – into partnership. The history of decolonization in francophone black Africa over the next thirty years would be punctuated by the *évolués'* efforts to break down this hegemonic system. As the emergence of Negritude suggests, this would be as much a cultural struggle as a political one. French Governors and their allies among local chiefs spoke the language of tradition, rural community, and customary law, the *évolués* the language of African cultural integrity, political engagement, civil rights, and economic modernization.[15]

Why, then, was associationism so popular among colonial officials? The answer lay in their academic training rather than in direct instructions from government. From the inception of modern French imperialism in the sixteenth century until the completion of further colonial conquests in Indochina and Africa in the late nineteenth century, the French Empire was centrally administered by the Ministry of Marine – a haven of conservatism and unreconstructed monarchism – and not by a dedicated Ministry of Colonies. It was not until March 1894 that an independent Ministry was finally established. For decades afterwards, this Ministry, often identified by its Paris location in the rue Oudinot, remained a weak reed, incapable of giving much direction to colonial policy. The formulation of associationist ideas and what French scholars call the 'territorialization' of colonies carved into discrete political and legal spaces owed far more to French ethnographers, geographers, and other enthusiasts for the 'new' social sciences popular at the turn of the century.[16] Individuals such as Maurice

Delafosse, one-time director of political affairs in the Dakar administration, and Henri Labouret, another former administrator in West Africa who, from 1929 onwards, became the driving force of the ethnographic courses taught at the Paris training college for Colonial Service appointees, the École Coloniale. Delafosse and Labouret were the pre-eminent voices among many long-serving officials in French Africa who regarded the fast developing 'colonial sciences' of anthropology and ethnology as key to effective administration.[17]

From 1926, the new director of the École Coloniale, Georges Hardy, gave concrete form to these ideas, ensuring that the upcoming generation of colonial officials saw their duty as the protection of 'authentic' African culture. Economic modernization, industrialization, and wider access to political rights were thus interpreted as dangerously disruptive; transitions to be approached with the utmost caution. Rather than widen access to citizenship, École Coloniale graduates in posts across black Africa in the 1920s and early 1930s focused instead on granting favoured status to conservative, rural elites based around the tribe and the village.[18]

What Frederick Cooper has dubbed 'the politics of retraditionalization' had other, more pecuniary motives.[19] If the principal objective of the French presence was to extract wealth and increase state power, why risk internal upheaval if colonial control could be accomplished in cooperation with influential indigenous elites?[20] Forging local political alliances to ensure the smooth operation of economic exploitation, military recruitment, and the preservation of rural order reinforced the power of tribal chiefs, Vietnamese mandarins, and village headmen who became adjuncts of the colonial state. Reduced to its barest minimum, the purpose of these crucial intermediaries was threefold. The first related to language. It fell to trusted elites and locally recruited clerical personnel to make sense of colonial edicts in the eyes of their own communities, literally translating what officials wanted into terms that were socially acceptable within their own communities. The second related to work. Heightened colonial export production required larger numbers of workers. In thinly populated regions especially, provision of an adequate labour supply became an essential task of colonial government – and of the local intermediaries to whom the job was delegated. Third was the matter of security. Keeping order in the rural interior of colonies where the colonial administrative or military presence was minimal might depend, in practice, on compliance and collaboration from local people of influence able to call upon networks of retainers, followers, or extended family relations.[21]

At root, associationism was a marriage of convenience. In return for their assistance, these intermediaries retained limited autonomy in matters of local justice, land disputes, tax collection, and military recruitment. The success of the policy rested in large part on colonial officials' understanding of clan hierarchies, religious affiliations, and the political economy of peasant societies still adjusting to the demands of export-driven colonial economic policies.[22]

The spread of wage labour throughout the Empire produced a small but recognizable indigenous industrial workforce largely confined to the major cities, ports, and commercial centres of individual colonies. This raised the worrying prospect for the French authorities of urban political dissent and industrial unrest of a type common in Europe. Fear of well-organized mass colonial protest was at the root of administrators' hostility to the urbanization and proletarianization of colonial societies. Anxious talk of 'detribalization' in black Africa was a coded expression of predictions that economic modernization would release social pressures in colonial cities that the French would be unable to withstand. Hence the tight confinement of African labour forces and the vigour with which the French authorities stamped out early African attempts to organize local unions in the 1930s. Not surprisingly, the first major strike waves to grip French West Africa immediately after the Second World War were signpost events at least as significant as the emergence of locally directed political parties.[23]

What about the position in other key imperial territories? The profound sense of isolation common among the French settlers (or '*colons*') of Tonkin within years of France's final conquest of Indochina in the 1880s suggests that, here at least, social divisions ran even deeper than in the 'bifurcated states' of French Africa.[24] Across the Indochina federation it was hard to find much community of interest between metropolitan imperialists, colonial officials, and the settlers at the forefront of local imperial consolidation. Here, again, terminology is revealing. '*Indochine*' was very much an artificial French construct, the more overtly colonial '*Indochine française*' even more so. The exoticism that Indochina evoked among the French public in the *belle époque* era bore little correlation to the economic and cultural segregation between French settlers and the indigenous populations of Vietnam, Cambodia, and Laos.[25] In many ways, the colonial state structures put in place by Governor General Paul Doumer at the turn of the century remained essentially unaltered forty years later when the Second World War began. As Pierre Brocheux and Daniel Hémery have noted, the federation's government was notable for its bureaucratic rigidity, or '*fonctionnarisme*'.[26]

One physical monument to the presence of colonial government in Indochina was Dalat. A hill station in the highlands of Annam (Central Vietnam), Dalat was supposed to become a summer capital in which the governor general, senior administrators, military officers, traders, and their families could escape the humidity of Saigon. In practice, the form and construction of Dalat said more about the shortcomings of imperial rule. For one thing, the resort took decades to take shape, its costs and alleged health benefits the subject of bitter acrimony. For another thing, Dalat's hotels and chalets, although built with local Vietnamese labour, were largely reserved for whites. These tensions between ambition and achievement, between exclusivity and inclusiveness, between Dalat as imperial summer capital and Dalat as Vietnamese-built oddity, exemplified the contradictions of the late colonial state.[27] Dalat indicated that the colonial authorities felt a widening obligation towards officials and settlers, but it raised unsettling questions about the limits of colonial responsibility to the peoples of Vietnam, Laos, and Cambodia. Here, the issue of emergency relief provides answers. In a region where natural disasters, harvest failure, and food shortage were endemic, the colonial state did not see itself as the ultimate provider of sustenance or shelter. Put differently, colonial treasury funds were not made available for welfare spending, even during periods of acute hardship and famine.[28] Yet, still colonial Indochina was idealized by writers, artists, and officials. Indochina's territories, like the African territories subjugated at much the same time, were treated, in historian Herman Lebovics' words, like 'blank sheets of paper'. Their indigenous cultures were judged to be either unworthy of record, or, as in the case of Vietnam and Cambodia, too decadent to survive the rejuvenating forces of French administrative rationalization and capitalist enterprise.[29] The job of government was not to offer remedial care for societies too hopeless to help themselves. It was, rather, to refashion those societies into something more vigorous, more valuable, more French.

The idea of an overarching unity between these South East Asian peoples catalysed by the centrifugal forces of colonialism made little sense to the populations concerned.

The consolidation of French control over Laos in the 1890s, for instance, partitioned ethnically Lao regions between Siam and France. The eastern sections of the country came under French rule, but the partition denied the Lao access to their traditional hinterland in the Khorat plateau further to the West. For the next fifty years, French officials consistently viewed Laos from the perspective of Vietnam. Laos was thus regarded as, at once, a strategic buffer, a hopelessly underdeveloped backwater requiring Vietnamese inward migration to make it profitable, and a quaint, museum-piece kingdom free from the political corruptions of Vietnam-style nationalist sentiment or communist ideology.[30]

Not surprisingly, the settler community envisioned Indochina's rural interior as a closed, forbidding environment. So, too, the city districts inhabited by Europeans were reconfigured on the assumption that a disease-bearing, seditious population must be kept at a safe distance.[31] Throughout Vietnam especially, the threat of civil unrest was never far from settlers' minds.[32] The insecure foundations of imperial cooperation between French officials and their indigenous elite collaborators had become painfully clear by 1918. A breakout of political prisoners, criminals, and mutinous local guards from the Thai Nguyen penitentiary in Tonkin (Northern Vietnam) on 31 August 1917 soon assumed the character of rebellion against the colonial state. The diverse regional, cultural, and political backgrounds of those involved anticipated the modern Vietnamese nationalism that would emerge more strongly during the interwar years.[33]

Vietnam represented the so-called *politique des races* in action: literally, a policy that favoured certain indigenous elites while excluding others. A variant of associationism and developed by General Joseph Gallieni, who consolidated the French hold over Tonkin during the late 1880s, the *politique des races* was subsequently adopted in numerous other colonial settings. Its inherent divisiveness and consequent political risks became apparent as French administration was implanted in Madagascar during the mid-1890s. Again, Gallieni was to the fore. He arrived on the island as France's first resident-minister in late 1895. His government wished to dispense with the native Merina dynasty with which the invading French forces had concluded a protectorate treaty on 1 October. Gallieni's advisers, including Louis-Hubert Lyautey, future imperial proconsul in Morocco, concocted an alleged royal conspiracy against French rule that served as a pretext to topple the monarchy and ostracize its followers, replacing them with more compliant indigenous partners marginalized under the old royal regime. Trampling over indigenous political culture in this way was ultimately counterproductive. Victimization of the Merina oligarchy – previously deeply unpopular in much of Malagasy society – made it a rallying point for proto nationalist opposition to the French presence.[34]

The divide and rule ethos of the *politique des races* reached its apogee in Syria and Lebanon, the two Middle East Mandates of which France took formal charge in 1920. Playing off different communities and economic interests against each another, and according various minorities privileged status at the direct expense of the Sunni Muslim majority, the Levant High Commission took both Syria and Lebanon down a path towards worsening interethnic friction and episodic communal violence. In the aftermath of a major revolt in Syria in 1925–6, Levant High Commissioner Henri Ponsot acknowledged that the country's nationalist leaders would not tolerate anything short of a treaty of national independence.[35] Other oppositional voices were emerging as well. Local women's movements challenged the French authorities to live up to the rhetoric of republican equality and the obligations of good governance written by League of Nations jurists into the terms of the Mandate.[36] Educators and Churchmen demanded fuller provision for ethnic and religious minorities, demanding that the region's rich cultural heritage be better served by French administrators who claimed to respect it.[37] Sect leaders and nomadic clan chiefs defied the restrictions of artificial geographical borders that ignored traditional rights of access to water, grazing, and other natural resources.[38] Little wonder that Ponsot was proved right: subsequent efforts to reconcile Syrians' aspirations with a continuing French presence ended in failure.

The experience of Gallieni and Lyautey in 1890s Madagascar, and the acrimonious parliamentary debates over the government of Syria thirty years later, point to something further: differing methods of colonial rule were contested between opposing political groups in mainland France.[39] By the late nineteenth century, assimilationist colonialism, rooted in the ideal of a colour-blind, unified empire of imperial citizens, was often identified with the French left. Conversely, associationism appealed to ultra-rightist thinkers such as Edouard Drumont, Gustave Le Bon, and Jules Harmond because it explicitly rejected racial equality. To these race theorists, segregation between colonizers and colonized mirrored the unbridgeable ethnic differences between Europeans and their colonial subjects.[40] By no means all associationists held such extreme views. Cost-conscious Paris governments were attracted to associationism by the economies inherent in an administrative practice that made use of pre-existing native power structures to impose colonial control.

This brings us to a final point: the resurgence of conservative associationism between the wars reflected the failure of schemes for colonial development, above all, the fifteen year investment plan proposed by Minister of Colonies, Albert Sarraut in 1921. Instead of long-term state funding of public works, welfare provision, and infrastructure construction, colonial development was conducted piecemeal – government by government, colony by colony. Where colonial economic growth was most pronounced, such as the North African territories of Morocco, Algeria, and Tunisia, wider access to citizenship and political rights did not necessarily follow. Greater economic opportunity, urbanization, industrial employment, and increased life expectancy among indigenous peoples fed demands for better educational provision, more jobs in government, and meaningful freedoms. And in dependent territories, like the North African protectorates of Tunisia and Morocco, in which colonial rule was constrained by surviving monarchical administrations, local people deftly exploited the clash of legal jurisdictions between the French and their royal partners in government – Tunisia's Bey and Morocco's Sultan.[41] As the menace of another World War loomed larger, the uncomfortable dynamic that confronted French imperialists was simple: as more colonial subjects became waged workers within stratified colonial economies, so popular disaffection grew.[42] The resulting dilemma was inescapable. Just how long could the Empire subsist without some effort to redress the growing imbalance between economic modernization and arcane colonial authoritarianism?[43]

The economics of France's interwar empire

The changing demographic profile of colonial populations made the racial segregation inherent in colonial economic organization even more apparent. Where statistically significant settler communities existed, as in French North Africa, Indochina, and the Antillean islands of Martinique and Guadeloupe, their rate of demographic growth did not match the increase in indigenous population. Furthermore, in most French colonial territories, net population increases outstripped the slow pace of imperial economic recovery after the Global Depression of 1929–36. Colonial subjects therefore faced a precarious economic future even after the depression lifted in 1937–8. Under employment and the emergence of a proletarian underclass in the first *bidonvilles*, or shantytowns, of the largest colonial cities – Algiers, Casablanca, Dakar, and Saigon – dominated official reportage of local economic conditions on the eve of war in 1939.[44] It was no coincidence that the colonial infants of the 1930s would become the nationalist supporters of the 1940s and 1950s. In 1937, Indochina's Governor General, Jules Brévié, issued a circular that forbade Vietnamese schoolchildren from discussing political questions or declaring any form of national allegiance other than to France. This followed warnings from officials in Central Vietnam (Annam) that the 'Popular Front generation' of school-aged children were acutely conscious of the discrimination and poor economic prospects they faced.[45]

The depression made a lasting impact on colonial economies and, hence, on the long-term origins of decolonization. Take the increased trade dependency between France and the colonies in the decade after 1927. In 1928 the colonial empire became France's most important trading partner. Yet this reflected the contraction of other overseas markets more than net growth in the volume of Franco-colonial trade. Once the depression hit the French economy in 1930–1, the empire served as a *réservoir colonial* providing raw materials and a captive market for home industries faced with empty order books. Profits generated by colonial export trade became vital to French economic stability. Some metropolitan manufacturers remained in business solely because they could sell their goods on their terms to colonial subjects. By 1939 over 40 per cent of French exports went to the empire, which, in turn, provided 37 per cent of France's imports.[46] In the longer term, however, this conferred few benefits on France or the colonies. Uncompetitive home industries limped on thanks to the colonial market. And diversification in colonial economies was stunted by reliance on overpriced French manufactured products. By 1930 the 'divorce' that historian Jacques Marseille identifies between France's long-term economic interest and its short-term preservation of closed colonial markets had begun.[47]

Other barriers to the growth of a vibrant colonial export economy also multiplied during the depression years. In the early 1930s most colonial governments lacked the funds, the communications infrastructure, or the administrative wherewithal to promote the emergence of secondary industries.[48] Nor was there strong metropolitan pressure for this to take place. Instead, year after year, the essence of colonial economic planning was the production drive: a concerted effort to augment colonial export volumes. The results were markedly different results for colonizers and colonized. Take Indochina. The spectacular growth of Vietnam's export output in the 1920s and the early development of an industrial sector concentrated primarily in Tonkin and Cochin China did not produce significant increases in general prosperity. Control of commerce and industry was largely confined to French joint stock companies, large industrial enterprises, the settler elite, Chinese traders, a small Vietnamese urban bourgeoisie, and the ubiquitous Bank of Indochina.[49] Working conditions for landless Vietnamese peasants, plantation labourers, miners, and textile workers remained dreadful.

Vietnamese smallholders, once regarded as key allies of the colonial state, faced retrenchment or ruin between 1930 and 1935. These peasant farmers possessed sufficient land to produce surplus rice for sale at market, but were severely affected by the crisis in Indochina's rice economy in the early 1930s.[50]

The pattern of minimal state aid to Vietnam's subject population was repeated in French North Africa, where a higher proportion of settlers in the resident population exacerbated the inequities of state welfare provision. Responsive to *colons'* demands, the French authorities were deaf to the needs of Muslim smallholders and landless labourers. At a macroeconomic level, the Ministry of Commerce in Paris, the North African administrations, French trading houses (notably in Lyons and Marseilles), and settler producers also regulated the terms of French North Africa's economic dependency on France to the exclusion of the Muslim majority.

Pre-war reforms

Uneven colonial economic distribution was replicated in patterns of cultural exclusion. Herman Lebovics has argued persuasively that the years 1900–45 witnessed a powerful shift towards cultural conformity within metropolitan France and its empire. Political, juridical, cultural, and anthropological definitions of what it meant to be truly 'French', and just how inclusive that category would be, became a critical ideological battleground between left and right. The result was a hardening of racial stereotypes, which left no room for any significant emancipation of France's subject peoples.[51] The experiences of immigrants from colonial territories in interwar France tend to confirm this shift towards more stringent racial, legal, and cultural distinction.[52] Nor was France alone in this regard. New restrictions on immigrant numbers and stricter regulation of interracial mixing was replicated in much of the industrialized 'white' world in which immigration quotas and exclusions, 'colour bars', and other forms of discrimination were widely reinforced in the decade following the First World War.[53]

The French state and the many pro-natalist organizations eager to replenish France's population after the First World War never looked on colonial immigrant workers favourably. Most of these arrivals came from France's North African territories, Algeria especially. Single men predominated. Most arrived from particular regions or communities in which labour migration and the payment of remittances to families back home were well established. These colonial workers were typically found in the worst urban housing stock of France's major industrial cities, particularly Paris, Lille, and Marseilles. Few brought their families with them; fewer still either acquired citizenship or intermarried with French women.[54] Both actions were frowned upon by the wider public and the state. Colonial immigrants were not encouraged to put down deep roots in metropolitan France, the argument being that their assimilation into the citizen body of France was infeasible. A common metaphor among pro-natalists was the blood transfusion: whereas Italian, Spanish, or Polish immigrant blood was compatible with French, Algerian, or Senegalese was not. Even some feminists committed to gender equality suggested that French women would debase themselves by marrying African or Asian men, particularly if this implied acceptance of Islamic cultural codes.[55]

Colonial immigrants were also closely monitored by police surveillance units, ostensibly there to ensure their welfare, but actually dedicated to preventing anti-colonial sedition or social transgression.[56] After the double murder in 1923 of two Parisian women on the Rue Fondary by a Kabyle immigrant, Camille Chautemps, Interior Minister in the Cartel des gauches coalition, introduced stringent measures to curtail North African immigration. Colonial immigrants were required to possess identity cards with photographs, medical certificates, and evidence of cash reserves in order to avoid arbitrary repatriation by the French judicial authorities. Additional legislation to restrict Muslims' freedom of movement and to prevent economic migration to France were introduced from 1924 onwards.[57] More formal regulation on the indigenous workforce served several objectives. For one, it met official anxiety about uncontrolled Algerian immigration to France, a concern that was, in turn, stimulated by more abundant signs of French blue-collar racism and union antagonism to employers' use of casual immigrant labour. Not surprisingly, colonial workers figured prominently among the first major lay-offs in French industry once the depression hit in the early 1930s.

The one government in France before 1940 that supported ground-breaking colonial reform was a product of this cultural milieu. This was Léon Blum's Socialist-led Popular Front coalition that held office for twelve months from May 1936. Its reforms were intended to strengthen the empire by correcting the worst abuses of colonial administration. Humanitarian measures, devised in response to observed conditions in the empire, also appeased the consciences of left-wingers uneasy about colonialism.[58] Certain targeted reforms were initiated immediately. With Blum's encouragement, Maurice Viollette, Socialist Minister of State and a former Governor of Algeria, resurrected a Bill he had first introduced in July 1931.[59] Tabled in December 1936, the so-called Blum-Viollette Plan proposed to grant French citizenship and attendant voting rights to some 25,000 Algerian elected officials, ex-servicemen, and lycée graduates without requiring them to abandon their statutory rights as Muslims under Koranic law.[60] Meanwhile, across North and West Africa, Madagascar, Syria, and the Indochina federation, amnesties for political prisoners were announced. Press restrictions were relaxed, political meetings were permitted, and French-educated colonial workers were allowed to join a trade union.[61] Detailed surveys of living conditions, women's rights, and child labour were also instituted in French West Africa and in Indochina, the intention being to accumulate the data necessary to improve legal protection and welfare provision for the most vulnerable. Most of these changes were short lived. The Blum-Viollette Plan was never put to the vote. The welfare surveys, though ultimately influential, remained incomplete when the Popular Front fell from power. Nationalist parties, colonial trade unions, and local language newspapers were outlawed in an empire-wide crackdown during 1937–8.[62]

What does this tell us? Avowedly committed to social and economic improvement for the colonial populations of French Africa and Indochina, the Popular Front remained trapped by two overlapping problems, one institutional, the other, conceptual. Take the institutional obstacles first. Resistance to reform pervaded colonial bureaucracy and was echoed by the government's most vociferous political opponents in the National Assembly. However, the conceptual barriers were stronger still. Even the supporters of reform in government and the Colonial Service regarded the racial and economic inequities of colonialism as problems to be reduced rather than ended.[63] In this sense, the Popular Front's contribution to decolonization was inadvertent and paradoxical. The limited scope and meagre results of Popular Front reformism lent greater urgency to nationalist opposition driven underground as France descended into another World War.

Locating French decolonization

Mention of the Second World War brings us to a central question with which any historian of French decolonization has to wrestle. When did France's colonial empire begin to fall apart? To an Anglocentric observer the answers may seem obvious. The crushing defeat of 1940, the traumas of occupation, and Vichy collaboration were surely prejudicial to colonial control. Above all, the Vichy-Free French rivalries played out across imperial territory from Africa through Syria to Indochina amounted to an undeclared civil war. What more obvious evidence of French disunity and inability to govern could there be? Yet the fact remains that for French imperial historians 1945 is not quite the watershed that we might imagine.

Perhaps four main elements help explain this French historiographical ambivalence. The first is the nature and outcome of metropolitan liberation. After Vichy's ignominious collapse in July 1944, the differing rates of liberation across southern and eastern France, and the provisional nature of republican government prior to the establishment of the Fourth Republic in October 1946, all added to the expectation that reconstruction of the French political system should mark a new beginning – both a deliberate rupture with the wartime past and a cherry-picking of the most attractive aspects of democratic republicanism. As a result, France's new leadership did not hold itself accountable for past colonial mistakes. The array of new political parties to emerge from the resistance, the long overdue enfranchisement of women, the unprecedented popular appeal of French communism, the discrediting of much of the French right, and the still untested power of Gaullism suggested that post-war politics would indeed be of a different stripe to the old days of Third Republic immobilism. Perhaps the new political elite would make a better job of the French Empire. Again, the enduring official emphasis on the imperative of cultural improvement as the core ingredient of colonial policy encouraged such optimism.[64] France might not have the money or the military power to reimpose old-style colonial order, but the new post-war Republic brought an abundance of new ideas, ambitious constitutional projects, and a commitment to a new-style republican imperialism. There are echoes here of the 'forward thinking' so apparent in Colonial Office planning during and immediately after the Second World War. The year 1945 presented an opportunity to correct past mistakes rather than merely pick up the reins of former colonial power.

A second reason for French imperial confidence in 1945 was less readily acknowledged, but no less significant. The Vichy state had paid more attention to colonial affairs than the Republic it replaced. This was partly circumstantial. The Vichy regime had freer rein to experiment in colonial territory than in metropolitan France. And policies designed to ensure that colonies did not fall under Gaullist or Anglo-American control were likely to gain German and Italian approval. But ardent Pétainists were also convinced imperialists. The certainty that the French Empire had been under poor management, at least since the election of the Popular Front in 1936, led to a more precise audit of colonial territory. For Vichy, proving the material value of empire was an essential step to creating the *hommes nouveaux* of the new France – patriots for whom a robust imperialism would be fundamental to French cultural identity.[65]

As Ruth Ginio's work on French West Africa reveals, Vichy was always more assiduous in its colonial propaganda, more fervent in its colonial legislation and more inclined to theorize about the nature and purpose of Empire, than its Free French rival.[66] During 1941 alone the Vichy government promulgated over 200 laws and decrees for application within the Empire. Taken as a whole, Vichy legislation created a distinct imperial order based upon a more explicit assertion of French racial supremacy and defence of settler interest. Yet, its anti-Semitic dimension apart, this 'racialization' of Vichy's colonial policies marked less of a new departure than might be imagined. Designated areas for whites-only and the conscripted use of African labour to ensure the profitability of European plantation agriculture did not represent an abrupt reversal of pre-war practice, merely the legal codification of long-standing practices.[67] Nor did *de facto* segregation and forced labour disappear from black Africa once the Gaullists took control.

Even so, Vichy rule was, in other ways, distinctive. In the fields of economic planning and judicial administration, new tiers of colonial administration were created. By May 1941 new controls were in place regarding the colonial press, labour service and employment provision, banking transactions, and individual freedom of movement. Colonial subjects within Vichy France were denied access to the occupied zone to the north. Elective institutions in overseas territories were either suspended or suppressed, nationalist parties and trade unions were proscribed, and, within Algeria, the 1919 Jonnart citizenship law was revoked. Aside from these rights denials, war brought other, more pressing hardships for colonial subjects. Living conditions declined in numerous French imperial territories from Morocco to Vietnam. Wartime inflationary pressure and market shortages made essential food and fuel harder to obtain. Standards of public health deteriorated. Malnutrition and epidemic illness (typhus and tuberculosis especially) reappeared among the poorest in colonial society.[68] Yet still Vichy's imperial planners ventured on. Remarkably, the corporatist ideas beloved of Vichy's colonial policymakers survived for a full year after the collapse of Vichy authority in North Africa, French West Africa (AOF), and Madagascar. Built around organizational committees set up for individual colonial industries and producers, Vichy's colonial *dirigisme* envisaged a systematic modernization of the economic structure and industrial organization of French Africa. This was to be carried out through a ten-year programme of investment, labour reform, and increased state direction. This ambitious scheme was never fully implemented. But what bears emphasis here is that the hangovers of corporatism and economic mobilization persisted in the minds of colonial officials (many of them ex-Vichyites) in post after 1943.

In terms of imperial propaganda, heightened state planning, and wider popular experience of colonial life, the Vichy years were exceptional. Empire was rammed down French throats during 1940–4 with vigour the like of which was unseen since the late nineteenth century. This, of course, had its Gaullist equivalent, a republican mirror-image colonialism, which, although in direct opposition to Vichy itself, shared many of its underlying imperial values. The success of Free France as an external resistance movement had an obvious colonial dimension. From the legendary *ralliements* of 1940 to the colonial campaigns so important to the resurrection of French martial pride, imperial territory provided an exotic and apparently loyal backdrop to Gaullist advance.[69] In less romantic terms, Brazzaville and Algiers became Free French administrative centres in which the day-to-day running of colonies occupied more time than the long-term planning of French liberation. On both sides of the Vichy-Free French divide then, imperial attachments acquired a new material and symbolic importance.

These considerations help account for the third element to the French imperialist outlook in 1945. This was what France's leading imperial historian, Charles-Robert Ageron, termed the 'colonial myth'. The metropolitan resistance movements and the civilian population living under occupation do not fit easily into comparisons of Vichy-Free French colonial rivalries. Did the members of Combat, the young *maquisards* evading labour service in Germany, the wives of prisoners of war, or the families struggling to make ends meet really care much about empire one way or the other? Ageron's shrewd answer is yes and no. No, Vichy's propagandizing had not turned France into a nation of empire enthusiasts. But yes, during 1944–5 the French public seem to have taken for granted that the empire should be preserved intact. Hence the colonial myth: control of empire, it was assumed, would enable France to reclaim its rightful place on the international stage. So much for Vichy's attempts at an imperial audit. By 1945 most French voters simply read possession of colonies as a necessary ingredient of national power. If anything, blissful ignorance of actual conditions across the empire was a more potent force for popular imperialism than the more deeply rooted colonialism that Vichy had tried to foster.

The paradox between limited domestic understanding of colonial societies and stronger public support for empire should not be taken too far. Even intellectuals, human rights activists, investigative journalists, and Church-based groups that eventually coalesced into an influential anti-colonial lobby in the early 1950s were by no means sure that empire had had its day at the end of the Second World War. And not until the clamour against army torture practices in Algeria from 1957 onwards did this intellectual opposition focus squarely on the injustices suffered by the mass of France's colonial subjects, preferring instead to champion the cause of particular high-profile individuals such as the Malagasy Deputies arrested in the immediate aftermath of the Madagascar uprising in April 1947.

From the right to the left of the French political spectrum in 1945 public opinion saw a future for the empire. As the Liberation of France and an eventual allied victory in the Second World War became increasingly likely, a new imperial optimism took root among the Free French leadership. Once Paris was liberated, a provisional government under General de Gaulle took office in July 1944. The new administration was 'provisional' because, once the war was won, the French public would have to decide what form of post-war regime they wished to see restored. It was widely anticipated that metropolitan and imperial constitution making would proceed hand in hand. Even as the provisional government and the first and second Constituent Assemblies made plans for France's new republic, they also produced a new schema for a more unified empire. Fourth Republic and French Union would be launched together in October 1946. The democratic legitimacy of the former was supposed to enhance the enlightened reformism of the latter. Old-style colonialism was dead, long live a new French imperialism uniquely grounded in the concept of federal partnership between metropolitan France and its dependent territories.

This was the Brazzaville spirit *par excellence* – a general belief that the generosity of intention behind colonial reform would somehow compensate for the actual French refusal to contemplate decolonization. The contrast between warm words and limited practical deeds had certainly been evident at the Brazzaville conference itself. The significance of the Brazzaville meetings in January and February 1944 derived from the French eagerness to be seen to make 'a new departure', underscoring de Gaulle's insistence upon the legitimacy of a post-war colonial order in Africa. Though Brazzaville held great symbolic importance, its proceedings were often uninspiring. There was an obvious contradiction between the sophisticated proposals formulated by Henri Laurentie and his subordinate officials at the Commissariat of Colonies, and the limited time allowed for the plenary conference of colonial Governors to debate

The Roots of French Decolonization

them. A series of meetings held over a ten-day period, with an agenda strictly regulated by a conservative Colonial Commissar, René Pleven, was never likely to produce a comprehensive plan for a revitalized relationship between France and its black African Empire. As the Free French Secretariat put it, the 'essential task' was to strike a balance between a spirit of generous reform and the need to produce viable, if 'modest', proposals.

Reform versus decolonization: The French Union scheme

France held its first post-war national election on 21 October 1945. This was no simple general election. The first of the many referenda that would be so much a feature of French – and French imperial – politics after 1945 was also scheduled alongside the choice of parliamentary representatives. Voters faced three choices. They had to elect national representatives. They also had to vote by referendum on whether the assembly they elected should draft a new constitution to replace the Third Republic that had been supplanted by the Vichy state in 1940. If, as they did, voters decided to give the new Parliament 'constituent powers' to devise a new constitution, their third and final choice was to accept or reject the provisional government proposal that the new assembly should only have authority for seven months at which point its constitutional plans should be voted on once more by referendum.

With these fundamental choices before them, and with several new or resurrected parties contesting the polls, including the Christian Democrat Mouvement Républicain Populaire (MRP), a revitalized Socialist Party, and a burgeoning Parti Communiste Française (PCF), it is little wonder that French voters had little time to dwell on the imperial implications of a new constitutional system. Revision of the metropolitan constitution would be accompanied by revision of the constitutional arrangements between France and its overseas dependencies. Partly in anticipation of this, sixty four of the 586 delegates to the Constituent Assembly elected in October 1945 were from overseas territories. However, forty of these delegates were elected by French citizens, mainly settlers, and were largely members of metropolitan French political parties. They sat in an assembly dominated by the PCF, the MRP, and the Socialists. These three parties controlled almost four-fifths of the seats in the first Constituent Assembly. They would share power until May 1947 in a series of short-lived administrations in which the balance of ministerial power between the three parties would gradually shift rightwards.[70]

It is a striking irony that numerous French politicians persistently argued that colonial peoples were incapable of running their own affairs and yet saw the same populations adapt perfectly well to the intricacies of French electoral procedure. In French West Africa and French Equatorial Africa, for example, between 1945 and 1948 voters not only went to the polls in three general elections but also selected three territorial assemblies and voted in four referenda. They thus had to choose delegates to the National Assembly, to the separate assembly of the French Union, as well as representatives for their own territorial assemblies and the Federation Grand Councils in Dakar and Brazzaville.[71]

Colonial problems, when discussed at all by the French public, seem to have caused a good deal of confusion. Uncertainty about the issues involved, and ambivalence about how best to tackle them, fostered a misleading impression of the scale of the challenge ahead.[72] The underlying belief that the empire could and should be preserved was by no means confined to the French right. Even the French Communist Party, increasingly dogmatic in its Stalinist loyalties, diluted the anti-imperialism supposedly at the heart of its ideological mission.[73] In the immediate post-war period, the Socialists, too, had little truck with anti-colonialism. Upon taking up his post in July 1946 as Minister of Food in Georges Bidault's coalition government, the Socialist Yves Farge briefly sought control over the Ministry of Colonies in an effort to ensure that the empire was entirely subordinated to France's most urgent supply needs.[74] Yet in a poll conducted in early 1946, 63 per cent of respondents agreed that a new constitution was necessary 'to give to the populations of the French colonies the same rights as French citizens'. Echoing this more generous mood, the oppressive-sounding Ministry of Colonies was relaunched as a Ministry of Overseas France on 26 January 1946. Three months later, on 19 March, a clutch of *anciennes colonies*, mainly island territories ruled by France since the seventeenth and eighteenth centuries, were accorded the status of overseas departments. As administrative outposts of France proper, albeit overseas ones, Guadaloupe, Martinique, Guyanne (French Guiana), and Réunion no longer came under rue Oudinot jurisdiction. It was thus with somewhat truncated responsibilities that the Ministry of Overseas France began its post-war work until its final dissolution on 4 October 1958 under the terms of the new constitution of the Fifth Republic.

Meanwhile, the French public's apparent support for fundamental colonial reform also reverberated through the Constituent Assembly in Paris. Take the declaration by Pierre Cot, the first Constituent Assembly's Reporter-General: 'The colonial empire is dead. In its place we are setting up the French union. France, enriched, ennobled, and expanded, will tomorrow possess a hundred million citizens and free men.'[75] In a speech to Parliament on 23 March 1946, the Minister for Overseas France, the veteran Socialist Marius Moutet, went further still. The era of colonial coercion was over: 'The maintenance of sovereignty on the basis of force alone is no longer possible. This period of colonization has passed. A nation, and ours in particular, will only maintain its influence in [its] overseas territories with the free consent of their inhabitants.'[76] This generous, confident mood soon dissipated. Another opinion poll conducted in April 1947 (within weeks of the vote of additional military spending for the Indochina War and the outbreak of the Madagascar revolt), revealed an almost equal split – 35 to 37 per cent – between those who thought the French Union would collapse and those who did not.[77]

During 1946 the structure of this French Union was discussed within the second Constituent Assembly's constitutional commission. MRP leaders vetoed the French Union proposals, although the commission tried to meet their objections. The party leadership ruled out a unicameral French Union Assembly. MRP ministers were buoyed up by rank-and-file support for a politically conservative but socially inclusive 'Catholic' colonial policy. In the Ministry for Overseas France backrooms where constitutional proposals were devised, Director of Political Affairs Henri Laurentie, who was instinctually reformist and certainly more creative than his political masters, eventually gave way.[78] Laurentie had little choice. MRP leader Georges Bidault threatened to resign the premiership in September 1946 to break the socialist and communist commitment to greater colonial autonomy.[79]

Bidault's MRP also left a lasting impression on colonial policy in the decade after 1944. The case of Algeria is instructive. In August 1947, MRP Ministers and Deputies pushed through the Statute that determined electoral representation and the distribution of fiscal powers within the colony. A year earlier, in late August 1946, the Constituent Assembly discussed autonomy proposals formulated by Ferhat Abbas's Union démocratique de Manifeste algérien. Georges Bidault, then premier and Foreign Minister, defended the more limited administrative reforms pursued in Algeria by Yves Chataigneau's government-general. As Odile Rudelle has shown, Bidault's insistence that agreement on an Algerian Statute should be postponed until after the October 1946 constitutional referendum had profound consequences. The intervening period allowed time for the mobilization of settler opposition in Algeria itself. The loudest protests came from the Radical Party's Algerian federations. Their leader, René Mayer, deputy for Constantine, agreed with MRP president Maurice Schumann on three core demands. The final Statute should preserve a double electoral college, French control over budgetary allocations, and the Governor's executive power. The Fourth Republic constitution also affirmed Algeria's status as three French departments (in other words, as a territorial extension of France overseas). Algeria would not be treated on nationalist or communist terms as a republic in the making. Bidault's original postponement of the debate on the Statute until after the new constitution was in place had served the MRP purpose by setting narrow confines to the scheme put forward. Infuriated by this constraint, all the Algerian Deputies abstained in the final Statute vote.[80] In line with the MRP demands, the reforms enshrined in the Statute for Algeria rehearsed tired assimilationist rhetoric by exhorting Algerians to 'fulfil the destiny of the French Community'.[81] The passage of the Statute was a triumph of settler pressure and MRP parliamentary manipulation. It suggests that the combination of powerful settler interests and a multiparty system of government in the new Fourth Republic widened the number of groups and political organizations with an effective power of veto over colonial reform. This, as Henrik Spruyt has recently demonstrated, was a major contributory factor to state intransigence and the slide towards anti-colonial violence as a negotiated path to decolonization was blocked.[82]

Just as the Algerian Statute suggested a French retreat from meaningful reform, so too did the complex constitutional apparatus of the French Union. A recent historian of the French Union scheme has seen beyond the fine details of the constitutional debates: "The endless parliamentary and party disputes over overseas policy that accompanied successive colonial crises were in reality struggles over the details of a single, fundamentally unsound policy of preserving colonial-style hegemony over the dependencies.'[83] Indeed, the French Union, as it emerged in its amended form in October 1946, is perhaps best understood as a constitutional project that never fulfilled its early promise as a vehicle of centralized imperial reform. Its most obvious feature was the altered titular status of dependent territories. The word 'colony' was meticulously avoided. Hence, below the Sahara, the territories of French West Africa and French Equatorial Africa, Madagascar, and French Somaliland became 'overseas territories', while the former mandates of Cameroon and Togo were made 'associated territories'. Overseas territory status was also applied to French possessions in the Pacific, St Pierre and Miquelon, and the French trading settlements in India. At the instigation of the black poet Aimé Césaire, then communist deputy for Martinique, the pre-1789 colonies of the French Antilles (Martinique, Guadaloupe, Guiana) as well as the Indian Ocean island of Réunion were designated 'overseas departments' of the French Republic. Those parts of the empire where indigenous political monarchies sustained the fiction of quasi-autonomy were made 'associated states'. This appellation was thus applied to the Morocco and Tunisia protectorates and to the component territories of the Indochina federation. Algeria was, as previously mentioned, regulated separately through its own Statute.

Table 1 Structure of the French Union

The French Republic	The overseas territories	The associated states	The associated territories
Metropolitan France	a. French West Africa: Senegal Ivory Coast(Côte d'Ivoire) Guinea Dahomey French Sudan Upper Volta (Haute Volta) Niger Mauritania	Vietnam Cambodia Laos	French Cameroon French Togoland
OVERSEAS DEPARTMENTS: Algeria Guadeloupe Martinique French Guiana Réunion	b. French Equatorial Africa: Moyen-Congo Gabon Oubangui-Chari Chad	Morocco Tunisia	
	c. Madagascar d. French Somaliland e. The Comores f. French India g. New Caledonia h. French Oceania i. St Pierre et Miquelon		

The fiction of a more equitable partnership extended to the administrative apparatus as well. In certain territories, former colonial Governors were overnight transformed into less authoritarian sounding high commissioners. The colonial wordage may have gone but the racial hierarchy of colonialism was, if anything, made more explicit. The demarcation between the value attached to white and non-white votes was most apparent in the arrangements made for the election of Deputies from overseas territories to the French Parliament. Only in the overseas departments, in French West Africa, as well as Togoland and French Somaliland, were single college elections to occur. Elsewhere, from Algeria to Congo, Cameroon, and Madagascar, where settlers were either more numerous, more powerful or both, a dual electoral college system was preferred. Separate electoral colleges for colonial subjects and French citizens ensured that *colon* representatives would still wield disproportionate influence in the selection of Deputies to sit in Paris. Evidently, French-style democracy was not for export in unadulterated form except to the few territories where the election of pro-French representatives could be safely assumed. Although some form of local assembly was set up in all of the former colonies, their form and composition, and the methods by which representatives were to be elected to them, differed.

In the overseas departments, that is Algeria (actually sub-divided into three *départements*), Martinique, Guadeloupe, Guiana, and Réunion, *conseils généraux* broadly equivalent to English county councils, were established much as in metropolitan France. In the overseas territories, local assemblies were created colony by colony. The principal power reserved to these overseas parliaments was the right of scrutiny over individual territory budgets. All former colonies and protectorates, whether designated as overseas departments, overseas territories, or associated states, were to send representatives to a separate assembly of the French Union. This was an imperial Parliament that sat in Paris, its combined membership consisting of overseas Deputies chosen by their local assembly as well as French members elected by the National Assembly.[84] However, imposing its name, this French Union Assembly was essentially a talking shop, always eclipsed by the National Assembly.

The Assembly's inaugural meeting took place on 10 December 1947. With some 230 elected members, termed 'conseillers de l'Union française', this was an unprecedented parliamentary gathering. Albert Sarraut, who chaired its opening session, was keen to stress the Assembly's symbolic importance as tangible proof the egalitarian partnership between France and its empire. His emphasis on the ceremonial was understandable. Although head of state, President Vincent Auriol presided over the French Union Assembly, it was little more than a colourful debating society. Its key power lay in the government's obligation to consult it regarding any legislation pertaining to imperial territory. The Assembly was also empowered to make recommendations to the government of the day about colonial policy. Pomp aside, within a year, the new Assembly had lost the battle to secure real influence within the new constitutional system. Its members failed to secure recognition as the authorized representatives of national communities, they were denied the right to challenge the government's Indochina policy, and their titular head, Vincent Auriol, was unable to impose his authority as French Union President to monitor colonial policy effectively. As part of the constitutional checks and balances on government management of the French Union, the new Assembly was a failure. Perhaps, as Marc Michel suggests, its most lasting contribution was to nurture a generation of future colonial leaders even if the successes they later achieved were largely accomplished outside the Assembly itself.[85]

Added together, this multilayered system was at once ambitious and deliberately obscure. The plethora of local and national assemblies did not amount to meaningful representative democracy except in the few island dependencies of the 'old' pre-revolutionary empire. The dichotomy between wide-ranging, if convoluted, constitutional liberalization and the reality of limited political change within the colonial territories themselves was also apparent in the reforms enacted preparatory to the launch of the Union scheme. In May 1946, the Senegalese Lamine Guèye, the leading black African within the upper echelons of the French Socialist Party, piloted an eponymously named citizenship law through the Constituent Assembly. At a stroke, the loi Lamine Guèye turned France's indigenous colonial populations from 'subjects' into 'citizens'. The immediate tangible benefit was to end the separate and arbitrary legal code – the indigénat – applied to colonial subjects. This complemented the end of forced labour for colonial subjects abolished by the Assembly a month earlier. To round matters off, Lamine Guèye's reforms were written into the October constitution.

It bears emphasis, however, that France's imperial citizens did not share the same rights of citizenship as their French cousins. Distinctions also remained within the colonial populations themselves. 'Citizens of common status', denoting those who had qualified for citizenship before 1946, were, for example, exempted from local customary law in matters such as inheritance and marriage. But customary law in civil matters continued to apply to the new 'citizens of local status' delineated in 1946. The situation was even more ambiguous for those of mixed race living in francophone Africa. In December 1946 a Bill was put forward advocating French citizenship for the so-called *métis non reconnus*. This applied to those of 'unrecognized' mixed race unable to provide legal proof of their French heredity. The fact that these people had already been granted such citizenship under Article 80 of the new constitution escaped many of the Deputies involved in scrutinizing the measure.[86]

Hardly surprising then that another legacy of associationist colonial reforms was the alienation of the Western-educated, politically active administrative cadres schooled in the French educational system. From Morocco to Vietnam, these Europeanized elites came to prominence in the interwar period. Contrary to French expectations, after 1945, few were reconciled to a subordinate, if privileged, role in colonial society. The majority were deeply frustrated by the reality of limited opportunities for economic, professional, or political advancement within a colonial regime.[87] Advocates of associationism and assimilationism elided the central fact of colonialism: racial domination precluded government by popular consent indefinitely. Aside from education, the growth and transformation of colonial cities proved another catalyst to elite opposition in dependent societies. The modernization and expansion of colonial cities proclaimed by urban planners in the early twentieth century, and most thoroughly pursued within Morocco, Indochina, and Madagascar, led to the creation of city administrative districts, public building complexes, and colonial 'new towns' which would become forcing grounds for local nationalist organization. In their attempts to marry modern urban design with a respect for existing local architectural forms, leading French colonial town planners were victims of their own success. As one historian of colonial urbanism has put it:

> Young people, trained in French institutions, in contact with the *villes nouvelles* and their own cultures' urban heritage, used *both* traditions as the basis for their demands. Their arguments for political independence, first put forth in the cities of these French colonies, relied in large part on cultural ideals: a synthesis of the Western concepts of *liberté* and *egalité* with the integrity and autonomy of their own traditions.[88]

Just as the rights and duties of colonial citizens in the French Union scheme caused widespread confusion, so, too, the precise economic implications of membership of the French Union were unclear. There was no French government statement defining the economic doctrine that the French Union would follow. Its economic institutions, whether in individual territories, in French government Ministries, or within the new technocratic bureaucracy of Jean Monnet's General Planning Commissariat, were scarcely integrated with one another. The one coordinating body that did exist – the French Union High Council – was a dead letter.[89]

Furthermore, France's specialist colonial bureaucracy was not eager to promote public debate about imperial reform or colonial economic development. The results were not edifying on the rare occasions when colonial matters were a major drain on parliamentary time. Between March and September 1947, Indochina, Madagascar, sub-Saharan Africa, and Algeria were all repeatedly discussed in the National Assembly. The most memorable aspect of these debates was that most Deputies did not bother to attend. The exception that proved the rule was the bitter parliamentary argument over policy in Vietnam between 14 and 18 March 1947. The parliamentarians' acrimonious exchanges over military policy in Indochina culminated in former minister Maurice Viollette being physically assaulted on the Assembly floor, an attack which the president of the session decided should be expunged from the official parliamentary record of proceedings.[90]

Conclusion

'Colonial reform was designed at every stage to consolidate and rationalize the empire.' Martin Shipway's observation certainly held true in black Africa. The Brazzaville conference proposals and the final terms of the French Union were in no way intended to begin the process of French withdrawal.[91] The irony, of course, was that reforms devised to increase African loyalty to France through gradual democratization and the steady improvement of living standards crystallized local political demands that France refused to meet. As ever, the essential contradiction of imperial reformism remained: no matter how liberal a reform might seem, it could not be truly democratic if it presupposed the continuation of colonial control. The 'liberal universalism' espoused by the architects of the French Union was at variance with social exclusion of subject peoples from the highest levels of political office.[92] The stultifying effects of colonial rule on indigenous cultures were clearly exposed in Professor O. Mannoni's *Psychologie de la colonisation* (1950), a psychoanalytical investigation of French-Malagasy interaction written by the head of Madagascar's Information Service. Mannoni identified a 'dependence complex' among colonial populations excluded from power and a fatal complacency among their French rulers. But even Mannoni rejected rapid decolonization, warning that the mass of the population was psychologically ill-prepared to exercise mature political judgement.[93]

Reluctant to cede genuine political power to African representatives, French Ministers and officials of every stripe took refuge after 1945 in a more clearly defined economic determinism. Even though France was to regulate African political life, the material benefits of increased life expectancy, falling infant mortality rates, better education, and long term infrastructure development justified the continued French presence. Even here, an inexorable logic of decolonization endured. If the post-war justification of empire rested squarely on improving the African's lot, then surely this was a finite process? If, as Colonial Ministry officials insisted, Africans had yet to acquire the political skills, the level of mass education, and the socio-economic sophistication necessary to run their own affairs, what could possibly justify colonial domination once reform conferred these very benefits? Put simply, popular political engagement within a colonial system was bound to undermine it.

CHAPTER 6
DECOLONIZING THE FRENCH AFRICAN FEDERATIONS AFTER 1945

In surveys of French decolonization, black Africa has too often received short shrift. Drawn by the violent upheavals of Indochina and French North Africa, historians, and latter-day French politicians have sometimes seen in the comparative lack of violence in sub-Saharan Africa proof that, here at least, France could regulate the decolonization process.[1] Some have gone much further, arguing that anti-colonial nationalism was peripheral in West Africa's transition to political independence. As Ebere Nwaubani puts it,

> For those who evaluate the significance of an anti-colonial movement by the magnitude of its ferocity and physical confrontation with the colonial authority, the nationalism of anglophone and francophone West Africa proves very disappointing indeed. At the best of times, the anti-colonial effort consisted of writings in newspapers, petitions and delegations to the metropolitan capitals, and attendance at constitutional conferences. … The conflation of this 'pen and paper' nationalism into a heroic anti-colonial struggle that ousted the colonial powers presumes an astonishing degree of cause and effect, which has not and cannot be convincingly demonstrated.[2]

It has even been suggested that so successful was France in perpetuating its political, cultural, and economic predominance over its former territories in western and central Africa that 'decolonization' is an inappropriate term for something actually closer to dependency.[3]

Writing in 1977, Richard Joseph identified an additional problem in the historiography of French black Africa. Interested in the fate of French Cameroon, where insurgency and violence took hold in the 1950s, Joseph pointed out that undue emphasis on the politics of Senegal and Ivory Coast as exemplars of decolonization in francophone Africa tended to distort the wider regional picture. The radical nationalism in Guinea, Niger, and Cameroon, for example, stood in marked contrast to the more conciliatory political alternatives pursued in other French African territories.[4] Historian Elizabeth Schmidt has taken up the challenge, highlighting the distinctiveness of grass-roots nationalist support in Guinea, the territory where demands for complete independence from France were pushed furthest during the late 1950s.[5] Frederick Cooper follows a different tack, reminding us how wrong-headed it is to presume that eventual decolonization was somehow inevitable and clearly foreseen. His starting point, quite rightly, is to consider West African politics after the Second World War on their own terms, not as a prelude to decolonization but, rather, as a moment in which multiple possibilities opened up, not just for divorce from France but for engagement with it. State-building, regional cooperation, and improved living standards were all objectives pursued within the framework of the French Empire, not in outright opposition to it.[6]

Whatever the extent of France's actual economic and strategic pull out from its sub-Saharan colonies, francophone Africa offers rich pickings to those interested in the constitutional mechanics of managed decolonization. It also presents the clearest example of cases in which indigenous leaders successfully turned the post-war language of colonial integration into an overseas French community against its architects.[7] Fastening on to talk of imperial citizenship, improved workers' rights, and welfare entitlements, party leaders and union organizers across West Africa challenged the French state to give substance to its rhetoric, demanding material changes to working conditions and political rights that would gradually loosen the apparatus of colonial control.[8]

While in no way minimizing these actors' achievement, it bears emphasis that their success was closely connected in the changing emphasis in colonial policymaking in post-war France. From the Brazzaville conference in 1944 through the French Union, to the launch of the *Communauté* of African states in September 1958, France's constitutional exercises in imperial redesign related principally to its black African territories. Hence the stereotype of a more or less orderly transfer of power from Dakar to the Congo formulated by stages and implemented without grave incident between 1956 and 1960. Scratch the surface and a different picture emerges – a collage that paints these metropolitan and African connections in more vibrant colours, reflective of local conflict, confrontation, and Africans' seizure of the political initiative. Seen in this light, several facets of the end of formal colonial rule in French West and Equatorial Africa acquire added significance. Among the most significant are the economic and industrial transformation of francophone Africa after 1945, the emergence of organized resistance groups prepared to fight for independence, and the importance of African trade unions and student groups in shaping the political culture of several West African territories.[9]

Similarly, the role of religion cannot be fitted into a binary model of conflict between popular nationalism and the colonial state. For one thing, the artificiality of French mental constructions of a distinct, black African Islam – one perceived as less dogmatic, not intrinsically anti-colonial, and more malleable than its North African and Middle Eastern counterparts – became more apparent in the post-war decades. What officials had, for years, patronisingly labelled '*Islam noir*' was exposed as little more than the product of their wishful thinking. If anything, the continuing pull of religious devotion with its implicit rejection of French values and integrationist ideas only amplified the authorities' inability to comprehend, still less to control, religious practice and forms of cultural expression in the West African interior.[10] In this sense, what Africanist scholars have dubbed an autonomous 'Islamic sphere' existed beyond the reach of the French colonial state in black Africa.[11]

Mutual connections and mutual incomprehension were also writ large at the level of French Africa's 'high politics'. There were, for example, several affiliations between francophone African political parties and their metropolitan partners in France. Some of these links help explain the splits among African politicians over the desirability of retaining federal structures across West Africa after a French withdrawal. Others merely emphasized the gaps – cultural, ideological, and racial – between supposedly client parties in France and West Africa.[12] The stronger cultural assertiveness evident among black African writers and artists also shaped the form that decolonization took. The concept of *négritude* refined in the poetry and essays of, among others, Senegalese socialist leader Léopold Sédar Senghor from the 1920s to the 1950s was as eloquent a challenge to the racialist assumptions of colonial authority as any political speech or street protest. Indeed, it informed Senghor's decision in September 1948 to break with the French Socialist Party to form the Bloc Démocratique Sénégalais (BDS), a more self-consciously African party with strong ties to Senegal's influential Sufi Muslim brotherhoods.[13] Clearly, the demise of French colonial authority in black Africa was no orderly process. To appreciate the speed with which the political climate in the French African federations changed, the colonial structure of these territories must first be described.

Colonial organization in black Africa

South of the Sahara, two huge colonial federations dominated the French Empire in Africa. Their ethnic, cultural, and economic diversity belied their supposed political unity. French West Africa (Afrique Occidentale Française – AOF, shown overleaf) was composed of seven territories: Mauritania, Senegal, Guinea, French Sudan (now Mali), Ivory Coast (Côte d'Ivoire), Niger, and Dahomey. In 1948, this number increased to eight with the re-establishment of Upper Volta (now Burkina Faso), an inland territory previously partitioned between its neighbouring colonies in 1932. French Togo, between the wars a Type B mandate, then designated a UN trusteeship territory in 1945, also fell within the economic and political orbit of AOF. The basic framework of federal rule in AOF was demarcated between 1895 and 1904, but its paternalistic administrative ethos owed much to William Ponty, governor general between 1908 and 1915.[14] His schema codified the responsibilities of individual colonial Governors to the French federal government-general at Dakar. The tidy hierarchy of centralized colonial authority, so appealing to metropolitan governments and colonial officials, belied the fact that AOF was neither culturally homogenous nor wholly pacified. Three of its colonies were landlocked, and could not be administered as autonomous economic units if they were to prosper. Bamako, Ouagadougou, and Niamey were the only towns inland where substantial urban growth occurred before 1945.[15] Contrasts between the poverty of the *Sahel* – the pre-Saharan northern grasslands – and the southerly rain forests, riverside settlements, and coastal towns were stark. Robert Holland identifies this economic polarization as a barrier to organized nationalism:

> The discontinuities between the coastal belts, where western-type activities had made some impact, and the 'traditional' interior, with its vast tracts of arid agriculture, were too sharp to allow anything other than a painfully slow approach to national integration. African political parties in French-ruled sub-Saharan regions, therefore, did not articulate their objectives in terms of constitutional independence, since to have done so would have been an economic and sociological nonsense.[16]

Perhaps inevitably, economic migration was central to AOF's socioeconomic structure. Peasant labourers headed south and westwards to work in the cash-crop and forestry sectors in Senegal, Guinea, Côte d'Ivoire, and Dahomey.[17] Army administration was firmest in the desert territories of Mauritania, Western Sudan, and Niger, but military repression was more widespread. The forest terrain of Ivory Coast and Guinea, for instance, made subjugation of the Dyula and Baule peoples very difficult.[18] In fact, the conquest of AOF continued well into the second decade of the twentieth century, despite Colonial Ministry determination to phase out military control. Across large parts of the AOF interior it was scarcely twenty years – no

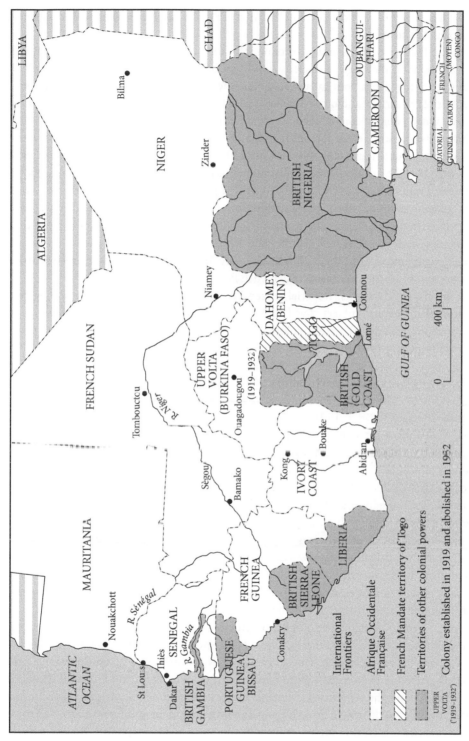

Map 3 French West Africa after the First World War.

more than a generation – between the implantation of French administration and the upheaval of the Second World War.

Senegal and Ivory Coast stood out as economic 'pearls' of the federation, which helps explain the greater attention they have attracted from historians of empire. Yet, much as these two colonies were, respectively, political and economic showcases of French rule, conversely, both were centres of the earliest and most significant African political mobilization against colonial abuses. An added political complication was that remnants of imperial reforms from the mid-nineteenth century survived in the original French colonial settlements in West Africa: the 'Four Communes' of Senegal (the three towns of Dakar, St Louis, and Rufisque, plus Gorée island). After 1848 the Communes' administration was modelled on the French system of local government. From October 1916 their inhabitants enjoyed 'citizen' status as opposed to that of mere colonial 'subjects'.[19] By 1936 there were some 100,000 black African and mixed-race (*métis*) citizens in the Four Communes, but only 2,400 throughout the rest of AOF.[20] Like other older colonies, such as the French Antilles and Réunion, residents of the Four Communes could elect representatives to the National Assembly. In 1912 they famously selected Blaise Diagne, the first black African to sit in the French Parliament.[21]

Aside from political rights, imperial citizenship conferred legal benefits, including two key exemptions. Colonial subjects lived under the *code de l'indigénat*, an agglomeration of legal regulations that differed from colony to colony but that was everywhere arbitrarily applied. Without arrest or trial, colonial administrators could punish subjects for a host of minor criminal infractions with short prison terms, fines, or corporal punishment. These infractions ranged from expressions of political dissent or grumbling over tax payments to littering, alcohol consumption, and unauthorized woodcutting. Devised in the early days of the Algeria conquest, after 1918 the *indigénat* was most vigorously applied in black Africa and New Caledonia.[22] As Gregory Mann has observed, for French *commandants* (colonial district officials) the *indigénat* 'was the most important element in the administrative tool kit'.[23] Applying its punishments, even for the most trivial or imagined offences reaffirmed the inferior status of the native subject. It is not difficult to see why the *indigénat* was loathed because, as Mann concludes, it was 'ultimately both a set of sanctions and a colonial state of being'.[24]

Colonial subjects were also bound by the *prestation* system to serve the colonial state through forced labour for a set number of days each year. It was *prestation* that ensured the upkeep of roads, railway lines, irrigation channels, and the like. And only those with citizen status were exempted from it. No surprise, then, that the Four Communes' uniquely assimilated status made them, at once, a model, a centre of African political activity, and a glaring proof of the inequity of colonial administration elsewhere in AOF.

In general terms, the higher the number of settlers the greater the likelihood that the local African population would face severe *indigénat* punishments and harsh labour conditions. In Ivory Coast, for example, rich hardwood resources and extensive plantation agriculture attracted the interest of French trading companies, white settlers, and Colonial Ministry planners. And, while the territory was notable for its large number of African-owned farms and plantations, even this privileged elite was subordinated, denied the same access to local labour and markets as white landowners. Among them was Félix Houphouët-Boigny, a Baule cantonal chief and future national leader of Ivory Coast. As a coffee grower rather than a political firebrand, Houphouët-Boigny spearheaded the organization of an African planters' association, the Syndicat Agricole Africain (SAA) in 1944. His call for substitution of forced

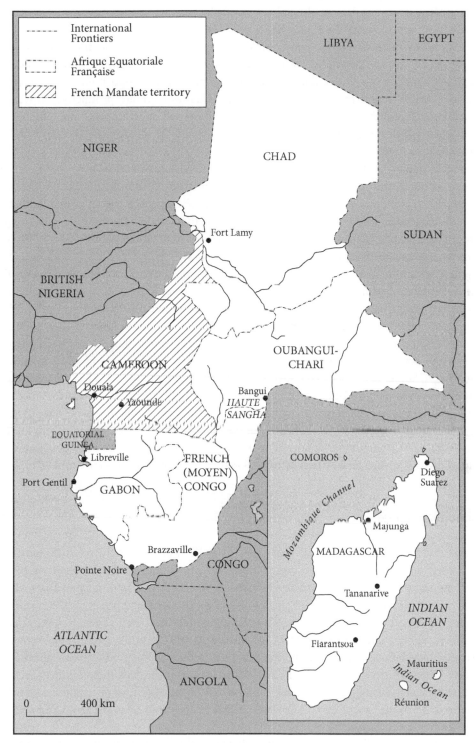

Map 4 French Equatorial Africa and Madagascar after the First World War.

labour with a competitive wage market in Ivory Coast's plantations drew broad support among African farmers. Unusually, it also won official backing. Ivory Coast Governor André Latrille sympathized with SAA grievances and realized that cooperation with its leaders served French interests better than confrontation. Latrille's views did not resonate with the resident European population or with the Dakar authorities, both of whom considered the SAA's challenge to settler dominance unacceptable. Their opposition was enough to ensure Latrille's replacement in August 1945.[25] This was counterproductive. Governor General Pierre Cournarie's hostility to the SAA hastened its transformation into Ivory Coast's first political party, the Parti Démocratique de la Côte d'Ivoire (PDCI), launched by Houphouët in 1946.

French Equatorial Africa (Afrique Equatoriale Française – AEF, shown on the preceding page) was poorer, more thinly populated, and less administratively complex than its West African counterpart. Four times the size of France, in 1945 AEF had a population of approximately 3.5 million; a mere 7,000 were Europeans.[26] Dubbed the 'Cinderella of the French Empire', it, too, was arbitrarily federated on the AOF model in 1910. Its four colonies, Gabon, Middle Congo (now Congo-Brazzaville), Ubangi-Chari (now the Central African Federation), and Chad were sites of some of the most unrestrained economic exploitation anywhere in the French Empire.[27] Much like Togo in West Africa, the former Type B mandate of Cameroon was placed under trusteeship in 1945, but remained economically and politically bound to AEF. It was not a happy marriage. The ruthless economic exactions in Equatorial Africa made bitter political confrontation more likely than in AOF. The region's indigenous élite of French-educated African politicians and junior officials were less numerous and much less influential than in AOF. Settler resistance to the African enfranchisement proposed under the Constituent Assembly's initial French Union scheme in 1945 was also strongest in AEF and Cameroon. Settler intransigence as well as the continuation of punishing labour-intensive development projects nurtured the ideological militancy of the one communist-type insurgency in French black Africa: in Cameroon, supporters of Ruben Um Nyobé's Union des Populations du Cameroun took up an armed struggle from 1956 till Um Nyobé's death in September 1958.[28]

Economic change

By war's end in 1945 the colonial economies of AOF and, even more so, AEF, were still dominated by export crop production, rubber extraction, and forestry.[29] Much as before 1939, the export market was controlled by large, long-established trading companies whose profits rested on their ability to sell French finished goods at inflated prices to Africans while purchasing export commodities at the lowest cost possible. Two such companies, the Société Commerciale de l'Ouest Africain (SCOA), founded in 1887, and the Compagnie Française d'Afrique Occidentale (CFAO), established in 1906, remained the undisputed giants of the French West African export trade. Each retained strong links with their original backers: venture capitalists from Lyons and Geneva in the case of the SCOA, more cautious Marseilles entrepreneurs in the case of the CFAO. Hard hit in the depression years of 1920–1 and 1931–5, these trading companies were commercially buoyant on the eve of war in 1939. The wartime boom in French and allied demand for strategic raw materials and tropical foodstuffs enabled the SCOA and the CFAO to expand their operations further. The former even issued new capital in 1941. Their commercial ties with British West African colonies suited AOF's conversion to the allied cause in December 1942.[30]

The immediate post-war period witnessed conflicting economic pressures on the major French corporations in AOF and AEF. On the one hand, growing industrial unrest among African wage earners, whose numbers were rapidly expanding, was matched by recognition in France that the exploitative nature of colonial commerce had to change. African farmers, largely engaged in cash-crop production, were understandably impatient to see an end to the requisitioning and price controls of the war years. Virtually all conceded that revocation of forced labour provisions and the *indigénat* legal code was long overdue.[31] Abolition of forced labour in 1946 and a surge in organized trade unionism across AOF produced more insistent demands for equitable terms of trade and employment regulation. Conversely, the creation in 1945 of a distinct currency, the franc CFA, eased the strong inflationary pressure in French Africa, improving the prospects for export growth. More significant in the short term, rising metropolitan demand for African commodities as France's reconstruction proceeded in the late 1940s was immediately followed by sharp increases in raw material prices, such as rubber and hardwood timber, triggered by the Korean war rearmament boom of 1950–3. Heightened international demand generated rapid expansion in these sectors of primary production. Black African colonies, for the first time, acquired economic importance as dollar earners, and were soon integrated into the US-directed bureaucracy of the Marshall Plan. This brought challenges of its own. Fears grew in French governmental circles from 1948 onwards of American corporate predation on West Africa's fledgling industries. These anxieties were sustained in the early 1950s by Washington's mounting interest in a rapid transition to self-government across the region, both to help stem communist infiltration and to facilitate US trade with emerging African economies.[32]

Mining activity across francophone Africa also increased after 1950. The extraction of iron ore in Mauritania, bauxite in Guinea, and uranium in Niger also became easier thanks to better road and rail communications. Slow at first, secondary industries from cement making to milling, gradually spread eastwards and inland from Senegal, Ivory Coast, Guinea, and Cameroon. Commodity trading companies jumped aboard the diversification bandwagon. SCOA helped fund a network of department stores across West Africa, the first of which – Printania – opened in Dakar in 1953. CFAO followed suit, teaming up with French supermarket chain, Monoprix, in 1954. The surviving trading companies of the colonial era slowly transformed themselves into recognizably modern, multinational corporations. Conducted in parallel with the political emancipation of French West and Equatorial Africa, this transition from colonial exploitation to neocolonial commercial dominance occurred largely without state direction.

The abiding importance of both private capital and the colonial business managers in charge of companies such as the highly influential Société Commerciale et Industrielle de la Côte d'Afrique bears emphasis because the years of the Fourth Republic are generally reckoned to have seen the first sustained programme of public investment in colonial development.[33] In late 1945 the Dakar government established a planning directorate to vet development projects put to the federal authorities. The first criterion for approval was that such programmes tangibly improve the welfare of the African population.[34] There was certainly more money available than ever before. Public funding for infrastructure modernization through the Economic and Social Development Fund (Fonds d'Investissement pour le Développement Economique et Social – FIDES), created on 30 April 1946, was quickly followed by some 10 billion francs of

Marshall Aid spending in AOF between 1948–52. At the outbreak of the Korean War in June 1950, $288.1 million in Marshall Aid funds was allocated to France's West African territories. Railway construction took the largest slice of this expenditure ($110 million), closely followed by other infrastructure projects to develop ports and road systems.[35] Hydroelectric schemes in Guinea and Cameroon promised cheaper power to industrial investors. Increasing export demand, combined with French governmental interest in infrastructure development, was also beneficial to the major corporations engaged in public works projects in AOF and AEF. A few of these companies were also anxious to expand their African operations to compensate for lost business in Indochina after the outbreak of the Franco-Vietminh war in 1946.

A typical example was the Société Française d'Entreprises de Dragages et de Travaux Publics. Although active in AOF since 1902, this conglomerate of businesses engaged in public works and port expansion only diversified its West African operations after 1945 when it was denied opportunities to complete long-term projects in Indochina.[36] Buoyant commercial interest in black Africa and the unprecedented influx of public funds produced dramatic results. The annual GNP of the AOF territories grew by an average 13.8 per cent between 1947 and 1951.[37] African wage earners and agricultural producers contributed to this expansion through increased per capita output, but public funding and foreign capital lay at its heart. Good economic news in the short term, this left former colonies vulnerable to external economic control after independence.[38]

Post-war politics

Little of the increased wealth in French Africa trickled down to the wider population, but the trade boom still had momentous social effects. It stimulated rapid urbanization, and it added to the numbers of politically active African wage earners. The new commercial prospects presented to adventurous capitalists also improved the opportunities for African workers to press claims for a decent wage, better working conditions, and employment protection. So much so that the greatest shift in the post-war balance sheets of the large trading companies was not the upturn in capital investment and annual profit, but the rising proportion of turnover allocated to wage payments. Demanding African workers were not attuned to the gradualism of imperial reform. Nor did they share the French political culture of *évolué* politicians such as Lamine Guèye and Léopold Sédar Senghor in Senegal or Félix Houphouët Boigny in Ivory Coast, each of whom claimed to speak on their behalf. The gulf between established local politicians and wage labourers in Senegal, Ivory Coast, and elsewhere became apparent in the emergence of disparate African political organizations towards the end of the Second World War. Still prohibited from organizing political parties or meetings, during the spring of 1945, *évolués* in the Four Communes, Dakar, and Abidjan flocked to join so-called Franco-African Study Groups (Comités d'Études Franco-Africaines – CEFA). These debating societies discussed the reforms necessary to achieve *évolué* assimilation. By contrast, trade union activists were attracted to the radical Communist Study Groups (Groupes d'Études Communistes), first established in December 1943.[39] Some of the fault lines in AOF politics were emerging before the restoration of peacetime political conditions.

Most of the ten deputies from AOF elected to the Constituent Assembly in October 1945 were alarmed by the rapid growth in African organized labour after union activity was legalized in

August 1944. Suspicion of African workers was only to be expected of the five deputies elected by citizens; in other words, principally by Europeans, other than in the one seat reserved for the Four Communes. But the other five deputies – Léopold Senghor (Senegal), Félix Houphouët-Boigny (Ivory Coast), Sourou Migan Apithy (Dahomey), Yacine Diallo (Guinea), and Fily Dabo Sissoko (Soudan-Niger) – elected by the 118,000 enfranchised African subjects also distanced themselves from the unprecedented industrial unrest that gripped French West Africa in the post-war decade.[40] One reason why certain French governments were temperamentally inclined to negotiate with these West African party leaders was that the shadow of grass-roots militancy loomed over all of them.

The African deputies in the Constituent Assembly had an immediate impact, profiting from the political eclipse of the French right in the immediate aftermath of the Liberation. Houphouët-Boigny piloted through legislation in April 1946 that finally abolished forced labour, cementing his reputation throughout sub-Saharan Africa in the process. A month later, Lamine Guèye secured citizenship rights for all populations within the French Union. Precisely what rights 'imperial citizenship' conferred remained unclear. After all, the first French Union scheme had just been rejected in a constitutional referendum held only days earlier on 5 May. Much like the Popular Front era ten years earlier, the Constituent Assembly interlude before the finalization of the Fourth Republic constitution proved to be an Indian summer of colonial reform. Following MRP gains in the elections to a second Constituent Assembly in June 1946, the final French Union scheme approved in October mirrored the rightward shift in the governing tripartite coalition of MRP, Socialists, and Communists. Georges Bidault's MRP acquired the dominant role in the formulation of colonial policy. The results were predictable – and unfortunate.[41] The reactionary lobby group, the États Généraux de la Colonisation Française, founded in Douala, Cameroon, in September 1945 to represent the interests of settlers in AEF and AOF, now found a more receptive audience in Paris.[42]

On 3 August 1946, in a rare acclamation of France's pre-war system, the *États généraux* implored the new government to recognize the Third Republic's achievement in building a strong, unified empire.[43] This was a coded plea for the preservation of settler privileges, including the dual college voting system. Although a single electoral college would be established in AOF for elections to the National Assembly, the number of African deputies to be elected was reduced from twenty-one to thirteen. Furthermore, in AEF and Madagascar the constitutional provisions of the French Union guaranteed *colon* dominance by preserving a dual college system in national and local elections.[44]

As the French Union became less a vehicle for reform and more a means to consolidate imperial authority, a new phase of African party politics began. In September 1946 Houphouët-Boigny led a group of African deputies who issued a manifesto calling for French adherence to the reforms promised under the earlier constitutional draft rejected in May. To support their case, they organized a congress in Bamako, French Sudan, between 19 and 21 October. The aim of the Bamako Congress was to unite differing black African parties into an inter-territorial grouping, the Rassemblement Démocratique Africain (RDA). Supported by the French Communist Party, the RDA quickly emerged as the foremost African political party in AOF and AEF. Houphouët-Boigny became party leader and used his power base in the PDCI to ensure RDA dominance in his home territory of Ivory Coast. For most of the RDA's founders, the party's communist links were not a matter of ideological conviction but a means to achieve a higher parliamentary profile in France. If anything, the RDA was as strongly assimilationist as the wartime CEFA. Take the first major RDA campaign to widen educational provision in AOF. It not only proposed additional primary and secondary schools and an AOF University, but, more significantly, the adoption of a French-style school curriculum.[45] Only in Senegal, where Senghor's BDS retained its links to the French Socialists, was opposition to the RDA particularly strong.

There was harsh reaction against the RDA's emergence in Paris. A political organization affiliated to the PCF, stretching across two colonial federations and with subordinate national parties in individual colonies, caused genuine alarm. The new party was identified as seditious, particularly as Cold War tensions hardened in France during the course of 1947. Once the French Communists left the tripartite coalition in May, a clampdown against the RDA was only a matter of time. The French Socialist Party (SFIO – Section Française de l'Internationale Ouvrière), smarting from the Communists' success in winning greater popular support in black Africa, despised the RDA. However, it fell to the MRP ministers holding the portfolios of defence, foreign affairs, and overseas France (colonies) to take the initiative. Bidault and his party colleagues entrusted the dirty work to selected colonial appointees who resorted to tried and trusted administrative tricks to undermine the RDA's bedrock of popular support.[46]

In 1948 Upper Volta was abruptly declared a separate AOF territory, the purpose being to detach it from the RDA-dominated Ivory Coast in readiness for elections in June. Here, and in other territories, French officials and MRP supporters encouraged African deputies to serve as independents. Their efforts soon bore fruit. In September 1948 Senegalese deputies broke with the French Socialists and joined former RDA supporters from Dahomey, Upper Volta, and Togo to form a new parliamentary bloc, the Indépendants d'Outre-Mer (IOM).[47] Soon afterwards the newly promoted Governor of Ivory Coast, Laurent Péchoux, set about the destruction of the RDA's grass-roots organization in its heartland. State repression peaked in 1949. In February senior PDCI activists were imprisoned without trial. In December several of them began a hunger strike supported by a party call for a boycott of European goods. Women, including the wives of the hunger strikers themselves, figured prominently in a series of further protests over subsequent weeks. These culminated in the death of thirteen protesters at Dimbokro in January 1950. By the end of that year some 3,000 RDA political prisoners were in AOF jails.[48]

African trade unionism in AOF

Party politics aside, much of the impetus for social change in French West Africa stemmed from African salaried workers, at least 25 per cent of whom were efficiently organized in trade unions modelled on their metropolitan equivalents. These African unions were sometimes actively supported by the Communist-affiliated Confédération Générale du Travail (CGT). The role of the French trade union confederation should not be exaggerated, however. French union bosses were generally slow to criticize the French Union. Furthermore, traces of paternalism, even racism, as well as a lack of understanding of French West Africa's predominantly rural economy, impeded the growth of effective working partnerships between French trade unionists and their West African counterparts.[49] None of this had much impact on the explosion of worker protest in AOF's major urban centres in the immediate post-war years. For all that, it is worth pausing to consider the scale of this trade union revolution. Indeed, before considering the impact of organized labour in French West Africa, we should remind ourselves that most of the labouring population across AOF, including the majority of working women, were engaged in 'customary labour' in agriculture. Few ever saw a union representative. Less than 5 per cent of the overall working population in French West Africa were wage labourers, perhaps no more than 70,000 by 1948.[50] This was smaller than the number of African ex-servicemen who drew army pensions from the French state after 1945. Many of these men were career soldiers who had completed lengthy terms of military service and acquired the much-prized *carte de combattante* that conferred additional pension benefits. These ex-servicemen, although not as well organized as sometimes assumed, were understandably ambivalent about colonial rule. While some joined the ranks of worker militants hostile to French control, others remained emotionally attached to, and financially dependent upon the colonial state.[51]

If former career soldiers of the *tirailleurs sénégalais* were often socially and politically conservative, unionized labourers were not. The key to understanding their influence lies less in the overall numbers involved than in consideration of three other factors. One was their urban concentration. Another was the accumulated experience of over twenty years of union organization, strike actions, and collective bargaining, something all too unusual in other European colonial settings. The third and final factor was also the most important. African trade union members were to be found in a few key strategic industries from transport and mining to plantation agriculture and the civil service. Union members dominated particular trades, industries, and corporations, most notably the dockyards, and West Africa's largest industrial conglomerate, its railway company, the Régie des Chemins de Fer de l'AOF or 'RAN'.[52] This concentration afforded the trade unions heightened influence in the towns of AOF – always the centres of federation politics.

Anxious to channel worker dissent into less confrontational groups, from mid-1946 the new governor general, René Barthes, one-time adviser to Marius Moutet, encouraged unions to build links with the pro Socialist CGT Force Ouvrière and the Catholic union federation, the Confédération Française des Travailleurs Chrétiens (CFTC). The AOF authorities therefore tried to cultivate moderate African trade unionism rather than to contest the power of labour organization *per se*. Central to this strategy was the Labour Inspection Service (*Inspection du travail*), which attempted to co-opt African trade unionism into the colonial order. Success hinged on an implicit recognition by both sides that industrial disputes were part of a modernizing capitalist economy that did not represent a challenge to the legitimacy of French rule. Notwithstanding official anxieties about communist subversion, French efforts to contain the West African workers' movement were also facilitated by the fact that several of AOF's trade unions were affiliated with their metropolitan equivalents under the aegis of the Communist-led CGT. African trade unionists typically sought parity in wages and conditions with their French counterparts rather than an outright break with France.[53] Even so, worker militancy was not easily tamed. Between 1946 and 1950 there was unprecedented industrial unrest in French West Africa, notably in Senegal and the Guinean capital, Conakry, where union organization was strongest.[54]

Spontaneous work stoppages in the port of Dakar in December 1946 soon escalated. In mid-January 1947 an eleven-day general strike paralysed the city as civil service staff, market women, and skilled and manual labours, joined the dockworkers in demanding equal pay for equal work regardless of race and a 300 per cent increase in the minimum wage then paid to African workers. Demands for French recognition of unions and family allowances showed that the strikers were well apprised of the power of modern trade unionism in France itself. The Dakar authorities confirmed the point by flying in an expert government industrial negotiator to conduct talks based on French-style collective bargaining agreements with representatives of the individual African labour unions at the forefront of the stoppages. The empire was striking back, emulating metropolitan example and the rhetoric of post-war reform to extract concessions from colonial authorities. By the time the final strikes petered out in the spring of 1947, Senegal's urban workforce had won substantial improvements in wages, working conditions, and allowances, all of which confirmed their status as 'workers' rather than merely contract labourers. Just as significant, rather than state repression, French practices of industrial relations, soon to be formally adopted by the AOF Inspection du travail, had been preferred to bring the strikes to an end.[55]

A railway strike across AOF between October 1947 and March 1948 confirmed the rising power of African trade unionism. The new governor general, the Socialist politician Paul Béchard, did not meet all the railwaymen's demands, but neither did he take any action against the strike leaders akin to official coercion of the RDA. Above all, he acknowledged that black railwaymen had the same negotiating rights as their white colleagues.[56] Here was assimilationism turned on its head. Union pressure had secured equivalent rights for black workers without any prior requirement to become 'French'. In 1950 Lamine Guèye championed legislation that set these principles in stone; welfare benefits, as well as wages, should be the same for all civil servants regardless of race.[57]

For all these successes, leading African political figures in AOF remained ambivalent about trade union power. Neither the Socialists, Lamine Guèye and Léopold Sédar Senghor in Senegal, RDA leader Félix Houphouët-Boigny in Ivory Coast, nor Fily Dabo Sissoko, leader of the Parti Progressiste Soudanais in French Soudan, sided with the strikers in 1946–8. By contrast, Ahmed Sékou Touré built his political career in the Parti Démocratique de Guinée as leader of the Guinean federation of CGT-affiliated unions. He and his fellow union leaders proved exceptionally capable as organizers and bargainers, particularly during a seventy-day general strike in Guinea between September and November 1953.[58] By 1956, around 35 per cent of AOF's wageworkers were union members. Ironically, herein lay the seeds of the downfall of trade unionism across much of francophone Africa. For the very success of internationalist trade unionism in AOF encouraged the French authorities to put responsibility for industrial relations in the hands of nascent national administrations that were set up under the aegis of the 1956 Gaston Defferre law. As we shall see, this enabling legislation created the framework for independent self-government. The salient point here is this: African national leaders, some of them former union officials, showed less sympathy for industrial unrest once they acquired real political power themselves. Even Sékou Touré, former champion of Guinean workers, would savagely repress trade unionism on his way to creating a one-party state in Guinea.

As independence neared, schisms emerged between those unions willing to maintain ties with the CGT or other, non-communist worker organizations in France and those determined to establish a new confederation better attuned to the needs of its African rank and file. As the CGT link dissolved, a new union confederation dedicated to African unity, the Union générale des travailleurs d'Afrique noire (UGTAN), took shape in January 1957. It was this new organization, potentially an alternative source of political power, which few African national leaders were prepared to tolerate. Trade unionism in French West Africa, shaped by its members, nurtured by activist leaders, and successful in winning substantial concessions from the French authorities, was ultimately undone by the insecurities of nationalist regimes unwilling to share power with worker interest groups. As Frederick Cooper concludes:

> The French move in 1956 to put significant resources in the hands of elected African politicians fundamentally changed the context of party-union relations. However much nationalist sentiments among the labor rank and files evolved from 1945 to 1956, the sharp break in 1956–1958 reflected the shift of state resources from a colonial power to African political leaders, eager to turn their complex political networks into an effective political machine.[59]

Political developments in AEF

French commercial penetration, industrial diversification, and African labour militancy were far less marked in post-war AEF than in the more populous West African federation of AOF. The leading historian of French Equatorial Africa, Elikia M'Bokolo, identified two reasons for the relative lack of militant nationalism and anti-colonialist protest across the federation. First and foremost was the decisive role of an educated African bourgeoisie – *évolués* in the official parlance of the 1940s, then renamed *lettres* in the equally condescending administrative vocabulary of the 1950s. As mentioned earlier, such individuals were few and far between. Across AEF as a whole, in 1939 only 300 Africans held certificates of primary school education. Until the establishment of an Ecole Supérieure Indigène in 1935, the federal administration in Brazzaville had done nothing to create locally educated and loyal administrative elites in AEF. This was soon to change. The Free French war effort, post-war development of the export economy, the expansion of state administration, and the minimum statutory requirements for public sector employees in the French Union all produced an explosion in the salaried employment of literate Africans. Ultimately, in 1955 AEF Governor General Paul Chauvet took this to its logical conclusion, 'Africanising' the civil service, the teaching profession, and commercial contract employment throughout the federation.[60]

If this helps account for *évolués*' dominance in AEF's post-war politics, it does not explain the part played by most of the African population. For most, formal schooling was unattainable, and lifelong work in agriculture, forestry, or mining remained the norm. By the time that de Gaulle's African Community was launched in 1958 only 13 per cent of school age children in Chad received any formal education; in the Moyen-Congo the figure was 8 per cent. Subsistence farming predominated in both countries.[61] The dual college voting system that applied in AEF gave literate *évolués* a greater voice in national politics but still excluded the silent majority, the '*pays réel*' of peasant agriculturalists, women, and unskilled workers. Their voices went largely unheard in debates over state independence.

The second characteristic of the decolonization process in AEF was thus the political demarcation between the minority of educated Africans and the majority working population. Unlike French West Africa, new political parties and labour activism did not bridge the gap between them. Party politics in the four Equatorial African colonies were more diffuse than in West Africa where the impact of the RDA was far greater. Privileged by the dual college system and less threatened by trade union disruption, across AEF Europeans retained a stronger grip on local politics. Between 1947 and 1955, for example, in the French Congo the struggle between the French Socialist Party and de Gaulle's Rassemblement du Peuple Français (RPF) for dominance of the first, settler-dominated electoral college had greater material consequences than the contest for African votes in the second electoral college between the RDA-affiliated Parti Progressiste Congolais and its opponents.[62]

The settler community was not about to surrender power to black African representatives, and particularly not to trade union militants. Little wonder then, that the first, violent clash in Equatorial Africa between reactionary settlers and trade unionists occurred soon after war's end in September 1945, not in AEF proper but in the port of Douala, Cameroon (effectively an adjunct to the AEF economy, although a trust territory). Powerfully armed white vigilantes shot down scores of striking African workers and unemployed African rioters.[63] The violence in Douala occurred in an urban environment typical of colonial cities throughout sub-Saharan Africa. It was marked by intense three-way antagonism between white settlers, an established urban community that retained strong tribal affiliations, and a burgeoning population of economic migrants that came to the port in search of casual labour or seasonal employment. What made Equatorial Africa stand out among France's sub-Saharan territories was the enduring strength and cohesion of the first of these groups: the settler community. AEF and the Cameroon trust territory were the focal point for the *colon* associations grouped together in 1945 as the Etats Généraux de la Colonisation Française. As we have seen, this coalition of settler groups defined itself in opposition to anything that smacked of Brazzaville-type reform. The *colons'* political dominance was apparent in the Cameroon administration's readiness to pervert or ignore metropolitan government directives as it saw fit. In 1946 the arrival as high commissioner of Robert Delavignette, Director of the École nationale de la France d'outre-mer and France's pre-eminent colonial theorist, was less of a new departure than might be imagined. A dedicated reformer committed to economic development, Delavignette's tenure in Cameroon between 1946–7 was too brief to undercut the settlers' hold over local politics.[64] Here at least, resident Europeans were authors of their own destruction.

Reactionary and overtly racist, the principal settler organizations of AEF and Cameroon were quite willing to use violence to crush any signs of African nationalism or worker protest. However, they were not successful in doing so. Trade unionists helped establish the nationalist Union des Populations du Cameroun (UPC) as the Cameroon *section* of the RDA in April 1948. But, when further rioting erupted across southern Cameroon in May 1955, the settler community, relieved to see the back of Delavignette, turned once more to a pliant local administration. Since his appointment in 1949, High Commissioner Roland Pré had followed Péchoux's example in Ivory Coast, resorting to official harassment and electoral manipulation to undermine the UPC. The 1955 riots gave Pré the excuse to ban the party outright. Denied political space, the party turned to armed insurgency in December of the following year. The radical nationalism of Um Nyobé's UPC drove the French authorities into closer cooperation with the party's more moderate rivals. Closer UN scrutiny from 1957 onwards eventually compelled the French to devolve power to a non-UPC government led by Ahmadu Ahidjo. By the time Cameroon acquired full independence on 1 January 1960, the irony was obvious. As Richard Joseph concludes, Cameroon's statehood 'arose not so much out of the realization of a national consciousness uniting diverse peoples into one movement against a colonial power but rather out of the suppression of such a movement'.[65]

The interracial violence that marked Cameroon's path to independence was the exception and not the rule. After 1945 political protest in rural AEF was more often directed at local chiefs than at the colonial authorities. Peasant opposition to chiefly power, in particular to alleged abuses of land tenancy, tended to neutralize the conservative political influence of the chiefs to the benefit of more progressive *évolué* politicians. Furthermore, the expansion of larger agricultural and logging enterprises, and the proliferation of public works projects under FIDES, brought larger numbers of casual labourers into the local wage economy. Unskilled workers on temporary contracts were poorly placed to organize politically next to their salaried counterparts in permanent employment. The decolonization debate was thus conducted on terms dictated by urban *évolués* to the virtual exclusion of AEF's unskilled African workforce. For the most part, the RDA politicians elected in AEF were self-consciously bourgeois and politically moderate. They also proved peculiarly susceptible to French neocolonialist control of economic activity in Equatorial Africa after the transition to formal independence during de Gaulle's first presidential term between 1958 and 1963.[66]

Nationalist politics in AOF, 1950–6

In the late 1940s West African trade unionism filled the political void left by state repression of the RDA. As union demands became more radical and their leaders more nationalist, so the official obsession with the RDA threat seemed less rational. Furthermore, in the three years of centre-right 'third force' coalitions in France between 1948 and the general elections of June 1951, government attitudes towards the RDA became confused. Was the party inherently dangerous because of its inter-territorial organization? Or was it a menace because of its ties to the PCF? Neither position made sense.[67] After all, the RDA's wide geographical reach was as much an opportunity for French negotiators as a threat. Shrewder analysts recognized that the party's earlier alignment with the Communists was a marriage of convenience, not a meeting of ideological minds. Since the RDA leadership had not called for outright independence and Houphouët-Boigny was clearly a good capitalist of pro-French views, surely negotiation with the RDA was preferable to dealing with the younger generation of union and student leaders coming to prominence in Dakar, Abidjan, and Conakry?

Nevertheless, the one symbolic gesture likely to convince France's governing coalition to change course was the severance of RDA links with the PCF. Only this would rupture the connections in the French official mind between the RDA's brand of populist nationalism and communist subversion. This turnaround took place between October 1950 and January 1952, and was largely the work of three men. Unsurprisingly, the first was RDA leader, Félix Houphouët-Boigny. Second was the Martinique-born Senator for Guinea, Raphael Saller. Third was François Mitterrand, appointed Minister for Overseas France by Prime Minister René Pleven on 12 July 1950. Houphouët-Boigny pushed through the RDA's disaffiliation from the PCF, splitting the party in the process, as a minority of communist diehards rallied to RDA secretary general, Gabriel d'Arboussier. For his part, Raphael Saller had been Pleven's chief colonial adviser since attending the Brazzaville conference in 1944 as Governor of French Somaliland. It was he who recognized that PDCI members were eager for a rapprochement with the French government. Saller's great achievement was to persuade Pleven's Cabinet to act on this.[68] Mitterrand duly abandoned the campaign against the RDA. To do so, he replaced its two most fervent advocates, Governor General Béchard and his deputy, Ivory Coast Governor Péchoux. The personal rapport between Houphouët-Boigny and his new ministerial patron was cemented when the RDA affiliated to Mitterrand's party, the centre-left Union Démocratique et Sociale de la Résistance (UDSR), in January 1952.[69]

The RDA was not alone in rejecting its old left-wing mentor. Léopold Senghor's Bloc Démocratique Sénégalais also distanced itself from their erstwhile backers, the French Socialists. Senghor and his ally, Sourou Migan Apithy from Dahomey, both former Socialist supporters, sat in the National Assembly as IOM independents instead. The increasingly independent stance of the RDA and the BDS signified more profound political changes. Most obviously, their refusal to work hand in glove with the PCF and the SFIO exposed the bankruptcy of the French left's colonial policies. Neither unequivocally anti-colonialist nor positively committed to progressive imperialism, France's two major left-wing parties had failed to carve out a viable position on colonial matters since the fall of the Popular Front in 1937. One might even take this criticism further, and suggest that neither party had ever managed to do so. Between the wars, the Socialists' nominal commitment to a reformist 'colonial humanism' and the Communists' tendency to read colonial politics through a Marxist ideological prism of incipient class formation and 'nations in the making' never made much sense to colonial leaders arguing for tangible liberties and national recognition.[70]

Despite the French left's chequered colonial history, the French African politicians that served in the National Assembly after 1945 were temperamentally inclined to see in French republicanism a worthy political ideal. By 1950 these African deputies faced a dilemma. The majority still favoured long-term political ties with France. Some, not least Houphouët-Boigny and Senghor, retained strong personal connections with 'establishment' figures in politics, the media, and the arts. Steeped in assimilationist values, they were ambiguous, almost schizophrenic, about the end of empire.[71] As more and more Africans won the vote and pressed their claims more effectively, their representatives in Paris risked losing popular support if they found new patrons in the National Assembly. Relations between the RDA and the trade union movement were also fraught; even more so those between the RDA leadership and West African student groups hostile to the cooperation with French officialdom, personified by the link between Houphouët-Boigny and Mitterrand's UDSR.[72]

By 1954, 1,320 black African students held bursaries to study in French universities. Perhaps four thousand more joined them with financial support from their families. Their student organization, the Fédération des étudiants d'Afrique noire en France, was a forcing ground for a new generation of nationalist politicians impatient for reform and sceptical of French rhetoric. Between 1952–6, the African student press, in particular L'Etudiant d'Afrique noire, and the RDA-backed La Voix de l'Afrique noire, became stridently nationalist.[73] In the six years preceding the introduction of self-government legislation in 1956, friction therefore mounted between the African deputies in Paris steeped in French culture and a younger, more radical constituency of nationalists both back home and in universities across France.[74] At the same time, tensions between the RDA and its opponents in Senegal intensified as the BDS competed more strongly for influence from 1949 onwards.

French governments capitalized upon these intra-African political divisions between generations, between territories, and between parties to control the pace and scope of reform in sub-Saharan Africa. At no stage in the early 1950s did popular discontent threaten to spiral out of administrative control as was occurring further north in the Maghreb territories.

However, these external events had an effect in black Africa too. French loss of Indochina in 1954, the Foreign Ministry's reluctant preparations to cede greater autonomy in Morocco and Tunisia, and the outbreak of the Algerian rebellion in November 1954 helped catalyse reform elsewhere. In 1955 Edgar Faure's Radical Party-led administration began studying proposals for constitutional reorganization in the black African territories. These plans emanated from a specialist advisory committee chaired by someone familiar: Robert Delavignette, still the pre-eminent specialist in African administration. Delavignette's committee was, in turn, born of the willingness of Pierre Mendès, France's preceding government, to contemplate fundamental change to France's relationship with black Africa.[75] Herein lay the origin of the enabling law, the *loi Gaston Deferre*, passed by the new National Assembly elected in February 1956.

Passage of the Gaston Defferre law was hugely significant. The French 'imperial nation state' turned its back on decades of assimilationist rhetoric. The ideal of making Africans more French in culture and practice gave way to recognition that independent African states should mould their own futures and devise legislation uniquely applicable to their local circumstances.[76] The law's author was mayor of Marseilles and a Socialist minister in Guy Mollet's 'Republican Front' coalition. Gaston Defferre was also the first Minister of Overseas France for eight years who did not come from MRP ranks. We should note though, that while the Socialists took the credit for the measures enacted, MRP and Radical Party ministers had previously approved the ideas in principle. Defferre's eponymous legislation, voted through on 23 June 1956, opened the door to constitutional reform in black Africa enacted by decree.[77]

The law thus made possible African self-government organized on a territorial, rather than a federal, basis. Indeed, the federal structure of AOF and AEF lost much of its administrative rationale as power was devolved territory-by-territory. Territorial (i.e. 'National') Assemblies were to be elected in each former colony by universal suffrage on a single electoral roll. In AEF especially, this deprived the European population of their earlier predominance under the dual college system. The new assemblies were to select government councils, the leader of which would serve as deputy to a French high commissioner in each territory. In the short term, the French government retained control of the essential troika of defence, foreign affairs, and financial policy. However, the Territorial Assemblies took on wide budgetary responsibilities. AOF High Commissioner Bernard Cornut-Gentille warned European members of the AOF executive council in June 1956 that the planned changes were irreversible. European representatives would have to 'become more African in thought while the Africans became more European in method'.[78]

This avalanche of administrative change was music to the ears of those African politicians such as Houphouët-Boigny who rejected federalism. Conversely, it was a body blow to West Africa's federalists, politicians like the IOM deputies Senghor and Mamadou Dia who envisaged differing levels of political and cultural attachment – or 'layered sovereignty' – between individual territories, a wider regional federation, and lasting connections with France.[79] Both men lambasted territory-based reform as the systematic fragmentation, or '*balkanisation*,' of francophone Africa. They warned that the creation of weak successor states would make French neocolonial dominance easier. In March 1956 they began campaigning in the French and AOF press against the '*territorialisation*' of black Africa. For his part, Houphouët-Boigny, by then a junior minister in Guy Mollet's Cabinet, had become the Socialists' new colonial darling. Enthusiastic RDA backing of government reform undermined the pro-federalists' campaign.[80] Over subsequent weeks and months the federalists failed to win mass support among African voters; in fact, quite the reverse: they found themselves losing the argument. AOF and AEF were derided as entirely French fabrications. The shift towards unitary states modelled on former colonial boundaries also brought to light long-standing local grievances about rapacious federal administration and the cross-subsidization of one territory by another. Resentments were especially strong in Ivory Coast, Dahomey, and Guinea. These were all 'richer' AOF territories whose leaders were eager to strike out on their own.[81]

With the federalists increasingly isolated, the first government councils were chosen in May 1957, two months after the election of the Territorial Assemblies. These new French African proto-governments were now the real centres of power, and the évolué politicians who had come to prominence in the post-war decade controlled most of them. Most shared elite backgrounds unrepresentative of the wider population. Of the ministers elected across AOF as a whole, thirty-three came from the liberal professions, twenty-three were bureaucrats, twenty-two were former teachers, and nine had worked in industry.[82]

The *Communauté* and independence in Afrique Noire

The impetus towards full self-government built up between 1956 and 1958 undercut the last French attempt to control the political evolution of black African states. But it did not dent the enduring faith among French ministers and colonial officials in their own prescriptions for African development. The Gaston Defferre law opened the door to local models of government and national citizenship in individual West African states but it did not mark the end of French involvement in the region. French officialdom and numerous francophone African political leaders retained their confidence in French political institutions and republican values. Phrased differently, French imperialism was specifically republican in its conception of empire as a spatial extension of French political culture. Not surprisingly, the 1956 legislation, and de Gaulle's proposals for a Franco-African Community two years later, presupposed that the political structures in former colonies would mirror those of France.

The *Communauté*, or Community, could be viewed as the wholesale export of the French Fifth Republic's constitutional model to black Africa; its fundamental purpose as being to reaffirm the politico-cultural ties between France and its overseas territories. It main architects were Houphouët-Boigny and the first prime minister of the *Cinquième*, Michel Debré. The fact that Houphouët-Boigny, like Senghor before him, was assigned a key role in drafting an imperial constitutional project attested to the acculturation of a francophone political elite without parallel in British Africa. So, too, the Community, like the French Union before it, would soon change beyond recognition. In one respect, though, Gaullist thinking made its mark. Most of the francophone African states that secured full independence in 1960 drew heavily on the Gaullist model of a strong executive presidency and tight constitutional restriction on parliamentary prerogatives.[83]

Whereas the RDA had welcomed the Gaston Defferre law, the party was profoundly divided over acceptance of de Gaulle's *Communauté*. The territories that signed up to this community stood to receive preferential French aid but not outright political independence. More serious in the long term, party politics in French West Africa cleaved between those still fearful of the region's '*balkanisation*' into unviable and antagonistic nation states and those that valued national independence above any kind of federal structure. In spite of these inter-African divisions, indeed, perhaps because of them, the *Communauté* was put forward in a new mood of French confidence, buoyed up by General de Gaulle's return to power on 1 June 1958. It was widely expected that a Gaullist regime would produce strong government at home, international leadership in Europe, and a rapid end to the Algerian War. At a Paris reception for African leaders held on 14 July, Bastille Day, de Gaulle jubilantly informed his guests that they would now serve as premiers, rather than as vice presidents, of their government councils.[84]

Yet, as the constitutional replacement for the French Union, the Community scheme was in some ways retrograde. The old distinctions between overseas departments (départements d'outre-mer – DOMs), overseas territories (territoires d'outre-mer – TOMs), and associated states were conserved and the powers devolved to Territorial Assemblies and governing councils were cut. Throughout the Community, France would retain its grip on those three essentials: finance, defence, and foreign affairs. At the apex of the system, all member states would be represented in an Executive Council supposed to determine Community-wide policies. (In fact, this Council only met on six occasions in total between February 1959 and March 1960.)[85] A French-administered, supra-national judicial authority was to be created. The entire monetary system of the *Communauté* would also stay under French control thanks to continued linkage of the franc CFA with the metropolitan currency. The entire project was to be voted on by referenda in all affected territories in black Africa, the Pacific, Occania, and the French West Indies on 28 September 1958. Voters had three choices. They could opt for continued status as an overseas territory within the *Communauté*, closer integration with France, or outright independence. De Gaulle's government warned that the latter choice would mean complete severance, including the immediate withdrawal of French aid, investment, and defence facilities.

Most African electorates followed the wishes of their national leaders, voting in support of *Communauté* membership. But Guinea's government council under Sékou Touré, the one militantly anti-French administration in AOF, defied the Gaullist threats. In doing so, Touré's government bent to strong pressure from below – RDA grass-roots activism leaving national leaders severely constrained.[86] Ultimately, over 95 per cent of Guinean voters supported Sékou Touré's call for immediate independence. The overblown show of French governmental fury at this outcome was meant to persuade other states of the consequences of such ingratitude. French officials departing from Guinea's capital, Conakry, ostentatiously shipped home all that they could. French financial support, technical assistance, and trade links were all cut off. It was a petulant display made more ludicrous by Khrushchev's willingness to fill the void as the principal backer of West Africa's one solidly pro-Soviet regime.

Communauté referenda elsewhere had other important, if less dramatic, consequences. In Senegal, the overwhelming 97.2 per cent vote in favour of *Communauté* membership gave added impetus to Senghor's new pro-federalist grouping, the Parti du Regroupement Africain (PRA), in its struggle against balkanization.[87] On 17 January 1959 representatives from Senegal, French Sudan, Dahomey, and Upper Volta agreed to create a new superstate. The four territories merged to become the Mali federation, as much an experiment in pan-African unity as a rejection of the RDA's support for unitary states.[88] The project came close to collapse within four months. Under strong RDA pressure, much encouraged by the local French administration, the Territorial Assemblies in Upper Volta and Dahomey refused to join the Mali federation, reducing it to Senegal and French Sudan. Clearly, France's capacity to shape the emerging political systems to its liking was far from spent.

Finn Fuglestad's analysis of the situation in Niger in the lead-up to the 1958 referendum provides another interesting case study of enduring French influence. Ultimately, the voters of Niger voted 76 per cent in support of Community membership, thereby defying the advice of their national representatives. Djibo Bakary led the Niger Cabinet at the time. He was an *évolué* with great political flair, apparent in the links he maintained with Niger youth movements, women's groups, the French Communist Party, and its trade union affiliate, the CGT. But these diverse political associations did him little good. Instead, by 1958 Bakary's government had come to rely on the conservative cantonal chiefs (*Sarkis*) of Hausaland in the east of the country. As Bakary discovered, this was too narrow a constituency to promote his preferred solution. To make matters worse, once it became clear that his government favoured a break with France, Bakary was coaxed and cajoled by Niger's last three colonial governors, notably Jean Ramadier, whose father Paul had been Socialist premier in France during early 1947.

Public rejection of Bakary's declared preference for a 'No' vote on the *Communauté* proposal is instructive on three counts. First, it confirmed the innate weakness of an African government that had failed to win over either educated African workers or peasant voters in a chronically poor colony reliant on subsidies from Dakar. Second, it revealed how much popular support the RDA still enjoyed in Niger. Finally, Bakary's humiliation suggests that even at this late stage in the colonial game, the French authorities, working largely through Houphouët-Boigny, who was, by then, Minister of Health, could undermine a leading African political figure with relative ease. Admittedly, the stakes in Niger were high. Had the territory followed Sékou Touré's Guinea in voting for immediate independence as Bakary wanted, the entire *Communauté* project might well have imploded.[89]

Guinea and Niger apart, in other states of AOF and AEF political parties with pro-French leaderships still dominated national politics. So the long-term fate of the Community rested on other differences between them. By 1959–60 the rapid march to independence in black Africa was inextricably linked with the long-running antagonism between the Senegalese federalists and the largely Ivorian territorialists. The government of the Mali federation pressed hard for independence, knowing that the Community provisions allowed for a negotiated transfer of power, even though its authors hoped that member states would see the benefits of continued membership and limited autonomy. The pace of political change in francophone Africa was also affected by the speed of European withdrawal from other former colonies, the Belgian Congo and the trust territories of Togo and Cameroon above all. Between April and September 1960 Senegal and Mali attained full independence from France. Both emerged as independent nation states once their earlier experiment with federation was formally dissolved on 20 August. There was an immediate domino effect. Not wishing to be trumped by his federalist rivals from Senegal and Mali, Houphouët-Boigny declared Ivory Coast independent on 7 August, not bothering to negotiate the detail until after the event. By November 1960 Djibouti, the four Comoros islands in the Mozambique Channel, and Réunion were the only remaining francophone African territories not to have become independent states.[90]

Thanks in part to a customs union between them established at Brazzaville in June 1959, the AEF governments approached independence more united than their counterparts in French West Africa. At the sixth and final session of the *Communauté* Executive Council in December 1959, the leaders of Chad, Gabon, Middle Congo, and the Central African Republic agreed to work in partnership during the talks preparatory to independence. French advisers played a key role in these discussions, even joining some of the negotiating teams designated to travel to Paris to settle the final terms in late 1960. Ethnic difference rather than ideological splits or party rivalries shaped the political process in AEF territories. For instance, Abbé Fulbert Youlou, mayor of Brazzaville and premier of the Middle Congo, rarely ventured into the north of his country, heartland of the M'Bochi people. Similarly, in Chad, Prime Minister François Tombalbayé, leader of the Parti Progressisite Tchadien, held little sway over the Muslim north of the country where political engagement in national politics was minimal. Indeed, the Arab dialect spoken in northern Chad contained no word for 'independence'.[91] It is hardly remarkable that French administrators and European settlers still wielded powerful backdoor influence in the former colonies of Equatorial Africa. But, neither should we be surprised at the violence of the eventual popular backlash against privileged whites and the multinational corporations in the Congo region during the early 1960s.[92]

Finally, it is little wonder that by November 1960 the old colonial federations and the complex constitutional arrangements that had succeeded them were swept away with virtually no opposition in France. De Gaulle's administration was more animated by the beginnings of negotiations to end the Algerian War. Shrewder observers also knew that the definitive break implied by national independence was more apparent than real. Most of the new black African nations were reluctant to risk losing essential French monetary and military support. Amid the horrors of the Algerian conflict, the French public seemed understandably content that a relatively peaceful end to sub-Saharan empire had taken place.

CHAPTER 7
PEOPLE'S WAR AND THE COLLAPSE OF FRENCH INDOCHINA, 1945–54

Ideology and people's war

One reason that political analysts have found the violence of French decolonization distinctive is that its two most protracted conflicts – in Vietnam and Algeria – are often characterized as 'people's wars'.[1] Clearly, both were part of the same historical process of the overthrow of European colonialism, a fact that Vietnamese and Algerian nationalist leaders were quick to appreciate, and keen to stress before, during, and after these wars of decolonization.[2] Each conflict pitted a nationalist political movement against a foreign occupying power thus fulfilling the essential criteria of 'people's war': a popularly driven military challenge to external control. Initially fought as guerrilla insurgencies, one key to victory in these conflicts lay in the control and eventual mobilization of the indigenous population, above all within the rural interior of both countries. Although the methods employed might be highly coercive – thereby casting doubt on just how 'popular' these movements really were – their ultimate capacity to mobilize mass support is hard to question. Only Portuguese Africa witnessed anything comparable.[3]

For all that, cracks begin to appear in the 'people's war' idea the closer one scrutinizes either the presumed unity or the momentum for overthrow of hated colonial regimes implied by the term. The conflicts in French Vietnam and, as we shall see, in French Algeria and Portuguese Africa, were notable for the irreconcilable divisions between anti-colonial rivals for power. Bitter internecine fighting was endemic. Indeed, terrorizing civilians became integral to these 'people's wars', assassinations and collective punishments being used to enforce popular compliance with the will of left-leaning nationalist movements. These conflicts were further distinguished by their lengthy duration. Far from achieving a rapid displacement of colonial rule, national movements in Vietnam, Algeria, and Angola faced many years of insurgent warfare, transnational propagandizing, and civil strife. But, in Vietnam's case especially, the hardship and sacrifice of fighting a colonial ruler did consolidate mass support for the struggle. More so than any other colonial conflict of the immediate post-war years, the Indochina War was totalizing in its effects and, by its closing stages in the 1950s, was closer to 'total war' than low-level insurgency.[4]

Within six months of the outbreak of the Indochina War on 19 December 1946, military operations by the League for the Independence of Vietnam (the Viet Nam Doc lap Dong Minh – commonly known as the Vietminh) had spread throughout the Vietnamese-speaking territories of the Indochina federation.[5] Yet the French expeditionary force that fought them argued justifiably that its counter-offensive had gone remarkably well in the same opening months of the war. French troops controlled the provincial centres of central and northern Vietnam and, by the end of February 1947, were also entrenched in the former imperial capital of Hue as well as in the north's most important city, Hanoi.

Driving Vietminh forces from the major urban centres was one thing, winning the loyalty of the civilian population entirely another. As 1947 unfolded, well-organized guerrilla attacks by the Vietminh's southern resistance led by Nguyen Binh in Cochin China, Vietnam's southern-most territory and the commercial heartland of French colonialism in Indochina, acquired a symbolic importance that outweighed their physical impact. These were actions conducted more for psychological effect than for short-term military gain. It was 'revolutionary war' in that the Vietminh selected targets by measuring their political, rather than their military, significance. To an extent, this was just expediency. The imbalance between French military strength and Vietminh forces, at least before 1950, compelled Vietminh cadres to avoid pitched battles where possible. But it was also much more. Vietminh tactics signalled the movement's capacity to strike anywhere, anytime, whether at French forces or at those who dared to work with them. These were facts no Vietnamese could afford to ignore. The Vietminh's aspiration to control the civilian population marked out the early stages of the Indochina War as an ideological struggle for hearts and minds rather than a classic military contest for territory.[6]

As we shall see in a later chapter, much the same could be said of the Algerian nationalist Front de Libération Nationale (FLN) during Algeria's war of independence between 1954 and 1962. The intense focus on civilian loyalties was at the root of the exceptional cruelty of these conflicts. The Algerian novelist, Mouloud Feraoun, surely spoke for a silent Muslim civilian majority when he recorded the following in his diary on 8 January 1956: 'The rebels' expectations are both excessive and disappointing. They include prohibitions of all kinds, nothing but prohibitions, dictated by the most authoritarian fist. In a way, this is true terrorism.'[7] Popular submission to the insurgents' will was critical to war's outcome in Vietnam and Algeria.

Self-perception was also important. The Vietminh and the FLN cast themselves as revolutionaries, uncompromising in their commitment to create a new political, economic, and social order rather than just seize the reins of power. However, it becomes difficult to sustain such comparisons in detail. The Vietminh's Marxist ideological grounding was absent from the FLN. Nor did the FLN's military wing, the Armée de Libération Nationale (ALN), develop into a mass 'people's army' in the way that the Vietminh, supplied with Chinese weaponry, did after 1950. In the early stages of the Algerian War, FLN commanders resorted to coercion as much as a distinct political programme to enforce popular compliance. Only gradually did the appeal of their socialistic nationalism win widespread support, perhaps less because of its intrinsic appeal than as a result of French military repression. Furthermore, as Matthew Connelly has argued so persuasively, the victory of Algerian nationalism owed as much to the FLN's cultivation of international support as to its internal operations against French forces.[8]

In colonial Indochina and Algeria it thus remains difficult to disentangle the threads of 'revolutionary nationalism'. The nationalist impulse in Vietnam and Algeria antedated the revolutionary groups that ultimately drove the process forward. The struggle for national independence acquired an almost visceral quality for many of those involved. Even among the Vietminh's leadership cadres, this basic nationalist impulse was sometimes stronger than the more intangible dream of socialist transformation. Long-standing suspicion of, and unresolved territorial disputes with, their major foreign backer, communist China, sharpened this underlying ethnocentric nationalism. One has to ask the most basic question: when they pulled the trigger, what were 'revolutionary nationalists' fighting for – revolution or nation? Simply to say both is to ignore the tension between internationalist ideology and ethnically rooted nationalism. It is also worth noting that the mobilization of an indigenous peasant majority to fight a colonial war did not result in the peasantry's dominance of post colonial politics in Vietnam, Algeria, or, for that matter, in Portugal's former African colonies. Marxist dictatorship in Vietnam and socialist republicanism in Algeria did not represent the fulfilment of what has been idealized as a 'revolutionary class alliance' between urban workers, bourgeois radicals, and the peasant masses.[9]

The Vietminh was, however, the first among France's colonial opponents to tie its ideological objectives to a clear military strategy. The leadership of Ho Chi Minh's Indochina Communist Party and, in particular, the Party's senior military strategist, Vo Nguyen Giap, cleverly melded Leninist anti-colonialism with the Maoist doctrine of a three-stage process of anti-colonial warfare to suit Vietnam's particular geopolitical conditions.[10] In the Chinese Civil War, Mao's communists had first withdrawn in the face of superior enemy numbers and then gradually achieved military equilibrium with their opponent. Only in the third and final stage of the conflict did they prosecute a general offensive. With this model much in mind, the Vietnamese Communists initially adopted a defensive military posture while at the same time consolidating their political grip on Vietnam's rural population. Urban centres were also critical in this first stage of revolutionary war. In Saigon especially, the Vietminh's supporters, many of them women, orphaned children, and commercial employees, listened in on French conversations, spirited away essential supplies, and identified suitable targets for attack.[11]

Growing stronger militarily and better informed about French movements and intentions, in the second stage of their revolutionary war Vietminh cadres throughout the rural interior and within the major cities began stretching the French expeditionary force units trying – and failing – to impose order. Bombings and assassinations in Saigon and Hanoi pinned down additional troops and exposed the limits of French claims to control.[12] During this second phase, Vietminh political representatives also built up an international supply network that channelled arms and other essential equipment from South East Asian states as far afield as Burma and the Philippines, overland via Thailand into southern Vietnam.[13] The partner to this economic consolidation was an intensive propaganda effort. By 1947, the Indochina Communist Party (ICP) envoys were proselytizing the Vietminh cause in Asian capitals and sending documentation to US diplomats to try to win the sympathy of President Truman's US administration.[14] Finally, from 1950 onwards, in a third phase of revolutionary war, Vietminh units abandoned guerrilla warfare in preference for larger, more conventional, military encounter-battles against a French force that was now outnumbered and often outgunned.[15] With the rare exception of General Jean de Lattre de Tassigny's inspirational year of command in 1951, the expeditionary force rarely dictated the terms of combat in the Indochina War.

By contrast, the supposed ideological coherence of the FLN was primarily an invention of French government propaganda. Attaching Marxist, pan-Arabist, or Islamist labels to the FLN marked the culmination of long-standing efforts by French ministers, colonial administrators, government officials, and press bureaux to demonize their nationalist opponents as implacably hostile to Western political and cultural values.[16] As Matthew Connelly has argued, by the time the Algerian War broke out such policies were anachronistic and counterproductive:

New means of communications, market integration, and mass migration had so complicated ties between metropole and colony, city and countryside, modernity and tradition as to make the relationships between these apparent dichotomies increasingly ambiguous. It was difficult, if not impossible, for the French to go on defining themselves against or through some colonial 'other' when Algerians, often living in their midst, appeared to be neither peasant nor proletarian, neither liberal nor communist, but French citizens, Algerian nationalists, and racial and religious separatists all at the same time.[17]

French-Vietnamese negotiations and the outbreak of the Indochina War

The appellation 'people's war' suggests a totalizing Vietnamese struggle to end colonial domination. But French inability to reimpose their authority over the Indochina federation after 1945 was perceived very differently in Paris. Several ministers and senior colonial officials were only dimly aware of Vietminh organization in the summer of 1945, a fact that made it much easier to dismiss the idea that the Vietnamese would also want to achieve national liberation. As we saw in a previous chapter, beyond PCF activists, public interest in the Indochina War was fitful.[18] With only professional soldiers, many of them African colonial troops, engaged in the fighting, the expeditionary force's rising losses were slow to influence public opinion back home.[19] That said, by 1950 media polling indicated growing popular disenchantment. Uncertainty about France's declared objectives fed irritation at the material costs of the war. Empathy for the expeditionary force's hardships emerged later, when the popular press and cinema newsreels glorified the valiant defence of the Dien Bien Phu fortress – le Verdun tonkinois – in 1954.[20]

In 1945 all of this was yet to come. Post-Liberation France embarked lightly on what A. J. Stockwell terms 'the second colonial occupation' of South East Asia.[21] Yet the reconstruction of the Indochina federation faced major obstacles. Japan's wartime domination of Indochina exposed the moral and material bankruptcy of French colonialism. The Vichy state's political accommodation with Tokyo, the importation of Pétain's 'National Revolution' to Indochina, and Vichy's promotion of Vietnamese traditionalism in opposition to nationalist politics, sapped France's credibility as a beneficent ruler.[22] By contrast, during the Pacific War the Vietminh had steadily increased its popular support among the Vietnamese peasantry and the small, but influential Vietnamese proletariat in the cities of Hanoi, Haiphong, Saigon, and Vinh. The Vietminh was conceived in May 1941 at the eighth plenum of the ICP. After fifteen years of revolutionary struggle and Leninist discipline, the ICP, founded in 1930, was a complex amalgam of worker, peasant, youth, and women's sections. No other Vietnamese political party could match its organizational prowess or its mass appeal from village to national level. A broad-based coalition, but always under ICP direction, the Vietminh was a front organization intended by its founders to advance the Vietnamese national cause as a prelude to the communization of the country.[23]

The Vietminh seemed to have another asset in these formative years: Indochina was the Asian focus of President Roosevelt's anti-imperialism.[24] The President gave vent to his feelings at a meeting of the US Pacific War Council on 21 July 1943: 'Indochina should not be given back to the French Empire after the war. The French had been there for nearly one hundred years and had done absolutely nothing with the place to improve the lot of the people.'[25] In its way, Roosevelt's assumption that it was for the Western powers to dispose of Asian colonies as they saw fit was as colonialist as the system he criticized. But the sincerity of his views cannot be doubted.[26] The President and his more liberal advisers condemned French colonialism in

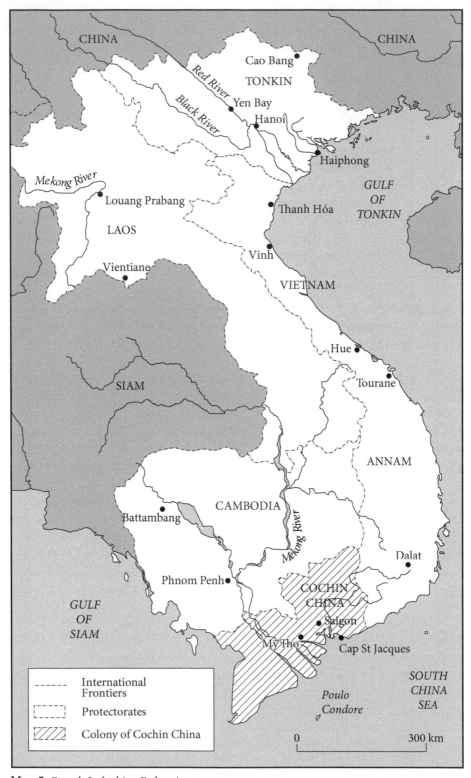

Map 5 French Indochina Federation.

the region as exploitative, inefficient, and a barrier to free trade. His administration disliked the Gaullist schemes to resume local control, and State Department analysts regarded the Indochina federation as a testing ground for American ideas of post-war trusteeship. However, by the time of Roosevelt's death in April 1945 Washington policymakers, still divided over the wisdom of allowing a resumption of French control, slid towards a policy of neutrality, refusing to give definitive US support to either the French or the Vietminh.[27] As a result, the restoration of French colonial sovereignty in Vietnam became part of a wider contest between European colonial powers anxious to regain their South East Asian possessions and nationalist groups that emerged from the war with unprecedented popular backing.[28] The Soviet Union, Nationalist China, and, above all, the United States all had vested interests in the outcome.

The year 1945 saw violent transitions in the territories of Indochina. First, Admiral Jean Decoux's isolated Vichyite regime in Hanoi finally succumbed to Japanese military domination in a ruthlessly executed coup in early March. The Japanese then opted to rule through local royalist elites. The Tokyo government sponsored nominally independent governments in Vietnam, Cambodia (renamed Kampuchea), and Laos, each under their historic royal sovereigns, Emperor Bao Daï, Prince Norodom Sihanouk, and King Sisavang Vong.[29] Six months later, new occupiers arrived. Following decisions taken at the Potsdam Conference in August, Chinese Nationalist and British military forces entered Vietnam from north and south to disarm the surrendered Japanese forces. Japan's surrender also triggered Bao Daï's abdication and the Vietminh's August 1945 revolution. In Hanoi, on 29 August, the ICP leader Ho Chi Minh announced the formation of a Democratic Republic of Vietnam (DRV) under Vietminh control.

Behind these events lay four issues of greater material importance to most Vietnamese. First and foremost was the spread of famine across northern and central Vietnam as the country's internal market and communications infrastructure collapsed during the winter of 1944–5. The Vichy authorities' acquiescence in Japanese grain exactions and their reduction in peasant entitlement to food aid exacerbated these famine conditions. Conversely, Vietminh efforts to secure control over granaries to facilitate famine relief won them widespread support.[30] It was not enough. Some estimates suggest that as many as two million Vietnamese starved to death.[31] The lessons of the famine help account for a second key factor: the DRV's imposition of draconian economic and fiscal controls over Vietnam's foodstuff supplies and land resources.[32] Third was the long-term importance of two political decisions taken for reasons of short-term expediency. One was the Japanese decision in March to incorporate the southern colony of Cochin China into a unified Vietnam under the titular authority of Bao Daï. The other was the arbitrary decision at Potsdam to divide allied occupation responsibilities between North and South Vietnam at the 16th parallel. Both set important administrative precedents for the future. The fourth consideration was that the events of 1945 proved time and again that the French were not masters of their own destiny, a fact that much of the Vietnamese population took to heart.

By the end of 1945 several elements of the coming Franco-Vietnamese war were in place. The ICP was not yet strong enough to rule without its nationalist partners in the Vietminh coalition. Nor did it command sufficient regular and militia forces to risk an open confrontation with the returning French military columns. These weaknesses made it essential for Ho and his senior military commander Vo Nguyen Giap to continue negotiations with French envoy

Jean Sainteny over a *modus vivendi* with France. The Vietminh won overwhelming support in elections to the DRV National Assembly in January 1946, but its component parties, some of which were ardently pro-Chinese, squabbled over the distribution of portfolios and over the optimum strategy to pursue with the French. Ho finally established a multiparty Government of Resistance and National Reconstruction on 2 March. Only after his hand was strengthened in Hanoi could Ho conclude discussions with Sainteny.[33]

French ministers and commanders also knew that their fragile hold on southern Vietnam made talks with Ho advisable. There was little respect in Paris or Saigon for Vietnamese nationalist aspirations or Vietminh military capability, yet, in hindsight, it is French weakness that stands out. The expeditionary force led by General Philippe Leclerc dispatched in autumn 1945 to restore military control across the Indochina federation was thinly spread, poorly equipped, and militarily exposed. In Cambodia, for example, Lieutenant-Colonel Paul Huard took over as chief commissioner in October 1945 with virtually no forces at his disposal, and precious little political legitimacy to underpin his authority.[34] Cambodia had escaped the famine conditions and political violence of neighbouring Vietnam in the immediate post-war period. Thanks, in part, to US diplomatic intervention, in November 1946 the Thai government surrendered sovereignty over the Cambodian provinces of Battanbang and Siam Reap, territories that it had forcibly annexed in 1941.[35] By this point, the Cambodian royal government under Prince Monireth had faced down opposition from the Khmer Issarak movement, making the country sufficiently stable to hold national elections. Yet it could hardly be said that Cambodia was a paragon of democratic virtue next to Vietnam. A truer picture of the political scene in Phnom Penh emerges in a report compiled in October 1946 by a member of the British military mission in Indochina:

> The [Cambodian] elections could hardly have been described as having been held under secret ballot. A large percentage of the population is illiterate and the election papers consisted of a disc showing a different design for each party, an elephant for the [pro-Monarchy] Democrats, for example; a pagoda and crossed arrows for other parties. The voters had to place one of these in the voting box. They were given considerable assistance in doing this by the Democratic Party whips who, in explaining the different discs to the illiterate, stated that the arrows were dangerous things and should be thrown away; the pagodas were sacred things and should be kept close to the heart by placing in the pockets – voters could then 'stable the elephant in the box.'[36]

Few people in Western capitals paid much attention to evidence of corruption in Cambodia; the situation in nearby southern Vietnam was far more alarming. The colony of Cochin China, centred on Saigon, was the heart of French cultural and economic influence in Vietnam. It was in political ferment for months after the DRV's creation in northerly Hanoi at the end of August 1945. Neither the British military units sent to police southern Vietnam after the Potsdam Conference, nor the expeditionary force that gradually replaced them over the winter of 1945–6 re-established order in Saigon and its outlying provinces. A year after the arrival of Leclerc's troops in September 1945, the ICP declared its newly formed Provisional Resistance Committee under Pham Van Bach, the sole legal authority in Cochin China. This move infuriated French negotiators who, quite understandably, rejected it, not least because one of their key political objectives was to consolidate a separate, pro-French-Vietnamese government in Saigon. The task would prove impossible and by October 1946 almost 75 per cent of southern Vietnam was under *de facto* Vietminh control.[37]

Earlier in 1946 the French suffered three other setbacks to their hopes of a swift return to power in Vietnam. First, de Gaulle's abrupt resignation as head of government in January 1946 fractured the political consensus in support of the reoccupation policy. Second, the Vietminh clearly disliked the outline structure of the French Union that emerged as talks over the new imperial constitution continued during the year. Vietminh leaders were certain that the French Union was intended to perpetuate imperial control, and they were not inclined to compromise with the French authorities over the long-term status of Vietnam within a rebranded colonial system.[38] However, on one occasion they did so. This was on 6 March 1946 when Ho and Jean Sainteny signed an interim agreement recognizing the DRV as a free state with its own parliament, armed forces, and budgetary powers within the Indochina federation (arguably, a contradiction in terms). The arrangement also promised an eventual referendum on Vietnamese national unification. In theory, French troop strength north of the 16th Parallel (in other words, in the Chinese zone of occupation) would not exceed 15,000 over the next five years. The 6 March accords, the third major reversal for the French, were actually the result of intense Chinese pressure, specifically the realization that the Chinese Nationalist occupation force would fight off a French military force sent to reoccupy Hanoi and Haiphong. As it did not serve the Vietminh's interest to entrench Chinese power in northern Vietnam, they, too, were pushed towards this temporary and ultimately fruitless compromise.[39]

As is well known, the 6 March accords never developed into a working agreement between the DRV and the French High Commission in Saigon. The 6 March accords did recognize the Republic of Vietnam. But just how much Vietnamese autonomy and how much French federation these arrangements entailed remained unclear. In particular, the allegiance of Cochin China remained unresolved, this being deferred until a plebiscite was held in the colony.

For the rest of the year, Franco-Vietnamese disagreement persisted over the unity of Vietnam's three component territories and French preference to treat Cochin China as a distinct entity. Historians Philippe Devillers, Stein Tønnesson, Martin Shipway, and, most recently, Mark Atwood Lawrence have shown that Admiral Georges Thierry d'Argenlieu's High Commission administration arrogated power from Paris during the summer of 1946 in a calculated attempt to preclude a definitive settlement with the DRV. The most glaring proof of this was d'Argenlieu's unilateral recognition of the 'Republic of Cochin China' on 1 June to supplant the pre-existing, and Vietminh-dominated, Saigon Committee of the South. Conscious that they enjoyed the tacit support of MRP ministers in Paris, d'Argenlieu, his key political adviser Léon Pignon, and other senior Saigon officials resolved to challenge the Vietminh claim to dominance over the whole of Vietnam whether other members of the Paris government approved or not.[40]

Having condemned the Ho-Sainteny accords as a 'Munich', d'Argenlieu's sponsorship of an anti-Vietminh separatist republic in Cochin China was the first in a series of gambits fabricated by the high commission team to weaken the DRV and tie the hands of the tripartite coalition in France.[41] Next on this Saigon clique's agenda was sabotage of the Franco-Vietnamese conference, convened at Fontainebleau near Paris between 6 July and 10 September 1946 to determine a final arrangement linking an autonomous Vietnam to the French Union.[42] Their spoiling tactics unfolded in stages. On 21 June French troops reoccupied the Moi Plateau in southern Annam, a move meant to signal to both sides at Fontainebleau that force of arms could accomplish more than negotiations. Even more blatant, on 1 August d'Argenlieu convened a rival conference at Dalat to settle the administrative structure of the Indochina federation. The Vietminh negotiating team led by Pham Van Dong walked out of the Fontainebleau talks in protest, leaving the French negotiations suspended for a month. Meanwhile, General Jean Valluy, Leclerc's hard-line replacement as expeditionary force commander, resolved to seize the military initiative by shifting the focus of French military preparations north towards Hanoi.[43] After a last-ditch private meeting at the Paris apartment of Socialist Minister for Overseas France, Marius Moutet, on 14 September, Ho did sign up to a resumption of the Fontainebleau conference early in 1947. This could not mask the fact that the talks had reached impasse, even if neither wished to admit it. Among other things, the Vietminh stood for Vietnamese national unification; by contrast, the French government and d'Argenlieu's High Commission were determined to keep control over the south. It was now a short step to war, a fact confirmed by heightened Vietminh insurgency in Cochin China and both sides' frantic military preparations from October to December 1946.

Military confrontation and failing French solutions

Skirmishes in and around Saigon were briefly halted by a tenuous ceasefire agreement on 30 October. The focus of tension between French and Vietminh forces then shifted to Tonkin: Hanoi, the port city of Haiphong, and Lang-Son, the northerly communications hub that linked Tonkin to China. The French decision to impose control over customs duties paid by Chinese traders in Haiphong provoked DRV fury and would become the occasion for violence between the two sides. What lay behind this was the contest for control over North Vietnamese trade, part of a wider scheme to lock the Hanoi government into a French-controlled customs union. This, in turn, was part of a more fundamental issue: money. Because the Vietminh government's Finance Minister Pham Van Dong ran the state Treasury in Hanoi, the French could only regain control over the national money supply by replacing those Vietnamese piastres in circulation with new issue notes valued against the franc. Their scheme to do so was well prepared. François Bloch-Lainé, the financial specialist sent to implement this monetary takeover, completed his work by December 1945.[44]

Outflanked in currency matters, the DRV was understandably incensed by the other French economic coup, the customs union set up during late 1946. This measure had a strong military dimension. General Louis Morlière, regional commander in northern Vietnam, and his senior in Saigon, General Jean Valluy, wanted to block DRV rice exports through Haiphong in exchange for which the Vietminh received weapons, supplies, and fuel. Confrontation between French troops and units of the Vietnamese 'National Army' (so designated in May 1946) quickly followed. Initial clashes sparked by the French seizure of banned imports in late November culminated in a murderous French naval and air bombardment of Haiphong's Vietnamese districts on 23 November. The nearby village of Kien An, to which thousands of Haiphong's civilian population fled, was also bombed, while refugees on the roads leading out of Haiphong were strafed by British-supplied aircraft.[45] The carnage was redolent of the destruction wrought by French shelling in Damascus eighteen months earlier, which had caused international outcry.[46] In Haiphong, as in the capital, the death toll became a matter of bitter dispute, but some observers accept a conservative figure of three thousand residents killed by bombs and shellfire.[47]

In one key respect, though, Vietnam was different. Unlike the bombardment of Damascus or the vicious repression of the Sétif uprising in eastern Algeria in May 1945, the severe French military response in Haiphong was not wholly endorsed in Paris. Why? Part of the answer lay in the changing dynamics of French coalition politics. Georges Bidault's outgoing government was at the time coming to terms with French Communist Party gains in the November 1946 general election after which PCF leader Maurice Thorez claimed the premiership. Only Socialist defections within the governing tripartite coalition prevented the first-ever Communist from occupying the prime minister's residence at the Hôtel Matignon. Veteran Socialist Léon Blum instead took charge of an all-Socialist transitional government. Only when Blum's Socialist colleague Paul Ramadier replaced him as Prime Minister in late January 1947 was tripartite government between the Socialists, Communists, and the MRP restored.[48]

During these months of political hiatus in France, key decisions fell to an inner-Cabinet committee, the Comité Interministeriel d'Indochine ('COMININDO'), set up at de Gaulle's behest in 1945 as the principal policymaking forum for Indochina. Bidault's fellow MRP ministers dominated this committee, drawing on highly partial advice from d'Argenlieu's Saigon team. Although Jean Sainteny and Ho Chi Minh briefly resumed their discussions, and the Vietnamese leader sent a last-ditch appeal to French premier Blum on 15 December, neither produced results. Significantly, Ho's cable to Blum did not reach Paris until 26 December. The crucial delay was attributable to d'Argenlieu and General Valluy's hawkish group in Saigon, by then resolved to provoke the Vietminh into hostilities in Hanoi.[49] As if this were not bad enough, on 18 December Blum had decided to send Minister for Overseas France on a peace mission to Hanoi, but this, too, was overtaken by events and the scheming of d'Argenlieu's circle.[50] War preparations were not all one-sided. The DRV government in Hanoi had made ready to abandon the north's major cities to pursue a revolutionary war coordinated from northern Vietnam's rural interior. And, irrespective of French provocation, Vo Nguyen Giap mobilized Vietnamese National Army units to strike against French positions in Tonkin in support of the local *Tu Ve* militia. After much confusion, this occurred in the evening of 19 December 1946. The attacks marked the formal, if chaotic, outbreak of the Franco-Vietnamese war.

The Saigon command was confident that the Vietminh could be quickly beaten. Their advice, combined with a spate of atrocities against French civilians in Hanoi, and Blum's genuine belief that the DRV had turned its back on a settlement, led the Paris government to preclude any dialogue until the French army established local control. To no avail, Ho made seven appeals for a ceasefire between 21 December 1946 and 5 March 1947.[51] Misinformation was therefore instrumental in the war's escalation. So, too, was the hard line maintained by MRP leaders anxious not to lose electoral ground to the Gaullists, who spent much of 1946–7 marshalling their support into a new political party, the Rassemblement du Peuple Français (RPF). RPF organizers, who regarded the MRP as their chief rival for centre-right votes, were sure to play the patriotic card if the MRP were to 'go soft' on colonial questions.[52] It is, however, doubtful that, after their collusion with d'Argenlieu in 1946, the MRP executive would have been any less uncompromising even if the RPF challenge had not existed. As it was, Paul Coste-Floret, MRP Minister of War and then Minister for Overseas France, led the party's charge towards bullets not talks. This MRP pressure bore fruit, helping to drive the Communists out of government in the process. Despite the Communists' departure and Socialist reservations, the multiparty coalitions in power backed the war throughout 1947.[53] Three changes of government during the year and a series of low-level exchanges between the Vietminh leadership and the much-respected regional specialist, Paul Mus, made little practical difference.[54]

If anything, party political attitudes to the Indochina War hardened even further during the course of the year. Centre-left tripartism finally collapsed in the spring of 1947. Nine months of bitter confrontation between Communists and their opponents – in parliament, in industrial relations, and on the streets – dominated French politics from March to December. Whereas 374,000 working days were lost to French strike action during 1946, in 1947 the figure leapt to a massive twenty-three million. The industrial unrest that convulsed France in 1947 was also significantly more violent than that of the pre-war Popular Front period. Communist sabotage of workplaces and transportation links culminated in December when former Communist resisters tried to sabotage a train carrying CRS riot police to Arras. Their actions misfired tragically, with the mainline Paris-Lille train derailed, causing the death of sixteen passengers. Worsening ideological polarization poisoned French political culture, making reasoned discussion of colonial abuses impossible.[55] PCF refusal to vote military credits for the Indochina War in early March had catalysed the Ramadier government's decision to break with the Communists on 5 May. A combination of factors made the Indochina conflict an acutely divisive issue in parliamentary politics. One was the increasing militancy of the PCF rank and file, epitomized by Communist dockworkers' refusal to load war supplies destined for Vietnam. Another was the closer identification of the centre-right 'Third Force' parties (especially the MRP and the Radicals) with support for outright military victory. There was, however, a contradiction here. While the National Assembly debates on Indochina were notoriously stormy, this rancour was slow to register in marked shifts of public opinion.[56] Perhaps the more urgent concerns of domestic reconstruction account for this, perhaps the escalation of Cold War in Europe. More likely, few people, aside from ardent Communists, were willing as yet to countenance the phased withdrawal from Indochina that a settlement with the Vietminh would have required.

Politicians acted in the knowledge that the general public, still quiescent about the deepening crisis in Indochina, would only tolerate so much. This effectively ruled out the dispatch of young national servicemen to a colonial war, but it also left room for an escalation of the campaign by the expeditionary force's professional cadres. The costs, both human and political, were profound. Continuing public apathy – maybe frustration or incomprehension are more accurate – about the war as it dragged on into later years alienated several expeditionary force officers from domestic opinion and the Fourth Republic system as a whole.[57] But, at the same time, the lack of public engagement with the trials of the expeditionary force until the final drama of Dien Bien Phu prevented the more serious domestic political fissures that would emerge over the army's role in the Algerian conflict after 1954.

There were other reasons for French public acquiescence in the war. For one thing, within eighteen months of the start of hostilities, France claimed to be fighting for something far more liberal than the mere reimposition of colonial authority. For another, there was at least a plan to install a new Vietnamese leadership, albeit one that ultimately proved hopelessly unrealistic. By December 1947 Robert Schuman's government, dominated like most 'Third Force' administrations by the MRP and the Radical Party, seemed wedded to the idea of restoring Bao Daï as ruler of a unified Vietnam. This was a watershed decision for several reasons. It suggested a realization in Paris that the policy of encouraging regional separatism in Cochin China was a dead letter. It allowed France to claim that its war effort was endorsed by a Vietnamese national government supportive of the French Union. Above all, it tied the success of French policy to Bao Daï's ability to win popular backing. To do this, his supporters had to capitalize on French recognition of Vietnamese national unity. They also had to prove their effectiveness as a bulwark against communism by building a working coalition from diverse nationalist parties and religious sects. Finally, they had to ensure that economic conditions outside Vietminh-controlled areas compared favourably with those inside. On all counts the Bao Daï solution failed.

Fraught exchanges with Bao Daï eventually bore fruit in the Along Bay convention, signed on 7 December 1947. Vietnam under Bao Daï was granted substantial internal autonomy within the framework of the French Union. The Vietminh and a remarkably wide spectrum of influential pro-French politicians within Annam and Cochin China dismissed the measure as a sham, not least because it was so strongly identifiable with Bao Daï personally. The former Emperor of Annam was a poor choice as national leader. His lack of credibility as an independent political actor was a more serious deficiency than his notorious playboy lifestyle. Within weeks a power struggle developed among the pro-French-Vietnamese of the south. It was a further six months before General Nguyen Van Xuan, premier of the Cochin Chinese government, signed up to a further Along Bay declaration by which France recognized the theoretical independence of a unified Vietnamese state. Yet, as before, this was to remain directly associated with Paris through the structure of the French Union.[58]

The divisions between the monarchical alternative of Bao Daï and the secular republicanism of General Xuan mirrored the policy differences in Paris between the two major parties involved, the MRP and the Socialists.[59] But the common defence plans, agreed under a subsidiary protocol to the second Along Bay Agreement, confirmed that both parties believed that France should spearhead the resistance to any Vietminh takeover. Where MRP and Socialist ministers parted company was over Bao Daï himself. The MRP could tolerate Bao Daï as a quisling head of state while the Socialists could not. In 1949 the incipient bitterness between the MRP and the Socialists over the wisdom of banking on Bao Daï or General Xuan was forced into the open by the so-called 'Generals' affair', a messy scandal originating in a leaked army report on the dire military position in Indochina. Whatever their internal bickering, publicly French governments still clung to the fiction that their forces were fighting to uphold a legitimate Vietnamese alternative to communist rule. The reasons were simple. The governing parties' disputes over Bao Daï in late 1948 did not become an open breach because of Mao Zedong's communists. Imminent communist victory in the Chinese Civil War strengthened Bao Daï's hand as the one anti-Communist option available in Vietnam. It also lessened the chances of broad negotiations with the Vietminh, an idea that tempted war-weary French Socialists and Radicals.

Cold War and the internationalization of Vietnamese liberation

The fact remained that the Bao Daï solution was fundamentally flawed. It was externally imposed, locally unpopular, and an untenable halfway house between colonial control and Vietnamese independence. However, in 1949 neither Henri Queuille's Third Force government nor the Truman administration saw things this way. As Mark Lawrence reveals, French officials persuaded policy hawks within the US government to back their two-pronged strategy of war against the Vietminh and consolidation of a pro-Western Saigon regime.[60] In mid-March the State Department reiterated Washington's support for the Bao Daï solution. French negotiators, meanwhile, traded on the ex-emperor's deepening hostility to the Vietminh to persuade him to head a national authority in a unified Vietnam.[61] This did not mark any real advance on the Along Bay conventions. By cajoling Bao Daï into accepting Vietnam's autonomy as an Associated State of the French Union, Queuille's government ensured that the new regime stood no chance of generating the mass following necessary to counter the Vietminh. The paradox was evident from the start. France claimed to back Bao Daï as the authentic representative of the Vietnamese nation, yet denied his government's right to authentic national independence. By early 1950, the Saigon regime under newly installed Prime Minister Nguyen Phan Long relied on elements implacably opposed to the Vietminh: the commercial classes, fervent anti-Communists, and Catholic and sect leaders hostile to communist atheism. These groups were no basis for a broad-based coalition.[62] Tied to a political solution for Vietnam lacking nationalist credibility or popular endorsement, the French military would increasingly find Bao Daï a millstone.

Meanwhile, the war intensified as the first major deliveries of Chinese communist aid to Giap's army flowed into northern Tonkin. After the foundation of the People's Republic of China in October 1949, Hoang Van Hoan, a member of the ICP central committee, visited China to consolidate ties with the new regime. In January 1950 Ho travelled on foot to meet Chinese leaders (the trip took seventeen days), following which he held discussions with the Moscow government. Ho requested military assistance from China and immediate diplomatic recognition from both Communist powers. In July and August 1949, Stalin had urged the Chinese leadership to play a larger role in supporting revolutionary movements in East Asia. Vietnam would be the test case. By the end of January 1950 a framework accord was signed providing for Chinese military aid, training camps, military advisers, and the construction of cross border roads to carry war material. Within a fortnight of signing of the accord, communist China and Soviet Russia also recognized the Vietminh as Vietnam's legitimate government. The American and British governments responded on 7 February by granting formal recognition to Cambodia, Laos, and Bao Daï's Vietnam as Associated States of the French Union. By the summer of 1950 a Chinese Military Advisory Group (CMAG) composed of seventy-nine senior Chinese officers under General Wei Gouqing was in place to train Vietminh forces and advise on their deployment.[63]

Far to the south, the first substantial delivery of US military equipment landed in Saigon a week after the outbreak of the Korean War on 25 June 1950. As planning for a stronger French military commitment to the defence of Western Europe took place, first under the so-called Pleven Plan and then through its successor, the European Defence Community (EDC), so the costs of fighting in Vietnam became harder for France to bear.[64] Only greater US funding and supplies could possibly fill the gap. The combination of escalating Asian Cold War, closer Vietminh alignment with the communist superpowers, and intensive French diplomacy convinced American policymakers to take this decisive step. Washington gambled on the creation of a non-communist political alignment in Vietnam that could somehow reconcile Western strategic and economic interests with nationalist demands for independence. It was a fatal mistake.[65]

The tit-for-tat escalation of international involvement was echoed in the fighting across Tonkin. By April 1950, hard-fought campaigning directed by the French regional commander, General Marcel Alessandri, appeared to have secured both the Red River Delta and the key border outpost of Dong Khe. These were short-lived victories. By the end of the year, the Vietminh had retaken Dong Khe and were threatening to evict French forces from Hanoi itself.[66] Most important of all, in the first week of October 1950 the expeditionary force suffered its heaviest military defeat in the war thus far. General Chen Geng, China's senior military adviser in Tonkin and a long-standing friend of Ho, persuaded the Vietminh executive that their utmost military priority should be to expel French forces from the Vietnam-China border region. Chinese military equipment could then be delivered uninterrupted. Facing sustained Vietminh attack, three French battalions were ordered by Commander-in-Chief General Georges Carpentier to withdraw from Cao Bang, the principal French garrison in North Eastern Tonkin. A further four battalions were sent to assist the retreat along the precarious *Route Coloniale 4*. The entire force was annihilated. By 13 October 1950 its losses totalled some 1,800 men either killed or missing.[67] Remaining French forces at Lang-Son were compelled to evacuate hurriedly, leaving nearly all of their equipment, including artillery, mortars, and several thousand rifles and machine guns to the Vietminh.[68] Tragic and politically explosive at home, the loss of Cao Bang and the pull out from Lang-Son also altered the strategic balance of the war. French withdrawal facilitated a further expansion of Chinese aid, paving the way for three separate Vietminh offensives along the Red River Delta mounted from December 1950 to June 1951.[69] (The extent of Vietminh control is shown in the map overleaf.)

In the parliamentary debate on the Cao Bang 'disaster', Radical Party leader Pierre Mendès France launched a withering attack on French policy, the futility of the Indochina conflict, and its appalling human and material costs. Why expend so much blood and treasure in Indochina when it was patently clear that it was still insufficient to secure victory? Why prosecute a war that the majority of the French population professed neither to understand nor to want? Why weaken French power in Europe for the dubious benefits of maintaining a Far Eastern presence?[70] It is hard to know how far Mendès's powerful rhetoric struck home. Opinion poll evidence from 1950 is ambiguous, suggesting a worrying shift in metropolitan attitudes to the Indochina War alongside growing opposition to it. A rising proportion of French voters had deliberately 'tuned out' from the subject, choosing not to read or to listen to media coverage of events in Vietnam. Few seemed clear about how the war should be ended.[71] The presence of settlers was not enough to change their minds. Still influential in Vietnamese politics, Vietnam's settler population never had the emotional impact in France of the far larger *colon* communities in North Africa.

By contrast, the events of 1950 marked a turning point in intellectual and religious opposition to the war. Numerous human rights groups, Church-affiliated organizations, and prominent literary figures questioned the wisdom, the methods, and the ethics of the Indochina War.[72] What of the politicians? Among the major parties in France, still only the PCF maintained a firmly anti-war line, besmirched in the eyes of many because it appeared ideologically driven rather than based on principled opposition to the war's violence. One could even argue that Communist espousal of anti-colonialism was, itself, a problem because it made it harder for other anti-communist parties to follow suit. The Socialists remained hopelessly caught between their rhetorical commitment to a negotiated solution, their reluctance to concede publicly that this meant dialogue with the Vietminh, and their

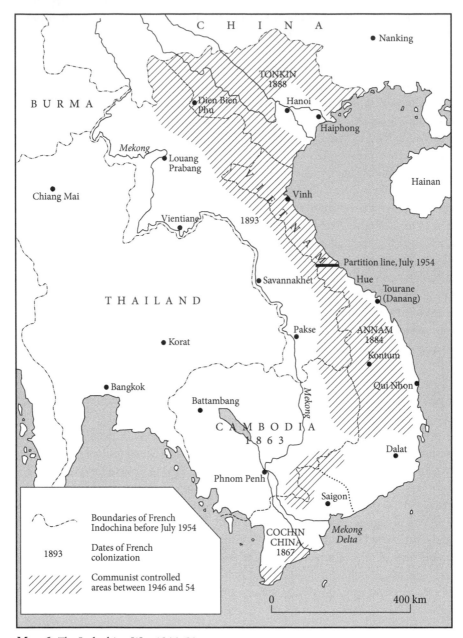

Map 6 The Indochina War, 1946–54.

endorsement of a continued French military presence. The MRP, the party most deeply immersed in the long-term running of the war, was still willing to sanction wider military operations without a coherent long-term political plan to accompany them. And from the safety of the opposition benches, the Gaullist RPF, opponents of the French constitutional system, criticized all the governing parties for their ineptitude without themselves offering a clear alternative.[73]

involvement in another ground war in Asia less than a year after the preceding one – in support of South Korea – had come to its inconclusive end. Nor did America's allies approve of the idea. Congress, the US service departments, and even Dulles's senior State Department advisers, knew that 'united action' and air strikes in support of the Dien Bien Phu garrison would have internationalized the Vietnam conflict.[91] But the project's failure left Dulles and Bao Daï's ministers sulking on the fringes at Geneva.[92] Their ill temper concealed the fact that the conference's real losers were the Vietminh.

The Geneva settlement restricted DRV authority to Vietnam north of the 17th parallel although the Vietminh controlled three quarters of the country when it signed a ceasefire accord on 20 July 1954. The monarchies of Laos and Cambodia now enjoyed international protection as neutral states. Worst of all, a South Vietnam state was formally recognized pending countrywide elections scheduled for July 1956. Neither side expected these to pass off as planned. In the interval, first the French, and then, far more so, the Americans did all they could to prevent outright Vietminh victory.[93] The movement of anti-communist Vietnamese into South Vietnam was encouraged, and the increasingly dictatorial South Vietnam government headed by Ngo Dinh Diem began its fatal dalliance with America. If French ministers and the Saigon High Commission may be blamed for conniving in schemes for war in 1945–6, after 1954 the French were bit players in seeding the ground for the more cataclysmic second Vietnam War. The advent of new protagonists in the Indochina conflict was tragic proof of the disastrous consequences of violent decolonization becoming subsumed in Cold War rivalry. Ironically, Charles de Gaulle, an original protagonist of the Indochina reconquest, realized only too well that American interventionism would probably end in disaster. Reinstalled as French presidential leader of the new Fifth Republic, he saw his 1964 proposals for Vietnam's neutralization rejected. Thereafter de Gaulle became an unlikely Vietnam War peacenik, proclaiming Vietnam's right to self-determination much to the annoyance of the French left, for whom such a complete Gaullist turnaround barely a decade after the original Indochina War seemed hard to credit.[94]

Conclusion

From the beginning of the first Indochina War to its dismal end, French governments never wholeheartedly pursued any of the objectives for which France was supposedly fighting. The initial war of colonial reconquest, allegedly integral to the reassertion of French international power, was all but abandoned by the end of 1947. It was, by then, evident that the Vietminh could not be entirely ousted from Tonkin. As for political initiatives, the Along Bay accords were always an unhappy compromise between restricted autonomy and the promise of eventual independence. There was an inherent contradiction between a French military campaign to guarantee the survival of a loyal Vietnamese state and the fact that the war itself sapped residual Vietnamese loyalty to any non-Vietminh alternative. Regardless of Bao Daï's shortcomings as a respected national leader and the instability of Cabinet government in Saigon, no Vietnamese regime could compete with the Vietminh for popular legitimacy.

Roosevelt's central criticism of France in Indochina was that the masses still lived in penury. In a fast-expanding population overwhelmingly tied to subsistence agriculture, French failure to enact substantial land reform after decades in charge was a searing indictment of colonial

Ironically, the French political crisis brewing over Indochina in late 1950 briefly simmered down in the coming year. This was in large part thanks to the remarkable military successes achieved by General Jean de Lattre de Tassigny. The General was a newcomer to Vietnam, sent there to assume civil and military command of the war in the wake of the Cao Bang defeat. The outstanding French commander of the war, de Lattre, thwarted the Vietminh's 1951 offensives in Tonkin and temporarily strengthened the French grip over Hanoi and its hinterland.[74] The impressive French military intelligence system was further improved. And de Lattre injected fresh impetus into the arduous process of building a Vietnamese army loyal to Bao Daï.[75] Buoyed by his reputation but terminally ill with cancer, de Lattre visited Washington in September 1951 to secure increases in military aid to French and Vietnamese army forces.[76] His spectacular, if fleeting, success in 1951 encouraged even Foreign Minister Robert Schuman, never much of an enthusiast for the war, to press the case for extended operations against the Vietminh.[77]

The French military impetus built up in 1951, the miraculous 'année de Lattre' dissipated in 1952. Neither of de Lattre's successors, Generals Raoul Salan and Henri Navarre, could emulate his success.[78] Nor did the French authorities sustain the consolidation of the Vietnamese army, the creation of which was pivotal to the survival of the Bao Daï régime. 'Vietnamization' of the war continued, but the Vietnamese army, although expanding and highly combative, was hamstrung by its French commanders who remained sceptical that it could operate independently.[79] In similar vein, French political intervention indicated time and again that the Associated States remained under neocolonial control. The abrupt decision of René Mayer's government to devalue the Indochinese piastre in May 1953 undermined all three Associated State governments. Infuriated by such high-handed French action, Prince Sihanouk seized the initiative, demanding and, in November 1953, securing full Cambodian independence.

By then the political climate in Paris was very different. War weariness had taken its toll among the parties previously committed to the war, the MRP especially. Public opposition to the conflict was also more vocal. Human rights campaigners, leading intellectuals, Church youth groups, and liberal journalists, particularly in the Catholic press, in Le Monde, and in the newly established weekly, L'Express, formed a cohesive anti-war lobby.[80] In late 1953 Dwight D. Eisenhower's Republican administration also pressed the new French government under Joseph Laniel to grant real independence to the governments in Phom Penh, Luang Prabang, and Saigon.[81] The Associated States idea imploded.

Meanwhile, Vietminh commanders and their CMAG advisers had learnt from the failure of their 1951 offensives. They resumed less costly guerrilla warfare and built up their arsenal of Chinese military supplies. With Ho Chi Minh still their president and Truong Chinh as General Secretary, the Vietnamese Communists, since February 1951 renamed as the Vietnamese Workers Party (VWP or Dang Lao Dong Viet Nam), were now openly committed to pursuit of the war within a Marxist-Leninist framework that prioritized eviction of the French over the revolutionary transformation of rural Vietnam.[82] The VWP Politburo agreed with the Beijing government that their first task was to secure North Western Vietnam and Upper Laos as a prelude to a further attack against the Red River Delta. As a result, after a series of advances southward from their Viet Bac stronghold, Giap's troops opened the Xam Neua offensive in Upper Laos in late March 1953. By the time of the Korean armistice on 27 July 1953, the Vietminh was in a commanding position.[83] Rural revolution was not entirely postponed. Within liberated zones, the VWP imposed a strict agrarian regime. In a highly effective propaganda campaign, the VWP publicized the fact that it would 'suspend' the distribution of communal land to peasants that served Bao Daï. Tightening VWP control over the countryside contrasted with the Emperor's attempt to win the loyalty of potential recruits through a series of land reforms in 1953. Bao Daï's efforts were undermined by the strength of opposition he encountered from Vietnamese landlords along the Red River and Mekong deltas.[84]

Dien Bien Phu, the Geneva conference, and the French withdrawal

The end of the Korean War permitted a further expansion in Chinese aid. But it also freed the United States to provision General Navarre's plan to secure Cochin China and southern Annam prior to an eventual advance on the north.[85] Furthermore, with the Korean War over and Soviet policy in flux after Stalin's death in March, the governments in Moscow and Beijing began diplomatic efforts in late September 1953 to convene a major East-West conference to ease Cold War tensions. In practice, the much-vaunted – and now better equipped – 'Navarre Plan' and the resumption of diplomatic efforts to end the war went together. Navarre's core objective, in other words, was not to defeat the Hanoi regime but to present it with the unwelcome prospect of a costly campaign of attrition to winkle out French forces.[86] Viewed from a French perspective, the diplomacy was to succeed where Navarre's military efforts failed. At the Berlin conference in January 1954, the Eisenhower administration and its French and British allies endorsed the Soviet proposal for a conference at Geneva to discuss peace in Korea and Indochina. The Vietminh's continuing military gains, Navarre's increasingly desperate schemes to slow them, and the entire outcome of the Indochina War, were likely to rest on the decisions of the superpowers. Here was Potsdam all over again. Just as the Vietminh neared definitive victory, international diplomacy conspired to thwart them.

For the French, the price of US aid was the integration of Indochina into American strategic planning in South East Asia, something in which France was bound to play a diminished role after the collapse of the Associated States project in late 1953. It was difficult for French political leaders to spurn Washington's requirements. American frustration with the course of the Indochina War added fuel to the Eisenhower administration's anger over fading French enthusiasm for the US-backed European Defence Community, a project designed, in large part, to facilitate West German rearmament and so ease the strategic burden carried by US forces in mainland Europe. With the eventual solution of West Germany's rearmament under NATO auspices yet to be devised, successive French governments in 1952–4 were poorly placed to question the advice that accompanied American assistance in Vietnam. It took Pierre Mendès France, who returned to office as premier and Foreign Minister on 19 June 1954, to break out of this vicious circle by rejecting further involvement in the EDC and Vietnam at a stroke.

The Geneva conference was scheduled to begin in April 1954. As conference preparations got underway a fortified garrison at the apex of communications between Tonkin, Upper Laos, and China became the Indochina War's focal point. Captured by French paratroops on 20 November 1953, the Dien Bien Phu fortress held as much symbolic as strategic importance. It signified a last French attempt to prevent Vietminh domination of northern Indochina. The ensuing battle was the one engagement of the war to dominate media coverage in France. As French fortunes worsened, so public fixation grew with the stoical self-sacrifice

of a doomed force. In a tragic case of life imitating art, the Dien Bien Phu garrison fulfilled all the stock requirements of colonial heroism that had dominated literary and cinematic depictions of empire for decades. Dien Bien Phu became 'le Verdun tropical', and France's leading photojournalism weekly, *Paris Match*, devoted an unprecedented five cover stories to the battle. As national interest heightened, press and newsreel reportage succumbed to racial stereotypes; the brave defenders resisting wave after wave of attacks by fanatical Vietminh hordes. The fact that the fortress garrison contained a large proportion of colonial troops was conveniently overlooked.[87]

Giap's attacking forces were anything but irrational. They systematically isolated Dien Bien Phu's hinterland by conducting subsidiary attacks in Upper Laos, Annam, and the Red River Delta. Giap's commanders then organized the delivery of unprecedented quantities of Chinese military supplies by truck and via lengthy columns of peasant irregulars that snaked their way through the surrounding jungle. It was a gargantuan effort and a triumph of mass mobilization. Thus equipped with everything from small arms to additional heavy artillery, Vietminh troops attacked Dien Bien Phu on 30 March 1954. Once Vietminh shelling destroyed the nearby airfield the defending garrison was in a hopeless position. French attempts to parachute in supplies were largely ineffective. By contrast, Chinese supplies to the Vietminh attackers included 2.4 million bullets, 60,000 artillery shells, and state of the art rocket launchers, used to devastating effect to breach the last French redoubts.[88] These logistical statistics point to a much bigger conclusion: the war's original asymmetry had been reversed.

At the military level, the key to Dien Bien Phu lay in the success of Vietminh strategy and supply. At the emotional level, the battle registered most immediately in the French media's obsession with the gallantry of the fortress defenders. But, at the political level, the protracted siege was painted on the larger canvas of international diplomacy. After the garrison fell on 7 May 1954, the main figures in this broader landscape were not the Vietnamese or the French, but the other parties to the Geneva conference: Chinese Foreign Minister Zhou Enlai, US Secretary of State John Foster Dulles, and British Foreign Secretary Anthony Eden.[89] The Chinese, Americans, and British each had distinct agendas. The Chinese delegation was anxious to end their country's international isolation. Zhou Enlai was prepared to see communism confined to northern Vietnam, with Laos and Cambodia made neutral buffer states adjacent to non-communist Thailand and Malaya. Zhou's moderation meshed with British efforts to secure a compromise peace in Indochina. Winston Churchill's government favoured a spheres of influence agreement that would preserve Britain's imperial interests in South East Asia through American protection and the assurance of Chinese non-intervention. For his part, French premier Mendès France forced the conference delegates to agree a decision swiftly. Mendès declared his intention to resign as Prime Minister unless a settlement was reached at Geneva within a month of his taking office in mid-June 1954.[90]

Together, the Chinese and British teams at Geneva stymied the more ambitious American project to resist any advance of communism in South East Asia. Dulles had earlier proposed the idea of 'united action' on 29 March 1954, in line with his wider support for 'Liberation' policies in areas of the developing world threatened by communism. Had the proposal succeeded, it would have required the French to fight on in Indochina as part of a new anti-communist alliance grouping the United States, Britain, France, Australia, New Zealand, the Philippines, Thailand, and the Associated States. In fact, the plan attracted little support either within Eisenhower's government or in Congress. It carried the obvious danger of American rule. Nor did Bao Daï fare much better, unable to overcome entrenched settler and landlord hostility to any reduction in their privileges. This made the Vietminh task far easier. The true meaning of people's war was apparent in the mobilization of DRV-controlled zones, first in the Viet Bac, and then far beyond it, in support of Vietminh operations. Frequently ruthless in tightening its grip upon the population, the ICP, and its later incarnation, the VWP, was, nevertheless, sustained by the Vietnamese peasantry's support. In sharp contrast, the political edifice built around Bao Daï was full of cracks, its foundations undermined by membership of the French Union with all the political, economic, and cultural subordination that this implied.

Finally, after Mao's victory in China and the massive increase in Vietminh military potential that followed, the French strategic position worsened rapidly. The year 1951 may have been the exception that proved the rule, but the *année de Lattre* was just that: a single year of achievement after which French fortunes declined once more. The expeditionary force certainly needed it, but the American military aid that sustained the last three years of the French war effort was always a source of friction in France's domestic politics. In 1953 alone, the war gobbled up some three thousand billion francs. It has been recently estimated that over the decade from 1946, France ploughed a yearly average of between 6 and 10 per cent of annual government expenditure into fighting the war in Indochina, a burden that impinged significantly on the rate of France's post-war reconstruction.[95] For what purpose? Apart from the high command in Saigon and the extraordinarily devoted professional cadres of the expeditionary force, from 1950 onwards it is hard to find any section of the French political community or the wider public that remained solidly committed to victory. Even Colonel de Castries, ill-fated commander of the Dien Bien Phu garrison, recognized that the nationalist ardour and revolutionary zeal of the Vietminh gave them the decisive edge over isolated professional troops honouring their contract of enlistment.[96] Much as it has been said by so many authors in so many contexts over so many years, the first Indochina War stands as one of the twentieth century's most costly and ultimately pointless conflicts, a sad testament to the futility of resisting decolonization.

CHAPTER 8
FROM FRENCH NORTH AFRICA TO MAGHREB INDEPENDENCE: DECOLONIZATION IN MOROCCO, TUNISIA, AND ALGERIA, 1945–56

The origins of colonial violence in French Algeria

The empire that France carved out in North West Africa began and ended in waves of violence. The port of Algiers and its surrounding coastal hinterland was swiftly captured during June and July 1830 by a 34,000 strong French expeditionary force dispatched in a 635-ship armada from Toulon. The fleet set sail at the behest of King Charles X following a diplomatic quarrel with the Algiers authorities. The expedition marked a last-ditch attempt to prop up the Bourbon regime against gathering opposition in France. In the event, the seizure of Algiers proved much more long lasting than the Bourbon Monarchy, which was ousted from power only days after the city was captured. The killings, army looting, sequestration of land and property, and general disregard for Muslim religious sensibilities that characterized this initial phase of the French conquest set the tone for the next forty years of military expansion and colonial settlement in Algeria.[1]

There was no long-term governmental scheme to colonize Algeria and make it the centrepiece of France's second colonial empire. But changes of regime in France drove the process forward. Throughout the 1830s and 1840s the Orléanist monarchy of Louis Philippe, anxious to legitimize its seizure of power, identified itself closely with the army's continuing Algerian conquest.[2] Yet, as the human and financial costs of conquering Algeria mounted, so, too, the colonial policy fragmented, becoming less a matter of royal decree or military fiat and more the result of competition between rival French stakeholders. In a pattern that would remain familiar until final decolonization a century later, what France did in Algeria – and how it justified its actions – reflected the interests of the French army, an expanding settler community, various land speculators and business interests, and the successive royal and republican regimes in office in nineteenth-century Paris.[3] Above all, the vigour and duration of Algerian resistance to French colonization drove the French military occupiers and the settlers that followed them towards increasing brutality and appropriation of Muslim lands.[4]

Localized armed resistance to the French presence continued in Algeria almost without interruption from 1830 to 1871. Its remarkable durability highlighted the integrity of Algeria's Muslim culture and confirmed that many Muslims recognized that they stood to lose everything.[5] The fight against colonization centred first on western Algeria where Emir 'Abd al-Qadir led a popular tribal uprising and established a proto-independent Algerian state from 1832 to 1847. In parallel to this, another rebellion, this time led by Ahmad ibn Mohammed (Ahmad Bey) of Constantine, denied the French control over much of eastern Algeria throughout the 1830s.

Determined to avert the humiliating failures of his predecessors, General Thomas Robert Bugeaud, appointed Governor in November 1840, crushed 'Abd al-Qadir's realm by the application of scorched earth tactics. Muslim civilians were targeted, homes and crops were burned, livestock slaughtered, and the rebellious population thereby denied the means of survival. In at least three cases, several hundred civilians were massacred by French troops, burned to death in caves where they had sought shelter. Such ruthlessness was as devastatingly effective in the short term as it was politically disastrous in the longer term.[6] 'Abd al-Qadir was driven into exile in Morocco and eventually surrendered to French forces in December 1847.[7] But his defeat brought with it a new wave of French land seizures that stirred implacable Muslim resentments. The end of 'Abd al-Qadir's nationwide movement shifted the focal point of indigenous unrest from the fertile plains and market centres to the more impenetrable highlands. In the 1860s and 1870s opposition to French rule became concentrated in two mountainous regions: the Aurès mountains in eastern Algeria, and Grand Kabylia, the main Berber region south-east of Algiers.

The pattern of French occupation set during the early conquest years remained intact for decades afterwards. Largely because of the intractable resistance encountered, the army remained at the forefront of administration and policymaking. From September 1834 a Government-General in Algiers reported directly to the War Minister in Paris. Even after the colonial government was opened up to civilian appointees, the colonial Governor ruled by decree. In other words, the Governor issued laws without prior parliamentary scrutiny of their content. This system continued, with some modification – consultative assemblies with limited powers of budgetary oversight were introduced in the early twentieth century – until 1946.

The scale of dispossession of Algeria's indigenous population was remarkable even by colonial standards. But the impact of settler land acquisition – for much of the nineteenth century, expropriation would be a more accurate term – on the indigenous population was uneven. In certain areas Muslims were entirely evicted from their ancestral lands. Around Blida, for instance, almost three quarters of cultivatable land was reallocated to the first wave of colonists that arrived in the 1840s.[8] Tribal populations that supported 'Abd al-Qadir's rebellion were punished by land confiscations and denial of grazing rights. Sedentary and nomadic clan groups linked to the Emir were driven from tribal lands into *cantonnements* policed by the army, usually in more arid, unfertile regions. Still more devastating was the 1863 *Senatus-Consulte*: a legislative code, the two central laws of which were passed on 22 April and 23 May of that year. With staggering disregard for the complexities of community allegiances in rural Algeria, the code delimited the territory of 709 officially designated 'tribes' and broke down landholding into recognized *douars* (rural administrative districts).[9] As intended, the measure hastened the detribalization of rural Algeria, facilitating another influx of *colon* farmers. A cholera epidemic in 1867 and a severe peasant famine the following year further decimated the Algerian peasantry.[10]

Algeria's importance to France was transformed by the impact of defeat in the Franco-Prussian War of 1870–1. The speed of Germany's victory and the punitive peace terms imposed, including loss of the French provinces of Alsace and Lorraine, provoked a change of regime in France. After its bloody suppression, the short-lived Paris Commune was succeeded by a new constitutional system: the Third Republic. Meanwhile, between January and October 1871 eastern Algeria was rocked by a major uprising centred on Grand Kabylia that triggered sporadic tribal violence and attacks on French interests that lasted for years. Following this rebellion, the

French colonial authorities embarked on a more systematic seizure of Algerian Muslim land. Former rebels saw their ancestral lands confiscated. Muslim farmers and absentee landlords lost their legal title to properties unless they could provide written proofs of ownership.[11] And huge areas of communally farmed Muslim common land were declared 'vacant' and therefore open to purchase by French agricultural settlers at nominal cost. One item of legislation was especially decisive: the Warnier Law of 26 July 1873 summarily introduced French property law to all transactions in Algerian land. It permitted dispossession of Muslim landowners who could not provide written proof of ownership – something rarely done under Muslim customary law.[12]

The coincidence of the loss of Alsace-Lorraine, the land sequestrations after the 1871 Algerian uprising, and the introduction of the Warnier Law together stimulated an unprecedented wave of French immigration to Algeria. Refugees from the two lost provinces, demobilized and unemployed soldiers from the recent Franco-Prussian War, former communards eager to get out of France, and French smallholders and peasant sharecroppers were all tempted by the prospect of cheap land and a new start in North Africa. In 1841 some 37,374 European settlers controlled only 40,000 hectares of land. After the suppression of the Kabylia insurrection and the Warnier Law, settler numbers rose to 412,435 and settler land ownership to 1.3 million hectares of land by 1881. By 1901 these figures climbed to 633,850 settlers in possession of 1.9 million hectares.[13]

The settler influx of the late nineteenth century, combined with the raft of laws, administrative discriminations, and land sequestrations that underpinned it, also provoked a sharper delineation of cultural identities – and the freedoms supposedly attached to them. As Lizabeth Zack notes, 'Assimilation-style colonization in the 1870s and 1880s reshuffled land, rights, and a sense of place in colonial Algeria, it accentuated distinctions and solidarities among "French," "Jews," "natives," "Algerians," and "neo-French/foreigners." The new laws and measures organized inhabitants into these groups and highlighted the boundaries around them.'[14] It would be going too far, though, to conclude that the social upheavals of the 1860s and 1870s tore at the fabric of Algerian rural communities so much that their capacity to resist colonial domination was broken. French attempts to impose European-style property rights, at odds with the communal farming practices and established Algerian patterns of landholding and transfer, were subverted by peasant cultivators who knew far better than French administrators the details of who farmed what, where, and for how long. Village assemblies, or *djemâa*, reorganized by French officials as part of the *Senatus-Consulte* reforms, exploited their position as intermediaries between colonial administration and local opinion to mitigate the impact of colonial edicts regarding rental payments and taxes. They, too, combined an intimate knowledge of farming patterns, livestock movements, and their community's food requirements with a unique understanding of local land ownership. This communal knowledge bank was often put to best use by setting clear limits to the changes that French administrators could safely impose. Limited cooperation with the demands of colonial government, sometimes depicted as a patron-client-style relationship, could thus be read differently: as a form of long-term resistance through which at least some of the long-established practices of peasant farming, community life, and village self-rule were upheld.[15]

These caveats aside, Algeria's place at the forefront of the French colonial system was assured in the 1870s. Furthermore, French imperial ambitions elsewhere were checked. The attempt to delimit a sphere of economic interest in Mexico during the 1860s failed. By 1881 the British

Ironically, the French political crisis brewing over Indochina in late 1950 briefly simmered down in the coming year. This was in large part thanks to the remarkable military successes achieved by General Jean de Lattre de Tassigny. The General was a newcomer to Vietnam, sent there to assume civil and military command of the war in the wake of the Cao Bang defeat. The outstanding French commander of the war, de Lattre, thwarted the Vietminh's 1951 offensives in Tonkin and temporarily strengthened the French grip over Hanoi and its hinterland.[74] The impressive French military intelligence system was further improved. And de Lattre injected fresh impetus into the arduous process of building a Vietnamese army loyal to Bao Daï.[75] Buoyed by his reputation but terminally ill with cancer, de Lattre visited Washington in September 1951 to secure increases in military aid to French and Vietnamese army forces.[76] His spectacular, if fleeting, success in 1951 encouraged even Foreign Minister Robert Schuman, never much of an enthusiast for the war, to press the case for extended operations against the Vietminh.[77]

The French military impetus built up in 1951, the miraculous 'année de Lattre' dissipated in 1952. Neither of de Lattre's successors, Generals Raoul Salan and Henri Navarre, could emulate his success.[78] Nor did the French authorities sustain the consolidation of the Vietnamese army, the creation of which was pivotal to the survival of the Bao Daï régime. 'Vietnamization' of the war continued, but the Vietnamese army, although expanding and highly combative, was hamstrung by its French commanders who remained sceptical that it could operate independently.[79] In similar vein, French political intervention indicated time and again that the Associated States remained under neocolonial control. The abrupt decision of René Mayer's government to devalue the Indochinese piastre in May 1953 undermined all three Associated State governments. Infuriated by such high-handed French action, Prince Sihanouk seized the initiative, demanding and, in November 1953, securing full Cambodian independence.

By then the political climate in Paris was very different. War weariness had taken its toll among the parties previously committed to the war, the MRP especially. Public opposition to the conflict was also more vocal. Human rights campaigners, leading intellectuals, Church youth groups, and liberal journalists, particularly in the Catholic press, in Le Monde, and in the newly established weekly, L'Express, formed a cohesive anti-war lobby.[80] In late 1953 Dwight D. Eisenhower's Republican administration also pressed the new French government under Joseph Laniel to grant real independence to the governments in Phom Penh, Luang Prabang, and Saigon.[81] The Associated States idea imploded.

Meanwhile, Vietminh commanders and their CMAG advisers had learnt from the failure of their 1951 offensives. They resumed less costly guerrilla warfare and built up their arsenal of Chinese military supplies. With Ho Chi Minh still their president and Truong Chinh as General Secretary, the Vietnamese Communists, since February 1951 renamed as the Vietnamese Workers Party (VWP or Dang Lao Dong Viet Nam), were now openly committed to pursuit of the war within a Marxist-Leninist framework that prioritized eviction of the French over the revolutionary transformation of rural Vietnam.[82] The VWP Politburo agreed with the Beijing government that their first task was to secure North Western Vietnam and Upper Laos as a prelude to a further attack against the Red River Delta. As a result, after a series of advances southward from their Viet Bac stronghold, Giap's troops opened the Xam Neua offensive in Upper Laos in late March 1953. By the time of the Korean armistice on 27 July 1953, the Vietminh was in a commanding position.[83] Rural revolution was not entirely postponed. Within liberated zones, the VWP imposed a strict agrarian regime. In highly effective propaganda campaign, the VWP publicized the fact that it would 'suspend' the distribution of communal land to peasants that served Bao Daï. Tightening VWP control over the countryside contrasted with the Emperor's attempt to win the loyalty of potential recruits through a series of land reforms in 1953. Bao Daï's efforts were undermined by the strength of opposition he encountered from Vietnamese landlords along the Red River and Mekong deltas.[84]

Dien Bien Phu, the Geneva conference, and the French withdrawal

The end of the Korean War permitted a further expansion in Chinese aid. But it also freed the United States to provision General Navarre's plan to secure Cochin China and southern Annam prior to an eventual advance on the north.[85] Furthermore, with the Korean War over and Soviet policy in flux after Stalin's death in March, the governments in Moscow and Beijing began diplomatic efforts in late September 1953 to convene a major East-West conference to ease Cold War tensions. In practice, the much-vaunted – and now better equipped – 'Navarre Plan' and the resumption of diplomatic efforts to end the war went together. Navarre's core objective, in other words, was not to defeat the Hanoi regime but to present it with the unwelcome prospect of a costly campaign of attrition to winkle out French forces.[86] Viewed from a French perspective, the diplomacy was to succeed where Navarre's military efforts failed. At the Berlin conference in January 1954, the Eisenhower administration and its French and British allies endorsed the Soviet proposal for a conference at Geneva to discuss peace in Korea and Indochina. The Vietminh's continuing military gains, Navarre's increasingly desperate schemes to slow them, and the entire outcome of the Indochina War, were likely to rest on the decisions of the superpowers. Here was Potsdam all over again. Just as the Vietminh neared definitive victory, international diplomacy conspired to thwart them.

For the French, the price of US aid was the integration of Indochina into American strategic planning in South East Asia, something in which France was bound to play a diminished role after the collapse of the Associated States project in late 1953. It was difficult for French political leaders to spurn Washington's requirements. American frustration with the course of the Indochina War added fuel to the Eisenhower administration's anger over fading French enthusiasm for the US-backed European Defence Community, a project designed, in large part, to facilitate West German rearmament and so ease the strategic burden carried by US forces in mainland Europe. With the eventual solution of West Germany's rearmament under NATO auspices yet to be devised, successive French governments in 1952–4 were poorly placed to question the advice that accompanied American assistance in Vietnam. It took Pierre Mendès France, who returned to office as premier and Foreign Minister on 19 June 1954, to break out of this vicious circle by rejecting further involvement in the EDC and Vietnam at a stroke.

The Geneva conference was scheduled to begin in April 1954. As conference preparations got underway a fortified garrison at the apex of communications between Tonkin, Upper Laos, and China became the Indochina War's focal point. Captured by French paratroops on 20 November 1953, the Dien Bien Phu fortress held as much symbolic as strategic importance. It signified a last French attempt to prevent Vietminh domination of northern Indochina. The ensuing battle was the one engagement of the war to dominate media coverage in France. As French fortunes worsened, so public fixation grew with the stoical self-sacrifice of a doomed force. In a tragic case of life imitating art, the Dien Bien Phu garrison fulfilled all the stock requirements of colonial heroism that had dominated literary and cinematic depictions of empire for decades. Dien Bien Phu became 'le Verdun tropical', and France's leading photojournalism weekly, *Paris Match*, devoted an unprecedented five cover stories to the battle. As national interest heightened, press and newsreel reportage succumbed to racial stereotypes; the brave defenders resisting wave after wave of attacks by fanatical Vietminh hordes. The fact that the fortress garrison contained a large proportion of colonial troops was conveniently overlooked.[87]

Giap's attacking forces were anything but irrational. They systematically isolated Dien Bien Phu's hinterland by conducting subsidiary attacks in Upper Laos, Annam, and the Red River Delta. Giap's commanders then organized the delivery of unprecedented quantities of Chinese military supplies by truck and via lengthy columns of peasant irregulars that snaked their way through the surrounding jungle. It was a gargantuan effort and a triumph of mass mobilization. Thus equipped with everything from small arms to additional heavy artillery, Vietminh troops attacked Dien Bien Phu on 30 March 1954. Once Vietminh shelling destroyed the nearby airfield the defending garrison was in a hopeless position. French attempts to parachute in supplies were largely ineffective. By contrast, Chinese supplies to the Vietminh attackers included 2.4 million bullets, 60,000 artillery shells, and state of the art rocket launchers, used to devastating effect to breach the last French redoubts.[88] These logistical statistics point to a much bigger conclusion: the war's original asymmetry had been reversed.

At the military level, the key to Dien Bien Phu lay in the success of Vietminh strategy and supply. At the emotional level, the battle registered most immediately in the French media's obsession with the gallantry of the fortress defenders. But, at the political level, the protracted siege was painted on the larger canvas of international diplomacy. After the garrison fell on 7 May 1954, the main figures in this broader landscape were not the Vietnamese or the French, but the other parties to the Geneva conference: Chinese Foreign Minister Zhou Enlai, US Secretary of State John Foster Dulles, and British Foreign Secretary Anthony Eden.[89] The Chinese, Americans, and British each had distinct agendas. The Chinese delegation was anxious to end their country's international isolation. Zhou Enlai was prepared to see communism confined to northern Vietnam, with Laos and Cambodia made neutral buffer states adjacent to non-communist Thailand and Malaya. Zhou's moderation meshed with British efforts to secure a compromise peace in Indochina. Winston Churchill's government favoured a spheres of influence agreement that would preserve Britain's imperial interests in South East Asia through American protection and the assurance of Chinese non-intervention. For his part, French premier Mendès France forced the conference delegates to agree a decision swiftly. Mendès declared his intention to resign as Prime Minister unless a settlement was reached at Geneva within a month of his taking office in mid-June 1954.[90]

Together, the Chinese and British teams at Geneva stymied the more ambitious American project to resist any advance of communism in South East Asia. Dulles had earlier proposed the idea of 'united action' on 29 March 1954, in line with his wider support for 'Liberation' policies in areas of the developing world threatened by communism. Had the proposal succeeded, it would have required the French to fight on in Indochina as part of a new anti-communist alliance grouping the United States, Britain, France, Australia, New Zealand, the Philippines, Thailand, and the Associated States. In fact, the plan attracted little support either within Eisenhower's government or in Congress. It carried the obvious danger of American involvement in another ground war in Asia less than a year after the preceding one – in support of South Korea – had come to its inconclusive end. Nor did America's allies approve of the idea. Congress, the US service departments, and even Dulles's senior State Department advisers, knew that 'united action' and air strikes in support of the Dien Bien Phu garrison would have internationalized the Vietnam conflict.[91] But the project's failure left Dulles and Bao Daï's ministers sulking on the fringes at Geneva.[92] Their ill temper concealed the fact that the conference's real losers were the Vietminh.

The Geneva settlement restricted DRV authority to Vietnam north of the 17th parallel although the Vietminh controlled three quarters of the country when it signed a ceasefire accord on 20 July 1954. The monarchies of Laos and Cambodia now enjoyed international protection as neutral states. Worst of all, a South Vietnam state was formally recognized pending countrywide elections scheduled for July 1956. Neither side expected these to pass off as planned. In the interval, first the French, and then, far more so, the Americans did all they could to prevent outright Vietminh victory.[93] The movement of anti-communist Vietnamese into South Vietnam was encouraged, and the increasingly dictatorial South Vietnam government headed by Ngo Dinh Diem began its fatal dalliance with America. If French ministers and the Saigon High Commission may be blamed for conniving in schemes for war in 1945–6, after 1954 the French were bit players in seeding the ground for the more cataclysmic second Vietnam War. The advent of new protagonists in the Indochina conflict was tragic proof of the disastrous consequences of violent decolonization becoming subsumed in Cold War rivalry. Ironically, Charles de Gaulle, an original protagonist of the Indochina reconquest, realized only too well that American interventionism would probably end in disaster. Reinstalled as French presidential leader of the new Fifth Republic, he saw his 1964 proposals for Vietnam's neutralization rejected. Thereafter de Gaulle became an unlikely Vietnam War peacenik, proclaiming Vietnam's right to self-determination much to the annoyance of the French left, for whom such a complete Gaullist turnaround barely a decade after the original Indochina War seemed hard to credit.[94]

Conclusion

From the beginning of the first Indochina War to its dismal end, French governments never wholeheartedly pursued any of the objectives for which France was supposedly fighting. The initial war of colonial reconquest, allegedly integral to the reassertion of French international power, was all but abandoned by the end of 1947. It was, by then, evident that the Vietminh could not be entirely ousted from Tonkin. As for political initiatives, the Along Bay accords were always an unhappy compromise between restricted autonomy and the promise of eventual independence. There was an inherent contradiction between a French military campaign to guarantee the survival of a loyal Vietnamese state and the fact that the war itself sapped residual Vietnamese loyalty to any non-Vietminh alternative. Regardless of Bao Daï's shortcomings as a respected national leader and the instability of Cabinet government in Saigon, no Vietnamese regime could compete with the Vietminh for popular legitimacy.

Roosevelt's central criticism of France in Indochina was that the masses still lived in penury. In a fast-expanding population overwhelmingly tied to subsistence agriculture, French failure to enact substantial land reform after decades in charge was a searing indictment of colonial rule. Nor did Bao Daï fare much better, unable to overcome entrenched settler and landlord hostility to any reduction in their privileges. This made the Vietminh task far easier. The true meaning of people's war was apparent in the mobilization of DRV-controlled zones, first in the Viet Bac, and then far beyond it, in support of Vietminh operations. Frequently ruthless in tightening its grip upon the population, the ICP, and its later incarnation, the VWP, was, nevertheless, sustained by the Vietnamese peasantry's support. In sharp contrast, the political edifice built around Bao Daï was full of cracks, its foundations undermined by membership of the French Union with all the political, economic, and cultural subordination that this implied.

Finally, after Mao's victory in China and the massive increase in Vietminh military potential that followed, the French strategic position worsened rapidly. The year 1951 may have been the exception that proved the rule, but the *année de Lattre* was just that: a single year of achievement after which French fortunes declined once more. The expeditionary force certainly needed it, but the American military aid that sustained the last three years of the French war effort was always a source of friction in France's domestic politics. In 1953 alone, the war gobbled up some three thousand billion francs. It has been recently estimated that over the decade from 1946, France ploughed a yearly average of between 6 and 10 per cent of annual government expenditure into fighting the war in Indochina, a burden that impinged significantly on the rate of France's post-war reconstruction.[95] For what purpose? Apart from the high command in Saigon and the extraordinarily devoted professional cadres of the expeditionary force, from 1950 onwards it is hard to find any section of the French political community or the wider public that remained solidly committed to victory. Even Colonel de Castries, ill-fated commander of the Dien Bien Phu garrison, recognized that the nationalist ardour and revolutionary zeal of the Vietminh gave them the decisive edge over isolated professional troops honouring their contract of enlistment.[96] Much as it has been said by so many authors in so many contexts over so many years, the first Indochina War stands as one of the twentieth century's most costly and ultimately pointless conflicts, a sad testament to the futility of resisting decolonization.

CHAPTER 8
FROM FRENCH NORTH AFRICA TO MAGHREB INDEPENDENCE: DECOLONIZATION IN MOROCCO, TUNISIA, AND ALGERIA, 1945–56

The origins of colonial violence in French Algeria

The empire that France carved out in North West Africa began and ended in waves of violence. The port of Algiers and its surrounding coastal hinterland was swiftly captured during June and July 1830 by a 34,000 strong French expeditionary force dispatched in a 635-ship armada from Toulon. The fleet set sail at the behest of King Charles X following a diplomatic quarrel with the Algiers authorities. The expedition marked a last-ditch attempt to prop up the Bourbon regime against gathering opposition in France. In the event, the seizure of Algiers proved much more long lasting than the Bourbon Monarchy, which was ousted from power only days after the city was captured. The killings, army looting, sequestration of land and property, and general disregard for Muslim religious sensibilities that characterized this initial phase of the French conquest set the tone for the next forty years of military expansion and colonial settlement in Algeria.[1]

There was no long-term governmental scheme to colonize Algeria and make it the centrepiece of France's second colonial empire. But changes of regime in France drove the process forward. Throughout the 1830s and 1840s the Orléanist monarchy of Louis Philippe, anxious to legitimize its seizure of power, identified itself closely with the army's continuing Algerian conquest.[2] Yet, as the human and financial costs of conquering Algeria mounted, so, too, the colonial policy fragmented, becoming less a matter of royal decree or military fiat and more the result of competition between rival French stakeholders. In a pattern that would remain familiar until final decolonization a century later, what France did in Algeria – and how it justified its actions – reflected the interests of the French army, an expanding settler community, various land speculators and business interests, and the successive royal and republican regimes in office in nineteenth-century Paris.[3] Above all, the vigour and duration of Algerian resistance to French colonization drove the French military occupiers and the settlers that followed them towards increasing brutality and appropriation of Muslim lands.[4]

Localized armed resistance to the French presence continued in Algeria almost without interruption from 1830 to 1871. Its remarkable durability highlighted the integrity of Algeria's Muslim culture and confirmed that many Muslims recognized that they stood to lose everything.[5] The fight against colonization centred first on western Algeria where Emir 'Abd al-Qadir led a popular tribal uprising and established a proto-independent Algerian state from 1832 to 1847. In parallel to this, another rebellion, this time led by Ahmad ibn Mohammed (Ahmad Bey) of Constantine, denied the French control over much of eastern Algeria throughout the 1830s.

Determined to avert the humiliating failures of his predecessors, General Thomas Robert Bugeaud, appointed Governor in November 1840, crushed 'Abd al-Qadir's realm by the application of scorched earth tactics. Muslim civilians were targeted, homes and crops were burned, livestock slaughtered, and the rebellious population thereby denied the means of survival. In at least three cases, several hundred civilians were massacred by French troops, burned to death in caves where they had sought shelter. Such ruthlessness was as devastatingly effective in the short term as it was politically disastrous in the longer term.[6] 'Abd al-Qadir was driven into exile in Morocco and eventually surrendered to French forces in December 1847.[7] But his defeat brought with it a new wave of French land seizures that stirred implacable Muslim resentments. The end of 'Abd al-Qadir's nationwide movement shifted the focal point of indigenous unrest from the fertile plains and market centres to the more impenetrable highlands. In the 1860s and 1870s opposition to French rule became concentrated in two mountainous regions: the Aurès mountains in eastern Algeria, and Grand Kabylia, the main Berber region south-east of Algiers.

The pattern of French occupation set during the early conquest years remained intact for decades afterwards. Largely because of the intractable resistance encountered, the army remained at the forefront of administration and policymaking. From September 1834 a Government-General in Algiers reported directly to the War Minister in Paris. Even after the colonial government was opened up to civilian appointees, the colonial Governor ruled by decree. In other words, the Governor issued laws without prior parliamentary scrutiny of their content. This system continued, with some modification – consultative assemblies with limited powers of budgetary oversight were introduced in the early twentieth century – until 1946.

The scale of dispossession of Algeria's indigenous population was remarkable even by colonial standards. But the impact of settler land acquisition – for much of the nineteenth century, expropriation would be a more accurate term – on the indigenous population was uneven. In certain areas Muslims were entirely evicted from their ancestral lands. Around Blida, for instance, almost three quarters of cultivatable land was reallocated to the first wave of colonists that arrived in the 1840s.[8] Tribal populations that supported 'Abd al-Qadir's rebellion were punished by land confiscations and denial of grazing rights. Sedentary and nomadic clan groups linked to the Emir were driven from tribal lands into *cantonnements* policed by the army, usually in more arid, unfertile regions. Still more devastating was the 1863 *Senatus-Consulte*: a legislative code, the two central laws of which were passed on 22 April and 23 May of that year. With staggering disregard for the complexities of community allegiances in rural Algeria, the code delimited the territory of 709 officially designated 'tribes' and broke down landholding into recognized *douars* (rural administrative districts).[9] As intended, the measure hastened the detribalization of rural Algeria, facilitating another influx of *colon* farmers. A cholera epidemic in 1867 and a severe peasant famine the following year further decimated the Algerian peasantry.[10]

Algeria's importance to France was transformed by the impact of defeat in the Franco-Prussian War of 1870–1. The speed of Germany's victory and the punitive peace terms imposed, including loss of the French provinces of Alsace and Lorraine, provoked a change of regime in France. After its bloody suppression, the short-lived Paris Commune was succeeded by a new constitutional system: the Third Republic. Meanwhile, between January and October 1871 eastern Algeria was rocked by a major uprising centred on Grand Kabylia that triggered sporadic tribal violence and attacks on French interests that lasted for years. Following this rebellion, the

French colonial authorities embarked on a more systematic seizure of Algerian Muslim land. Former rebels saw their ancestral lands confiscated. Muslim farmers and absentee landlords lost their legal title to properties unless they could provide written proofs of ownership.[11] And huge areas of communally farmed Muslim common land were declared 'vacant' and therefore open to purchase by French agricultural settlers at nominal cost. One item of legislation was especially decisive: the Warnier Law of 26 July 1873 summarily introduced French property law to all transactions in Algerian land. It permitted dispossession of Muslim landowners who could not provide written proof of ownership – something rarely done under Muslim customary law.[12]

The coincidence of the loss of Alsace-Lorraine, the land sequestrations after the 1871 Algerian uprising, and the introduction of the Warnier Law together stimulated an unprecedented wave of French immigration to Algeria. Refugees from the two lost provinces, demobilized and unemployed soldiers from the recent Franco-Prussian War, former communards eager to get out of France, and French smallholders and peasant sharecroppers were all tempted by the prospect of cheap land and a new start in North Africa. In 1841 some 37,374 European settlers controlled only 40,000 hectares of land. After the suppression of the Kabylia insurrection and the Warnier Law, settler numbers rose to 412,435 and settler land ownership to 1.3 million hectares of land by 1881. By 1901 these figures climbed to 633,850 settlers in possession of 1.9 million hectares.[13]

The settler influx of the late nineteenth century, combined with the raft of laws, administrative discriminations, and land sequestrations that underpinned it, also provoked a sharper delineation of cultural identities – and the freedoms supposedly attached to them. As Lizabeth Zack notes, 'Assimilation-style colonization in the 1870s and 1880s reshuffled land, rights, and a sense of place in colonial Algeria, it accentuated distinctions and solidarities among "French," "Jews," "natives," "Algerians," and "neo-French/foreigners." The new laws and measures organized inhabitants into these groups and highlighted the boundaries around them.'[14] It would be going too far, though, to conclude that the social upheavals of the 1860s and 1870s tore at the fabric of Algerian rural communities so much that their capacity to resist colonial domination was broken. French attempts to impose European-style property rights, at odds with the communal farming practices and established Algerian patterns of landholding and transfer, were subverted by peasant cultivators who knew far better than French administrators the details of who farmed what, where, and for how long. Village assemblies, or *djemâa*, reorganized by French officials as part of the *Senatus-Consulte* reforms, exploited their position as intermediaries between colonial administration and local opinion to mitigate the impact of colonial edicts regarding rental payments and taxes. They, too, combined an intimate knowledge of farming patterns, livestock movements, and their community's food requirements with a unique understanding of local land ownership. This communal knowledge bank was often put to best use by setting clear limits to the changes that French administrators could safely impose. Limited cooperation with the demands of colonial government, sometimes depicted as a patron-client-style relationship, could thus be read differently: as a form of long-term resistance through which at least some of the long-established practices of peasant farming, community life, and village self-rule were upheld.[15]

These caveats aside, Algeria's place at the forefront of the French colonial system was assured in the 1870s. Furthermore, French imperial ambitions elsewhere were checked. The attempt to delimit a sphere of economic interest in Mexico during the 1860s failed. By 1881 the British usurped France's place in Egypt, taking unilateral control of the Suez Canal in the process. By contrast, possession of Algeria facilitated French expansion into neighbouring Tunisia in 1881, and into Morocco in the early twentieth century, paving the way for the formal establishment of the French Moroccan protectorate in 1912.

The protracted violence and societal dislocation that characterized the French conquest and colonization of Algeria was not replicated to anything like the same extent in Tunisia. In Morocco, however, even under the governorship of France's near-legendary first Resident-general, Marshal Louis-Hubert Lyautey, the extension of French control over the mountainous interior took decades of low-intensity warfare against Berber clans and other tribal communities.[16] This task of 'pacification' was formally declared over in 1934 by which time organized urban protest was fast becoming the major challenge to French imperialism in the Moroccan protectorate. Rural opposition to French rule was always weaker in Tunisia, a far smaller country and a predominantly Arab society in which most political activity centred on the town. It was in Tunisia's major urban centres, for example, that Arab trade unionism first became firmly established among the industrial labour force.[17] A bitter dock strike in the ports of Tunis and Bizerta in late 1924 saw the rise to prominence of the French empire's first Arab trade union confederation. The Confédération Générale du Travailleurs Tunisiens (CGTT) was modelled on, though not supported by, its French counterpart, the CGT. The movement's founders, M'hamed Ali and Tahar Haddad, were committed to the advancement of Arab workers' rights. Both men were jailed in 1925 for their activities. Their detention highlighted the racial discrimination characteristic of North African industrial relations and the colonial shop floor.[18] More broadly, the development of indigenous trade unionism across interwar French North Africa suffered a body blow in the late 1930s. After the bloody industrial confrontations of the Popular Front era in 1936–8, trade union activity was proscribed, remaining outlawed throughout the Second World War. By the early 1950s, however, mass trade unions had recovered lost influence and were a major factor in nationalist politics in Tunisia and Morocco.

Clearly then, in the Maghreb's three French-ruled territories, collectively given the administrative appellation of French North Africa, the encounter with French colonialism varied markedly. Yet for all their differences, the development of anti-colonial nationalism in each territory followed a similar trajectory. In Morocco and Tunisia the dominant nationalist parties, the Istiqlal (Constitution) Party and the Neo Destour, had interwar roots among young Arab students, intellectuals, and bourgeois junior *fonctionnaires*.[19] In Algeria too, nationalist groups of various stripe emerged in the interwar period. Many of their supporters also drew inspiration from the powerful reaffirmation of Algeria's cultural identity as a Muslim nation articulated by the country's leading Koranic scholars, organized into the Association of reformist 'ulama.[20] As became apparent during the putative uprising in and around the eastern towns of Sétif and Guelma in May 1945, 'ulama leaders lent the power of moral authority to nationalist resistance.[21] Throughout the post-war decade 'ulama clerics decried the iniquities of colonialism and rejected the possibility of compromise with French authority. The logical culmination of their assertion that true Algerians were inalienably Muslim was a *fatwa* declaring it impermissible for true believers to accept French citizenship through naturalization.[22] It bears emphasis, however, that, before 1940, there were two poles of attraction in Algerian nationalism – one strongly cultural and located in Algiers, the other overtly political and centred in France. The most radical among these early nationalist groups – Messali Hadj's Etoile Nord-Africaine and its 1930s' progeny, the Parti Populaire Algérien – originated in the squalid tenements of northern Paris among the Algerian community of immigrant workers.[23]

If political longevity was one aspect of post-war Algerian nationalism, generational change was another. The Front de Libération Nationale (FLN), the organization that would mount a violent challenge to French authority, was characterized by its youthful membership, few of whom had direct links with the Messalists. This was evident in the FLN's forerunner, the Organisation Spéciale (OS), developed in the late 1940s as the PPA's paramilitary wing. In 1949 the average age of OS 'general staff' members was only twenty-seven.[24] Many of these young militants, such as Hocine Ait Ahmed, future international spokesman for the FLN, drew inspiration from the Vietminh's armed struggle, as well as from Nasser's assertion of secular pan-Arabism.[25] In their recognition of the necessity both for external aid and the mobilization of international support, several of the tenets of OS thinking would later come to fruition in the transnational strategy of the FLN so well documented by Matthew Connelly.[26] Not surprisingly, the French army and police cracked down hard against the OS from 1950 onwards, with Maurice Papon, erstwhile Vichy collaborator and future Paris police chief, playing a central part in the formulation and implementation of the colonial authorities' repression.[27] But the FLN would prove a different proposition for Papon and his successors.[28] Part ruthless terrorist group, part socialist front, part defender of Muslim rights, and, albeit only in the latter stages of the Algerian War, a genuine mass movement, the French authorities never got the measure of the FLN.[29] But, before discussing the course of nationalist protest and rebellion in the three North African territories, it is worth considering the nature of the colonial cities in which, for the most part, these activities occurred.

Urban growth and communal division in French North Africa

Historians of French urbanism demonstrate that the colonial cities of the Maghreb were laboratories in which ambitious official schemes of urban regeneration were first enacted. The formalization of metropolitan town planning regulations immediately after the First World War drew directly on the earlier ideas of Lyautey's urban planners in the Moroccan protectorate and a century's accumulated experience of demolition and redesign in colonial Algiers. In official rhetoric, the housing projects, public hygiene systems, new boulevards, and settler towns that sprang up from Casablanca to Tunis were lauded as concrete proof of imperial benevolence. In practice, colonial urban planning was driven by several overlapping concerns. It was imperative that French security forces gain easier access to Muslim urban space to establish control over the indigenous populations of casbahs and, from the late 1930s, the shantytowns, or *bidonvilles* that encircled the major cities. In Morocco especially, the Lyautey administration also imposed a more formal racial and economic segregation between affluent and spacious settler new towns and the densely populated Muslim quarters of the old cities. This was a practice emulated and extended in Algiers where the main casbah was effectively hemmed in by settler-dominated suburbs and the main administrative and commercial districts near the city's old port.[30]

After his appointment in 1946, Michel Ecochard, director of French urban planning in Morocco, continued the tradition established by Lyautey and his chief architectural planner,

Henri Prost, in the first years of the protectorate. Morocco thus remained a favoured experimental location in which ambitious urban design could be implemented free of the legal restrictions and special interests that constrained French local government. More important, the regulation of urbanization in the Maghreb's fast-expanding post-war cities mirrored settler demands for space, exclusivity, and protection of their property.[31] Morocco's settler-dominated *villes nouvelles*, set apart from the more densely populated Muslim and Jewish quarters, certainly marked an improvement on the wholesale destruction of Muslim housing in the early phases of French colonization in Algeria. But they reinforced a racial segregation between Europeans and the Muslim majority. As wealth was the surest route to improved housing, a class divide was superimposed onto this racial division.[32] Economic disparities and spatial segregation between rich and poor, settlers and Muslims, were never total. Europeans and Muslims interacted on a daily basis at work, in the streets, on farmland, and even in shared apartment blocks. Settlers in Algeria especially were conflicted between their desire to preserve their social superiority over the Muslim majority and their immersion in an adopted French-Algerian culture that was, in part, assimilated to the Arab-Berber lifestyle. Often lampooned by the metropolitan French as uncultured and crude, in Ali Yedes's words,

> The European Algerians thrived on opposites and contradictions: they wanted to be Algerian but did not want to be associated with the indigenous Algerian character, nor did they accept the Metropolitan French conception of themselves as 'Pied Noir'; on the other hand they wished to be French, while insisting on their being different from the French of France. ... Alienated in Algeria, alienated in France, the European Algerians were in the end perfect foreigners ... remaining in constant search for an ever-elusive identity.[33]

As the pressures of urbanization increased from the 1930s onwards, the marriage between the aesthetics of French urban design and the requirements of social and political control broke down. Casablanca's population of Moroccan Arabs and Berbers grew by over 300 per cent between 1936 and 1952, many of them only able to find accommodation in the city's fast-growing shantytowns to which many were effectively confined.[34] One consequence of this colonial 'urban apartheid' was more chronic overcrowding in the Muslim quarters of French North Africa's principal cities, not just Casablanca, but also Rabat, Oran, and, above all, Algiers.[35] These urban districts became forcing grounds for nationalist ideas.

By 1949 as many as 64,000 Algerians were crammed into the thirty-eight hectares of the Algiers upper casbah that would become the nerve centre of FLN operations in the impending war of independence. *Bidonvilles* also grew dramatically during the 1950s, particularly as migrants fled the violence and economic hardship of rural areas such as Kabylia.[36] The casbah acquired legendary status on both sides of the political divide in the Algerian War. To the city authorities, it symbolized the failure of previous urban planning. To the military, it was shorthand for Muslim sedition. To the wider French public it still represented the exotic impenetrability of Muslim society. By contrast, for the Algerians themselves, the Algiers casbah was the beating heart of the national revolution, at once an enduring symbol of defiance in the face of French military ruthlessness and a monumental testament to the inequity of colonial dominance.[37] Hardly surprising then, that the last major economic modernization schemes of the colonial era, Algiers Mayor Jacques Chevallier's 'Agence de Plan' devised in 1954, and the

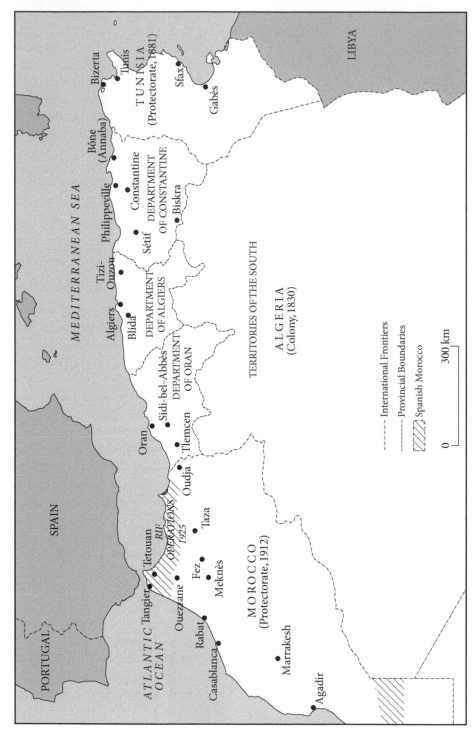

Map 7 French North African territories.

Constantine Plan launched by General de Gaulle in October 1959, focused on new housing projects and basic educational provision as ways to overcome the ethnic segregation and social exclusion that blighted urban politics in French North Africa.[38]

The struggles for independence in Morocco and Tunisia, 1950–6

These internal dynamics of colonial society cannot alone explain decolonization in the Maghreb. Historians of the final years of France's rule in its two North African protectorates agree that the march towards independence resulted, in part, from nationalist protest and, in part, from external pressures. Some pay most attention to local politics, making the North African peoples the principal agents of their own political freedom. Others suggest that, while internal factors were vital, wider international changes determined the rhythm and content of negotiations and the final form that national independence took. It makes no sense to impose a rigid dichotomy between these two approaches, partly because decolonization is rarely reducible to a single cause, and partly because North African nationalist leaders actively sought the involvement of the international community to bolster their demands for French concessions. Even so, in the Morocco and Tunisia of the early 1950s, it does seem that decolonization was acutely sensitive to outside pressure. Of these extraneous factors, perhaps three stand out. First were the stress fractures in the French body politic caused by the loss of the Indochina War in 1954 and the outbreak of the Algerian conflict soon after. Second was the gathering weight of international opposition to French colonialism in North Africa, expressed primarily through the United Nations, the Arab League, and various meetings of the Non-Aligned Movement in the early 1950s. In each case, fellow Muslim countries and former colonial states led calls for accelerated reform and French withdrawal, demands that were deftly exploited by Moroccan and Tunisian nationalists eager to internationalize their cause. Closely related to these first two factors was the third: the US' growing interest in the long-term stability and pro-Western orientation of the Arab world in general and North West Africa in particular.

By 1950 the basic lines of division between French authority and nationalist opposition in Morocco and Tunisia were clear. At the level of high politics in Rabat and Tunis, there was an uneasy coexistence between dominant nationalist parties, the French Residencies, and the indigenous monarchical administrations of the Moroccan Sultan and the Tunisian Bey. Most of the time, each of the participants in these triangular relationships recognized that political progress could only be achieved by co-opting at least one of the other two. Furthermore, the two monarchical regimes and most nationalist politicians accepted the wisdom of close relations with France after independence. A French presence in Morocco and Tunisia – economic, strategic, political, and cultural – endured, albeit in reduced form, after final independence terms were agreed in early 1956. What did change after 1950 was the basic conception of Moroccan and Tunisian self-government at issue. Seen in this light, the narrative of Franco-Moroccan and Franco-Tunisian negotiations in the early 1950s is one of widening parameters. From initial discussion of limited internal autonomy with continuing French control over the troika of foreign affairs, defence, and finance, talks eventually encompassed full independence and something approaching amicable interstate relations between France and its former protectorates. To use the French political jargon of the time, 'co-sovereignty', a code for limited autonomy and enduring French influence, gave way to 'partnership'.

From our perspective, the more interesting dimension to this shift is whether it may be counted a successful decolonization. Here, the temptation to draw comparisons with the descent to violence in Algeria may be misleading. Admittedly, the French administrations in Morocco and Tunisia avoided full-blown national rebellion and managed to retain important privileges for France in the ultimate independence settlements. But to measure events in the two North African protectorates against the scale of colonial breakdown in Algeria is unsatisfactory for several reasons. For one thing, it makes light of the extent of popular protest and inter-communal violence that punctuated the course of negotiations over Moroccan and Tunisian self-rule. For another, it suggests that the two protectorates were on different political trajectories to that of Algeria. This last point deserves closer attention.

Similarities in the socioeconomic and political structures of Morocco, Tunisia, and Algeria also concealed important differences. Morocco shared Algeria's heterogeneous demographic composition with large Arab and Berber populations rubbing shoulders, but Tunisia remained a more singularly Arab country. All three contained substantial settler populations as well as established urban Jewish communities. In each case, settlement was predominantly confined to northern cities and their fertile hinterlands while, in Morocco and Algeria, lasting opposition to colonization remained strongest in the mountainous interior. However, the social structures and political engagements that developed from Franco-Muslim interaction in Morocco and Tunisia differed fundamentally from those in Algeria. Morocco's powerful *caïds* and other urban notables and Tunisia's highly organized trade unionism set them apart. Algeria also lacked an indigenous monarchical administration to bridge the gap between imperial conservatism and radical mass nationalism. Here we return to the triangular relationships mentioned earlier. Their importance becomes apparent if we consider the final steps to negotiated independence in the early 1950s.

In June 1950 a new Resident-general, Louis Périllier, took up his post in Tunis. Acting in tune with Foreign Minister Robert Schuman, Périllier rekindled stalled negotiations over Tunisian internal autonomy. Disagreement persisted over extensions to the franchise, the relative weight of Arab and settler influence in local and national assemblies, and restrictions on the power of French advisers within Tunisia's government. The French strategy was to focus on municipal, rather than national, reform. By contrast, the Tunisian Bey and the Neo Destour executive preferred to discuss issues of national importance, in particular, the creation of a democratically elected Constituent Assembly and an end to French powers of oversight over Tunisia's existing government.[39] One side or the other would have to give ground if progress were to be made.

Talks over constitutional reform followed a similar path in Morocco. Here, Sultan Mohammed V played the decisive role in pushing matters forward. His appointment of an Imperial Moroccan Cabinet in September 1950 enabled the country's major nationalist party, the Istiqlal, to assume a decisive role in Moroccan government. Whereas Tunisia's Bey kept Neo Destour at arm's length during the reform process, Mohammed V embraced Istiqlalist nationalism wholeheartedly. This was confirmed on 11 October when the Sultan issued three core demands reflective of Istiqlal policy: increased educational opportunities for young Muslims; greater Moroccan control over internal administration; and the right for Moroccan workers to organize trade unions. Met with an evasive French reply, the Sultan stunned René Pleven's Paris government on 2 November 1950 by suggesting immediate talks on abolition of the 1912 Treaty of Fez. The treaty was the protectorate's legal foundation stone and, so the French mistakenly presumed, the basis of the Sultan's political authority.[40]

Deadlocked over permissible reform, during 1951 to 1953 the Moroccan and Tunisian paths to independence diverged. In Morocco French efforts to break the alliance between the Sultanate and the Istiqlal took a fatal turn. In January 1951 France's Resident-general, General Alphonse Juin, an Algerian-born hardliner, threatened Mohammed V with deposition unless he moderated his demands. Meanwhile, French regional administrators worked up Berber resentment against the predominantly Arab Istiqlal, making the most of their ties with conservative pachas and *caïds* who stood to lose influence in any Istiqlal-dominated Sultanate. During 1951 the French Foreign Ministry also pressed ahead with plans to widen the franchise for elections to the Moroccan section of the country's Government Council, exploiting franchise reform as a means to increase rural and Berber influence in government at the expense of the Istiqlal heartland in the cities of the north. Finally, the Residency called a snap election in a bid to deny the Istiqlal time to mobilize its supporters. This was classic divide and rule, and it was typified by French investment in Si T'hami el-Glaoui, pacha of Marrakesh and southern Morocco's most revered *grand caïd*.[41]

The greater urgency evident in French actions in Morocco received further stimulation from the block of Arab-Asian states at the United Nations. Their efforts from 1951 onwards to engage both the UN General Assembly and the Security Council in North African affairs caused profound alarm in Paris. It had long been an article of faith for imperial powers that the United Nations had no jurisdictional competence to interfere in internal colonial affairs. But the UN's successful supervision of Libya's transition to full independence in 1950, as well as the communist bloc's interest in promoting anti-Western self-rule across the colonial world, made it hard to remain sanguine about UN non-intervention.[42] The key variable here was the United States. Since Roosevelt's death in April 1945, America's deepening strategic commitment to its Western European allies overshadowed the residual attachment to historical anti-colonialism. However, while Washington dug deeper in support of the French position in Indochina after 1950, it had less reason to do so in North Africa where the principal representatives of nationalist opinion seemed relatively moderate and pro-Western. With Arab neutralism gathering impetus after Gamal Abdel Nasser's seizure of power at the head of Egypt's Free Officers Movement in July 1952, it was clearly to America's advantage to cultivate a long-term working relationship with the Istiqlal and the Neo Destour, political parties which, whatever the French arguments to the contrary, seemed to speak for the majority of their Moroccan and Tunisian compatriots. If, for reasons of strategy, economics, culture, and creed, France took precedence over North Africa in US governmental calculations, for much of the 1950s, first the Truman and then the Eisenhower administrations nonetheless favoured a more rapid transition to independence for the Maghreb states than French opinion would tolerate.[43]

Little wonder that Antoine Pinay's centre-right conservative coalition government was furious when, in October 1952, the Arab-Asian block lobbied successfully for UN General Assembly consideration of the Tunisian situation. Worse still, the American delegation, anxious not to lose friends in the developing world, defended the UN's right to discuss such colonial matters.[44] In fact, the US decision, due in part to sophisticated Neo Destour propaganda in Washington and New York, made excellent sense. With Neo Destour's talismanic leader, Habib Bourguiba, held in detention throughout the early 1950s and with Tunisia's Bey, Sidi Lamine, disinclined to follow Mohammed V in championing the nationalist cause, it was closer international scrutiny of French behaviour in Tunisia that eventually kick-started the reform process back into life. This did not come about overnight, nor was it exclusively attributable to UN pressure. It took the advent of a new French government in January 1953 led by a Radical Party stalwart René Mayer, a boycott of May 1953 local elections by both Neo Destour and the Tunisian Socialist Party, and the appointment of another reformist Resident-general, Pierre Voizard, before the French conceded broader reforms. But the prospect of condemnation in the General Assembly's autumn 1953 session undoubtedly encouraged the promulgation of a package of concessions on 26 September.

Announced by Voizard in Tunis these measures ranged from the lifting of press censorship and the transfer of responsibility for local policing to the release of political prisoners (though not Bourguiba). Their underlying purpose was twofold: to foster dialogue with nationalist moderates and to deflect UN criticism of French repression.[45] Additional concessions followed on 4 March 1954, when Voizard promised to broaden Tunisian participation in local and national government, although the Residency retained its ultimate veto over all major policy decisions. To sweeten the pill, Bourguiba was also transferred from the Tunisian island of Galite to more congenial enforced residency on Groix, an island off the Brittany coast. It made no difference. Unlike the Bey who was willing to negotiate on Voizard's terms, the Neo Destour leader urged his followers to reject the latest proposals and insist on full independence. Meanwhile, a popular and predominantly rural insurgency covertly supported by the Neo Destour intensified over the early summer months with targeted attacks on soldiers, police, and settlers, and a boycott of French products and businesses.[46] By mid-1954 then, the most burning questions in Tunisian politics were these: When would Bourguiba be freed? When would the Residency concede control over Tunisia's internal affairs? And when would a French government accept that only face-to-face negotiations with Neo Destour and the Bey could achieve real progress?

Dialogue over internal autonomy in Morocco had collapsed earlier and even more dramatically than in Tunisia. The failure of the 1951 elections and the threat of a renewed UN General Assembly debate on Morocco in late 1952 made little impact on Rabat Residency policy, by this point directed by Juin's replacement, another army appointee, General Augustin Guillaume. Municipal reforms were preferred to national democratization and settler privileges were to be safeguarded.[47] The Istiqlal and the Sultan therefore redoubled their efforts to mobilize domestic support and win international sympathy for Moroccan independence. They were joined in this by Morocco's one legalized trade union, the Union Générale des Syndicats Confédérés du Maroc (UGSCM), which organized demonstrations in Casablanca as part of a wider strike action on 7 and 8 December 1952 to protest against the murder of the Tunisian trade union leader, Ferhad Ached, three days earlier. The ensuing clashes between demonstrators, riot police, troops, and settlers left untold numbers of Moroccans dead in what was immediately dubbed 'the Casablanca massacre'.[48] The killings provoked a Residency ban on the Istiqlal as a seditious organization, a move decried in a formal UN appeal for the resumption of Franco-Moroccan negotiations issued on 17 December.[49] Locking up Istiqlalist leaders not only triggered wider public protests but also intensified the rivalry between the leading urban nationalist movement and supporters of an incipient insurgency in the Berber-dominated regions of the High Atlas Mountains, the Armée de Libération Marocaine (ALM). Competition and violence between the Istiqlal and the ALM would become an increasingly significant facet of Morocco's internal politics as the country neared independence, something that imperial administrators were, on occasion, willing to exploit.[50] But during 1953 the political focus remained on the high politics of the Sultanate.

During the early months of that year Mohammed V faced concerted pressure from the Residency and a loose coalition of Muslim Brotherhoods and conservative *caïds* led by Abdelhaï el-Kittani and el-Glaoui, the pacha of Marrakech, to sever all ties with the nationalists. The alternative was deposition. Although other notables and Muslim religious leaders rallied to the Sultan's defence, Guillaume and Foreign Minister Georges Bidault were determined to press home their advantage, hoping to corner Mohammed V into acceptance of the very municipal reforms the Sultan had previously rejected as inadequate. This was dangerous brinkmanship, which made light of the civil disorders that erupted as sectarian divisions deepened. The Sultan behaved more responsibly than his French adversaries and their local clients. After weeks of deadlock, on the evening of 13 August 1953 he gave way, accepting the Residency's municipal reform plan in order to avert further violence between his supporters and those of his opponents.[51]

It was now that the extent of the French gamble – miscalculation might be more accurate – became clear. Guillaume, Bidault, and French Interior Minister, Léon Martinaud Déplat, acting without the full assent of either Prime Minister Joseph Laniel or the full French Cabinet, had used the conservative Moroccan opposition to impose their will on the Sultan.[52] But the manipulators were, in turn, manipulated. Unimpressed by Mohammed V's concessions, el-Kettani and el-Glaoui redoubled their demands for the Sultan to go, pushing his uncle, Sidi Moulay Mohammed Ben Arafa, as replacement. Meanwhile, clashes between both sides' supporters worsened, with Europeans often targeted. In the worst of these incidents, on 16 August rioters slaughtered at least forty-three settlers in the eastern border town of Oujda.[53] More protracted violence between el-Glaoui's predominantly Berber forces and those loyal to the Sultan looked possible, meaning that the French army would have to intervene. Guillaume was therefore compelled to act. On 20 August he forced Mohammed V and his two sons into abdication, dispatching them by plane to Corsica.[54] By nurturing el-Glaoui's conservative opposition, the Residency, the Foreign Ministry, and a coterie of senior ministers first in René Mayer's and then in Joseph Laniel's 1953 governments had created a monster they could not ultimately control. Far from removing an obstacle to Residency policy, Mohammed V's deposition cemented his reputation as a nationalist champion, making it impossible to proceed with meaningful reforms in his absence. Internationally, the deposition united critics of Residency policy and destroyed France's reputation as a 'protecting power' in Morocco. The events of August 1953 were truly a watershed that hastened the French exit from Morocco.

As in Tunisia, so in Morocco, a decisive political breakthrough required fundamental alteration in the triangular relationship between French government, royal house, and the leading nationalist groups. In practice, this meant that little could be accomplished until a genuinely reformist coalition took office in Paris; until Bourguiba was allowed to participate in Tunisian independence talks; and until the ban on the Istiqlal was lifted and Mohammed V restored to the throne in Morocco. The first of these changes occurred when Radical Party leader Pierre Mendès France assumed the French premiership on 19 June 1954. Mendès France was as impatient as he was visionary. Acting as his own Foreign Minister, he was determined to break the logjams that had marred French foreign and colonial affairs since 1950. A new phrase entered the French political lexicon – *Mendésisme* – a term that connoted the dynamic, centrist modernism heralded by the new administration.[55] Committed to negotiating France's final withdrawal from Indochina and jettisoning the long-stalled EDC project, his government was equally resolved to achieve a breakthrough in the North African protectorates. Indeed, the cult of Mendès France as the great last hope of the Fourth Republic is most persuasive when one makes a reckoning of his colonial policies.

Christian Fouchet, one of the 'first hour' resisters who had accompanied de Gaulle to London in June 1940, was appointed to head a new Ministry of Moroccan and Tunisian Affairs. His brief was to restart negotiations over the transition from autonomy to independence. Inevitably, Neo- Destour, the Istiqlal, and the deposed Sultan would have to figure large in this final disavowal of the old 'co-sovereignty' concept. Tunisia, where peasant *'fellagha'* insurgency continued and the local government had just collapsed, took first priority. Mendès France asked his close associate, the Socialists' chief North Africa specialist, Alain Savary, to open a backchannel to Bourguiba to keep him abreast of government thinking.[56] Within weeks the French government was ready to act. During a visit to Tunisia, on 31 July Mendès France issued the 'Carthage Declaration' conceding full internal autonomy and promising talks over the transition to independence.

Five weeks later, on 4 September 1954 negotiations began in Tunis between Fouchet and his new Resident-general, Pierre Boyer de Latour, and members of Tahar Ben Ammar's Tunisian government. With four Neo Destour ministers in this administration, the party endorsed the talks despite the vocal opposition of its radical, pan-Arabist wing led by Bourguiba's chief rival for power, Salah Ben Youssef. The exchanges stalled over the thorny issues of settlers' rights and the creation of a Tunisian national army and police force. The outbreak of the Algerian rebellion on 1 November 1954 made these security issues harder to resolve; indeed, they dogged Franco-Tunisian relations in the sixteen months remaining before full independence on 20 March 1956. But Bourguiba's willingness to work with Mendès France and their mutual support for an amnesty for *fellaghas* in return for an end to their campaign opened the door to final agreements over control of national finances, public services, and education. In France, however, it would be Edgar Faure's successor government, and the new Minister for Moroccan and Tunisian Affairs, Pierre July, that carried negotiations forward after the Mendès coalition lost a no-confidence vote in an acrimonious parliamentary debate on North African affairs in early February 1955.[57]

With Mendès France ejected from office and the Algerian situation deteriorating, the prospects receded of a swift breakthrough over Moroccan independence comparable to that achieved in Tunisia. Other complications also suggested that Morocco would be a tougher political proposition. One was the Istiqlal's outlaw status. Another was Ben Arafa's position as titular Sultan and the fact that el-Glaoui's supporters as well as French government hardliners including Interior Minister Maurice Bourgès-Maunoury and Minister of National Defence General Pierre Koenig seemed determined to keep him there. After all, Faure's administration took power on the back of a conservative reaction against Mendès France's readiness to enact colonial reform. This left the new premier with scant room for manoeuvre. Meanwhile, a shadowy insurgency gradually took hold across Morocco. Assassinations of notoriously pro-French notables became commonplace and what ultimately became known as the Moroccan Liberation Army mounted attacks on army and police targets. Settler violence also assumed new guises as Présence Française and the Organization de Défense Anti-Terroriste, a related counterterrorist group, determined to defend settler privileges, began killing their opponents. Anthony Clayton notes that in the twelve months from July 1954, 41 Europeans and 254 Moroccans died in terrorist attacks.[58] Underlying all of this was *la question dynastique*: when and in what circumstances would the rightful ruler be restored? The problem was not going to go away. On 20 August 1954, the first anniversary of Mohammed V's deposition, police reported over 300 terrorist-related 'incidents' in Casablanca and Rabat alone.[59]

Faure tried to resuscitate the Moroccan reform process by appointing a progressive Gaullist, Gilbert Grandval, as Resident-general on 20 June 1955. The following day, the Prime Minister announced a mirror image of the Carthage Declaration, promising full Moroccan autonomy and offering talks on 'genuine inter-dependence' between France and Morocco. It was left to Grandval to flesh out the details.[60] Implicit in the so-called 'Grandval Plan' was a recognition that nothing could be made to stick without the involvement of Morocco's two major nationalist parties, the Istiqlal and their weaker rival, the Parti Démocratique de l'Indépendance (PDI). This, in turn, required the restoration of the Sultan. With the second anniversary of his deposition approaching, the threat of an upsurge in violence added urgency to the problem.[61] By this stage, neither Faure and Grandval, nor the nationalist leadership were obstacles to progress. All of them favoured Mohammed V's return. The fault lay elsewhere: with former Laniel government ministers and other diehards who refused to budge over settler privileges, and with the pro-Ben Arafa conservative tribal chiefs who stood to lose authority if the rightful Sultan were reinstalled.

As so often in French North Africa it took renewed bloodshed to effect change. As predicted, on 20 August 1955, the second anniversary of Mohammed V's deposition, widespread urban rioting and an orgy of killings occurred across Morocco and Algeria. In both territories, scores of settlers were massacred, provoking savage French reprisals. With police, army, and press reports still revealing the extent of the violence, on 22 August direct negotiations over the constitution of a democratically elected Moroccan government at last began in the resort town of Aix-les-Bains between French government representatives and Istiqlal and PDI leaders.[62] Meanwhile, the former Free French General, Georges Catroux, directed more surreptitious talks with Mohammed V, then in exile on Madagascar, to establish terms for the Sultan's return to Rabat.[63] General Boyer de Latour, the former Resident-general in Tunis, was sent in as replacement to Grandval to ensure Ben Arafa's removal and prepare for final independence. However, it was a spectacular about-face by T'hami el-Glaoui, who ostentatiously withdrew his support from Ben Arafa on 25 October and called for Mohammed V's prompt restoration that ensured there would be no repeat of the clashes between his supporters and those of the Sultan and the Istiqlal.[64]

If the pacha of Marrakech could swallow his pride, his political allies in Paris could not. Members of Laniel's government that had sanctioned Mohammed V's deposition as well as the most ardent Gaullists in Faure's administration refused to sanction the Aix-les-Bains accords, the Sultan's return, or the end of French Morocco that they implied. On 5 October 1955 the National Committee of the Gaullist Movement called for the formation of 'a government of public safety' to deal with the North African crisis. This first attempt to lever de Gaulle into power was a flop. Forced into a corner, Faure acted decisively. He dismissed the Gaullist intransigents, Pierre Koenig and Veterans' Minister, Raymond Triboulet, from his government. In doing so, he removed the final political obstacle to Mohammed V's triumphal return to Rabat on 16 November.[65] Meanwhile, the National Assembly voted overwhelmingly – 462 to 132 – in favour of Moroccan self-government.[66] As with Tunisia, this was finally conceded in March 1956 with abrogation of the protectorate Treaty of Fez and a formal announcement of

Moroccan independence.[67] Right-wing opposition to colonial withdrawal from the Maghreb focused henceforth on Algeria.

Conclusion

Could we read the events in Morocco and Tunisia as successful decolonization? Hardly, on the basis of the evidence offered above. But here again we return to the challenges inherent in studying the end of empire comparatively. French extrication from both territories without a complete breakdown of civil order owed much to skilled negotiators on all sides. However, it was the forbearance of ordinary Moroccans and Tunisians in the face of enormous provocation – internal and external – that prevented a descent into anarchy. Tit-for tat killings of AML guerrillas and Istiqlalist activists rumbled on before and after independence, marring what might otherwise have been French North Africa's most peaceful decolonization. But still the country avoided the kind of inter-party warfare that would become so prevalent in Algeria.[68] Furthermore, the essential moderation of the Istiqlal and the Bourguiba loyalists of the Neo Destour as well as the statesmanship of Mohammed V also stood in marked contrast to the opportunistic and reactionary policies pursued by elements of the French right.

A relatively peaceable negotiated withdrawal was always possible because of the willingness of Moroccan and Tunisian nationalists to sustain some form of privileged, post-independence relationship with their former colonial master. The question had always been whether the French political community had the vision to seize this opportunity, much as the Afro-Asian block and the United States urged them to do. Mendès France did so, making it virtually impossible for its successors to backtrack. But if the final years of French rule in the North African protectorates were a stop-start story of negotiation, protest, and eventual compromise, the violence that punctuated these phases paled in comparison with that unleashed in the neighbouring colony of Algeria. As we shall see, only by viewing events through the prism of the Algerian War could one consider France's departure from Morocco and Tunisia a relative political success.

CHAPTER 9
ALGERIA'S VIOLENT STRUGGLE FOR INDEPENDENCE

The magnitude of the Algerian War

The Algerian war of independence was unique. Those historians who have compared the Algerian conflict with British colonial emergencies tend to concede that, whatever similarities may exist, the destruction and divisiveness of the Franco-Algerian War set it apart. As Jean-Pierre Rioux notes, metropolitan divisions over the war reanimated the 'Franco-French' conflicts between republicans and anti-republicans characteristic of the Vichy years.[1] And the increasingly extreme lengths to which the French Republic was prepared to go to 'maintain order' in its North African *départements* raised the most fundamental questions about French values, individual rights, and permissible state violence. The severity of the war was imprinted in the numerous official euphemisms through which French government agencies concealed the reality of French oppression. Whatever the term used – *les événements d'Algérie* (the Algerian events), police actions, restoration of order, or pacification operations – all amounted to an undeclared colonial war of unprecedented brutality. An army strategy of intensive psychological warfare that forced civilians to take sides in the conflict hastened Algerians' alienation from the colonial state while, in France, military escalation triggered deeper domestic divisions.[2] The tragic irony was that from 1956 onwards, in opinion poll after opinion poll, a clear majority of the French public registered their support for negotiated withdrawal.[3] This silent majority view – and herein the problem: it was silent for much too long – remained rock solid until the final army pull out in July 1962.

Many among the estimated 2.5 million French servicemen sent to Algeria harboured similar reservations. The armed forces were never monolithic in social composition or in political attitudes, and, as Martin Alexander points out, one of the rare points of agreement among French soldiery in Algeria was a shared dislike of the settler community they were called upon to protect.[4] There is, however, no escaping the fact that the French army's resort to dirty war practices in Algeria not only antagonized the mass of Algerian Muslims, but precipitated a crisis of national confidence in state legitimacy in France as well. Some historians have gone further, noting the parallels between what Henri Rousso dubbed France's 'Vichy Syndrome', meaning the country's post-war struggle to come to terms with the extent of Second World War collaboration, and the nation's reluctance to acknowledge the savagery and scale of the Algerian conflict. Just as France took decades to admit to its behaviour under Pétain, France has only recently begun to exorcize the demons of the Algerian experience.[5]

Not surprisingly, the exact death toll in the conflict has been bitterly contested. Algerian historians and most of their French colleagues suggest that the number killed was far higher than the French government has ever conceded. But few would go so far as the FLN itself. As early as 15 October 1959, the party's official newspaper, *El Moudjahid*, claimed that estimates of 'between nine hundred thousand and one million victims' underestimated the total numbers killed. After independence, Ahmed Ben Bella, FLN leader and first president of the Algerian Republic, formally confirmed that the Algerian death toll was over a million, possibly as much as 1.5 million.[6] These figures are certainly exaggerated. At the other extreme, French 'official figures' admitted to 'about' 143,000 'rebels' killed between All Saints Day, 1 November 1954, date of the first spate of FLN terrorist attacks, and 19 March 1962, which marked the signature of the Evian peace accords. According to these official figures, 47 per cent of these died *after* de Gaulle took office in May 1958. In 1974 Algeria's Ministry of War Veterans produced a figure of 152,863 FLN dead, or 45 per cent of all party activists and ALN fighting units combined.[7] But how many were purged, and what about those who were not party members? Analysis of demographic statistics, although imprecise, suggests a significantly higher figure for the Algerian Muslim population as a whole: somewhere between 300,000 and 400,000 dead.[8] Perhaps even more shocking than the bald – and still disputed – figures is the fact that so many were civilians. French government statistics suggested 19,166 civilians killed (16,378 of them Muslims) in terrorist attacks, plus a further 13,671 'disappeared' (of which 13,296 were Muslims). For their part, the diehard French terrorists of the Organization de l'Armée Secrète (OAS) appear to have murdered well in excess of 3,000 people, many of them after the 1962 ceasefire.[9]

The manner in which so many combatants and civilians died also remains deeply disturbing. This was dirty war in the most visceral sense. Its weapons were as likely to be the knife, the razor, the strangulation cord, and the homemade bomb, as the professional soldier's rifle. Discoveries of mass graves, both of victims of French army torture and summary killings and of Algerian families butchered by nationalist cadres, have further complicated the calculation of overall losses. In addition, it is at least debatable whether war victims should only include those killed between November 1954 and March 1962. The Algerian conflict defies such neat periodization. Some suggest that the rebellion began in May 1945 with the Sétif massacres of French settlers in eastern Algeria, and the subsequent French military repression in which upwards of 6,000 Algerian Muslims lost their lives.[10] Apart from certain FLN militants, most observers agree that war victims should include the tens of thousands of indigenous auxiliaries (*harkis*) that had worked with the French army during the war, a significant proportion of whom, including relatives and children, were massacred over the spring and summer of 1962 in a wave of retributive bloodletting.[11] And what about the thousands of Algerian immigrants killed during the murderous contest for political supremacy between the FLN and supporters of Messali Hadj's Mouvement National Algérien (MNA) in both Algeria and mainland France?[12] The recent conservative estimates of approximately 300,000 total war-dead do not take the Sétif victims, the *harkis*, or those killed inside France into account.[13]

The massive imbalance between Algerian Muslim and European casualties, so much a feature of asymmetric warfare between a weakly armed opponent and a professional military force, needs no emphasis. But it should be stressed that demonstrative killing also was integral to FLN strategy. The nationalist front never shied away from the political utility of extreme brutality, whether to eliminate opponents, to tie down French forces, or to intimidate the civilian population. Sometimes entire village populations were killed to enforce the party's will on local Muslim communities through 'compliance terrorism'.[14] Yet such ruthlessness also had a grim, twisted logic of its own.[15] The FLN/ALN's recourse to extreme violence, which, in turn, bred vicious security force reprisals, was, in part, designed to repel the French public, convincing metropolitan opinion that the human costs of the war and the traumatization of young recruits was simply not worth it. Seen in this cold, amoral light, the strategy worked.[16] By any standards, the Algerian conflict was the dirtiest of colonial wars.

What lay at the root of this bitterness? It has become increasingly fashionable to emphasize cultural difference alongside the perennial culprit of French political intransigence, but perhaps it is time to return to socioeconomic structures. Put crudely, there is surely a case for viewing the war through the prism of class, of rural deprivation, of gender discrimination, as well as through those of race and constructions of ethnic identity. What is certain is that the conflict's violence must be investigated at these deeper levels of causation rather than simply pinning meaningless labels of 'savagery' or 'cruelty' onto the war's protagonists.[17]

Four months after the outbreak of the war, in a March 1955 appeal to the non-aligned states then meeting in Bandung, Indonesia, Messali Hadj, the veteran leader of integral Algerian nationalism and head of the MNA, identified several aspects of the colonial oppression of Algeria's Muslim population. Significantly, Messali placed economic factors above the denial of political rights. The scourge of long-term unemployment and the fact that over 80 per cent of Algerian Muslim families lived in poverty, scraping by on less than 1,200 francs per month, were singled out as the two most glaring proofs of French misrule. For those among the Algerian peasantry and the unskilled labour force able to find work, underemployment remained a perpetual concern. The availability of seasonal labour kept these workers off the unemployment roll. Still, they could not find enough remunerative employment to provide an income sufficient for a full twelve months. In 1955 Robert Delavignette acknowledged that the combination of long-term unemployment and unviable seasonal labour was fundamental to the social crisis unfolding in Algeria.[18] Furthermore, even ostensibly encouraging statistics could easily mislead. By 1956 the number of Muslim winegrowers across Algeria was almost equivalent to the number of settler viticulturalists, apparently a significant advance. In total, however, these Algerian-owned vineyards amounted to only 40,000 hectares next to 341,000 hectares under *colon* management. So, in spite of the gradual emergence of a 'middle class' of Algerian farmers, the agricultural sector was still dominated by settler landowners employing landless labourers.[19]

In his appeal to the delegates at Bandung, Messali also depicted an illiteracy rate of close to 95 per cent, and the systematic confinement of Algerian Muslims to the lower tiers of the employment market, as searing indictments of settler privilege and government neglect of the majority population. Only in his fifth and final point did Messali turn from the socio-economic situation to the political. Settlers controlled the instruments of administrative power from departmental to municipal assemblies. Those Algerians elected alongside them were French 'puppets'. Distilled to its essence, the MNA leader's argument was devastatingly simple: economic marginalization, the inescapable consequence of colonial inequality, mattered most to Muslim families struggling to make ends meet.[20]

The course of the war

Contrary to popular belief, the outbreak of widespread Algerian disturbances in November 1954 did not take Pierre Mendès France's government entirely by surprise. Intelligence, both covert and open-source, had indicated the likelihood of terrorist attacks. What did cause astonishment was the scale of the disorder these attacks unleashed. So, too, did the identity of its perpetrators. By the autumn of 1954 the French security forces were certain that they had broken the Organisation Spéciale (OS), a paramilitary group linked to the major pre-1954 nationalist party, the Mouvement pour la Triomphe des Libertés démocratiques (MTLD), hitherto regarded as the principal rebel threat.[21] The fact that the MTLD was tearing itself apart in bitter faction fighting only added to French complacency. So the most striking aspect of the official response to the outbreak of rebellion was the uniform refusal to accept that a colonial war had begun against a new and better-organized opponent: the Front de Libération Nationale (FLN).[22]

One reason for the swiftness of the FLN's rise to prominence was the totality of the MTLD's demise during 1953–4. Pro and anti-Messalist factions, the former based in France and soon to coalesce into the MNA, the latter in Algiers, refused to work with one another. Both were also increasingly at odds with the other leading Algerian political parties, Ferhat Abbas's Union démocratique de Manifeste algérien (UDMA) and the Parti Communiste algérien (PCA). Not surprisingly, young FLN militants, many trained in the OS, were impatient with the internecine squabbling of the older generation of political leaders. From the outset, the FLN showed little inclination to work with any of them. Aside from its war against the French in Algeria, the FLN therefore fought an increasingly murderous contest against Messali Hadj's MNA, its main rival for popular support among the Muslim population inside Algeria and, even more so, within the immigrant community in urban France. In 1957 alone almost 4,000 Algerian immigrants died in the FLN-MNA feuding.[23]

The Algerian War, then, was played out within France – above all, in the working class immigrant neighbourhoods of the Seine prefecture, home to 115,000 registered Algerian immigrants by 1958. It was also in the greater Paris region that French police countermeasures went furthest.[24] The MNA could never replicate the revolutionary zeal and single-minded ruthlessness of the younger generation of FLN leaders.[25] Nor did it secure the backing of Algeria's respected Muslim clerics, organized into Association des 'ulama musulmans algériens (AUMA). From early 1956, the AUMA provided funds and the authoritative voice of religious edict, at home and abroad, in support of the FLN's nationalist vision.[26] The MNA, by contrast, could neither match its FLN rival's dominance of Algeria's political culture nor the FLN's growing ideological influence within the Arab world.[27] Instead, the MNA's stronghold remained that of its intellectual forebears, the Étoile Nord-Africaine, the Parti Populaire Algérien, and the MTLD, namely Algerian industrial workers in Paris' 11th *arrondissement*, in the Seine prefecture, and in the Nord and Pas-de-Calais regions of Northern France. As Messali put it, since the 1920s, Algerian emigration to France had been the 'arsenal' of Algerian popular nationalism.[28] Northern industrial towns such as Lille, Roubaix, Valenciennes, and Lens all remained MNA strongholds, but, by 1958, the FLN had eclipsed its rival in the Paris region. Within Algeria, an MNA guerrilla force, the Armée Nationale du Peuple Algérien, briefly held sway in eastern Kabylia under its notorious leader Si Mohammed Bellounis.[29]

On 1 September 1957 Messali issued a public appeal for an end to fratricidal killings. The spectre of so much feuding among Muslims was alienating world opinion from the Algerian national cause.[30] In fact, by this stage, the MNA had already lost the battle for influence with the FLN. Its popular support inside Algeria ebbed away as the FLN targeted MNA supporters, most notably in Kabylie and the Ouarsenis Mountains. Suspected Messalists, their throats cut, were put on display to remind waverers that the FLN brooked no opposition. These massacres peaked on 28 May 1957 when an ALN unit slaughtered over 300 villagers at Mechta Kasba near Sétif. In France, too, MNA activists faced worsening FLN retribution and Messali himself remained confined under house arrest. The crushing blow came in 1958 with the killings of key MNA military leaders in Algeria, some of whom, including Si Mohammed Bellounis and Belhadj Djilali, had begun working with the French security forces against the FLN's military wing, the ALN.[31] In France, too, the MNA was in terminal decline. In January 1958 the French secret police reckoned that some 1,700 MNA supporters remained active in and around the French capital. FLN supporters in the Paris region were estimated at 40,000.[32]

The FLN-MNA conflict remains, to a degree, Algeria's (and France's) forgotten civil war, but what of the better-known inter-communal conflict between French and Algerians? As suggested above, it was several months before the severity of the Algerian disorders and the FLN's directing hand struck home to politicians and public in France.[33] But this period of uncertainty was abruptly ended. The nature and scale of the Algerian War was utterly transformed between August 1955 and October 1957. On 20 August 1955, second anniversary of Mohammed V's deposition, FLN commanders in eastern Algeria ordered their ALN cadres to impose a reign of terror in the Constantine and Philippeville regions. Seventy-one settlers and at least sixty-one Muslims suspected of loyalty to the French were butchered, sometimes in front of former workmates, farmhands, and other bystanders. Many were mutilated. There was widespread evidence that female victims were raped before being put to death. Horrified by the massacres, the security forces went on a rampage comparable to that which followed the nearby Sétif massacres a decade earlier. Although a French cameraman working for Fox-Movietone news caught a gendarme on film murdering an Algerian in the streets, the incriminating footage did nothing to curb the repression.[34] The colonial government admitted to 1,273 Muslims killed; the FLN claimed upwards of 12,000. It was the first decisive escalation of the war and the clearest indication of the FLN's unswerving commitment to the terrorist methods of revolutionary warfare.[35] Both sides crossed the nebulous boundary between warfare and murder. Algeria's dirty war had begun.

After the August 1955 killings, state of emergency measures were put into force region by region. Troop reinforcements, already announced by Edgar Faure's Cabinet in April and May 1955, were also hurried through.[36] Yet the most critical decisions: to send conscripts to the war, and to employ increasingly ruthless, inhumane tactics to dismantle the FLN-ALN command structure, were still to come. Both occurred during a period of centre-left 'Republican Front' administration from February 1956 to June 1957.[37] The irony was that this left-leaning coalition, headed by Socialist Party leader, Guy Mollet, was elected on a platform of bold administrative reform in Algeria.[38] The Mollet government's turnaround – from liberal reformers to protagonists of a massive war effort – was fatal to the future of France in Algeria. It was during this period that the critical shift in the balance of power between civilian government in Paris and military leadership in Algiers took place.[39] The introduction of special powers legislation in March 1956 extended the state's capacity to wage war against the FLN, most importantly by designating French national servicemen to serve in the conflict, something hitherto precluded.[40] An opinion poll conducted in the aftermath of this vote recorded that 63 per cent of the French public now estimated Algeria to be France's gravest problem.[41]

Conscripts poured into Algeria during the latter half of 1956. By the time France and Britain embarked on their disastrous Suez intervention in October, French forces in Algeria stood at 476,279.[42] The failure to oust Nasser's regime, always the FLN's pre-eminent Arab supporter, only increased French military resolve to smash the Algerian rebellion. Senior French commanders now had the resources to drive the FLN from its rural hideouts and to strike at its networks of urban underground support. The paradox was that in doing so they lost two other, more important struggles: for Algerian hearts and minds and for international support of their actions. FLN recruitment continued unabated. Women assumed increasingly significant roles within the movement, whether as *moudjahidate* fighters in the countryside or as *fidaiyates* waging urban guerrilla warfare by planting bombs and ferrying supplies.[43] Countless rural women provided the food, shelter, and silence essential to enable FLN/ALN members to survive. At tremendous personal risk, these women defied increased intrusion into their lives by the security forces and the network of government agencies working to turn rural populations against the rebellion.[44] But the praise accorded to women's heroism and purity in FLN-ALN pronouncements carried the implication that the patriarchal norms of Muslim society should be upheld.[45] Agents of social and cultural reproduction, women were required to conform to the FLN vision of Algeria's future.[46] Penalties for transgression and, most especially, for perceived fraternization or disloyalty, could be severe.[47] Perhaps not surprisingly, many of the women who made sacrifices for the FLN in cities or villages were ultimately disillusioned by the war's outcome, which saw traditional patriarchal structures reasserted and women's critical roles downplayed.[48]

Meanwhile, the French population, responding to the war's seemingly unstoppable momentum, would also gradually turn away from the war, its costs, and those who fought it. Why was this so? One reason was that the greater availability of conscripts (as well as helicopter transport) released professional troops to conduct more ambitious operations: search and destroy missions in the hilly upcountry and along Algeria's land frontiers, and, more famously, an aggressive counter-terror campaign against the FLN's support network in Algiers. These actions had devastating social consequences. Military success was achieved by 'dirty war' practices, so much so that army actions are remembered for the methods employed, not for the objectives sought. From 1957, even more so than before it, executions without trial, torture of suspects, and maltreatment of civilians became the markers of the French army in Algeria.[49] The sustained efforts of some, such as the doctors, administrators, engineers, and Arab specialists of the army's Sections Administratives Spécialisées to improve the lives of Algerian Muslims could not compensate for these horrors.[50] The French army, whose resurrection after the 1940 defeat was rooted in the struggle against Nazi tyranny, was now an occupying force whose 'elite' units employed similar methods of torture and reprisal.[51] Even the French legal system became tainted, with some 1,500 nationalists condemned to death, of whom almost 200 were executed.[52]

Another new development from 1957 onwards was the greater stress placed on depriving ALN bands of essential weapons, supplies, and reinforcements. This was to be achieved by constructing a network of barbed wire fences, minefields, and observation towers along Algeria's frontiers with Morocco and Tunisia.[53] Sensible in theory and, again, militarily effective, the frontier fortification scheme must be counted a failure because of its human costs: in this case, the forcible relocation of tens of thousands of Algerians from border regions and other known ALN hotspots to the infamous *camps de regroupement*. These were holding centres reminiscent of the squalid British 'concentration camps' of the South African War. Eviction, incarceration, and refugee hardship were persuasive recruiters for the FLN.[54]

Two further results followed from this dichotomy between the army's apparent success in sapping ALN military capacity inside Algeria and the Muslim antagonism provoked by army methods. First was the FLN's greater concentration on the international stage as the primary arena in which to fight a propaganda war against French colonialism. Second was the deepening alienation of French professional soldiery in Algeria from their political masters in Paris and from a wider French public increasingly appalled by the army's behaviour.[55] Meanwhile, the war's financial costs spiralled out of control, imperilling France's surging economic growth. War costs, in turn, threatened Gaullist projects to enhance French international influence and construct an independent nuclear deterrent.[56] It was the combination of all these factors, more than far-sightedness or generosity, which impelled de Gaulle to contemplate French withdrawal.

Supporters and opponents of French Algeria: Settlers versus intellectuals?

Before resuming the chronological history of the Algerian conflict after General de Gaulle's spectacular return to power in May 1958, we should dwell a little more on the idea of 'French Algeria'. The role of integrationist ideas at the heart of Algérie française thinking, sometimes dismissed as, at best, irrelevant and unachievable, at worst as reactionary and racist, are now attracting renewed academic interest. From 1955 'integration' was the most-often cited official justification for France's attachment to North Africa. Yet it was also the mantle behind which colonial domination was concealed, and the concept that divided French people the most.[57]

Algérie française traded on a myth of a distinctive new society built by settlers, developed by the importation of French political institutions and cultural practices, and refined into a uniquely Mediterranean society by the adaptive genius of its hardy colonists. Algeria's history, according to the settler myth, began with Roman rule before stagnating under the Arabs and Ottomans. In this reading of the past it took French colonization to revive a polity stifled by the decadence of successive Muslim rulers.[58] As one observer puts it, 'As far as the ethics of occupation were concerned, it was the Arabs who had started the process by usurping what should have been an extension of the Christian world.'[59] An axiom of republican imperialism in Algeria was that a new society had been forged by the combination of pioneering military conquest and settlers' toil.[60] Neil MacMaster captures the underlying fragility of this construct:

French Algeria was a frontier-society, which, like the American West, produced a mythical self-image of the settler as a virile hero, the breaker of virgin land, the energetic and indomitable farmer, who with bloodied hands created wealth from a harsh and unforgiving land. However, the Franco-Algerian myth was perpetually undermined or ran up against the reality of an indigenous society that not only refused to go under, but which – in spite of massacre and colonial-induced famine – began to grow so fast that the *colons* felt outnumbered and vulnerable.[61]

In this context, the widening disparity between settler and Muslim population growth, a feature of Algeria's demography throughout the early twentieth century, bears emphasis. In 1926 the ratio between *colons* and Muslims was 1: 5.5. By 1948 the figure stood at 1: 7.3, and, by 1960, it was 1: 8.7. Nowhere was the relative growth of the Muslim population more apparent than in the major cities. By 1954 only Oran retained a European majority. As we saw in the previous chapter, on the eve of the Algerian War, the largest urban centres in France's North African territories were ringed by shantytowns filled with new arrivals exhausted by scratching a living in an impoverished countryside. Increasingly permanent and ever expanding, for the colonial authorities these labyrinthine '*bidonvilles*' were some of North Africa's most impenetrable political spaces, intrinsically threatening because their inner dynamics defied control.[62] On the eve of de Gaulle's return to power in May 1958, Jean Vibert, future director of the government's long-term investment plan for Algeria (the Constantine Plan), noted that the eclipse of the French majority in cities like Algiers, Bône (Annaba), and Oran would spell the end of French Algeria.[63] It seems then that in Algeria, colonial subjugation is best understood as the defensive response of a settler society convinced of its racial supremacy and cultural integrity but fearful of being swamped, even exterminated, by the Arab majority. State violence in colonial Algeria became a reflex response to the perceived threat of a Muslim 'other'.

Five elements fundamental to the downfall of settler dominance in Algeria are implicit in this model of a minority community under siege. First, the connection between French colonialism, economic growth, and a rapid increase in indigenous population growth trapped French Algeria in a vicious circle. The greater the monetary investment in colonial Algeria, the more pronounced became the demographic imbalance between the European and Muslim populations. The consequent underemployment and social marginality of young Algerians spurred a more militant Algerian nationalism that came to fruition in the FLN. Second, settler insistence that Algeria owed its national cohesion and economic modernization to French initiative was used to justify exclusionary policies that radicalized Muslim opposition. Third, the tendency in settler society to see any Muslim political organization as inherently seditious stifled the development of a more conciliatory Algerian nationalism predicated on sharing power with the European population. Fourth, the growing social and economic divisions between the few rich settler proprietors and the majority of poorer *petits blancs* sapped the settlers' capacity to act in unison against the emerging nationalist challenge. Finally, the glaring maltreatment of Algerian Muslims over generations of European settlement normalized discrimination as an aspect of Algeria's – and France's – political culture, blunting French sympathy for a colonial war fought, at least in part, in defence of unjustifiable settler privilege.[64]

To leave matters here, though, would be to misunderstand the depth of the attachment that many settlers felt, not only to the Algerian soil, but also to the idea of a uniquely forged Franco-Muslim community in North Africa.

'What luck to have been brought into the world on the hills of Tipasa, and not in Saint Etienne or in Roubaix. I appreciated my good fortune and accepted it with gratitude.' Written seven weeks after the start of the Algerian War, these were the words of Albert Camus, the most famous literary figure of the *colon* community.[65] Camus was no defender of colonialism, but his Algiers upbringing drove him to accept the myth that Algérie française stood for a uniquely hybrid society moulded from the daily interaction between Muslims and Europeans. Like many other settlers, most of them from modest, urban backgrounds, Camus resented French media characterization of pampered *colons* as the root cause of the Algerian War.[66] The imputation of collective guilt onto the settler community was based on a gross distortion of their socioeconomic status.

An oligarchy of '*grands colons*' certainly existed. Wealthy settlers owned the bulk of prime agricultural land, ran the country's major industrial consortia, controlled the Algiers press, and exerted undue influence over policymakers in Paris. FLN propaganda made the most of this. Young conscripts were serving the interests of these settler fat cats – 'insatiable parasites' with strong Vichy connections. France was wasting its young men in defence of a corrupt, reactionary minority.[67] Whatever the grains of truth in this caricature, it was not a fair representation of Algeria's European community. In 1957 the leading ethnographer Germaine Tillion estimated that these rich *colons* comprised about 12,000 of a settler population of 1,042,409.[68] As these figures suggest, the vast majority of Algeria's settlers were neither landowners nor managers. Most were small traders, urban workers, or public sector employees. More settlers were to be found working as post office clerks or schoolteachers than as owners of large estates. Government population statistics compiled in 1958 revealed the settler community's strongly urban profile, particularly in the department of Algiers. The capital had 296,041 registered non-Muslim residents; a further 63,588 lived in the districts of Maison-Blanche and Blida. Oran registered 204,393 non-Muslims, Bône 50,753, and the Constantine urban district 44,015. These were the forgotten majority that Camus defended. As Jeannine Verdès-Leroux has suggested, these *petits colons* could not win. Either they were misrepresented as wealthy capitalist exploiters or they were criticized for their poor education, ignorance of Muslim custom, and inability to see beyond their limited urban horizons.[69] The dilemma for Camus and others was that defence of settlers' rights to remain in Algeria inevitably meant rejection of Algerian independence. For so long identified with colonial oppression of the Muslim majority, the settlers could not be assimilated into an FLN-controlled Algerian state.

Aside from those with direct experience of life in Algeria, others were slower to appreciate the conflict's seismic consequences. Take France's intellectuals, potentially influential opinion makers in a country that attached such value to learning and literature. The time lag between the war's beginning and intellectuals' voicing opposition to it was echoed among Algerian writers, too. Several of Algeria's leading novelists struggled to reconcile their creative autonomy with their social conscience and the belief that they should somehow contribute to the struggle against colonial rule. For some, such as Mouloud Marreri and Kateb Yacine, writing about anything other than the war and colonial oppression seemed frivolous and irresponsible. And for those who composed their novels in French, there were additional problems to confront, particularly those relating to Algerian identity, the integrity of Arab and Berber culture, and their primary audience.[70] Algerian students felt the same conflicting pressures, this time in the context of classes delivered in French and determined by French curricula. On 19 May 1956 the General Union of Algerian Muslim Students called for a boycott of all French-run schools and universities. Students were urged to join the liberation struggle instead.[71]

Meanwhile, in France, the first major forum for French anti-war intellectuals, the Comité d'Action des Intellectuels contre la poursuite de la guerre en Afrique du nord (Intellectuals' action committee against the war in North Africa), was founded in November 1955, twelve months after the war began. The committee grouped together leading writers and academics opposed to French actions in the Maghreb. But during 1956 it fractured. Its members divided as much over leftist ideology as over questions of anti-colonialism. French academics with an intimate knowledge of Algeria were similarly divided. For some ethnographers, such as Germaine Tillion, Camus' economic determinism made sense: French funds and expertise would heal the inequities of colonial rule.[72] But for the sociologist Pierre Bourdieu, whose foundational research was conducted among the Berbers of rural Kabylia, Algerian society was devastated by colonialism, the majority population having been impoverished and subordinated for so long.[73]

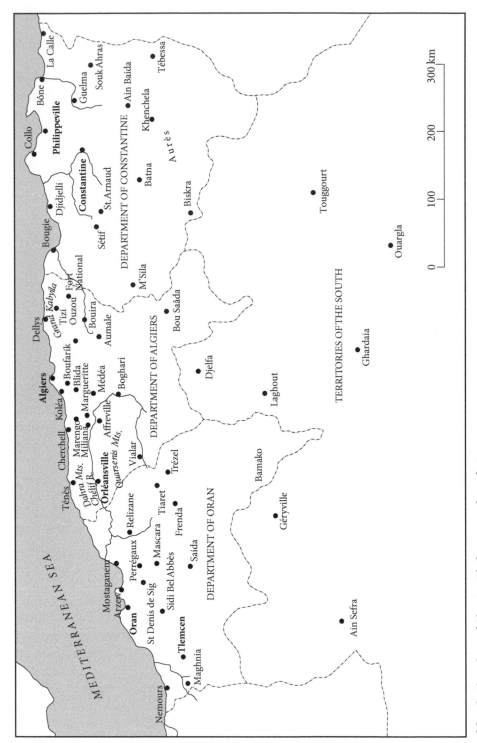

Map 8 The colony of Algeria with department boundaries.

Despite these differences of view – indeed, perhaps because of them – literary, academic, and cinematic criticism of French actions shaped wider public opposition to the war's indefinite continuation.

On the far left, contributors to the magazines *Les Temps Modernes* and *Esprit*, such as Jean Rous and Claude Bourdet, were quick to draw parallels between French army atrocities in Algeria and Nazi persecution of French civilians. French anarchists, Trotskyites, and leading members of the surrealist movement (the surrealist movement had always been a radical voice at the margins of leftist intellectualism) distinguished themselves as the first to take issue with the war, protesting against government censorship and colonial repression in December 1954.[74] The novelist-philosopher Jean-Paul Sartre added his voice to this critique in the following year. More moderate (and more influential) leftist and liberal Catholic writers, notably François Mauriac, Jean-Jacques Servan-Schreiber, Maurice Duverger, and Camus himself, also attacked the human rights violations committed in Algeria. Servan-Schreiber's journal, *L'Express*, the 'new left' *France-observateur*, the newspaper *Le Monde* (founded in 1946), and the review *Le Nef*, were the principal outlets for this loosely connected group. These publications were held in higher esteem by the reading public than the outspoken *Les Temps Modernes*, which wore its radical politics on its sleeve.[75]

It bears emphasis that French Communist politicians and intellectuals did not strongly oppose the war from the outset. The PCF built bridges with Mollet's Socialists in the months of Republican Front government during 1956–7, the critical period in which the war effort expanded.[76] Much as with the intellectual community, the fall of Mollet's Ministry and the war's worsening excesses provoked greater Communist engagement from 1957 onwards. During that year, the battle of Algiers exposed the extent to which professional army units used techniques reminiscent of the Nazis. The revelations of torture and killings by General Jacques Massu's tenth parachute division during its 'clean-up' of FLN cells within Algiers shocked and divided public opinion back home. A stream of condemnatory writings appeared. In *Lieutenant en Algérie*, serialized in *L'Express* from March 1957, Servan-Schreiber evoked army malpractice in a fictionalized record of his experiences as a reservist officer. An even more powerful account was a collection of soldiers' testimonies, Des Rappelés témoignent (*Reservists testify*), compiled by an anti-war committee composed of academics. Des Rappelés témoignent recounted numerous military abuses, including on-the-spot execution of Algerian suspects and shootings of unarmed civilians during village searches. The Catholic essayist Paul-Henri Simon also collected first-hand testimony from policemen and soldiers in an incendiary pamphlet, Contre la Torture, publicized in *Le Monde*.[77] If, by 1957, the comparison with the Nazi Occupation of France was impossible to ignore, it had also been slow to register. The flipside to the upsurge in popular outrage from 1957 onwards was the public's relative quiescence in earlier years. William Cohen notes that literary juxtaposition between French army and Gestapo methods was made as early as January 1955 by former *résistant* journalists appalled at the fast accumulating evidence that torture was already a commonplace within the colonial security forces. So widespread were these accusations that two government investigative missions were sent to Algeria to verify them in 1955.[78]

The fact remains that it was not until 1957 that the flood of allegations hit home across France. Perhaps this was because, like all human – or, in this case, inhuman – interest stories, they needed a focus, a face, a name. All were provided by the scandal over the torture of two French Communists, Maurice Audin and Henri Alleg, arrested by Massu's forces in June 1957.

Audin disappeared, and was presumed murdered. Editor of the outlawed Communist daily *Alger Républicain*, Alleg survived. His account of his experiences under torture, *La Question*, caused a media sensation. The book was printed in February 1958 by *Éditions de Minuit* (*Midnight editions*), the French publishing house identified with resistance writings during the Nazi occupation. True to its origins, *Édtions de Minuit* would go on to publish several other texts highlighting military crimes, miscarriages of justice, and other civil rights abuses in Algeria. Interest in Alleg's recollections intensified as Félix Gaillard's government first attempted to ban publication of *La Question*, and then stood helpless as foreign newspapers, including the *Manchester Guardian*, took up the story and serialized Alleg's account. For all this, it is worth recalling that most mass circulation French newspapers chose not to take issue with army practices. Anti-war sentiment did not yet span the political spectrum.[79]

Mounting evidence that Algerian women, some of them detained during the battle of Algiers, some of them afterwards, were subjected to torture, including beatings, electric shock treatment, sexual degradation and rape, had a cumulative, rather than an immediately transformative impact on French opinion. Revulsion and outrage there certainly was, but its force was blunted by two countervailing factors. One was predictable: the official insistence, matched in some quarters of the French press, that torture victims, regardless of their age or gender, were also killers (something that, whether factually accurate or not, was not, of course, an intrinsic justification for torture.) The other was less predictable and, in a way, more disturbing. The writer-philosopher Simone de Beauvoir captured its essence when she petitioned on behalf of Djamila Boupacha, a young Algerian woman who, while awaiting trial on terrorist offences in 1959–60, sought legal redress against her army torturers in the infamous El Biar prison in Algiers. De Beauvoir lamented that the excruciating details of Boupacha's sexual torture had acquired an air of banality in the eyes of French readers. Put simply, the French nation had become used to hearing or reading graphic accounts of maltreatment by security forces in Algeria. To be fair, there were thousands prepared to protest against human rights abuses conducted in their name. De Beauvoir was surely right, though, in pinpointing the deadening effects of repeated exposure to brutality – whether for the soldiers who perpetrated it or the civilian population back home who encountered it on their news stands.[80] Just as revelations about state violence provoked some into anti-war activism, in others they induced a numbing silence.[81]

From May '58 to Evian '62

It is sometimes assumed that General de Gaulle's return to power during the 'May crisis' of 1958 heralded the beginning of the end of the Algerian crisis (although, as we have seen, not an end to torture). The fact that the first official, though abortive, offer of negotiations with the FLN – de Gaulle's so-called 'peace of the brave' – followed in October 1958 has strengthened this impression. Yet, to see war's end written in the General's reascendancy is misleading on several counts. First, it attributes undue influence to de Gaulle personally, ascribing to him alone remarkable singularity of purpose in bringing the conflict to a close. This takes too narrow a view of history, not to mention an inaccurate one. Second, it presupposes a direct link between de Gaulle's return to office and the manner in which the war ended. Put bluntly, in this interpretation, the General gets most of the credit. Yet, it seems that de Gaulle had no clear Algeria policy when he took office, and was willing to countenance an expansion of military operations provided that those officers in charge remained loyal to the new Fifth Republic. Admittedly, it remains tempting to read more into this lack of clarity; specifically, a masterful presidential obfuscation, fabricated to keep both the FLN and disgruntled French commanders opposed to talks guessing until the government issued firm proposals for Algerian self-determination on 16 September 1959.[82] But, on close analysis, such a grand design becomes harder to sustain. Third, too Gaullist a view of the last years of the Algerian War underplays the extent to which the FLN seized the political, if not the military, initiative. Building on its existing political bases in Tunis and Cairo, on 19 September 1958 the party announced the creation of a provisional government-in-exile with functioning ministries and accredited overseas representatives. The FLN had found a new way to fight a war of decolonization beyond the reaches of the colonial power. Its internationalization of the conflict exploited Cold War divisions and the non-aligned movement's anti-imperialism, leaving France ever more exposed as one colony after another achieved full independence in the years 1958 to 1962.[83] Finally, to regard the May crisis as the start of the 'home stretch' towards the finishing post of Algerian decolonization is to ignore two uncomfortable facts: the war had longer to run after May 1958 than before and at a cost of even more Algerian and French lives in these last four years of struggle than in the three and a half that preceded de Gaulle's return.

So what did mark out these last four years of the Algerian War? There is much to be said for Raymond Betts' succinct appraisal. He notes the mounting distrust between settlers and French army commanders immediately before May 1958. Yet they were united by a common fear: that Paris officialdom, alarmed by events running out of control in Algiers, would cave in to FLN demands. After May 1958 these tensions between Algiers and Paris persisted but in different form. During 1959–60 the French armed forces, led by de Gaulle's appointee, the air force General, Maurice Challe, struck hardest at the ALN and came closest to winning the war on the ground. But, in the same period, de Gaulle's administration edged towards negotiated withdrawal as the sole solution to the crisis.[84] Another irony: the refusal of army 'ultras' and settler diehards to accept this turn in government policy only deepened state attachment to it. With the Muslim majority by now lost to the French cause, the key constituency of undecided opinion was in France. In this sense, de Gaulle's greatest contribution to ending the Algerian War was as a media performer, a reassuring presence who persuaded fellow politicians, serving conscripts, and the general public in landmark television and radio addresses that the wisest course of action was to leave the quest for a negotiated settlement in his hands. Seen in this light, the last two years of the war were as much a Franco-French war as a French-Algerian one.

After the military victories of the 'Challe Plan', de Gaulle's public endorsement of Algerian self-determination in September 1959 came as a bitter shock to the elite units, mainly parachutist and other specialist colonial regiments, that led the fighting against ALN bands. Hardened campaigners isolated from mainstream civilian society in France, it was from within this 'warrior caste' that rebellion against state policy and OAS counter-terrorism would emerge.[85] On 24 January 1960 some of these army 'ultras' and their settler sympathizers erected street barricades in Algiers in open defiance of government policy. Defiance turned to violence when troops and their settler supporters shot dead fourteen of the gendarmes sent to clear the streets. 'Barricades week' ended after de Gaulle renewed his commitment to Algerian self-government in a famous television address on 29 January. But the whiff of army revolt was still detectable. Anti-government plotting, some of it involving the French intelligence services, became endemic. The government countered with special powers legislation in late February, a purge of dissentient officers, and the disbandment of the psychological warfare bureau, the intellectual 'brains' of army militancy.

Meanwhile, preparations for negotiation with the FLN continued, although senior party leaders, including Ahmed Ben Bella, held in detention since October 1956, were not released. Not surprisingly, the first direct exchanges between the French government and FLN representatives, held at Melun near Paris in late June 1960 seemed unproductive. At a deeper level, however, the momentum for withdrawal increased. De Gaulle referred to his expectation of an Algerian Republic in another television address on 4 November. The raft of new African states that joined the UN in 1960, and the prospect of an incoming Kennedy presidency in Washington committed to faster reform, added to the international pressure for an end to the war. Most important, in a referendum on 8 January 1961, 75 per cent of French voters endorsed de Gaulle's proposal for Algerian self-determination.[86]

The ultras' response was twofold: the abortive general's putsch of 22–25 April 1961 led by four erstwhile commanders in Algiers – Maurice Challe, André Zeller, Edmond Jouhaud, and Raoul Salan; and, once that coup attempt collapsed, the intensification of the OAS campaign of murder and intimidation against supporters of a pull out.[87] Discredited and desperate, OAS violence was always counterproductive. It cemented French public support for the resumption of talks with the FLN, and it strengthened the FLN's provisional government-in-exile as the sole legitimate voice of Algerian opinion. In another ironic twist, these final months of the conflict witnessed a further intensification of violence at the very moment that the French administration and the FLN's government-in-exile in Tunis edged towards agreement. It is at least questionable whether the majority of the French population willed an end to the war out of principle rather than fatigue or even boredom.[88]

Even in these later stages, the conflict's brutality was not always apparent to the voting public back home. For many, this must have surely have been deliberate, a tuning out. Jim House and Neil MacMaster have highlighted the extent to which police beatings and murders of Algerians suspected of FLN activism became part of a pattern of 'routinized state violence' in France in the latter stages of the war, particularly in Paris whose infamous police chief, Maurice Papon, orchestrated much of the repression. Determined to expose police brutality, over the summer of 1959 *Éditions de Minuit* and *Les Temps Modernes* each published the testimonies of five Algerian men – Bachir Boumaza, Mustapha Francis, Benaïssa Souami, Abdel Kader Beljadj, and Moussa Khebali – tortured by police in France.[89] Some French observers were appalled. Anti-racist groups, in particular, drew unsettling parallels between the police actions and the round-ups of Parisian Jews a generation earlier. This 'radical comparativism' was blunt and hard-hitting. But it was also slow to register with the wider public.[90] The minimal popular reaction to the gathering evidence of Algerians systematically maltreated by government authorities in France prefigured what was to come.

Few Parisians seem to have been especially animated by police killings of well over a hundred Algerian immigrant protesters during a night of bloody demonstrations in the capital on 17 October 1961. A large proportion were murdered by killing squads of the *compagnies d'intervention* riot police, many of them hardened ex-servicemen.[91] Up to that point, as House and MacMaster point out,

> Contesting state repression remained a politically marginal activity, undertaken by numerically small groups, often addressing or reaching the converted few. Campaigning

had not enabled a realization of the widespread extent of such abuses, their inter-relatedness (systemic nature), their motivation (counter-revolutionary warfare), and impact on Algerians' daily lives. The dominant version of the war propagated by the state and right-wing media and other colonial discourses presented Algerians as a collective danger and the Paris police as the victims, never the perpetrators, of terror. … The vast majority of Parisians simply did not understand the lived experience of Algerians and, after seven years at war, few were willing to make the effort to do so.[92]

Only in the 1980s and 1990s did the 'Paris massacre' resurface in public debate as a criminal cover-up, a national shame, and pivotal moment in the racialization of France's North African community.[93] As Jean-Paul Brunet remarks, at the time, many Parisians were astonished the FLN 'enemy' had the audacity to show itself in public. Most were inclined to forgive any police 'excesses'.[94]

Not everyone was so blinkered. Some French people were so bitterly opposed to the war that they were willing to go beyond legal protest. A small minority lent active support to the FLN by, for example, encouraging conscripts to desert, raising funds, and distributing pro-FLN literature. Here, too, women made exceptional sacrifices. Some, particularly those in mixed-race relationships with Algerian men, even worked alongside the FLN's French Federation as liaison agents and *porteuses de valises*, literally, 'suitcase carriers' who transported funds to the movement's activists.[95] Their actions and those of Frenchmen of like mind amounted to what Martin Evans has identified as a resistance movement. The best known such group was 'the Jeanson network', twenty-three of whose members were put on trial on 5 September 1960. In December 1955 Colette and Francis Jeanson had published a devastating attack on French colonialism in Algeria, *L'Algérie hors-la-loi* (literally *Outlaw Algeria*). In the following year Francis Jeanson began working with FLN supporters in France, convinced of the justice of their cause, and the need to hasten their victory and so end the war.[96] In 1958 he established a journal, *Vérités pour...*, that gave voice to this pro-Algerian resistance.

Jeanson typified *avant-garde* leftist intellectualism, but many of those who worked with him, and the soldiers who chose to avoid the draft, did not. Their willingness to break French law and risk lengthy imprisonment took to its ultimate conclusion the more widespread intellectual view that vocal opposition to the war had become a moral imperative. The Jeanson network treason trial therefore took place under an intense media spotlight. On the eve of proceedings, 121 writers and artists issued the 'Manifesto of the 121', defending the individual's right to resist immoral state action and insisting that desertion, although illegal, was morally courageous. Signatories included Sartre and Simone de Bouvoir, the pioneer of the surrealist movement André Breton, the novelist Marguerite Duras, and the historian Pierre Vidal-Naquet.[97] Intellectuals' anti-war activism had come a long way since 1955.

On the Algerian side of the divide, Mouloud Feraoun stands out as a particularly sensitive observer of the war's impact on ordinary Algerians. Feraoun was a French-educated Kabyle who returned to school teaching in Algeria during the conflict. It was a remarkable act. By 1954 he was perhaps the best known Algerian novelist of his generation. His books, penned in French, won him plaudits in North Africa and France.[98] Feraoun acknowledged that he was an intellectual hybrid: part Kabyle, part Algerian, part French. He saw virtue in Franco-Algerian cultural exchange, if not in French colonialism. This put him at odds with Frantz Fanon, the Martiniquan psychiatrist whose writings on the Algerian War, *A Dying Colonialism* (1959), and, most famously, *The Wretched of the Earth* (*The Damnés de la Terre*) (1961) extolled the FLN's revolutionary violence.

Fanon insisted that only through a cataclysmic rupture from French control could Algerians fashion a national identity wholly their own. His characterization of a total socioeconomic-cultural gulf between colonizer and colonized appealed to the French intellectual left, and continues to fascinate postcolonial scholars. But it left little room for the lived experience of interaction between Algerians and French. As Feraoun knew only too well, most Algerians found themselves caught between the violent extremes of FLN compliance terror and French army repression. This was no choice at all. Colonial war had dehumanized its protagonists as both sides increasingly preyed on innocent civilians to win advantage. Tragically, the cruel logic of the Algerian War left no scope for such a moderate voice. The OAS murdered Feraoun, the most eloquent critic of violence, only days before the March 1962 ceasefire.[99]

Insulated from this turmoil, high-level talks resumed in May 1961; this time in the spa town of Evian. Again, progress was slow. Only after the French government yielded in October over the retention of mineral-rich Saharan territories (by then, France's favoured nuclear test site), did later negotiations, first at Les Rousses and later back at Evian make real progress towards final agreement. In the last week of the war prior to signature of the Evian accords on 18 March 1962 the ALN launched a general offensive against the eastern frontier barrage, pounding French army emplacements with Soviet-made artillery.[100] It was final proof of FLN resilience, of the extent of the Party's international connections, and a warning that the months following the March 1962 ceasefire would be fraught with danger.

On first reading, the Evian accords seemed a triumph of compromise, with provision made for an orderly transfer of power and a transitional French administration prior to a final Algerian referendum on independence. French strategic and commercial privileges remained, as did guarantees for settler life and property.[101] In practice, Evian was overtaken by events. The FLN rode to power on a wave of popular enthusiasm. OAS attacks continued in Algeria and France. And the final declaration of Algerian independence on 3 July 1962 heralded a vast refugee exodus as some 650,000 settlers and 130,000 Muslim *harkis'* families flooded into an ill-prepared France.[102]

Conclusion: Legacies of North African decolonization

The Algerian War of independence may be over, but its bitter heritage lives on. The aftershocks of the loss of *Algérie française* reverberated through de Gaulle's Republic in the 1960s. It was most immediately apparent in the campaign of OAS terrorism that nearly claimed the General's life at Petit Clamart on 22 August 1962 and the subsequent trials of its perpetrators, including Colonel Jean-Marie Bastien-Thiry, the one OAS commander executed for crimes against the state. Yet the OAS was already an anachronism. Public approval for de Gaulle's Algerian policy registered in the consolidation of presidential power approved in a French constitutional referendum on 28 October 1962.[103] Other, lasting effects were more insidious. Most obvious was an Algerian polity socially and economically devastated by the conflict and a population scarred by war, routine brutality, and personal loss. Another was the hundreds of thousands of French ex-servicemen left traumatized by their experiences.[104] Yet another was the rise of a recidivist French ultra-right motivated by xenophobic hostility to immigration, hatred of the Parisian political elite, and a rejection of the increasing liberality of the times.[105]

Ironically, it was de Gaulle's confrontation with student new leftism in May 1968 that heralded a reconciliation between the Gaullist state and the ultra-rightist imperialist diehards of both Jean-Louis Tixier-Vignancourt's Alliance républicaine pour les libertés et le progress and Pierre Poujade's Union de défense des commerçants et artisans. This uneasy compromise was cemented after de Gaulle's infamous trip to West Germany at the height of the Paris student protests in late May 1968 to consult General Jacques Massu, former strategist of the Battle of Algiers, then serving as commander of the French Rhine Army. Following the meeting, troops took up positions around the French capital to crush any leftist insurrection. And Massu's loyalty was later rewarded with a general amnesty for senior OAS leaders including Raoul Salan and Georges Bidault, as well as Pierre Fenoglio, killer of the Socialist mayor of Evian, the town where the Algerian peace talks concluded six years earlier.[106]

Beyond the realm of high politics, hostility and racial prejudice towards North African residents in metropolitan France, people of Algerian descent above all, was evident in several aspects of the immigrant experience in France long after 1962. From the common usage of racist descriptors to the identification of North African immigrants with high levels of criminality in the urban public housing blocks (cités-HLM) of the outer suburbs (banlieues), the colonial past still shapes France's social and political environment.[107] Since the Front National achieved its first significant electoral breakthroughs in the 1980s, for the extreme right the very terms banlieues and cités have become buzzwords for social deprivation, street crime, and the 'colonization' of France by immigrants from former colonial territory. In this rhetoric, the shantytowns of urban Algeria have been transplanted to post-colonial France.[108] Most French people reject such racism, but few could claim that social cohesion has been achieved. The resilience of postcolonial cultures among France's immigrant population seems in part a defensive reaction and in part an attempt to escape the marginalization of minority groups in a country still dominated by a republican elite attached to integrationist ideals rather than multicultural diversity.[109]

CHAPTER 10
TERRITORIES APART: MADAGASCAR, THE TOGO TRUSTEESHIP, AND FRENCH ISLAND TERRITORIES

One answer to an inquisitive reader unsure why the vast island of Madagascar and the tiny West African territory of French Togo should be treated side by side would be that both were administered separately of the francophone African federations. Another might be that local opposition to French rule emerged strongly in Madagascar and Togo immediately after the war, in large part because of the hardship that the Free French war effort had imposed on the mass of the population. Politics in post-war Madagascar were dominated by the causes and consequences of a bloody uprising in 1947. By contrast, in Togo, opposition to French authority was largely peaceful and uniquely focused on the United Nations, thanks to French Togo's status as a Trusteeship territory. If the differences seem manifest, the commonality between the two requires explanation. In Madagascar and French Togo the struggle against foreign domination was inextricably linked to communal politics. Long-standing ethnic rivalries among Madagascans and Togolese determined the course of decolonization in both territories.

French Togo

At the end of the Second World War, the administration of Togoland was still divided between France and Britain in accordance with the partition of this former German colony agreed under the Treaty of Versailles in 1919. The key difference was that whereas the French and British escaped tight League of Nations scrutiny before 1939, from 1945 each became answerable to a more intrusive authority: the United Nations Trusteeship Council. Composed of equal numbers of representatives from colonial and non-colonial powers, the Trusteeship Council was the arm of the UN General Assembly that supervised administration in the assortment of former mandates and Italian colonies redesignated UN Trust Territories. The United States and the Soviet Union, never active players in the mandate system, were intimately involved in trusteeship regulation. This stronger external pressure on French administration in Lomé, French Togo's capital, was matched internally by the political mobilization of the territory's main ethnic group.[1]

Colonial partition had left the Ewe people spread across three distinct territories. According to John Hargreaves, in French Togo there were some 174,000 Ewe, in British Togoland 137,000, and in the Gold Coast to the immediate west, some 376,000.[2] During the war, large numbers of Ewe had crossed into British territory. Among those that returned to French Togo, many retained a sense that British administration was preferable to French, a view that would be sharpened as the Gold Coast edged closer to self-government. The solidarity among the Ewe enhanced by transmigration was bolstered by local economic factors and common political demands. Thus, the Ewe's commercial dominance in southern Togoland added strength to their calls for bureaucratic office and substantial educational provision in the Ewe language. Links between Ewe businessmen and the British multinationals, the United Africa Company and Unilever, increased the Anglophilia among Ewe leaders in French Togo. The result was predictable. The first major African political grouping in French or British Togo advocated the unification of Ewe-dominated regions into a single Ewe state rather than independence for a reunified Togoland based on old colonial frontiers. Ewe tribalism was a more precocious force than Togolese nationalism.

The Ewe of French Togo found a shrewd leader in Sylvanius Olympio, member of an elite cosmopolitan family of southern traders. From 1946 Olympio voiced Ewe fears of Togo's gradual absorption into the structures of French West Africa and the French Union. Locally, the All Ewe Conference, the organization representing the Ewe across Togoland and the Gold Coast, articulated demands for a Ewe state. But the UN Trusteeship Council became the focal point of the Ewe campaign after an initial appeal to the UN Secretary General in April 1947 for a plebiscite on the issue. Numerous Ewe petitions, backed by Olympio's personal appearance before the Trusteeship Council were followed by a UN inspection mission to Togo in December 1949. By this point, the neighbouring French and British administrations had stemmed the tide of Ewe tribalism, if not the impetus towards African self-rule in Togo that the Ewe campaign had generated. Franco-British colonial cooperation across West Africa as a whole was by then well established, spurred on by mutual interest in economic and technical collaboration. It was also sustained by shared concern over growing nationalist pressure, heightened Cold War tensions, and international criticism of colonialism.[3]

The UN's involvement from 1947 onwards compelled French and British colonial officials to devise common strategies to justify their rejection of All Ewe Conference demands. Robert Delavignette, newly appointed Director of Political Affairs in the Ministry of Overseas France, and Andrew Cohen, his counterpart in the Colonial Office Africa Division, liased regularly over 'the Ewe question'. So, too, did Gold Coast Governor, Sir Charles Arden-Clarke, and the high commissioner in French Togo, Jean Cédile. By 1948, however, their greatest asset was the division within the Ewe leadership between the supporters of an ethnically modelled state and those that favoured an independent Togo. As the All Ewe Conference split, French and British delegates persuaded UN observers that any new partition along ethnic lines would only provoke inter-communal conflict. The introduction of self-government in the Gold Coast in 1951 further undermined support for a Ewe state. Ironically, it would be as the leader of Togo nationalism rather than as spokesmen for the Ewe that Olympio would achieve greater success, eventually becoming President of Togo on independence in 1960.

Madagascar from uprising to independence

In Madagascar political debate over eventual independence was also bound up with historic ethnic divisions between Malagasy populations of Malay and Bantu origin. As we saw in the first chapter in the French Empire section, after the French conquest began in 1895, Madagascar became a laboratory in which the island's first colonial governor, Joseph Gallieni, tested his hugely influential *politique des races*. Its central tenet was that colonial authorities should exploit existing divisions between differing ethnic groups, building alliances with some while ostracizing those whose dissent was strongest. In practice, French administration in Madagascar capitalized on the economic discrimination between Malagasy social groups and the acute provincial suspicion of the old Merina elite in the capital Tananarive (now Antananarivo), centre of the pre-colonial state of Imerina. For those Malagasy formerly subjugated to the Merina, the French arrival was, at worst, another colonialism, at best, liberation from Merina oppression. But among the displaced, the members of local secret societies, and the communities hostile to the exactions of the colonial state, the French arrival gave rise to a kind of proto-nationalism that coalesced into support for indigenous political parties in the inter-war period.[4] Meanwhile, Gallieni and his successors advanced the interests of the non-Merina population, whose broad geographical distribution led to their collective appellation as *côtiers*: 'coastal peoples'. The French tendency to administer Madagascar through a racially conceived policy of divide and rule survived beyond 1945. Ironically, the first manifestation of this was the recognition that the antagonism between the island's ethnic groups might facilitate the introduction of a federal political system that would limit Merina power.[5]

As in French West and Equatorial Africa, after 1939 the pressures of wartime requisitions, intensified production drives, and arbitrary colonial government fed popular resentment against French rule. To the pre-war frustrations among Madagascar's educated elite regarding limited access to French citizenship and the colonial state's alternate repression and toleration of indigenous political groups and trade unions, were added specifically wartime hardships deriving from the island's subordination to French war needs.[6] From 1943 the Gaullist governor, General Paul Legentilhomme, harnessed Madagascar's economy to the war effort, augmenting Free French currency reserves by boosting the island's export output. His administration drained Madagascar's internal market of essential foodstuffs, imposed additional forced labour obligations, and made full use of the harsh *indigénat* native judicial code, unusually, applying it to women.[7] After these acute hardships, the Brazzaville Conference's vague reformist proposals made less impact than abolition of the *indigénat* in February 1946 and of forced labour two months later. Relaxation of wartime controls over rice supply within the island was also welcomed. These material improvements looked set to continue with the appointment in May 1946 of a reformist high commissioner, the Socialist Marcel de Coppet. The selection of an experienced governor and former Popular Front supporter whose reputation was built on introduction of a labour inspection service in French Africa promised a good deal.[8] At minimum, it heralded the overhaul of what had become a woefully inefficient colonial administration. Moreover, constitutional reform was making itself felt. New representatives were elected to Parliament in Paris, a system of two electoral colleges having been retained that assured the election of settler and Malagasy deputies in 1945. By October of the following year provincial assemblies were also in place across the island.[9]

The first two Malagasy deputies to the French Constituent Assembly issued from Madagascar's indigenous elite. Dr Joseph Ravoahangy-Andrianavalona was descended from the old Merina nobility in Tananarive. His colleague, Dr Joseph Raseta, issued from a clan historically tied to the Merina dynasty. During 1945–6 their actions and speeches received wide local coverage thanks to unprecedented press freedom in Madagascar. This increasingly vocal nationalism was matched by the rapid growth of political parties. Of these, the Mouvement démocratique de la rénovation malgache (MDRM), founded in Paris in February 1946, seemed strongest. The MDRM's local structure and collegiate leadership style drew on the precedent of the Madagascan Communist Party that was created in response to Popular Front reform in 1936–7. Ravoahangy and Raseta, both MDRM members, had also been active in the Communist Party, and could trace their opposition to French rule back to the First World War.[10] Much to French (and American) irritation, the two men renewed old acquaintances with fellow colonial comrade Ho Chi Minh during the Vietnamese leader's stay in Paris during 1946.[11]

Prior to this, in 1945, the two doctor-deputies also received backing from other groups, including the southern-based Parti nationaliste malgache (PA.NA.MA.) and the 'JINA', the most influential of the secret societies that emerged in Madagascar politics during the Second World War. A more moderate nationalist group, the Parti démocratique malgache, was somewhat set apart, drawing its principal support from the protestant community and the bourgeoisie of Tananarive. However, the MDRM's rapid growth elicited most comment. By 1946 it claimed 300,000 supporters, grouped into local sections nationwide. As the MDRM expanded, so Raseta and Ravoahangy became more exclusively identifiable with it, the former becoming the party's first President. In an ebullient mood, on 21 March 1946 both men called for the abrogation of the 1896 law that established French colonial control and immediate French recognition of Madagascar as a Free State within the French Union with its own government, legislature, and armed forces.[12] But there were storm clouds gathering to change Madagascar's seemingly brighter political outlook.

On the island itself old political rivalries endured between the peoples of the western and north-western coastal provinces and the Merina of the high plateaux around Tananarive, still closely identified with the pre-colonial monarchy. Within these communities MDRM success was readily interpreted as the resurgence of Merina domination. This was mirrored in the abiding bitterness towards Merina elitism among the Hova Mainty, formerly a slave caste under the Merina dynasty in the nineteenth century. These two anti-Merina constituencies formed the core support of the provocatively named Parti des déshérités de Madagascar (Party of the Disinherited of Madagascar – PADESM), a political party founded in June 1946 in direct opposition to the MDRM. Where the MDRM stressed the unitary quality of Malagasy nationalism, the PADESM played on the regional and tribal basis of its support, arguing that MDRM government would mark a return to the Merina oligarchy of the pre-colonial period.[13] Irrespective of these political divisions, the repatriation of large numbers of Malagasy ex-servicemen during the course of 1946 provided a new reservoir of potential MDRM supporters with recent military experience.

Meanwhile, the settler population, envious of white power in nearby South Africa, demanded stronger French measures to contain the alarming upsurge in organized Malagasy nationalism. One obvious means to do so was to lend administrative support to the PADESM, particularly at election time. In November 1946, settlers' anxieties increased following the election of a third MDRM deputy, Jacques Rabemananjara, as the island's representation increased in the first legislative elections of the Fourth Republic. Facing widespread attacks on government and settler property, much of it MRDM-inspired, High Commissioner de Coppet reverted to a single college electoral system in provincial elections in January 1947 to ensure the defeat of MDRM candidates by a coalition of PADESM and *colon* groups.[14]

Calls for a return to sterner colonial ways found a receptive audience in Paris. In the Ministry of Overseas France, Henri Laurentie, Delavignette's predecessor as Director of Political Affairs, agreed with de Coppet's analysis that the MDRM was running out of control.

On 5 January 1947 Laurentie therefore approved plans for a ban on the party.[15] Overtaken by events on the ground, the ban was eventually imposed by decree on 10 May. At governmental level, tensions within the centre-left tripartite coalition worsened over the winter of 1946. As we saw in earlier chapters, the MRP put its conservative stamp on the final provisions of the French Union and blocked negotiations with the Vietminh. The outbreak of war in Indochina in December impacted on Madagascar in three ways. First, it hastened the departure of the French Communists from government in spring 1947, the prelude to a steady rightward shift in French government as the year proceeded. Second, the Indochina War hardened governmental determination to suppress signs of colonial dissent elsewhere lest the working partnership between Socialists and MRP break under the strain. Finally, the war in Vietnam meant that around 20,000 French reinforcements would pass via Madagascar soon after a nationalist uprising erupted.

Just as controversy persists over the extent of French manipulation of the PADESM, so also there is little consensus over the precise origins of the outbreak of the Madagascar revolt on the night of 29 March 1947. The MDRM appears to have been split over the wisdom of a popular uprising. The party executive even sent a telegram on the 27th warning its supporters against acts of violence. Nonetheless, this was no spontaneous outbreak, nor did it come as a surprise to the French authorities.[16] Using information from local police chief Marcel Baron, de Coppet's initial report on the uprising made much of two things: the choice of date, which coincided with the annual Fandroana festival, and the insurrectionists' primary focus on disrupting arterial rail communications.[17] Both suggested careful preparation.

Bloodshed occurred first in the districts of Manakara and Moramanga. This was largely by default as planned insurrections in the towns of Tananarive, Fianarantsoa, and the port of Diego-Suarez were blocked at the last moment. Even so, the colonial infantry garrison stationed in Diego-Suarez mutinied. But at no stage did the uprising cover the entire island; Madagascar's far south and west never joined the rebel cause.[18] As with so many French colonial conflicts, the subsequent escalation of violence followed a familiar nauseating cycle. Vicious attacks on isolated police and army outposts and settler families were cited as justification for far larger massacres by military forces. Police torture became commonplace and, in some of the most egregious instances of colonial brutality, captured prisoners were thrown from aircraft over rebel-held zones.[19] Under the command of Generals Pellet and Garbay, Foreign Legion, North African, and, especially, West African infantry units (a *tirailleur sénégalais* garrison had been attacked on the first night of the rebellion) showed little mercy towards the indigenous population despite the obvious fact that their opponents rarely had access to firearms. Without radios or motorized transport, most rebel groups struggled to maintain communication with one another, making it easier for French forces to isolate and eliminate them once the 1948 dry season began.[20] In fact, the rebellion had lost its momentum soon after the initial wave of French military violence. By late December 1947 the area under rebel control had contracted by over two-thirds. At least 200,000 Malagasy nationalists submitted to government authority, and the MDRM was utterly broken, with some 2,500 of its members imprisoned on treason charges.[21]

The impact of state coercion was as much ethnic as party political. French repression had particularly devastating effects on the Betsimisaraka people in eastern Madagascar. The scale of the killings and the attendant social disruption not only decimated the Bestsimisaraka, but disrespected their customs such as the observance of a traditional mourning period. French actions left an enduring legacy of acute suspicion towards central government authority among Betsimisaraka leaders.[22] Cultural insensitivity was one thing, mass murder quite another. Suffice to say that even the official death toll in the Madagascan revolt calculated in February 1949 admitted the killing of 89,000 Malagasy, making this one of the most awful chapters in the history of European colonialism. The government figure was almost certainly an underestimate, and it made little of the obvious fact that the dead included huge numbers of women and children in addition to young males only loosely identified as rebels. With so many MDRM organizers behind bars, the movement increasingly relied on its lower tier supporters, many of them Merina women with familial as well as political ties to the party, to sustain grass-roots nationalist organization and journalistic output in the immediate aftermath of the rebellion. Inevitably, their focus shifted from nationalist mobilization towards campaigning on behalf of Malagasy political prisoners.[23]

Back in France, the three MDRM deputies became the focal point of what little public interest events in Madagascar stirred either during or after the revolt.[24] With the outbreak of hostilities in Indochina so recent, the parliamentary mood was unforgiving. In spite of vociferous Communist opposition, the National Assembly voted by 342 to 195 to lift the deputies' parliamentary privileges. The MDRM representatives were then prosecuted for alleged incitement of the revolt. Their trial, held in Madagascar before a strongly biased jury, was little more than a kangaroo court. All three were convicted. Two received the death sentence, although this was later commuted to life. Ironically, between 1953–6 a campaign in France to free Malagasy political leaders drew strong support among Catholic intellectuals and left-wing politicians outraged by the imprisonment of North African politicians. Directed by Louis Massignon, professor of Islamic Studies at the prestigious Collège de France, a Committee for the Release of Colonial Political Prisoners lobbied for the release of the MDRM deputies. Guy Mollet's Socialist-led government acceded to this in 1956 but refused to allow the former deputies back to Madagascar before independence in 1960.[25]

The ban on the MDRM, and the killing or incarceration of much of its regional leadership, cast a long shadow over politics in Madagascar after the embers of revolt died down. Aside from restricting party political activity, in October 1947 the High Commission imposed severe press censorship, reversing the swift liberalization of political expression of the immediate post-war period. Suspected MDRM sympathizers were also purged from the local bureaucracy. As before, High Commission policy deliberately conflated the MDRM with Merina exclusivity and rebel violence. De Coppet's successors denied that the party represented an authentic nationalism. Yet nationalist sentiment persisted, albeit in less strident form, particularly in Tananarive. During the early 1950s Malagasy politicians and nationalist journalists were careful to state that their objective was Free State status within the French Union.[26]

External events also rekindled hopes of independence. Between 1954–6, the retreat of French colonialism from Indochina and North Africa was matched by the growing power of the non-aligned movement in international politics. The extension to Madagascar of the Gaston Defferre law, devised to cover West and Equatorial Africa, did not therefore come as a surprise. Introduction of universal suffrage underpinned a raft of measures built around administrative decentralization, communal reform, and the transfer of additional powers to regional assemblies. Faced with tangible prospects of national sovereignty, the PADESM split. Led by Philibert Tsiranana, a French-educated *côtier*, PADESM progressives formed a powerful coalition with the Front national malgache, the party that had filled the void left by the MDRM in the Merina heartland. In December 1956 the two groups fused into the Parti social démocrate (PSD), a moderate grouping with genuine interethnic appeal. A host of more sectarian parties were also formed to contest municipal elections in December 1956. None could supplant the PSD. Under Tsiranana, the PSD leadership profited from its willingness to sustain long-term links with France. The departing French administration did much to facilitate PSD dominance of the first Madagascar government installed in 1958.[27]

Official support was especially important in preparation for the September 1958 referendum on membership of the French *Communauté*. Although nationally 83 per cent of Malagasy voters said 'oui-oui' to the new constitutional arrangements and membership of de Gaulle's new imperial club, in the province of Tananarive a narrow majority (50.5 per cent) voted 'non'. The capital and its hinterland remained a bastion of militant nationalism, unconvinced by Tsiranana's programme of cooperation with Paris.[28] PSD success also affected attitudes to decolonization in the four Camoros islands in the Mozambique Channel, where the party courted support among the islands' majority Muslim population. Like their larger island neighbour, the Camoros opted to join the French Community in the 1958 referendum. (The four islands are Grande Comore, Anjouan, Moheli, and Mayotte.)

In a meticulously orchestrated ceremony, the Republic of Madagascar was proclaimed on 14 October 1958 in the Place d'Andohalo, the forum in which the Merina dynasty's royal decrees were announced to the populace of Tananarive in the nineteenth century. Twenty-one months later, on 26 June 1960 Philip Tsiranana, the *côtier* outsider who had risen to become first President of independent Madagascar, proved equally keen to identify himself with the grandeur of pre-colonial rule. He announced French recognition of the island's full independence from the former palace of Prime Minister Rainilaiarivony, husband to two successive Merina Queens, whose career had been dominated by the struggle against French imperial domination.[29]

French island territories I: The Pacific and Indian Oceans

The French Empire in the South West Pacific was diverse and widely scattered. Tahiti, French-controlled since 1842, and the other territories of French Oceania (Établissements Français d'Océanie – EFO) along the eastern margins of Polynesia formed one administrative cluster. To the west lay Wallis and Futuna, also Polynesian but geographically isolated from the EFO and ruled as protectorates since the 1880s. Still further west, and therefore closer to Australia's Pacific coast was New Caledonia, originally a penal colony and the largest of the Pacific dependencies, as well as the other Melanesian islands of the New Hebrides, which were jointly governed as a condominium with Britain. All would find their administrative designations changed under the terms of the French Union in October 1946.[30] By this point, the strategic and economic significance of these tiny colonial states had become more obvious to Paris and Washington, thanks to their role in the war against Japan. New Caledonia, in particular, became a vital supply centre for US forces and remained a key component in the Free French Empire throughout the years 1940–4. Perhaps inevitably, it was also the scene of some of the bitterest political and cultural clashes between two supposed allies: a weakened yet unremittingly colonial France and a super-powerful United States dismissive of French pretensions to imperial grandeur in the Pacific.[31]

That is not to suggest, however, that the value of Pacific possessions only struck home to French opinion makers during the Second World War. Like other more extensive and populous dependencies, by the early twentieth century France's Pacific territories had fervent backers in Paris. They were grouped together in one of the most coherent lobby groups of the Parti Colonial: the French Oceania Committee.[32] Its members, a cast of leading officials, diplomats, businessmen, journalists, and ethnologists, favoured the rapid consolidation of French influence in the Pacific and were undeterred by the islands' geographical remoteness. They focused instead on the temptations of rich mineral deposits, deep-water ports, settlement opportunities, anthropological investigation, and tourist development.[33] In this sense, the Second World War did change matters. In its aftermath the official rationale for retention of France's Pacific Empire was altogether simpler: the islands added to French international prestige, enhancing the capacity to project power globally. Furthermore, the Pacific territories had proven their loyalty to France, ranking among the first to 'rally' in General de Gaulle's cause in 1940. For much of the late 1940s and 1950s local pressure for any loosening of French control also seemed nugatory.[34]

To these abstract calculations, other, more practical considerations could be added. White settler communities – the loudest political voices on most of the islands – were not about to concede their privileged social status either to indigenous Polynesians and Melanesians or to other non-European immigrant populations, mainly Asian contract labourers. There were also valuable mineral resources, principally New Caledonian nickel that could be exported for precious dollars. And, in later years, after the loss of the Algerian Sahara, French Oceania would become the favoured site for French nuclear testing.

As this list suggests, most of the critical post-war decisions of long-term political and economic significance to the French Pacific territories were made in Paris and not in the island capitals. The terms of the French Union, for example, redesignated all of France's island possessions as either overseas departments or territories. The old Caribbean colonies Martinique, Guadaloupe, and Guyane, as well as Réunion in the Indian Ocean – became départements d'outre-mer (DOMs); the French Pacific territories, in common with other, newer colonies in francophone Africa, became territoires d'outre-mer (TOMs). Unlike the DOMs, these territories were not integrated into the French administrative or legal systems. Instead, TOMs retained their colonial governmental structure with a governor at its apex. Voting rights also remained narrowly confined and strongly biased in favour of white settlers. Local assemblies were established, but their decision-making powers were confined to consideration of budgetary spending and local social provision.[35]

Just as significant as these political changes was their economic counterpart: state-backed investment through the Overseas Territories' Economic and Social Development Fund (Fonds d'Investissement pour de Développement Économique et Social des Territoires d'Outre-Mer – FIDESTOM). Established in 1947 to promote economic modernization through public works and infrastructure development, the FIDESTOM represented a major source of capital investment throughout the French Pacific.[36] Together, the new-style administrative arrangements, gradual franchise extensions, increased industrial development, and growing numbers of wage workers precipitated fundamental changes in the political economy of the Polynesian and Melanesian islands. Behind these lay an abiding tension: between the administrative centralization characteristic of French colonial governance and the politicization of indigenous islanders impatient for greater independence.[37]

In Tahiti and New Caledonia especially, locally powerful party-based independence movements would dominate the political scene from the late 1940s to the 1980s and beyond. In the former case the Tahitian Peoples' Democratic Union (Rassemblement Démocratique des Peuples Tahitiens – RDPT) and its charismatic leader Pouvanaa a Oopa became the major force in island politics from the 1950s onwards with a mass membership of between eight to ten thousand organized into over a hundred local sections.[38] In New Caledonia it was the Union Calédonienne (UC) that set the agenda for relations with France. Both parties prioritized the interests of the indigenous majority population, and both followed similar political trajectories. However, from 1959 Pouvanaa and the RDPT faced crippling government sanctions, including a lengthy party ban imposed in 1963 just as French government plans for a nuclear test site in Polynesia took shape. When French Polynesia eventually won self-government in 1984, successor groups and rivals to the RDPT took much of the credit.[39]

In New Caledonia the UC remained the principal actor in New Caledonia's politics from its inception soon after the 1951 enfranchisement of the island's Melanesian majority. It, too, became increasingly radical over time, controlling the island's territorial assembly until 1958. Much like the RDPT, the UC later faced legal challenges after two of its leaders were found guilty in 1962 of bombing the assembly building and their own party headquarters in an effort to 'frame' their Gaullist political rivals. Unlike the RDPT, however, the UC escaped a ban. By the late-1970s imminent independence agreements in French Indian Ocean territories, as well as the Comores islands and the French Somali enclave of Djibouti, plus a final independence settlement closer to home in the New Hebrides, fired more radical UC opposition to French rule in New Caledonia. Here, again, it was not the UC but a successor group that drove this more radical independence movement forward. As its name implied, the foundation in 1976 of the Kanak Liberation Party (Parti de Libération Kanak) signified greater anti-colonial militancy among New Caledonia's Melanesian population.[40] The 1980s witnessed a descent into political violence and confrontation between the French state and this Kanak independence movement.[41]

French island territories II: The French West Indies

Ruled by France since the 1630s, the two Antilles islands of Martinique and Guadeloupe ranked among the oldest parts of the French colonial empire. French Guiana (rendered in French as Guyane), a tiny dependency on the South American mainland, was annexed even earlier – in 1604 – although effective French administrative control was only established in the late seventeenth century. Originally a strategic outpost protecting the southern flank of the French Antilles, Guiana's administrative role, its political utility to France, indeed, its very identity, was transformed by its development as a prison colony from 1851 onwards.[42]

If Guiana was unique, Martinique and Guadeloupe were not. In the words of one commentator, their demographic composition fitted 'the classic profile of a sugar-based colony resting on three components': a slave labour force that remained at the bottom of the socioeconomic spectrum after abolition in 1848, an intermediate social stratum of mixed-race mulattoes, and a dominant group of white Creoles, known, on Martinique, as *Békés*.[43] In the port cities especially, social and ethnic divisions were more complex. Poor whites, many of them indentured servants, rubbed shoulders with poor persons of colour in the slum dwellings of the urban underclass. As the social anthropologist Michel Laguerre observes regarding the Martinique capital: 'The history of Fort-de-France during the colonial period is fundamentally the history, on the one hand, of social inequality between the colonists and their slaves and, on the other, of the control of urban space by the European segment of society.'[44]

A key question that confronts us is whether these differing communities shared any interest in decolonization. Certainly, after 1945, issues of ethnicity and language usage became closely identifiable with the construction of islander identity and an emergent nationalism. Furthermore, the focal points for these sentiments were autonomist movements that promoted indigenous Creole culture while rejecting the dominance of a white, francophone settler elite. In other ways, however, the two French West Indies islands were less comparable.

In Martinique, the *Békés*, an elite of wealthy, white Creole landowners, dominated the island's economy and politics for much of the nineteenth and twentieth centuries. Their continuing influence reflected a crucial historical difference between the sugar economies on the two islands that arose from their differing experience of the French Revolution and the Napoleonic Wars during which the British occupied Martinique but not Guadeloupe. As a result, the Martiniquan planter class remained *in situ*. By contrast, Guadeloupe's planters were largely driven into exile, making way for metropolitan corporations to take control of the bulk of the island's sugar production.[45] A substantial mulatto middle class also became gradually established within Martinique's more heterogeneous population.[46] Guadeloupe's demographic composition was less diverse, and its Creoles were far poorer. Many abandoned plantation agriculture to work on estates and in industries owned by French and Martiniquan interests. In Guadeloupe, therefore, neither the local sugar industry, nor the service sector and tourist trade remained under local control. By contrast, among the island's poorer social groups, memories of slavery and an African cultural heritage remained a more powerful political instrument than in the more Europeanized atmosphere of Martinique. Although slavery had been abolished in 1848 and the trajectory of colonial rule was always towards closer administrative integration with France, these islands, Guadeloupe especially, remained socially stratified.[47]

The impact of colonialism also transformed patterns of land use on Martinique and Guadeloupe. In both cases, the best available agricultural land was, and is, devoted to export production, with sugar cane (partly for refining into rum) and banana cultivation predominating. By the early 1950s sugar cane production in particular was highly capitalized but still labour intensive. On Guadeloupe, the largest of the Lower Antilles island chain, comprising some 570 square miles, by 1951 nine commercially run plantations occupied over half of the land given over to sugar cane production. Owner-occupied farms, usually of less than three acres, and sharecropper holdings were marginal by comparison. And sharecroppers typically supplemented their farming income by working as day labourers on the larger plantations.[48]

The major political reorganization of the French Union in 1946 is relevant here. Legislation passed on 19 March 1946 reclassified France's four 'old colonies', Martinique and Guadeloupe, along with Guiana and Réunion, as overseas departments. Erstwhile colonial governors became Prefects and local assemblies took the same appellation – Conseil Général – as their equivalents in metropolitan *départements*. French labour legislation was also made applicable to the DOMs. As Eric Jennings points out, these reforms were promoted both as a 'reward' for the territories' efforts to back Free France and as an explicit rejection of Vichy's colonial racism. Guadeloupe Governor Ernest de Nattes announced that 'Guadeloupeans are now

French to the same degree as Basques, Bretons or Lorrains. They have the same rights, but also the same duties.'[49] This was not wholly empty rhetoric. Employment rights were improved and local wage rates increased, although the metropolitan minimum wage was differentially applied in the French Caribbean. Perhaps not surprisingly, 'departmentalisation' was generally popular. However, disillusionment quickly set in.[50] As production methods did not become commensurately more efficient overnight, state subsidies that artificially inflated the prices of French West Indies exports became essential to enable agricultural employers to pay their workers the increased wages to which they were now entitled.[51] Thus, a paradox: if one result of the 1946 legislation was to ameliorate labour conditions, another was to increase the French Caribbean's economic and commercial dependency on France.[52]

Departmentalization was perhaps most significant of all to Guiana, a territory whose previous status and terrifying reputation as a deathly penal colony, had been confirmed by near total neglect of the economic needs of its small population (still less than 100,000 in the 1980s). Little wonder, then, that Guiana could not be transformed into 'a department like the others' by the stroke of a legislator's pen. Social conditions certainly improved markedly in the post-war years, but, alongside this, the territory became utterly dependent on French state support. By 1974 over 60 per cent of Guiana's working population were employed in the tertiary sector, mainly in commerce, transport, and financial services. Despite the revenue generated by Guiana's forestry industry and the prestige attached to its well-publicized European Space Centre at Kourou, it is hard to view the territory as a viable economic unit capable of standing alone.[53] Again, the picture is rather different on the French Caribbean islands.

During the 1950s and 1960s the historic roots of ethnic and socioeconomic division between the haves and have-nots in Martinique and Guadeloupe gradually resolved themselves into two distinct strands of political confrontation. One was between those eager to assert the islands' Creole identity in the face of a growing reliance on French investment and an expansion in tourism. Another was a broad left-right split between those political groups that advocated greater island autonomy and those who supported the strongest possible links with France as the essential guarantee of rising prosperity. With public spending apparently critical to economic stability and welfare relief for an expanding underclass of unemployed or underemployed islanders, arguments would persist into the 1960s and 1970s over whether dependency on France was, in some ways, defensible. Hence the persistence in support for greater island autonomy as opposed to outright independence.[54]

By the late 1950s, local Communist parties and trade unions on both islands emerged as protagonists of island autonomy. However, the Parti Progressiste Martiniquais (PPM), dominated by Aimé Césaire, a founding father of the Negritude movement, steered majority opinion towards a moderate autonomism, a course that mirrored Césaire's intellectual journey in the 1950s and 1960s from Marxism to supreme respect for the individuality of colonized cultures.[55] By contrast, on Guadeloupe, the political scene was more complex. It was only in the mid-1960s that a full-blooded independence movement – the Groupe d'Organisation Nationale de la Guadeloupe (GONG) – took shape. GONG proved short-lived. It was outlawed in 1967 for the incitement of riots in the cities of Basse-Terre and Pointe-à-Pitre during a bitterly contested building workers' strike.[56] Yet, in spite of GONG's demise, the link established between trade unionists and pro-independence politicians continued in the guise of the Union Populaire pour la Guadeloupe (UPLG). From its inception in 1978, the UPLG became the dominant voice – and emphatically a Creole, and not a French, voice – in island politics.[57]

Socialist victory in the 1981 French elections heralded a shift towards decentralization of administrative power in the DOMs. The Mitterrand government also endorsed greater cultural and linguistic autonomy. Meanwhile, in the same year, final recognition of an independent state of Belize meant that French Guiana remained the sole European dependency on the Latin American mainland. In February 1983 the Socialists' devolution of power in the French Caribbean gathered pace. Local Conseil Généraux were replaced with Conseils Régionaux, equipped with budgetary authority and extended decision-making powers. Abstention rates and support for the French right had been especially high on Martinique during the 1981 elections.[58] Nonetheless, the PPM broadly welcomed the subsequent reforms. Their reception on Guadeloupe was much different. Far from defusing Creole-led demands for outright independence, socialist policies were lambasted as a conjuring trick, devised to conceal surreptitious French domination. During the early 1980s Creole militants on Guadeloupe mounted a series of small-scale terrorist attacks against public buildings, large tourist hotels, and other symbols of the French presence. These bombings suggested that the issue of autonomy versus independence was bound up with deeper problems of Creole status within island society, a complicated matter that defied any easy solution.[59]

Perhaps, as William Miles records in his study of Martinique electoral politics, the administrative assimilation inherent in 'departmentalisation' is the root problem:

> As individual units of a highly centralized bureaucracy and form of government, yet distantly scattered from the administrative headquarters in Paris, the overseas departments have suffered even *more* from bureaucratic inefficiency, red tape, and communications lapses than they did formerly, and more than do the Metropolitan departments. They may now vote directly for the presidency and participate in the French Parliament as equals, but as vastly outnumbered equals. ... Over the years, the futility of their numerical weight, and the indifference of the Parliament as a whole concerning overseas affairs, have raised doubts about the real gains of having been so well assimilated into a large, centralised, often bureaucratically blind system.[60]

Whatever its faults, since 1946, the French response to increasing popular pressure for structural change has lain in departmentalization as an alternative to decolonization. If results have been mixed and, in some respects, disappointing, it is worth bearing in mind that the economic prosperity and communal stability of numerous other islands and 'mini-states' that secured independence in the early 1960s has also remained precarious.

PART III
DUTCH DECOLONIZATION
Bob Moore

INTRODUCTION TO PART III: THE DUTCH EMPIRE

Although the discussion of the modern Dutch Empire and its decolonization has largely been confined to Dutch writers and historians, it cannot be entirely divorced from the wider history of European imperialism. Some of the contradictions apparent in the French case could also be applied to the Netherlands, but there is also an argument for a certain particularity when discussing Dutch conceptions of colonialism and their enforced retreat from empire after 1945.

The history of the Dutch overseas Empire in the modern era owes much of its origins to merchant capitalism the merchant capitalism of Dutch cities and adventurers from the sixteenth century onwards. Indeed, with the possible exception of southern Africa, none of their possessions were settler colonies but were driven by business and mercantile interests. This exploitation of trade with the East Indies and along the African coast was later augmented by the riches to be gained through voyages to the West Indies. To trade was to engage in the politics of the regions involved and also to develop the means to protect that trade from piracy and the exigencies of war. Over time this led to the amalgamated Dutch trading companies acquiring both territorial rights and military potential, a process that saw a continued growth in their geographical scope as their financial power increased – both a product of and a driving force behind the golden age of the Dutch Republic. By the end of the eighteenth century, however, their fortunes were decidedly on the wane, having to compete with other trading nations and lacking the military and (especially) naval power to defend their interests alone. The death knell finally sounded when the Republic itself was overrun by the French in 1795 and this might have been the end of Dutch colonial ambitions had it not been for the settlement brokered after the defeat of Napoleon, where the victorious powers deemed it necessary wherever possible to have strong states bordering France. The creation of a Kingdom of the Netherlands in 1815 and the restoration of some formerly Dutch overseas possessions was one outcome of this policy – in some respects a European colonial power created by default.

However, to claim that the Dutch were reluctant or accidental imperialists would be to deny the strong psychological bond that associated the Indies, both East and West, with Dutch prestige and the Kingdom's claims to status as a European power. Indeed it was this belief that the colonial Empire somehow defined the Netherlands that was to remain an important *leitmotif* in Dutch diplomatic and political behaviour, and in public opinion even beyond the mid-twentieth century. This was reinforced by cultural and social interactions developed over 400 years which created a hybridity perhaps even more profound than in imperial France. The long-term Dutch presence was personified by elite families, multiple generations of which were born in the colonies. They regarded the Indies as their home. Over the centuries, the arrival of employees of the trading companies and adventurers also gave rise to intermarriage and concubinage that created a mixed-race class of Eurasians to add to the multiplicity of peoples and languages already present in these colonial domains.

During the nineteenth and early twentieth centuries, Dutch policies towards their colonial possessions went through a number of stages – mirroring perhaps the changing attitudes and political climate of the times, but always having a distinctive Dutch element. Thus Crown control was gradually replaced by government oversight and economic exploitation was initially geared towards transforming the colonies from being a drain on the exchequer to becoming a major contributor to the country's well-being. As the detrimental effects of these policies on the indigenous populations became known, changes were made to economic policies and the first modern social reforms were initiated. These were driven by two competing political perspectives in the metropole; Liberalism and Orthodox Calvinism, the latter giving rise to the so-called 'ethical' policy, introduced by the Prime Minister and theologian Abraham Kuyper in the first decade of the twentieth century. Put another way, the public and international justifications for Dutch rule changed with the wider political and social landscape, a process made easier because, unlike most of its European counterparts, the Dutch had no part in the aggressive imperialism of the later nineteenth century, preferring to consolidate what they already held. That said, the sheer scale of the territories claimed meant that their dominion in many parts of the East Indies was more nominal than real and there was little formal administration of the outer islands even in the twentieth century.

Unlike the belligerent powers during the Great War, the four years of conflict were more of an inconvenience than a major issue for the Dutch, but the 1920s and 1930s can be characterized as an era of conservative modernization used to justify the idea of an enlightened colonialism, coupled with repression of perceived nationalist, Islamic, and communist subversion. The fact that the Dutch rulers saw these movements as unrepresentative of popular opinion across the Indonesian archipelago allowed for the creation of a dangerous delusion that would colour opinion and government behaviour in the metropole after 1945. The Japanese conquest of the Indies was as much of a shock to Dutch opinion as the capitulation to the Germans in May 1940 and deprived the Netherlands of any weight in the Allied councils of war. This powerlessness became even more evident after the defeat of Germany in 1945 when the Dutch had no effective resources to deploy in recovering their colonial territories from the Japanese.

A failure to understand or to accept the changed political realities of the emerging post-war world seems to have characterized Dutch behaviour, both among the returning political classes in the metropole and among the military and colonial administrators charged with restoring Dutch rule. They signally failed to recognize the power of anti-colonial sentiment and assumed that the removal or defeat of the nationalists, who owed all their prominence to the Japanese, would mean that the Dutch would be welcomed back by the majority. When this belief proved illusory, the Dutch were forced into ever more belligerent policies until their freedom of action was curtailed by pressure from the United States and international opinion. This made plain the impotence of the Dutch as an imperial power and forced a public and academic re-examination of 'empire'. How little was learnt in the 1950s can be seen from the stubborn attempts to retain New Guinea at the end of the decade, but even after this, the debates on the loss of the Indies remained internal and essentially political in nature. Only in the 1970s was there a greater concern with the social and cultural history of the colonies as a potentially important explanatory factor and the first proper analysis of the growth of Indonesian nationalism and its leadership. In spite of this more considered analysis, many recent texts on the decolonization process are still criticized for their traditional empiricist approach – centred on the diplomatic and colonial negotiations – where the Indonesian leaders are relegated to mere cyphers and the conflicts within nationalism not afforded their rightful position as defining parts of the narrative. That said, Indonesian affairs continue to be reported in the Dutch press, in part to inform those resident in the metropole who had their origins in the East Indies, but also perhaps as an echo of the hybridities built over several centuries. It could be said that the colonial past and the decolonization process have never been fully historicized – either in the academic or in the public sphere. Soldiers who fought in the campaigns to restore Dutch rule after 1945 were bitter when their sacrifices were largely ignored in a Netherlands increasingly focused on its role within Europe. In the same vein, successive Dutch governments were unwilling to countenance close examination of the conflict between 1945 and 1949, and public debate and apologies for crimes committed during those hostilities have only occurred in recent years.

Although much less important in a colonial narrative dominated by Indonesia, the Dutch possessions in the West Indies have experienced a rather different trajectory. While Surinam opted for independence in the 1970s, with some ostensibly disastrous results, the six Caribbean islands have seen advantages in continued links with the European Netherlands and have retained their status, albeit in different constitutional forms, within the Kingdom of the Netherlands into the twenty-first century.

CHAPTER 11

AN 'ETHICAL IMPERIALISM'? THE DUTCH COLONIAL EMPIRE BEFORE 1945

The background to Empire: Origins and structures from the nineteenth century

The Dutch Empire in the nineteenth century is unusual insofar as scholars have seldom considered it in debates about the development of imperialism or used it as a comparison with the policies pursued by other European states.[1] This omission has been explained by the focus given in such debates to the aggressive expansion of European states into Africa from the 1880s onwards, a process from which the Netherlands was conspicuously absent, and the fact that the Dutch were ostensibly concerned only with imperial consolidation – hanging onto what they already had rather than promoting expansion – either for domestic or international reasons.[2] More recent scholarship has sought to highlight the similarities of the Dutch case, especially in the key period between 1880 and 1914 when ideas about a civilizing colonial mission were in vogue, but criticisms of this approach remain. Dutch expansion remained contiguous – confined to territories adjacent to existing possessions – unlike the expansionist policies of their European neighbours. Likewise the formal occupation of territories already claimed – especially where those claims had been accepted by the major powers – was not portrayed as an attempt to prevent their falling into other imperial hands but as 'consolidation' of what already existed.[3] However, these interpretations do not alter the fact that the Dutch state took a much more active role in dictating the development of its colonies during the final decades of the nineteenth century, including the use of military force where it was deemed necessary.[4]

The Dutch colonial Empire originated in the explorations and exploitations of the Verenigde Oostindische Compagnie (United Dutch East India Company, VOC) and the Westindische Compagnie (WIC) of the United Provinces when they built substantial trading dominions over territories in both the East and West Indies during the seventeenth and eighteenth centuries. Towards the end of this period, both companies came under increasing threat from outside competition; the WIC went into liquidation in 1791 when its patent expired, and the VOC was nationalized during the Batavian Republic in 1798 – leaving the government with a debt of 140 million guilders.[5] Occupation by the French destroyed most of what remained of Dutch overseas power when other territories such as Zeylan (Ceylon) and the Cape Colony were taken into protective custody by the British, and it was only after the defeat of Napoleon that the newly formed Kingdom of the Netherlands was able to reassert claims to the former mercantile patrimony. What remained was the bulk of East Indies that had been nominally in the hands of the VOC, and the scattered islands and territories in the Caribbean and South America formally controlled by its West Indian counterpart, territories that also included the WIC settlement of Elmina on the Gold Coast of Africa. British collusion in the restoration of these Dutch possessions by the Treaty of London in 1814 was predicated on the belief that a strong Kingdom of the Netherlands would be capable of holding neighbouring France in check.[6] There is no doubt that the Dutch belief in the importance of 'empire' mirrored that of other imperial states, but the former rulers, the Dutch East and West India Companies had ceased to exist, and there were no obvious administrative or commercial structures to replace them. As in the past, colonial possessions were viewed as a potential asset to the Kingdom, but, initially at least, they proved to be a major drain on the new state's resources.[7]

The East Indies

In 1816, three Dutch Commissioners-General were sent to take possession of the colonies from the British, but there were still no clear policy guidelines regarding their future administration or economic exploitation. All these decisions were controlled directly by the Crown and were not within the remit of the Cabinet or of Parliament. The most pressing problem was that the East Indies were a drain on the Dutch exchequer. This was exacerbated in 1825 when a revolt broke out in Java, a war described as the last stand of the Javanese elite but one that encompassed all levels of society. This took five years to suppress and necessitated a substantial deployment of men and resources.[8] To combat the rapidly increasing debt, the King Willem I instituted a scheme suggested by one of his leading advisers, the soldier Johannes van den Bosch. The so-called *cultuurstelsel* (culture system) involved the remission of peasant taxes in exchange for use of proportions of their land and labour. These revenues were then directed by government agents into the cultivation of crops suitable for sale in the European market. The assumption was that the revenues generated from these export crops would exceed the remitted taxes and costs of administration.[9] The scheme was to succeed beyond the wildest dreams of its proponents. In 1830, the East Indian debt was around 30 million guilders, yet by 1877 the Asian colonies were estimated to have contributed 832 million guilders to the Dutch exchequer, helping to clear all the outstanding debts in the process.[10]

Whatever the advantages to the Dutch exchequer, the *cultuurstelsel* was undoubtedly damaging to the colonial territories. The peasants were severely exploited, being paid only a fraction of the value of their crops and deprived of time to cultivate food for themselves or for the domestic economy. Land was often exhausted in the effort to meet production targets exclusively for the benefit of the motherland. Crown control over the colonies prevented any parliamentary scrutiny and this was reinforced by strict government censorship. Change began only with the growth of political liberalism in the Netherlands and the effects of the revolutionary year of 1848. Dutch liberals took issue with exclusive Crown control over the colonies, and this brought about greater parliamentary oversight of colonial affairs and paved the way for the East Indian Government Act of 1854.[11] This new legislation did not, of itself, bring immediate change to the colonial economic system, but it did stimulate debate about the unlimited exploitation of colonial peoples and its compatibility with liberal and Christian principles.

While it might be argued that the first cracks in the colonial system stemmed from domestic political change, some individual reformers also espoused the cause of the Javanese. Two in particular had a profound impact on Dutch society. The first was W. R. Baron van Hoëvell, who had served as a minister of the Reformed Church in Batavia for eleven years before returning to the Netherlands. He published extensively and argued that the Indies should be opened up to private enterprise and to missionary activity in order to better the lot of the indigenous populations. His position was largely inspired by guilt at the levels of exploitation and the need for the Dutch to adopt a 'civilising mission' to their Asian territories.[12] Still more important in highlighting the plight of the colonies to the Dutch public was the author Eduard Douwes Dekker. A civil servant in the Indies until 1856 when he resigned over a conflict with his superiors, Douwes Dekker returned to the Netherlands and, in 1860, under the pseudonym Multatuli, published *Max Havelaar, of de koffijveilingen der Nederlandsche Handel-maatschappij*, a novel that exposed widespread colonial abuses.[13] Neither author opposed the *cultuurstelsel* outright, but both insisted that it should be reformed.[14]

The struggle for control of colonial administration and colonial policy continued in the Netherlands throughout the 1860s. The year 1864 saw the East Indian Auditing Act and, in 1867, the East Indian budget came under annual parliamentary scrutiny. This established the general principle that Cabinet Ministers were responsible to parliament and not to the Crown, enabling the Liberals to finally wrest control of government from the monarch. However, liberal colonial policies took longer to develop, the problem being that many of the Liberals' proposed domestic reforms could only be funded from the profits of the *cultuurstelsel*.[15] As a result, it was only in 1870 that the Agrarian Law abolished all state-imposed cultivation, save that of coffee, although by then, most crops had already been abandoned as unprofitable so the law only really affected the cultivation of sugar. Coffee cultivation was deemed less objectionable as it occurred on virgin land rather than at the expense of existing peasant holdings. Compulsory production of coffee endured until 1915 by which time it, too, had become unprofitable.

Ironically, the gradual decline of unrestricted government exploitation in the Indies was offset by increased private investment. The Agrarian Law of 1870 sought to resolve the vexed question of land ownership. This was done by recognizing the indigenous Javanese rights to the land they cultivated, while leaving all the waste and common land to the state, which it, in turn, made available to entrepreneurs at favourable rates. This opening of the Indies to European planters, and to missionaries and social reformers heralded the beginning of a more progressive colonial policy. The taxation system was reformed from the 1880s onwards and there was greater state investment in education and the development of a railway system.[16] Dutch steamship companies benefited from the opening of the Suez Canal in 1869 and competed with the British for shipping contracts in South East Asia. There was also some evidence that the indigenous population benefited from the new system as the value of imports to the East Indies increased threefold between 1870 and 1890. As for the Dutch, the losses of revenue from the *cultuurstelsel* were offset by reforms in the domestic taxation system spearheaded by the introduction of death duties (1878) and a graduated income tax (1893).[17]

Ostensibly, this new-style colonial policy was successful, but falling prices during the 1870s and injudicious lending policies rapidly brought the entire system to the brink of collapse. It was only salvaged by the Dutch commercial banks in the 1880s following the incorporation of many plantations into limited liability companies. This marked a decisive economic shift. Henceforward it was large-scale Dutch capitalist interests that controlled the East Indies' plantation economy.[18] Moreover, whatever short-term benefits might have accrued to the indigenous population were soon eroded as the effects of the initial reforms wore off and the international economy went into decline.

The territory claimed by the Dutch in the East Indies was colossal. It included the colonized larger islands of Java and Madura, but also the 'outer possessions' of Borneo, Bali, and Celebes, and many thousands of smaller islands. Traditionally, The Hague's claims were largely accepted by the other European colonial powers, but the extent of Dutch control of these territories was nominal, and, in some cases, non-existent. The Dutch had neither the resources nor the political will to impose their suzerainty over such a large area by force, opting instead to impose protectorates where indigenous princes had defined and recognized territorial control. This strategy of informal empire remained tenable while Dutch claims went unchallenged, but became unsustainable in the latter half of the nineteenth century. British complaints about Achinese pirates in the Straits of Malacca led to a classic colonial bargain in 1872 whereby the Dutch conceded all their rights on the Gold Coast of Africa (Elmina) in exchange for a free hand against the Sultanate of Aceh. Guarantees of equal treatment for British trade in the area were also made.[19] These arrangements paved the way for a declaration of war against the Sultanate, followed by a military expedition in 1873. There was little domestic popular enthusiasm for the war, either from the Liberals in government or the confessional opposition who saw it is an 'unjust' war of conquest driven by international pressures. The hope was that a single expedition would be sufficient to impose Dutch control and minimize the costs involved. These hopes were soon disappointed and various other methods were attempted between 1873 and 1885 but with little immediate success.[20]

It could be argued that Dutch policy in the East Indies during the last quarter of the nineteenth century was reactive: driven by external considerations and not geared to any specific economic or political agenda. Seen as a 'defensive' form of imperialism by the Dutch, it was contrasted with the aggressive and economically driven imperialism of other European states. This 'abstentionism' of the 1880s was 'strictly adhered to … by the government and the colonial administration because they had no choice, and by the Dutch parliament and the general public more as a matter of principle'.[21] However, official attitudes began to change in the 1890s as the Court, military circles, and broad sections of Dutch political opinion adopted a more interventionist stance.[22] This heralded a more active policy of military pacification and the imposition of direct rule over the outer East Indian territories. Governor Van der Wijck's successful Lombok expedition in 1894 brought him widespread public acclaim, and Johannes Van Heutsz was greeted as a hero in the Netherlands after his forces went onto the offensive and finally brought the Aceh war to a conclusion.[23]

The extension of Dutch influence into its colonial territories was also evident at another level. In the mid-nineteenth century, there had been some ambiguity about extending the provision of education beyond the white and Eurasian communities. A widespread belief existed that this would mark the beginning of the end for colonial rule. Progress was slow and it was only in 1880 that a number of schools were established to train the sons of senior local rulers for administrative careers. This broadening of education policy was given an added impetus towards the end of the century by the growth of Islam across the whole archipelago. Inherently opposed to the 'infidel' Dutch, local Muslim teachers could not be allowed to operate unchecked.[24] However, the language and mode of colonial education remained a matter of dispute, and schooling was only ever available to the rich and well connected.[25] Dutch fear of Islam was long-standing and they were suspicious of the Haj pilgrimage, but the influence of Christiaan Snouck Hurgronje, the government advisor for Native and Arabic Affairs between 1896 and 1906, brought about a change in policy that allowed for freedom of worship but suppressed any elements of Islamic political protest.[26] This realization that change was urgently required was subsumed into the adoption of what became known as the 'ethical policy' towards the Indies at the beginning of the twentieth century.[27]

'Ethical policy' had been championed by Conrad Theodor van Deventer whose writings demanded restitution to the East Indies for the ravages of the *cultuurstelsel* and a greater interest in the moral, economic, and welfare position of the indigenous peoples. It was given political weight by the strong Calvinist principles of the Anti-Revolutionary Party led by Abraham Kuyper, who became Minister-President in 1901. Their ideas took concrete form in 1905 when East Indies government debts to the Netherlands totalling 40 million guilders were written off on the understanding that the money released would be spent on the improvement of economic conditions in Java and Madura. The traditional policy of non-interference in the outer islands was also abandoned, as planters in Sumatra demanded greater administrative intervention.[28]

Two factors were at work here. The first was an increasing separation between the government in the Netherlands and the government of the Indies, with the latter acquiring greater freedom to act independently. This culminated in 1912 when the finances of the two were separated and the Government of the East Indies acquired its own juridical status. The second factor was the implicit, and sometimes explicit, assumption that the ultimate outcome of the 'ethical policy' would be the independence of the Indies from the mother country. Whereas some exponents of the policy saw this in terms of centuries, other interested parties, including an increasingly vocal independence movement, perceived it as an attainable, if not imminent, goal.

Another factor worthy of note in this period relates to the Netherlands' international position at the end of the nineteenth century. Watching European Great Power diplomacy from the sidelines, the Dutch developed a sense of themselves as a second rank or 'middle' power, a nation unable to compete with the major industrial and military nations that surrounded them, but one that nevertheless had a more important role to play in the world than other small states.[29] This became manifest in Dutch leadership in the development of international law and their hosting of the conference which led to the Hague Conventions of 1899 and 1907.[30] To some extent, this signified an abandonment of the studied 'aloofness' that had characterized Dutch foreign policy since the 1830s, although it was recognized in some quarters that maintaining this status relied heavily on the attitudes of the other European powers.

In summary, while the Dutch continued to see their extension of colonial control during the later nineteenth century as defensive, and thus different from the aggressive policies of other European states, they were drawn into a more interventionist policy as the century progressed. Moreover, while there were echoes of the 'civilising mission' idea in the pacifications of Aceh and Lombok, it is also clear that these successful military adventures provoked new forms of patriotism and nationalism.[31] This change should be emphasized as there had been little initial political support for intervention generally, even less for the specific military expeditions. Some had objected on grounds of cost, but others had taken a more ideological or ethical stand. Liberals opposed intervention on principle, while the confessional elements (both Calvinist and Roman Catholic) within Dutch politics saw it as immoral and unjust. In other imperial states, these qualms were drowned out by the imperatives of international politics, but in the Netherlands, the importance of the liberal and confessional political parties as the cornerstones of an increasingly *verzuild* (pillarized) Dutch polity [32] meant that the ideologies and principles they espoused played a key role in the development of colonial policies.

Attempts to decentralize the administration of the Indies in the early twentieth century were seen by many as a mere façade, not least because transfers of authority were so gradual, and the transfers of funds to cement that authority were slower still. In many regions of Java and Sumatra, and even more so in the outer islands, the Dutch continued to work with indigenous hereditary ruling elites. There had never been the manpower or resources for direct rule by Europeans, but shortages were offset by the existence of a Eurasian population sufficiently large to provide civil servants and a large proportion of the manpower for the Dutch colonial army (Koninklijk Nederlands Indisch Leger, KNIL). Nevertheless, the trend towards greater education for the Eurasians and elements of the indigenous population soon provoked frustration that clerical and higher administrative posts were not made available to those who benefited from these improvements in provision. At the same time, there were debates about the future governance of the Indies, whether it should be unitary or federal. A unitary system would amount to domination by the more numerous Javanese, but many nationalists saw the federal alternative as a form of divide and rule by the colonial power.[33]

The outbreak of the Great War can also be seen to have had some impact on the Dutch East Indies. Although the Kingdom maintained a strict neutrality during the conflict, its trading relationships were severely disrupted and lines of communication became irregular, especially after the Germans began unrestricted submarine warfare in 1917. This often forced both the colonial authorities and commercial interests to act without reference to their masters in the Netherlands. Islam, which had been seen as a motivating and unifying force for opposition to Dutch rule throughout the nineteenth century, once again came to be feared.[34] The first indigenous political movement, Boedi Oetomo, arose on Java in 1908 and was composed of the upper classes, local government officials, and intellectuals. It was soon eclipsed by Sarekat Islam, a less elitist movement that focused on safeguarding economic welfare and used Islam as its unifying force against increasing Christian missionary activity. The apparently increasing popularity of Sarekat Islam raised Dutch fears about the loyalty of elements within the indigenous population and, although these were not justified in the early months of the conflict, unease remained when support was later voiced for fellow Muslims in the Ottoman Empire fighting in alliance with the German Empire. As the war continued, Indonesian nationalism became more radicalized and, unsatisfied with the limited steps towards greater autonomy and wider participation in government and administration, it also assumed a markedly socialist character.[35] The movement also developed a more overt consciousness of racial divisions within the population. For example, the Chinese were targeted both as a non-Islamic minority and also because of their presumed role as capitalists and middlemen, exploiting the peasants.[36] Its increasing popularity in a wider constituency beyond the upper classes and intellectuals can be seen in the 450,000 members claimed by 1918.

Meanwhile, the Dutch further extended their control over the outer islands. During the first two decades of the twentieth century, these princely states were required to accept direct Dutch sovereignty through the so-called 'short declaration'. As a result, in 1922, the term 'colonies' was replaced by 'overseas territories', the idea being to strengthen direct rule while at the same time developing (suitably pliable) representative organizations.[37] The most visible manifestation of political reform was the creation of a *Volksraad* (People's Council) that met for the first time on 18 May 1918. Although largely consultative, it had certain budgetary oversight and its composition was split between indirectly elected members and others directly appointed by the governor general. Almost for the first time, the problems of an ethnically and geographically diverse polity had to be addressed. This was most marked in the rules dictating the ethnic composition of the *Volksraad*, insofar as the rights of European (non-Dutch) and non-indigenous Asiatics required protection. A series of further revisions took place meaning that, by 1927, electoral districts had been drawn up to ensure a reasonably fair distribution of seats according to the ethnic make up of the colony.[38] Although made into a more co-legislative body in 1925, the *Volksraad* still exercised only limited powers, with the Minister for the Colonies able to veto amendments or curtail discussion altogether. Yet the *Volksraad* was not as weak as is often portrayed, not least because it acted as a safety valve for discontent and a forum for moderate nationalists, and conflicts were sometimes resolved by a process of mutual concessions. Nonetheless, it proved largely powerless when the government pursued policies of rigorous financial stringency during the depression years of the 1930s, with an inevitable detrimental effect on the colony's economic welfare.

The interwar period saw an exacerbation of a number of trends. The relatively small number of Western-educated Indonesians found it difficult to secure employment commensurate with their perceived status and it appeared that the Dutch did not trust them with any important posts. Increasingly, their aspirations became tied to ideas about political and social modernization.[39] Economic conditions also remained discriminatory in spite of the ethical policy, with the tax burden increasing year-on-year. This led to pauperization of small farmers and other rural populations whose incomes were stagnant if not falling. European rubber planters earned between six and twelve times more for their product than their indigenous counterparts, this being a function of discriminatory taxes and allocations of export quotas.[40] Economic modernization served to break down traditional patterns of village life in parts of the colony, leading to the displacement of many people into new working environments and new locations. This also had an effect on local government as centralized agencies assumed a greater role in organizing the colonial economy. This modernization also created tensions that erupted in a series of strikes and violent attacks that began in 1920 and culminated in rebellions in West Java in November 1926 and in West Sumatra in January 1927.[41] Although successfully suppressed by the authorities, these insurgencies were widely assumed to be communist inspired, but may have been equally motivated by religious issues.[42] Blaming Marxist subversion betrays the deep-seated Dutch fears of communism, both at home and in the Empire.

The colonial government's response to the continuing crisis was to establish an internment camp at Boven-Digoel, deep in the interior of New Guinea. This was soon populated by over 800 alleged subversives and remained in use throughout the interwar period.[43] It contained many known communists, but not their leader Tan Malaka who had published the influential *Naar de Republieke Indonesia* and who managed to evade capture. Others held there included trade union leaders and Indonesian nationalists.[44] While Dutch policies undoubtedly weakened the communist movement in the Indies by locking up many of its leaders, it was not entirely eliminated.[45] Objective judgements of the real threat posed by communism are difficult. Sarekat Islam seems to have resisted infiltration, but it was undoubtedly weakened in the struggle.[46] Its leaders, and even those of the more moderate Indische Partij, were victims of a more hard-line government policy in the post-war years and suffered terms of imprisonment and exile.[47]

It has been argued that the Dutch policy in the East Indies after the 1870s was primarily to preserve order and this led to a 'state of violence' and a regime based on fear enforced by colonial police and, in cases of exceptional need, by the colonial army.[48] The apogee of this policy seems to have come in the suppression of the 1927 rebellion when a photograph of KNIL soldiers parading the corpse of a communist leader hanging from a pole through a kampong appeared in a Batavia periodical. The following year, government policy was revised to require that resistance be dealt with 'forcefully, but humanely'.[49] In some respects, the show of force used in 1926 and 1927 was employed to mask a potentially fatal weakness in Dutch colonial control as the state had only around 35,000 policemen and 32,000 soldiers to control a population estimated at more than sixty million by 1930.[50]

This should not suggest that Dutch rule was entirely concerned with repression. There were members of the administration, such as Karel Creutzberg, the Vice President of the Council of the Netherlands East Indies, who were critical of the policies being followed and sought greater accommodation with nationalism.[51] For its part, the post war colonial government made serious attempts to inculcate 'western' values through the (sometimes rudimentary) education system and through the establishment of a network of 2,500 public libraries (Balai Pustaka) containing books and magazines translated into local languages.[52] While enjoying some success and persisting until the Japanese occupation in 1942, even an initiative on this scale could not compete with the spread of nationalist sentiments.

The Partai Nasional Indonesia (PNI), formed at Bandung in 1927 by Sukarno, represented a different strand of nationalist thought emanating from those Indonesians educated in the Netherlands, and an increasing number, not all of them from the wealthy elite, who were now gaining their higher education at home. Although Governor General Jonkheer Andries C. D. de Graeff had some sympathy for more moderate nationalist sentiment, rumours of imminent revolt in late 1929 drove the government to take action. Sukarno and the other PNI leaders were arrested on 29 December. Sukarno was tried in August 1930 and, although sentenced to four years' imprisonment, was able to make a lengthy statement in mitigation, in which he condemned Dutch imperialism and its 'ethical' policy.[53] His early release in 1931 heralded a limited realignment of nationalist political forces, but little in the way of unity, with Sukarno still seeing the masses as an instrument to gain political power, while others such as the intellectuals Mohammed Hatta and Soetan Sjahrir, both of whom had spent some time in the Netherlands, saw their role primarily as political educators.[54]

In the 1920s, therefore, the Dutch felt they were faced with a twin threat, from radical Islamic ideas and from the communists. De Graeff's successor Bonifacius C. de Jonge took a harder line and was willing to imprison radicals to counteract the politicization of the masses. After May 1933, he was backed by a more conservative regime in The Hague led by Hendrik Colijn, a politician who had served with the colonial army, the KNIL, in the 1890s before returning to business and political life in the Netherlands. The situation was also exacerbated by the global depression that made severe inroads into the Dutch economy. Henceforward, compromise with anything more than the most moderate of nationalist aspirations was ruled out. Continuing instability prompted the authorities to insist that all schools and places of education be subject to licensing, a deliberate ploy to curb nationalists' attempts to educate wider sections of the community. The resultant unrest provoked a further government crackdown on nationalist leaders. Sukarno was exiled to Flores in August 1933 while Hatta, Sjahrir, and others were committed to the internment camp at Boven-Digoel in February 1934.[55]

The degree of Dutch nervousness over the Indies can be seen in the reaction to a mutiny on board a Dutch naval vessel, *De Zeven Provinciën*, stationed in north-west Sumatra in January 1933. Pay cuts imposed on naval personnel led to refusals to obey orders at the Surabaya base.

Although the mutiny stemmed from poor conditions and ineffective leadership within the Dutch Navy, the wider public reaction pinned the blame on nationalism and even communist agitation among the mutineers. This may help to explain both the government's violent reaction to the mutiny itself and conservative responses to other problems of colonial governance later in the 1930s.[56] That said, even after the detention of leading nationalist figures, moderate Indonesian nationalist groups continued to function within the *Volksraad* and even the more radical Mohammed Husni Thamrin was able to use his membership to criticize colonial abuses without fear of retribution.[57] These privileges made him more dangerous than the nationalists who rejected cooperation with representative democracy and whose institutions and leaders continued to be harried by the Dutch security services. Boven-Digoel continued in operation until 1943 but changes to the regime were made in 1936 when it was decided that it was not an appropriate location for university-trained 'intellectual nationalists' such as Hatta and Sjahrir, who were moved to Banda Neira, and there was a comprehensive case review of those who had been or remained in the camp.[58]

By the end of the 1930s, there was increasing disenchantment among moderates as their loyalty to the colonial state had not been rewarded with significant reform in the face of Dutch political intransigence. As a result, Thamrin was able to engineer a new coordinating alliance of political groups, the Gabungan Politik Indonesia (GAPI). This new organization owed its establishment to the realization of the worsening European situation and real possibility that, in the event of a European war, there was little chance that the Netherlands would be able to remain neutral.[59] The response of de Jonge, and his successor Jonkheer Alidius W. L. Tjarda van Starkenborgh-Stachouwer, was to promote provincial councils rather than any centralized autonomy as a means of limiting the impact of nationalist agitation.[60]

It seems clear that GAPI did represent a new alliance of nationalist groups in the archipelago, but, even if all the politically organized Indonesians could be brought under a single umbrella, they represented only a very small percentage of the total population. Estimates suggest that there were only 80,700 who were members of political groups, and this in a total population of about sixty million, of whom perhaps six million were literate.[61] To some extent, the more repressive policy of interwar colonial governments had borne fruit. While nationalist leaders could drum up huge support at rallies and meetings, this was not translated into mass action, and their arrest and incarceration usually led to the collapse of the movements they led. This was true of Sukarno, Sjahrir, and Hatta, each of whom was variously imprisoned or interned for much of the 1930s, but who later emerged as leaders of the nationalist revolution during and after 1945. In 1940, however, the nationalist movement was not publically perceived to represent a threat to continued Dutch colonial rule and Colijn had famously described nationalist support as 'thin as the silver skin on a grain of rice'.[62] That said, the archival record paints a rather different picture and demonstrates that the Dutch officials had a very clear idea of the depth and breadth of the nationalist movement.[63] The assumption must be that they thought their policies sufficient to control the more radical elements and that with leaders exiled or interned, there was no real threat to continuing Dutch hegemony. At the same time, Dutch rule remained 'superimposed' on the East Indies and with few active supporters beyond the European community – the 200,000 Eurasians who furnished most of the manpower of the KNIL, police and administration – and the Chinese business class. In the early years of the twentieth century there had been a concerted attempt to extend formal rule across the archipelago, and this had brought increased monetary benefits to the colonial treasury and to European enterprise now able to access the region's rich resources.[64] Yet even this gradual process of administrative modernization and cultural penetration failed to make much difference to the huge differences in the pace of change and impact of colonial rule between the urban centres of heavily populated Java on the one hand, and the vast rural expanses of other major and many hundreds of smaller islands that made up the Dutch imperium in the East Indies.[65] These differences were to have an impact on both colonists and Indonesian nationalists alike in the years to come.

The West Indies

The continental territory of Suriname and the six islands comprising Curaçao, Aruba, and Bonaire off the coast of Venezuela, and the Leeward Islands of St Eustatius, St Maarten (divided with the French), and Saba were all reoccupied in early 1816 when the British withdrew their forces. Like the East Indies, the post-1816 era brought these territories directly under the Dutch Crown, and required the creation of a new administrative and governmental apparatus. A degree of consultation with the local population existed through an appointed *Raad* (Political Council) in both Curaçao and Paramaribo, the capital of Suriname, but while the Governors General enjoyed a good deal of independence in domestic matters, all important decisions had to be ratified in The Hague.

While the political and diplomatic issues of this restoration period were to have some long-term effects on the Dutch West Indian colonies, economic factors were a more important determinant of the colonies' fortunes in the subsequent 150 years. It could be fairly said that the end of the Napoleonic wars had left both Suriname and the Dutch Islands without an economic role. The islands had traditionally operated as trading and victualing centres for the West India trade, with additional wealth in both Suriname and the islands generated from a slave-based plantation economy. However, the beginning of the nineteenth century saw the collapse of the sugar trade and increasing prohibition of the trade in, and use of, slaves in European colonial territories. These two factors were destined to have the greatest effects on the economic, demographic, and, ultimately, the political development of the territories. Curbs on the use of slaves had a detrimental effect on a plantation economy, which struggled to survive in the nineteenth century as its products were available more cheaply elsewhere. The net effect was to make government revenues in all the West Indian colonies insufficient to meet the costs of administration and defence, but there was a marked reluctance on the part of the government in The Hague to spend any more than was absolutely necessary on its ailing West Indian possessions.

However, it was the emancipation of the slaves in Suriname, which was destined to have the greatest long-term impact on the colony. The slave population in 1853 was reputed to be in the region of 33,000; thus, their numbers dwarfed the European population of the colony that amounted to no more than a few thousand. Political control was therefore perceived as difficult to maintain, and pressure on the Dutch for reform came from all quarters. Even before slavery was abolished on 1 July 1863, plans were afoot to alter the basis of the plantation sector and that of the agricultural economy as a whole. A state commission under former governor general of the East Indies, Jean Chrétien Baud reported in 1855 that the only future for the territory was as a farming colony. Ultimately, the former slaves were given the choice of where to work and put under very limited short-term supervision. The costs of compensation to the former slave-owners of 300 florins per slave were paid out of revenues from the East Indies.[66]

This left the problem of how the remains of the plantation economy could be maintained. Even before the emancipation had been put in train, schemes were under way to bring new labour into the colony. 500 indentured Chinese labourers were brought from Macao in the 1850s, but were insufficient to meet the need for plantation labour. Salvation came from a scheme to promote Hindustani emigration to Suriname and, between 1873 and 1917, some 34,000 immigrants from British India arrived in the colony.[67] Offered five-year contracts, free medical care, and protection by a British agent, the labourers could either return home at government expense when their contracts expired, renew their contracts, or use the transportation money to buy land in designated plantations - an option that was encouraged through preferential loans. Around two-thirds of the Indian immigrants chose this last option, creating the basis for a large permanent Hindustani population in the colony. Ironically, this created permanent demand for plantation labour as immigrants moved on to become small farmers. The success of Indian labourer immigration led to a further scheme to import labourers from Java on much the same basis. It had the advantage that the newcomers were already Dutch subjects, familiar with Dutch administration, and in some cases, the language as well. As with the Chinese in the mid-nineteenth century, the majority of the contract labourers chose to stay in Suriname, but took up alternative livelihoods when their contracts expired. In this way, large minority groups of (ultimately) free settlers were introduced to the colony and immigration from Java continued until 1939. This ethnic diversity is fundamental to understanding the twentieth century politics of Suriname. The effects of these successive waves of contract labour can be seen in the table below; yet even the very small European community was far from homogeneous as the relative tolerance of the earlier colonial Governors had allowed the establishment of refugee Huguenots and Roman Catholics in addition to the Dutch protestant and small Jewish community.

During the first half of the twentieth century, Suriname, Curaçao, and Aruba all underwent a process of population concentration, albeit for different reasons. In Suriname, the lack of opportunity for a younger generation in the rural areas led to an increasing migration to Paramaribo in search of paid work. In both Curaçao and Aruba, the lure was the wealth created by the oil refineries that provided new employment in a whole range of sectors,

Table 2 Suriname: Population Census 31 December 1939[68]

		%
Europeans born in the Netherlands	1,032	1.1
Europeans born elsewhere	1,044	
Negroes and Mulattoes (Creoles)	69,817	39.2
British Indians (Hindustanis)	45,674	25.7
Indonesians (Javanese)	32,840	18.5
Chinese	2,242	1.3
Bush Negroes (Maroons)	19,032	
Amerindian	2,616	14.2
Others	3,682	
Total	177,979	100.0

encouraging Europeans to enter the colonies in search of better employment. Both the islands and Suriname elected representatives to their colonial assemblies, but on a very limited and tax-based franchise. Even after the last pre-war reform in 1936, only around 2 per cent of the population were actually entitled to vote.[69] Thus, salaried and educated Europeans had the potential to wield decisive influence over the composition of the elected elements in the assemblies.

If plantation agriculture dominated the West Indian colonies for the first 300 years, adaptation to changing markets delayed, but did not reverse, the decline in the agricultural sector. Growing international competition made the plantations less and less profitable and, by the end of the 1930s, the Suriname economy was in severe difficulties. The only new element in the equation was the discovery and export of bauxite (aluminium ore), but the colony's initial returns from this were limited as the ore was exported directly to the United States for smelting. Even when aluminium increased in importance as a strategic raw material immediately before the Second World War, the only revenues that accrued directly to the colonial exchequer came from taxes on the exported tonnages of unprocessed ore.[70] In terms of economic growth, Curaçao fared better in its transition from a plantation economy at the end of the nineteenth century. The discovery and exploitation of oil reserves in Venezuela led to the construction of oil refineries in both Curaçao and Aruba. This changed the economies of both islands with a new influx of European workers, both from the Netherlands and elsewhere. Their wages went into the local economy while duties and taxes on the import and export of oil also meant that in 1924 the colonial budget went into surplus for the first time since the restoration of 1816.[71] This rapid economic development was not consistent, as the depression of the 1930s was to prove, nor without its consequences, as old forms of culture, behaviour, and employment were swamped by the new wealth and a far more transient population – made even more mobile by the arrival of regular KLM flights after 1934.

After the abolition of slavery, the governance of the West Indian colonies was vested in colonial Governors and leading civil servants appointed by the Crown, and the *Koloniale Staten* (Colonial Estates). This latter body was made up of thirteen and later fifteen members, some of whom were appointed by the Governors and the remainder elected. In Suriname it was an oligarchy of planters who controlled the elective seats, and on the islands, a small group of (mainly European) people with the necessary income and education to qualify. While the relationship between Governor and *Staten* was often fraught with difficulties, there were also major rifts between the colonies and the government in The Hague. These arose primarily because the colonies required increasing levels of central government subsidy to balance their budgets and politicians in the motherland would often cut spending plans of interest to the colonial community while prioritizing their own economic projects which had little local backing.[72] Like the East Indies, the Antilles and Suriname were redesignated as overseas territories in 1922, and major changes took place in 1936 when the assemblies were renamed as the States of Curaçao and the States of Suriname. Each had fifteen members, ten of whom were to be elected. On the islands, some attempt was also made to extend the franchise, but even after this measure, the electorate was no more than 3 per cent of a total population of 90,000.

These modernizations were really of limited effect, as the electorates remained small and the Governors were not obliged to consult the assemblies about legislation. Yet there had been little organized political activity in the Dutch West Indies before the 1930s. There was only one insurrection of any note, when in 1911 a former police inspector conspired to overthrow the government in Suriname by mobilizing the discontent among the poor and unemployed in Paramaribo. Attempts at formal planter and middle class political organizations in Suriname were largely absent before 1940. Of greater impact were organizations created to represent the interests of the lower (disenfranchised) classes. The Surinaamsche Volksbond (Suriname People's Federation) was formed to press for electoral reform and indigenous rights to public office, but only in the 1930s did political activism become more noticeable when, as in Indonesia, small numbers of non-European young men went to the Netherlands to be educated and returned imbued with new political ideologies, especially socialism and communism.

Unrest caused by widespread unemployment in the early 1930s led to the creation of a trade union organization, the Surinaamsche Arbeiders en Werknemers Organizatie (SAWO) in 1932.[73] SAWO developed close contact with a left-wing Surinamese schoolteacher in the Netherlands, Anton de Kom, who returned to Paramaribo in January 1933 after spending thirteen years in the Netherlands as a soldier and commodity dealer. During that time he made contact with Indonesian nationalists, contributed articles to radical journals, and gave regular lectures on Suriname. His radical solutions to the country's perceived social and economic problems meant that the government regarded de Kom as a communist agitator although he denied this. His arrival in Suriname served to mobilize working class Creole opinion. He was also popular among sections of the Indonesian immigrant population who heard rumours that they might be allowed to return to Java, and among the Hindustani workers who saw him as a Gandhi-like figure. In February, the then Governor banned one of his mass meetings, but further protests threatened to get out of hand and on 7 February, a mass demonstration in the centre of Paramaribo was fired on by police leaving two dead and twenty-three injured. This was used as a pretext to arrest and later deport de Kom and his family to the Netherlands.[74] Other new workers' organizations were created and there were further disturbances and fatalities; occurrences that served to frighten the authorities and led to the adoption of new 'anti revolutionary' statutes in Suriname as the state assumed greater powers to preclude any further unrest by imprisoning or expelling activists.[75] SAWO continued, but its constituency remained limited by two factors: many workers involved in mineral extraction were based outside the main population centres, and contract labourers often chose to become small farmers when their contracts expired.[76]

The wider political fears engendered by this unrest coincided with the appointment of Colijn as Prime Minister in The Hague. He appointed Johannes C. Kielstra as Governor of Suriname in August 1933.[77] Both men believed in reinforcing Dutch control in the colonies and opposed measures likely to lead to political or administrative autonomy. To that end, Kielstra departed from previous policies, which had been directed towards assimilation of the various ethnic groups in the colony, opting instead for the separate development of each group through a system of vertical integration.[78] The intention here was to strengthen the political position of Javanese and Hindustani groups, (who were regarded as a potential backbone of small farmers within the colony), and also to promote local democracy through community councils. This might help to sideline demands for greater democracy at the centre. However, Kielstra also believed that could only be administered at district and central levels by colonial civil servants who had linguistic and practical experience of the East Indies. To that end, he insisted on recruiting only those with experience in the Dutch East Indies or with training in the mother country at the expense of candidates from the upper echelons of the lighter-skinned Creole population who had traditionally filled these posts. The net effect was to severely curtail the opportunities of this group who had traditionally been the candidates for such jobs. This did nothing to endear Kielstra to the Creole population, and his unpopularity in this quarter was compounded after the constitutional changes of 1936 by his appointment of three members of Asian extraction to the *Staten* which had heretofore been dominated by Creole interests.[79] In the late 1930s, the Creole majority in the *Staten* increasingly viewed Kielstra as a dictatorial figure who ignored their opinions and although his policies took time to take effect, their impact was felt during the Second World War when Kielstra faced increasing domestic opposition from the colony's non-European elites.

In international terms, the Dutch West Indian territories were a backwater. The one key issue was the oil trade between Curaçao, Aruba, and Venezuela, where the Dutch islands had benefited from the oil companies' worries about Venezuela's political stability, port facilities, and healthiness for Europeans. The fact that refining took place outside their borders was a constant irritation to the Venezuelans, who resented the loss of revenues. The issue acquired greater importance in September 1939 when the Dutch proclaimed their traditional neutrality. The British rapidly came to realize the importance of the Dutch-controlled refineries on Curaçao and Aruba as one of the few secure sources of aviation spirit for the RAF. Thus, when the Netherlands was invaded on 10 May 1940, the British and French lost no time in garrisoning the two islands with their own troops. Although the two Dutch Cabinet Ministers sent to London that same day sanctioned this retrospectively, the suspicion remains that this might have been done without Dutch permission. Although this might also technically be interpreted as a breach of the Monroe doctrine, for the moment at least, Washington chose to take no action.[80]

Conclusion

The Dutch received some very positive comments about their colonial policy in the interwar period. For example, British colonial administrator Sir Hesketh Ball complemented the Dutch in Java for their 'steadfast policy of prudent, gradual and judicious progress which has made the Netherlands Indies the admiration of all colonizing nations'. However, this could not altogether disguise the internal and external threats to imperial security.[81] Internal subversion remained very much at the forefront of colonial concerns. Worries about the growth of nationalism combined with an almost pathological fear of communism, as epitomized by the reaction to the mutiny on *De Zeven Provinciën*. The government in Batavia, and by extension the politicians and bureaucrats of the Colonial Ministry, used restrictions and internment to counter the influence of dangerous individuals but also had to react to changing economic circumstances, not least the increased unemployment among European as well as local workers.[82] Although there were no outright challenges to Dutch rule before the arrival of the Japanese, the colonialists' fear of the kampong and its potential for internal subversion remained.

The East Indian colonies' external security was also a matter for particular concern. In the aftermath of the First World War, politicians, the military and even mercantile interests all expressed fears about the ability of the motherland to secure its eastern empire in the face of a growing threat from Japan. During the interwar period, there was a permanent tension between defence and spending on the internal development and welfare of the colonies. This was accentuated by anti-war sentiments and opposition to defence spending in the motherland and reinforced by ministers' pessimism about the efficacy of further outlay. For example, the then Minister for the Colonies, Simon de Graaff wrote privately in 1929 to the governor general suggesting that the building of a third cruiser for colonial defence would only lead to it being blown away in its first encounter with the enemy.[83] If (self) defence was untenable, then the Dutch government might be able to rely on a commonality of interest with the other European colonial powers, but its best guarantee was some form of understanding with the United States. However any hopes in this direction were likely to be complicated by an increasingly anti-colonial attitude in Washington that mirrored American public opinion at large.[84]

Whatever the problems of colonial control might have been, there was overwhelming popular support for maintaining the Empire, and even modest proposals for political and social reform could guarantee opposition from certain quarters; based on worries that any loosening of ties between metropole and colonies would be damaging. The imperial idea remained strong in Dutch discourse about the future of the Kingdom, and the East Indies in particular were seen as central to the well-being of the Dutch exchequer.[85] Although first coined in 1914, the maxim 'Indië verloren, rampspoed geboren' (Indies lost, disaster born) continued to inform and epitomize Dutch opinion until disaster did strike in 1942.[86]

CHAPTER 12
INDONESIA: THE POLITICS OF DELUSION, 1940-7

The devastating effects of the Second World War

The inward-looking attitude that characterized the Dutch and their Empire came to an abrupt halt on 10 May 1940 when the mother country was overrun by the German armed forces. It had been a continuing source of frustration for the British in the later years of the 1930s that although the Dutch were totally reliant on British goodwill in the maintenance of their Empire, and indeed for their own domestic security, The Hague insisted on a policy of independence and strict neutrality, and haggled over every last clause of a British-inspired War Trade Agreement.[1] For London, it brought back unhappy memories of the mendacious attitudes of the Dutch in the First World War when they had been regarded as having played off the belligerent powers against each other in order to maximize their political and commercial advantage. While their future allies may have despaired, the position for the Dutch government was parlous. The basis of Dutch policy was thus to accept the reality of having far too many defence commitments, but to work on the principle that in the case of a threat to any part of the Empire, their armed forces would be sufficient to hold out until help from putative Allies could arrive. In theory, this gave the Dutch the best of all worlds but was completely undermined by the country's rapid capitulation to German arms.

Almost as soon as the German invasion began, the Foreign and Colonial Ministers (Eelco van Kleffens and Charles Welter respectively) had made their way to Britain to coordinate Defence and Imperial matters with London. Within days they were joined by the majority of their Cabinet colleagues as the Dutch military position collapsed. For the duration of the war, the Dutch Empire would be controlled from the capital of another power, although the reality was that the *Volksraad* in Batavia retained substantial autonomy in both internal and external affairs. The external protection of the East Indies fell to the Dutch Navy, while internal security was handled by the relatively small Koninklijk Nederlands Indisch Leger (KNIL), made up of around 35,000 Eurasians from the colonies, and volunteers from the mother country.[2] Like the British and the Americans, the Dutch government had been aware of the potential Japanese threat to the East Indies for some time, yet there was little practical remedy in the short term. The severe economic depression during the 1930s meant that defence had been one of the areas hardest hit by government attempts to balance the budget. Thus although substantial steps were taken to increase spending in the late 1930s (from 9.1 per cent of national expenditure in 1936 to 22.6 per cent in 1939),[3] this came too late to have much impact on the modernization or expansion of either the European or the colonial Dutch armed forces.

Nationalists within the Dutch East Indies took differing views on the motherland's plight. The veteran former nationalist leader Tjipto Mangoenkoesoemo, exiled in Macassar, issued a press appeal: 'Now we stand beside the Dutch, now that the Japanese danger threatens. Bury the differences with the Netherlands, a greater danger threatens.'[4] However, his was a lone voice. Other leaders such as Hatta, Sjahrir, and Sukarno remained in exile and kept their own counsel.[5] Even after May 1940 and with the threat from Japan becoming ever greater, the Dutch found it difficult to arrange arms purchases[6] and their troops were eventually incorporated into ABDA command a few days after the Japanese had begun their invasion of the East Indies with attacks on Borneo, Celebes, and the Moluccas on 20 December.[7] Even in coalition, the Allied powers proved unequal to their task. The oil refineries at Palembang (Sumatra) were attacked on 16 February 1942 and within a fortnight General Wavell's ABDA command was forced to disband after the defeat of the combined naval force under Rear-Admiral Karel Doorman. Soon afterwards, the Dutch administration in Batavia began to lose its authority; records were destroyed and employees were sent into the countryside for safety. Military and civilian installations were also destroyed (doing far more damage than Japanese bombs), and there were outbreaks of violence and looting, first in the countryside and then spreading to the cities, directed primarily at European homes and offices. Although not apparently prompted by the nationalist movement, this disorder demonstrated a widespread outpouring of anti-European and anti-colonial sentiment.[8] The remaining military forces on Dutch soil were transferred to the command of the Dutch governor general on Java, Tjarda van Starkenborgh Stachower, who finally surrendered on 8 March.[9] By this stage, Singapore had fallen, Palembang had been occupied,[10] and Japanese forces were making substantial progress from their beachheads on the northern coast of Java towards Bandoeng. Some 37,000 Europeans and 55,000 Indonesians of the KNIL were taken into captivity,[11] thus paving the way for almost total defeat in the Dutch East Indies. Only parts of New Guinea were to remain outside Japanese control.[12]

Apart from the obvious economic importance of the Dutch East Indies, the Japanese were also determined to use their presence to remove all traces of Western influence once stability had been ensured. This included cultural changes that removed most aspects of racial discrimination, with hotels and cinemas being made available to all.[13] At the same time all Dutch civil servants were dismissed and replaced by Indonesians, and Europeans and Eurasians generally were excluded from society, with the majority interned in camps.[14] Education in the Dutch language was prohibited, as were all publications and radio broadcasts in the colonial tongue. Japanese calendars, customs, and holidays were introduced. Teachers arrived from Japan in May 1942 to replace the Dutch, and Japanese became the language of instruction for all schoolchildren, with an emphasis on military training and learning the words of the Japanese national anthem by heart.[15] In replacing the Dutch, the Japanese sought to demonstrate the superiority of the Asiatic over the European, by demeaning the former colonial power at every opportunity.[16] Their prime source of evidence was, of course, the rapid defeat of the Dutch when faced with the might of Japan. However, the new conquerors did make conscious efforts to ingratiate themselves with local populations. Many of the Indonesian soldiers taken prisoner as part of the KNIL were soon released as part of an amnesty for the Emperor's birthday on 29 April 1942. Thousands then volunteered or were pressed into becoming *heiho* (auxiliary soldiers) who were then employed on road building, transport, and loading duties.[17] In addition, the Japanese created two further paramilitary organizations, the Keibodan as an auxiliary police and air raid protection service, and the Seinendan, a scouting organization. Together, they had hundreds of thousands of Indonesian members and, beyond official duties; they occupied themselves with military drill and meetings.[18] There were also attempts to mobilize labour in different ways through the use of *rōmusha* ('work soldiers'), these included skilled workers taken overseas to work and much larger numbers of poor labourers forcibly employed on specific projects.[19] While estimates for the total numbers vary widely, more than 300,000 were shipped from Java to work in other parts of South East Asia and even on the Japanese home islands.[20] Mortality rates among these workers were horrendous. For example, of the 120,000 *rōmusha* sent to Sumatra, less than 23,000 survived.[21] Later, when Japanese manpower resources were stretched by Allied incursions elsewhere in the Pacific, they also created a volunteer army to defend Java. By the end of the war, it consisted of 70 battalions of 1,600 Japanese-trained officers and NCOs, and around 37,000 men.[22] As a consequence, much larger numbers of Indonesians were exposed to military training and weapons than the Dutch would ever have considered expedient. By 1944 its members were characterized as 'strongly nationalist, anti-Japanese, anti-Dutch but for the most part favourably disposed towards the other Allies, particularly the United States'.[23] Later, this same force was to become the backbone of the Indonesian Army.

Resistance to the Japanese occupation was limited. Europeans could not 'hide' among the indigenous population and the Japanese were ruthless in stamping out any attempts at underground military organization or intelligence gathering. In addition, the Japanese Secret Police (Kempetai) arrested around 6,500 Dutch, Chinese, and Indonesian civilians for resistance activities. How many of these were really involved in illegal work is difficult to ascertain, but all met 'the most horrible martyrdom'.[24] Many of the Indonesians had initially greeted the Japanese as liberators, a result of their increasingly virulent anti-Dutch sentiment and a reflection of the commonly held belief that the Dutch would be driven out by 'a yellow race from the North'.[25] Others saw the Japanese as a modernizing force,[26] although most were soon disenchanted as it became clear that changes were only intended to benefit Japanese interests and the myth of the co-prosperity sphere gave way to the reality of economic deprivation and forced labour. Cutbacks in cultivation combined with Japanese requisitioning of food staples led to shortages and some local uprisings, often prompted by Islamic leaders.[27] Initially, the Japanese had suppressed any form of revolutionary change and forbade any Indonesian political activity. This prohibition was later reconsidered. Certain nationalist figures, such as Soetan Sjahrir and Amir Sjarifoeddin,[28] refused to be drawn into any relationship but others, such as Sukarno and Mohammed Hatta did agree to work with the Japanese, although their participation has subsequently been portrayed as tactical rather than principled.[29] Initially, they were no more than puppets, organizing propaganda and the Pusat Tenaga Rakjat (Centre of People's Power, PUTERA) to encourage work and production for the Japanese war effort.[30] At one level, PUTERA deflected criticism away from the Japanese for the unpopular measures introduced, but it also served as a means whereby these leading nationalists could re-establish contact with the mass of the Indonesian population. The Japanese also organized the Indonesian Pembela Tanah Air (Volunteer Army of Defenders of the Homeland, PETA) as an auxiliary defence force against a possible Allied attack.[31] This, too, soon became imbued with nationalist principles.[32] Once it became apparent that the Japanese were losing control, PUTERA was dissolved but as the tide of war turned against them, the Tokyo government was prepared to make more fundamental concessions. On 7 September 1944, the Japanese Prime Minister Lieutenant-General Kuniaki Koiso told the Japanese parliament that progress would be made towards Indonesian independence.[33] Permission was granted for the use of the Indonesian flag and national anthem, and a new paramilitary youth organization, the Barisan Pelopor, was established. This new body was different from the Keibodan or Seinendan in that it offered a platform for nationalist rather than Japanese ideas and propaganda.[34] However, nationalist euphoria at this turn of events was tempered by the tardiness of Japanese actions as it was not until May 1945 that Tokyo authorized a constitutional congress to discuss statutes for future independence.[35] However, the significance of these new youth formations was in their mobilization of large numbers of young men who were thus exposed to nationalists' ideas and who would form the basis for the so-called *pemudas*, or ultra-nationalist youth groups in the immediate post-liberation period.[36]

Seen from the Dutch perspective, the Indonesian nationalist movement was widely perceived as a Japanese creation, and its main protagonists as no more than craven collaborators. However, many Indonesians had had their eyes opened to the possibilities of independence and were thus unwilling to countenance the possibility of a return to colonial rule. This Dutch misreading of the depth of popular nationalism hid the fact that the Japanese had merely been the catalysts for the awakening of nationalist feeling. The wartime damage done to Indonesia's economic structures and to general living standards had been substantial and although there was little in the way of popular resistance, the idea that nationalism was infinitely preferable to colonial rule by either the Japanese or the Dutch took root. Generalizations also served to mask the great variety of nationalist opinion across the archipelago. In particular, there emerged a much more radical, intransigent, youth-oriented movement that demanded immediate independence and rejected the compromising nature of the older generation of nationalists.[37]

At the outbreak of war, the vast majority of the Dutch were still wedded to the idea of empire with only the left-wing parties dissenting. However, the shock of 1940 did provoke some changes – albeit more by compulsion than by choice. The Colonial Minister, Charles Welter, had suggested some reforms to the imperial structure after the Dutch government had gone into exile but these had been widely opposed, both in London and Batavia.[38] The Atlantic Charter of 1941 included a recognition of the 'right of all peoples to choose the form of government under which they will live' yet the Dutch government in London showed genuine surprise when the East Indies *Volksraad* asked how this would apply to Indonesia. Its reply was that the Charter did not concern itself with empires 'whose existence [had] proved itself in history'.[39] In the spring of 1942, the Colonial Minister Hubertus J. van Mook had travelled through the United States on his way to London from Australia and had come to realize that American opinion believed that the days of the colonial system were numbered.[40] He reported this to the Dutch government-in-exile in London, but it was a message that most ministers were unwilling to hear. Foreign Minister van Boeyen described Indonesia as 'politically still a child', and even Prime Minister Gerbrandy thought it would bring nothing but trouble.[41] Nonetheless, van Mook was asked to devise a new colonial policy statement, which was then broadcast by Queen Wilhelmina on 6 December 1942, the first anniversary of the outbreak of war in the Far East.[42] Perversely, the broadcast was not heard in Indonesia and its contents did not become known there until much later. It hardly mattered as the real purpose of the broadcast was to influence American opinion, not to appeal to the Indonesian population.[43] The government-in-exile certainly did not see the declaration as heralding a radical alteration of the imperial structure when the war ended and it remained adamant that there should be no dialogue with nationalists.[44]

By the time the Pacific War ended in August 1945, the Kingdom of the Netherlands was severely weakened: economically, politically, and internationally. The European motherland had undergone five years of German rule and most of the Indies had been subjected to three-and-a-half years of Japanese occupation. Only the Dutch West Indies had escaped enemy control, but the Netherlands' allies had garrisoned even these outposts of Empire to protect the strategic raw materials they produced. What remained of the Dutch armed forces were the few who had escaped the Germans and Japanese together with the limited numbers raised from the West Indies and from Dutchmen living abroad. The Dutch European economy had been severely run down by the Germans, and there was no means of knowing what damage the Japanese had wrought in the East Indies. Dutch resources overseas had been harnessed for the Allied war effort and all but exhausted. Immediate reconstruction was essential. Politically, the Queen and her government-in-exile had to re-establish their authority in the Netherlands and the country had to be reunited after five years of social fragmentation under national-socialist rule. It was against this background that the Dutch tried to resume their role as a European colonial power in the immediate post-war era.

The aftermath of Japanese rule

British and American decisions were to play a key role in the ultimate fate of the Dutch East Indies. In April 1944, the Dutch established an East Indian government-in-exile near Brisbane[45] and, from October, they applied considerable pressure in Washington, London, and via their representatives at South East Asia Command (SEAC) Headquarters in Kandy to ensure that some of their troops would be available to reoccupy the East Indies as soon as the war with Japan ended. A total of 5,000 marines had been trained in the United States but attempts to prepare still more met with a negative American response. Likewise, after initial approval from Canberra, plans to move 30,000 troops to Australia in preparation for transfer to the East Indies were blocked by the Australian Prime Minister as a result of domestic opposition. Moreover, the extension of SEAC's boundaries at the Potsdam Conference in July 1945 to include Java and the other Dutch territories to the east in his area forced Admiral Lord Louis Mountbatten to reconsider his original plans.[46] While work to aid prisoners of war and internees would take place in all liberated territories, Java was low on his list of priorities. This was partly a matter of geography but when it became politically expedient to have British, rather than American or Chinese, forces take the Japanese surrender on Hong Kong, a naval task force was rapidly dispatched to stake a claim for continued sovereignty. No such expedition was considered necessary for the Dutch possessions as their future was not in dispute among the Allies and even the United States was apparently amenable to a resumption of imperial control.[47] Roosevelt had been heavily influenced by Queen Wilhelmina's radio broadcast of December 1942, and was on record as saying that he believed that the Dutch would grant democracy and dominion status to their possessions.[48] However, his legacy did not extend to providing the necessary transport for a rapid resumption of colonial control.[49]

When Java had been considered part of the American SWPA, the Dutch had been able to negotiate a Civil Affairs Agreement with the United States' planners whereby all civilian matters were to be the responsibility of a new Netherlands Indies Civil Administration (NICA). This suited the Americans, who had no organization or resources to carry out such a task. It also distanced them from any potential difficulties arising from the resumption of colonial rule. The arrangement also suited the Dutch, promising them a free hand and access to American supplies.[50] With the transfer of responsibility to SEAC, the Civil Affairs arrangements for Sumatra were applied to all the Dutch territories. However, this meant that for an interim period, NICA would remain subordinate to Mountbatten's military command structure, and would also have to operate alongside the British civil affairs organization.[51] At the same time, Mountbatten was to be advised on internal matters by the Dutch, and specifically by van Mook, by this time appointed lieutenant governor general.[52] This, it was assumed, would be for a short period only, while the military reoccupation of the islands took place and the Dutch augmented their forces in the region. The reality was to be rather different. These administrative changes also disrupted van Mook's strategy for the resumption of Dutch control. He had cultivated a relationship with the American commander in the Pacific, General Douglas MacArthur, only to find the Americans belatedly transferring all responsibility for Dutch imperial territories to the British.[53]

Allied military occupation of the Dutch East Indies was delayed not only by a shortage of manpower, but also by General MacArthur's wish that no military actions should be taken before the Japanese had actually signed the instrument of surrender in Tokyo. His reasoning was that there could be no assumption that all the Japanese would surrender, that precipitate action by a theatre commander might jeopardize the whole process, and that Japanese field commanders might not obey the orders of an incoming Allied force. Although Mountbatten disagreed, he was powerless in the face of wider support for this stance from the American and the British Chiefs of Staff. Thus when the Japanese surrender came, the Dutch were militarily unprepared to resume their colonial role. Five battalions of 800 men were due to be deployed in late September 1945, reinforced by a further twelve in the following two months, but none of these units would arrive early enough to provide immediate replacements for the Japanese.[54]

With no external forces at their disposal, the Dutch looked for alternatives. Their eyes alighted on the 18,000 prisoners of war thought to be in camps on Java who had been members of the KNIL. The fact that many were non-European Ambonese and Manadonese was conveniently disregarded and it was blithely assumed that they would be capable of returning to military service almost immediately, taking care of internal security until other forces arrived. No account was taken of the possible toll that three and a half years of Japanese captivity might have taken on these men. The disparity between Dutch aspirations and their actual military position was never greater than at this crucial moment, or as Peter Dennis describes it, 'Ignorance and self delusion were a potent mixture, and the Dutch were yet to appreciate the enormity of the situation facing them and the limits of their own power.'[55]

In part, this ignorance regarding actual conditions in the East Indies reflected the inadequacy of the Dutch intelligence service. Admiral Helfrich's Corps Insulinde worked in tandem with Britain's SOE, but was hamstrung both by British restrictions on its operations in Sumatra and by the poor quality of its senior staff.[56] Its agents were few and far between, and attempts to increase their numbers were opposed by the British who did not want to encourage the Japanese to strengthen their forces on Sumatra, something that might happen if Tokyo became aware of an increased British and Dutch presence on the island. Even the agents who were sent into occupied territory reported a good deal of hostility from local populations, yet there was little sense that the Dutch authorities recognized this as an ill omen for the future.[57] Intelligence from civilian sources was equally sparse and neither the Dutch nor the British had much idea of internal conditions or the burgeoning independence movement prior to the Japanese surrender. If it was considered at all, it was thought of as a small group of fanatics with a larger group of fellow travellers.[58] Although Dutch East Indies Chief Commissioner Charles Olke van der Plas, then based in Melbourne, had cautioned in February 1944 that the

Japanese might grant 'independence' to some sort of government of quislings, his warnings went unheeded. Even in September 1945, when Dutch intelligence reported the existence of a Republican Army of 40–50,000 men, it was assumed that such a force could not mount any effective opposition to a Dutch military reoccupation.[59] It has also been suggested that one further contributory element to Dutch ignorance of the true situation was the late transfer of Java from SWPA to SEAC and the Americans' failure to hand over any of their intelligence reports before the end of the war.[60]

The premise behind the Anglo-Dutch agreements was that any resistance to the reoccupation would come from renegade Japanese commanders unaware or unwilling to carry out orders from Tokyo. Moreover, it was thought that the re-establishment of law and order would be rapidly accomplished, thus facilitating a prompt transition from military to civilian rule. This view had been based on experiences in New Guinea, where Dutch rule had been rapidly restored, and on assumptions about conditions in Java and Sumatra.[61] While the less developed nature of the New Guinea population made any comparisons somewhat spurious, van Mook wrote to Johann Logemann, the Minister for Overseas Territories, on 12 August 1945 as follows:

> I expect no great difficulties on Java, with the exception of the chance of local brigandage as a result of the temporary absence of authority and the problem of the reorganization of the police; this is perhaps the most difficult. In Sumatra, I expect greater problems as a result of the different disposition of the population and the mutual controversies.[62]

These expectations underestimated the strength of popular support for the independence movement, the strength of its leadership and also the continuing military weakness of the colonial power. Only in September 1945 did van Mook and the leading Dutch officials begin to comprehend that they were not going to be dealing with a political vacuum, but with an indigenous movement that had already proclaimed an independent Republic of Indonesia on 17 August 1945, only two days after the Japanese surrender.[63] The declaration of independence may have been nothing more than token, but the delay in the arrival of Allied forces allowed the spirit of revolution to take hold. Sukarno was chosen as the first President of the fledgling Republic, with Mohammed Hatta as his Vice President. A cabinet of ministers was formed and a constitution drawn up. The new state even began the process of creating its own armed forces using Dutch or Japanese-trained officers.[64] Perhaps more importantly, the Republic also extended its control across substantial areas of Java in those first crucial days and weeks.[65]

Although facilitated by the absence of Allied forces, Sukarno and Hatta's success also owed something to the Japanese authorities that were left in place by Mountbatten to maintain law and order. The new government's control in Java, the most populous and richest of the islands, rested on a formidable alliance between nationalists, the indigenous bureaucratic elite, and orthodox-Islam. This was reinforced by support from broad sections of the politically aware population, and especially from the ranks of the young who had been most influenced by Japan's anti-Western propaganda. This alliance of majority Indonesian opinion was reflected in the creation of an interim committee of 137 members, the Komitee Nasional Indonesia Pusat, which contained individuals who had cooperated with the Japanese, such as Sukarno and Hatta, alongside those who had not, such as Sjahrir and Sjarifuddin.[66] Together they took control of the press and radio, and also acquired weapons, both from the Japanese police and by storming the Japanese arsenal at Surabaya. This allowed the creation of an army, the Tentara Keamanan Rajkat (TKR), or People's Security Army. The nomenclature was significant: Sukarno was keen to impress upon Mountbatten that the force existed to guarantee law and order in a period of potential chaos.[67] Only the minority groups, primarily the Chinese, the Eurasians, and the many Christians (for example from Ambon), still looked favourably on Dutch rule as guaranteeing their protection from the majority.[68]

In the light of these developments, the Dutch meeting with Mountbatten at the latter's headquarters in Kandy on 4 September became a crucial element in determining the speed and nature of their return to the East Indies. Discussions centred on how to deal with the existence of the Republic. The Dutch had originally drafted leaflets instructing the population to obey neither the Japanese military nor the Indonesian Republic pending the Allied arrival, but this was clearly a recipe for anarchy and disaster. Yet van Mook remained adamant that no recognition should be afforded to the Sukarno regime and the final text vested temporary control in the hands of the Japanese commander of the Southern Army, Field Marshal Count Terauchi. RAPWI (Recovery of Allied Prisoners of War and Internees) units were also instructed to deal exclusively with the Japanese. Mountbatten refused to take a position over the recognition of the Republic, as this was a political matter and the question was therefore referred to London. Thus it was left to the Dutch to issue their proclamation and a matter for London whether to instruct Mountbatten to enforce its terms.[69]

Mountbatten's original plan had been to delay the military reoccupation of Java until the arrival of the 26th Division in early October. In the interim, Terauchi was instructed to maintain law and order. Van Mook's insistence that no recognition could be given to the idea of an Indonesian Republic presented a potential conflict with his, and the Allies', other objective, namely the identification, location, and liberation of prisoner-of-war and civilian internment camps. Initial reports indicated a much larger number of camps and internees than had been expected, and Mountbatten therefore advanced his plans and sent in a small expeditionary SOE force to Batavia. Its report on the conditions in camps prompted the despatch of an advance naval force on 15 September to put a RAPWI Control Office on the island.[70] The latter's arrival in Batavia and contact with the Japanese military authorities demonstrated the extent of previous miscalculations. The Japanese had attempted to maintain order, but admitted that *de facto* control had already passed to the nationalists. Anti-Dutch feeling was already running high and the reappearance of the colonial power and display of the flag was perceived to be an extremely inflammatory gesture.[71] Mountbatten, under pressure from London to resolve the question of British and European prisoners still in camps, became anxious to dissociate the RAPWI mission from the arrival of the Dutch. The mission was only likely to be successful if it could negotiate with the nationalists who ostensibly controlled much of the interior. At the same time he was also under pressure from the Dutch to deploy British troops in order to maintain security and pave the way for a Dutch military reoccupation in due course. To that end, he restructured SEAC military priorities and dispatched two brigades from the 23rd Division from Malaya, the first to Batavia and the second to the other nationalist stronghold on Java: Surabaya.[72]

Commanded by Lieutenant-General Philip Christison, these first British forces were required to walk a very fine line. Their primary purpose was to facilitate the recovery and repatriation of prisoners of war and internees, yet it soon became clear that van Mook and the Dutch expected them to do much more, namely keeping order until Dutch forces could arrive in sufficient numbers. Meanwhile, speaking in Singapore on 28 September, Britain's Secretary of State for War, Jack Lawson confirmed that no British soldiers would be used to intervene in Java.[73] Christison too, in a bid to assuage nationalist opposition, had said explicitly that there were no Dutch soldiers under his command. He went on to imply that the Dutch should engage in a round table discussion with the nationalists. These statements incensed the Dutch who felt that the British were reneging on their commitment to facilitate Dutch reoccupation of their colonial territories. Van der Plas had been active in trying to split the nationalists and persuade 'moderates' to become part of the civil affairs structures under the military government, but without success. For their part, the nationalists saw all Dutch soldiers, however small in number, as a provocation that might result in further violence and military intervention by the Indonesian armed forces.[74] While London did its best to pour oil on troubled waters, instructions to Christison continued to insist that he should not take sides.[75]

As the realities of the situation on the ground became clearer, Mountbatten entered the fray. He suggested that the Dutch would have to enter some form of dialogue with the nationalists, as their existing stance would lose them the Indies altogether.[76] To that end he brought pressure to bear on van Mook and the Dutch government to issue some clear-cut statement about the future of the Netherlands East Indies. Outraged by Mountbatten's offering of political advice, van Mook nonetheless pressed the British to continue their efforts to maintain control. In exchange, he was prepared to enter discussions with the Indonesian leaders provided that this was not taken to imply any recognition of the Republic of Indonesia.[77] This was a major step for the Dutch lieutenant governor general to take and one for which he was excoriated at home in the Netherlands. If the Dutch officials trying to expedite the resumption of control in the East Indies were considered intransigent by their British allies, this was as nothing to the attitudes taken by the government, politicians, and the general public in the Netherlands.

In essence, Dutch domestic opinion had taken no account of the radically changed realities of international politics. Their British allies had been all but bankrupted by the war effort and geostrategic power now lay primarily with the United States and the Soviet Union. Both had good reasons to oppose the restoration of European colonial empires. The post-liberation Dutch government was inevitably concerned primarily with domestic readjustment and reconstruction after the occupation by the Germans, but also adopted a hard line over the fate of the colonies. No one questioned the presumption that victory for the Allies over the Japanese would mark a return to colonial rule in the Indies. What other outcome was possible?

To some extent, van Mook was responsible for this misconception at home having advised there would be few problems in restoring Dutch control in Java and that only Sumatra was likely to require greater military intervention.[78] This was in spite of the fact that Abdulkadir Widjojoatmodjo, a member of the Netherlands Indies Government-in-exile, had arrived in Java on 15 September and reported that Sukarno and his group were much better supported than had been thought, and that the best course of action was negotiation.[79] Van Mook nonetheless continued to portray the popular support for nationalist home rule as Japanese inspired, and suggested either that the entire edifice of nationalist administration would disappear once normality was restored, or that it could be expunged by military force if necessary. Perhaps inevitably, the Dutch were not inclined to treat with the likes of Hatta and Sukarno, both of whom were demonized as pro-Japanese collaborators. At a time when many thousands of Dutch citizens were being tried and imprisoned or punished for collaboration with the Germans, the idea of negotiating with the nationalist leadership was unthinkable.[80] Furthermore, a resumption of control in the Indies was also judged essential to Dutch economic reconstruction, a view encapsulated in the continuing restatement of Sandberg's maxim: *Indië verloren, rampspoed geboren*.[81]

This is not to say that Dutch attitudes were entirely reactionary. During the war, the Dutch Indies government-in-exile had attempted to recruit Indonesian Muslims in Saudi Arabia for training in propaganda and other forms of subversion. This produced only seventy-two volunteers and was ultimately adjudged a failure. Most of those approached had argued that the struggle had nothing to do with them. More important and more remarkable was the attempted harnessing of Islamic leaders who had been imprisoned in Boven-Digoel by the Dutch as subversives in the 1930s. This internment camp never fell into Japanese hands but its 'liberation' by Allied forces in 1943 allowed the transport of former inmates to Australia where they could be used for propaganda work and radio broadcasts to occupied Indonesia. Their help was enlisted on the basis that Japanese rule was inimical to Islam and that Muslims would be better served by a Dutch colonial power prepared to countenance wholesale religious, social, and educational reform. The contradiction here is stark. These were men whom the Dutch had previously regarded as sufficiently inimical to their colonial ambitions that they had to be imprisoned in faraway New Guinea. Now they were seen as a possible asset.[82]

In a broader context, it was widely accepted in Dutch circles that the promises made in Queen Wilhelmina's radio broadcast of 7 December 1942 would have to be given some substance. There was inevitably some resistance from hard-line elements within the Dutch administration, but Logemann, as Minister for Overseas Territories, (itself a re-branding of the former Colonial Ministry) insisted that changes had to be made.[83] A reconstituted *Volksraad* would have an Indonesian majority, legal discrimination against Indonesians would be removed, Indonesians would have more chances for advancement in the civil service, and the very name Nederlands-Indië would be replaced by Indonesië. At home, the Schermerhorn-Drees Cabinet received almost unanimous support for its policies both from the interim Second Chamber of the Dutch parliament and most of the press.[84] However, imperial authority still had to be restored before any of this could be accomplished.

Backing for the Dutch government's position increased as reports filtered back from the Indies. These chronicled what became known as the *bersiap* period,[85] the months of chaos immediately following the Japanese surrender, when tens of thousands of young Indonesians waged a conflict against the Japanese, the Dutch, the British and even their indigenous 'feudal' leaders. Unsure of what the British and Dutch reaction might be to the declaration of the Republic, the *pemudas* began a campaign of terror against anyone considered inimical to the new regime.[86] Pro-Dutch Indonesians as well as Dutch nationals and Eurasians were targeted. In one such case, fourteen people were taken from a train at Tjikampek and murdered, and the wives and children of loyal Ambonese were especially badly treated. Many others were imprisoned and released only when British troops arrived. In Buitenzorg (Bogor) some 1,400 people had to be freed from the police station and local prison.[87] In Surabaya there were objections when returning former internees attempted to raise a Dutch flag – an incident that led to bloodshed.[88] Amid the chaos, large quantities of Japanese arms fell into *pemuda* hands. There were innumerable cases of kidnapping and murder in the major towns and cities as the Dutch, pro-Dutch Indonesians, and even the Japanese found themselves the targets of indiscriminate persecution and violence.[89] This was also true in the interior where many thousands of Dutchmen and women were still in the internment camps where the Japanese had left them. With no other protection, they were entirely at the mercy of the *pemudas*.[90]

In many respects therefore, the battle lines of Indonesia's decolonization were drawn before a single Allied soldier had set foot on either Java or Sumatra. The Dutch political leadership clearly underestimated the nature of burgeoning Indonesian nationalism, and remained dismissive of the reports received by NICA indicating widespread antipathy and, sometimes, virulent hatred of the Dutch, even among sections of the population where it had not existed before.[91] The administrators dealing with the British and the Americans felt that Dutch interests were being overlooked while the major powers pursued their own interests, failing to take advice, even when it was proffered with the best of motives. For their part, the Indonesians saw opportunities in the period of Japanese occupation for greater (albeit not complete) freedom in administration, education, and the public discussion of new ideas; all of which had been far more restricted under Dutch rule.[92] Both the real and the psychological impact of these changes on nationalists and new classes inside the country were to become a major mobilizing factor in the following months and years.

The British military occupation

While the political negotiations in Kandy continued, the first sizeable British imperial contingents under Christison's command arrived on Java on 28 September 1945. As the commander had promised, Dutch forces were excluded from these early landings and held in Malaya to preclude any conflict with Indonesian nationalists.[93] Political problems arose for the British when Reuters news agency reported on 29 September that Christison had given a *de facto* recognition to the Indonesian regime. This provoked a storm of protest from The Hague and from van Mook, forcing Mountbatten to have Christison deliver a statement clarifying that only the Dutch were recognized by the British and their delay in arriving was purely a question of preparedness.[94] To some extent, it was the British who were embarrassed by this situation. There was no possibility of accelerating the movement of Dutch forces from Europe without sacrificing the interests of the French in getting their troops to Indochina, or more importantly of British civilians and soldiers being transported home from service overseas or long-term captivity. A change in priorities was considered unacceptable in London, but the alternative was to deploy more British forces, which were likely to encounter armed resistance and suffer casualties and would in any case have to be withdrawn from tasks elsewhere. As a result, it was decided that Japanese forces on Java would be remobilized temporarily to maintain law and order. A second issue was to elucidate the purpose of British involvement. Was it merely to hold a few strongholds and major cities, or was the remit to extend direct control into the interior? Mountbatten looked to the Chiefs of Staff and his political masters for a definitive answer.

In the meantime, van Mook had finally arrived in Batavia but his position accurately mirrored that of the colonial power he represented. He had arrived at 5pm on 2 October 1945 and was greeted by an escort of KNIL soldiers cobbled together from locally based former POWs. One description commented that he had,

> arrived in Batavia in the most miserable and almost shameful manner. At that moment, he was in charge of a powder keg, formerly a well run and major colony for the whole

world. Never in the history of the Dutch East Indies had an acting governor confronted so many and such important problems and questions on his arrival.[95]

In a private letter he himself noted that the governor's palace was in reasonably good order, although taps were leaking and the telephone and electricity supply took time to restore. Food could be had at the Hotel des Indes where the RAPWI headquarters was based and where there were many familiar faces – all malnourished and with the grey 'camp' pallor.

Dutch political intransigence continued unabated at a meeting in Singapore on 10 October. The minutes included a deconstruction of the Christison broadcast and a restatement of each side's position.[96] Both van Mook and Admiral Helfrich remained suspicious of the British and refused to be won over by Mountbatten into a more accommodating and 'realistic' attitude.[97] For his part, Mountbatten refused to countenance the idea of British troops being used to destroy the Indonesian Republic,[98] but in the event, he did concede more than van Mook, and additional troops were commissioned to occupy areas where there were known to be prisoners, internees, and large concentrations of Japanese soldiers. At the same time, van Mook insisted that he should decide with whom he would negotiate – still adamantly refusing to have anything to do with either Sukarno or Hatta.

The only Dutch forces to have arrived in Batavia thus far were a single battalion of soldiers made up of former POWs and seven Internal Security Companies,[99] yet even the behaviour of these small contingents caused concern for the British. They seemed to go out of their way to be provocative towards the local population and Christison was soon forced to confine those not required for active duties in Batavia to the garrison of Tanjong Priok, some seven miles away. Even then there were problems. When a car backfired outside the Dutch headquarters, the guards outside the building reacted by shooting the driver. All the Indonesians in the street were then rounded up and some Republicans and Eurasian 'collaborators' were summarily executed. In mid-November a group of Ambonese soldiers attacked an Indonesian police post to the south of Batavia and killed its entire cohort in direct retaliation for the earlier massacre of their wives and children.[100] This picture of an insensitive and trigger-happy colonial power was reinforced by British reports about the Dutch troops to be sent to the Indies who were considered 'indifferent and semi-trained'.[101] One officer reported that:

> The Dutch are behaving like reactionary exiles or neurotic prisoners of war and internees. The former refuse to admit that Indonesians did declare their independence and assume power on 17 August, the latter are hysterically frightened that they will all be massacred.[102]

One of Christison subordinates saw Dutch excesses as deliberate policy to force the British to move beyond their policy of political non-interference.[103] For his part, Christison feared that if Dutch troops arrived on Java, civil war would ensue, which would inevitably involve the British and Indian troops stationed there. He also wanted all Dutch forces withdrawn from RAPWI work on the grounds that they were reputedly using this humanitarian work to smuggle arms and agents into the interior.

In his reports to Mountbatten, Christison was more outspoken about what the Dutch ought to do. On 4 October, his advice was straightforward.

Van Mook should fly to Holland to give the Dutch Government the true picture. He must be realistic. He must face the fact that Indonesia did declare her independence on 17 August 1945 and that since then, with or without Japanese support, Java has been run by the Sukarno Cabinet. It is such a shock to the Dutchmen coming in that I have had the greatest difficulty in dragging the ostriches' heads out of the sand.[104]

However logical this may have appeared to Christison, getting van Mook to accept the realities of the situation was one thing, having him persuade his countrymen at home to accept those same realities was something else entirely. The Schermerhorn-Drees Cabinet in The Hague had consistently refused to issue a statement on the future of Indonesia and had precluded van Mook from opening talks with Sukarno and Hatta, men who were still derided as terrorists and 'fascist Japanese puppets'.[105] In early October, the Dutch government even asked the British to arrest Sukarno and Hatta as war criminals. In this climate, compromise seemed impossible.

British frustration was palpable, but the Dutch had additional reason to prevaricate. The Republic was far from united politically and existed economically on a hand-to-mouth basis. In Dutch eyes there seemed a real chance that, if and when conditions worsened, their prospects of being welcomed back might improve. This left aside the possibility of more radical (communist) political elements taking over in the interim, but even that would increase the probability of British and American aid to assist Dutch ambitions. How much wishful thinking was involved here cannot really be estimated. In the event, the Republic's survival through these early months can be attributed to several factors; the unity of purpose between hard-line and moderate elements in Indonesia in seeking their shared objective of full independence; the Republic's leaders not being blamed for the shortcomings of the new regime – in the short term at least; the fact that most international opinion seemed to be on the side of the Republic, and most importantly of all, the loyalty of the people to Sukarno as the embodiment of the Republic.[106]

Later in October, the British did engineer a meeting with the Republic's leaders, but only after receiving grudging agreement from van Mook. Thus, the two parties were both present at an informal gathering on 25 October.[107] The intention was to clarify the British position with Sukarno and Hatta to facilitate the work of the RAPWI units in reaching the 100,000 POWs and internees still reputed to be scattered across the country. Maberly Esler Dening, Mountbatten's Chief Political Adviser, became the spokesman and reported that the Indonesians were disappointed with British support for Dutch sovereignty. However, Dening did make some progress. The nationalists agreed in principle to meet van Mook. There is no doubt that the lieutenant governor general was changing his mind about the situation, influenced primarily by stories of massacres, the situation in Batavia where the KNIL and Ambonese soldiers were undoubtedly trigger-happy, and the fact that a continuing absence of dialogue played into the extremists' hands. Van der Plas had already noted that 'there was a general unanimous hatred against the Netherlands and such a desire for freedom that the only chance to avoid bloodshed is to concede independence to Sukarno and Hatta'.[108]

The British occupation of Surabaya bore out all Mountbatten's and Christison's worst fears. The arrival of the 49th Brigade, 23rd Indian Division, on 25 October 1945 led to the local nationalists erecting barricades. This was countered by a show of air power and a tentative ceasefire agreement between the two sides that broke down within days. An RAF mission on

27 October dropped leaflets on the city calling on all Indonesians to lay down their arms and claimed that the British military administration was now replacing the nationalists who had run the area since August. This was ill advised, but the excuse given was that the leaflets were intended for general use and took no account of the specific circumstances in Surabaya. The effect was immediate. Moderate nationalists were ousted from leading roles and replaced by extremists, whose troops then mounted attacks against British positions.[109] It soon became clear that the nationalists had access to large quantities of modern weaponry acquired from the Japanese, including armoured cars and light tanks.[110] On 29 October, Sukarno and Hatta were flown in by the British to organize a truce and help restore order. Although they achieved some success, their efforts were immediately undone on 30 October when the British Commander, Brigadier Aubertin Mallaby, was shot in the street.[111] It was later discovered that two of his subordinates had also been tortured and killed by extremists.[112] Van Mook had received explicit instructions from The Hague not to meet Sukarno or other 'irreconcilables',[113] but after Mallaby's murder he went ahead and met the nationalists, including Sukarno, on 31 October, in spite of his government's objections.[114] For him, this was preferable to no negotiations at all. News of the meeting was greeted with horror in the Netherlands and van Mook was threatened with dismissal by his political masters but reprieved by the Queen on the grounds that to replace him 'in the midst of battle' would be a mistake.[115] He was instructed instead not to repeat his mistake. There was some concession that meetings with nationalists might have to take place, but that any contact with Sukarno (who had become the focus of Dutch public hatred) had to be broken off.[116]

News of the disorder destabilized many areas of Java, leaving Christison with huge problems, not least the prisoners and internees still in camps in the interior nominally protected by the Japanese but now potentially hostages of the nationalists.[117] It took nearly two months, further reinforcements and some heavy fighting, to bring Surabaya under control.[118] The imperial and international implications of the events in Surabaya were lost neither on the British, nor on the Americans. Although the United States had effectively withdrawn from SEAC by September 1945, it was still a major force in determining the future of the Dutch East Indies. In Washington, attitudes towards the Dutch remained mixed. The Dutch marine brigade training in the United States was not permitted to receive any volunteers from the liberated Netherlands, and armaments sales from American stockpiles were vetoed. Lease lend for SEAC was rapidly terminated and the identifying marks on trucks and other equipment painted out, but the United States did allow the transit of some Dutch armaments and its Foreign Liquidation Commission in Manila sold surplus C-47 aircraft to the Dutch – albeit without consulting Washington first.[119] Certainly, the Truman administration was anxious not to take sides between the Dutch and the nationalists, and while the Dutch were partners in Europe, they could not be aided in colonial ventures when such a policy was so inimical to American public opinion.

The limits of Sukarno's local political control were now apparent and he knew that the British would not allow their forces to be driven off the island, but would merely reinforce them to the point where the existence of the Republic might be threatened.[120] Uncontrolled *pemuda* violence continued nonetheless, spurred on by radio propaganda about the treatment of Indonesians. In Semarang, Japanese soldiers and some three hundred Japanese citizens were tortured and murdered. At the end of November, a British transport plane made an emergency landing near Bekassi. Local *pemuda* captured and killed all twenty-two British Indian soldiers on board.[121] For their part, the British soon realized that the Indonesians' dogged resistance derived primarily from fear that the Dutch would come in on British coattails. Yet, this was exactly what was timetabled to happen once the British, whose agreed task under the Civil Affairs Agreement was to round up the Japanese and free all the POWs, decided that their work was complete.[122]

International tensions eased in mid-November 1945 when political developments within the Indonesian Republic culminated in a new cabinet under a social democratic Prime Minister, Sutan Sjahrir, who was responsible to a provisional parliament.[123] Six of the eleven Cabinet Ministers had studied in the Netherlands and four were Christians. Sjahrir was perceived as more 'respectable', having had no dealings with the occupying Japanese, and according to van Mook, his Cabinet were 'representatives of a better type'.[124] Van der Plas was also enthusiastic, arguing that it was important to 'avoid everything which may cause or hasten Sjahrir's fall and do everything which could, without damaging the Netherlands, strengthen Sjahrir's position'.[125] Both his friends and his enemies in Dutch political circles regarded him as a socialist. Although Sukarno remained Head of State, this 'peaceful coup' now meant that he could be sidelined, allowing further tripartite talks to take place almost immediately.[126] All this could be interpreted as a deliberate attempt by the Republic to display its most acceptable face in order to facilitate agreement with the Dutch.[127] The situation for the Republican government nevertheless remained precarious as British troops extended their control over the islands, but at the same time prompted major resistance from the nationalists. There was severe fighting in Bandung (Bandoeng) at the end of November 1945 as well as British reprisal raids against Bekassi on 13 December. As the net slowly tightened, the government's base in Jakarta (also known as Djakarta) became increasingly exposed and both Sjahrir and Sjarifuddin were subject to assassination attempts. Thus in early 1946, the Cabinet moved inland to Yogyakarta (also known as Jogjakarta).[128]

In spite of the changes, subsequent discussions produced no tangible results, as Sjahrir seemed evasive on most issues.[129] A further meeting was cancelled after Dutch colonial troops went on the rampage in Jakarta and attacked several Indonesian leaders, a political calamity that Christison blamed on his Dutch counterpart, General Ludolph van Oyen. Christison wanted his removal but van Mook made it clear that his own position was already heavily criticized at home and that van Oyen's removal would be the last straw.[130] This highlighted a major problem for van Mook, namely that his military commanders did not view the crisis in the same way. Van Oyen and the Commander-in-Chief Helfrich held views typical of the pre-war elite; that the nationalists had little real mass support and that Dutch rule could be reimposed through military action. Helfrich was anything but subtle and the British suggested that his solution to most problems amounted to 'shoot the lot'.[131] Others, including van Mook's senior adviser Petrus J. A. Idenburg, Internal Affairs Director van der Plas, and the Dutch military commander on Java General Wybrandus Schilling, all presented reports suggesting that such a solution was impossible. The idea that the Dutch political and military representatives thought or spoke with a single voice had now visibly broken down.[132]

Although van Mook's position was extremely precarious, the British knew that only he might be able to broker a peaceful settlement of the dispute – at least long enough for the British forces to withdraw. The pressure from Dutch opinion not to compromise became both public and explicit in an interview given by the Dutch Minister for Overseas Territories, Logemann. He indicated that, while the Dutch would negotiate, they were also prepared to use force to keep Java inside the Kingdom. Moreover, he insisted that his representatives would parley with Sjahrir, but only as leader of the Indonesian nationalists and not as Prime Minister of the Indonesian Republic.[133] This ill-timed and poorly phrased public utterance provoked outrage within Indonesia and internationally. In Indonesia, it was interpreted as a declaration of war, and Christison warned that without a categorical retraction of the statement and Logemann's immediate resignation, he would not be answerable for the military consequences.[134] Yet Logemann was merely voicing a common position held in the Netherlands. By November, there were almost daily protest meetings in the The Hague, with figures such as Welter, Gerbrandy, Frederik Carel Gerretson, and Jan W. Meyer Ranneft at the centre.[135] Large sections of Dutch opinion (including many who had relatives, contacts, or property in the Indies) had been so influenced by the stories of 'bersiap' atrocities that they were pathologically opposed to any negotiations with the Republic as an institution, and Sukarno in particular, as he was regarded as personally responsible.[136] Even though he and Hatta had little control over the *pemudas*, the Dutch needed someone to blame. The problem for Logemann and his colleagues was that they could not alter their negotiating partners and had to react to domestic opinion, even if it only showed the degree to which this was at odds with the realities of the situation.

By November, van Mook decided on an alternative plan. If the reoccupation of Sumatra and Java were bound to be troublesome, this should not divert attention from areas of the Empire that could be retaken with minimal cost. This meant concentration on Borneo and the Great East where reoccupation was already occurring under Australian tutelage. Van der Plas reported that it would take no more than 5,000–8,000 soldiers to establish Dutch authority in these regions, as opposed to the 75,000 expected to be required for Java and Sumatra. Successful reoccupation of the other territories would give the Dutch a more secure foothold in their former Empire, permitting a different approach to the nationalist threat. The replacement of Australian troops in Borneo, Celebes, the Moluccan Islands, and the lesser Sunda Islands took place with little opposition, but on Bali and Celebes, there was more or less continual fighting between the Dutch and Republicans well into 1948. This included the mission of Captain Westerling, who was responsible for the brutal 'pacification' of Celebes and the execution of anywhere up to 30,000 guerillas and civilians.[137] This new approach did not go unchallenged, as the returnees from internment did not understand van Mook's prevarication. They thought that the 'Brisbane' Dutch (named after the wartime Dutch administration of the Indies based there) could just crush the nationalists – not realizing how precarious the Dutch position actually was.[138] At much the same time, the government in The Hague had been alerted to an unwelcome truth, namely that it would be impossible to find more than 30,000 troops for the East Indies before October 1946.[139]

The fact that the Republic had survived its first months of life gave it a credibility that the rest of the world could not ignore. Battle lines were drawn and national sympathies established either for the new state or for the colonial power. For some, such as the United States, the choice remained a complicated one, and best avoided if possible. However, even though much of world opinion was ranged against the Dutch from an early stage, this was not the prime reason for their inability to restore their control in the Indies. The answer lay elsewhere: in their lack of political and military resources to bring about a resumption of colonial rule.[140]

By December diplomatic bridges had been sufficiently rebuilt to enable talks to resume.[141] Although the content of the discussions was meant to deal with immediate practical matters in an informal manner, it became clear that, just as van Mook had to deal with intransigent opinion at home, so Sjahrir was more outspoken on the question of independence with his

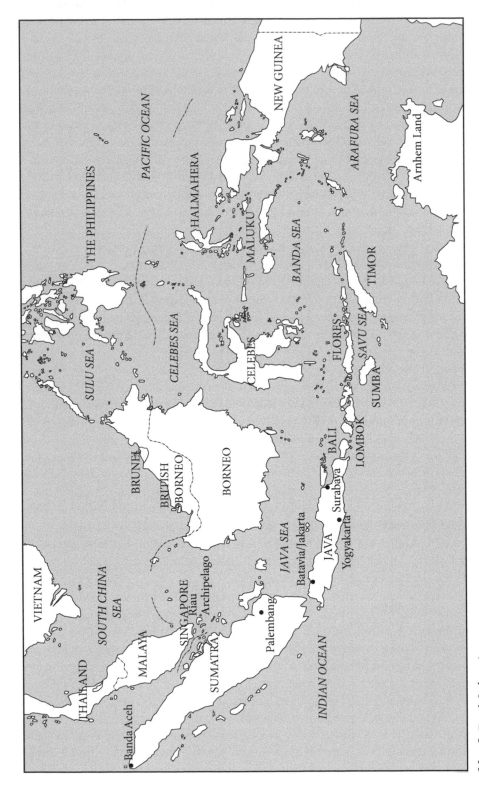

Map 9 Dutch Indonesia.

people than in conversations with the British and Dutch. His position as Prime Minister was dependent on support from the Komite Nasional Indonesia Pusat which, although overwhelming in November 1945, was subject to changing alliances within the movement and increased radicalism among a substantial section of its supporters.[142] Against this background, the political assassinations in Jakarta continued and there was annoyance in Dutch quarters that the British maintained contacts with the Republican Army to expedite the return of former prisoners and internees from the interior of Java, thus granting the Republic what amounted to *de facto* recognition. An even more serious breach occurred when Dutch forces burned two villages, ostensibly as reprisals for unspecified acts of sabotage. British observers were adamant that no resistance had come from the villages, nor were there signs of Indonesian military activity. Mountbatten took this as yet another example of Dutch indiscipline and insisted that Helfrich deal with it stringently. This he did to Mountbatten's satisfaction, but there was outrage in The Hague at the severity of the British reprimand and the perceived slight to their commander.[143]

In a meeting on 6 December in Singapore, Mountbatten had made clear to the Dutch that he would not allow Dutch troops in until their government agreed to negotiate with the Indonesian Republic. This also remained Mook's prime objective but he needed further guidance and travelled to the Netherlands for talks with his political masters. There, he was castigated as a traitor and an oriental despot who, without consulting Queen or parliament, was conspiring to destroy the Kingdom by giving Indonesia independence. However, his position was safe, if isolated, and the Cabinet agreed a more liberal formula as the basis for discussions with the nationalists.[144] Thus by the end of the year there were grounds for optimism. The Dutch had decided to replace van Oyen, Helfrich, and other members of the 'old guard', and Christison mounted an operation to pacify Jakarta.[145] By the beginning of 1946 the most pressing issue was Dutch insistence that their troops be brought to Indonesia, a matter of urgency in their eyes if they were to establish control and so carve out a bargaining position for future talks. There was no meeting of colonial minds here. Mountbatten and the British commanders still viewed the arrival of Dutch troops as a recipe for violence and disorder.[146] Ultimately, the British agreed to permit the deployment of the Dutch Marine Brigade if van Mook requested it.

What cannot be ignored here is the pressure that Dutch public opinion placed on its government. Stories of the *bersiap* continued to appear in the Dutch press and many sought a speedy reckoning with the Republic. To try to calm unrest within political circles, Prime Minister Schermerhorn and some of his senior ministers briefed influential members of both parliamentary chambers regarding what had been agreed with the British. They doubtless also made clear the problems that prevented any substantial military intervention; namely the existence of the Civil Affairs Agreement that gave overall control to Mountbatten and the British, the absence of a merchant fleet to transport troops, and the bankruptcy of the Dutch economy after five years of war.[147] Thus, despite some noisy opposition, the government secured majority acceptance of Indonesia's right to secede from the Kingdom. This was historic. Prior to this, the Dutch had never conceded Indonesia's right to self-determination. Forced onto the defensive, opponents of this policy insisted that a parliamentary commission should visit the Indies, alleging that the Cabinet had misinformed parliament about the true state of affairs.[148] As we shall see in the next chapter, this conflict between hawks and doves framed Dutch governmental behaviour in the tortuous negotiations that lay ahead.

CHAPTER 13
INDONESIA: CONFLICT AND DIPLOMACY

Dutch return, British departure, and the Linggadjati Agreement

In February 1946, the Netherlands' position in the East Indies was still precarious with few Dutch troops on Javanese soil. Their British allies largely confined themselves to keeping order in Batavia and the attempts made to remove or disarm Indonesian nationalists in other major cities under their control often merely exacerbated the violence. The nationalist government had meanwhile moved to Yogyakarta, and Sukarno and Sjahrir had to contend with militant elements among the *pemudas* and the activities of the communist party under Tan Malaka who had managed to forge a 'United Front' alliance of 141 different organizations that encompassed the whole political spectrum, and included even extreme right orthodox Muslim groups.[1]

Separate British-Dutch and British-Indonesian negotiations had begun in the same month, based on Dutch plans for a transitional Commonwealth of Indonesia within the Kingdom of the Netherlands, after which the parties would decide on their future relationship.[2] The British dismissed Indonesian demands for immediate Dutch recognition of the Republic as a precondition for future negotiations as untenable. For his part, Sjahrir was prepared to negotiate but required the sanction of the interim Indonesian parliament.[3] This he obtained, despite widespread support for outright independence from the United Front which tried but failed to unseat him.[4] However, there remained major differences between the Dutch and Indonesians on the timescale involved. Whereas Sjahrir talked of a ten-year transition period, van Mook was known to favour the twenty-five years proposed by his government.[5]

It was only in early March 1946 that the British finally expedited the arrival of appreciable numbers of Dutch troops in Java. At the same time, Sjahrir introduced counterproposals to those of the Dutch but they were again predicated upon Dutch recognition of the Republic, something that The Hague would not countenance. Van Mook responded in June with a proposal that drew heavily on the Franco-Vietnamese accords of 6 March 1946.[6] This envisaged Dutch recognition of an Indonesian Republic on Java that would remain part of a Federal Indonesian state that would, in turn, be a constituent part of the Kingdom of the Netherlands. The Indonesians' response was to insist that Sumatra be included alongside Java as part of the Republic's territory, partly for prestige reasons, but also because the island's raw materials would guarantee the economic viability of the new polity. The remaining islands were to have a subordinate status. However, the main difference in the nationalist draft was to represent the treaty as one enacted between equal sovereign states rather than one between a metropole and a former colony.[7] This formulation became the basis for an interim agreement between the delegates, but it remained for van Mook to consult with The Hague.

The subsequent discussions in the Netherlands were marked by van Mook's effective disavowal of many aspects of the terms he had agreed in Jakarta. Challenged about this in later years, he referred to a meeting with the social democrat Willem Drees where the latter had adopted such a negative attitude that van Mook came to believe there was no chance of the proposals being accepted as they stood. Formal meetings nevertheless took place between the Dutch and an Indonesian delegation at St Hubertus in the Hoge Veluwe in the Netherlands, but the Dutch refused to accept some of the central tenets agreed earlier and left the Indonesians with no mandate to renegotiate matters that their government regarded as already settled.[8] Blame for this breakdown was placed firmly at the feet of the Dutch who had appeared deliberately obstructive.[9] A draft instruction to van Mook from Logemann, then Minister for Overseas Territories, indicated that if negotiations failed then the government would look to military action for a solution.[10] Dutch troops were now arriving in Indonesia in substantial numbers and they had already garrisoned Surabaya and Semarang, but their effectiveness was somewhat diluted by the need to replace the British and Australian forces being rapidly withdrawn from the outer islands.[11] At the same time, Dutch military indiscipline continued when, on 17 April, their troops attacked the village of Pesing, in direct defiance of orders from the British not to occupy areas where opposition might be encountered.[12] The British were genuinely appalled by the actions of the Dutch and their subsequent treatment of twenty-seven Indonesian prisoners taken during the action, but attempts to insist that the Netherlands forces adhere to the operational agreements between the two powers met with a blunt refusal from their commander, Colonel Simon de Waal.[13] This continued provocative behaviour by the Dutch troops and the apparent collusion of their senior officers was to sour relations with the British and make any prospect of a negotiated settlement with the Republic all but impossible.[14]

In the months following the conference at the Hoge Veluwe, the Dutch continued to protest every time the British had any dealings with the Indonesian leadership. They nonetheless allowed van Mook to return to Jakarta and continue negotiations. By this stage, Sjahrir's position within Republican circles was weakening. Sukarno appeared to have rejected a settlement and many local Indonesian military commanders were now acting independently. Conversely, many members of the Dutch Cabinet now favoured an agreement, realizing that the passage of time and the eventual withdrawal of all British forces would inevitably strengthen the Indonesians' hand. Ostensibly, however, the Dutch were regaining some elements of power in the summer of 1946, most notably with the hand over of all former NEI territories except Java and Sumatra to their military control from 1 July.[15] For their part, the British were prepared to remain as a neutral third-party broker, calculating that if they withdrew, the two sides would move further apart and provoke the Indonesians to call for outside intervention, with all the consequences that might then ensue. The Attlee government wanted to use the impending withdrawal of their troops to browbeat the Dutch and so cut through the arguments between Indonesian and Dutch protocols by insisting that the former agree to the Republic becoming a constituent part of the Kingdom and the latter to concede the inclusion of Sumatra as part of the Republic.

More pertinent to Dutch attitudes was the general election that took place in the Netherlands on 16 May 1946. Less than two weeks earlier, the parliamentary commission report had been presented to the Second Chamber. It had no good words for the Republic, and reflected at length on the atrocities of the *bersiap* period. It also implied that van Mook had given too much attention to the Republic and that it had been the British who had dropped the Dutch into the mire.[16] The elections ultimately produced a new, but potentially more conservative government led by the Catholic politician Louis J. M. Beel, an outcome that did nothing to improve the possibility of compromise. The leader of the Catholic Party, Carl P. M. Romme, did not join the Cabinet, but had previously insisted that the empire was indivisible, and the new Minister for Overseas Territories, Jan A. Jonkman, was adamant that the Netherlands should remain a world power.[17] However, this new government took two months to form, leaving van Mook with no mandate to continue discussions in Jakarta.[18]

The stalemate continued when the new Cabinet decided to form a Commission-General led by the former Prime Minister Schermerhorn to act alongside the lieutenant governor general. Its status was complicated by the fact that its precise function vis-à-vis van Mook was not clarified and all three of its members had to agree on measures to be taken, giving each of them a power of veto over the Commission's work.[19] Progress towards direct negotiations was slow but began with a ceasefire agreement on all British/Dutch and Indonesian fronts from 14 October onwards.[20] The basic disagreements obstructing a final settlement remained the same. The Dutch were prepared to recognize the Republic, but only as a part of an Indonesian federation that was itself a constituent part of the Kingdom of the Netherlands. For the Indonesians, it was the link to the Dutch crown that was the sticking point as this could not be reconciled with the idea of an independent sovereign Republic.

Negotiations eventually resumed in early November in the resort of Linggadjati in Central Java and culminated in an agreement that exceeded the earlier Dutch concessions at the Hoge Veluwe. The *de facto* authority of the Republic of Indonesia over Java, Madura, and Sumatra was at last recognized and the Republic and the Netherlands' governments were to cooperate in the establishment of a 'sovereign democratic state on the basis of a federation called the United States of Indonesia'.[21] The inclusion of the word 'sovereign' had served to undermine the objections to a Netherlands-Indonesian Union headed by the Queen of the Netherlands. The agreement was initialled by both parties on 15 November 1946, but remained subject to ratification by both parliaments.

The prospects for ratification were unclear. On the one hand, the Dutch Commission-General had been headed by Schermerhorn, the former Prime Minister, whose involvement gave weight to its decisions at Linggadjati. On the other hand, breaches of the military truce continued, for which the Dutch were widely condemned. Admiral Albertus S. Pinke, the naval Commander-in-Chief, had deployed aircraft armed with rockets against shore batteries, contrary to the orders of the Allied Forces' military commander.[22] More seriously, Dutch Ambonese soldiers had searched a train and left the passengers kneeling on the ground for some hours. Among them was then Indonesian Minister of Justice Susanto Tirtoprodjo. Van Mook was incensed by this and insisted that the Ambonese were replaced by Dutch troops and the officer involved arrested.[23] It was clear to all concerned that the situation was deteriorating with both the Indonesian and the Dutch politicians finding it hard to control their respective armed forces and commanders in the field. It was against this background that the last British troops withdrew from the region and SEAC came to an end on 30 November 1946.[24]

At home, the Dutch government had to obtain parliamentary approval for the agreement, whose terms it had 'dressed up' (*aangekleed*).[25] Initial optimism about its possible reception soon evaporated.[26] Initially, public opinion had been almost equally divided, with 38 per cent in favour, 36 per cent against, and 26 per cent undecided.[27] Details of the agreement only served to polarize political and public opinion still further as the issue was debated in parliament on 16 December 1946. The Partij van de Arbeid (PvdA) was prepared to vote in favour, as were the communists, albeit for tactical reasons. However, while Katholieke Volkspartij (KVP) support was delivered by Romme he nevertheless tabled an amendment limiting the Dutch government's commitments in signing the agreement. This kept the coalition government alive and also allowed the KVP to be seen as progressive.[28] Even Schermerhorn, in voting for the agreement, commented: 'It's a rotten thing, but you have to do it.'[29] The opposition Conservative Anti-Revolutionary Party (ARP) and Christian Historical Union (CHU) were committed to retaining the unity of the Kingdom, albeit with some greater rights and freedoms for the Indonesians,[30] and railed against the spirit and content of the agreement, including in their list of objections the possibility that the terms were in breach of the Dutch constitution. There was also talk of differences between the 'phantom' agreement that had been presented to the public, and the 'real' agreement.[31] However, none of their speakers could suggest a viable alternative, save refusing to sign the agreement and calling an Imperial Conference instead.[32] After they lost the vote, elements within the CHU leadership took a more pragmatic line by trying to convince their constituency that they had 'to make the best of it'.[33]

Beyond parliament, a new National Committee for the Maintenance of Imperial Unity (Nationaal Comité Handhaving Rijkseenheid) led by former Prime Minister Gerbrandy and including many former senior ministers and the former Commander-in-Chief, General Winkelman, campaigned against the agreement, collecting around 300,000 signatures for a petition. A huge gulf remained between the perceptions of the situation in government offices in The Hague on the one hand and the realities in Batavia on the other. In the Indies, nearly all the Dutch and Eurasian populations were unimpressed by the agreement.[34] They, as well as the colonial civil servants, the Dutch armed forces, and van Mook, all thought that they were being sold down the river.

Within the Republic too, the population required some degree of convincing about the merits of the agreement. In a speech to students on 3 December 1946, Hatta described it as a springboard for the next phase in the campaign to create a sovereign Indonesian Republic that controlled the entire Dutch East Indies. This failed to dampen opposition, not least in the interim Indonesian parliament. Sukarno resolved this dilemma by extending parliamentary representation to include all areas of the NEI, and appointing governors for Borneo and the Great East. In practice, the representatives were nearly all resident on Java and the governors based in Yogyakarta. The result was an assured pro-agreement majority but also gave a clear signal that the regime would not be content with a final agreement confined to Java and Sumatra.[35]

Both parties signed the basic terms of the Linggadjati Agreement on 25 March 1947. Yet even before this, the Dutch took steps to create other 'states' of Borneo and East Indonesia in the former NEI to act as a counterweight to the Republic in the proposed United States of Indonesia. The Dutch military even tried to create a separate state of Pasundan in West Java, in spite of the fact that, under Linggadjati, the Dutch had recognized the whole territory as a *de facto* part of the Republic. This did nothing to reduce the level of Indonesian suspicion. The Dutch Navy also continued its blockade of Republic ports and was incensed that the Indonesians had expanded their diplomatic relations in apparent contravention of Article 1 of Linggadjati which the Dutch had assumed left foreign relations in their hands. Again, it was recognition of the sovereign status of the Republic to which the Dutch objected. At home, conservative opposition to the agreement continued. For example, radio broadcasts spoke of the Republic as 'established by the Japanese, grown stronger by the terrorism of extremists, helped by the British and now recognized by the Commission-General'. In addition, both Helfrich, as Head of the Navy, and Lt. General Hendrik J. Kruls as Chief of the Army General

Staff both petitioned the Queen for an audience to express their fears about the threat of mutilation to the empire.[36]

Implementation of Linggadjati was therefore deadlocked, but a visit by Prime Minister Beel and Minister for Overseas Territories Jonkman on 7 May 1947 led to a series of discussions, which revealed just how weak Sjahrir's position as Prime Minister was becoming.[37] He was forced to refer every decision back to his capital and his recommendations were usually rejected.[38] On returning home, the Dutch politicians attempted to break the stalemate with a series of proposals designed to give substance to the Linggadjati terms. These were transmitted to the Republic on 27 May 1947 and stipulated the formation of an Interim Federal Government including representatives from the Republic, the other Indonesian 'states' as well as from the crown. This Dutch representative would chair the government and have a 'special position with the power of decision'.[39] A Council for Foreign Affairs would be similarly constructed, and a Directorate of Internal Security with a joint Indonesian-Dutch gendarmerie would maintain law and order across the Indonesian archipelago. The plan was submitted as an ultimatum with the stipulation that the Republic should respond within fourteen days. Further discussions were ruled out if the response was negative or unsatisfactory.

This high-handed approach could be understood in terms of the lack of progress achieved in implementing Linggadjati, but could also be interpreted as part of the Dutch government's efforts to placate the diehard minority at home. Forces opposed to the agreement packed meetings across the Netherlands. Gerbrandy and the Nationaal Comité Handhaving Rijkseenheid even contemplated a coup d'etat against the government which they felt was betraying the Kingdom. They went so far as to recruit strike-breakers to counteract an expected general strike by the labour unions in the event of such a coup. Ultimately, their activity was limited to a further petition, this time with 240,000 signatures.[40] Against this background, the government had to tread carefully. Implementation involved constitutional changes that required a three-fifths majority in parliament, and this proved impossible to achieve even though the Catholic and Labour parties had sufficient seats between them to carry the day.[41] Nonetheless, this harder line left the Dutch government with little further negotiating room and the leadership were keen to enlist British and American help to persuade the Indonesians. They openly admitted that their only alternatives were either complete withdrawal from Java and Sumatra or recourse to 'limited' military action.[42] Meanwhile, Sjahrir's readiness to discuss the latest Dutch plan aroused bitter parliamentary opposition in Indonesia. He lost a vote of confidence and resigned on 27 June 1947.[43]

It has been argued that the Dutch still had four possible courses of action in the aftermath of the Linggadjati Agreement. The first was to implement it in full and concede total control of Java, Sumatra, and Madura to the nationalists by removing Dutch troops from those areas. The second was to try to persuade the Republican government that a United States of Indonesia would best fulfil the nationalists' aims. A third possibility was to use the armed forces at Dutch disposal to expunge the Republic from the political map, and the final option was to surrender the entire problem to the United Nations for settlement. As the first and final options represented major political and military 'defeats' for the Dutch and would be unacceptable to conservative elements at home, and the second was unlikely to find any favour with the Indonesian Republicans, the only course left was direct military action. It has been suggested that this had probably been decided when Beel and Jonkman visited Indonesia in May 1947, but it had been left for van Mook to find the optimum moment to carry it out.[44]

The first 'police action', the beginnings of US involvement, and the good offices commission

Following the announcement of the Truman doctrine on 12 March 1947, the American response to the ongoing crisis in the Dutch East Indies changed. Faced with the possibility of an all-out war in the archipelago, the Americans abandoned their traditional policy of neutrality in favour of a more proactive approach. US anti-colonialism was now tempered by an anti-communist policy of containment. In this respect, the Linggadjati Agreement was a godsend – a negotiated settlement between a colonial power and an indigenous independence movement – and the Americans were keen to make it work. In concert with London, they suggested modifications to the Agreement to make the details acceptable to both sides and even offered financial aid to assist Indonesia's economic rehabilitation.[45]

This US intervention forced the Dutch to delay their proposed military action scheduled for 30 June. Negotiations continued with Sjarifuddin, the new Prime Minister, but on 7 July, the Dutch insisted on unequivocal answers to five questions about the Republic's position. Perhaps surprisingly, Sjarifuddin replied positively to four of them on 8 July, but refused to concede the fifth, which concerned the composition and role of the gendarmerie. Nor did the Republican government accede to the Dutch demand that the Indonesians proclaim a ceasefire order and withdraw 10 kms – thus giving the impression that only their forces had violated the treaty.[46] It seems likely that the Indonesian response was not conditioned by the attitudes of the politicians – as most were known to favour a compromise – but the result of pressures from their military commanders.[47] In the days that followed, it became clear that The Hague intended to use the Indonesian refusal on these last issues to justify military intervention and Dutch forces duly launched their 'police action' on 21 July.[48]

Operating from the enclaves inherited from the British, the Dutch action was remarkably successful.[49] The Indonesians were forced to retreat into the mountains by opponents superior in weaponry and organization, if not in numbers. Within two weeks, the Dutch controlled large swathes of Java including most of the export-crop-producing areas. Similarly on Sumatra, they extended their control over Medan (tea, rubber, and tobacco) and Palembang (oil and coal).[50] For both strategic and political reasons, the area around Yogyakarta was left untouched.[51] This success gave ammunition to the hawks in The Hague, whose insistence that colonial rule in Indonesia could always be reimposed by military means seemed to have been affirmed, but the political ramifications of the police action extended way beyond the boundaries of the Dutch Empire. Particularly vehement protests came from Ben Chifley's Australian Labor government and the Nehru regime in India. Both were instrumental in bringing the Indonesian question before the UN General Assembly on 30 July.[52] Locally, the picture of rapid Dutch advance was more confused. Retreating Republican fighters used scorched earth tactics, making the resumption of colonial economic activity harder. Plantations and their white owners became obvious targets for further attacks. Local guards were recruited, some of whom ultimately turned on their employers.[53]

Meanwhile, within hours of the initial Dutch military action, the British had made an offer of 'good offices' to both parties. London was concerned that this demonstration of naked colonial power would destabilize the whole region, threatening many British and other European colonial interests. Dutch responses were evasive and attempts to involve the United States in possible arbitration came to nothing.[54] As the State Department suspected, the ebullient Dutch were in no mood to accept British overtures particularly after Britain's arms shipments to them had been suspended under pressure from domestic public opinion. In the meantime, the government in The Hague vetoed van Mook's request to continue the military action against Yogyakarta, ostensibly because of rank-and-file opposition within the Partij van de Arbeid that threatened their coalition with the Catholics and could thus bring down the government.[55] Although the Dutch continued to see Indonesia as a purely internal matter, UN interest was impossible to ignore. As a result, both Yogyakarta and The Hague were impelled to assent to a Security Council Resolution calling for an end to violence and a return to peaceful negotiations.[56]

The involvement of the United Nations forced the hand of the American State Department. Although it was dubious about the 'good offices' proposal, the alternatives on offer were worse. The Americans did not relish having to oppose the Dutch in the United Nations. Nor did they favour a UN Commission to deal with the issue, which would open the door for communist interference 'in a manner prejudicial to the Netherlands and to the interests of the Western Democracies in the Far East'.[57] At this stage, it was clear that the United States continued to have sympathy with the Dutch – not least in relation to the wider issues of security in the region.[58] At the same time, the Republic's politicians thought they had far more to gain from UN mediation than from bipartite negotiations with the Dutch brokered by Washington. In order to prevent further internationalization of the issue, the Americans produced a revised proposal for a UN Committee of Good Offices (CGO).[59] Each party would nominate one member and these two would nominate the third. Thus the Dutch nominated Belgium, the Republic nominated Australia, and these two then brought in the United States. The State Department thereby achieved its key objective in keeping the communist bloc out of the process. Even for the nationalists, whose control over territory had been severely curtailed by the Dutch 'police action', the diplomatic initiatives provided a welcome boost in profile and prestige. The Republic was recognized as a 'party' to the international dispute at the United Nations and its representatives, including Sjahrir himself, played a full part in the debate. Even more pleasing to them was the exclusion of representatives from the other Dutch-inspired (puppet) 'states' of East Indonesia and West Kalimantan.[60]

On the ground, the Dutch continued mopping-up operations even after the ceasefire, provoking renewed hostilities. Their intention was to reinforce their control over these newly recovered areas and establish defensible boundaries (known as the van Mook line). This would be preparatory to the creation of new 'states' in these areas. Both van Mook and General Simon Spoor felt that outside intervention had cheated them of a solution to their Indonesian problem, arguing that a decisive strike against the leaderless Republic in Yogyakarta would have settled the issue. However, the Beel government could not ignore a Security Council Resolution and the threat of sanctions. While van Mook and Spoor continued to press for a military assault on the Republican capital, they were finally thwarted by an explicit warning from the American ambassador in The Hague against any further military operations. The Dutch actions had severely curtailed the areas in Republican hands, but this did not imply that the colonial power had any real control. Many elements of the Indonesian forces had gone underground to continue a guerrilla war. The Dutch found it hard to get local Indonesian civil servants to work with them, a problem compounded by their continuing military activity to root out activists inside occupied territory. An infamous incident was the Dutch attack on the village of Rawahgedeh on 9 December 1947 where 150 villagers were killed and a further twenty executed after questioning on the orders of the commanding major.[61] Summary killings and persistent maltreatment of detainees suggested that such security force violence was not atypical but 'business as usual'.[62] Although militarily inconclusive, this first 'police action' effectively left the Netherlands' international position and reputation much weakened.[63]

The CGO had arrived in Jakarta on 27 October 1947 and a further Security Council Resolution, passed on 1 November, had attempted to bolster the ceasefire.[64] It was agreed that the negotiations should take place at a neutral venue, and the US ship *Renville* was sent from Okinawa.[65] Dutch negotiators approached the talks in buoyant mood, but they soon stalled. The Hague was already openly talking of new states in the areas they had occupied and of creating a Republic of the United States of Indonesia (RUSI) with or without the Republic of Indonesia.[66] The choice for the Yogyakarta politicians was either to comply and enter the RUSI in their economically weakened position or face the possibility of a further 'police action' in the future. While this gung-ho attitude may have played well in the Netherlands, the United States saw substantial problems, both for the Dutch and for the future of the region. If the Republic refused to accede to Dutch demands, as intelligence suggested they might, then further military action would create a situation where the Dutch would face a long-term, very expensive, and possibly unsustainable military commitment that would probably produce a second, and much more radical revolution sometime in the future.

The prospect of the negotiations collapsing threatened the efficacy of the CGO and the UN's status as a peacemaking institution. Thus Frank Porter Graham, the US representative on the CGO devised a new set of proposals on 25 December. The Republic agreed to this so-called Christmas programme, albeit with some misgivings, but the Dutch countered with 'Twelve Principles' on 2 January 1948. These embodied some elements of the CGO document, but kept open the possibility of the creation of new states.[67] The Dutch regarded these proposals as final and 'reserved their liberty of action' if they were not accepted. Their increasing truculence suggested that the Dutch thought they now had a winning hand.[68] As the Republic could not accept these terms, the most likely outcome was a further Dutch 'police action'. While this might represent a Dutch victory and be welcomed in The Hague, the damage to international security, the reputation of the UN, and most importantly to the United States as a key peace broker was bound to be severe. In consequence, Frank Graham tabled 'six additional principles' that were designed to protect the interests of the Republic. These proposals would have been unacceptable in The Hague but for the fact that the Americans now decided to wield the big stick to bring the Dutch into line.[69] On 8 January, the State Department made 'strong informal representations' to the Dutch Embassy in Washington, inviting the government in The Hague to consider and accept Graham's proposals. Underlying this request was a threat: if the Dutch did not comply, US economic help to the Netherlands would be summarily withdrawn.[70] Although this represented a major departure from the principles of 'good offices', the United States successfully brokered an agreement that was signed on the *Renville* by both sides on 17 and 19 January 1948.[71]

Although portrayed in public as a settlement, the Renville agreements provided only a framework for the two sides to achieve a more permanent solution to the Indonesian question. Opposition to the agreement led directly to Sjarifuddin losing political support at home and to his replacement as Prime Minister by Mohammed Hatta on 23 January 1948. This represented a change in more ways than one, as the new Cabinet was presidential and responsible to Sukarno rather than to the representative institutions.[72] In territorial terms, the Republic was substantially weaker than it had been after Linggadjati. Much depended on the six additional principles that allowed for plebiscites, which, it was hoped, might lead to some territorial readjustments of the van Mook line. For their part, the Dutch were anxious to delay matters, as this would give more time for the creation of further states under their control that could then be used to ensure their dominance of the proposed RUSI. For the Americans, Renville met all their policy aspirations for South East Asia, with continuing European control tempered by a timetable for eventual self-government.[73] Thus their new representative on the CGO, Coert duBois, fought to implement the terms of the agreements in full, but this remained a distant prospect.[74] Over time, duBois became increasingly disillusioned about the Dutch and better disposed towards the Republic, but his masters in Washington were still committed to supporting their European ally as the best guarantee of stability and the supply of strategic war materials. Thus the $506 million Marshall Aid given to the Netherlands included $84 million for the rebuilding of the Dutch East Indies. This was greeted warmly in The Hague, but denounced by the Republic.[75] In some respects, the Dutch had done well. American participation in the CGO appeared to strengthen their hand and rumours of political splits within the Republic encouraged a belief that persistence would allow them to 'succeed in the end'. Certainly, there were some grounds for viewing the increasingly intransigent attitudes coming from Yogyakarta as a result of different factions attempting to out-do each other by playing up their nationalist demands.[76]

For their part, the Dutch perception of the Republic was epitomized by the views of their leading delegate, Jonkheer Heinrich van Vredenburch. He regarded the entire leadership as untrustworthy rebels and it soon became clear that the Dutch intended to go on with the creation of the RUSI with or without the Republic.[77] A further attempt at mediation in June 1948, through the duBois-Critchley proposals, was undermined when the text was leaked to the press.[78] The Dutch blamed duBois, but the likelihood is that they themselves were responsible in order to prevent having to discuss any of the substantive issues the proposals addressed.[79] DuBois and van Vredenburch both left the scene in July. The former on health grounds, the latter recalled by The Hague.[80] Van Vredenburch's departure created the opportunity for a more conciliatory execution of Dutch policy.[81] At home, general elections in the Netherlands produced a new cabinet. It was dominated by the PvdA and Catholic parties that had first formulated Indonesia policy after 1945, but had also produced intransigent statements on the Indonesian question for the benefit of the electors – a bifurcation that made political compromise even more unlikely.[82]

The breakdown of negotiations and continuing Dutch procrastination alarmed the Americans, who feared that the Hatta government might go the way of its predecessors and be replaced by a much more left-wing, or even communist-dominated, regime. The spectre of the communists extending their power in Indonesia had to be resisted if at all possible, especially given events in Europe and the first indications of an incipient Cold War in South East Asia as troubles became evident in Malaya during the summer of 1947. The political situation in the Republic was radically altered by the return of the communist leader Musso. He had been in exile in the USSR since the abortive coup of 1927, but returned on 11 August and was received by Sukarno. The result was a reformed and expanded communist party PKI that was to include both labour and socialist parties.[83] Its objective was a complete rejection of all existing treaties and the overthrow of the existing Hatta regime. This also created a potential conflict with the anti-communist Indonesian armed forces. US policy was aimed towards a political settlement between the Dutch and the Hatta regime that would bolster the latter's credibility and reduce the communist threat, but their revised (Cochran) plan[84] of 10 September ran into the same problems as all earlier solutions. Dirk Stikker, the Dutch Foreign Minister, was scathing: 'Do you really believe that the advice of a handful of people who have been in Indonesia for three months is of more worth than the experience that we have gleaned there in more than three centuries?'[85] Nonetheless, the Americans remained adamant that the revitalized PKI posed a major threat to the region and insisted that nothing should be done to undermine a regime that could be an ally in the Cold War.[86]

In fact the communist threat was dealt with largely from within. Hatta had ordered the demobilization of all communist-controlled army units and this provoked a localized coup in the city of Madiun. The national PKI leadership under Musso attempted to exploit the situation by offering a peaceful settlement to the crisis in exchange for their participation in the government. When this was rejected, the communists threw their weight behind the coup and attempted to extend it across the country. This ended in dismal failure. Musso was killed in a skirmish and former Prime Minister Sjarifuddin, who had joined the new organization, was captured and executed.[87] Greeted with relief in Washington, this outcome bolstered American support for the Sukarno/Hatta regime. Ironically, however, the excision of the communist threat also served to remove the Dutch obligation to reach an immediate settlement with the Republic.[88]

Worn out by trying to balance the demands of his office with the realities on the ground in the East Indies and intransigent opinion at home, van Mook had ceased to believe that a solution was possible and tendered his resignation as Governor to the Queen. Too many factors were now ranged against him; the American shift to greater support for the Republic, the inability to pursue a military strategy, and international opinion heavily weighted against the Netherlands. Having asked to be relieved of his office as early as February 1946, he remained the key Dutch representative until domestic political bargaining in the formation of a new Dutch government in August 1948 saw Emmanuel (Maan) Sassen appointed as Minister for Overseas Territories. One of the new Minister's first acts was to invite van Mook to step down and replace him with former Minister-President Louis Beel, who took office as Representative of the Crown on 4 November 1948.[89]

The second 'police action' and the diplomatic isolation of the Netherlands

In some respects, the parties returned to the *status quo ante*. The Republic expressed itself willing to negotiate on the basis of the Cochran Plan but the Dutch continued to prevaricate and became increasingly convinced that the United States was favouring the Hatta regime.[90] At the same time, Catholic, right-wing, and military opinion inside the Netherlands was opposed to a political settlement because it felt that a military solution was not only practicable, but also desirable to wipe out the Republic completely.[91] Even at this late stage, a contemporary American observer noted that the Dutch continued to believe that hard-line sanctions against the Republic (in contravention of the Renville Agreement) would bring about the downfall of the 'left wing extremists' in Yogyakarta that had misled the population.[92] By this time, American government sympathy did indeed lie with Hatta, as the State Department recognized how many concessions he had been prepared to make in order to achieve a settlement. An American *aide-memoire* to the Netherlands government on 7 December 1948 urged the government to resume negotiations and while it accepted that the Dutch could probably overrun the Republic militarily within a few weeks or even days, this 'would come as a profound shock to the American people'.[93] Moreover it noted that such action would be a drain on resources and 'tend to nullify the effect of appropriations made to the Netherlands and Indonesia under the Economic Cooperation Administration (ECA), or jeopardize the continuance thereof'.[94] The text also outlined US policy if the problem returned to the Security Council of the United Nations, namely that the Americans would back the original Cochran Plan, and would seek to withdraw from the CGO so that they could resume their freedom of action in the affair.

Herein lay the real threat to the Dutch: the withdrawal of future ECA funds. Strangely, two days later this *aide-memoire* was withdrawn and replaced by a modified version that removed the implied threat to funding. It was explained as a 'misunderstanding' but probably reflected wider US worries about threatening a member state of the Western Union so soon after the Berlin Airlift had begun.[95] In spite of further concessions from Hatta, the Dutch found themselves unbound once more. Free to proceed with their plans, they published their proposals for *Bewind Indonesië in Overgangstijd*.[96] These would essentially give the Dutch crown power over all salient matters and reduce the Republic to one of fifteen other states or 'special regions'. The Republic was also to concede all political and military powers to Beel as the High Representative of the Crown. This was an impossible step for any Republican administration and the Dutch ultimatum for the acceptance of their terms unsurprisingly expired on 18 December without a response from the Hatta regime.[97] The Dutch then informed the powers that they would take immediate action to deal with Republican terrorism, and 'to re-establish conditions of peace and security in the whole of Indonesia'.[98] Dutch haste reflected the fact that the UN Security Council would not meet between 15 December and mid-January 1949. If the military intervention could be completed before then and an interim federal government created, the international community would be faced with a *fait accompli*. Such a solution drew support across the Netherlands' political spectrum, with even the PvdA openly advocating a military solution. This 'loss of temper and balance' in the Dutch government was almost complete.[99]

The planned Dutch military assault, Operation Kraai, began on 19 December and swept aside any initial Republican military resistance. Yogyakarta was taken within hours; most other cities fell quickly. The Republican government allowed itself to be captured and was then interned by the Dutch. However, any expectation that the Dutch would be greeted as liberators and that more 'moderate' leaders would emerge to cooperate with Dutch plans proved illusory. Instead, an 'orgy of destruction' took place and civil servants refused to cooperate in upholding any semblance of order and administration.[100] In spite of Dutch denials, there was widespread public support for the Republic based not only on nationalism, but also on a sense of shared purpose in combating Dutch control and engineering a social revolution.[101] The Republican army, far from disbanding, retreated into the mountains from where it mounted a successful guerrilla campaign.[102] Even the governments of some of the states created by the Dutch in other parts of Indonesia resigned in protest at this second 'police action'.[103] Most serious of all was the adverse international reaction to Dutch military intervention.

In concert with the Australians, the Truman administration arranged an emergency session of the UN Security Council in Paris on 22 December. The day before, Washington had announced that Marshall Aid for Dutch use in Indonesia was to be suspended, as there were doubts about whether the funds were to be used for reconstructive assistance. However the United States stopped short of including aid to the European Netherlands in the embargo. This measured response highlighted the problems of the American position. On the one hand, they did not want a major break with a Western European state that was part of a key security alliance.[104] On the other, they were incensed by Dutch behaviour, condemning it as totalitarian and morally unjustified.[105] In their eyes the military intervention and the removal of the Hatta regime was a crass example of Western capitalist imperialism that had merely opened the door for the communists. There was some justification for this claim on the ground, as the power vacuum in the Republic had been the cue for the Trotskyist, Tan Malaka, to begin a major propaganda offensive, although he was ultimately caught by Republican forces in East Java and shot in April 1949.[106]

Protests from other governments also came thick and fast.[107] Two Security Council Resolutions on 24 and 28 December 1948 called for an immediate cessation to hostilities and the release of the Republic's leaders.[108] The Dutch refused to comply and continued with plans to create a Dutch-dominated RUSI, in spite of their inability to find any 'reasonable' elements to represent the Republican state. The Dutch refusal to comply with the Security Council Resolutions necessitated a further UN debate as its prestige was now at stake. The Dutch rejected a draft resolution put forward by the United States on the grounds that it required the restoration of the Republican regime. This was seen as a slap in the face for the Dutch and that although the United States did have the means to drive them out of Indonesia, they would prefer to go down fighting.[109]

Determined to reassert its authority, the UN Security Council approved a much stronger resolution on 28 January 1949. While welcoming the Dutch timetable for the creation of RUSI and for the transfer of sovereignty on or soon after 1 January 1950, it nonetheless insisted on a ceasefire and the release of all political prisoners taken since 17 December 1948.[110] The resolution also created a new United Nations Commission for Indonesia (UNCI) to replace the CGO. The new body was invested with much broader powers to facilitate and direct negotiations. Faced with a resolution that had passed through the United Nations unopposed and with only three abstentions, the pressure on the Dutch was intense.[111] Both the United States and Britain, while accepting that the Dutch should have time to comply with the resolution, nonetheless insisted that they would not be allowed to circumvent it. The United States pointed out that a meeting of African and Asian states in January 1949 had been highly critical of Dutch actions in Indonesia, and had created the basis for an anti-Western Asiatic bloc of countries.[112] On 7 February, UNCI representative Cochran also explained to the Dutch Prime Minister Willem Drees that a large section of US domestic opinion was ranged against the Dutch and that this was bound to have an impact on the congressional hearings on ECA aid.[113]

In private, the Dutch were more candid about their position. Stikker admitted that Dutch acceptance of the UN resolution would bring down the government, yet the costs involved in continuing the 'police action' were unsustainable beyond a further five or six months. Moreover, there was some admission that serious mistakes had been made in aspects of the campaign. It was clear that the swift military solution planned by the Dutch had not come to fruition. Substantial forces had become engaged in an extensive guerrilla war with the Indonesian TNI, which saw 1,275 of their men killed – more than all those lost in the previous three years. The 'dirty war' continued until an armistice in June 1949, with estimates of 150,000 civilian casualties amid stories of torture, prisoners being indiscriminately shot, and villages being wilfully destroyed. General Spoor pursued his objectives with little regard for the realities of the situation, failing to grasp that his men were in a struggle they could not hope to win, either militarily or politically.[114]

Conditions were less than promising for the next Dutch move, the so-called Beel Plan. Before the second police action and the UN resolution, Beel and his Catholic colleague Sassen had been in agreement on how to deal with Indonesia, but Sassen's refusal to accept the UN resolution under any circumstances drove Beel to devise some form of compromise that might take matters forward. Sassen's resignation on 11 February 1949 gave Beel the opportunity to announce his plan in the Netherlands at the end of that month.[115] It accelerated the creation of RUSI and the transfer of sovereignty, leaving the representative states and the Republicans to agree upon an interim government.[116] Opposition came from the United States and Britain, who both took the view that the plan could not replace compliance with the Security Council Resolution and in any case allowed the Dutch too much latitude to gerrymander the process to their own advantage.[117] In essence, the Dutch did not think there was much difference between their plans for the transfer of power, and that proposed by the resolution. All that was at issue was the means by which this was to be achieved. This was not strictly true, as full compliance with the resolution in stopping military action and releasing Republican leaders would have weakened any future Dutch negotiating position. Yet The Netherlands' prestige was at stake, both in terms of its international position, but also in relation to domestic opinion. Any retreat would be seized upon by hard-line elements in the Dutch political establishment, and this group had sufficient parliamentary and public support to hamstring the government of the day. The UN Security Council therefore flexed its muscles once again in a 'ruling' of 23 March 1949 that demanded Dutch compliance with the resolution of 28 January.[118]

Van den Doel suggests that there was already a greater sense of realism in Dutch circles about their position even before the 'ruling', in part prompted by Herman van Roijen, their ambassador at the UN, making it clear to his political masters that they really did not have a leg to stand on (*geen been om op te staan*).[119] No one would take a Republic of the United States of Indonesia or a Round Table Conference seriously if it did not include the leaders of the Republic, and even hard-line politicians like Romme had accepted that they would need to be released. Thus as a way out, van Roijen and his Canadian colleague Andrew McNaughton drafted a proposal whereby the UNCI brokered a resumption of talks in Jakarta on 14 April. After more than three weeks of discussion, an agreement was reached. Republican leaders were allowed to return to Yogyakarta in exchange for certain guarantees, and the outlines for the Round Table Conference and future RUSI were confirmed.[120]

The settlement was greeted with protests in The Hague and regarded as a disaster by the Republic's leaders. Inevitably, there was some fall out from this. Among the Republicans, there remained a strong view that the Dutch could not really be trusted. On the Dutch side, Beel resigned as Crown Representative and General Spoor succumbed to a heart attack.[121] Their going, coupled with the earlier resignation of the hawkish Emmanuel Sassen as Minister for Overseas Territories in February, paved the way for more moderate opinions to hold sway.[122] As US Ambassador Baruch commented:

Since the departure of Sassen from the Overseas Territories portfolio, the Ministry under van Maarseveen seems to have pursued a straightforward course and did not endeavour to torpedo the course of Drees and Stikker, as was Sassen's habit. ... We have not in any of our contacts with the Government or Foreign Office officials encountered any indication of Machiavellian plans. ... The Dutch have seen a steady drain on their resources, guerrilla warfare and no real progress made since the war ended. They have now resigned themselves to the inevitable and want the Indonesian question cleared up as quickly as possible.[123]

In early July 1949, the Republican leaders were finally able to return to Yogyakarta. Soon afterwards, the Inter-Indonesian Conference was convened so that representatives of all the Indonesian states could meet to present a common front at the forthcoming Round Table Conference. The result was domination by the Republic's leaders, primarily because the other states relied on Dutch support, which was soon to disappear, making some accommodation with Sukarno and Hatta essential. These two figures also enjoyed the international reputations that other Indonesian leaders lacked, and they alone controlled their own military force, which would inevitably become the backbone of any future RUSI army.[124]

The Round Table Conference and the final settlement

The Round Table Conference finally convened on 23 August 1949 in the Ridderzaal in The Hague. President Truman had set out a series of 'cardinal elements of US policy' for Cochran, as US UNCI representative, to ensure in the coming negotiations. These centred on civil rights, the protection of private property, and foreign access to the Indonesian economy. Beyond these, he was to facilitate the negotiations and to suggest solutions but not engage with the detail of the settlement. Arguments centred on the character of the Netherlands-Indonesian Union, which the Indonesians feared was intended as some form of super-state that would retain powers to intervene in the domestic affairs of the newly independent state.

The statutes governing this were finally hammered out after members of the delegation spent a weekend in discussions in the Belgian city of Namur. A second element of contention was the question of the debts to be assumed by the new state. Both sides agreed that the pre-1942 debts would be an Indonesian responsibility, but the Dutch were anxious that the debts up to 1949 also form part of this 'patrimony'. As this would include the costs of the two 'police actions', the Republicans, not surprisingly, raised vehement objections. The Dutch refused to reduce their demands and the Indonesians claimed that their financial position was so bad that unless there was some compromise, sovereignty might just as well be transferred directly to the communists.[125] In the event, this matter was transferred to a Debt Commission, whose recommendations were to be binding. In effect, the Dutch backed down in the face of pressure from outside not to jeopardize the negotiations as a whole. This same manoeuvre was applied to the question of New Guinea (West Irian) when it came up for discussion. Although largely ignored in earlier negotiations, the Dutch now made an issue of its transfer, but again a decision was deferred in order to achieve an overall settlement within the designated timescale for the conference. The transfer of sovereignty finally took place on 27 December 1949 with the newly formed Republic of the United States of Indonesia being granted immediate recognition by many of the great powers, including Britain and the United States.

The end of an era

The history of the Dutch attempts to regain control of their East Indian territories after the end of hostilities in 1945 seems, to the outside observer, to have been littered with lost opportunities. On more than one occasion, the colonial power was on the brink of achieving most of its stated aims, only to press its case too far and precipitate a breakdown in communications and foster further ill-will with the Indonesian nationalists. Understanding this propensity for snatching defeat from the jaws of victory requires a detailed examination of the forces at work, both in the domestic sphere and internationally.

In domestic politics there is no doubt that many Dutch citizens saw their control over the Indies as an intrinsic and non-negotiable element of an imperial mission – even to the point of claiming it to have been ordained by God. Three hundred years or more of history could not be lost overnight. If anything, this imperial focus became even stronger during the German occupation of the European Netherlands, and there seems to have been no question that the restoration of colonial control after the defeat of Nazi Germany and Imperial Japan would be one of the country's first post-war tasks. Moralistic and formalistic aspects loomed large in Dutch thinking on the issue. More pragmatically, the Indies also represented a major source of potential income and presumed international prestige to the Netherlands, commodities that were both in short supply in the aftermath of war and occupation. Thus in 1945 all parties across the political spectrum with the exception of the communists supported the return of empire.

That said, few people inside the European Netherlands including the country's leading politicians or those who had spent the previous five years in exile had much idea of what this task might entail. At the war's end in the summer of 1945, the degree of destruction to Dutch control and prestige in the region wrought by three and a half years of Japanese rule was difficult to ascertain. In reality, the damage had been extensive. There had been an almost complete removal of the colonial bureaucracy, with the surrendered Dutch and Eurasian armed forces, civil servants, and civilians all interned in camps. Their subsequent ill treatment decimated their numbers and limited their potential contribution to a reconstruction of Dutch rule after the Japanese were driven out. The rapid collapse of the Dutch and other European powers in South East Asia had also destroyed once and for all the myth of white supremacy over the Asiatic races – a factor heavily stressed in wartime Japanese propaganda. Economic control over the Indies was also lost and not easily regained, as civilians were unable or unwilling to return to their pre-war occupations. Above all, the Japanese also created space for the flowering of an Indonesian nationalism that had been largely suppressed by the Dutch before 1942. Not all Indonesians were prepared to believe or buy into the Japanese ideas and some deliberately avoided any contact with the occupying power, but others did so to advance the nationalist cause, even though they were no more convinced of Japanese intentions.

Perhaps the greatest Dutch failing was to dismiss or at least to underestimate this growth of indigenous nationalism. The fact that it had been 'managed' in the period up to 1942 was no guarantee that it would never be a force in the region. Yet Dutch politicians, opinion formers, and the general public in the Netherlands continued to dismiss nationalist demands as a creation of the Japanese or the product of a few populists and gangsters long after the Republic's leadership had won international recognition and had demonstrated its strength 'on the ground' for all but the most myopic observer. This blinkered attitude spanned almost the entire political spectrum and bolstered hawkish elements within the government and the military who assumed that the use of force – once it could be mustered in the region – would be sufficient to restore European rule. These opinions died hard. Thus the second police action was seen as a remedy for the untimely cessation of the first – before a complete military victory had been won. Yet, what emerged from the police actions was a colonial power being drawn into a guerrilla war against forces with widespread popular support. The subsequent experiences of the British, French, and Americans in South East Asia bear testimony to the dangers of this, but in the early post-Pacific War years, the Dutch seemed remarkably unconcerned about where such an approach might lead. One telling remark comes from Hendrik Tilanus, the leader of the CHU in the crucial post-war years. In talking of his internment by the Germans during the war he noted the importance of contact with Meyer Ranneft and Logemann who were experts on the Indies:

> Most of the politicians, myself included, knew almost nothing of the Indies, in spite of the fact that we passed judgement on the colonial budget every year. … In discussions with Logemann and Meyer Ranneft, I began to realize that there were social developments there about which we in the Netherlands knew nothing. Certainly, we shouted loudly in the chamber – but with hindsight – what did we know about the Indies?[126]

What they were aware of was the increasing impact of international opinion. Whereas before 1942, they had been able to deal with their colonies more or less in any way they saw fit, the post-war world proved a very different place. After 1945, the United States was clearly going to take a much closer interest in the South East Asia region, as were the Australians. Moreover, the threat of communist insurgency was perceived to be ever-present. This Cold War agenda loomed large in the minds at the White House and the State Department. Another issue unfamiliar to the Dutch was the democratization of international politics through the United Nations. While the permanent members of the Security Council still wielded the greatest power, the Cold War was fought here as well, bringing other states, sometimes themselves newly independent, to the forefront in championing the cause of indigenous nationalism.

Individuals, too, were important. The man who had to balance all these factors and then try to execute Dutch policy on the ground was the Lieutenant Governor General van Mook. From 1945 until his resignation in late 1948, he played the pivotal role in trying to match the decisions of his political masters in The Hague with the increasing stridency of nationalism within the Indies. Alongside this he had to take account of objective realities – something that both sides could ignore in their demands – and also measure Dutch policy against a background of increasing international interest, involvement, and intervention. He was hamstrung by the unrealistic aspirations of the Dutch public and politicians whose belief in their inherent right to empire proved remarkably impervious to their collapsing imperial position. In the end, van Mook's quest to save the East Indies as part of the Dutch Empire failed. However, it is arguable if anyone else could have done better in the circumstances. His successors, albeit with different titles, could do no more than oversee a further diplomatic disaster followed effectively by a wholesale capitulation to the demands from Yogyakarta.

A final line of enquiry might be to question the nature of the personalities involved. Could van Mook detach himself from the role of paternalistic administrator in the 1930s who thought he knew best what was good for the indigenous population? Could the succession of military commanders really break free from the idea that their prime purpose was to confront the enemy within? Put another way, were there structural reasons that help to explain the failure of the Dutch to adapt to the changed conditions in Indonesia after the Japanese surrender in August 1945?[127]

The impact of the loss of Indonesia on the Netherlands should not be underestimated. It had been very much the jewel in the Dutch colonial crown. The internal political debates on how to retain control after 1945 were seen as crucial to the long-term well-being of a Kingdom ravaged by five years of war, yet the compromises forced on successive governments split the nation and left a lasting legacy. Only the rapid recovery of the Dutch economy and a reorientation towards Europe helped to heal the wounds.[128] The conflict involved over 170,000 men, 100,000 of them conscripts, in the largest military operation ever carried out by the Dutch armed forces. The capitulation in 1949 served to make it a forgotten war, rediscovered only when stories of atrocities surfaced later, but with no great public discussion about the wider role of the soldiers who had fought in the campaigns.[129] There had been some contemporary recognition of their service, but this was soon buried as peace with Japan in 1951 became the main focus of Dutch policy. The same was true of the estimated 250,000 Dutch and pro-Dutch Indonesians repatriated after 1945, many of whom had never been to the Netherlands before.[130] Among these, it was the 12,000 Ambonese South Moluccans who proved to be the most intractable political and social problem; refusing to integrate into Dutch society and ultimately resorting to acts of terrorism in 1975, 1976, and 1978 in order to publicize their case for a homeland in South East Asia independent of Indonesia.[131] On a broader scale, there were specific events that brought the Japanese occupation and Dutch loss of Indonesia back into the spotlight. These included the first public discussion of Dutch 'war crimes' in Indonesia after a controversial television programme in 1969, and the unofficial visit of the Emperor Hirohito to the Netherlands in October 1971. This was combined with the first formal commemorations of the Japanese surrender and an increasing interest in the effects of war trauma and the extension of state welfare provision to all those affected. Later still, the publication of the official history of the war in the East Indies again led to fierce public debate, as did a Dutch royal visit to Japan in 1986 and a campaign for a separate monument for the victims of the war in the Indies which was finally unveiled in The Hague on 15 August 1988.[132] Monuments in other municipalities have since followed, all of which include the Japanese occupation, the *bersiap* period, and the police actions.[133] At the same time as these debates on Dutch victimhood have taken place, the country's loss of its East Indian empire has remained a hotly debated subject that, in spite of the voluminous literature, continues to the present day.

CHAPTER 14
UNFINISHED BUSINESS: NEW GUINEA AS A LAST OUTPOST OF EMPIRE

The exclusion of New Guinea from the Indonesian settlement

The various negotiations that finally brought about independence for Indonesia in 1949 failed to resolve the fate of Netherlands New Guinea. Although the leaders of the Indonesian Republic insisted that the territory was an integral part of the new polity, the Dutch had seemingly gone to great lengths to exclude it from the negotiations. Neither the Linggadjati nor the Renville agreements provided the basis for a solution.[1] Linggadjati had ruled that all the territories of the Netherlands Indies would be transferred to Indonesia, but that account had to be taken of the wishes of the indigenous population. In the case of New Guinea, the General Commission thought this impossible and had stipulated that an alternative solution should be found.[2] In practice, further negotiations did not take place for nearly a year, and a meeting in December 1950 again failed to provide a resolution. Indonesian representatives insisted that the territory belonged to Indonesia, while the Dutch resisted any attempts to loosen their continuing control. With the Republic in its infancy and with any number of pressing issues to consider, Mohammad Hatta, as the country's lead negotiator, had taken the view that New Guinea's status could probably be resolved in more peaceful times and was prepared to allow the issue to be carried over, with the stipulation that the two sides 'remained in dispute'.[3]

The crucial question therefore is why the Dutch went to such lengths to hang onto this least important element of their East Indian dominions with such tenacity in the negotiations during and after transfer of power elsewhere in South East Asia.[4] The contemporary literature contained a panoply of justifications; historical, juridical, geographical, ethnological, and ethical. Taken individually, none of them were particularly convincing or compelling and even taken together they did not really make an overwhelming case. While expressing an overt belief in their continued colonial role as beneficial to the indigenous Papuans, this claim to guardianship over underdeveloped peoples carried little real weight when the Dutch had neither the economic nor the political power to promote their interests in the region.[5]

The subsequent dispute between the Netherlands and Indonesia was conducted under a number of headings. There were disagreements about the historical origins of Dutch dominion over New Guinea, disagreements over its geographical position – as part of the Indonesian archipelago or as part of Australasia, disagreements over the cultural origins of its peoples, and arguments about the rights of the Dutch and their record as a colonial power.[6] None of these disputes could be said to have been clearly delineated. Dutch control over the western half of the second largest island in the world had somewhat obscure origins and had been based on the Dutch East India Company vesting sovereignty of the 'Papuans or all of their islands' on the Kingdom of Tidore in 1660.[7] When the Company increased its control of the East Indies in the seventeenth and eighteenth centuries, New Guinea was included, but even after its formal inclusion as part of the Netherlands' colonial Empire after 1815, the Dutch government paid little attention to this huge, but largely unexplored land mass. Direct rule was instituted only in 1872, but this remained nominal until 1898 when the first permanent government posts were established at Manokwari and Fak-fak.[8] In fact, Dutch control remained superficial in the extreme and many inhabitants of the interior had little or no knowledge of their supposed colonial masters, even in the 1930s.[9]

The economic rationale for retaining New Guinea was unconvincing. Although both Marxist and non-Marxist writers had made claims about the mineral importance of the area and its potential for immigration, little empirical evidence existed to substantiate this. There had been suggestions that the colony might become an area for intensive colonization for Dutchmen and especially Eurasians 'who would wish to live under their own administration'.[10] In reality however, the climate and environment put off most settlers, and the schemes put forward and tried in the interwar period were poorly thought out and under-funded. Most of the Eurasian settlers who did arrive came from white-collar rather than agricultural backgrounds but it was assumed that land ownership would transcend any practical difficulties that the colonists might experience. Thus all the schemes were 'a dismal tale of mismanagement, frustration and failure',[11] and nearly all the remaining colonists were either killed fighting the Japanese or executed after the surrender.

The proclamation of Indonesian independence in August 1945 brought the plight of the Eurasians back into stark relief. Their status in the former colony was as Dutchmen, and they had been treated as such by the Japanese, occupying the same camps and suffering the same fate as their European counterparts. Thus their future in the newly independent state was at least precarious. Relocation to the Netherlands held few attractions, but racially ordered immigration policies also disbarred them from movement to many other parts of the Europeanized world. Hence, the idea of New Guinea as a new home for the dispossessed Eurasians was rekindled. Colonization associations re-emerged and received strong support from Eurasian organizations, and many other interests inside the Netherlands.[12] Beyond the colonial lobby, there was also the Comité Openlegging Nieuw-Guinea door Politieke Deliquenten formed by Koos Vorrink, a well-known social democrat and resistance leader, which promoted the idea of using New Guinea as a dumping ground for the former Dutch national socialists and SS volunteers, the 'Teutonic lackeys' who were a 'sick, incurable spot in our social body'.[13] They would be removed from the European motherland and be punished by having to provide the essential labour for a future full-scale Dutch colonization of the territory. As the debate on New Guinea took place within wider discussions on the future of the Dutch East Indies as a whole, isolating the various strands of the argument is difficult. However far-fetched the colonization schemes were, they garnered some support and were predicated on the idea that New Guinea should remain in Dutch hands and not be handed over to Indonesian control. Indeed, as early as the end of 1949, the Dutch ship Waebalong had dropped anchor in Dorehbaai and disembarked 1,400 Indo-Europeans from Java as colonists for Manokwari.[14]

Economic and commercial activity in the colony had also been minimal during the interwar period. Indeed, it was largely foreign interest in the colony's potential that prompted the Dutch government to 'influence' its major East Indian companies into further exploration and exploitation. As one Dutch resident officer put it, 'We only showed concern when others let their eyes fall on it.'[15] The German Phoenix Company had applied for agricultural exploitation rights in the 1920s and there were also negotiations for a German chartered company in the region. These initiatives (showing evidence of German desires to rebuild a colonial empire) were all rebuffed by the Dutch. More worrying was the Japanese interest that began to manifest itself in the 1930s. However, by mobilizing banking, shipping, and mining companies into a Nieuw Guinea Comité for 'the promotion of the development of Netherlands New Guinea', the Dutch largely succeeded in keeping foreign interests out of the colony prior to 1942. At this stage, and in the years immediately after 1945, it was still possible for those determined to hang onto New Guinea to believe that there remained huge unexplored potential in the colony. Thus resources that were as yet *onbekend* (unknown) could easily become *ongekend* (unprecedented) in the minds of those wanting to be persuaded – or to persuade themselves.[16]

The influence of civil servants and governmental structures also needs to be taken into account. The majority of bureaucrats in the territory were 'conservative and anti-Indonesian',[17] many having come from other parts of the East Indies in 1949. At the metropolitan centre, the civil servants were also often former colonial administrators and were better placed to influence government policy. Thus in December 1952, B. J. Krijger, Head of the New Guinea Section of the key Ministry of Union Affairs and Overseas Territories, reiterated many of the justifications for a continued role in New Guinea.

> When one considers the New Guinea problem, one will have to weigh not only the … ethical task of the education of a backward people, but also the following. Holland is saddled with its problem of overpopulation and with obtaining the raw materials that the country itself does not produce. As long as there is no convincing evidence that the overseas parts of the realm do not offer any possibility of absorbing a part of Holland's overpopulation and producing the raw materials necessary for the Netherlands, one might ask whether it is really justified to leave these overseas parts of the realm unexplored. The answer to the question involves a heavy responsibility of the Dutch people towards their descendants, particularly if the decision on this question should be irrevocable.[18]

The role played by civil servants in New Guinea in propounding and maintaining the arguments for continued Dutch involvement in the early 1950s has been characterized as a form of late empire-building and explained either by the concepts of the 'turbulent frontier' or of 'collaboration theory'.[19] Essentially, they saw their role as empire builders, even as revanchists harking back to a previous imperial age, but now determined to create a model colonial construct. While this may seem entirely revisionist in outlook, their longer term ambitions were to see themselves as colonial administrators who would ultimately transform into development workers over time,[20] a conception that had echoes of the 'ethical policy' at the beginning of the twentieth century. Their influence in the short term was considerable and was aided by the procession of Ministers who passed through the Ministry but were not in post long enough to influence policy.[21] This changed only after 1952 when relations with Indonesia were transferred to the Foreign Ministry and consistent ministerial oversight of their actions was much stronger.

Even taken together, these issues cannot entirely explain the tenacity of the groups in the Netherlands who were committed to retention of New Guinea. Beyond the practical, there were also the subjective and psychological factors. The first of these is the most obvious, namely that retaining New Guinea could act as a palliative for the loss of the other parts of the South East Asian empire and allow the Netherlands to retain a foothold in the region – with all the implications this had for the prestige of the country and her ability to continue as a colonial, and therefore a 'middle ranking' (*middelgrote*) power rather than just as a small state in continental Europe.[22] Although the territories in the West Indies were as yet unthreatened, they were barely considered as adding to Dutch 'weight' in international terms, whereas New Guinea was part of 'the' Dutch colony, the Netherlands East Indies.

A second element was the shock at the growth of nationalism in the East Indies and the inherent criticism of Dutch colonial rule that this implied. The Dutch self-image as benign, progressive rulers became unsustainable in the face of such evidence. Retention of New Guinea offered a means to disprove the international critics and demonstrate the advantages of Dutch colonial rule. In such justifications, there was often a strong element of nineteenth-century paternalism – of a mission to civilize. It remained an article of faith for many in Dutch society in the early 1950s that, had they been left to handle the Indonesian crisis without outside interference, then the whole colonial Empire might have been retained by the use of military force against the nationalists. Such ideas traded on the fiction that nationalism was purely a Japanese creation. Dutch inability to secure a military solution to the Indonesian crisis was attributed, in part, to the country's moral and political weakness, and to the attitudes of the other major powers. In this construct, the British could be condemned for their lack of help in the early stage of the crisis, while the United States was similarly castigated for a policy of intervention and exerting pressure on the Netherlands to settle the dispute. As we have seen, the agreements with Indonesia in 1949 for the transfer of power failed to solve the question of New Guinea. However, the colony's exclusion from the immediate transfers of power was also politically decisive, enabling the government to achieve the necessary two-thirds majority in both Chambers of the Dutch parliament to ratify the agreements.[23]

Most opposition came from the extreme left (Communists) and the extreme right (Anti-Revolutionary Party, Political Reform Party, and Catholic National Party), albeit for very different reasons. A split in the Calvinist Christian Historical Union meant that four of its members voted for the agreements and five against. Had New Guinea been included then the party would almost certainly have taken a solid stance in opposing the agreements and the government victory would have been in doubt. Similarly, the government needed the support of the Liberal Volkspartij voor Vrijheid en Democratie (VVD). Some party leaders were uneasy about the settlement, having opposed conciliation in the 1948 election campaign, and a poll in November 1949 had indicated that 52 per cent of Liberal voters were also opposed, a much higher proportion than any other groups save the Anti-Revolutionaries. Their leader, Dirk Stikker, nonetheless persuaded his fellow representatives and the party at large of the need to support the agreements, and used the New Guinea issue as a means to mask what was essentially a political *volte-face*.[24] In other words, the exclusion of New Guinea from the transfer of sovereignty was the price paid by the government to ensure the necessary parliamentary majority for the rest of the deal.[25]

Holding on after 1950: The material arguments

It might have been expected that the settlement with Indonesia would have allowed sentiment over New Guinea to calm down, even though the fate of the territory remained undecided. However, the subsequent actions of the Jakarta regime served only to exacerbate Dutch feelings. Soon after formal independence, the Indonesian government dismantled its federal constitutional structure, replacing it with a unitary alternative. All the guarantees that the Dutch thought had been built in for the minority populations within the archipelago disappeared at a stroke.[26] Legal they may have been, but these Indonesian measures were seen in the Netherlands as an act of bad faith.[27] They served to colour the putative negotiations over the future of New Guinea, whose transfer to Indonesia would not now include any of the guarantees implicit in a federal constitution. Dutch misgivings were given further impetus by the actions of the Ambonese, who had been staunch supporters of Dutch rule. Alarmed by the erosion of regional autonomy, Ambonese leaders proclaimed their own 'Republic of the South Moluccas' and carried on a guerrilla war against the Indonesian government for a number of years.[28] Some 13,000 Ambonese also fled to the Netherlands where their plight drew widespread sympathy. This combination of factors stoked the Dutch sense of obligation towards the inhabitants of New Guinea and a desire to frustrate the Indonesians and their future ambitions if at all possible.[29]

Two other issues served to strengthen Dutch resolve. First, the outbreak of the Korean War reinforced the sense of moral obligation to anti-communism and the Western Alliance. In these circumstances, Indonesian neutralism appeared even more suspect, and encouraged a Dutch belief that New Guinea would serve as a strategic stronghold. Australian policy, aided in part by a change in government, evolved along similar lines. From being traditional opponents of Dutch colonial rule, the Australians in the later 1940s became more keenly aware of New Guinea's importance to their own security at a time of international uncertainty.[30] In sum, the Dutch were no longer alone in their quest to keep New Guinea out of Indonesian hands. However, any objective assessment of the colony's strategic importance would have noted that the Dutch garrisons on the island were totally inadequate to withstand any sustained incursions, and also that if the Netherlands' alliance partners genuinely regarded New Guinea as a key element in hemisphere defence, they would have backed the Dutch case more strongly. In fact, neither the United States nor the South East Asia Treaty Organization (SEATO) states provided much support for the Dutch in the various UN debates during the 1950s and early 1960s. Only Australia saw continued Dutch rule as a bastion against a possible communist takeover in Indonesia, but even its expressions of national interest were never translated into practical support.[31]

Dutch intransigence and Sukarno's increasingly strident statements that Indonesian national aspirations could not be fulfilled until New Guinea (West Irian) was in the fold[32] meant that discussions held at the end of 1950 to resolve the New Guinea question stood little chance of success. When Foreign Minister Stikker appeared willing to concede a transfer of sovereignty to the Netherlands-Indonesian Union, he was repudiated by his party, an event that precipitated the fall of the Drees Cabinet on 24 January 1951.[33] Although talks did continue into 1952, common ground proved hard to find. Not surprisingly, there was no improvement in Dutch-Indonesian relations during the early 1950s. Instead, the case for retaining New Guinea assumed an increasingly political complexion. The colony's economic value appeared minimal, especially after newly discovered mineral resources proved to be of little value. As a result, the colony consistently produced budget deficits that had to be underwritten by the Dutch government. An official shortfall of fl.15, 572,099.38 in 1950 had grown to fl. 84,175,500 by 1960 and the actual figures may have been over twice those officially reported.[34] The value of imports invariably exceeded exports and oil production, by far the most important export commodity, peaked in 1954 after which it showed a consistent decline in both volume and value between 1957 and 1961.[35] Moreover the oil company concerned, the NV Nederlandsche Nieuw Guinea Petroleum Maatschappij, was allowed to retain its foreign currency balances so that these also did not benefit either the colony or the Dutch exchequer.[36] It has also been argued that the NNGPM, which was 60 per cent American and 40 per cent Royal Dutch Shell-owned, deliberately withheld knowledge of major oil resources discovered at the Sele field just before the Japanese invasion. The charge is that the company did not share this knowledge either with the Dutch or with the American and Indonesian governments until after the end of Dutch rule and the overthrow of Sukarno in 1965, when the arrival of General Suharto as President was seen as a propitious moment to announce the new 'find'. Thus, a company partly owned by Royal Dutch Shell was complicit in keeping the oil deposits a secret from the Netherlands' government when its exploitation might have made a substantial difference to the economic viability of New Guinea as a colony.[37]

If actual benefits were minimal beyond providing work for some 9,000 Papuans, it is nonetheless important to ask whether the Dutch thought the colony had any future real economic potential. Commercial prospecting for viable new oilfields was more or less abandoned by the end of the 1950s, and deposits of metal ores were deemed insufficiently large or too low grade for commercial exploitation. This suggests that there was little belief in a future Eldorado of raw materials that would make the colony a desirable possession in the modern world. The Dutch government also categorically denied claims that the territory possessed appreciable quantities of uranium or gold. Although New Guinea was not fully explored and the interior might still have contained some secrets, it was generally held that the only major economic benefits lay in timber and, perhaps, hydroelectric schemes.[38] However, the poor infrastructure and the mixture of tree types hindered commercial exploitation of the former, while the latter had no obvious market or purpose. The soils were considered too poor for intensive agriculture and there was a shortage of viable labour for such projects, the indigenous population being used to extensive subsistence farming and totally unfamiliar with 'western' labour discipline. Capital was also in very short supply and any improvements were hindered by the continued uncertainty over the colony's political future. Finally, any commercial economic interests that might have continued private Dutch interest in the colony were compromised by the fact that they often had much larger investments in Indonesia, and to make an enemy of Indonesia over New Guinea would have seemed perverse in the extreme.[39] The Dutch had clearly overestimated the economic and agrarian potential of the colony.[40] Lijphart is unequivocal on the issue.

> The view of New Guinea as an economically advantageous area was completely false. New Guinea was a liability rather than an asset to the Dutch treasury: it offered no rich source of raw materials, no trade advantages, no investment opportunities, and no possibilities for immigration either by Eurasians or by white Dutchmen.[41]

In sum, New Guinea was certainly no Belgian Congo.

Colonization associations also lost interest as the commercial and agricultural potential of the territory was exposed as a myth, although they continued to champion the idea of Dutch rule. More outspoken was the ex-servicemen's organization Veteranen Legioen Nederland. In theory open to all military veterans, those who had fought in the Indonesian campaign dominated it. In their eyes the retention of New Guinea helped justify what had otherwise been a lost war.[42] Although supposedly apolitical, the armed forces also held pronounced opinions. Thus the Royal Dutch Navy saw continued control over New Guinea as strategically critical for its future as an oceanic force.[43] Missionary societies also joined the debate, as both the major churches had operated on the island, the Dutch Reformed from 1855 and the Roman Catholics from 1895.[44] By 1953 it was estimated that around 30 per cent of the indigenous population had been Christianized. However, the missions and their mother churches did not follow a consistent line on the New Guinea issue. The Dutch Reformed lobby was split between those who saw New Guinea as a complication to better relations with Indonesia, and those who attached primary importance to their assumed moral obligation to the native Papuans. Given that the East Indies was just about the only area of missionary operations for the Dutch Reformed Church, it is hardly surprising that the colony loomed large in its calculations. However, divided opinions on the issue cancelled out any impact its intervention might have had. Although equally split, the more global interests of the Roman Catholic Church led it to support continued Dutch sovereignty in New Guinea in the Netherlands, while championing the cause of transfer in Indonesia.[45]

The strategic and political value of the colony was also debatable. While the Dutch controlled the Indonesian archipelago, the possession of New Guinea provided a block to any incursions from the Empire's Eastern flank. However, the loss of the East Indies rendered this argument worthless and its only residual value was as a contribution to the defence of the Western Alliance in the burgeoning Cold War.[46] At a political level, the case is even more obscure. It has been argued that the Dutch could have used their continued control over New Guinea as a bargaining counter to protect and even enhance commercial interests inside Indonesia by offering the possibility of a gradual transfer of sovereignty. Certainly, there were economic associations that pressed for changes in Dutch-Indonesian relations in order to promote a better trading environment for Dutch concerns in the archipelago,[47] but there is no evidence that the Dutch Foreign Office ever pursued such a policy. The Indonesians could always counter with the threat of expropriation or nationalization of Dutch assets. Indeed, most commercial concerns had conceded defeat in the early 1950s and scaled down their activities accordingly.

Holding on after 1950: The internal politics

However unconvincing the pragmatic arguments were for the Dutch retention of New Guinea, there is no doubt that political opinion on the subject hardened after the Round Table Agreement and the failure of the conference talks in 1950. The attitudes of parties that had opposed the Round Table Conference were unsurprising. The Anti-Revolutionaries opposed any concessions to Indonesia and Pieter Gerbrandy, the former wartime Prime Minister of the government-in-exile was on record as saying that New Guinea was a chance to retain 'a small fragment of Holland's former greatness'. He referred to 'totalitarian Jakarta' and government policy as 'perfidious and dishonourable'.[48] Other protestant parties took a similar, if less extreme, line as did the Catholic National Party whose spokesman, the former Minister for the Colonies, Charles Welter, bemoaned the fact that nationalist arguments no longer held sway in government circles. Yet even the parties that had supported the Round Table Conference became increasingly obdurate in response to the behaviour of the Indonesian regime. Thus large sections of the Liberal and Catholic Parties shifted to supporting the status quo, both in defence of the Papuans' right to self-determination and in protest against the 'neutral' stance of the Indonesians.[49] Only the Partij van de Arbeid (Labour) remained split on the issue. While its parliamentary party was still prepared to consider the secession of the territory to Indonesia with certain guarantees, their Ministers in government, including Prime Minister Drees, opposed any further concessions.[50] This remained the trend in Dutch politics throughout the early 1950s.[51] Informal talks in 1951, 1952, and 1954 failed to reach any meaningful conclusions beyond the abrogation of the Netherlands-Indonesian Union.[52] Thereafter the Dutch refused to discuss the future of New Guinea, a position that came to be known as the *ijskastformule* (deep freeze solution).[53]

This attitude was exacerbated by the behaviour of the Indonesian leadership and the toleration and even sponsorship of anti-Dutch protests that took place periodically.[54] Also of importance were heightened Cold War fears, coupled with the British and French fighting extended colonial wars in Malaya and Indochina respectively. Amendments had to be made to the Dutch constitution in line with the changed political realities left by the lack of a final resolution in 1950, but it was not until 1956 that New Guinea was formally included and Indonesia removed from Article 1 that delineated the Kingdom of the Netherlands.[55]

The tenacity with which the Dutch hung onto their last remaining South East Asian colony diminished only with the passing of time. The open wound of losing Indonesia began to heal and Dutch attention was increasingly focused on the various treaties and arrangements that culminated in the Treaty of Rome and the founding of the European Economic Community. With increasing economic prosperity emanating from post-war reconstruction, imperial possessions seemed less important.[56] The international situation also provoked new fears. The Dutch could not fail to observe Belgium's traumatic and rapid loss of the Congo, and the increasingly belligerent behaviour of an Indonesia, now being aided and even armed by the United States, the United Kingdom and the Soviet Union. This would pose a potentially disastrous problem for the Dutch if they were ever forced to defend their New Guinea territories alone. The Indonesian government made a number of attempts to raise the New Guinea question at the United Nations. In the sittings of 1954 and 1956–7, it failed to obtain the two-thirds majority required for a resolution.[57] Thus in spite of continued Indonesian pressure, no further progress was made towards a settlement. This was to change only in the late 1950s when the instability of the new Indonesian state prompted a change in tactics.

The final stages of the dispute

Late in 1956, Indonesia was rocked by insurrections in Sumatra and Eastern Indonesia led by regional military commanders discontented with the central government. In early 1957, Sukarno began the process of dismantling parliamentary government in favour of a National Council that would provide a national consensus under presidential guidance. Opposition dissatisfaction was exacerbated after the summer of 1957 when regional parliamentary elections in Java saw major gains for the communist PKI. From then on, Sukarno was seen as working with the communists in order to implement his new system of government. This served to further alienate the rebel leadership. Western fears of a communist takeover prompted plans in Washington to create an alternative seat of government, thus potentially breaking up the Republic altogether. In the event, Sukarno opted to appoint a 'working cabinet' and rearm and remobilize the armed forces loyal to his regime in order to suppress the rebellion once and for all. Appeals to the United States for military aid went unheeded and so he turned to the Eastern Bloc states of Poland, Czechoslovakia, and Yugoslavia to buy approximately $100 million of Soviet armaments. In response, the United States began supplying the rebels with armaments, but the scale of Soviet bloc help for the Indonesian Armed Forces and their successes in the field led to a Western reappraisal of the realities of the situation.[58] Henceforward, Washington began to think of the Indonesian Armed Forces as a possible alternative to Sukarno and his communist support. More worrying for the Australians and the Dutch in New Guinea was the undoubted success of Indonesian amphibious operations against the rebels, indicating their potential to mount similar operations in disputed territories.

A UN resolution on the question of West New Guinea was tabled on 16 August 1957. Sponsored by a number of non-aligned states, its intention was to produce a 'peaceful solution' to the long-standing dispute. Although debated in the Assembly the following November, it once again fell short of the required two-thirds majority to be implemented.[59] Its failure led to an almost immediate outbreak of violence, with attacks against Dutch citizens still in Indonesia becoming more commonplace. In the same vein, the regime began expropriating Dutch property and expelling the remaining Dutch nationals from the country.[60] There was a good deal of internal Indonesian opposition to this move, but in a political climate that was rapidly descending into civil war, there was little room for protest. At the same time there were renewed demands from Jakarta for the transfer of New Guinea to Indonesia. This was part of the platform of the powerful communist PKI, and to keep their support, Sukarno felt impelled to adopt a more aggressive stance as the decade came to a close.[61]

In the Netherlands, the height of anti-Indonesian feeling probably occurred at the end of 1957 when the Jakarta government had completed the expulsion of the remaining 50,000 Dutch and Eurasian people and news of the expropriations reached Europe.[62] It was therefore the expellees that bore the brunt of the failure of the two states to settle the New Guinea question. Apart from the physical harm many of them experienced, they also collectively lost between 4 and 5 milliard guilders in destroyed or confiscated property.[63] Although seen at that time as the nadir of Indonesian-Dutch relations, the actions of the Sukarno regime served to clear away many areas of friction. The Dutch in Indonesia were no longer an issue, and the increasing prosperity of the Netherlands allowed their rapid absorption into the labour market. Moreover, those individuals, organizations, and institutions that had championed the cause of continued colonial control in New Guinea either lost their influence or changed their minds. Colonization societies became impotent as the Eurasians' interest in New Guinea waned and they looked elsewhere for permanent homes. During 1956, the Synod of the Dutch Reformed Church attempted to re-examine the possibilities of a permanent solution for New Guinea in the form of a 'Call to Reflection' on the tensions caused in Dutch-Indonesian relations. This became less relevant after the expulsions had taken place and the Church's missionary work was curtailed. Although the question of its role inside New Guinea remained, much of its energies were perforce focused elsewhere.[64] The civil service in New Guinea also changed its view as the 'refugees' from Indonesia who had been sent there as administrators after 1945 were gradually replaced by a new generation of men who had not served in the Netherlands Indies and were more concerned with promoting self-determination 'than to conceptions of colonial grandeur'.[65] In the second half of the decade, various Dutch economic interest groups began pressing for New Guinea to be transferred to Indonesia. They were motivated, in part, by the possibility of compensation or a resumption of trade between the two nations, and partly by a desire to avoid being seen as representatives of a colonial power in a rapidly changing international political climate.[66]

Shifts in public opinion were also beginning to be manifest in certain sections of the press during the late 1950s. While the majority of mainstream national newspapers continued to support the government line until 1961 and were highly critical of those who advocated change, including the authors of the 'Call to Reflection',[67] some commentators in left-wing and liberal newspapers began to argue for a more permanent solution to the New Guinea question. The fear was that the Netherlands might be drawn into a conflict on the other side of the globe to defend an outpost of Empire that few now believed was viable. Moreover, she would have to do this unsupported by any of her European or NATO allies, and perhaps in the teeth of their opposition. At this stage, internationalization was the preferred option, involving the transfer of sovereignty to either Australia or the United Nations. This shift in thinking was accentuated after January 1961 as more newspapers began to question the idea of continued control of New Guinea. Some went so far as to suggest transfer to Indonesia as the best available solution. Ultimately, even the Anti-Revolutionary daily *Trouw* began advocating reconciliation.[68]

At a political level, this shift towards decolonization was predicated on two conditions being met: that self-determination of the Papuans would be protected and that Indonesian aspirations in the area would be thwarted. In this sense, all the reasons put forward to justify continuing Dutch control of New Guinea were essentially negative and designed primarily to prevent a transfer of power to Indonesia. Large swathes of opinion in the Netherlands remained convinced that the country should not give in to the increasingly belligerent attitude emanating from Jakarta.[69] Nevertheless, much energy was expended during the late 1950s in accelerating the moves towards self-determination. Thus Governor Jan van Baal suggested that New Guinea should be ready for full independence (*volledig zelfstandigheid*) by around 1980 and pioneered the creation of village councils as a form of local democracy. In addition, there were the beginnings of political parties. The Democratische Volkspartij was formed in 1957, but consisted entirely of Indo-Europeans. The first indigenous Papuan party, the Partai Nasional, did not emerge until 1960.[70] Party politics fostered a limited climate of nationalism and thus little enthusiasm for union with Indonesia. The possibilities of UN supervision were also explored. UN involvement might have enabled the Netherlands to shed her responsibilities without compromising the original justifications for retaining the territory in the first place. Conversely, the growing threat of Indonesian military intervention and consequent regional destabilization encouraged a more 'flexible' approach to self-determination.[71]

This tendency was first manifest within the Partij van de Arbeid during the Drees Cabinet of 1956–8, but not followed by the other coalition members, the Anti-Revolutionaries, Catholics, and Christian Historical Union who all remained committed to the idea of self-determination under Dutch sovereignty. Towards the end of 1958, the perceived military threat from Indonesia led to plans for increased Dutch garrisons on the island but this measure would have meant the use of conscripts, something that required parliamentary approval. Attempts to change the military service law evoked strong opposition from the PvdA in government and an immediate crisis was only averted by the use of volunteers.[72] Changes were made in 1959, but only after the PvdA had left government. Not until 1960 was the decision taken to further reinforce the colony in the face of a continuing threat from Indonesia. In an act designed to bolster Dutch military prestige in the area, The Hague also sent the aircraft carrier *Karel Doorman* to South

East Asia.[73] On 17 August 1960, the Indonesians broke off all diplomatic relations with the Netherlands, thus further escalating the crisis.[74] By this stage, the government led by Jan De Quay had received pleas from two of the largest Dutch multinationals, Philips and Unilever, to normalize relations with Indonesia by resolving the New Guinea question once and for all.[75]

Both countries indulged in increasingly belligerent rhetoric, but the Dutch position was much the weaker. The Indonesians interpreted the arrival of the Dutch aircraft carrier in the region as a direct challenge and moved closer to taking the territory by military force. The Soviet Union lent its support by providing $1,000 million of arms and equipment.[76] For their part, the Dutch had received backing as late as 1959 from an Australian government still concerned about security on its northern frontier and Prime Minister Robert Menzies had made clear to Indonesian Foreign Minister Subandrio that Australian-Dutch cooperation would continue until the Papuans were capable of deciding their own fate.[77] By 1961, however, the Australians shifted their position and, in further discussions with the Indonesians, intimated that no military agreement with the Dutch existed. Nor would Canberra insist on Papuan self-determination as a precursor for any future talks.[78]

The United States increasingly regarded New Guinea as more than just a regional question, as other countries across the globe achieved independence and opted for non-alignment to maximize the benefits of being courted by both sides in the Cold War.[79] In the later 1950s Washington voiced increasing concern about Indonesia's attitude towards communism,[80] and there were rumours that the CIA had been involved in the 1957 insurrections against Sukarno.[81] This judgement was revised in the later stages of the Eisenhower presidency when the United States came to see the Indonesian army as the key bulwark against communist insurgency in the region.[82] As early as 1958 it became evident that the United States was actually supplying armaments as well as food to the Indonesians. The Dutch had already taken steps to prevent the Italians and Germans from selling military materiel to Jakarta but this news made any further restraint irrelevant and led to a stormy meeting between Netherlands Ambassador J. Herman van Roijen and Secretary of State John Foster Dulles in Washington.[83]

Eisenhower's successor, John F. Kennedy, shared Australia's concern about communist incursions into South East Asia and, like Canberra, was keen to improve relations with Indonesia.[84] Washington was also adamant that it wanted a permanent solution to the problem and not just another tactical victory at the United Nations.[85] Pressure was mounting as it became apparent that the Indonesians had agreed a deal for the supply of heavy weapons from the Soviet Union and it was at this stage that Washington informed the Dutch that unless they came up with a plan to resolve the situation, the United States would impose one. There was no question that majority opinion in the Netherlands by this time favoured a retreat from the imperial commitment in New Guinea, but there was a reluctance to cave in to the demands of the Sukarno regime or to give way to international pressure. Steps had been taken to hasten the drive towards self-determination in New Guinea, with the creation of a New Guinea Council on 5 April 1961 as a first step to a full legislative body, but this gradualist approach found little favour in international circles and even the Dutch chose to downplay its authority.[86] At the same time, Carl Romme, the long-serving leader of the Catholic People's Party (KVP) and opponent of further concessions to the Indonesians, gave up his office, allowing a reshuffle of the Dutch Cabinet.[87] Following this, a new formula was attempted. This was the so-called Luns Plan, presented to the United Nations in September 1961.[88] Essentially, it transferred sovereignty to the Papuans and administration to an international executive authority under the United

Nations. The plan was discussed at the UN General Assembly on 28 November 1961 and, although supported by a broad coalition of parties inside the Netherlands, the defeat of two 'less far-reaching' resolutions in the General Assembly led to its withdrawal.[89] Thus, at the very moment when Dutch opinion had come to accept that change was necessary, international backing evaporated, leaving the Dutch without a viable policy. Meanwhile, increasing US involvement in Vietnam made it essential for the Americans to reduce the number of potential flashpoints across South East Asia.[90]

Washington therefore insisted that Sukarno be given the space and time to control his country's communist party and to meet its objectives with regard to New Guinea. Failure would mean a conflict that, even if localized, would inevitably involve the United States on the side of its NATO ally the Netherlands, with Indonesia being supported by the anti-imperialist communist and non-aligned states. White House pressure elicited an agreement from the Dutch through their Ambassador van Roijen, to re-enter negotiations, but with the stipulation that Papuan self-determination remained central to their position.[91] Meanwhile, statements from Jakarta became increasingly belligerent, culminating on 19 December, with Sukarno's speech in which he gave his 'final order' for the Indonesian people to prepare for general mobilization to free West Irian 'from the claws of Dutch imperialism'.[92] This was no idle threat. From the beginning of 1962 Indonesian military incursions against New Guinea increased, involving casualties on both sides.[93] The Dutch military build-up also continued. As military tension mounted, Kennedy sent his brother Robert to The Hague to explain the US position. His comments were reiterated when Josef Luns, by that time Foreign Minister, met the President on 3 March. Although he waved 'a flabby forefinger' in the President's face, Kennedy remained intransigent. The De Quay government duly accepted the resumption of negotiations with the Indonesians without the precondition of safeguards for Papuan self-determination.[94] American views of public Dutch intransigence had been coloured by other sources of information. Sympathetic journalists, and even Prins Bernhard, had intimated that the majority of the Dutch public were now in favour of a settlement and Dirk Stikker, by that time secretary general of NATO and a man whom the Americans thought spoke for the Dutch business community, vouchsafed the fact that US leadership on an international trusteeship arrangement would be welcomed.[95]

US policy on New Guinea cannot be seen in isolation but as part of much wider Cold War calculations. Thus American backing for a UN-brokered solution soon evaporated when claims about self-determination threatened to undermine independence settlements elsewhere. If Papuan claims to be a separate entity from the rest of the Indonesian archipelago were accepted, then this might prompt separatist claims elsewhere, for example in Africa. From being a stick with which to beat the colonial powers, Washington now saw self-determination as something of a two-edged sword and shifted its ground accordingly towards the end of 1961. This change was perhaps epitomized by a memorandum from Robert Komer (who served on the staff of the National Security Council) to Walt Rostow (then Deputy National Security Adviser) where he intimated that it was time 'to take the gloves off and adopt a frankly pro-Indonesian stance while there's still time to get some political capital out of it'.[96]

By this stage, the Indonesian government was justifiably confident that it had the tacit backing of the US administration and could therefore hold out for an American rather than a UN mediator.[97] The talks that began in March 1962 were brokered by the US diplomat Ellsworth Bunker on behalf of the United Nations with the blessing of the Kennedy administration. Their outcome was the creation of a 'temporary executive authority' under the aegis of the United Nations that would first take over the sovereignty of the territory from the Dutch, preparing the ground for a hand over to Indonesian authority in the following year.[98] Meanwhile, the Dutch government faced increasing pressure from its domestic political parties and the country at large to find a solution to the crisis, amid widespread fears that it might otherwise lead to war. Predictably, the PvdA proposed a series of motions to the Second Chamber, all of which were defeated, but their attempts at extra-parliamentary pressure produced a petition with more than half a million signatures in little over a month. However, it was the changing stance of the Anti-Revolutionaries and the Catholic Parties that was to prove crucial. Both pressed for a moderate solution and acceptance of the Bunker Plan as a basis for negotiation. The Indonesians also ratcheted up the pressure, invading the island with parachute troops on 12 July.[99] Subsequent negotiations took place the same month and led directly to a Dutch-Indonesian agreement on 15 August 1962 that embodied the terms of the Bunker Plan. Even at the last minute, there were points when the negotiations almost broke down as the Indonesians tried to wrest every last concession in their favour. There were disputes about the proposed plebiscite, about the length of UN administration, even about the date and time when the Indonesian flag was to be raised.[100]

The arrangement to transfer the sovereignty of New Guinea to the Indonesians thus took shape, but left few guarantees of self-determination for the Papuan peoples.[101] Even so, the Dutch parliament's two chambers ratified the agreement on 7 and 14 September 1962 with only a few dissenting voices. The transfer of power to the United Nations proceeded on 1 October 1962 and thence to Indonesian control eight months later on 1 May 1963. Even before this process was completed, relations between Jakarta and The Hague picked up. Diplomatic relations were restored in March 1963 and trade resumed in July of the same year. A year later, Luns was able to visit Indonesia bearing a million guilders in credit guarantees.[102] Something like normal relations had been restored.

Conclusion

Luns' 'flabby forefinger' proved to be the last vestige of Dutch colonialism in Asia.[103] The puzzle remains as to why the Netherlands was apparently prepared to go to the brink of war over an admittedly large territory, but one that was largely unknown to Western eyes. The economic and strategic arguments had never stood close scrutiny after 1950. Nor was the moral commitment to oversee the development to self-government of the Papuans deeply felt, judging by the speed with which the issue disappeared from Dutch public discourse after 1962. Conversely, there is no doubt that the Dutch insistence on remaining in New Guinea damaged both the country's international reputation and its material interests.[104] In the absence of pragmatic reasons for the Dutch resistance to decolonization of New Guinea, Lijphart is forced to fall back on the subjective and psychological factors of a frustrated nationalism, 'the search for national self-esteem, feelings of moral superiority, egocentric altruism and deep resentment against Indonesia'.[105] Only towards the end of that decade did domestic opinion begin to change. This allowed the government, facing international isolation, to move to a settlement, albeit one that abandoned the principles that had been used to justify continued sovereignty over New Guinea since 1949.

Esterik draws a broader set of conclusions. First, he argues that Dutch intransigence constituted a last attempt to pursue a policy independent of NATO. As such, it was a reflexive response to the inevitable downgrading of a former middle-ranking colonial power to little more than a delta on the edge of the North Sea or a province of Europe. Second he notes that the retention of New Guinea allowed the confessional political parties in the Netherlands to maintain the idea of a colonial ideology against the industrial and political modernization of the state. In this respect, New Guinea was seen as a new colony, virgin territory in which the civilizing mission of the Dutch could continue. Finally, diehard attitudes were a reaction against Indonesia's aggressive pursuit of sovereignty over New Guinea and her insistence on being non-aligned when the world was ideologically divided by the Cold War.[106]

Ultimately, the Dutch could not buck the trend evident among other European colonial states. The French were mired in the Algerian civil war and Harold Macmillan's 'wind of change' speech in 1960 had set the tone for British decolonization in Africa. More important was the realization that it was impossible to stand alone against world opinion in general, or against the United States in particular. This was the hard truth finally brought home to Dutch politicians early in 1962. In that respect they had learnt little from the US threats during the Indonesian crisis, the only difference being that, whereas in the late 1940s they could still count on majority public support for the idea of empire, by 1962, all such justifications had ebbed away.

CHAPTER 15
DECOLONIZATION BY DEFAULT: DUTCH DISENGAGEMENT IN SURINAME

Colonial rule before 1940

Suriname and the islands of the Dutch West Indies were unusual as colonial territories in that there was never a strong popular consensus in favour of independence. The ethnic diversity of the colonies' population and its translation into political representation meant that many social and political groups saw continued Dutch stewardship as a guarantee of their rights and a bar to the untrammelled dominance of political rivals. Also unusual, given the location of the colonies on the periphery of the Caribbean and the interest taken by the United States in the region, is the relatively minor role played by international factors in undermining colonial rule. Ultimately, independence did come for Suriname: driven in part by gradually increasing internal political pressures, in part by international considerations, but ultimately by Dutch fears of a continued colonial commitment and what this might entail.

Until the late 1940s, the relationship between the European Netherlands and her West Indian colonies conformed essentially to the traditional imperial model. The Dutch state was forced to address problems associated with colonial governance in the 1930s, but the 'shock' of 1940 and the occupation of the motherland led to the West Indian colonies' economic dependence on the United States and the arrival of an American military presence in Suriname to assure that colony's security. While these factors may have played some role in loosening ties with the European motherland, the fears of Dutch imperialists were not realized in the immediate post-war years. Instead, a series of steps were taken during and after the war to 'modernize' the Netherlands' constitutional relationship with her remaining imperial territories after the loss of Indonesia, most notably the three Round Table conferences of 1948, 1952, and 1958. More important in the post-war period were the internal political developments that went hand in hand with this modernization – the emergence of political parties based on ethnic divisions and the extension of the franchise to include most of the adult population for the first time. However, even in the 1960s, it could be argued that the political structure of the colony militated against support for increased independence, and it was ultimately only the conjuncture of a particular set of internal political circumstances combined with a sea change in Dutch attitudes towards empire in the early 1970s which brought full independence.[1]

The effects of the Second World War

The defeat and occupation of the European Netherlands had brought new social and economic pressures to the West Indian colonies. In the summer of 1940, there were rumours of German troops ready to invade the Guianas from Brazil and the chairman of the US War Resources Board, Edward R. Stettinius, voiced fears about the security of bauxite shipments. With the cessation of colonial trade with the motherland, it was estimated that some 80 per cent of Suriname's imports now came from the United States, and even the Governor was forced to admit 'the greatly increased dependence on the US'.[2] Anglo-American observers evinced a fairly low opinion of Dutch colonial administration in general and the Governor in particular. Anti-colonialist sentiment was to be expected from the Americans, but even the British, who were more sympathetic to the plight of a weakened colonial power, saw the regime as inefficient and inadequate to the task of defending the colony effectively.[3] In truth, the Dutch position was pitiful. Manpower was at a premium, and it proved impossible for the Dutch to find sufficient forces to replace even the relatively small British garrisons sent to Curaçao and Aruba in 1940.[4]

On 1 September 1941, the United States contacted the Dutch with a view to assisting with the defence of Suriname in line with the procedure agreed at the 1940 Havana Conference. Negotiations dragged on into November, and even then split the Dutch Cabinet and caused the resignation of two ministers, including Minister for the Colonies, Charles Welter. There remained a strong feeling within Dutch government circles that the Netherlands should still try and look after its own defence without outside help. Governor Kielstra was among those who thought that Suriname could still be defended, but this may have stemmed from fear of the alternative rather than any empirical evidence. He certainly fretted that any American military presence in the colony might result in annexation. The Dutch ambassador in Washington agreed, and warned that a US force in Suriname 'would have a detrimental effect on [the Netherlands] prestige as a colonial power'.[5] Ultimately, these objections were overridden as events in the East Indies assumed paramount importance. On 24 November 1941, a joint communiqué was issued and US troops arrived the following day.

The precise effects of the American presence in the colony between 1941 and 1945 are difficult to gauge. At an economic level, the colony produced a trade surplus for the first time in 1941 as a result of the demand for bauxite,[6] but this masks the fact that imported American goods had replaced those from the colonial power. As in French-controlled New Caledonia, the arrival of around 2,000 US troops with money to spend tended to skew the local economy, and the employment of non-white workers by the American garrison at wages way above local rates further exacerbated the situation. It has been estimated that the total investment in the colony plus the money brought in by the American soldiers during the war amounted to Sfl.65 million (Surinamese guilders), of which approximately Sfl.50 million went to local workers and the purchase of local goods. The net effect was an improvement in living standards among many in the colony who had previously existed only at subsistence levels, while the inevitable inflation tended to impoverish those on fixed incomes, such as government servants.[7]

The arriving American troops also brought with them an entirely different culture and value system which inevitably percolated into the society of the colony.[8] More apparent challenges to Dutch colonial rule came when the Americans decided to replace their existing 'white' soldiers with 'coloured' Puerto Ricans. It is probably true to say that the Dutch were unnecessarily touchy about many of the assumed slights on their colonial prestige and *amour propre*, but there were nonetheless one or two occasions when the Americans upset the political balance by being implicated in internal matters.[9] In the event, few if any of the Dutch fears about American involvement in Suriname came to fruition, and even the hard-line policies of Governor Kielstra during the Second World War did little immediate damage to colonial rule.[10] In the immediate post-war era however, Suriname's survival as a Dutch colony became inextricably tied up with international politics and the fate of the Dutch East Indies.

This did not mean that Suriname's internal political development was irrelevant. New organizations began to appear in the later 1930s and early 1940s based on occupational or social democratic groups. Queen Wilhelmina's December 1942 speech received a warm welcome in Suriname, especially from the Creole community who saw the prospect of local autonomy as a means to bolster their position and so undermine the increasingly autocratic rule of Governor Kielstra.[11] The term 'baas in eigen huis' (boss in your own home) became common parlance.[12] However, they were less enthusiastic about another possibility, namely that reform might bring about pressures for universal suffrage, which would certainly remove their majority position in the *Staten*.[13] Kielstra was replaced towards the end of the war, and the prospect of negotiated constitutional change encouraged new political organization among all sections of the community, a step that had seemed irrelevant before when the colonial Governor had exercised so much power. The result was the establishment in the immediate post-war years of a whole raft of political parties, divided more or less along ethnic lines. Four were of major importance: The lighter-skinned Creole elite transformed its previous representative organization, the Unie Suriname,[14] into the Nationale Partij Suriname (NPS). Ostensibly a party for all groups irrespective of race or religion, it attracted support only from the urban Creole elite, largely because it espoused only a limited franchise. However the increased general wealth generated by wartime economic expansion and better access to education led to wider political mobilization, albeit usually led by the upper social echelons. This gave rise to a Catholic-based Suriname Progressive People's Party (Progressieve Surinaamse Volkspartij, PSV) that drew support from the Creole lower classes, and two parties that represented the Asiatic communities: the United Hindu Party (Verenigde Hindostaanse Partij, VHP), for those whose origins lay in British India, and the Indonesian Farmer's Party (Kaum Tani Persatuan Indonesia, KTPI) for those from the East Indies.[15] While the ethnic base of each party was clear, there were also socioeconomic distinctions, with the Hindu and Javanese populations being largely rural and the Creoles of all classes being more urbanized.[16]

Political developments after 1945

Discussions over the autonomy of the Dutch West Indian possessions were sidelined and all but forgotten in the post-war crisis that engulfed the Netherlands and its East Indian possessions. Dutch government commissions to the West Indian colonies discovered that there was little or no interest in independence but a desire for autonomy within a reconstructed Kingdom of the Netherlands.[17] Discontent was focused on the powerlessness of local councils and the overweening powers of the Governors rather than on the relationship between the colonies and The Hague.[18] A delegation from the West Indies visited the Queen in July 1946 with a petition containing the ideas of a quadripartite kingdom (the Netherlands, Indonesia, Curaçao, and Suriname) based on her speech of December 1942, and there was outline agreement that reform would be discussed as soon as possible.[19] Thus there was anger in Suriname when the Dutch, desperate for something to hold the Indonesians, negotiated the Linggadjati Agreement in November 1946 that provided for a Netherlands-Indonesian Union with no reference to the position of the West Indies.[20] Statutes to facilitate the autonomy of the West Indian territories were discussed by the Dutch parliament at the end of 1947 and became law in May 1948. In the meantime January 1948 saw the first Round Table Conference to discuss the future constitutional relationship between the Netherlands, Suriname, and the Antilles.[21] In spite of some initial problems, caused mainly by the representatives from the Antilles,[22] there was little argument about full legislative and budgetary powers over internal affairs or about increases in the size of the *Staten*, but the major disagreements came in relation to the precise responsibilities of future ministerial cabinets and the vexed question of universal suffrage. Thus when the Conference adjourned, the drafting of a constitution was left to the heads of the three delegations.[23] Ultimately, the Dutch government rejected their draft constitution as it gave the West Indian representation far too much say in the internal administration of the Netherlands and as a result of this stalemate, the Kingdom had to be run on the basis of an interim regulation (*interimregeling*) from January 1950 onwards.[24]

Negotiations to create a Kingdom-wide legislative body were conducted at a second Round Table Conference, beginning in April 1952. There had been some prior discussion between the representatives of Suriname and the Antilles, with the former deliberately adopting a more extreme line.[25] However, this alliance was rapidly broken when the Dutch suggested that the Antilles bear some of the costs of foreign representation and defence.[26] The objections from the Surinamese were nonetheless serious: on the question of the Dutch Prime Minister having the casting vote in cases of dispute within the new body, and the lack of any statement in the preamble to the new constitution which conveyed the right of self-determination – and therefore technically also the right to secession.[27] These reservations were unacceptable to the Dutch and a stalemate ensued. The Dutch threatened to abandon aid for economic development, and the Surinamese countered with a threat to take their grievances to the United Nations. This had serious ramifications for the Dutch as they were already under pressure from the United Nations, and the international community in general, over the self-governance of their Caribbean possessions.[28] When the Minister for Union Affairs and Overseas Territories Willem Kernkamp attempted to secure Dutch parliamentary approval for the right of self-determination, he was defeated in both houses and labelled a traitor to his country by a member of his own party.[29] The memories of Indonesia were far too fresh in the minds of most Dutch politicians.

Ironically, the Round Table was quietly reconvened on 20 May 1954 and, in the space of five days, agreement was reached. The Charter of the Kingdom of the Netherlands was then approved by all colonial legislatures, and was implemented on 29 December 1954.[30] Given the acrimonious debate in 1952, this is perhaps surprising, but it seems that all sides in Suriname recognized that the territory needed continuing financial help from the Netherlands, which was, in turn, prepared to gild the lily by offering to sponsor a major hydroelectric programme at Brokopondo on the Suriname River and a ten-year plan for development assistance.

The new statute did provide for autonomy in most internal affairs. Only elements judged as important to the Kingdom as a whole were excluded, of which defence, foreign relations, the judiciary, and civil rights were the most prominent. The Governor now fulfilled a dual role; as constitutional head of government and as representative of the Crown with the latter giving him control over the armed forces. Thus, even though the colonies had been granted internal autonomy and a supposed equality within the Kingdom, the strength and power of the Netherlands meant that this equality 'was in fact an illusion'.[31] Nevertheless, the Charter did have important advantages for the Netherlands. Reaction in the United States to the settlement was generally positive and in 1955, the United Nations dropped its requirement for the country to report on progress towards decolonization.[32]

The adjournment of the Round Table Conference was the catalyst for internal political change. Johan Adolf (Jopie) Pengel, one of the NPS leaders, split the party by espousing a more nationalist course. This created new political alliances, the most important being the cooperation (*verbroederingspolitiek*) between the rump NPS under Pengel and the VHP led by Jagernath Lachmon. This grouping came to power in 1958, and from then until 1967 became the dominant political alliance.[33] Politics during the period were not only shaped by cooperation between the parties, but also relied heavily on the personal relationship between Pengel and Lachmon.[34] The need to maintain this alliance helped to keep Pengel's ideas on independence in check, as Lachmon and the VHP were wary of what their position might be in an independent Suriname and felt that Dutch influence was the best guarantee of their continuing security.[35] Nationalist demands did not disappear entirely once the NPS-VHP alliance took power. In the late 1950s, buoyed up by the successes of Castro in Cuba and the gathering momentum of European decolonization, nationalist sentiment became increasingly evident among the Creole lower classes and gave rise in 1959 to the Nationalistische Beweging Suriname (NBS), which called openly for independence.[36] Nonetheless, the object of the NPS-VHP coalition in this period was to promote national unity though new symbols such as a national flag and a national anthem even though these produced some major and often acrimonious political debates.[37]

With half an eye on the 1963 elections and anxious to limit defections from the NPS to the NBS, but keen to seize other opportunities which greater autonomy might create, Pengel began to promote moves towards greater independence. Even Lachmon, with all his deep-rooted objections to such a course, was prepared to consider a more autonomous Suriname with dominion status, perhaps primarily to try and protect his coalition partner.[38] This prompted demands for a third Round Table Conference.[39] Dutch political leaders were well aware that there was little support in Suriname or the Antilles for outright independence, but only for some limited dominion status.[40] In the event, the Round Table Conference of May-June 1961 produced nothing of substance. Pengel realized that he had overreached himself and gave way in order to protect the NPS-VHP alliance.[41] Likewise, Lachmon had also found himself under great pressure at home from his VHP supporters, neither to pursue independence nor to accept any further changes to the Charter unless there were reforms to the electoral system to provide a more equal distribution of seats.[42] In the event, a working group was set up to discuss the three modifications of the Charter passed down from the Round Table Conference.[43] All three related to foreign affairs, but the Dutch rapidly undermined them. Demands for independent diplomatic representation were met with estimates of the costs of foreign missions, for example in Washington and London, and demands for independence in foreign policy were countered by the view that this was impossible within the existing constitutional structure.[44] Moreover, Pengel could not count on support from the representatives from the Antilles. They were well aware that their territories were not sufficiently large or well populated to be entirely independent.[45]

In spite of this, independence remained on the political agenda. In 1961 elements within the NBS formed the Partij van de Nationalistische Republiek (PNR) led by the writer Eddy Bruma,[46] a grouping with an overtly separatist stance, but elections in 1963 showed that there was only limited support for out-and-out independence.[47] The PNR gained just over 3,000 votes overall and remained unrepresented in the *Staten*.[48] The ruling coalition also benefited from economic changes, with Suriname being granted associate status within the European Economic Community but relations with the United States and the Caribbean territories remained strong.[49] The NPS-VHP alliance remained intact until 1967 when it foundered, ostensibly on VHP demands for greater influence that were unacceptable to the NPS as it would limit their powers of patronage.[50] Thus, during the period of rapid decolonization by Britain and France, although Pengel and the NPS aspired to greater autonomy if not independence, their need for political accommodation with the VHP who were opposed to further loosening of ties with the European motherland meant that moves in this direction were minimized.[51]

The final stages

Shifts in the coalition politics of the territory in the years after 1967 were the catalyst for more radical change. The NPS government under Pengel was initially allied with the Hindu Actie-Groep. However, this was brought down in 1969 by a strike wave, and a VHP coalition with the smaller Creole-based Progressieve Nationale Partij (PNP) took office under Jules Sedney. In this way, the ethnic diversity of governing coalitions was retained, but the traditional cooperation between the two largest Creole and Hindustani parties had been decisively broken. There appear to have been few tears shed in The Hague when the Pengel administration collapsed. His conduct had been erratic and unpredictable at times. This was something of an embarrassment for the Dutch but more serious had been his escalation of a border dispute with Guyana and his attempt to call for Dutch monetary and practical assistance to settle the strikes in his country. At much the same time, strikes in Curaçao in 1969 had led to widespread violence and the burning of part of Willemstad. This necessitated the intervention of Dutch marines stationed locally and the despatch of others to restore order. Pengel's maverick behaviour brought home to the Dutch government the possibility that they might consistently be forced to intervene under the terms of the Charter if serious political crises continued to beset the West Indies. Intervention in Curaçao smacked of neocolonialist behaviour and had left an unpleasant taste in many Dutch mouths, fostering a desire to reform or rescind such constitutional obligations. This became apparent when the issues were discussed in the Dutch parliament and press in the summer of 1969. Moreover, the stark images of armed Dutch marines patrolling the streets of Willemstad conveyed the impression of a colonial power using force to impose its will. Until the late 1960s, the Netherlands government and people seem to have been reactive rather than proactive in the debate on the status of the West Indian territories. In part at least, this was a legacy of the seismic shock that was the loss of the East Indies in the immediate post-war period. If demands for change came from Suriname or the Antilles, successive Dutch governments were prepared to enter into discussions, but seldom made the running.[52] Nevertheless, the shifts in public opinion evident over the New Guinea issue in the early part of the decade also played some role.

As a result of the crises of 1969 and a general view that the relationship between the European Netherlands and its West Indian territories was outmoded, discussions began in 1970, and while there was little pressure for an immediate change from the West Indian side, it became clear that the Dutch took the view that independence for all the territories should be granted within a limited timeframe. A Royal Commission was set up in 1972 to investigate how this could be achieved.[53] It visited the Caribbean on three occasions but its suggested compromises to facilitate independence were rejected by the representatives of the West Indian states. This can be explained primarily by the fact that none of the colonies really perceived themselves as viable economic entities, capable of assuming all the responsibilities of full statehood. In the case of Suriname, the VHP-dominated government still opposed full independence on the grounds of the threat it might pose to the Hindustani electorate. However, at the same time, all the Dutch political parties were beginning to give the issue more consideration. The PvdA was traditionally the most vociferous advocate of independence in the short term,[54] and received backing from a number of centre parties. Thus when the PvdA under Joop den Uyl became the major party of government, it more or less coincided with political changes in Suriname, with both sides then committed to seeing the country made independent sooner rather than later.

In many respects, 1973 could be regarded as the turning point for Suriname. Elections in that year produced a win for a broad electoral coalition of Creole-based parties (NPK), as it secured twenty-two of the thirty-nine seats.[55] This was more than enough to unseat the government previously dominated by the VHP.[56] This anti-VHP 'marriage' of the NPS, PSV, and KTPI with the smaller nationalist PNR, and its small majority meant that the PNR obtained a degree of influence that far exceeded its electoral strength. The other parties in the coalition, the more moderate NPS and the traditionally anti-independence PSV and KTPI, all felt it necessary to adopt the cause of independence, if only to retain the support of the PNR whose four seats effectively held the balance of power.[57] The new Prime Minister was Henck Arron, who continued the party's tradition of preaching cultural integration, but was far more outspoken on demands for independence. On 15 February 1974 he stated that Suriname would accept independence before the end of 1975.[58] This sat ill with VHP leader Lachmon's contemporary statement that independence was out of the question for at least another twenty-five years.[59]

Essentially, the 1973 elections had produced exactly the nightmare scenario that the Hindu population most feared, a Creole government moving towards outright independence.[60] In the event, progress to independence took place without the expected interethnic violence. Arron and Lachmon were able to negotiate a settlement, but with the latter making most of the concessions and with no formal agreement on electoral reform to give the Hindus better proportional representation. Most commentators give credit to the two men for their ability to compromise and to engineer the unanimous adoption of the new constitution by the *Staten*. However, this apparent stability and goodwill to some extent masked the feelings of the people concerned. In the months leading up to independence, many thousands of Hindustanis chose to leave Suriname, fearing that Creole domination unfettered by Dutch influence would leave them open to economic and social discrimination. It has been argued that the desire for independence itself was never a major issue within Suriname even among the Creole population and 'remained a matter for the intellectual upper crust'.[61] Indeed, there is evidence to suggest that many of the ideas for increased independence and separatism had their origins among Surinamese students who had studied in the Netherlands and had absorbed the anti-colonial and pro-independence ideas current in Europe in the 1960s and 1970s.[62] Events in neighbouring British Guiana also had an effect, demonstrating both the possibilities and the pitfalls of pressing for independence.

It seems that the final moves for independence were begun when Arron wrote to den Uyl asking about a possible timetable. André Haakmat notes that this was done primarily to please the PNR leader, Eddy Bruma (and thus reinforce his support for the coalition), rather than from any strong personal desire to accelerate the process. Arron was even more surprised at the speed with which The Hague replied – inviting him for immediate talks.[63] When Arron's Cabinet put forward a formal resolution for independence to the Dutch, there were few obstacles placed in its way. Political disputes over the issue in Paramaribo were regarded as internal matters and the only questions to be resolved were whether the Netherlands could transfer sovereignty without concrete guarantees about the maintenance of democracy and human rights, and how the new constitution was to be approved. In the event, the Royal Commission decided, with only the VHP representatives dissenting, that the timetable for independence was the Netherlands' only responsibility.[64] Buddingh' notes that the den Uyl Cabinet wanted Suriname's independence as soon as possible, and this overrode all other considerations. Debate centred on three elements: improving social and economic conditions, bettering relations between the ethnic groups, and stemming the flow of people from Suriname to the Netherlands. Few thought that much could be done in the short term to affect the first two, so discussion centred on the third element.[65] Indeed, it has been argued that the speed of final decolonization was largely attributable to Dutch government fears about the probable scale of Surinamese immigration and the racial and social tensions that it would unleash in the metropole.[66] In the event, the government had little room for manoeuvre. Restrictions were deemed unenforceable without border controls with EEC neighbours and, in any case, undesirable because they would have an overtly racial basis.[67] Thus, continuing immigration was permitted in spite of worries that it would cause a social and housing crisis. Conversely, the net outflow of people helped to act as a safety valve in Suriname after it became an independent state on 25 November 1975. With a failing economy and mounting unemployment, the Arron government came to rely on emigration to keep social tensions in check.[68]

Some issues remained outstanding. These included the creation of a constitution, external defence, levels of development aid, and the question of nationality and migration between the republic and the Netherlands. The first was resolved by a new constitution based on the Dutch model being presented to the Surinamese Parliament immediately before it voted to end the Charter.[69] The Dutch also wanted rid of responsibility for defence, but compromised by providing additional payments for Suriname to arm and pay its new armed forces. The other problems remained in abeyance. The political process continued to gather pace and the Dutch parliament actually approved the transfer of sovereignty before it was debated in the colony. The debate in the Netherlands from 21 to 23 October 1975 included the Surinamese deputies and was heated, with the colony's political opposition implying that they had been 'abandoned [by the Dutch] and pushed into the gas chambers of terror and fascist suppression'.[70] Summing up on the third day of debate, Premier den Uyl glossed over the criticisms, implying that there was no crucial difference of opinion on the desirability and inevitability of independence. The subsequent vote was 106 in favour and only 5 against. The majority in the Dutch senate (Eerste Kamer) was only slightly smaller.[71]

The speed with which independence was finally agreed left many questions unresolved. The amendment of the Charter had to be completed in such a hurry that, rather than motions to delete every reference to Suriname in the text, a final clause was appended that the Charter would no longer apply to Suriname. The new state did not even have internationally agreed borders. These had technically been in dispute since colonial times and many remained unresolved. The question of development aid was finally settled with grants, guarantees, and debt write-offs totalling 3.5 billion Dutch guilders over ten years. This was much more than the Dutch had originally considered necessary, but only about a third of what Suriname originally asked for.[72] In effect, the Dutch bought themselves out of their colonial commitment.

Conclusion

In conclusion, it seems appropriate to reflect both on the factors that hindered moves towards independence and those that finally brought it to fruition. The major retardant was undoubtedly the suspicion and uncertainties that existed between the various ethnic groups in Suriname and their political representatives from the 1940s onwards. The Hindu VHP was permanently on guard against moves towards greater autonomy by the Creole NPS. Frictions within the NPS produced divisions and the formation of the Eenheitsfront ensured that Creole interests were never represented by a single party. Thus, Pengel's ambitions for independence were curtailed in the period 1958–67 by the need to maintain his political alliance with Lachmon and the VHP in order to stay in power. However, reading the documentation it is difficult to escape the conclusion that domestic politics in Suriname during this period were very much of the 'parish pump' variety. Nevertheless events in the outside world also played some part in the story. The development of international aid and development organizations in the 1950s provided Suriname with possible alternative sources of financial assistance which might, in time, have allowed the breaking of colonial economic ties. Yet for the most part, these remained tantalizingly out of reach. Cold war politics also had some impact. The Cuban crisis and the turmoil in British Guiana did not go unnoticed, either in Paramaribo or in The Hague, but the effect was to make both sides wary of precipitate action for fear of bringing about the chaos and disorder they could see happening elsewhere.

On the Dutch side, it seems that the psychological shock of losing the East Indies in the late 1940s took some time to subside. In certain quarters, it merely increased the determination to hold onto the remaining vestiges of empire at all costs, and this can be seen in many of the parliamentary debates on the Imperial Statute of 1954 and in relation to the West New Guinea crisis in the early 1960s. In characterizing the Dutch political and administrative handling of the West Indian colonies, one could compare it to comments made about the Colonial Ministry in the interwar period, namely that it was reactive and strove to administer and manage rather than to initiate any new policies.[73] This imperial tendency remained apparent until the centre-left Cabinet of Joop den Uyl took office in 1973 and replied almost immediately to what had been no more than a tentative enquiry about a timetable for independence. This response was coloured not only by the ideological commitments of the PvdA in general and Joop den Uyl in particular, but also by a shift in Dutch public opinion that had come to terms with the disastrous way Indonesia had been decolonized and wanted a more enlightened form of retreat from the remaining elements of empire that were now seen as anachronistic.[74] The Dutch focus was now on the European Union and on the primacy of domestic concerns. Criticisms of Dutch behaviour surfaced, both at the time and subsequently, although these were inevitably conditioned by the chaos that ensued in the former colony, culminating in the military coup of 1980.[75] Den Uyl was accused of acting with indecent haste in pushing the process forward, primarily to serve the interests of the Netherlands rather than to ensure a peaceful and orderly transfer of power, yet given the international circumstances and opinion at the time, he had little real room for manoeuvre. Thus there were important retarding factors on both sides of the Atlantic that served first to delay the process of decolonization until the 1970s, and then, when more or less simultaneous changes in political circumstances took place in both countries, finally brought about the end of Dutch rule, at least on the South American mainland.

The Antilles: The persistence of Empire

It was undoubtedly the plan of the den Uyl Cabinet that the transfer of sovereignty in Suriname would be closely followed by a similar transfer of power for the Antilles, thus finally ending the existence of overseas territories within the Kingdom of the Netherlands. However, there had been no great pressure in the six islands for secession, and assumptions that the Antilles were only viable as a single entity were dashed when Aruba insisted on a separate status in 1986. It was subsequently granted such a role as a country in its own right within the Kingdom of the Netherlands in 1996. Even the 'Antilles of five' (Curaçao, Bonaire, St Eustasius, St Maarten, and Saba) did not manage any degree of political coherence and remained riven by disputes.

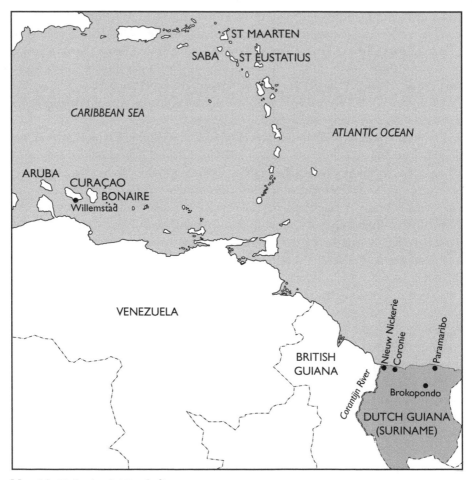

Map 10 Netherlands West Indies.

At the same time, the Netherlands became more and more involved in the administrative and economic development of the islands. In effect, overseas decolonization remained incomplete because there was no means of creating a viable state from the remaining Dutch territories, there was no political will within those territories for outright independence, and the decolonizing imperative that had marked left-leaning Dutch governments in the early 1970s disappeared as the country was ruled by a series of centre right coalitions. Moreover, the example created by Suriname was not an edifying one. The military coup in 1980 had precipitated a complete breakdown of law and order, civil war, and economic collapse.[76]

By the 1990s, the problems were there for all to see, and the Dutch were unwilling to be blamed for similar political and economic chaos in their remaining dependencies if the issue of independence was forced. In the meantime, The Hague had reluctantly been pressured into enacting supervisory 'special measures' in St Maarten during 1992–3, where the local administration was widely regarded as corrupt and there were even rumours of connection with the Italian mafia. This supervision was ended in 1996 but Dutch concerns were rekindled in 1997 when a report was published which showed that organized crime was using Aruba as a centre for money-laundering. Similar concerns about Dutch responsibilities arose when adverse reports about the treatment of prisoners in the Curaçaoan penal system began to appear.[77] The problem for The Hague was how far it could or should interfere in the affairs of the other constituent parts of the Kingdom, even though the Antilles had become more closely linked to the Netherlands, economically and administratively, than at any time since 1954.[78]

At the end of 2008, the Netherlands Antilles Federation was broken up and Bonaire, St Eustatius, and Saba were given the status of separate municipalities within the administration of the European Kingdom. Elections on 20 April 2007 had led to St Maarten adopting a status similar to that of Aruba as a separate constituent part of the Kingdom. Finally on 10 October 2010, and after many years of uncertainty and dispute, Curaçao followed suit.[79] This marked the end of the Netherlands Antilles as a single entity and the end of the decolonization process. The desire for local autonomy and self-determination had to be balanced with political realities and the need to create viable economic units. In the event, the solution was to keep all the islands within the Kingdom – with all the economic and political security benefits which that conveyed. While no longer a colonial empire, the Kingdom of the Netherlands in the twenty-first century nonetheless retained responsibilities for these territories beyond the European motherland.

PART IV
CONTRASTING PATTERNS OF DECOLONIZATION
Martin Thomas

INTRODUCTION TO PART IV
THE BELGIAN AND PORTUGUESE EMPIRES

Why did Belgium, a small country with a vast central African colonial domain, leave its Congo colony so abruptly in June 1960? And why did that withdrawal provoke such severe destabilization that the apparatus of central state authority disintegrated into secession, civil war, and wave after wave of foreign intervention. Was the Rwandan genocide of 1994 somehow written in the country's Belgian colonial past? The signal importance of these questions needs no amplification. What does bear emphasis, as will become apparent in this final chapter, is that Belgium's colonial collapse, like those investigated earlier in this book, occurred within a global system in which transnational connections, international rivalries, and changing normative standards made imperial rule much harder to sustain. Patrice Lumumba, Congo's presumptive national leader at independence, drew inspiration and encouragement from pan-Africanist networks in West Africa. Yet, his efforts to situate Congolese statehood within a discursive framework of African liberation were, in practice, belied by his growing reliance on backing from the Soviet bloc. Meanwhile, Belgium, working closely with the United States, conspired to remove him. Tragically, the growing intolerance of European colonialism at the United Nations, among the world's press, and in the wider public sphere of international politics was not enough to save the Congolese Republic from destructive foreign interference. Thus did Belgian decolonization in 1960 come to be described in more vivid shorthand as the Congo Crisis.

Shining a light on the Belgian experience in some ways makes Portugal's decolonization from Africa seem even stranger. The geriatric dictatorial regime of António de Oliveira Salazar was already losing its grip over its African dominions of Angola, Mozambique, and Guiné-Bissau as the meltdown in the Belgian Congo unfolded. Full-blown rebellions engulfed each of these Lusophone African territories between 1961 and 1964. It would take a decade of war, worsening refugee crises, and gross humanitarian violations before the Portuguese Empire in Africa finally crumbled. Even then it is at least arguable whether the final implosion of the Lisbon dictatorship was the cause or the consequence of this long-delayed colonial withdrawal. Meanwhile, the ethnic particularities and sectarian divides characteristic of the anti-colonial movements in Angola and Mozambique resurfaced in protracted civil war. Just as Congo would long remain a battleground between regional powers and Cold War antagonists, so, too, the former territories of Portuguese southern Africa became enmeshed in proxy wars in which Cuban revolutionaries and South African reactionaries joined the superpower rivals in combat over the outcome of another bitter decolonization.

CHAPTER 16
CONTRASTING PATTERNS OF DECOLONIZATION: BELGIAN AND PORTUGUESE AFRICA

Breakdown in Belgian Africa

The tiny nation of Belgium has been characterized as Western Europe's 'reluctant imperialist'.[1] In geopolitical terms its very existence as an independent state was, from the 1830s onwards, peculiarly dependent on two external factors: the relative strength of France and Germany and the depth of international support for Belgian claims to statehood. Culturally and, to varying degrees, politically the country was internally divided between its Flemish-speaking and broadly Dutch-facing provinces and the more heavily industrialized francophone regions of Wallonia, or southern Belgium. These regional and linguistic divisions ultimately mapped onto Belgian colonialism. Flemish speakers disparaged the predominance of French and francophone officials within colonial administration. Some Flemish nationalists even claimed to be suffering under the yoke of a form of internal Walloon colonialism.[2] And, as decolonization neared, some Belgian social commentators even predicted that the break-up of overseas territory prefigured the end of Belgian national unity.[3]

The extent of Belgian popular, communal, or party political engagement with empire should not be overdrawn – at least in this first phase of colonial expansion. It was royalty rather than industrial expansion or public pressure that drove Belgium to acquire imperial territory in Africa. King Leopold II, who ascended the throne in 1865, shared the interest of geographical societies and eager-eyed investors in the few regions of Africa and Eastern Asia yet to be claimed by Europe's established imperial powers. Commercially astute and politically interventionist, Belgium's ambitious monarch became obsessively interested in the hinterland of the Congo basin, an area whose exploration in the 1870s by Henry Morton Stanley and others he actively sponsored.[4] It was, however, the prospect of a French takeover in this vast region that gave Leopold the opportunity to advance his claim as guardian of a central African free trade zone, an alternative much preferred by Britain and Bismarck's Germany in particular. The resultant Congo Free State, its foundation confirmed during the Berlin Congress of European imperial powers in 1884–5, was always a misnomer. Never free, nor, technically, was it a colonial state. Neither the Belgian government nor the Belgian public had any direct involvement in running what was, in effect, an overseas royal domain. Anachronistic even by the imperial standards of the late nineteenth century, the Congo Free State was a triumph of international expediency. Neighbouring colonial powers quickly secured preferential trading and navigation rights in the Congolese interior in a series of commercial treaties signed with the King.

The Congo Free State, almost from its inception, has been reviled as the most egregious example of untrammelled colonial exploitation. Central to its grim reputation for ruthless extraction, environmental spoliation, and cruel punishment of coerced labourers was the *système domanial* introduced in the territory during 1891–2. At its core, a legal sleight of hand that summarily rendered all uncultivated Congolese soil Crown property, what made this royal land grab a 'system' was the rising global demand for the Congo's resources, red (wild) rubber and ivory prominent among them. The *système domanial* opened the door to private companies to purchase exclusive 'concessions' to exploit particular products in particular regions. In addition, those unfortunate Congolese unable to prove their title to farmland were declared liable to work in the newly created 'domains'. The 'system' thereby inaugurated a forced labour regime of devastating severity.[5] What shocked its critics, most famously the British humanitarian activist, E. D. Morel, was the appalling treatment of rubber workers, many of them children, within a system whose economic rationale was to satisfy the growing demands of Western consumers for affordable luxuries. It was the dissociation between the cruelty of the production process and the end products purchased and consumed that would come to define twentieth-century arguments over the ethics of globalized consumption.[6]

Three points perhaps deserve emphasis here. One is that the *système domanial* left a bitter cultural legacy that soured inter-communal relations in the Congo throughout the colonial period. It was no coincidence that the official 'celebration' of Congolese independence on 30 June 1960 was hijacked by newly installed Prime Minister, Patrice Lumumba, who angrily refuted the fatuous claims made by King Baudouin, Leopold's great-grandson, of Belgian munificence in their dealings with the Congolese. Related to this is a second point. The excesses of the rubber industry provoked transnational opposition serious enough to compel the Belgian state to assume the mantle of colonial administration in 1908.[7] Thus did the most highly privatized colonial regime to emerge from the African scramble of the late nineteenth century give way to more conventional state-driven, direct rule. While governmental and party political support for the Congo venture remained, at best, lukewarm, the 'reluctant imperialist' characterization was, by the turn of the twentieth century, less applicable to the Belgian public.[8] Indoctrination to colonialism, evident in school curricula, in Church teaching, in military service, and, perhaps above all, in public ceremony, exhibitions, and imperialist propaganda affected Belgians much as it did the British and the French.[9] Pro-empire lobbyists, some of them affiliated with academic institutions and geographical societies, others with commercial interest groups and banking consortia, encouraged Belgians to see the Congo as both a source of wealth and a cultural space to which Belgian values should be transmitted.[10] Here we come to the third point. Central to understanding the decolonization of the Belgian Congo is the tension between a domestic public unwilling to accept the flaws of their colonial system and the resultant shockwave that rippled through Belgian society and politics once it became incontrovertibly clear that the Belgian Congo was nothing like they had been told it was.[11]

The Belgian Congo and the neighbouring colonies of Rwanda-Burundi were certainly poorly equipped to manage an abrupt transition to independence. Theirs would be what one analyst termed a 'precipitous decolonization'.[12] The Congo was a sprawling central African state with a large heterogeneous population. Although relatively numerous when compared with other colonial authorities, Belgian administrators had done precious little either to develop a national infrastructure and an indigenous bureaucracy or to educate the Congolese to whom such tasks would eventually fall. Substantial primary education there certainly was, but most of it took place in Catholic and Protestant missions in which vocational training and spiritual discipline were instilled at the expense of genuine academic inquiry.[13] The Church also dominated the minimal advanced educational provision available to Congolese. Missionaries were sometimes torn between respect for the faith communities they oversaw and disdain for non-Christian practices and traditions.[14] At the insistence of Catholic lobby groups and their Belgian Christian Democrat allies in government, the Catholic University of Louvain established a university in Léopoldville (Kinshasa) in 1953, to which the Christian Democrats' Liberal and Socialist opponents added a separate, and secular, university of the Belgian Congo in Elisabethville (Lubumbashi) three years later.[15] Even so, seminarians rather than university students figured as the only discrete group to benefit from higher learning before 1960.[16] Relatively few Congolese students travelled to Belgium for advanced study when compared with the numbers of colonial students from the British and French empires in London, Paris, and elsewhere, making it impossible to speak of a substantial intelligentsia with a stake either in colonial administration or its overthrow.[17] Despite these limited educational opportunities – or perhaps because of them – access to white-collar employment for native Congolese depended on the acquisition of the infamous 'civil merit card', a precious certificate that was virtually impossible to obtain. Among those denied the card were many of the writers and early political organizers who used the local press and journals such as *Conscience Africaine* to voice their anger over social marginalization and Belgium's failure to match the pace of reform in nearby French Equatorial Africa.[18]

It bears emphasis, however, that such voices were few and far between. African women were still largely excluded from the political process and, although classified discretely as objects of state taxation, generally figured in colonial administrative discussion only when issues of moral panic, of 'declining' colonial behaviour figured large.[19] In the absence of substantial African educated elites, political parties, most of which were communal and regional rather than nationalist in orientation, only took shape after 1956. Their emergence coincided with a severe economic downturn in the colony's economy. Declining export revenues in the late 1950s soon translated into higher unemployment and worsening urban poverty among the thousands of economic migrants that had flocked from the countryside to the cities since 1945. Rather than turning towards economic development to assuage popular anger, the focus of colonial government's survival strategy lay elsewhere.

The ethnic, religious, and linguistic diversity of the Congo peoples had long been exploited by the colonial power to entrench Belgian control.[20] In Rwanda and Urundi, too, Belgian manipulation of ethnic differences between Hutus, Tutsis, and Twa peoples facilitated colonial dominance, and stored up quite devastating long-term consequences. Belgian colonial administration during the interwar period constructed the Hutu majority as indigenous Bantu people, and the Tutsi minority as a migratory Hamitic race that originated in Ethiopia. The racialization of Rwandan society was a colonial invention.[21]

Race theory, propagated by ethnographers within the Catholic missionary establishment, was therefore central to colonial state formation in Rwanda where legal codes, forced labour regulations, educational provision, and local administration were all predicated on the political difference asserted between civilized Tutsi *évolués* and uncivilized Hutu *sujets*. With the strong support of the Catholic Church, during the 1920s colonial officials installed Tutsi chiefs as key agents of local government and customary law throughout Rwanda. As a result, these customary chiefs – and the Tutsi minority more generally – became identifiable in the eyes of Hutu agriculturalists with the enforcement of the most coercive aspects of colonial power: forced labour, arbitrary punishments, compulsory cultivation of designated crops, and payment of unfamiliar taxes.[22] Ironically, the colonial preference accorded to the Tutsis both stirred their opposition to the colonial system and fired a deeper and, ultimately, cataclysmic

Hutu resentment against an ethnic group exempted from the worst impositions of the colonial state. Tutsi antagonism had different causes. Denied any opportunity to ascend beyond the lower rungs of colonial administration or commercial employment, educated Tutsis, much like other *évolué* groups in the French Empire, became a key source of opposition to the colonial system.[23]

However, it was the post-independence consequences of the colonial construction of Tutsi-Hutu difference that were so catastrophic. As Mahmood Mamdani has argued, the Rwandan genocide of 1994 was rooted in the Hutus' conviction that the Tutsis, a relatively privileged minority under the Belgian colonial system, were an alien presence, a different race more akin to hostile settlers than fellow Rwandans. What made the genocide possible was what Mamdani terms a 'race branding' that originated in the late colonial period. This racial stigmatization was reanimated by the Hutu-dominated governments of the First and Second Rwandan Republics after 1959 to mobilize the Hutu population as killers of their Tutsi neighbours.[24] At least 130,000 Tutsi fled into exile during 1961 alone. By the time that Rwanda and its neighbour Urundi secured final independence in July 1962, enmities between Tutsi and Hutu had become so deeply embedded that they would dominate the region's politics for generations.

The history of colonial manipulation of ethnic groups in the Belgian Congo was different, conditioned in large part by the levels of economic wealth and European settlement in particular provinces rather than by the systematic advancement of one indigenous community over another. Across the colony as a whole, it was the inadequacy of state institutions, bureaucratic systems, and legal structures that proved critical to the postcolonial future of the Congolese people. As we have seen, so rare had been the opportunities to acquire administrative positions or advanced education that only a handful of Congolese in the capital could claim any political experience or university education at independence in June 1960. By then, only sixteen Congolese students had graduated from the colony's two universities.[25] Most Congolese that did organize politically rallied support with appeals to communal hegemony and regional interest rather than with calls for a Congolese nation state.

It was against this backcloth that rioting broke out in Leopoldville, the colonial capital on 4 January 1959. The immediate trigger for these clashes was a ban imposed by the colonial authorities on a political meeting of the Association des Bakongo, or ABAKO cultural association. By then transformed into a fully fledged political party, ABAKO was the principal mouthpiece of the Bakongo people throughout Lower Congo. The Association had performed impressively in municipal elections held in December 1957, and this electoral breakthrough added a new edge to ABAKO's demands for Bakongo self-rule. The Association also claimed to be the successor of a long-running messianic movement loyal to Simon Kimbangu, a self-appointed prophet who had died nine years earlier in a colonial prison. Thus linked to the Kimbanguist Church, ABAKO's potential for rapid expansion as an anti-colonial movement helps explain why the security forces wanted to stamp on it. The Leopoldville riots were quickly and savagely put down by the army and police. Official figures admitted to forty-nine fatalities and over a hundred wounded. The disturbances nonetheless catalysed Belgian public opinion and legislators in Brussels into a hasty retreat.[26]

Until then, Belgian preparations for a transfer of power had been nugatory. But with the numerous territories of French black Africa close to final independence, and the terrible consequences of colonial war in another French-speaking colony, Algeria, becoming ever clearer,

Belgium's population, itself split along ethnolinguistic lines, had no appetite for a last-ditch effort to cling on in Africa. The result was what came to be known as 'the Congolese wager' (*le pari congolais*): a headlong rush towards decolonization that was as rapid as it was ill-judged.[27] A new constitution – la Loi Fondamentale – was hastily compiled in early 1960 following a Round Table Conference in January between nationalist leaders and senior colonial officials. The Fundamental Law made provision for a bicameral parliament, Cabinet government, and a president serving in a largely ceremonial role as head of state. Most remarkably, everything was to occur within a few months: final independence was scheduled for 30 June. Speedy it may have been, but, as Robert Holland notes, this was no conventional 'transfer of power'. With hardly any trained Congolese officials in place, with state revenue still largely derived from Western corporations, and with the maintenance of order dependent on the Belgian-officered Force Publique, the Brussels government envisaged a central role for Belgian civil servants, businesses, and soldiers in a post-independence regime.[28] Perversely then, Belgium's previous reluctance to prepare the Congo for self-government became the justification for the continuation of a Belgian administrative, commercial, and military presence after the 30 June deadline.

Elections on the eve of independence in May 1960 produced a coalition government. Its two main components were the Mouvement National Congolais (MNC), the one party with genuinely inter-communal support, and ABAKO, whose support was still largely confined to the Bakongo community. MNC leader Patrice Lumumba, a former postal clerk and trade union organizer from south-western Congo, became the new country's first Prime Minister. The ABAKO leader Joseph Kasavubu took the presidency.[29] They did not get on. The UN observer at the independence-day celebrations reported that the two men 'studiously ignore each other', their relations 'strained, even hostile'.[30]

Lumumba's government had a mountain to climb. Within days of independence the latent instability in the Congo exploded into violence. As the Belgians had foreseen, once the apparatus of the colonial state began to disintegrate, viable central administration became impossible. To make matters worse, the forces of order compounded the problem. Incensed by the actions of their last Belgian commander, General Emile Janssens, who seemed determined to keep junior and middle-ranking Congolese officers from ascending the military hierarchy, in the first week of July the army mutinied against its remaining Belgian commanders. The Force Publique, for decades the instrument of a brutal 'pacification' in the Congo, rapidly disintegrated as its Belgian officers fled.[31] News of the mutinies and Belgian naval shelling of the port of Matardi provoked widespread panic among the remaining European population, torpedoing the earlier scheme for a smooth transition of power under Belgian guidance. With the country's security forces in turmoil, Congo's fragile national unity fractured. Lumumba's utopian vision of a unified socialist nation state, inspired by his admiration for Kwame Nkrumah's Ghana, was no match for the countervailing pressures of ethnic self-interest, the massive economic disparities between Congolese provinces, and powerful regional separatism in the richer areas.

These factors alone might not have caused civil war – at least not so quickly. But there were others prepared to exploit Congo's internal social divisions: disgruntled Belgian officials reluctant to accept the postcolonial order; neighbour states anxious about their Congolese frontiers and eager to advance their own strategic or economic interests; and powerful multinational mining interests determined to protect their stake in the Congo's vast mineral wealth.[32]

On 11 July 1960 the country's wealthiest province, Katanga in south-eastern Congo, seceded from the newly independent state. This was no spontaneous event.[33] The former colonial administration, local Belgian settlers, and the Congo's largest mining concern, the Union Minière du Haut-Katanga, conspired to deny the Lumumbist government control over the Congo's economic powerhouse: Katanga's mines.[34] The neighbouring white-ruled Central African Federation, another key mineral producer, also became immersed in this effort.[35] The Katanga constitution, its gendarmerie, even its new government led by local businessman Moïse Tshombe, were, to varying degrees, sustained by Union Minière funds and Belgian civil and military advisers. As soon as Katanga seceded, Union Minière representatives provided an advance of 1,250 million Belgian francs. Indirect monetary support was also forthcoming from Belgium's central bank, which, in agreeing to help manage Katanga's foreign currency transactions, offered the secessionist province a measure of financial stability. By the end of 1960 there were 1,133 Belgian advisers of the Mission Téchnique Belge (known as Mistebel) in Katanga's political centre, Elisabethville, almost double the number present in the Congolese capital of Léopoldville/Kinshasa.[36] It might seem ironic, then, that Belgium never officially recognized Katanga's independence until we recall that no other country did either. For all that, Belgium, the United States, and South Africa in particular worked closely with the Katangese authorities to ensure that the Union Minière's mineral exports continued to flow.[37]

Tshombe cannot, though, simply be characterized as a stooge – far from it. Married to the daughter of the Lunda King, the Mwant Yav, Tshombe was closely connected both to southern Katanga's elites and to the region's chiefly authorities. Both shared genuine – and mounting – grievances about the immigration of large numbers of workers from Kasai, many of whom secured favoured jobs in the provincial capital of Elisabethville. For Tshombe, Katangese secession did not represent co-option by the former colonial power but, rather, the reassertion of ethnic self-determination by the Lunda. They had, after all, enjoyed substantial regional autonomy from central colonial government in the early years of the twentieth century. More to the point, their demands and grievances, rooted in Katanga's distinct political economy, were simply not those of Lumumba's supporters. Working first through an organization founded in 1957, the Groupement des associations de l'empire lunda (known as Gassomel), then through a broader alliance, the Confédération des Associations Tribales du Katanga (or Conakat for short), Tshombe and his fellow Conakat leaders, Godefroid Munongo and Evariste Kimba, pledged to defend the interests of Katanga's Lunda and Yeke peoples against those of 'outsiders' from elsewhere in the Congo.[38] Like many Katangese, what Conakat's leadership foresaw in the unification of a vast Congolese state was the inevitable subsidization of the country's poorer regions with the revenues generated in their home province. Katanga's secession was, in part, driven by the conviction that the province's wealth should not be leached away by a remote central government.[39] (That remoteness is apparent in the map on the next page.)

Wider international involvement also lurked in the shadows. The United States, British, and French governments were alarmed at the wider ramifications of leftist government in such a huge state strategically located at the heart of Africa, and the CIA provided covert funding to those leaders judged to be pro-Western, Tshombe included. US determination to safeguard Western access to the Congo's mineral wealth, underpinned the CIA's covert intervention from the early 1950s onwards.[40] The Congo's invaluable resources of uranium – essential to America's atomic programme – were, quite naturally, regarded as strategically critical.[41] Seen from Washington's perspective, it was imperative to prevent Lumumba, a dangerous political

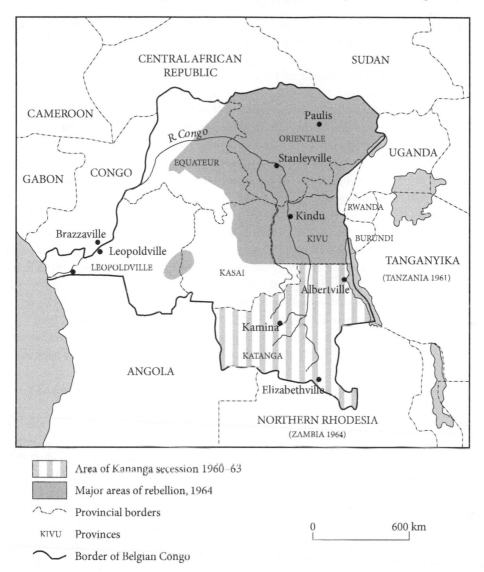

Map 11 The Belgian Congo, 1960.

maverick, from obtaining Soviet assistance to reunify the country. Were he to succeed the Soviet Union might secure access to Katanga's strategic raw materials, copper and uranium above all. In these circumstances, virtually any anti-Lumumba figure became an acceptable partner for the United States.[42]

Tshombe and Conakat were the first to ride this anti-communist wave to advance their own claims to Katangese self-determination. In doing so, their supporters seized *de facto* control of public space in the province's major towns before the secessionist government purged the local Force Publique garrison of its non-Katangese troops to create a distinct Katangese gendarmerie.[43] Whether operating within Katanga during the period of secession (July 1960 to January 1963) or working as an insurgent force from bases across the border, this gendarmerie would remain the principal military supporter of Katangese self-rule for decades to come.[44]

Ultimately, however, the principal recipient of American munificence was Colonel Joseph-Desiré Mobutu. His effectiveness as the key officer in the Congolese National Army depended on his unique access to dollars with which to pay the men under his command. At the time, however, the more obvious evidence of US financial intervention lay in its support for the United Nations peacekeeping force, which began to arrive in the Congo three days after Lumumba and Kasavubu issued a joint appeal for UN assistance on 12 July.

It soon became apparent that neither the UN's roving Secretary General Dag Hammarskjöld, nor the UN troop commanders on the ground were prepared to assist in achieving Lumumba's key objective of the forcible reunification of the Congolese state. Within weeks US determination to prevent a pro-Soviet regime from becoming established in Leopoldville coalesced into a CIA plan to assassinate Lumumba. In the event, Mobutu's seizure of power in an army-led coup d'état on 14 September 1960 resolved the problem. The self-appointed Colonel, whose government lasted until February 1961, curried American favour by expelling the Soviet and Czechoslovak aid missions that Lumumba had invited to assist him. Lumumba, meanwhile, took shelter in his residence under UN guard. Still calling for international support to defeat his many opponents, he clung to the hope that he might regain power by escaping to the north-eastern city of Stanleyville, the regional heartland of Lumumbist support. It was while trying to escape there that Lumumba was captured by Mobutu's troops on 1 December 1960.[45] His fate was sealed by Mobutu's decision six weeks later to transfer the troublesome Prime Minister and two of his associates, Maurice Mpolo and Joseph Okita, from detention in Leopoldville to the Katangan capital of Elisabethville. Soon after arriving there, Lumumba was tortured and murdered, actions, which, it appears, occurred with the connivance of the Belgian secret police and the CIA.[46]

Lumumba's death did not, however, signal the end of the Congo Crisis, far from it. Katanga had broken away. Separatism had also taken hold in another mineral-rich province: South Kasai, home to the country's diamond mining. And soon after Lumumba's capture in December 1960, his former deputy, Antoine Gizenga, created what he claimed was the Congo's only legitimate government in far-off Stanleyville, the capital of Orientale province. It was a view shared by several left-leaning African states as well as by China and the Soviet Union.[47] Gizenga's external backers watched with approval as he built up substantial military forces that advanced into neighbouring Kivu and northern Katanga in early 1961.[48] By contrast, for all the underhand CIA involvement in the Congo's labyrinthine politics, John F. Kennedy's new administration remained deeply pessimistic about the country's post-independence prospects. One of the first regional security assessments to cross the President's desk in January 1961 concluded as follows:

> There is no indication that the Congo is developing a national leader, a national party or a national consciousness. Political instability on a grand scale, probably leading to increased violence and other excesses, both organized and disorganized, appears to be the most likely prospect for the Congo for some time to come.[49]

In these difficult circumstances, wider questions loomed large. Was the Congo to be reunited or divided? Could the Congolese ever establish a government acceptable to the many outside interests pulling the country's economic strings? And what role would the United Nations play in the eventual outcome? Could UN peacekeepers achieve the three main objectives set for them by their political masters in New York, namely, the removal of Belgian forces, the restoration of order, and the preservation of Congo's territorial unity?[50]

The murky circumstances of Lumumba's grizzly demise aside, the nature, scale, and impact of the UN deployment dominate the historiography of the Congo crisis. One reason for this is that the country's political meltdown exposed the limitations of the UN's peacekeeping power. This was tragically exemplified by Hammarskjöld's death in an air crash while shuttling between Congolese delegations in September 1961. Another reason to focus on the UN's Congo force is that arguments over its role and purpose drove a wedge between the US government and the UN Secretariat in New York.

Between January and September 1962 troops loyal to the Leopoldville government ousted Gizenga from Stanleyville and then defeated the South Kasai secessionists. But Katanga was a different proposition. A multinational UN contingent largely comprised of non-Western troops supplanted Congo's fractious army in the effort to bring an end to Katangan separatism. This, in turn, raised deeper questions about whose interests the United Nations was supposed to serve, especially as its membership swelled in the early 1960s with the addition of numerous newly independent nations determined to oppose what vestiges of Western colonialism remained around the globe.[51] It was only in January 1963, thanks to a combination of diplomatic persuasion and UN military muscle in Elisabethville, that Tshombe at last renounced secession. Six months later he left for exile in Europe.[52]

In spite of these political victories, by 1963 the pro-Western government under Cyrille Adoula faced a deepening economic crisis across the country. By October two thirds of Leopoldville's population were unemployed. An International Monetary Fund rescue package cut government spending, but caused further short-term decline in living standards. Protesters took to the streets. A government crackdown against trade union demonstrations was soon followed by widespread disorder and looting by poorly paid soldiers. Even more serious, opponents of Adoula and Mobutu organized a National Liberation Committee in Brazzaville. Their insurgent forces swept through northern and eastern Congo over the summer of 1964, capturing Stanleyville in August. There a 'People's Republic' was declared. Widely supported but politically chaotic, the Stanleyville government seemed to herald a fresh descent into civil war that might culminate in the victory of a pro-Communist regime. With Katanga back in the Congolese fold, international attention focused on this so-called 'Stanleyville pocket', actually a vast swathe of territory in north-eastern Congo.[53]

'Salvation' came from an unexpected quarter. Backed by the Union Minière and other Belgian corporations, Moise Tshombe returned from exile to Leopoldville in July 1964. President Kasavubu offered the former secessionist the premiership. Although President Lyndon Johnson's administration had grave doubts about Tshombe, the CIA helped organize South African and Rhodesian mercenary forces to assist Belgian troops and Mobutu's Congolese National Army in crushing the Stanleyville regime. Gradually the eastern insurgency was rolled back, often to the accompaniment of horrendous massacres committed by both sides. Belgian paratroopers, dropped from US air force planes, recaptured Stanleyville in November 1964, and the country was ostensibly reunified by March 1965. In fact, rebel 'Simbas' continued to operate in the remotest sectors of Congo's north-east until the end of the decade.[54] This was not a problem for Tshombe, who was ousted from power in October 1965. Fighting the Simbas' insurgency fell instead to Mobutu, who again seized power in a military coup on 25 November 1965.

In sum, the Congo Crisis was both the first and perhaps the most complex of all the proxy wars that crackled into life from the dying embers of colonial rule in sub-Saharan Africa. Its violent escalation was a sad reflection on the condition of the Cold War by the early 1960s.[55] Just as it revealed US willingness to back any non-communist alternative in a strategically important colonial state, so it exposed the Soviet Union's inability to project its power effectively in black Africa. Ultimately, it would be other communist states, and Fidel Castro's Cuba in particular, that would lend support to the left-wing insurgents fighting to overthrow the pro-Western regime installed in Leopoldville.

Colonial in origin, the internationalization of the Congo Crisis, the ruthless 'kleptocracy' of the Mobutu regime, and the horrors of the 1994 Rwanda genocide are sometimes viewed in isolation from their roots in the deliberate intensification of inter-communal rivalries and regional particularities during Belgium's rule of this great swathe of Central Africa. That is not to lay the blame for Mobutu's dictatorship or the mass murder of Rwanda's Tutsi population at Belgium's door, nor is it to absolve the Congolese and Rwandans of responsibility for their own destinies. More simply, it is to stress the connections between patterns of colonial rule, the circumstances of decolonization, and the hatreds and political abuses that endured for years afterwards.

War and revolution: The end of 'ultra-imperialism' in Portuguese Africa

If Belgian Africa was the first site of the new-style proxy wars in black Africa, Portugal's sub-Saharan territories were to witness even more protracted and widespread international intervention as decolonization gathered pace. The hollowness of French assimilationist doctrine found echoes in the colonial policies of Dr António de Oliveira Salazar's Portuguese dictatorship, which took shape after the former Finance Minister's elevation to Prime Minister in 1932 and his promulgation of a new Portuguese constitution in the following year. Anxious to give substance to his quasi-fascist authoritarianism, Salazar's regime insisted that Portugal's African colonies, Angola and Mozambique above all, were tangible proof of Portugal's historic greatness and civilizing mission. In a Portuguese variant of a common foundational myth of European colonialism, the Salazarist state maintained that Portuguese settlement had transformed African dependencies from inchoate, backward geographical spaces into uniquely integrated territories that had transcended their colonial origins.[56] Indeed, the Salazarist dictatorship went further, tying its conception of Portuguese national identity to the country's long-standing and ostensibly integrationist imperial tradition. Thus, even in the tiny West African colony of Guiné-Bissau the Lisbon regime insisted that talk of colonial exploitation and racial inequality made no sense. Despite abundant evidence of colonial discrimination, whether legal, educational, economic, or political, the administration maintained that Guiné comprised part of a united Lusophone 'community of peoples'.[57] Meanwhile, in Portugal, a country where public debate about the value of, and ethical justifications for, overseas possessions would remain severely constrained from the 1930s until the early 1970s, officially at least, empire and nation were two sides of the same coin.[58]

In practice, such grand-sounding rhetoric was shadow, not substance. Modest colonial development plans as well as limited collaboration with indigenous elites that had taken shape in the preceding Republican era of Portuguese imperialism were quickly abandoned.[59] Portuguese colonial oppression would, instead, continue for decades after Salazar's initial consolidation of power between 1928 and 1932.[60] Like other imperial nations, Salazarist Portugal insisted that its colonial administration was a 'scientific occupation'. It was supposedly informed by the rational study of dependent peoples, the maximization of their economic potential, and benevolent, albeit authoritarian, government.[61] Where the Portuguese Empire differed was in its stubborn adherence to this ideology of domination after 1945, at a time when other imperial states were adopting strategies of modernization and greater political inclusion in an effort to assuage international criticism and breathe new life into their empires.

Undeterred by decolonization's momentum elsewhere, the Salazarist regime developed an entire political vocabulary to justify continued Portuguese control of African territory. As in the French case, black African colonies were redesignated as 'overseas possessions'. The colonial power, Portuguese colonial settlers, and the colonized peoples formed a single 'pan-Lusitanian' community linked by shared language, acquired European customs, and the imposition of Portuguese civil and criminal law. The very designations 'Angolan' or 'African' were declared outmoded. In Salazar's conception of 'Lusotropicalism', a term appropriated from the Brazilian sociologist Gilberto Freyre, the entire empire was composed of Portuguese, albeit of various colours and aptitudes and with markedly different political rights and economic opportunities. In Salazar's characterization, this was a post-imperial meritocracy. Portuguese control was justified because it promoted the civilization of native populations by assimilating them to Portuguese culture.

The lived experience for black Africans was much different. The Salazarist colonial state was, if anything, more stringent in its application of rigid racial categories than the other European empires whose practices it derided. Designation of the terms *'civilisado'* and *'indigena'* was formally codified in two decisive legislative instruments: the Colonial Act of 1930 and the Organic Charter of the Portuguese Empire, promulgated in 1933. Taken together, these laws set out the juridical framework for differential rights and legal punishments in Portugal's African territories. Their cumulative effect was to formalize the distinctions between Portuguese citizens and colonial natives. The Colonial Act, in particular, entrenched the empire's structural inequality by judging African native populations to be at a primitive stage of cultural development and, therefore, racially and legally inferior to their Portuguese overseers. In this sense, the *indigenato* legal code built upon an earlier law, the Labour Code for Indigenous Peoples from the Portuguese Colonies of Africa, passed in December 1929. At first glance, this legislation seemed to offer legal protection to subject populations against labour abuses but, in practice, its primary purpose was the exact reverse: to guarantee a cheap supply of African workers for public works and settler enterprise, often through coercive means.[62]

Salazar's 'New State' thus responded to the global economic crisis of the 1930s by imposing more rigid social stratification in its colonies while at the same time justifying these measures as aspects of a long-term development programme predicated on closer state control over economic activity in general and export production in particular.[63] Paradoxically, then, Salazarist colonial officials defended harsher labour discipline and the forcible relocation of workers as integral to the cultural 'elevation' of dependent peoples. Armed with this cultural defence of heightened colonial extraction, the New State was disinclined to alter political course. International criticism notwithstanding, the *indigenato* and the Labour Code retained their racially coded coercive power. Although the legislation was theoretically no longer recognized after 1961, this situation persisted long after other colonial powers had turned away from overt legal discrimination and forced labour.[64]

With all of this in view, we should not be surprised that Portugal had the unfortunate distinction of being involved in three intractable African colonial wars simultaneously – in Angola from 1961; in Portuguese Guinea (Guiné-Bissau) from 1963; and in Mozambique from 1964. As in the case of France and the Algerian conflict, Portugal's colonial wars ultimately brought down a metropolitan regime following a revolt by its colonial army. Redolent of the exodus of *pieds noirs* from Algeria over the chaotic summer of 1962, in the spring of 1975 tens of thousands of Portuguese settlers flooded out of Angola after fighting broke out in the capital, Luanda, between rival nationalist and Marxist factions in the wake of Portugal's decision to pull out.

Historian Norrie MacQueen discerns two dominant historiographical trends regarding European decolonization since 1945. The first depicts colonial collapse as the consequence of successful colonial nationalism – Africans and Asians seized the unprecedented opportunities to build transnational networks of support available to them in the new international system of the Cold War. The second represents decolonization as more orderly, a mixture of conflict and reform, but one in which European imperial nations generally managed to negotiate transfers of power. As MacQueen puts it:

> Within this reductive framework the general assumption has been that, however problematic the cases of, say, France or the Netherlands, the Portuguese example appeared unambiguous. A clear victory for the political and military forces of radical African nationalism had, it seemed, brought imperial collapse. Moreover, in the Portuguese case, colonial nationalism appeared to precipitate not just African independence but metropolitan revolution as well. In reality, though, the end of Portuguese imperialism in Africa, no less than that of the other European colonial empires, can be comprehended only in terms of *both* insurgent nationalism in Africa *and* the logical conclusion of long-term change in the metropole.[65]

Final Portuguese withdrawal from southern Africa is thus commonly attributed to events at the metropolitan centre of colonial power: the army coup in Lisbon that overthrew the remnants of the Salazarist regime; mounting public exasperation with the human and material costs of the African wars; and a fast-expanding Portuguese economy whose future development lay in EEC membership rather than an outdated and declining colonial commercial sector. Premier Marcello Caetano, who had succeeded an increasingly infirm Salazar in September 1968, presided over a country with a booming economy fired by recent industrial modernization. Upholding a colonial empire to buttress what had been a closed and stagnant economy no longer made economic sense. Admission to the European Community, with all its attendant trade benefits, also rested squarely on an end to Portugal's colonial wars. It was the pull of EEC membership that made regime change in Lisbon appear imperative to influential constituencies of domestic opinion, from the educated middle class to business leaders and the junior officers that orchestrated military opposition to Caetano's government. In short, the survival of a discredited, authoritarian regime became inextricably associated in the public mind with the continuation of unpopular colonial wars that promised only further human misery, financial waste, and the ostracism of European partners.[66]

Political scientist Hendrick Spruyt adds another dimension to this metropolitan explanation for the final disintegration of Portugal's African empire. Focusing on key institutions and social groups with vested interests in the colonies, he sees the abrupt abandonment of empire after the Lisbon regime change in April 1974 as a reflection of the differing degrees of influence exercised by those constituencies caught up in the colonial maelstrom. Of the groups he identifies – the armed forces, Portuguese trading companies, settler agriculturalists, and Salazar loyalists – only the army was strong enough to impose its will on government. Once it became politically fragmented, with its officer corps no longer united in defence of empire, there was no going back. As for the business sector, its prosperity lay in the consolidation of trade within Europe, not Africa. For their part, the settlers were poorly organized politically, lacking a political party or other interest group to put their case in Lisbon. In short, the authoritarianism of the Salazarist regime was ultimately the instrument of its own downfall. By vesting so much power in the army, outlawing multiparty politics, and so denying a political voice even to pro-imperialist settlers, the regime's backers had no one else to turn to when elements in the armed forces turned against the further prosecution of colonial war.[67]

An influx of returning settlers, many of them recent migrants that had settled in Angola and Mozambique since the late 1950s, added to the impression that Portuguese Africa was a lost cause. Some three quarters of the 335,000 white settlers in Angola and the 200,000 or so in Mozambique decided to leave.[68] Many chose to do so during the final years of the Caetano regime in the early 1970s. Some 40,000 settlers quit Mozambique between 1971 and 1973.[69] Their cousins in Angola would follow a similar path. Generous state allocations of cultivable land to incoming settlers – typically made at African expense – made little difference. Only a tiny minority of European *colonos* had established viable farms and ranches in the Angolan countryside by 1969.[70]

These factors were all critical to Portuguese withdrawal from Africa. But excessive concentration on socioeconomic changes in Portugal, or on the April 1974 coup alone, masks the fact that the Portuguese grip on Mozambique and Angola was rendered untenable by the oppressive nature of Lusophone colonialism and the violent opposition it engendered.[71] Even before the 'formal' outbreaks of rebellion in their African territories, Portuguese suppression of worker unrest and other protests in their African territories was extraordinarily violent. At least fifty strikers were killed during the August 1959 confrontations with police at Pidjiguiti docks in Guiné-Bissau. Up to 600 members of local agricultural cooperatives were cut down following a demonstration outside colonial administrative buildings in Mueda, Mozambique, in June 1960. An untold number of educated or Western-dressed Angolans in the capital Luanda were targeted by settler vigilantes during reprisal killings against potential nationalist supporters following a spectacular attempt in February 1961 to free political prisoners from the municipal jail in the capital, Luanda.[72]

Little wonder that insurgent movements found large reservoirs of popular support among urban workers and landless labourers from which to draw. Take the colony of Guiné-Bissau – at only 36,000 square kilometres, one of Africa's smallest territories. Within months of the January 1963 outbreak of guerrilla warfare in Guiné-Bissau, the colonial authorities lost their grip over the rural interior. Seventy-five days of aerial bombardment, including sustained use of napalm, later that year failed to dislodge the insurgents from their southern stronghold.[73] Nor were an administrative clear-out and the unification of civil governorship and military command in the hands of former Interior Minister Arnaldo Schultz in mid-1964 enough to slow the loss of colonial control. By 1965, production of groundnuts, the colony's one export staple, had collapsed; essential foodstuffs had to be imported, and the colony's single state-backed commercial conglomerate, the Companhia União Fabril, had virtually ceased trading.[74] Never much of an asset, Guiné-Bissau's material worth to Portugal was far outstripped by the military expenditure wasted in trying to keep it. The supreme irony was that the Salazarist state was driven by its own twisted constitutional logic to fight on.

Since 1951 all the Portuguese African territories had been redesignated 'overseas provinces' (Províncias Ultramares) of the indivisible Portuguese state. Having tried and failed to open a dialogue with Lisbon in the late 1950s, Amílcar Cabral, the inspirational Cabo Verdean leader of the Guinean guerrillas, calculated that only violent resistance could ever evict the Portuguese.[75] Better concealed among the rural population, Cabral's fighters blended bush warfare techniques with Marxist re-education, the provision of basic healthcare and low-cost food made available through 'people's stores'.[76] The emerging generation of nationalists in Angola and Mozambique followed similar paths, typically leaving the major cities where the Portuguese security presence was strongest to conduct rural insurgencies from 'safe zones' in which their writ ran furthest. If anything, Salazar's intransigence increased in reaction to the Congo crisis, which, he felt, confirmed the perils of decolonization in ethnically divided African societies. There was, admittedly, some connection. A northern rebellion launched by Holden Roberto's Union of the Peoples of Angola in March 1961 sought to emulate pre-independence unrest in the Congo, hoping to shock the Portuguese state into changing course. Instead, the severity of security force repression sent tens of thousands of refugees fleeing northwards across the Congolese frontier.[77]

Even the Kennedy and Johnson administrations, the most influential of the foreign governments urging Portugal towards accelerated reform, were rebuffed. Kennedy, in particular, was persuaded in his first months as President in 1961 that continuing US tolerance of Portuguese colonialism was politically self-defeating and ethically indefensible. The strategic benefits that accrued from Portugal's membership of NATO, its staunch anti-communism, and its provision of mid-Atlantic airbases in the Azores were useful. But they paled into insignificance next to the damning impression that Washington connived in the worst excesses of Portuguese rule in black Africa. Anti-colonialists throughout the global South could hardly be expected to take seriously the Democrats' protestations of respect for civil rights and racial equality at home and abroad if the new administration failed to signal its displeasure at Portugal's unreconstructed imperialism. Joining the UN's vocal condemnation of colonialism confirmed this shift diplomatically. But Washington's changed position registered more strongly in geostrategic terms.[78] Lisbon's rejection of American entreaties (and its turn to France and West Germany for military supplies to fight its African wars) drove Kennedy's advisers towards covert backing for the UPA's successor movement, the Frente Nacional de Libertação de Angola (FNLA).[79] George W. Anderson, US ambassador in Lisbon, recounted a typically fruitless exchange with the Portuguese dictator in April 1964 as follows:

> Regret I must report that Salazar remained adamantly opposed [to] any public statement on self-determination. ... On balance I could perceive no real give or hint of prospective change in Salazar's position. He made clear and explicit his belief that US G[overnment] efforts are misdirected and that morally and realistically we should be pressing African states to withdraw support from terrorists who impede [the] political, economic and

social evolution of Portuguese Africa rather than pressing Portugal to take steps which could only lead to instability and retrogression.[80]

Named after the Lisbon ambassador, a subsequent US-brokered peace proposal, the Anderson Plan, got nowhere. Presented to the Portuguese in September 1965, the plan built on an earlier scheme devised by Tanzanian President, Julius Nyerere. The Anderson Plan proposed a timetable for internationally monitored plebiscites on self-determination in the Portuguese African states, NATO diplomatic support for Portugal, and long-term development aid to its former colonies. Salazar's government rejected it and by March 1966 this American negotiation effort was dead.[81]

In its refusal to open up political space for Africans to participate in colonial decision-making, the Salazarist state radicalized dependent populations who were left with no alternative between subjugation and armed revolt. With labour movements and political parties outlawed, nationalist leaders forced underground or into exile, and little prospect of substantial economic liberalization, it seems fair to conclude that the Portuguese state was wholly responsible for the violence of decolonization in its African territories.[82]

As we discussed in Chapter 4, Portugal's anti-colonial conflicts were conceived by many of those who led them as people's wars: popular liberation struggles against one of the most repressive colonial systems of the late twentieth century.[83] However, their courses ran very differently. Why? Patrick Chabal has argued that the relative success of the people's war in Portuguese Guinea, next to the much greater difficulties facing the nationalist uprisings in Angola and Mozambique was determined by three factors. One was the extent to which the dominant nationalist groups achieved uncontested political control over the territory they sought to liberate. In this respect, Amílcar Cabral's Partido Africano para a Independência da Guiné e Cabo Verde (PAIGC) in Portuguese Guinea was the most successful. By contrast, the leftist MPLA (Movimento Popular de Libertação de Angola) and FRELIMO (Frente de Libertação de Moçambique) never established unilateral control over the much greater geographical expanse and more ethnically diverse populations of Angola and Mozambique.[84] In both cases, the elite, urban backgrounds of their leadership cadres frustrated their efforts to claim they were 'of the people' they professed to represent. Long spells in exile, albeit essential in consolidating the support of key neighbour states, added to this impression of distance between bookish leftists in fatigues and the dirt-poor village populations whose socialist futures they were planning.[85]

This brings us to the second prerequisite for the success of people's war in Portuguese African territories, which was to establish a viable economy and effective administrative system in those liberated areas under insurgent control. Orderly government and organized economic activity were critical if popular support was to be retained and international recognition of the claim to independence won. Here, again, the PAIGC was the outstanding performer. To a degree, this was simply a matter of demography and geography. With only a tiny population, short supply lines, and friendly states across the Guinean border, the PAIGC's task in attracting recruits, sustaining campaigns, and evading the Portuguese security forces was far easier than that of its nationalist colleagues in Angola and Mozambique. That said, the PAIGC was undoubtedly popular in town and countryside. It achieved that most difficult of objectives: pursuing a radical socialist agenda while staying true to the popular will.[86] Mozambique's FRELIMO was less united, less effective militarily, and therefore less able to sustain effective political control over large tracts of territory, at least until 1969–70 by which time its new leaders were beginning to overcome the movement's earlier divisions and military deficiencies. Meanwhile, Portuguese psychological warfare and a hearts and minds strategy focused on persuading northern Mozambique's Muslims to reject FRELIMO's Marxism were not enough to halt the movement's advance.[87] Indeed, it is at least questionable whether the massive social dislocation consequent upon the security force strategy of corralling villagers in Mozambique's most highly contested provinces into *aldeamentos*, or 'protected villages', did not in fact compel larger numbers of peasant farmers into opposing colonial authority for fear of losing access to land.

If FRELIMO's story is one of gradual consolidation, the predominant nationalist groups in Angola, the MPLA, the Frente Nacional Libertação de Angola (FNLA), and the União Nacional para a Independência Total de Angola (UNITA) remained bitter rivals incapable of establishing a hold over large tracts of territory – or, at least, not for long. Admittedly, the MPLA controlled a strategically important zone in eastern Angola and UNITA kept a hold over parts of the Bié-Moxico district in the south.[88] But neither was ever close to evicting the Portuguese completely from the Angolan interior. Denied undisputed control of substantial liberated areas, Angola's nationalist movements could not build up an efficient alternative administration to the central colonial government.[89]

Here we come to the third determinant of success – the nature of the nationalist movement and the social, ethnic, and regional composition of its support. The Balante people of Guiné-Bissau dominated the PAIGC rank and file, but many of the movement's leaders, Cabral included, were *mestiço* (mixed race) Cabo Verdeans who had spent time as students in Lisbon. In practice, this basic ethnic split between the PAIGC leadership and its ordinary cadres was not a barrier to success. The organization, although in some ways elitist, eventually mobilized support across all ethnicities and socioeconomic groups in Portuguese Guinea. By contrast, neither the MPLA nor FRELIMO managed to grow into multi-ethnic and broadlybased popular movements. The MPLA executive remained a closed grouping, many of whose leaders were educated in mission schools in and around Angola's colonial capital, Luanda. Their mainstay of support was the intellectuals and workers of Luanda and its hinterland. Even after the movement opened its Eastern Front in Angola's thinly populated eastern flatlands in 1966, the party leadership under MPLA President, Agostinho Neto, operated from bases in Zambia and the movement's foreign headquarters in Tanzania. Local MPLA commanders on the Eastern Front had often spent most of their lives abroad and had little knowledge of the cultural dynamics within the communities they administered. This lack of local knowledge compounded the rivalries among MPLA leaders frustrated with the slow pace of advance towards independence.

Not surprisingly, despite intensive indoctrination efforts by the MPLA's educational centres (Centro de Instrução Revolucionário), support among the peasant communities in MPLA controlled south-eastern Angola for the party's Marxist vision of secular modernization was as much a product of coercion and the lack of viable options as of genuine popular commitment. Acute economic hardship, the war's destruction of village communities, and near-starvation conditions inevitably meant that large numbers of civilians simply did their best to avoid becoming caught in the crossfire between the MPLA, its nationalist rivals, and the colonial state. Growing popular opposition to the Portuguese colonial regime developed more in reaction to the government's forced resettlement of over a million Angolans from 1967 onwards than from any ideological commitment to either the MPLA or its principal rivals.[90] Moreover, as Inge

Brinkman has shown, the persistence of such decidedly non-Marxist practices as summary executions of alleged witches and reliance on chiefs previously promoted by the Portuguese authorities suggest that the movement did what it deemed necessary to retain its grip over the civilian population in the south-east.[91] (We should note, however, that the MPLA's principal challenger, Jonas Savimbi's UNITA, terrorized Angola's south-east even more.[92])

Elsewhere, the MPLA enjoyed even less success. MPLA recruiters signally failed to draw much support among Angola's Bakongo people in the north of the country. The conflict in northern Angola was exceptionally disruptive. Fighting between insurgents, settler vigilantes, and Portuguese military units to control communications routes and village centres led inexorably to the militarization of the rural interior and the targeting of civilians. As we saw earlier, beginning in 1961, local people continued to flee in huge numbers across the border into newly independent Congo/Zaire. There, Angolan refugee numbers already exceeded 100,000 by June 1961 and grew to over half a million by 1972.[93] Little wonder that the MPLA message of Marxist salvation registered little impact in the north. But the MPLA's limited national appeal could also be attributed to the structures of the colonial state and the distribution of influential Christian missions, both of which heightened Angola's innate regional differences and ethnic particularities.[94] To make matters worse, splits later emerged between the MPLA's civil and military leaders after the Portuguese military offensive against the Eastern Front in 1972. These culminated in the defection of senior MPLA military commanders to the third nationalist party competing for power in Angola, the FNLA.[95] As for Jonas Savimbi's UNITA forces, they were solidly backed by Angola's largest ethnic group, the Ovimbundo. This largely Protestant community had fought especially hard against Portuguese colonial penetration and favoured UNITA throughout the war.[96]

In Mozambique, too, inter-communal friction weakened the Marxist FRELIMO coalition that was established on 25 June 1962 and led from September by Eduardo Mondlane, a UN employee. Although FRELIMO was the product of the merger of three ethnically based parties, it took time for its overarching anti-colonialism to subsume the tensions between its constituent groups. It was only after Mondlane's 1969 assassination, part of the bloody aftermath of a FRELIMO purge, that the movement's younger leaders, Samora Machel and Marcelino dos Santos, made real progress in reducing the regional and ethnic rivalries among its northern and southern supporters. In their case, the adoption of a more doctrinaire, class-based vision of a Marxist one-party state helped overcome local particularism.[97]

Another critical feature common to the wars in Angola and Mozambique was that their long duration, from 1961 to 1975, ensured that both became bound up with escalating Cold War rivalries in southern Africa. Internationalization of the wars of decolonization in Portuguese Africa had other causes, too. One was that both Angola and Mozambique had extensive land frontiers with southern African states still committed to white minority rule. While Angolan and Mozambican insurgents found sanctuary in other, more sympathetic neighbour states – Zambia, the Congo/Zaire, and Tanzania for example – white-ruled South Africa and Rhodesia each became important players in the proxy wars fought out in these Portuguese colonial territories.[98] (These regional neighbours are indicated in the map inserts overleaf.) Geographical situation alone cannot account for the spread of proxy war to Portuguese Africa; chronology was also vital.

Whereas France and Britain were well along the road to African decolonization by the time the Soviet Union, the People's Republic of China, and Fidel Castro's Cuba took a close strategic

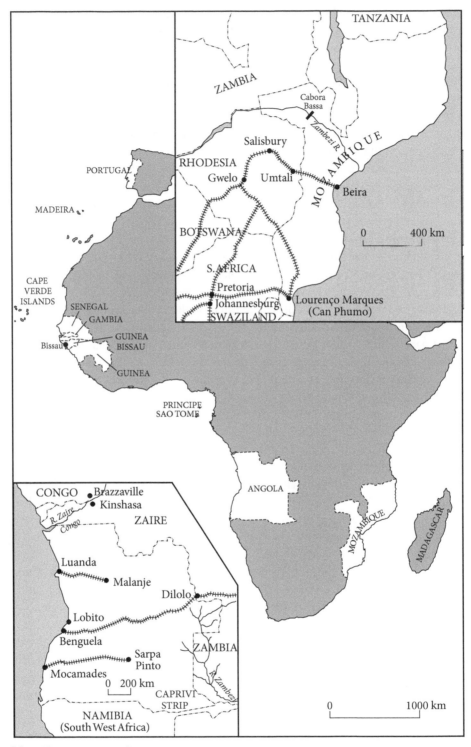

Map 12 Portuguese Africa.

interest in African affairs, counterinsurgencies in Portugal's African colonies had barely started. Faced with nationalist militias trained by Soviet advisers, equipped with Soviet and Chinese military hardware, and supported by Cuban-armed forces and medical volunteers, Portugal eventually secured United States and, especially, South African support to stem what could henceforth be convincingly portrayed as communist rebellions.[99] By 1970 the Soviet Union had joined Cuba in lending military support to the PAIGC and the MPLA. And once Portuguese forces pulled out in 1975, the CIA coordinated aid to both the FNLA and UNITA as civil war engulfed post-independence Angola. Often, the military hardware delivered had a major strategic impact as, for example, when PAIGC fighters acquired Russian-built surface-to-air missiles (SAM-7s) capable of downing the Portuguese army helicopters that ferried troops to the Guinean interior.[100]

To sum up, Portuguese decolonization married all the most explosive aspects of earlier anti-colonial struggles in French and British Africa. Reactionary settler militancy that intensified as local security deteriorated; the army's deepening alienation from the civil power; increasing recourse to locally recruited, ill-disciplined colonial forces; and dirty war practices that provoked a chorus of international protests from the UN General Assembly, independent African states, and the European Community.[101] A simple tally of UN Security Council votes during Caetano's term of office is revealing: sixteen in total between July 1969 and July 1973 in none of which did the United States, Britain or France choose to support the Portuguese position.[102] As we have seen, there were other, more distinctive elements to Portugal's situation as well: a declining dictatorial regime at odds with a rising generation of educated, liberal opinion, and a developing Cold War front line in southern Africa that transcended the requirements of colonial rule.

After the first major rebellions in Angola, Salazar's government tried to mollify its African colonial populations. A package of social reforms was belatedly rushed onto the statute book in 1961 and 1962. The measures introduced in the early 1960s swept away the legislative instruments of state coercion introduced since the 1930s. The native statute of 1954 was abolished, thereby conceding legal equality – at least on paper – between settlers and subjects. An end to forced labour obligations and liberalization of the wage economy followed. Government compulsion of peasant cultivators, forced to grow export crops traded at government prices, had been integral to the outbreak of rebellion in Angola and Mozambique.[103] So the removal of this requirement, as well as new laws to promote African land tenure, might have been expected to pacify rural populations in the worst affected areas of Portuguese Africa.[104] Not so. The reforms were simply too little, too late. Registering few positive results from its reformist initiatives, the Salazarist government saw no alternative to the pursuit of its military campaigns against the nationalists.

Much the same logic applied in Guiné-Bissau even though the colony had hardly any settlers to protect and precious little economic resource to exploit. What, then, was the point of prosecuting a colonial war there? According to General António de Spínola, who took over from Arnaldo Schultz as colonial commander in May 1968, Salazar was adamant that the colony be held. His reasoning was simple, and immune to counterargument. Even if the loss of Guiné were insignificant in itself, it could precipitate colonial collapse in Angola and Mozambique. As Norrie MacQueen comments, 'This imperial domino theory, justified on the basis of national destiny and economic benefit, was to emerge as the basis of the entire Portuguese endeavour in Guiné.'[105]

Ultimately, Portugal's colonialist diehards among the settler population and within the regime were eclipsed by a coalition of professional officers and conscripts opposed to fighting on. As Spruyt puts it, 'More and more elements within the army started to question the wisdom of continuing a war that led, at best, to stalemate (as in Angola), protracted withdrawal (in Mozambique), or imminent defeat (in Guiné-Bissau).'[106] It was this Armed Forces Movement (Movimento das Forças Armadas – MFA) that seized power in Lisbon in a coup on 25 April 1974, staking 'its legitimacy on the delivery of the three Ds: Decolonization, Democracy and Development'.[107] Army opposition represented the confluence of several long-held grievances, some more principled than others. Many were unsurprising. War fatigue, annoyance over service terms and conditions, and a growing sense of abandonment were, for example, complaints familiar to any student of France's wars of decolonization. But the growing generational gap between Portugal's ageing leadership and its junior officer corps was more distinctive. So, too, was the widely held fear among more senior commanders that Caetano's government might blame the army for Portugal's inability to cling onto its colonial possessions. Salazar's vilification of the army's performance after Indian military forces reoccupied the Portuguese enclave of Goa in 1961 bred lasting antagonism towards the Lisbon regime. These grievances simmered on in mess tents and command centres on the African front line for the next fifteen years.[108] The colonial army officers grouped around Spínola in Guiné never forgot that Goa's Governor and his senior military commanders were first court-martialled and then expelled from Portugal despite having faced an impossible task against a vastly superior Indian force. To cap it all, a July 1973 law that bypassed regulars by offering accelerated promotion to loyalist officer recruits stirred renewed resentment among long-serving soldiers, some of whom had considered the possibility of an anti-regime coup as far back as 1958.[109]

Just as tensions between the Lisbon regime and its colonial commanders increased over time, so, too, did the military problems on the ground. Here again the case of Guiné-Bissau is instructive. Soon after his arrival in May 1968, Spínola adopted a hearts and minds strategy designed to sow division in PAIGC ranks. Spínola nurtured tribal assemblies, grandly called 'people's congresses', and held out the promise of a referendum and eventual autonomy. Devastating search and destroy missions continued, typically involving saturation bombing, but the army command knew its forces were too thinly spread to achieve outright military victory. Spínola turned instead to a locally recruited militia, the Frente Unida de Libertação (United Liberation Front), in an effort to turn the tide against the PAIGC. His hope was that abiding resentments about Cabo Verdean dominance of the anti-colonial movement could be decisively turned against it.[110] More important, from early 1970 onwards, Spínola's staff kept open a back channel to the PAIGC leadership based in the neighbour state of former French Guinea. The resultant exchanges were sporadic, frequently interrupted by factions on both sides determined to derail them, but they pointed the way to a negotiated solution. Unfortunately, Caetano's government was too fragile and too deeply split between hardliners and modernizers to opt unequivocally for diplomacy over force.[111] They were not alone in this.

Spínola and his key military backer in Lisbon, Chief of Staff General Costa Gomes, were not wholeheartedly committed to phased withdrawal.[112] On 22 November, nine months after the PAIGC's spectacular assassination of three army negotiators, Portuguese commandos launched a raid on Conakry, the capital of francophone Guinea. Acting on the advice of the Portuguese security service, the Direcção Geral de Segurança, their objectives were apparently threefold:

to destroy the PAIGC's headquarters, to kill Amílcar Cabral, and, perhaps, to overthrow Sékou Touré's regime in the process.

The attack turned out to be something akin to Portugal's Suez. Its most immediate outcomes were a massive propaganda coup for Cabral and his pro-Soviet ally Touré, plus a strongly worded UN Security Council condemnation of Portugal's invasion of a sovereign state. With direct Portuguese-PAIGC talks stymied, during 1971, attention turned to Senegalese premier Léopold Senghor's long-standing offer to act as an intermediary. Much like his more radical French-speaking rival, Sékou Touré, Senghor saw an opportunity to make political capital out of Portugal's mounting crisis in Guiné. But he also wanted to stabilize a dangerous situation along Senegal's frontier with the embattled colony. This time it was the PAIGC that spoiled things; correctly calculating that Senghor's peace plan would only propose autonomy, not full independence. Guerrilla attacks in border areas intensified, their purpose being to provoke vicious Portuguese reprisals, and renewed UN criticism of army actions. Senghor's diplomatic efforts limped on until, in May 1972, the Lisbon government, still in thrall to unreconstructed Salazarists, pulled the rug from under Spínola's feet.[113]

Although hidden from the domestic population, the contradictions of Portugal's colonial war in Guiné-Bissau were beginning to tear the regime apart. Prime Minister Caetano claimed to favour 'progressive autonomy'; yet he had stifled the talks designed to achieve it. Hardliners, such as Colonial Minister, Joaquim da Silva Cunha, and Portugal's President, Admiral Américo Tomáz, expected the army to keep fighting, but they lacked the means to reinforce it. Although relatively low, Portugal's military losses of 8,290 (4,027 of whom were killed in action) in its African colonial wars since 1961 affected critical front-line units most severely.[114] Hard-pressed military commanders in Angola and Mozambique fought tooth and nail to prevent the diversion of additional forces to the Guiné enclave. For his part, Spínola was determined to avoid the fate of his predecessors in Goa, who had been expected to uphold a position that was as much politically, as militarily, indefensible.[115]

In the event, peripheral pressure, as well as the impending collapse of the Lisbon regime, brought matters to a head. Neither the murder of Amílcar Cabral during a failed kidnap attempt in Conakry on 20 January 1973 nor the mystery surrounding it did much to halt the PAIGC's political advance. Cabral's half-brother Luis took over the leadership and quickly garnered stronger support at the United Nations. During early 1973 the movement's estimated 7,000 guerrilla fighters also received their first shipments of heavy weaponry, including the all-important SAM missiles. These weapons soon brought a halt to Portuguese bombardment of PAIGC 'liberated zones'. It was here that elections were organized with UN blessing. Their outcome was the PAIGC's unilateral declaration of an independent Guiné Republic in September 1973.[116] Much like their FLN forebears in Algeria, the PAIGC had won the political battle for international recognition before the colonial power came to terms. In Guiné-Bissau at least, the people's war had been won, thereby rupturing the supposed indivisibility of the Portuguese colonial state.

Wider international developments also played a role in Portugal's final withdrawal from Africa. By the early 1970s the geopolitics of Cold War in Africa left no room for a Portuguese colonial presence. As East-West détente gathered strength, American and UN pressure on Lisbon to pull out intensified. By this point, the Portuguese territories in southern Africa were already edging closer to postcolonial civil strife as the leading Marxist insurgent groups in Angola and Mozambique, the MPLA and FRELIMO, confronted their Western-backed nationalist opponents, UNITA and RENAMO (Resistência Nacional Moçambicana).[117] The intensification of anti-colonial insurgency in white-ruled Rhodesia further destabilized the territory's already porous frontier with Mozambique. The warring parties in the conflicts in both countries criss-crossed the frontier, whether chasing down opponents or seeking refuge and recruits.[118] RENAMO exemplified this transnational turn in the last stages of Mozambique's fight for independence. A shadowy, unaccountable group, it originated as the bastard child of the Portuguese secret police and the Rhodesian military. Each recruited former Portuguese colonial special forces personnel (the infamous *flechas*) and 'turned' insurgent prisoners to serve as a brutal vanguard in their war against the MPLA.[119]

Even before RENAMO was established (in 1976), the growing internecine complexity of the conflicts in Mozambique and Angola encouraged MFA organizers within the colonies to negotiate local ceasefires where possible. Seen as the prelude to self-determination, such accords made sense to these reformist Portuguese Army officers who, in the immediate aftermath of the 25 April 1974 coup in Lisbon, felt they had freer rein to negotiate their withdrawal.[120] It is therefore unsurprising that the elaborate formulas for final Portuguese departure from Guiné, Mozambique, and Angola devised by General Spínola, who became Portugal's post-coup transitional leader, and pursued by Mário Soares, Socialist Party leader and Foreign Minister in Portugal's transitional government, had to be fundamentally revised during 1974–5 to take account of the chaotic situation on the ground. Crucially, against his better judgement, Spínola caved into MFA demands. His 27 July 1974 declaration conceding self-determination to Portugal's African territories proved irreversible.[121]

Important realignments also occurred within the Portuguese government during early 1975 as an increasingly radical MFA leadership forged closer ties with the Communist Party. In many ways, this represented the ultimate transnational 'blowback' from decolonization: leftist army officers and militant workers drew inspiration from the ideological struggles and insurrectionist ideas of the anti-colonial movements with whom they now sought peace.[122] Portuguese negotiators, many drawn from MFA ranks, conceded independence swiftly in Guiné and Mozambique. MFA leaders, influenced by a combination of Europe's leftist student radicalism and broad ideological sympathy for the liberationist ideals of African guerrilla movements, saw much to admire in the PAIGC and FRELIMO. But, despite a comparable sympathy for the MPLA, in mineral-rich Angola, events took a different turn.[123] Portuguese negotiators did secure an accord – the 15 January 1975 Alvor Agreement – that envisaged a transfer of power to a coalition of the Angolan liberation movements before the end of the year, but this settlement never came to fruition. Determined to pre-empt their rival's seizure of power, on 23 March FNLA forces stormed MPLA headquarters in Luanda.[124] The skirmishing between Angola's opposing groups had escalated into full-blown civil war. Each side received foreign supplies, from the United States, the Soviet Union, from apartheid South Africa, and from Mao's China, ensuring that the conflict would be especially bloody. Indeed, Angola's colonial conflict transmogrified into something else: a contest for political supremacy and precious economic resources between rival nationalist groups backed by external Cold War sponsors.[125]

Where the Soviet Union had conspicuously failed to intervene effectively in the Congo, it succeeded in the initial stages of Angola's postcolonial conflict. A huge influx of Cuban troops transported and equipped with Soviet assistance to western Angola in late 1975 ensured the survival of Neto's MPLA regime. In two months of intense fighting during November and

December 1975 the MPLA's Cuban-dominated units first defeated a US-equipped FNLA force that entered the country from Zaire, and then a South African-led UNITA army advancing from the south-east.[126] By May of 1976 the FNLA no longer existed as a viable guerrilla army and South African Defence Force troops had been withdrawn. But, if these MPLA victories brought the first phase of Angola's proxy war to a close, they did not signal the end of the conflict between Angola's nationalist forces and their external sponsors.[127] Thus did the extreme violence of Portuguese decolonization shade into a new nightmare of civil strife, inter-communal violence, and foreign intervention that would decimate the Angolan population over the next two decades. In spite of Portugal's sustained efforts since 1975 to conciliate former colonial dependencies, the last major European decolonization from Africa must rank among the most tragic.[128]

CONCLUSION
CHANGING ATTITUDES TO THE END OF EMPIRE

Europe's overseas colonial empires disintegrated in a thirty-year period stretching from the end of the Second World War in 1945 to the final collapse of the settler regimes of southern Africa after 1975.[1] It was a remarkably quick end to empires that had been centuries in the making. The rapidity and near totality of Europe's withdrawal from empire was rarely anticipated either by governments and colonial political elites or by their anti-colonial opponents. But can we ascribe such a complex process as decolonization to a mere thirty years of sociopolitical change? What about its long-term origins in two World Wars and in the twentieth century's most protracted economic crisis – the Global Depression of the 1930s? What of the inherent self-destructiveness of colonial rule, whose violence and exclusionary practices stirred fear and loathing among the majority populations of dependent territories? What, finally, of the 'suicidal tendency' among late colonial states? By advocating development, preaching greater political inclusivity, and laying the foundations for post-imperial partnerships with dependable leaders in politics, the military, and business, the more reformist colonial administrations negated the rationale for their existence.

Just as we should question when the process of decolonization began, so we might rethink its ending. Decolonization was not as finite as dusty analyses of constitutional 'transfers of power' might suggest. Informal imperial networks – some in commerce and the world of money, others cultural and family based – remained long after formal colonial withdrawal. Colonialism left enduring, and often acutely divisive, cultural impacts ranging from language, religion, media, and the arts, to judicial systems and educational curricula, architecture and the urban environment of postcolonial states. As newly independent states, former colonies somehow had to reconcile their sense of national identity with the colonial past that shaped it. The first generation of rulers in these countries often sought to define that national identity in opposition to their own struggles with the former colonial power. Many writers and artists did, too, refusing in their own work to use the language or media of their erstwhile colonial masters. For all that, the apparent rupture with foreign overseers was sometimes belied by economic realities. Former colonial dependencies were constrained by patterns of industrial and agricultural output, restrictive currency alignments, and trading partnerships established under European rule. These would, in turn, make trade dependency, crippling loan payments, and chronic deficits a common feature of political economy in the developing world. Elsewhere, the former colonizers withdrew only to return in the guise of political and scientific advisers, military missions and aid providers, bankers and lenders of last resort.[2] 'Self-determination' for many former colonies was sometimes more apparent than real, particularly in the realm of economic sovereignty.[3] In other territories such as the oil-producing states of North Africa and the Middle East or the rainforest regions of South East Asia, multinational conglomerates and foreign governments desperate for valued raw materials made a mockery of sovereign economic independence. The heightened extraction of such goods constituted what Rob Nixon describes as a 'slow violence' of environmental spoliation whose roots are traceable to the late colonial years.[4]

The precedent of self-government for the Dominions helped cushion the impact of decolonization on Britain. More than a convenient constitutional fig leaf, this came to be seen by successive British governments as the key to successful colonial withdrawal. Provided that former colonies could be coaxed into joining an expanding and evolving Commonwealth, the trappings of formal empire might be surrendered while its substance would remain intact. It was an optimistic reading on the part of policymakers, and one ultimately to result in disappointment. New Commonwealth members were understandably reluctant to accept British leadership or guidance. The persistence of white minority regimes in Rhodesia and South Africa remained an acutely divisive issue, even after the miscreant governments in Salisbury and Pretoria no longer had links with the Commonwealth.[5] Spurred by their visceral loathing of apartheid, black Commonwealth leaders could be bitterly critical when British double standards on matters of racial discrimination at home or in the wider world were laid bare. Moreover, British expectations of Commonwealth compliance appear to have been based on the assumption that it would be possible to substitute continuing, 'informal' influence for formal colonial rule, placing Britain's overseas interests on a secure footing, one acceptable to international opinion. Britain's aim, according to one view, was 'not that Britain should sustain the Empire but that the Empire, in a new form, should continue to sustain Britain'.[6]

Yet, as soon became apparent, maintaining an informal empire required degrees of financial pre-eminence, military power, and diplomatic leverage, that, by the 1960s, Britain no longer possessed. The record of Britain's presence in the Middle East after 1945 demonstrated just how taxing could be attempts to maintain informal influence on a shoestring budget without active American support. Furthermore, if such a 'blueprint' for decolonization existed in the minds of Britain's policymakers, the reality proved far more complex and less manageable than had been hoped. Time and again, Britain found itself responding to crises rather than anticipating them. Any sense that the process was under control was an illusion sustained for metropolitan public consumption and to assuage Britain's allies.

The French retreat from empire began in Asia in 1945, but the dismantling of its North and sub-Saharan African Empires is concentrated at the apogee of the decolonization era in the later 1950s and early 1960s when it was paralleled by rapid changes to the British Empire. Conversely, the Dutch case study provides examples from the beginning, middle, and end of the process. A similar post-Second World War expulsion from the Far East, albeit over a shorter time span, followed by a relatively minor crisis over the future of New Guinea in the 1960s that was almost overlooked in the massive changes that were being engineered elsewhere, and, finally, the loss of what was, by then, a relic of empire in the form of Suriname in the mid-1970s. The smaller European empires were among the most intransigent. Belgium's retreat from the Congo in 1960 was as abrupt as it was calamitous. Secession, competing international and regional interventions, and social dislocation followed within a matter of months.[7] Portugal refused to quit its African territories until a combination of draining colonial warfare and domestic revolution compelled it to do so, much to the relief of most Portuguese. These were some of the most chaotic and bloody decolonizations and, unsurprisingly, they left a legacy of violence and inter-communal enmity that lasted beyond the end of the twentieth century.

The French and Dutch paths to decolonization intersected in some ways, diverged in others. Before comparing these experiences in the post-1945 period, it is important to survey underlying similarities and differences between the two imperial states. To begin with, the empires themselves were of different chronological origins and geographical locations. The Dutch had been a presence in South East Asia and the Caribbean since the beginning of the seventeenth century whereas the French Empire in Africa was largely a creation of the post-Napoleonic period. Only in the Caribbean and in South East Asia were there clear geographical parallels between the two states. Both had to rebuild their empires after 1815, but from very different starting points. Ironically, the Dutch did so only after a French occupation of the mother country, and relied on British cooperation and goodwill to do so. French construction of a 'second' colonial empire began in earnest with the invasion of coastal Algeria in 1830, with this and subsequent expansion into Africa being conducted in the teeth of bitter inter-European rivalry.[8] For both the French and the Dutch, the upheavals of the early nineteenth century compelled them to find new justifications for colonial governance and economic exploitation that would colour the nature of their colonial rule for the following hundred years.

In certain respects, parallels with other European empires make more sense. The growth of the Eurasian population in the Netherlands East Indies shared much in common with Portuguese Africa where mixed-race Luso-African communities developed over centuries in Senegambia, Cape Verde, and Guinea-Bissau. Similar integration occurred in other parts of Portugal's *thalassocracy*, a maritime and commercial empire built around coastal trading settlements and slaving. Although the overall numbers of mixed-race descendants were smaller than in Dutch Indonesia, the impact on Portuguese conceptions of empire and colonial identity in the 'Lusotropical' world was, if anything, greater.[9]

Ideas of race are, of course, integral to understanding changing conceptions of imperialism. Underpinning the existence of all European colonial empires was an assumption of the inherent superiority of the white races over their non-white counterparts. As a result, the 'civilising mission' of the colonial power loomed large in the British, French, and Dutch public justifications for empire in the later nineteenth century. Doctrines of the 'right to rule' had more of a religious basis in the Netherlands and Belgium where confessional politics held sway. Equally, in the French Third Republic the internal clashes between secular republicans and their Catholic opponents were often put to one side within colonial territories where religious missions and colonial administrations typically closed ranks against domestic critics or local opponents of French hegemony.[10] The compulsion to justify colonialism as ethically imperative and culturally benevolent was common to all three states. It chimed with liberal and social democratic doctrines that refused to accept colonies merely as territories to be exploited for the economic benefit of the mother country. Just as in Britain at the turn of the century the idea of 'constructive imperialism' gained adherents, so the concept of 'mission' led to an overt espousal of what was called an 'ethical' policy by the Netherlands which saw the educational and social development of colonial peoples as part of the task given by God to the colonizers. During the early part of the twentieth century, it was the extent and purpose of this mission that was the subject of debate.[11] Presumptions about their alleged unpreparedness for social and political leadership levelled against the populations of black Africa were less persuasive when applied to the South Asian, Javanese, and Indo-Chinese elites who had ruled large polities – even empires of their own – before the Europeans arrived in Asia. Yet even where it was considered expedient to train small numbers of indigenous people for tasks within colonial government, their aspirations for advancement were usually thwarted by the existence of 'glass ceilings' blocking promotion and preferment. In this context, education and the integration of elements of the indigenous population into colonial administration produced benefits, but also potential dangers for long-term stability. Many of those considered worthy of further education were sent to the metropole, where they encountered a wealth of new ideas and ideologies, including critiques of imperialism. The colonial powers were thus complicit in helping to educate men who would later become their fiercest political and, in some cases, military opponents.

Colonial rule also required armed forces and gendarmeries to assure security, law, and order. All European colonial powers produced their own models for this. The British had a long tradition of identifying so-called 'martial races' among their colonial subjects, ethnic groups supposedly characterized by a warlike temperament and robust masculinity, whose menfolk were recruited into imperial armies in large numbers. In South Asia, for example, the Punjabi population was singled out as a group which appeared to fit British requirements admirably.[12] The French developed separate colonial armies for their Asian and black African colonies and for their North African territories, relying heavily on recruits from one colonial region to police another. The Dutch, too, depended on recruits from specific regions of their empire, such as the Ambonese. They also drew upon the large numbers of Eurasians created by 300 years of colonial rule who saw military service as one way of breaking the social shackles created by their mixed-race backgrounds.[13] In the Congo, the Belgians turned what had been a private army into a fearsome enforcer of state authority – the Force Publique. The Portuguese were pioneers of colonial army organization. They had employed African troops since the sixteenth century, and their colonial forces, though always white-officered, were often predominantly black. In 1973, the last full year of campaigning in Angola and Mozambique, official figures indicated that at least 60 per cent of Portugal's serving soldiers were Africans.[14]

One major expression of the frustration felt by educated or militarized indigenous elites excluded from the higher reaches of colonial administration was the growth of nationalism in the twentieth century, but it would be entirely wrong to suggest that this was a coherent or homogenous movement in any British, French, or Dutch imperial territory. Some early manifestations were essentially pleas for greater (local) self-government. Others were better described as cultural defence, the effort to sustain moral economies of belief, languages, inheritance rights or legal practices, or religious (often Islamic) opposition to the Christianizing missionary work carried out under the aegis of colonial rule. Locally diverse, these forms of cultural resistance implicitly rejected Western ideas of the nation state rather than affirming a distinct 'national' identity in competition with it. While we should not overplay the political unrest created by nationalism in the interwar period, neither should we underestimate the fears that nationalist sentiment created in the minds of the imperialists – especially when combined with the spectre of communism. In the wake of Europe's 'Greater War' and the accompanying Russian revolution, fear of 'the masses' being mobilized by unscrupulous agitators was commonplace among the Continent's ruling elites.[15] It required little imagination to see this phenomenon transferred to the colonies.

In economic terms, relationships between European imperial states and their colonies changed profoundly during the 1930s. In some cases, the collapse in colonial commodity prices during the global economic crisis led exporters to drive their workers harder in an effort to increase overall output and thereby compensate for falling revenues. In South-East Asia's rubber-producing territories, in the plantation economies of the Caribbean, and in the mining settlements of black Africa, this provoked major unrest.[16] Conditions of Depression at home meanwhile increased metropolitan reliance on reserved colonial markets, which were seen in British and French attempts to construct protected trading blocs to the annoyance of other countries, not least the United States.[17] Greater interdependence between home and colonial markets was not necessarily a good thing. Increases in the colonies' share of French exports during the 1930s reflected a crippling mutual dependency between failing metropolitan industries and the colonial purchasers denied any alternative to overpriced French goods.[18] In strategically exposed regions such as the Dutch East Indies and the Indochina federation, the costs of defence protection became prohibitive, making *de facto* dependency on foreign allies more likely. In this context, one only needs to mention America's lengthening economic and strategic reach across the Pacific region, and the looming military threat posed by the Japanese on the Asiatic mainland and beyond.[19] Inevitably, with the partial exception of neutral Portugal, domestic economic and security concerns dominated the politics of the European colonial powers in the 1930s as economic crisis gave way to the growing likelihood of European war, and imperial defence was seen as less of a priority when there were so many other pressing demands on the public purse.[20]

The impact of German victories in Western Europe was, of course, a disaster for the Dutch, Belgians, French, and British. Almost overnight, the Dutch were forced to move their whole government apparatus to London, as did the Belgians after a period of administrative and political chaos. In the French case, the armistice and advent of the Vichy regime heralded an undeclared civil war across the empire. In the Dutch case, the damage done to imperial power was compounded when the Japanese overran the East Indies and systematically dismantled all vestiges of Dutch rule. Japanese hegemony in South East Asia wrought havoc with the ingrained ideas of white superiority, both on the part of the colonizers and of the colonized. Whether local nationalist leaders saw advantage in cooperating with the Japanese, as in Indonesia, or assumed prime responsibility for resisting them, as in Vietnam, Burma, and Malaya, the damage done to European colonialism proved irreparable. Years of wartime control from Tokyo coupled with the structural problems of restoring colonial authority post-war proved overwhelming, not least as both the Dutch and French were compelled to turn to the resource-strapped British and the uncommitted Americans for help. For Britain, the defeats inflicted by Japan represented an intolerable loss of the prestige essential to colonialism, making it vital that the South East Asian territories be regained *without* external help. In the meantime, indigenous political movements established themselves as *de facto* rulers, achieving a degree of credibility that made them difficult to dislodge. Formally negotiating with people regarded as collaborators of the Japanese, as communist insurgents, or as terrorists proved a step too far for successive Dutch and French governments, and strained British resources and ingenuity to their limit. This intransigence was compounded by the lack of hard information, or deliberate misinformation, received about actual conditions in the colonies. To some extent, this served the purposes of those intransigents that disparaged a negotiated settlement, favouring a military solution instead. Yet, even they were misled by their own propaganda, mistakenly assuming their armed forces' superiority in the ensuing conflicts.

Military intervention in Indonesia and Indochina became a practical proposition from 1946 onwards, by which time sufficient forces had been shipped in. The Dutch and French recourse to arms was disastrous nonetheless. Initial victories did not win over hearts and minds, nor did they prevent Indonesian and Vietnamese forces from continuing a guerrilla campaign from the interior that would ultimately sap Dutch and French resources. Yet even before this became an issue, the troops themselves proved difficult to control. Loyalist colonial soldiers had their own agendas and scores to settle with the nationalists; some European troops were poorly trained, others underequipped. Whereas in earlier colonial campaigns European military conduct rarely drew sustained international criticism, media reportage of the conflicts in South East Asia meant that their every aspect was examined round the globe. The atrocities carried out by both sides rapidly entered the international public domain, making it less likely that other Western states, even those temperamentally inclined to assist the Dutch in Indonesia, would do so. American opinion remained avowedly anti-colonial and the reporting of Dutch actions did nothing to alter this view.

US intervention proved critical to the outcome of decolonization in South East Asia, but in markedly different ways. There is no question that it was American and international pressure that forced Dutch acquiescence in a negotiated retreat from empire in Indonesia in 1949.[21] Opinions at home had not really changed since 1945, but the pressures brought to bear on successive Dutch Cabinets ultimately meant that even the most intransigent imperialists were forced to recognize that hegemony in the Indonesian archipelago was over. Withholding Marshall Aid was not the only stick used by the Americans to beat the Dutch, but it was a compelling threat for a country still struggling to rebuild its ravaged economy.

Almost the exact reverse applied with regard to Indochina. President Truman's administration put aside long-standing dislikes of French colonialism as the Asian Cold War recast Vietnam as a dangerous, potentially communist front-line state. The result was a *volte-face* in US policy in 1949–50. It was prefigured by French adoption of a military-diplomatic strategy that sought to build up a non-communist alternative to the Vietminh. Whereas external pressure hastened the end of European rule in Indonesia, foreign involvement in the first Indochina War extended the agony of decolonization for another twenty years after France's decisive military defeat at Dien Bien Phu in 1954.[22]

In Britain's case, a critical colonial policy goal was to defeat the communist insurgency in Malaya after 1948. Victory was essential to ensure the uninterrupted flow of profits and dollars earned by Malaya's exports that were pivotal to Britain's, and the Sterling Area's, post-war economic recovery. Vigorous action in Malaya also enabled Britain to argue convincingly, not least to the United States, that it was sharing responsibility for containing communism. Measures that served British imperial and economic interests therefore played the important ancillary function of bolstering the 'special relationship' with Washington.[23] More broadly, it might be argued that American help, as evidenced in Marshall Aid and the security guarantee enshrined in common NATO membership, enabled post-war Britain to divert scarce resources into its colonial empire and so delay decolonization.[24]

Even though most decolonization took place over a twenty-year period, within that brief time span the dynamics of domestic politics and a rapidly changing international situation make direct comparisons between case studies problematic. In the late 1940s European governments could count on public support for empire and the Cold War was still in its infancy. By the late 1950s, that support was fast diminishing, and Cold War attitudes had become more deeply entrenched across the globe. The bitter conflict between Western capitalism and communism had reached a new, more dangerous pitch with the outbreak of the Korean War in June 1950. Alongside this direct confrontation, the US vision of European imperialism underwent fundamental revision. Thus, while Washington's public rhetoric retained its anti-colonial flavour, there was an increasing acceptance that decolonization might open the door to communist infiltration and that colonial rule might be the best guarantee of stability on new Cold War front lines in Asia and Africa. In this context, the French struggle in Indo-China captured most attention. Other contemporaneous conflicts were secondary. One such was New Guinea, which, in spite of its size, had little to offer as a strategic or economic prize. However, the Dutch process of detachment from New Guinea does show how domestic opinion slowly shifted after the traumas of Indonesia. Stern refusal to concede anything further to the Indonesians initially held sway, but gradually dissipated as economic interests and some confessional groups came to see this intransigence as a hindrance to their long-term presence in the region.

There are strong echoes of these sentiments in changing French official and corporate assessments of formal political control in the sub-Saharan federations of French West and Equatorial Africa. In both cases, opportunities clearly existed to cement viable working relationships with former colonial dependencies. That is not to say, however, that in francophone black Africa independence did not have to be fought for and won. The experience of African trade unionists, RDA activists, and opponents of the 1958 French 'Community' project suggests otherwise.

Some recent commentators have ascribed the dramatic acceleration of British decolonization during the early 1960s to the wider international context, specifically the deepening Cold War, rather than to colonial nationalism as such. The issue here is one of degree; namely, the extent to which the geopolitical background of Cold War lent colonial nationalists their enhanced bargaining position during this period. We do not have to accept the view that decolonization was ultimately 'a gigantic footnote to the Cold War' to recognize the impact East-West rivalries might have had on rapidly changing relationships between the colonial powers and their overseas territories.[25] A recurring theme in London's discussions was the importance of 'harnessing' the energy of nationalism, identifying new, pro-Western groups willing to cooperate with the British, in order to forestall the ascendancy of potentially hostile groups that were likely to be supported by Moscow or Beijing.

The fear that communist influence would escalate into outright intervention crystallized during the Congo crisis. But the re-emergence of 'metropolitan' explanations of decolonization, which recent stress on the Cold War might suggest, does not, in fact, imply any reduction in the significance of the agency of colonial actors. On the contrary, against the background of Cold War tensions, and mounting international condemnation of colonialism, seen particularly in the deliberations of the expanding United Nations, the extent of nationalist mobilization (amounting in some instances to all-out insurrection) could prove decisive in persuading a colonial power to withdraw. Equally, the Cold War offered nationalists from Indonesia to Algeria a wider framework for their activities as well as opportunities to exploit East-West rivalries to ensure external backing for their newly independent states.[26]

Attitudes towards empire in the immediate aftermath of the war were also conditioned by the urgent requirements of domestic reconstruction. In Britain's case, this reconstruction was meant to ensure the country's ability to act independently, or failing that, to regain a stature sufficiently great for the country to be taken seriously as the United States' most important ally. Only briefly did London contemplate a joint West European approach to questions of reconstruction through colonial development.[27] For countries like France, the Netherlands, and Belgium, however, central to the vision of post-war reconstruction was deeper economic and political cooperation between Western European states. In spite of official arguments to the contrary, over time it became harder to see where colonies might fit into this more integrated Western Europe.[28] There was an obvious disjuncture between France's adoption of a stronger leadership role in Western Europe from 1947 onwards and growing internal opposition to its imperial control overseas. Herein lay the central paradox of the Fourth Republic's international history. The dichotomy between foreign policy success and colonial policy failure should be set alongside what William Hitchcock dubs 'the paradox of French recovery'. A regime beset with political divisions pursued an innovative modernization programme that laid the foundations for almost thirty years of spectacular economic growth.[29] It was thus doubly ironic that colonial problems ultimately overwhelmed the Fourth Republic at the very moment that its success in transforming the French economy deprived the country's colonial connections of their material importance to national prosperity. If anything, the costs of colonial war in Algeria and the reliance of otherwise uncompetitive exporters on reserved colonial markets suggested that empire was a net economic burden that allowed outmoded industrial practices to survive.[30]

Official estimates of military expenditure in Algeria during 1956 and 1957, for example, ranged from 344 to 700 billion francs per year, or between two and four times the budget of the French rail network, SNCF.[31] The financial costs of the Algerian conflict highlighted uncomfortable facts that leading economists such as Maurice Allais, as well as *Paris Match* journalist Raymond Cartier, had pinpointed earlier: maintaining empire was a drain on the exchequer and an impediment to the modernization of industry essential to French competitiveness on the open market.[32] Even more disquietingly, these costs were incurred after military expenditure in Indochina had averaged 10 per cent of state expenditure in each year from reoccupation in late 1945 to the final repatriation of the colonial expeditionary force in 1955. Little wonder then that, as the Algerian War weighed heavier on the French defence budget, senior Finance Ministry officials such as Director of Overseas Finance Guillaume Guindey, Budget Director Roger Goetze, and Treasury Chief François Bloch-Lainé became influential voices in government debate over imperial policy.[33]

Richard Kuisel, Kristin Ross, and, most recently, Barnett Singer, have highlighted the speed and enthusiasm with which post-war French society embraced American-type consumerism in the 1950s. It was ironic that as French colonial domination was coming to an end, France faced unprecedented cultural domination by the United States. Ross links economic modernization and the growth of consumerism to public attitudes to decolonization, the Algerian War in particular. More significant to us here, consumer culture generated a preoccupation with hygiene, exemplified by bright homes complete with new kitchen appliances and electrical goods. In this brave new world of consumerist aspiration and self-consciously 'modern couples', empire seemed irrelevant and alien to metropolitan life.[34] The suburbanization of French cities, marked by the movement of workers and colonial immigrants to housing projects around city limits, added to the clinical separation between bourgeois culture and those removed to its physical margins, many of them from former colonial dependencies.[35] In Britain, meanwhile, it has been suggested that the middle classes, riding a similar wave of post-war consumerism, and benefiting from the extended welfare provision after 1945, became anxious that government should not embark on potentially expensive colonial adventures, especially if these jeopardized funding for the welfare state.[36]

In France, the turning away from all things colonial was apparent in several facets of republican political culture. In 1961 de Gaulle's government transferred the remains of France's greatest imperial proconsul, Marshal Lyautey, from his burial place in Morocco's capital, Rabat, to the Invalides in Paris. It was a gesture loaded with symbolism.[37] The memorialization of empire through museums, monuments, and ceremonial dedications of public spaces and buildings tells us much about changing attitudes to colonialism. As Robert Aldrich has shown, imperial memorializing peaked in the years after the First World War, combining celebration of France's colonial achievements with concerted state efforts to foster popular imperialism. Iconic representations of martial valour and colonial loyalty to France were erected across the country just as territories from Morocco to Vietnam slid into violence and rebellion during the 1920s. Such overt celebrations of imperial grandeur fell out of favour after 1945. On the one hand, colonial war and imperial withdrawal was too raw an experience to be publicly recognized in statues or museum cabinets. On the other, a new myth of France, opponent of US 'imperialism', champion of Third Worldism, and cradle of a vibrant francophone culture took hold to the exclusion of anything that smacked of erstwhile colonial oppression.[38]

There are parallels to be drawn here with social changes under way in the Netherlands. At the dawn of the 1960s, a time of rapidly accelerating decolonization, the Dutch transfer of New Guinea reflected a similar public disengagement from matters of empire. While not everyone in the Netherlands was prepared to forget the atrocities of the 1945–9 period, most had lost their commitment to empire and merely sought to save face in the process of colonial detachment. Between the loss of Indonesia and the transfer of New Guinea, the Dutch state and its people had made the mental transition from an imperial state to a vital constituent of the new Europe. At the same time, the UN's growing role, coupled with the continuing centrality of the United States and wider international opinion in decolonization issues, once again demonstrated the inability of the Dutch as a 'middling' European power to pursue an independent course of action in a large colonial territory.

Not so in the smaller territories. The smallest European dependencies – the islands and coastal enclaves dotted around the world's oceans – produced some of the most idiosyncratic patterns of decolonization. At the very end of the twentieth century several of these oceanic outposts of colonial rule, the 'confetti of empire', endured across the globe. The one element of the 1946 French Union scheme that far outlived the demise of the Fourth Republic in 1958 was the DOM-TOMs of the French Caribbean and the French Pacific. In some cases, such as French Guiana, formal separation from France threatened economic unviability. In others, decentralization assuaged demands for full independence. In several island territories, from New Caledonia to Guadeloupe, the very question of decolonization proved acutely divisive. Perhaps, however, it is Dutch withdrawal from Suriname that presents the strangest case of all. While there was no internal demand for self-government, successive Dutch regimes had no real justification for change. While the West Indian colonies were a drain on resources, independence alone would not change the financial commitments that the Dutch state would have to make to ensure their viability. Moreover, the political balance of three racially discrete groups generated positive pressure to uphold the status quo. It was only an unusual set of electoral circumstances that enabled a Social-Democrat-led Cabinet in The Hague to act. In this context, decolonization was driven, not by popular pressure within the colony, but by a metropolitan government keen to shed a burdensome imperial tie. The fact that no such circumstances occurred in the internal government of the Antilles has meant that these few remaining islands have, somewhat anachronistically, remained part of the Dutch state into the twenty-first century.

Governmental and public efforts to come to terms with difficult imperial pasts have produced mixed results. Take the French case. In a striking bid to 'decolonize' aspects of Paris's architectural history, during the 1970s the names of imperial conquistadors were sandblasted off the exterior walls of the former Ministry of Colonies, and the triumphant murals and frescos of the École Coloniale and the Musée Colonial were hidden from view. Not until the 1980s did the French authorities make sustained efforts to address the contested nature of the colonial past, the sacrifices of colonial peoples and of French soldiers sent to fight colonial wars. After the election of the Socialist President, François Mitterrand, in 1981, central government showed greater willingness to confront the physical losses, psychological scars, and national divisions caused by wars of decolonization. Noted opponents of slavery and of colonial oppression were, for the first time, officially commemorated. Such acknowledgement was no easy task for politicians, let alone for the many veterans, displaced *pieds noirs*, and marginalized *harki* exiles, for whom decolonization, and the Algerian War especially, remained the defining moment of their lives. Jacques Chirac's conservative administration continued the commemorative process, but shifted its emphasis towards the contributions and sacrifices of the French in their former colonial territories.[39]

Facing up to recent colonial actions was – and is – an incremental process signposted by a series of commemorative landmarks.[40] Some of these were material, such as the belated 1974 conferment of veterans' benefits to returned soldiers from Algeria. Others were cultural: Benjamin Stora's 1991 television documentaries on 'the Algerian years'; Bertrand Tavernier's film, '*La Guerre sans nom*' (*The War without a name*), recording interviews with traumatized former soldiers; an increasing number of books and press articles revisiting dirty war practices and the use of torture against FLN suspects.[41] Some were simply unavoidable: the acknowledgement of past colonial crimes brought to light once more during the sensational 1997 trial of Vichy collaborator and former Pairs police chief, Maurice Papon; the eventual government declaration two years later that the conflict in Algeria had indeed been a 'war'.[42] Still others were monumental: the opening in 1993 of a national monument and museum centre in Fréjus to the Indochina War; a North African war memorial on the Paris Quai Branly unveiled by President Chirac in 2002.[43] In other official gestures, the provenance of overtly colonialist monuments and public buildings that had been 'rebranded' or allowed to fall into disrepair was acknowledged once more as national and municipal authorities made genuine attempts to confront and explain France's colonial legacy. In May 2004 mayor of Paris Bertrand Delanoë even renamed a Paris square, the Place Maurice Audin, in recognition of a University of Algiers academic tortured and killed by the French army in 1957 for his opposition to the Algerian War.[44]

As with France and Algeria, public memory of the East Indies in the Netherlands was coloured by the traumatic final collapse of Dutch hegemony. This memory is also highly selective, spotlighting certain events, concealing others. In this context, nationalist atrocities and economic losses loomed large in public discussion, whereas Dutch military excesses during the police actions were overlooked. The returning soldiers, already antagonized by what they perceived to have been a political 'sell-out', were further incensed by society's lack of recognition of their sacrifices. Public memory was also shaped by an influx of former colonial administrators, professional troops, and their families that needed to be rapidly integrated into Dutch society. Only over time did the historiography shift from its early hostile preoccupation with Indonesian nationalism towards a more benign view of the colonial past. In the words of Frances Gouda,

> Most of the historical imaginings of 'Our Indies', whether they are conjured up by elderly … scholars, former government officials and private Indies residents, or even by an occasional modern-day historian, frequently boil down to a story grounded in a natural sense of superiority and a simple faith in the right to rule. Even if these narratives are modulated by a self-imposed ethical duty to 'civilize' and 'uplift', they nonetheless devise a tale that is a far cry from the renowned Dutch habit of compromise.[45]

Britain's public memory of decolonization appears equally selective. While nationalist 'atrocities' are emphasized, the handling of the British response has, until very recently, been curiously muted. This is particularly striking, given the concern shown by successive British governments over possible domestic reactions to colonial counterinsurgency methods, and the real political repercussions felt in Britain when excesses were revealed.

The fact that decolonization is closely bound up with contested historical memories reminds us that its effects still reverberate among the societies touched by it. Put another way, the history of decolonization is also the history of the contemporary world. It is an often violent and frequently tragic story in which the interaction of imperial powers, superpowers, and Third World states generated some of the most intractable conflicts, the longest wars, and the bitterest clashes of the Cold War and post-Cold War eras.[46] It is also a two-way history in which the actions of colonial peoples and colonial nationalist movements were every bit as significant as the decisions and opinions of European governments and their allies. In the case of Portuguese Africa, for instance, local contests for power were every bit as significant as the overarching fight to be free of colonial domination. Left-wing nationalist movements in Mozambique and Angola were the first to mobilize the rural population in the independence struggle. Meanwhile, their ideological confreres in Guiné-Bissau adapted existing political structures to create a form of people's government in those areas liberated from Portuguese control. In nationalist-held zones, insurgent groups even organized elections to select representative governing bodies that would assume control of the state apparatus at independence. With broad popular support, once independence was won, the dominant nationalist coalitions in Mozambique and Guinea-Bissau – FRELIMO and the PAIGC – were thus in a position to replace the colonial state rather than simply to inherit it. By contrast, in Angola, the Marxist MPLA was never able to mobilize, still less to unite, the nation against the Portuguese. Dogged by conflict with its UNITA rivals and unable to transcend its essentially urban power base, the MPLA 'never overcame the ethnic, political, and military obstacles which stood in the way of nationalist and socialist ambitions'.[47]

What these examples suggest is that the collapse of Europe's colonial empires cannot be reduced to simple 'metropolitan' or 'peripheral' explanations, quite the reverse. Colonial subjects and complex internecine rivalries were as critical to colonial withdrawal, and the form that national independence took, as were the actions of colonial masters, who frequently departed amid social chaos and a loss of political control. Little wonder then that periods of sociopolitical instability, some transitory, some near permanent accompanied the end of empire.[48] Little wonder, too, that decolonization became such a volatile international issue, capable of disturbing the alignments and political certainties of Cold War. From this it is only a short step to the conclusion that decolonization and Cold War are closely related, if not quite two sides of the same coin then certainly parts of the same historical legacy.[49]

Few would challenge the conclusion that decolonization's impact was global. If that was indeed the case, why did so many critical decisions about the future of colonial peoples arouse relatively little public interest in Europe? It is easy to counter here that events as diverse as the Dutch police actions in Indonesia, the 1958 May Crisis in France, and the Lisbon revolution of April 1974 prove that decolonization precipitated fundamental political change in Europe too.[50] And Europe's 1968 – a shorthand for the civil rights protests, radical leftism, and political activism that spread across the continent and beyond in the late 1960s – was in many ways bound up with growing revulsion among young people for the racist and authoritarian reflexes of their ruling elites.[51] Nonetheless, there are numerous occasions in which colonial policy choices with devastating human consequences made little impact 'back home'. In some ways, this reveals more about public engagement with politics than anything else. Many of the events recounted in this book took place after universal suffrage had been introduced to the European imperial nations. With French women at last enfranchised in April 1945, only in Salazar's Portugal was there no democratic accountability.

Yet surely this tells us nothing. Trying to explain patterns of decolonization, and especially the incidence of war and violence within it, by reference to metropolitan regime type is problematic. While 'democratic peace theory', essentially the argument that democracies are less likely to wage war (particularly with one another) than non-democratic regimes, has some traction in the analysis of decolonization, it does not offer any comprehensive answers.[52] Democratically elected politicians answerable to their publics signed off on acts of colonial violence, even war, with alarming frequency. Again and again, the connections between the metropolitan political process and decolonization struggles reveal no such accountability whatsoever. The opening stages of the Indochina conflict provide one such example. France went to war in Vietnam without full Cabinet approval, let alone a popular mandate. The architects of this policy, from Admiral d'Argenlieu in Saigon to Georges Bidault in Paris, were never sanctioned for what amounted to a criminal abuse of power. Similar analogies could be drawn with the repression of the Madagascar uprising in 1947 or the deposition of the Moroccan Sultan Mohammed V in August 1953. These instances cannot simply be dismissed as evidence of flawed constitutional arrangements, in this particular case, the Fourth Republic's lack of clear executive control. They were also part of a deeper problem: the fact that Europe's political elites were rarely held to account for their colonial actions. In Britain, this process may have been assisted by the broad, cross-party consensus on colonial issues, which is commonly claimed to have held for much of the decolonization period. The consensus was not unconditional: it was severely strained over the future of the settler colonies in East and Central Africa. Nevertheless, British policymakers were perhaps fortunate that domestic attention tended, as in earlier periods, to focus on issues with a more direct bearing on everyday life, such as employment, health, and housing.[53] Equally, although the 'process' of decolonization could seldom be controlled from London, its presentation to the metropolitan public was something that preoccupied all post-war British governments, the common theme being that independence implied no abrupt change either in Britain's world status, or in its relations with its former colonies.

Nor should the politicians and colonial governors shoulder all the blame. If decolonization should remind Europeans of one thing, surely it is their obligation as citizens to interest themselves in vital overseas policy decisions and hold their governments to account for them. Unfortunately, there is scant evidence that this occurred in the Europe of the 1940s and early '50s. The prevailing political cultures of the day, the relative obscurity of some colonial problems, and the existence of more pressing worries closer to home suggest that, as historians, we should appreciate why this was so. But the fact remains that popular indifference or, at best, a sluggish public realization of what was being done in their name in colonial territories created a permissive atmosphere in which political violence against colonial peoples went frequently unobserved and generally unpunished. Recent revelations about the scale of torture, rape, and arbitrary killing by British security forces during the Mau Mau emergency point to the fact that for all of Europe's colonial powers the gulf between lofty ideals and colonial practices was staggering.[54] The Foreign and Commonwealth Office's recent 'discovery' of over twenty-thousand British colonial government files in a Buckinghamshire storage facility is a case in point.[55] Many of these records relate to army and police actions, punishments and killings, providing a stark reminder of how systematic colonial repression could be.[56] Linked to this, the belated offer of limited compensation to Kenyans abused by the security forces, while intrinsically welcome, only highlights the fact that the traumas of empire remain issues of bitter, contemporary dispute.[57] If there is a didactic purpose to the study of decolonization, it must be that it behoves the citizen to look beyond the domestic horizon and take a closer interest in their government's overseas involvements.

Finally, historians and other commentators have become increasingly aware of the possible legacies of empire for the former colonial powers. Among all of Europe's former colonial powers, there are those who see the empire (and their own country's post-imperial condition) as a potent influence on questions of national identity, ethnicity, gender relations, and even constitutional make up. From this perspective, arguably, decolonization has not been matched by 'de-colonialization' in the imperial mindset. Britain, in particular, has yet to resolve fully some aspects of its former world role, suggesting that the empire continues to influence not only Britain's reading of its own past, but its future, too. We face the possible paradox that whereas former colonial populations see the colonial period as of diminishing relevance to them, some Europeans are yet to discard it wholeheartedly, and live on in its shadow.[58]

NOTES

Introduction

1. Michael A. Reynolds, *Shattering Empires: The Clash and Collapse of the Ottoman and Russian Empires, 1908-1918* (Cambridge: Cambridge University Press, 2011), 1–8, 252–3.

2. Ronald Grigor Suny, 'The Empire strikes out: Imperial Russia, "national" identity, and theories of empire', in Ronald Grigor Suny and Terry Martin (eds), *A State of Nations: Empire and Nation-Making in the Age of Lenin and Stalin* (Oxford: Oxford University Press, 2001), 24–32.

3. Reynolds, *Shattering Empires*, 17.

4. For the impact of empire on metropolitan society in the decades surrounding decolonization, see Andrew Thompson (ed.), *Britain's Experience of Empire in the Twentieth Century: OHBE Companion Series* (Oxford: Oxford University Press, 2011); and, for the effect of a particular crisis of empire – the Algerian War – on French society, see Raphaëlle Branche and Sylvie Thénault (eds), *La France en guerre 1954-1962: Expériences métropolitaines de la guerre d'indépendance algérienne* (Paris: Autrement, 2008).

5. Gary Magee and Andrew S. Thompson, *Empire and Globalisation: Networks of People, Goods and Capital in the British World, c.1850-1914* (Cambridge: Cambridge University Press, 2010).

6. United States National Archives (USNA), RG 59, Bureau of African Affairs, Lot file 63D393/Box 4, Bureau of Intelligence and Research paper, 'Remnants of the colonial system', 25 June 1962.

7. See, for example, Alain Rouvez, *Disconsolate Empires: French, British and Belgian Military Involvement in Post-Colonial Sub-Saharan Africa* (Washington, DC: University Press of America, 1994).

8. William Eckhardt, 'Civilizations, empire and wars', *Journal of Peace Research*, 27:1 (1990), 12–15.

9. For examples of this in French-speaking Africa, see John F. Clark and David E. Gardinier (eds), *Political Reform in Francophone Africa* (Boulder, CO: Westview Press, 1997).

10. John Darwin, 'Decolonization and the end of Empire', in Robin W. Winks (ed.), *The Oxford History of the British Empire Volume V Historiography* (Oxford: Oxford University Press, 1999), 545; Martin Thomas, 'A path not taken: British perspectives on French colonial violence after 1945', in L. J. Butler and Sarah Stockwell (eds), *The Wind of Change: Harold Macmillan and British Decolonization* (Basingstoke: Palgrave Macmillan, 2013), 159–79.

11. See Darwin, 'Decolonization and the end of Empire', 542; Robin Winks, 'On decolonization and informal Empire', *American Historical Review*, 81:3 (1976), 540–56.

12. Frederick Quinn, *The French Overseas Empire* (Boulder, CO: Westview Press, 2000), 230.

13. Odd Arne Westad, 'The new international history of the Cold War: three (possible) paradigms', *Diplomatic History*, 24:4 (2000), 562–3.

14. Roger Kanet, 'The superpower quest for Empire: the Cold War and Soviet support for "wars of national liberation",' *Cold War History*, 6:3 (2006), 331–52.

15. Nzongola-Ntalaja, 'Bureaucracy, elite, new class: who serves whom and why in Mobutu's Zaire?' *Canadian Journal of African Studies*, 18:1 (1984), 99–102.

16. Martin Shipway, *Decolonization and its Impact: A Comparative Approach to the End of the European Colonial Empires* (Oxford: Blackwell, 2008), 115.

17. Robert H. Jackson, *Quasi-States: Sovereignty, International Relations and the Third World* (Cambridge: Cambridge University Press, 1993), 5, 21–31.

18. Westad, 'The new international history of the Cold War', 563.

19. See the illuminating discussion in John Darwin, *The End of the British Empire: The Historical Debate* (Oxford: Blackwell, 1991), 3–7.

20. For analysis of recent perspectives on development, see Corinna Unger (ed.), 'Modernizing missions: approaches to "developing" the non-western world after 1945', *Journal of Modern European History*, 8:1 (2010). For important case studies of development policies and their various impacts, see Joseph M. Hodge, Gerald Hödl and Martina Kopf (eds), *Developing Africa: Concepts and Practices in Twentieth-Century Colonialism* (Manchester: Manchester University Press, 2014).

21. Corinna R. Unger, 'The United States, decolonization, and the education of Third World elites', in Jost Dülffer and Marc Frey (eds), *Elites and Decolonization in the Twentieth Century* (Basingstoke: Palgrave Macmillan, 2011), 241–52.

22. For two expressions of this self-destructive tendency, see Suny, 'The Empire Strikes Out', 30–1; John Darwin, 'What was the late colonial state', *Itinerario*, 23:3–4 (1999), 73–82.

23. Julius Nyerere, the architect of Tanzanian Socialism, is often identified as the honourable exception to this general rule; see Andreas Eckert, 'Julius Nyerere, Tanzanian elites, and the project of African socialism', in Dülffer and Frey, *Elites and Decolonization*, 216–18, 226–8.

24. Partha Chatterjee, *Nationalist Thought in the Colonial World: A Derivative Discourse* (Minneapolis: University of Minnesota Press, 1993), 30, 50–1; also cited in Gary Wilder, *The French Imperial Nation-State: Negritude and Colonial Humanism between the Two World Wars* (Chicago: University of Chicago Press, 2005), 203.

25. Cited in Orde Arne Westad, *The Global Cold War: Third World Interventions and the Making of Our Times* (Cambridge: Cambridge University Press, 2005), 90.

26. For a thoughtful discussion of these differing theories, see Ebere Nwaubani, *The United States and Decolonization in West Africa, 1950-1960* (Rochester, NY: University of Rochester Press, 2001), 1–25.

27. Crawford Young, 'The colonial state and post-colonial crisis', in Prosser Gifford and Wm. Roger Louis (eds), *Decolonization and African Independence: The Transfers of Power, 1960-1980* (New Haven: Yale University Press, 1988), 5; see also the editors' trenchant comments on pages ix–xiii.

28. Judith M. Brown, 'Gandhi and civil resistance in India, 1917-47: key issues', in Adam Roberts and Timothy Garton-Ash (eds), *Civil Resistance and Power Politics: The Experience of Non-Violent Action from Gandhi to the Present* (Oxford: Oxford University Press, 2011), 43–56.

29. Mary L. Dudziak, *Cold War and Civil Rights: Race and the Image of American Democracy* (Princeton, NJ: Princeton University Press, 2000); Brenda Gayle Plummer, *In Search of Power: African Americans in the Era of Decolonization, 1956-1974* (Cambridge: Cambridge University Press, 2012).

30. David C. Engerman, 'The Second World's Third World', *Kritika*, 12:1 (Winter 2011), 183–211.

31. Miles Larmer, 'Historicising activism in late colonial and post-colonial sub-Saharan Africa', *Journal of Historical Sociology*, 28 (2014), 1–8.

32. Frederick Cooper, 'Possibility and constraint: African independence in colonial perspective', *JAH*, 49 (2008), 167–96.

33. Frederick Cooper, 'Alternatives to Nationalism in French Africa, 1945-60', in Dülffer and Frey, *Elites and Decolonization*, 110–19.

34. Elizabeth Schmidt, 'Top down or bottom up? Nationalist mobilization reconsidered, with special reference to Guinea', *American Historical Review*, 110 (October, 2005), 975–1014.

35. Raymond Betts, *France and Decolonization, 1900-1960* (London: Macmillan, 1991), 128.

36. An important new work on Fanon's thought is Leo Zeilig, *Frantz Fanon: The Militant Philosopher of Third World Liberation* (London: I.B. Tauris, 2014).

37. Frederick Cooper, 'The dialectics of decolonization: nationalism and labor movements in postwar French Africa', in Frederick Cooper and Ann Laura Stoler (eds), *Tensions of Empire: Colonial Cultures in a Bourgeois World* (Berkeley: University of California Press, 1997), 406–35.

38. Chris Tiffin and Alan Lawson (eds), *De-Scribing Empire: Post-Colonialism and Textuality* (London: Routledge, 1994), 3–6, 230–4.

39. See the excellent introduction to Alec G. Hargreaves and Mark McKinney (eds), *Post-Colonial Cultures in France* (London: Routledge, 1997), 14–16; Ann McLintock, 'The angel of progress: pitfalls of the term "post-colonialism"', *Social Text*, 10:2 (1992), 84–98.

40. Frederick Cooper and Ann Laura Stoler, 'Between metropole and colony: rethinking a research agenda', in Cooper and Stoler, *Tensions of Empire*, 29.

41. Alice L. Conklin, 'Boundaries unbound: teaching French history as colonial history and colonial history as French history', *French Historical Studies*, 23:2 (2000), 220.

42. Johannes Fabian, 'Missions and the colonization of African languages: developments in the former Belgian Congo', *Canadian Journal of African Studies*, 17:2 (1983), 165–87.

43. Alan Isaacman, 'Peasants, work and the labor process: forced cotton cultivation in colonial Mozambique, 1938-1961', *Journal of Social History*, 25:4 (1992), 815–56; M. Bowen, *The State against the Peasantry: Rural Struggles in Colonial and Postcolonial Mozambique* (Charlottesville: University of Virginia Press, 2000); Miguel Bandeira Jerónimo, 'The "Civilisation Guild": race and labour in the third Portuguese Empire, c. 1870-1930', in Francisco Bethencourt and Adrian Pearce (eds), *Racism and Ethnic Relations in the Portuguese-Speaking World* (New York: Oxford University Press, 2012), 173–99.

44. Witness what Laurent Dubois terms the 'republican racism' to emerge in the French Caribbean after slave emancipation in the 1790s: Dubois, *A Colony of Citizens: Revolution and Slave Emancipation in the French Caribbean, 1787-1804* (Chapel Hill: University of North Carolina Press, 2004), 3–4, 166–8.

45. Jonathan K. Gosnell, *The Politics of Frenchness in Colonial Algeria, 1930-1954* (Rochester, NY: University of Rochester Press, 2002), 218.

46. Ronald Hyam, 'Bureaucracy and "Trusteeship" in the Colonial Empire', in J. M. Brown and Wm. Roger Louis (eds), *Oxford History of the British Empire (OHBE) Volume 4: The Twentieth Century* (Oxford: Oxford University Press, 1999), 255–79. For a useful survey, see John Darwin, 'What was the late colonial state?', *Itinerario*, 22:3-4 (1999), 73–82.

47. W. B. Cohen, 'The Colonized as child: British and French colonial rule', *African Historical Studies*, 3:2 (1970), 427–31.

48. Benoît de l'Estoile, 'Rationalizing colonial domination? Anthropology and native policy in French-ruled Africa', in Benoît de l'Estoile, Federico Neiburg, and Lygia Sigaud (eds), *Empires, Nations, and Natives: Anthropology and State-Making* (Durham, NC: Duke University Press, 2005), 49–54.

49. Keith Panter-Brick, 'Independence, French style', in Prosser Gifford and Wm. Roger Louis (eds), *Decolonization and African Independence: The Transfers of Power, 1960-1980* (New Haven: Yale University Press, 1988), 73, 77.

50. J. Darwin, 'British decolonization since 1945: a pattern or a puzzle?', *JICH*, 12:2 (1984), 187–209; Ronald Hyam, 'Winds of change: the Empire and Commonwealth', in W. Kaiser and G. Staerck (eds), *British Foreign Policy 1955-64: Contracting Options* (Basingstoke: Macmillan, 2000), 190–208.

51. See, e.g., Ronald Hyam, *Britain's Declining Empire: The Road to Decolonisation 1918-1968* (Cambridge: Cambridge University Press, 2006), 301–4; Wm. Roger Louis and Ronald Robinson, 'The imperialism of decolonization', *JICH*, 22:3 (1994), 462–511; and Ronald Hyam and Wm. Roger Louis (eds), *British Documents on the End of Empire Series A, Volume 4 The Conservative Government and the End of Empire 1957-1964* (London: The Stationery Office, 2000).

52. The classic statement of this concept is R. Robinson, 'Non-European foundations of European imperialism: sketch for a theory of collaboration', in R. Owen and B. Sutcliffe (eds), *Studies in*

the Theory of Imperialism (London: Longman, 1972), 117–40. For a rebuttal, see A. Adu Boahen, *African Perspectives on Colonialism* (Baltimore: The Johns Hopkins University Press, 1987), 41.

53. Darwin, 'Decolonization and the End of Empire', 542–3, 549.

54. Hafid Gafaiti, 'Nationalism, colonialism, and ethnic discourse in the construction of French identity', in Tyler Stovall and Georges van den Abbeele (eds), *French Civilization and its Discontents: Orientalism, Colonialism, Race* (Lanham: Lexington Books, 2003), 198–210.

55. See, for example, Robert Bourgi, *Le Général de Gaulle et l'Afrique noire* (Paris: LGDJ, 1980); John Chipman, *French Power in Africa* (Oxford: Blackwell, 1989), and, less convincingly, David Chuter, *Humanity's Soldier: France and International Security, 1919-2001* (Oxford: Berghahn, 1996).

56. Hargreaves and McKinney, *Post-Colonial Cultures in France*, 3–4, 11.

57. See, for example, A. J. Stockwell, 'British decolonisation: The record and the records', *Contemporary European History*, 15:4 (2006), 573–83.

58. Crawford Young, *The Politics of the Congo: Decolonization and Independence* (Princeton, NJ: Princeton University Press, 1965); Mahmood Mamdani, *When Victims Become Killers: Colonialism, Nativism, and the Genocide in Rwanda* (Princeton, NJ: Princeton University Press, 2001); Patrick Chabal, *A History of Postcolonial Lusophone Africa* (Bloomington: Indiana University Press, 2002), 41–50.

Chapter 1

1. John Darwin, *Britain and Decolonisation: The Retreat from Empire in the Post-War World* (Basingstoke: Macmillan, 1988), 28–9; Kent Fedorowich and Carl Bridge, 'Mapping the British World', *JICH*, 31:2 (2003), 1–15.

2. John Darwin, *The Empire Project: The Rise and Fall of the British World-System, 1830-1970* (Cambridge: Cambridge University Press, 2009), 1–20.

3. J. M. Mackenzie (ed.), *Imperialism and Popular Culture* (Manchester: Manchester University Press, 1986).

4. S. Howe, *Anticolonialism in British Politics: The Left and the End of Empire, 1918-1964* (Oxford: Oxford University Press, 1993); Nicholas Owen, 'Critics of empire in Britain', in Brown and Louis (eds), *OHBE IV: The Twentieth Century*.

5. See esp. Barbara Bush, *Imperialism, Race and Resistance: Africa and Britain, 1919-1945* (London: Routledge, 1999), 203–47.

6. Christian Hogsbjerg, *C.L.R. James in Imperial Britain* (Durham, NC and London: Duke University Press, 2014); Leslie James, *George Padmore and Decolonization from Below: Pan-Africanism, the Cold War, and the End of Empire* (Basingstoke: Palgrave Macmillan, 2014).

7. See, e.g. Howe, *Anticolonialism in British Politics*, 89.

8. Richard Whiting, 'The Empire and British politics' and Andrew Thompson, 'Afterword: the imprint of empire', in Andrew Thompson (ed.), *Britain's Experience of Empire in the Twentieth Century* (Oxford: Oxford University Press, 2012), 337.

9. Partha Sarathi Gupta, *Imperialism and the British Labour Movement; 1914-1964* (London: Macmillan, 1975); D. Goldsworthy, *Colonial Issues in British Politics 1945-1961: From 'Colonial Development' to 'Wind of Change'* (Oxford: Oxford University Press, 1971). Despite their age, these two works remain unsurpassed in their coverage.

10. A. Clayton, '"Deceptive might": imperial defence and security, 1900-1968', in Brown and Louis (eds), *OHBE IV: The Twentieth Century*, 282; A. Clayton, *The British Empire as a Superpower, 1919-39* (London: Macmillan, 1986).

11. S. R. Ashton and S. E. Stockwell (eds), *Imperial Policy and Colonial Practice, 1925-1945: British Documents on the End of Empire Series A, Volume I* (London: HMSO, 1996), xciv n18.

12. W. David McIntyre, 'Australia, New Zealand, and the Pacific Islands', *OHBE IV*, 673.

13. Ashton and Stockwell, *Imperial Policy and Colonial Practice*, xxxiv. Clayton, *OHBE IV*, 283.
B. R. Tomlinson, *The Political Economy of the Raj, 1914-47: The Economics of Decolonization in India* (London: Macmillan, 1979), 114–17. See also R. J. Blyth, *The Empire of the Raj: India, Eastern Africa and the Middle East, 1858-1947* (Basingstoke: Palgrave Macmillan, 2003), esp. 132–69.

14. N. Owen, 'Critics of Empire in Britain', *OHBE IV*, 192.

15. Clayton, *OHBE IV*, 290; D. E. Omissi, *Air Power and Colonial Control: The Royal Air Force 1919-1939* (Manchester: Manchester University Press, 1990); Priya Satia, 'The defense of inhumanity: air control and the British idea of Arabia', *American Historical Review*, 111:1 (2006), 26–30.

16. Antony Best, *British Intelligence and the Japanese Challenge in Asia, 1914-1941* (Basingstoke: Palgrave Macmillan, 2002), 45–7.

17. J. Darwin, 'A third British Empire? The Dominion idea in imperial politics', *OHBE IV*, 69.

18. S. Constantine (ed.), *Emigrants and Empire: British Settlement in the Dominions Between the Wars* (Manchester: Manchester University Press, 1990).

19. Darwin, *OHBE IV*, 72–3, 86; J. M. Mackenzie, '"In touch with the infinite": the BBC and the Empire, 1923-53', in J. M. Mackenzie (ed.), *Imperialism and Popular Culture* (Manchester: Manchester University Press, 1986), 165–91.

20. Simon Potter, *Broadcasting Empire: The BBC and the British World, 1922-1970* (Oxford: Oxford University Press, 2012); Thomas Hajikowski, *The BBC and National Identity in Britain, 1922-53* (Manchester: Manchester University Press, 2010).

21. D. K. Fieldhouse, 'The metropolitan economics of empire', *OHBE IV*, 101.

22. Ashton and Stockwell, *Imperial Policy and Colonial Practice*, lxiii.

23. R. F. Holland, 'The end of an imperial economy: Anglo-Canadian disengagement in the 1930s', *JICH*, 2:1 (1983), 159–75.

24. I. M. Drummond, *Imperial Economic Policy 1917-1939 Studies in Expansion and Protection* (Toronto: University of Toronto Press, 1997), 29–32. Patricia Clavin, *The Failure of Economic Diplomacy: Britain, Germany, France and the United States, 1931-36* (Basingstoke: Macmillan, 1996), 117–41.

25. Ashton and Stockwell, *Imperial Policy and Colonial Practice*, lxiv.

26. P. J. Cain and A. G. Hopkins, *British Imperialism 1688-2000*, 2nd edn (Harlow: Longman, 2001), 464–88.

27. Fieldhouse, *OHBE IV*, 97.

28. P. J. Cain and A. G. Hopkins, 'Afterword: the theory and practice of British Imperialism', in R. E. Dumett (ed.), *Gentlemanly Capitalism and British Imperialism: The New Debate on Empire* (Harlow: Longman, 1999), 210–11.

29. S. Constantine (ed.), *Emigrants and Empire: British Settlement in the Dominions between the Wars* (Manchester: Manchester University Press, 1990).

30. Marjory Harper and Stephen Constantine (eds), *Migration and Empire* [Oxford History of the British Empire Companion Series] (Oxford: Oxford University Press, 2010); Robert Bickers (ed.), *Settlers and Expatriates: Britons over the Seas* (Oxford: Oxford University Press, 2010).

31. Clayton, *OHBE IV*, 284.

32. Ashton and Stockwell, *Imperial Policy and Colonial Practice*, xxx, xxxiv–xxxv, xciv n22.

33. M. J. Cohen, 'British strategy in the Middle East in the wake of the Abyssinian Crisis, 1936-39', in M. J. Cohen and M. Kolinsky (eds), *Britain and the Middle East in the 1930s: Security Problems, 1935-39* (Basingstoke: Macmillan, 1992), 21.

34. Ashton and Stockwell, *Imperial Policy and Colonial Practice*, xciv n26.

35. C. M. Bell, 'The "Singapore strategy" and the deterrence of war with Japan: Winston Churchill, the Admiralty and the dispatch of Force Z', *English Historical Review*, 112 (2001), 608–34.

36. D. Reynolds, *Britannia Overruled: British Policy and World Power in the Twentieth Century* (Harlow: Longman, 1991), 131.

37. K. Jeffery, 'The Second World War', *OHBE IV*, 306–7.

38. Ashton and Stockwell, *Imperial Policy and Colonial Practice*, xxxvii.

39. A. Jackson, *The British Empire and the Second World War* (London: Hambledon Continuum, 2006), 21–40.

40. M. Cowen and N. Westcott, 'British imperial economic policy during the war', in D. Killingray and R. Rathbone (eds), *Africa and the Second World War* (London: Macmillan, 1986), 20–67.

41. Fieldhouse, *OHBE IV*, 92.

42. J. M. Lee, '"Forward thinking" and war: the Colonial Office during the 1940s', *JICH*, 6:1 (1977), 64–79.

43. Tim Harper and Christopher Bayly, *Forgotten Wars: The End of Britain's Asian Empire* (Harmondsworth: Penguin, 2008); B. R. Tomlinson, *New Cambridge History of India Volume 3: The Economy of Modern India, 1939-1970* (Cambridge: Cambridge University Press, 1993), 156–213.

44. David Killingray, *Fighting for Britain: African Soldiers in the Second World War* (Woodbridge: James Currey, 2010), 35–81.

45. Hal Brands, 'Wartime recruiting practices, martial identity and post-World War II demobilization in colonial Kenya', *JAH*, 46:1 (2005), 103–25.

46. Jeffery, *OHBE IV*, 323–4; A. Jackson, *Botswana 1939-1945: An African Country at War* (Oxford: Clarendon Press, 1999); Killingray, *Fighting for Britain*; Brands, 'Wartime recruiting practice', 103, 122; Ashton and Stockwell, *Imperial Policy and Colonial Practice*, xc–xci.

47. Christopher Bayly and Tim Harper, *Forgotten Armies: The Fall of British Asia 1941-1945* (London: Allen Lane, 2004), 106–55.

48. Bayly and Harper, *Forgotten Armies*, 208–30, 315–21.

49. A. J. Stockwell (ed.), *British Documents on the End of Empire Series B, Volume 3 Malaya* (London: HMSO, 1995).

50. John Darwin, 'Imperialism in decline? Tendencies in British imperial policy between the wars', *Historical Journal*, 23:3 (1980), 674.

51. D. George Boyce, 'From Assaye to the *Assaye*: reflections on British government force and authority in India', *Journal of Military History*, 63:3 (1999), 643–64.

52. J. M. Brown, 'India', *OHBE IV*, 432.

53. B. R. Nanda, *In Search of Gandhi: Essays and Reflections* (Oxford: Oxford University Press, 2002), 74–81.

54. Nicholas Owen, *The British Left and India: Metropolitan Anti-Imperialism, 1885-1947* (Oxford: Oxford University Press, 2007), 106–96; Nicholas Owen, 'Critics of empire in Britain', in Brown and Louis (eds), *OHBE IV: The Twentieth Century* (Oxford: Oxford University Press, 1999).

55. On Gandhi's visit, see Judith M. Brown, *Gandhi and Civil Disobedience: The Mahatma in Indian Politics 1928-1934* (Cambridge: Cambridge University Press, 1977), 242–62.

56. Owen, *The British Left*, 235–70.

57. Wm. Roger Louis, 'Introduction', *OHBE IV*, 432.

58. S. Ball, *Baldwin and the Conservative Party: The Crisis of 1929-31* (New Haven: Yale University Press, 1988), 115.

59. Ashton and Stockwell, *Imperial Policy and Colonial Practice*, xlvi.

60. R. J. Moore, 'India in the 1940s', in Winks (ed.), *The Oxford History of the British Empire Volume V Historiography*, 233; J. Darwin, 'Decolonization and the end of empire', *OHBE V*, 545.

61. Darwin, 'Imperialism in Decline?', 677.

62. M. Misra, *Business, Race and Politics in British India, c.1860-1960* (Oxford: Oxford University Press, 1999), chs 5 and 7; M. Misra, 'Gentlemanly capitalism and the Raj: British policy in India between the wars', in Dumett (ed.), (1999), 169–70.

63. D. E. Omissi, *The Sepoy and the Raj: The Indian Army, 1860-1940* (Basingstoke: Macmillan, 1994); Brown, *OHBE IV*, 439–40; Clayton, *OHBE IV*, 285.

64. Louis, *OHBE IV*, 33.

65. Brown, *OHBE IV*, 430.

66. F. Robinson, 'The British Empire and the Muslim World', *OHBE IV*, 410–11.

67. P. Clarke, *The Cripps Version: The Life of Sir Stafford Cripps 1889-1952* (London: Allen Lane, 2002), 292–322; N. Owen, 'The Cripps Mission of 1942: a reinterpretation', *JICH*, 30:1 (2002), 61–98.

68. Brown, *OHBE IV*, 436.

69. Bayly and Harper, *Forgotten Armies*, 248, 277; J. W. Cell, 'The Indian and African freedom struggles: some comparisons', in R. D. King and R. Kilson (eds), *The Statecraft of British Imperialism: Essays in Honour of Wm. Roger Louis* (London: Frank Cass, 1999), 116–17.

70. A. Jalal, *The Sole Spokesman: Jinnah, the Muslim League and the demand for Pakistan* (Cambridge: Cambridge University Press, 1997); A. S. Ahmed, *Jinnah, Pakistan and Islamic Identity: The Search for Saladin* (London: Routledge, 1997), 61–115.

71. R. J. Moore, 'India in the 1940s', *OHBE V*, 237.

72. Jalal, *The Sole Spokesman*, 133–5, 138–9.

73. Jeffery, *OHBE IV*, 324.

74. B. R. Tomlinson, *The Political Economy of the Raj, 1914-1947: The Economics of Decolonization in India* (London: Macmillan, 1979), 92–100.

75. Paul Greenough, 'Indian famines and peasant victims: the case of Bengal in 1943-44', *MAS*, 14:2 (1980), 205–35; Bayly and Harper, *Forgotten Armies*, 251–3, 281–91.

76. See Peter Clarke, *The Last Thousand Days of the British Empire: Churchill, Roosevelt and the Birth of the Pax Americana* (London: Bloomsbury Press, 2008).

77. G. Balfour-Paul, 'Britain's Informal Empire in the Middle East', *OHBE IV*, 503.

78. G. H. Bennett, *British Foreign Policy During the Curzon Period, 1919-24* (Basingstoke: Macmillan, 1995).

79. K. Jeffery, *The British Army and the Crisis of Empire, 1918-22* (Manchester: Manchester University Press, 1984).

80. Martin Thomas, *Empires of Intelligence: Security Services and Colonial Control after 1914* (Berkeley: University of California Press, 2007), ch. 4.

81. J. Darwin, 'An undeclared empire: the British in the Middle East, 1918-39', in R. D. King and R. Kilson (eds), *The Statecraft of British Imperialism: Essays in Honour of Wm. Roger Louis* (London: Frank Cass, 1999), 169.

82. P. Sluglett, 'Formal and informal empire in the Middle East', *OHBE V*, 425–6.

83. D. K. Fieldhouse, *Western Imperialism in the Middle East 1914-1958* (Oxford: Oxford University Press, 2006), 260.

84. C. Tripp, *A History of Iraq* (Cambridge: Cambridge University Press, 2000), 61–76.

85. Louis, *OHBE IV*, 33.

86. Jeffery, *The British Army and the Crisis of Empire*, 141; J. Darwin, *Britain, Egypt and the Middle East: Imperial Policy in the Aftermath of War 1918-1922* (London: Macmillan, 1981).

87. Sluglett, *OHBE V*, 431.

88. Heather J. Sharkey, *Living with Colonialism: Nationalism and Culture in the Anglo-Egyptian Sudan* (Berkeley: University of California Press, 2003), 76–85.

89. I. Gershoni and J. P. Jankowski, *Egypt, Islam, and the Arabs: The Search for Egyptian Nationhood, 1900-1930* (Oxford: Oxford University Press, 1986); see also I. Gershoni and J. P. Jankowski, *Redefining the Egyptian Nation, 1930–1945* (Cambridge: Cambridge University Press, 1995), 14–15, 95, 141–2.

90. Darwin, 'An undeclared empire', 170–1.

91. Darwin, 'An undeclared empire', 169.

92. Y. Porath, *The Palestinian Arab Movement Volume Two: 1929-1939 From Riots to Rebellion* (London: Frank Cass, 1977); C. D. Smith, *Palestine and the Arab-Israeli Conflict*, 2nd edn (New York: St Martin's Press, 1992).

93. Clayton, *OHBE IV*, 292–3.

94. Jeffery, *OHBE IV*, 318.

95. Balfour-Paul, *OHBE IV*, 504.

96. Darwin, *Britain and Decolonisation*, 55.

97. Ashton and Stockwell, *Imperial Policy and Colonial Practice*, xliii–xliv.

98. Darwin, *OHBE V*, 545.

99. Ashton and Stockwell, *Imperial Policy and Colonial Practice*, xxvii.

100. Bush, *Imperialism, Race and Resistance*, 101–28.

101. A body of theory drawn from Lord Lugard's experience as northern Nigeria's governor, 1912–19.

102. J. W. Cell, 'Colonial Rule', *OHBE IV*, 235; Ashton and Stockwell, *Imperial Policy and Colonial Practice*, xlviii.

103. Ashton and Stockwell, *Imperial Policy and Colonial Practice*, xlviii. On the contribution of anthropology to colonial policymaking, see Jack Goody, *The Expansive Moment: Anthropology in Britain and Africa 1918-1970* (Cambridge: Cambridge University Press, 1995) and H. Kuklick, *The Savage Within: The Social History of British Anthropology 1885-1945* (Cambridge: Cambridge University Press, 1991).

104. Cell, *OHBE IV*, 235.

105. T. Falola, 'British imperialism: Roger Louis and the West African case', in King and Kilson (eds), *The Statecraft of British Imperialism*, 132.

106. Cooper, 'Writing the history of development', 9–10.

107. Ashton and Stockwell, *Imperial Policy and Colonial Practice*, li.

108. Ashton and Stockwell, *Imperial Policy and Colonial Practice*, lxi; Cooper, 'Writing the history', 9.

109. H. Johnson, 'The British Caribbean from demobilization to constitutional decolonization', *OHBE IV*, 609; H. Johnson, 'The West Indies and the conversion of the British official classes to the development idea', *Journal of Commonwealth and Comparative Politics*, 15:1 (1977).

110. Cooper, 'Reconstructing Empire', 198.

111. Ashton and Stockwell, *Imperial Policy and Colonial Practice*, xxviii. On the evolution of thinking on development, see Joseph M. Hodge and Gerald Hödl, 'Introduction', in Joseph M. Hodge, Gerald Hödl, and Martina Kopf (eds), *Developing Africa: Concepts and Practices in Twentieth-Century Colonialism* (Manchester: Manchester University Press, 2014), 1–34.

112. Darwin, *Britain and Decolonisation*, 45.

113. Darwin, *OHBE IV*, 84; Darwin, *Unfinished Empire: The Global Expansion of Britain* (London: Allen Lane, 2012), 343–6.

114. Ashton and Stockwell, *Imperial Policy and Colonial Practice*, lv–lvi.

115. Wm. Roger Louis, *Imperialism at Bay: The United States and the Decolonization of the British Empire, 1941-1945* (Oxford: Oxford University Press, 1978), 121–97.

116. J. E. Flint, '"Managing Nationalism": The Colonial Office and Nnamdi Azikiwe, 1932-43', in King and Kilson, *The Statecraft of British Imperialism*, 152.

117. *Hansard*, 5th series, 391, 48–69, 13 July 1943.

118. John Gallagher, *The Decline, Revival and Fall of the British Empire* (Cambridge: Cambridge University Press, 1982), 142–3.

119. J. M. Lee and M. Petter, *The Colonial Office, War, and Development Policy: Organisation and the Planning of A Metropolitan Initiative* (London: Maurice Temple Smith, 1982), 147–99.

120. H. Johnson, 'The Anglo-American Caribbean Commission and the extension of American influence in the British Caribbean, 1942-1945', *Journal of Commonwealth and Comparative Politics*, 22 (1984), 180–203.

121. Jeffery, *OHBE IV*, 321.

122. K. M. de Silva (ed.), *British Documents on the End of Empire, Series B, Volume 2: Sri Lanka Part I, The Second World War and the Soulbury Commission 1939-1945* (London: HMSO, 1997).

123. Louis, *OHBE IV*, 34; S. R. Ashton, 'Ceylon', *OHBE IV*, 460.

124. J. Flint, 'Planned decolonization and its failure in British Africa', *African Affairs*, 82:328 (July 1983), 389–411; C. Sanger, *Malcolm MacDonald: Bringing an End to Empire* (Liverpool: Liverpool University Press, 1995), 146–9.

125. J. W. Cell, *Hailey A Study in British Imperialism, 1872-1969* (Cambridge: Cambridge University Press, 1992), 254–65.

126. R. Robinson, 'British imperialism: The Colonial Office and the settler in East-Central Africa, 1919-63', in E. Serra and C. Seton Watson (eds), *Italia E Inghilterra Nell'Eta Dell Imperialismo* (Milan: Franco Angeli, 1990), 195–212.

127. TNA: CO 967/57/46709, 'A federal solution for East Africa', July 1942.

128. M. Chanock, *Unconsummated Union: Britain, Rhodesia and South Africa, 1900-1945* (Manchester: Manchester University Press, 1977).

129. Ashton and Stockwell, *Imperial Policy and Colonial Practice*, lvi–lvii.

130. Ashton and Stockwell, *Imperial Policy and Colonial Practice*, lviii.

131. A. N. Porter and A. J. Stockwell (eds), *British Imperial Policy and Decolonization, 1938-64 Volume 1: 1938-51* (Basingstoke: Macmillan, 1987), 37–8.

132. N. Tarling, 'The British Empire in South East Asia', *OHBE V*, 412.

133. A. J. Stockwell, 'Imperialism and Nationalism in South-East Asia', *OHBE IV*, 477.

134. M. Nicholson, *The TUC Overseas: The Roots of Policy* (London: Allen & Unwin, 1986).

135. Jeffery, *OHBE IV*, 327. On the war's impact on Britain's capacity to maintain its empire, see Clarke, *The Last Thousand Days of the British Empire*.

Chapter 2

1. R. Hyam (ed.), *British Documents on the End of Empire Series A, Volume 2: The Labour Government and the End of Empire 1945-1951* (London: HMSO, 1992), xxiii; Darwin, *Unfinished Empire: The Global Expansion of Britain*, 342–85.

2. John Darwin, *Britain and Decolonisation: The Retreat from Empire in the Post-War World* (Basingstoke: Macmillan, 1988), 69; Frederick Cooper, 'Reconstructing empire in British and French Africa', *Past and Present*, 210 (suppl 6) (2011), 196.

3. Hyam, *The Labour Government*, xlii–xliii; A. Cairncross, *Years of Recovery: British Economic Policy 1945-51* (London: Methuen, 1985), 123–30.

4. Hyam, *The Labour Government*, xliii.

5. Reynolds, *Britannia Overruled*, 162–3, 168–9, 173.

6. Hyam, *The Labour Government*, xliii–xliv; Reynolds (1991), 179–80.

7. Hyam, *The Labour Government*, xxiv–xxv, lxviii–lxix; A. Inder Singh, 'Keeping India in the Commonwealth', *Journal of Contemporary History*, 20 (1985), 469–81.

8. N. Mansergh, *The Commonwealth Experience* (London: Macmillan, 1982), ii, 158.

9. Darwin, *Britain and Decolonisation*, 153.

10. Hyam, *The Labour Government*, lxviii.

11. A. J. Stockwell, *British Documents on the End of Empire Series B, Volume 3 Malaya* (London: HMSO, 1995), lxxix.

12. W. David McIntyre, 'Commonwealth Legacy', *OHBE IV*, 696.

13. Christopher Andrew, *The Defence of the Realm: The Authorized History of MI5* (Harmondsworth: Penguin, 2010), 443; Paul M. McGarr, '"A serious menace to security": British intelligence, V. K. Krishna Menon and the Indian High Commission in London, 1947-52', *JICH*, 38:3 (2010), 460–1.

14. S. Constantine, 'Waving Goodbye? Australia, Assisted Passages, and the Empire and Commonwealth Settlement Acts, 1945-72', *JICH*, 26:2 (1998), 176–95.

15. W. David McIntyre, *Background to the ANZUS Pact: Policy-Making, Strategy and Diplomacy, 1945-55* (London: Macmillan, 1995).

16. Hyam, *The Labour Government*, lix–lx; D. Devereux, 'Britain, the Commonwealth, and the Defence of the Middle East, 1948-56', *Journal of Contemporary History*, 24:2 (1989), 327–45. See also R. Ovendale, *The English-Speaking Alliance: Britain, the United States, the Dominions and the Cold War, 1945-1951* (London: George Allen & Unwin, 1985), 231–3; TNA CAB 21/1786, minutes of meeting of Commonwealth Defence Ministers, June 1951.

17. Wm. Roger Louis, 'Hong Kong: the critical phase, 1945-1949', *American Historical Review*, 102:4 (1997), 1052–85.

18. Cooper, 'Reconstructing empire', 202–3.

19. Sarah Ansari, 'Subjects or citizens? India, Pakistan and the 1948 British Nationality Act', *JICH*, 41:2 (2013).

20. J. Darwin, 'British decolonization since 1945: a pattern or a puzzle?', *JICH*, 12:2 (1984), 187–209.

21. Hyam, *The Labour Government*, xxv; T. Burridge, *Clement Attlee: A Political Biography* (London: Jonathan Cape, 1985). For a perceptive study of the wider implications of Asian nationalism for Britain, embracing both South Asia and Indochina, see T. O. Smith, *Vietnam and the Unravelling of Empire: General Gracey in Asia 1942-1951* (Basingstoke: Palgrave Macmillan, 2014).

22. R. J. Moore, *Escape from Empire: The Attlee Government and the Indian Problem* (Oxford: Clarendon Press, 1983).

23. Reynolds, *Britannia Overruled*, 165.

24. Hyam, *The Labour Government*, lvii–lviii; B. R. Tomlinson, *The Political Economy of the Raj, 1914-47: The Economics of Decolonization in India* (London: Macmillan, 1979), 147; R. Aldrich and M. Coleman, 'Britain and the strategic air offensive against the Soviet Union: the question of South Asian air bases', *History*, 242 (1989), 400–26.

25. Anita Inder Singh, *The Limits of British Influence: South Asia and the Anglo-American Relationship, 1947-56* (London: Continuum, 1990), 47.

26. W. Gould, *Hindu Nationalism and the Language of Politics in Late Colonial India* (Cambridge: Cambridge University Press, 2004).

27. Reynolds, *Britannia Overruled*, 165; N. Mansergh and P. Moon (eds), *Constitutional Relations between Britain and India: The Transfer of Power, 1942-1947 Volume IX, The Fixing of a Time Limit*, 41, Wavell to Sec of State for India, 11 November 1946. For a reassessment of Wavell's Viceroyalty, see Irial Glynn, '"An Untouchable in the presence of Brahmins": Lord Wavell's disastrous relationship with Whitehall during his time as Viceroy to India, 1943-7', *MAS*, 41:3 (2007), 639–63.

28. Hyam, *The Labour Government*, xxv; Darwin, *Britain and Decolonisation*, 92.

29. TNA: CAB 128/8, (46) 108, Confidential annex, 31 December 1946, cited in Louis, *OHBE IV*, 328.

30. Hyam, *The Labour Government*, xxv; Reynolds, *Britannia Overruled*, 168.

31. S. Wolpert, *Shameful Flight: The Last Years of the British Empire in India* (Oxford: Oxford University Press, 2006), 153–82; For a discussion beyond 'high policy', exploring the development of Muslim identities, see D. Gilmartin, 'Partition, Pakistan and South Asian history: in search of a narrative', *Journal of Asian Studies*, 57:4 (1998), 1068–95; I. Talbot and S. Thandi (eds), *People on the Move: Punjabi Colonial, and Post-Colonial Migration* (Karachi: Oxford University Press, 2004).

32. Owen, *The British Left and India*, 271–98.

33. N. Mansergh and P. Moon (eds), *Constitutional Relations between Britain and India: The Transfer of Power, 1942-47 Volume X: Mountbatten Viceroyalty, Formulation of a Plan*, 329.

34. P. Darby, *British Defence Policy East of Suez, 1947-1968* (London: Oxford University Press, 1973), 10–31.

35. Frederick Cooper, 'Reconstructing empire in British and French Africa', *Past and Present*, 210 (supplement 6) (2011), 199.

36. A. Jackson, *The British Empire and the Second World War* (London: Hambledon Continuum, 2006), 307–19.

37. Hyam, *The Labour Government*, xxvi.

38. TNA: CAB 128/9, 44(47), 6 May 1947, cited in Darwin, *Britain and Decolonisation*, 105.

39. S. R. Ashton, 'Ceylon', *OHBE IV*, 463–4.

40. Christopher Bayly and Tim Harper, *Forgotten Armies: Britain's Asian Empire and War with Japan* (Harmondsworth: Penguin, 2005), 156–61, 170–80.

41. S. R. Ashton, 'Burma, Britain, and the Commonwealth, 1946–56', *JICH*, 29:1 (2001), 65–91.

42. R. B. Smith, 'Some contrasts between Burma and Malaya in British policy in south-east Asia, 1942-6', in R. B. Smith and A. J. Stockwell (eds), *British Policy and the Transfer of Power in Asia: Documentary Perspectives* (London: School of Oriental and African Studies, University of London, 1988), 46–8, 68–72.

43. P. W. T. Kingston, *Britain and the Politics of Modernization in the Middle East, 1945-1958* (Cambridge: Cambridge University Press, 1996). See also Johan Franzén, 'Development versus Freedom', *JICH*, 37:1 (2009), 77, 82–3, 84–5.

44. Franzén, 'Development versus Freedom', 90–1.

45. Hyam, *The Labour Government*, xxviii, xlviii; Reynolds, *Britannia Overruled*, 190.

46. TNA: CAB 131/4, DO(47)23, memorandum by Chiefs of Staff, 7 March 1947.

47. J. Kent, 'Informal empire and the defence of the Middle East 1945-56', in R. Bridges (ed.), *Imperialism, Decolonization and Africa: Studies Presented to John Hargreaves* (Basingstoke: Macmillan, 2000), 114–52.

48. Steven G. Galpern, *Money, Oil and Empire in the Middle East: Sterling and Postwar Imperialism, 1944-1971* (Cambridge: Cambridge University Press, 2013). See also Nicholas J. White, 'Reconstructing Europe through rejuvenating empire: the British, French and Dutch experiences compared', *Past and Present*, Supplement 6 (2011), 215.

49. Kent, 'Informal empire'.

50. Wm. Roger Louis, *The British Empire in the Middle East 1945-1951: Arab Nationalism, The United States, and Postwar Imperialism* (Oxford: Clarendon Press, 1984), 9–10.

51. J. Kent (ed.), *British Documents on the End of Empire Series B, Volume 4: Egypt and the Defence of the Middle East* (London: The Stationery Office, 1998), xlvi–lxxxiv.

52. Reynolds, *Britannia Overruled*, 166.

53. Hyam, *The Labour Government*, xxvi.

54. M. J. Cohen, *Palestine and the Great Powers, 1945-1948* (Princeton, NJ: Princeton University Press, 1982), 392.

55. Hyam, *The Labour Government*, xxvi–xxviii.

56. TNA: CAB 129/21, CP(47)259, memorandum by Foreign Sec.

57. R. Holland, *The Pursuit of Greatness: Britain and the World Role, 1900-1970* (London: Fontana, 1991), 224.

58. Saul Kelly, *Cold War in the Desert: Britain, the United States and the Italian Colonies, 1945-52* (London: Macmillan, 2000).

59. Louis, *The British Empire in the Middle East*, 666, 688; R. Hyam, 'Africa and the Labour Government, 1945-1951', *JICH*, 16:3 (1988), 158. Ironically, the British and US secret services had previously colluded to overthrow Mossadegh: Galpern, *Money, Oil and Empire*.

60. R. Hyam, 'Africa and the Labour government, 1945-1951', *JICH*, 16:3 (1988), 158.

61. White, 'Reconstructing Europe', 215–16.

62. Hyam, *The Labour Government*, xxix, xxxv.

63. R. F. Holland, 'The imperial factor in British strategies from Attlee to Macmillan, 1945-63', *JICH*, 12:2 (1984).

64. Cooper, 'Reconstructing Empire', 206.

65. Hyam, 'Africa and the Labour Government', 153.

66. Benjamin Grob-Fitzgibbon, *Imperial Endgame: Britain's Dirty Wars and the End of Empire* (Basingstoke: Palgrave Macmillan, 2011).

67. Hyam, *The Labour Government*, xxiv, lv, lii; S. L. Carruthers, *Winning Hearts and Minds: British Governments, the Media and Colonial Counter-Insurgency 1944–1960* (Leicester: Leicester University Press, 1995), 1–24.

68. Hyam, *The Labour Government*, liii–liv.

69. R. Heinze, '"Decolonising the mind": nationalism and nation building in Namibian and Zambian radio', *Archiv für Sozialgeschichte*, 48 (2008), 295–316.

70. Hyam, *The Labour Government*, xlii, li.

71. A. J. Stockwell, 'British imperial policy and decolonization in Malaya, 1942-52', *JICH*, 13:1 (1984), 68–87. See also White, 'Reconstructing Europe', 214.

72. Hyam, *The Labour Government*, xlii.

73. D. K. Fieldhouse, 'The Labour governments and the Empire-Commonwealth, 1945-51', in R. Ovendale (ed.), *The Foreign Policy of the British Labour Governments 1945-1951* (Leicester: Leicester University Press, 1984), 83–120; P. S. Gupta, 'Imperialism and the Labour government of 1945-51', in J. M. Winter (ed.), *The Working Class in Modern British History* (Cambridge: Cambridge University Press, 1983). See also L. J. Butler, *Industrialisation and the British Colonial State: West Africa, 1939-1951* (London: Frank Cass, 1997), 187–228.

74. Hyam, *The Labour Government*, xlvi–xlvii; L. J. Butler, 'Reconstruction, development and the entrepreneurial state: the British colonial model, 1939-51', *Contemporary British History*, 13:4 (Winter 1999), 29–55. See also Joseph M. Hodge, *Triumph of the Expert: Agrarian Doctrines of Development and the Legacies of British Colonialism* (Athens: Ohio University Press, 2007), 207–53.

75. Christophe Bonneuil, 'Development as experiment: science and state building in late colonial and postcolonial Africa, 1930-1970', *Osiris*, 2nd series, 15 *Nature and Empire: Science and the Colonial Enterprise* (2000), 263–4.

76. M. M. van Beusekom and D. L. Hodgson, 'Lessons learned? Development experiences in the late colonial period', *JAH*, 41 (2000), 29–53; F. Cooper, *Decolonization and African Society: The Labor Question in French and British Africa* (Cambridge: Cambridge University Press, 1996), 451;

Joseph M. Hodge, '"British colonial expertise," post-colonial careering and the early history of international development', *Journal of Modern European History*, 8 (2010/1), 29–30.

77. Reynolds, *Britannia Overruled*, 188. On the concept of the 'second colonial occupation', see 'Introduction', in D. A. Low and A. Smith (eds), *History of East Africa Volume III* (Oxford: Oxford University Press, 1976); White, 'Reconstructing Europe', 223–4.

78. Hyam, *The Labour Government*, xlviii–xlix.

79. White, 'Reconstructing Europe', 225–6; L. J. Butler, *Copper Empire: Mining and the Colonial State in Northern Rhodesia, c.1930-1964* (Basingstoke: Palgrave Macmillan, 2007), 146–93. See also White, 'Decolonisation in the 1950s: the version according to British business', in Martin Lynn (ed.), *The British Empire in the 1950s: Retreat or Revival?* (Basingstoke: Palgrave Macmillan, 2006), 101.

80. Andreas Eckert, 'Late colonial rule' *Archiv für Sozialgeschichte*, 48 (2008). For a discussion which makes useful comparisons between the situations in British and French Africa, see Frederick Cooper, 'Decolonization and citizenship: Africa between empires and a world of nations', in Els Bogaerts and Remco Raben (eds), *Beyond Empire and Nation: The Decolonization of African and Asian societies, 1930s-1960s* (Leiden: KITLV Press, 2012), 39–67.

81. Andreas Eckert, 'Regulating the social: social security, social welfare and the state in late colonial Tanzania', *JAH*, 45:3 (2004), 468–9.

82. Cooper, 'Writing the history of development', 1, 11–12; S. Bose, 'Instruments and idioms', in Frederick Cooper and Randall Packard (eds), *International Development and the Social Sciences: Essays on the History and Politics of Knowledge* (Berkeley and Los Angeles: University of California Press, 1997), 45–63.

83. Hodge, 'British colonial expertise', 29–30; see also Hodge, *Triumph of the Expert*, 207–53.

84. See, e.g., Emma Hunter, '"The history and affairs of TANU": intellectual history, nationalism, and the postcolonial state in Tanzania', *International Journal of African Historical Studies*, 45:3 (2012), 366.

85. Good, complementary studies, which highlight the inherent instability in the development strategy, include Rohland Schuknecht, *British Colonial Development Policy after the Second World War: The Case of Sukumaland, Tanganyika* (Berlin: Lit Verlag, 2010) and Monica M. Van Beusekom, *Negotiating Development: African Farmers and Colonial Experts at the Office du Niger 1920-1960* (Martlesham: James Currey, 2002).

86. Corinna R. Unger, 'The United States, decolonization and the education of Third World elites', in J. Dülffer and M. Frey (eds), *Elites and Decolonization in the Twentieth Century* (Basingstoke: Palgrave Macmillan, 2011), 254–5.

87. Frederick Cooper, *Africa since 1940: The Past of the Present* (Cambridge: Cambridge University Press, 2002), 85–6.

88. D. L. Hodgson, 'Taking stock: state control, ethnic identity and pastoralist development in Tanganyika, 1948-1958', *JAH*, 41:1 (2000), 55–78; see also R. Grove, 'Colonial conservation, ecological hegemony and popular resistance: towards a global synthesis', in J. M. Mackenzie (ed.), *Imperialism in the Natural World* (Manchester: Manchester University Press, 1990), 15–50.

89. A. J. Stockwell, 'Southeast Asia in war and peace: the end of European colonial empires', in N. Tarling (ed.), *The Cambridge History of Southeast Asia: Volume Two: The Nineteenth and Twentieth Centuries* (Cambridge: Cambridge University Press, 1996), 355–6.

90. T. N. Harper, *The End of Empire and the Making of Malaya* (Cambridge: Cambridge University Press, 1999).

91. A. J. Stockwell (ed.), *British Documents on the End of Empire Series B, Volume 3 Malaya* (London: HMSO, 1995), lviii.

92. Darwin, *Britain and Decolonisation*, 109; Bayly and Harper, *Forgotten Wars: The End of Britain's Asian Empire* (London: Allen Lane, 2007), 98–100, 130–5, 209–17; C. M. Watson, 'Reconstructing Malay identity', *Anthropology Today*, 12:5 (1996), 10–14.

93. Bayly and Harper, *Forgotten Wars*, 213–17.

94. Hyam, *The Labour Government*, xxxviii.

95. A. J. Stockwell, 'British imperial policy and decolonization in Malaya, 1942–52', *JICH*, 13:1 (1984), 68–97.

96. Stockwell, *Malaya*, lxi.

97. Stockwell, *OHBE IV*, 485.

98. Stockwell, *Malaya*, lxiii–lxvi; Harper, *The End of Empire*, 140–8; White 'Reconstructing Europe', 232.

99. Hyam, *The Labour Government*, xxiv.

100. Hyam, *The Labour Government*, xxvii.

101. Kumar Ramakrishna, '"Bribing the reds to give up": rewards policy in the Malayan emergency', *War in History*, 9:3 (2002), 332–63; Stockwell, *Malaya*, lxvii.

102. Lee Kam Hing, 'A neglected story: Christian missionaries, Chinese new villagers, and Communists in the battle for the "hearts and minds" in Malaya, 1948–1960', *MAS*, 47:6 (2013), 1977–2006.

103. Hyam, *The Labour Government*, xxvii.

104. Carruthers, *Winning Hearts and Minds*, 90–5.

105. K. Hack, *Defence and Decolonisation in Southeast Asia: Britain, Malaya and Singapore 1941-68* (Richmond, Surrey: Curzon, 2000).

106. Peter Lowe, *Contending With Nationalism and Communism: British Policy Towards Southeast Asia, 1945-65* (Basingstoke: Palgrave Macmillan, 2009), 73–96.

107. On labour problems, see especially Frederick Cooper, *Decolonization and African Society: The Labor Question in French and British Africa* (Cambridge: Cambridge University Press, 1996), 234–40, 248–60.

108. M. Sherwood, *Manchester and the 1945 Pan-African Congress* (London: Savannah Press, 1995), *passim*; H. Adi, 'Pan-Africanism and West African nationalism in Britain', *African Studies Review*, 43:1 (2000), 69–82.

109. TNA: CO 847/25/47234, memorandum by G. B. Cartland, 'Native Administration Policy', 1946; R. D. Pearce, 'Morale in the Colonial Service in Nigeria during the Second World War', *JICH*, 11:2 (1983), 175–96.

110. Hyam, *The Labour Government*, xxx; R. D. Pearce, *The Turning Point in Africa: British Colonial Policy 1938-1948* (London: Frank Cass, 1982), 162–84.

111. Hyam, *The Labour Government*, xxx–xxxi.

112. Pearce, *The Turning Point in Africa*, 162–84.

113. Emma Hunter, 'Dutiful subjects, patriotic citizens and the concept of "good citizenship" in twentieth-century Tanzania', *Historical Journal*, 56:1 (2013), 257–77.

114. White, 'Reconstructing Europe', 234.

115. Hyam, *The Labour Government*, xxxv.

116. Fieldhouse, 'The Labour governments and the Empire-Commonwealth, 1945-51', 106–10.

117. Fieldhouse, 'The Labour governments and the Empire-Commonwealth, 1945-51', 106–10.

118. Hyam, *The Labour Government*, lii.

119. Richard Rathbone (ed.), *British Documents on the End of Empire, Series B Volume I: Ghana Part 1* (London: HMSO, 1995), xliv–xlv.

120. David Birmingham, *Kwame Nkrumah: The Father of African Nationalism* (Athens: Ohio University Press, 1998); R. Rathbone (ed.), *British Documents on the End of Empire Series B, Volume 1: Ghana* (London HMSO, 1992), xliv–xlv.

121. Hyam, *The Labour Government*, 155, citing TNA: CAB 128/17, CM 30(50)6, 11 May 1950.

122. Hyam, *The Labour Government*, xxxvii.

123. Hyam, 'Africa and the Labour Government', 156.

124. Darwin 'British decolonization since 1945'; White, 'Reconstructing Europe', 215; see also Butler, *Copper Empire*, 198–209.

125. Hyam, *The Labour Government*, lxv.

126. Hyam, *The Labour Government*, lxv.

127. G. Berridge, 'Britain, South Africa and African defence, 1949-55', in M. Dockrill and J. W. Young (eds), *British Foreign Policy, 1945-1956* (Basingstoke: Macmillan, 1989), 101–25; G. R. Berridge and J. E. Spence, 'South Africa and the Simonstown Agreements', in J. W. Young (ed.), *The Foreign Policy of Churchill's Peacetime Administration 1951-1955* (Leicester: Leicester University Press, 1988).

128. Hyam *The Labour Government*, lxiv–lxv; Ovendale, *English-Speaking Alliance*, ch. 9.

129. Hyam, *The Labour Government*, xxxvi; R. Hyam, 'The geopolitical origins of the Central African Federation: Britain, Rhodesia and South Africa, 1948-1953', *Historical Journal*, 30 (1987), 145–72. Settlers in Central Africa, who had long campaigned for territorial 'amalgamation', may have exaggerated the extent of the Afrikaner threat: see P. Murphy, '"Government by blackmail": the origins of the Central African Federation reconsidered', in M. Lynn (ed.), *The British Empire in the 1950s: Retreat or Revival* (Basingstoke: Palgrave Macmillan, 2006), 53–76.

130. S. Marks, 'Southern Africa', *OHBE IV*, 567–8.

Chapter 3

1. D. Reynolds, *Britannia Overruled: British Policy and World Power in the Twentieth Century* (Harlow: Longman, 1991), 181; John Darwin, *The Empire Project: The Rise and Fall of the British World System, 1830-1970* (Cambridge: Cambridge University Press, 2009), 640–5.

2. J. Kent, 'Informal empire and the defence of the Middle East 1945-56', in R. Bridges (ed.), *Imperialism, Decolonization and Africa: Studies Presented to John Hargreaves* (Basingstoke: Macmillan, 2000), 133–4.

3. D. Goldsworthy (ed.), *British Documents on the End of Empire Series A, Volume 3: The Conservative Government and the End of Empire 1951-1957* (London: HMSO, 1994), xxix.

4. Holland, 'The imperial factor', 173.

5. W. David McIntyre, 'Admission of small states to the Commonwealth', *JICH*, 24:2 (1996), 256–7.

6. Goldsworthy, *The Conservative Government*, l; W. David McIntyre, *British Decolonization, 1946-1997* (Basingstoke: Macmillan, 1998), 40.

7. Goldsworthy, *The Conservative Government*, li, lxvi n47.

8. Goldsworthy, *The Conservative Government*, lxv n18.

9. S. Brooke, 'The Conservative Party, immigration and national identity, 1948-1968', in M. Francis and I. Zweiniger-Bargielowska (eds), *The Conservatives and British Society, 1880-1990* (Cardiff: University of Wales Press, 1996), 147–70.

10. T. Hopkins, 'Macmillan's Audit of Empire, 1957', in P. Clarke and C. Trebilcock (eds), *Understanding Decline: Perceptions and Realities of British Economic Performance* (Cambridge: Cambridge University Press, 1997), n49.

11. See, e.g., A. Hinds, *Britain's Sterling Colonial Policy and Decolonization, 1939-1958* (Westport, CN: Greenwood Press, 2001).

12. Catherine R. Schenk, *The Decline of Sterling: Managing the Retreat of an International Currency, 1945-1992* (Cambridge: Cambridge University Press, 2013), 83–116.

13. R. Holland, *The Pursuit of Greatness: Britain and the World Role, 1900-1970* (London: Fontana, 1991), 260–1.

14. Goldsworthy, *The Conservative Government*, lvi.

15. Catherine R. Schenk, 'Decolonization and European economic integration: the Free Trade Area negotiations, 1956-58', *JICH*, 24, 3 (1996), 445-7; see also James Ellison, *Threatening Europe: Britain and the Creation of the European Community, 1955-58* (New York: St Martin's, 2000).

16. C. H. Feinstein, 'The end of empire and the golden age', in Clarke and Trebilcock, *Understanding Decline*, 227-8.

17. Nicholas J. White, *Decolonization: The British Experience since 1945*, 2nd edn (Abingdon: Routledge, 2014), 34-6.

18. Bonneuil, 'Development as experiment', 265-9.

19. Hodge, 'British Colonial Expertise', 33-4.

20. Rohland Schuknecht, *British Colonial Development Policy after the Second World War: The Case of Sukumaland, Tanganyika* (Berlin: Lit Verlag, 2010); cf. John McCracken, 'The ambiguities of nationalism: Flax Musopole and the northern factor in Malawian politics, c.1956-1966', *Journal of Southern African Studies*, 28:1 (2002), 78.

21. Cooper, 'Writing the History of Development', 14-15.

22. Cooper, 'Writing the History', 21; Richard Waller, 'Rebellious youth in colonial Africa', *JAH*, 47:1 (2006), 92; Crawford Young, 'The end of the post-colonial state in Africa? Reflections on changing African political dynamics', *African Affairs*, 103:410 (2004), 28.

23. Frederick Cooper, 'Reconstructing empire in British and French Africa', *Past and Present* 210 (suppl 6) (2011), 208.

24. R. Hyam, 'The parting of the ways: Britain and South Africa's departure from the Commonwealth, 1951-61', *JICH*, 26:2 (1998), 158.

25. Eugene L. Rogan and Avi Shlaim (eds), *The War for Palestine: Rewriting the History of 1948* (Cambridge: Cambridge University Press, 2007), 100.

26. M. Mason, '"The decisive volley": the Battle of Ismaelia and the Decline of British Influence in Egypt, January-July 1952', *JICH*, 19:1 (1991), 45-64.

27. J. Kent (ed.), *British Documents on the End of Empire Series B, Volume 4 Egypt and the Defence of the Middle East* (London: The Stationery Office), 570-1; M. W. Daly, *Imperial Sudan: The Anglo-Egyptian Condominium, 1934-56* (Cambridge: Cambridge University Press, 1991), 352-99.

28. Roger Louis, 'The Tragedy of the Anglo-Egyptian Settlement of 1954', in Wm. Roger Louis and R. Owen (eds), *Suez 1956: The Crisis and its Consequences* (Oxford: Clarendon Press, 1989), 43-72.

29. Goldsworthy, *The Conservative Government*, 101-2.

30. N. J. Ashton, *Eisenhower, Macmillan and the Problem of Nasser: Anglo-American Relations and Arab Nationalism, 1955-59* (Basingstoke: Macmillan, 1996).

31. K. Kyle, *Suez: Britain's End of Empire in the Middle East* (London: IB Tauris, 2003).

32. S. J. Ball, 'Banquo's ghost': Lord Salisbury, Harold Macmillan, and the high politics of decolonization, 1957-1963', *Twentieth Century British History*, 16:1 (2005), 74-102.

33. P. Murphy, *Alan Lennox-Boyd: A Biography* (London: IB Tauris, 1999), 192.

34. Quoted in D. Goldsworthy, 'Keeping change within bounds: aspects of colonial policy during the Churchill and Eden governments, 1951-57', *JICH*, 18:1 (1990), 92.

35. Goldsworthy, *The Conservative Government*, lii.

36. H. Johnson, 'The British Caribbean from demobilisation to constitutional decolonization', in Brown and Louis (eds), *OHBE IV: The Twentieth Century*, 618; S. R. Ashton and David Killingray (eds), *The West Indies: British Documents on the End of Empire Series B Volume 6 (London: The Stationery Office, 1999).

37. Goldsworthy, *The Conservative Government*, liii.

38. Stephen Howe, *Anticolonialism in British Politics: The Left and the End of Empire 1918-1964: The Left and the End of Empire, 1918-64* (Oxford: Oxford University Press, 1998); Josiah Brownell,

'The taint of communism: the Movement for Colonial Freedom, the Labour Party, and the Communist Party of Great Britain, 1954-70', *Canadian Journal of History*, 42:2 (2007), 235–58.

39. Richard Whiting, 'The Empire and British politics', in Andrew Thompson (ed.), *Britain's Experience of Empire in the Twentieth Century* (Oxford: Oxford University Press, 2011), 161–210; Gregory Claeys, *Imperial Sceptics: British Critics of Empire, 1850–1920* (Cambridge: Cambridge University Press, 2012), esp. 21–46.

40. See, e.g., Jeffrey Cox, 'From the Empire of Christ to the Third World: religion and the experience of empire in the twentieth century' and Andrew Thompson and Meaghan Kowalsky, 'Social life and cultural representation: empire in the public imagination', in A. Thompson (ed.), *Britain's Experience of Empire in the Twentieth Century* (Oxford: Oxford University Press, 2012), 76–121, 251–97.

41. See esp. John Stuart, *British Missionaries and the End of Empire: East, Central and Southern Africa, 1939-64* (Cambridge: Wm. B. Eerdmans, 2011), and David Maxwell, 'Decolonization', in Norman Etherington (ed.), *Missions and Empire* (Oxford: Oxford University Press, 2005), 285–306.

42. F. Furedi, *Colonial Wars and the Politics of Third World Nationalism* (London: I.B. Tauris, 1994).

43. D. Killingray and D. M. Anderson, 'An orderly retreat? Policing the end of empire', in D. M. Anderson and D. Killingray (eds), *Policing and Decolonization: Politics, Nationalism, and the Police, 1917-65* (Manchester: Manchester University Press, 1992), 5.

44. Benjamin Grob-Fitzgibbon, *Imperial Endgame: Britain's Dirty Wars and the End of Empire* (Basingstoke: Palgrave Macmillan, 2011), 377.

45. Emma Hunter, 'Dutiful Subjects, Patriotic citizens, and the Concept of "Good Citizenship" in Twentieth-Century Tanzania', *Historical Journal*, 56:1 (2013), 267.

46. See, e.g., J.-B. Gewald, M. Hinfelaar, and G. Macola (eds), *One Zambia, Many Histories: Towards a History of Post-Colonial Zambia* (Leiden and Boston: Brill, 2008). For a concise but shrewd analysis of African nationalism, see Jean Allman, 'Between the present and History: African Nationalism and Decolonization', in John Parker and Richard Reid (eds), *The Oxford Handbook of Modern African History* (Oxford: Oxford University Press, 2013), 224–40.

47. For a detailed recent study of an important example, see Miles Larmer, *Rethinking African Politics: A History of Opposition in Zambia* (Farnham: Ashgate, 2011), 1–20.

48. John McCracken, 'The ambiguities of nationalism', 76–7.

49. Goldsworthy, *The Conservative Government*, xlvii, 100; Holland *The Pursuit of Greatness*, 261–2.

50. Sir Ralph Furse, *Aucuparius: Recollections of a Recruiting Officer* (London: Oxford University Press, 1962), Appendix I.

51. Goldsworthy, *The Conservative Government*, li–lii; Goldsworthy, 'Keeping Change', 86.

52. A. J. Stockwell, 'Imperialism and nationalism in South-East Asia', in Brown and Roger Louis (eds), *OHBE IV: The Twentieth Century*, 486.

53. R. Stubbs, *Hearts and Minds in Guerrilla Warfare: The Malayan Emergency 1948-1960* (Singapore: Oxford University Press, 1989).

54. A. J. Stockwell, 'British imperial strategy and decolonization in South-East Asia, 1947-1957', in D. K. Bassett and V. T. King (eds), *Britain in South-East Asia* (Occasional Paper 13, Centre for South-East Asian Studies, University of Hull, 1986), 88.

55. See esp. Nicholas J. White, '"A waste of time and money"? The Colombo Plan in Malaya, Singapore and the Borneo Territories during the 1950s', in Shigeru Akita, Gerold Krozewski, and Shoichi Watanabe (eds), *The Transformation of the International Order of Asia: Decolonization, the Cold War, and the Colombo Plan* (Abingdon: Routledge, 2015), 72–90.

56. Simon C. Smith, *British Relations with the Malay Rulers from Decentralization to Malayan Independence 1930-1957* (Kuala Lumpur: Oxford University Press, 1995).

57. A. J. Stockwell (ed.), *British Documents on the End of Empire Series B, Volume 3 Malaya* (London: HMSO, 1995), lxxix–lxxx.

58. Nicholas J. White, 'Reconstructing Europe', 232.

59. Technically, Sudan took precedence by becoming independent in 1956, but this territory had a unique status, and was not a 'colony' in the conventional sense.

60. Goldsworthy, 'Keeping Change', 88.

61. Goldsworthy, *The Conservative Government*, xlviii.

62. R. Rathbone (ed.), *British Documents on the End of Empire Series B, Volume 1 Ghana* (London: HMSO, 1992), lix–lx. See also M. Lynn, 'The Nigerian self-government crisis of 1953 and the Colonial Office', *JICH*, 34:2 (2006), 245–61.

63. Richard Rathbone, *Nkrumah and the Chiefs: The Politics of Chieftancy in Ghana 1951-60* (Oxford: James Currey, 2000), 29–47.

64. Richard Rathbone, 'Things fall apart: the erosion of local government, local justice and civil rights in Ghana, 1955-60', in Martin Lynn (ed.), *The British Empire in the 1950s: Retreat or Revival* (Basingstoke: Palgrave Macmillan, 2006), 122–43.

65. Sarah Stockwell, *The Business of Decolonization: British Business Strategies in the Gold Coast* (Oxford: Clarendon Press, 2000).

66. See Jean Marie Allman, 'The youngmen and the porcupine: class, nationalism and Asante's struggle for self-determination, 1954-57', *JAH*, 31:2 (1990), 263–79.

67. Rathbone, *Ghana*, lxii, lxviii; Goldsworthy, *The Conservative Government*, liii–liv.

68. John Lonsdale, 'Mau Maus of the mind: making Mau Mau and remaking Kenya', *JAH*, 31:3 (1990), 393–421; Joanna Lewis, *Empire State-Building: War and Welfare in Kenya 1925-52* (Oxford: James Currey, 2000), 370–3.

69. Frederick Cooper, *Africa since 1940: The Past of the Present* (Cambridge: Cambridge University Press, 2002), 71–4; see also M. Chege, 'Mau Mau rebellion fifty years on', *African Affairs*, 103:410 (2004), 123–36.

70. A. F. D. Mackenzie, *Land, Ecology and Resistance in Kenya, 1880-1952* (Edinburgh: Edinburgh University Press, 1998).

71. L. Thomas, '*Ngaitana* (I will circumcise myself): the gender and generational politics of the 1956 ban on clitoridectomy in Meru, Kenya', in N. R. Hunt, Y. P. Liu, and J. Quataert (eds), *Gendered Colonialisms in African History* (Oxford: Blackwell, 1997), 4.

72. S. Geiger, *TANU Women: Gender and Culture in the Making of Tanganyikan Nationalism, 1955-1965* (Oxford: James Currey, 1997).

73. S. Howe, 'Mau Mau judgement', *JICH*, 39:5 (2011), 697; D. Anderson, 'Mau Mau in the High Court', *JICH*, 39:5 (2011), 699.

74. D. Anderson, *Histories of the Hanged: Britain's Dirty War in Kenya and the End of the Empire* (London: Weidenfeld and Nicolson, 2005), 326–31.

75. Murphy, *Alan Lennox-Boyd*, 154.

76. Anderson, *Histories of the Hanged* and C. Elkins, *Britain's Gulag: The Brutal End of Empire in Kenya* (London: Jonathan Cape, 2005).

77. See Anderson, 'Mau Mau in the High Court', 699, 701, 713. For valuable correctives to the traditional rosy consensus, see B. Grob-Fitzgibbon, *Imperial Endgame: Britain's Dirty Wars and the End of Empire* (Basingstoke: Palgrave Macmillan, 2011); Bennett, 'Soldiers in the court room: the British Army's part in the Kenya Emergency under the legal spotlight', *JICH*, 39:5 (2011), 727; Huw Bennett, 'Minimum force in British counterinsurgency', *Small Wars and Insurgencies*, 21:3 (2010), 459–75 and the same author's *Fighting the Mau Mau: The British Army and Counter-Insurgency in the Kenya Emergency* (Cambridge: Cambridge University Press, 2013).

78. N. Owen, 'Decolonization and postwar consensus', in H. Jones and M. Kandiah (eds), *The Myth of Consensus: New Views on British History, 1945-64* (Basingstoke: Macmillan, 1996), 168–9.

79. K. Kyle, *The Politics of the Independence of Kenya* (Basingstoke: Macmillan, 1999).

80. Daniel Branch, *Defeating Mau Mau, Creating Kenya: Counterinsurgency, Civil War, and Decolonization* (Cambridge: Cambridge University Press, 2009), esp. 117–47.

81. T. Kanogo, *Squatters and the Roots of Mau Mau 1905-63* (London: James Currey, 1987); D. W. Throup, *Economic and Social Origins of Mau Mau 1945-53* (London: James Currey, 1987).

82. B. Berman, *Control and Crisis in Colonial Kenya: The Dialectic of Domination* (London: James Currey, 1990), 111, 369–71, 387–8. See also Cooper, 'Writing the History of Development', 13–14, and Hodge, 'British Colonial Expertise', 30–4.

83. Myles Osborne, 'The Kamba and Mau Mau: ethnicity, development and chiefship, 1952-1960', *International Journal of African Historical Studies*, 43:1 (2010), 63–87.

84. P. Murphy (ed.), *British Documents on the End of Empire Series B, Volume 9, Central Africa* (London: The Stationery Office, 2005).

85. J. Darwin, 'British Decolonization since 1945', 190.

86. Christopher J. Lee (ed.), *Making a World After Empire: The Bandung Moment and its Political Afterlives* (Athens: Ohio University Press, 2010), 196–7.

87. Gerard McCann, 'From diaspora to Third Worldism and the United Nations: India and the politics of decolonizing Africa', *Past and Present*, 218 (Supplement 8) (2013), 258–80.

88. Goldsworthy, *The Conservative Government*, xlii–xliv.

89. R. Holland, *Britain and the Revolt in Cyprus 1954-1959* (Oxford: Clarendon Press, 1998), 42.

90. Reynolds, *Britannia Overruled*, 204; Holland, *The Pursuit of Greatness*, 272.

91. Goldsworthy, 'Keeping change', 103.

92. Goldsworthy, *The Conservative Government*, xxxiv; Reynolds, *Britannia Overruled*, 204.

93. Steven G. Galpern, *Money, Oil, and Empire in the Middle East: Sterling and Postwar Imperialism, 1944-1971* (Cambridge: Cambridge University Press, 2010), 166–77.

94. Wm. Roger Louis and Roger Owen (eds), *Suez 1956: The Crisis and Its Consequences* (Oxford: Clarendon Press, 1989), 173–88.

95. D. Mackenzie, 'Canada, the North Atlantic Triangle, and the Empire', in Brown and Louis (eds), *OHBE IV: The Twentieth Century*, 593.

96. Reynolds, *Britannia Overruled*, 205; McIntyre, 'The admission of small states to the Commonwealth', 259; Louis and Owen, *Suez 1956*, 257–318.

97. Galpern, *Money, Oil and Empire*, 277–8.

98. See especially A. J. Stockwell, 'Suez 1956 and the moral disarmament of the British Empire', in Simon C. Smith (ed.), *Reassessing Suez 1956: New Perspectives on the Crisis and Its Aftermath* (Farnham: Ashgate, 2008), 227–38.

99. R. Holland, *Britain and the Revolt in Cyprus*.

Chapter 4

1. P. E. Hemming, 'Macmillan and the end of the British Empire in Africa', in R. Aldous and S. Lee (eds), *Harold Macmillan and Britain's World Role* (Basingstoke: Macmillan, 1996), 101.

2. Wm. Roger Louis and R. Robinson, 'The Imperialism of Decolonization', *JICH*, 22:3 (1994), 462–511.

3. A. Horne, *Macmillan 1957-1986* (London: Macmillan, 1989), 204.

4. R. Holland, *The Pursuit of Greatness: Britain and the World Role, 1900-1970* (London: Fontana, 1991), 179; D. Reynolds, *Britannia Overruled: British Policy and World Power in the Twentieth Century* (Harlow: Longman, 1991), 211.

5. S. Constantine, 'Waving goodbye? Australia, assisted passages, and the Empire and Commonwealth Settlement Acts, 1945-72', *JICH*, 26:2 (1998), 176–96.

6. J. Darwin, *Britain and Decolonisation: The Retreat from Empire in the Post-War World* (Basingstoke: Macmillan, 1988), 237–9.

7. T. Hopkins, 'Macmillan's audit of empire, 1957', in P. Clarke and C. Trebilcock (eds), *Understanding Decline: Perceptions and Realities of British Economic Performance* (Cambridge: Cambridge University Press, 1997), 255.

8. N. White, 'Liverpool and the end of empire: the Ocean Group in East and Southeast Asia, c.1945-73', in Sheryllynne Haggerty, Anthony Webster, and Nicholas J. White (eds), *The Empire in One City? Liverpool's Inconvenient Imperial Past* (Manchester: Manchester University Press, 2008), 182–3.

9. TNA: CAB/134/1555, 28 January 1957.

10. Hopkins, 'Macmillan's audit', 249–50.

11. Reynolds, *Britannia Overruled*, 225–6.

12. D. Percox, *Britain, Kenya and the Cold War: Imperial Defence, Colonial Security and Decolonization* (London: I.B. Tauris, 2004).

13. Holland, *The Pursuit of Greatness*, 292–4.

14. TNA: CAB 128/30 pt.2, CM4(57), 9 January 1957.

15. R. Ovendale, *Britain, the United States and the Transfer of Power in the Middle East, 1945-1962* (Leicester: Leicester University Press, 1996), 183, 192–4. For a recent reassessment, see S. C. Smith, ' "America in Britain's Place?": Anglo-American relations and the Middle East in the aftermath of the Suez Crisis', *Journal of Transatlantic Studies*, 10:3 (2012), 252–70.

16. M. Joyce, 'Preserving the sheikhdom: London, Washington, Iraq and Kuwait, 1958-61', *Middle Eastern Studies*, 31:2 (1995), 281–92.

17. Wm. R. Louis, 'Harold Macmillan and the Middle East crisis of 1958' (Elie Kedourie Memorial Lecture), *Proceedings of the British Academy*, Volume 94 (1996) *Lectures and Memoirs*, 207–28.

18. R. A. Fernea and Wm. Roger Louis (eds), *The Iraqi Revolution of 1958: The Old Social Classes Revisited* (London: I.B. Tauris, 1991); M. Eppel, 'Degrees of accommodation with Britain: the decline of British influence and the ruling elite in Iraq', in M. Cohen and M. Kolinsky (eds), *Demise of the British Empire in the Middle East: Britain's Responses to Nationalist Movements 1943-1955* (London: Frank Cass, 1998), 196; see also Johan Franzén, 'Development versus freedom', *JICH*, 37:1 (2009), 91–4.

19. L. Tal, 'Britain and the Jordan Crisis of 1958', *Middle Eastern Studies*, 31:1 (1995), 39–57.

20. N. J. Ashton, 'A microcosm of decline: British loss of nerve and military intervention in Jordan and Kuwait, 1958 and 1961', *Historical Journal*, 40:4 (1997), 1082; N. J. Ashton, 'A "special relationship" sometimes in spite of ourselves': Britain and Jordan, 1957-73', *JICH*, 23:2 (2005), 221–44.

21. Nicholas J. White, 'Reconstructing Europe through Rejuvenating Empire: the British, French and Dutch Experiences Compared', *Past and Present*, Supplement 6 (2011), 215–16.

22. Ashton, 'A microcosm of Decline', 1072–3.

23. M. Farouk-Sluglett and P. Sluglett, *Iraq Since 1958: From Revolution to Dictatorship* (London: KPI, 1987), 50, 100.

24. Simon C. Smith, *Britain's Revival and Fall in the Gulf: Kuwait, Bahrain, Qatar, and the Trucial States, 1950-71* (London: Routledge-Curzon, 2004).

25. Ashton, 'A Microcosm of Decline', 1073.

26. N. Ashton, 'Britain and the Kuwaiti crisis, 1961', *Diplomacy and Statecraft*, 9:1 (1998), 163–81.

27. TNA: PREM 11/3430, Brook to Macmillan, 13 September 1961, cited in R. Ovendale, 'Macmillan and the Wind of Change in Africa, 1957-60', *Historical Journal*, 38:2 (1995), 235.

28. P. Murphy, *Alan Lennox-Boyd: A Biography* (London: I.B. Tauris, 1999), 194.

29. S. Mawby, *British Policy in Aden and the Protectorates 1955-67: Last Outpost of a Middle East Empire* (Abingdon: Routledge, 2005).

30. S. R. Ashton and D. Killingray (eds), *The West Indies British Documents on the End of Empire Series B, Volume 6* (London: The Stationery Office, 1999).

31. Ashton and Killingray (eds), *The West Indies British Documents on the End of Empire Series B*, 1999.

32. J. Darwin, 'Decolonization and the end of empire', in Winks (ed.), *The Oxford History of the British Empire Volume V Historiography*, 545.

33. Ovendale, 'Macmillan and the Wind of Change in Africa'.

34. S. Howe, *Anticolonialism in British Politics: The Left and the End of Empire, 1918-1964* (Oxford: Clarendon Press, 1993); see also review of same by R. Holland in *International Journal of African Historical Studies*, 28:3 (1995), 673–6, and Josiah Brownell, 'The taint of communism', 235–58.

35. J. Turner, *Macmillan* (Harlow: Longman, 1994), 199.

36. TNA: PREM 11/2587, Macmillan to Lloyd, 2 July 1959.

37. Ovendale, 'Macmillan and the Wind of Change', 463; S. R. Ashton, 'Keeping change within bounds: a Whitehall reassessment', in M. Lynn (ed.), *The British Empire in the 1950s: Retreat or Revival?* (Basingstoke: Palgrave Macmillan, 2006), 45.

38. Ovendale, 'Macmillan and the Wind of Change', 477.

39. Louis and Robinson, 'The imperialism of decolonization', 487–9.

40. M. Lynn (ed.), *British Documents on the End of Empire Series B, Volume 7 Nigeria* (London: The Stationery Office, 2001).

41. M. Lynn, '"We cannot let the North down": British policy and Nigeria in the 1950s', in M. Lynn (ed.), *The British Empire in the 1950s: Retreat or Revival?* (Basingstoke: Palgrave Macmillan, 2006), 144–63.

42. Wm. Roger Louis, 'The dissolution of the British Empire', in Brown and Louis (eds), *OHBE IV: The Twentieth Century*, 350.

43. Hemming, 'Macmillan and the end of the British Empire', 101.

44. Wm. Roger Louis, 'Introduction', *OHBE IV*, 30.

45. Louis, *OHBE IV*, 351.

46. 'Trouble in Africa', *The Spectator*, 31 January 1964.

47. J. Ramsden, *The Winds of Change Macmillan to Heath 1957-1975* (Harlow: Longman, 1996), 147.

48. TNA: PREM 11/3075, minute, 28 December 1959; Holland, *The Pursuit of Greatness*, 299.

49. Louis and Robinson, 'The imperialism of decolonization', 489.

50. L. J. Butler and Sarah Stockwell (eds), *The Wind of Change: Harold Macmillan and British Decolonization* (Basingstoke: Palgrave Macmillan, 2013), 1–19.

51. S. J. Ball, 'Banquos's ghost', 74–102; Ramsden, *The Winds of Change*, 5–6.

52. Hemming, 'Macmillan and the end of the British Empire', 112.

53. Wm. Roger Louis, 'Public enemy number one: the British Empire in the dock at the United Nations, 1957-71', in M. Lynn (ed.), *The British Empire in the 1950s: Retreat or Revival?* (Basingstoke: Palgrave Macmillan, 2006), 186–213.

54. R. Hyam, 'The primacy of geopolitics: the dynamics of British imperial policy, 1763-1963', in R. D. King and R. Kilson (eds), *The Statecraft of British Imperialism: Essays in Honour of Wm. Roger Louis* (London: Frank Cass, 1999), 45.

55. Louis and Robinson, 'The imperialism of decolonization', 489–90.

56. Emma Hunter, 'Dutiful subjects, patriotic citizens', 270; see also the same author's 'The history and affairs of TANU', 369–70.

57. Murphy, *Alan Lennox-Boyd*, 228–32; Louis, *OHBE IV: The Twentieth Century*, 352.

58. Miles Larmer, *Rethinking African Politics: A History of Opposition in Zambia* (Farnham: Ashgate, 2011), 1–3, 14; Toyin Falola and Matthew M. Heaton, *A History of Nigeria* (Cambridge: Cambridge University Press, 2008), 158–80; Chibuike Uche, 'Oil, British Interests and the Nigerian civil war', *JAH*, 49:1 (2008), 111–35; Chinua Achebe, *There was a Country: A Personal History of Biafra* (London: Penguin, 2013); Frank Schubert, 'The Colonial Roots of Post-Colonial Violence: The Making of Martial Tribes and Political Ethnicity in Uganda', *Archiv für Sozialgeschichte*, 48 (2008); Phares Mutibwa, *Uganda since Independence: A Story of Unfulfilled Hopes* (London: C. Hurst, 1992), 22–103.

59. Darwin, *Britain and Decolonisation*, 188–9.

60. J. D. Hargreaves, *Decolonization in Africa*, 2nd edn (Harlow: Longman, 1996), 178.

61. Ovendale, 'Macmillan and the Wind of Change', 471.

62. See especially Camilla Schofield, *Enoch Powell and the Making of Postcolonial Britain* (Cambridge: Cambridge University Press, 2013), 121–38.

63. Murphy, *Alan Lennox-Boyd*, 220–7.

64. David M. Anderson, 'Yours in struggle for Majimbo'. Nationalism and the party politics of decolonization in Kenya, 1955-64', *Journal of Contemporary History*, 40:3 (July 2005), 547–64.

65. K. Kyle, *The Politics of the Independence of Kenya* (Basingstoke: Macmillan, 1999), 113–15, 130.

66. J. Darwin, 'British decolonization since 1945', 204.

67. Margret Frenz, 'Swaraj for Kenya, 1949-1965: the ambiguities of transnational politics', *Past and Present*, Supplement 8 (2013), 151–77.

68. Frenz, 'Swaraj for Kenya', 173–5.

69. McCracken, 'The ambiguities of nationalism', 67–82. A particularly valuable corrective to previous assessments of Anglican involvement in decolonization is Sarah Stockwell's ' "Splendidly leading the way"? Archbishop Fisher and decolonization in British colonial Africa', in Robert Holland and Sarah Stockwell (eds), *Ambiguities of Empire: Essays in Honour of Andrew Porter* (Abingdon: Routledge, 2009), 199–218.

70. Murphy, *Alan Lennox-Boyd*, 184.

71. Julia Tischler, *Light and Power for a Multiracial Nation: The Kariba Dam Scheme in the Central African Federation* (Basingstoke: Palgrave Macmillan, 2013); see also Andrew Cohen, 'Dams and the dilemmas of development', *African Historical Review*, 46:1 (2014), 70–81.

72. McCracken, 'The Ambiguities of Nationalism', 72–5.

73. C. Baker, *State of Emergency: Crisis in Central Africa, Nyasaland 1959-1960* (London: I.B. Tauris, 1997); J. Darwin, 'The Central African Emergency, 1959', *JICH*, 21:3 (1993), 217–34.

74. Giacomo Macola, 'Harry Mwaanga Nkumbula and the formation of ZANC/UNIP', in Jan-Bart Gewald, Marja Hinfelaar, and Giacomo Macola (eds), *Living the End of Empire: Politics and Society in Late Colonial Zambia* (Leiden: Brill, 2011), 49.

75. L. Butler, 'Mining, nationalism, and decolonization in Zambia: interpreting business responses to political change, 1945-1964', in Anja Kruke (ed.), *Dekolonisation: Prozesse und Verflechtungen 1945-1990* (Bonn: Dietz, 2009), 317–32.

76. Ovendale, 'Macmillan and the Wind of Change', 476.

77. Holland, *The Pursuit of Greatness*, 299.

78. Louis and Robinson, 'The imperialism of decolonization', 489.

79. L. J. Butler, 'Britain, the United States and the demise of the Central African Federation, 1959-1963', *JICH*, 28:3 (2000), 131–51.

80. P. Murphy, *Party Politics and Decolonization: The Conservative Party and British Colonial Policy in Tropical Africa 1951-1964* (Oxford: Clarendon Press, 1995), 184–90.

81. Darwin, 'British Decolonization since 1945', 204–5.

82. Ovendale, 'Macmillan and the Wind of Change', 474.

83. S. R. Ashton, 'British government perspectives on the Commonwealth, 1964-71: an asset or a liability?', *JICH*, 35:1 (2007), 73–94.

84. Harper and Constantine, *Migration and Empire* (Oxford: Oxford University Press, 2010), 189–90.

85. Ian Spencer, *British Immigration Policy since 1939: The Making of Multi-Racial Britain* (London: Routledge, 1997), 98–102.

86. Marjorie Harper and Stephen Constantine, *Migration and Empire*, 198.

87. J. D. B. Miller, *Survey of Commonwealth Affairs: Problems of Expansion and Attrition 1953-1969* (London: Oxford University Press, 1974), 341–4.

88. Harper and Constantine, *Migration and Empire*, 198–99, 208–9; Spencer, *British Immigration Policy*, 135–51.

89. See, e.g., Panikos Panayi, *An Immigration History of Modern Britain: Multicultural Racism since 1800* (Abingdon: Routledge, 2014), 200–58; Winston James, 'The black experience in twentieth-century Britain', in Philip Morgan and Sean Hawkins (eds), *Black Experience and the Empire* (Oxford: Oxford University Press, 2004), 347–86.

90. Harper and Constantine, *Migration and Empire*, 199, 207–8.

91. Jim House and Neil MacMaster, *Paris 1961: Algerians, State Terror, and Memory* (Oxford: Oxford University Press, 2009).

92. Simon Holdaway and Megan O'Neill, 'Institutional racism after Macpherson: an analysis of Police views', *Policing and Society*, 16:4 (2006), 349–69.

93. See, e.g., Panikos Panayi, 'Immigration, multiculturalism and racism', and Katherine Watson, 'Education and Opportunity', in Francesca Carnevali and Julie-Marie Strange (eds), *Twentieth Century Britain: Economic, Cultural and Social Change*, 2nd edn (Abingdon: Routledge, 2014).

94. See, e.g., Elizabeth Buettner, 'We don't grow coffee and bananas in Clapham Junction you know!: Imperial Britons back home', and John Darwin, 'Orphans of empire', in Robert Bickers (ed.), *Settlers and Expatriates: Britons over the Seas* (Oxford: Oxford University Press, 2010).

95. S. Dockrill, *Britain's Retreat from East of Suez: The Choice between Europe and the World?* (Basingstoke: Palgrave Macmillan, 2002); see also S. R. Ashton and Wm. Roger Louis (eds), *British Documents on the End of Empire Series A, Volume 5 East of Suez and the Commonwealth* (London: The Stationery Office, 2004), xxxiii–xlii.

96. M Jones, *Conflict and Confrontation in South East Asia, 1961-1965: Britain, the United States and the Creation of Malaysia* (Cambridge: Cambridge University Press, 2001).

97. A. J. Stockwell, 'Malaysia: the making of a grand design', *Asian Affairs*, 34:3 (2003), 227–42; see also A. J. Stockwell (ed.), *British Documents on the End of Empire Series B, Volume 8 Malaysia* (London: The Stationery Office, 2004).

98. Clayton, '"Deceptive might"', 303; J. D. B. Miller, *Survey of Commonwealth Affairs Problems of Expansion and Attrition 1953-1969* (London: Oxford University Press, 1974), 82–98.

99. Harold Wilson, speech to the Labour Party Annual Conference, Scarborough, 1963, in H. Wilson, *Purpose in Politics: Selected Speeches* (London: Weidenfeld and Nicolson, 1964), 27.

100. Miller, *Survey of Commonwealth Affairs*, 302–5.

101. Darwin, 'A third British Empire?', 85.

102. Peter Lowe, *Contending With Nationalism and Communism: British Policy Towards Southeast Asia, 1945-65* (Basingstoke: Palgrave Macmillan, 2009); Darwin, *Britain and Decolonisation*, 287.

103. S. Mawby, *British Policy in Aden and the Protectorates 1955-67: Last Outpost of a Middle East Empire* (Abingdon: Routledge, 2005); S. C. Smith, 'Rulers and residents: British relations with the Aden Protectorate, 1937-59', *Middle Eastern Studies*, 31:3 (1995), 509–23.

104. Holland, *The Pursuit of Greatness*, 332.

105. Shohei Sato, 'Britain's decision to withdraw from the Persian Gulf, 1964-68: a pattern and a puzzle', *JICH*, 37:1 (2009), 99–117.

106. P. Sluglett, 'Formal and informal empire in the Middle East', in *OHBE V*, 434.

107. Wm. Roger Louis, 'The British withdrawal from the Gulf, 1967-71', *JICH*, 31:1 (2003), 83–108.

108. Simon C. Smith, *Britain's Revival and Fall in the Gulf: Kuwait, Qatar, and the Trucial States, 1950-71* (London: Routledge-Curzon, 2004).

109. P. Murphy (ed.), *Central Africa, Part I: Closer association 1945-1958 British Documents on the End of Empire* (London: The Stationery Office, 2005), xcviii–cvii; see also Carl P. Watts, *Rhodesia's Unilateral Declaration of Independence: An International History* (Basingstoke: Palgrave Macmillan, 2012).

110. Carl P. Watts, 'Killing kith and kin: the viability of British military intervention in Rhodesia, 1964-5', *Twentieth Century British History*, 16:4 (2005), 382–415.

111. Carl Watts, 'Britain, the Old Commonwealth and the problem of Rhodesian Independence, 1964-65', *JICH*, 36:1 (2008), 75–99.

112. See especially, Andrew Thompson (ed.), 'Introduction', in *Britain's Experience of Empire in the Twentieth Century* (Oxford: Oxford University Press, 2012), 1–32.

113. Philip Murphy, 'Britain as a global power in the twentieth century', in Thompson, *Britain's Experience*, 33–75.

114. Jim Tomlinson, 'The Empire/Commonwealth in British economic thinking and policy', in Thompson, *Britain's Experience*, 211–50.

115. Whiting, 'The Empire and British politics', in Thompson, *Britain's Experience*, 161–210.

116. Andrew S. Thompson, *The Empire Strikes Back?: The Impact of Imperialism on Britain from the Mid-Nineteenth Century* (Abingdon: Routledge, 2005), 240–1.

117. Thompson, *The Empire Strikes Back*, 201, 213, 239, 242.

118. Wendy Webster, 'There'll always be an England: representations of colonial wars and immigration, 1948-1968', in Stephen Howe (ed.), *The New Imperial Histories Reader* (Abingdon: Routledge, 2009).

119. Wendy Webster, 'The Empire comes home: Commonwealth migration to Britain', in Thompson, *Britain's Experience*, 122–60.

120. Thompson, *The Empire Strikes Back*, 87–8, 137–8; see also David Arnold, *Colonizing the Body: State Medicine and Epidemic Disease in Nineteenth-Century India* (Berkeley and Los Angeles: University of California Press, 1993).

121. E.g. Mahmood Mamdani, *Citizen and Subject: Contemporary Africa and the Legacy of Late Colonialism* (Princeton, NJ: Princeton University Press, 1996).

122. Hunter, 'Dutiful Subjects', 271.

123. Crawford Young, 'The end of the post-colonial State in Africa? Reflections on changing African political dynamics', *African Affairs*, 103:410 (2004), 23–49.

124. Gita Subrahmanyam, 'Ruling continuities: colonial rule, social forces and path dependence in British India and Africa', *Commonwealth and Comparative Politics*, 44:1 (2006), 84–117; see also Leander Schneider, 'Colonial legacies and postcolonial authoritarianism in Tanzania: connects and disconnects', *African Studies Review*, 49:1 (2006), 93–118 and Nandini Gooptu, 'The political legacy of colonialism in South Asia', in Douglas M. Peers and Nandini Gooptu (eds), *India and the British Empire* (Oxford: Oxford University Press, 2012), 334–56.

125. Frederick Cooper, *Africa Since 1940: The Past of the Present* (Cambridge: Cambridge University Press, 2002), 88–9.

126. Hunter, 'History and affairs of TANU', 367, 382–3.

127. Eckert, 'Late colonial rule, decolonization and international order. Introductory remarks', *Archiv für Sozialgeschichte*, 48 (2008), 3–20.

128. Eckert, 'Regulating the social', 467–89.

129. Giacomo Macola, '"It means as if we are excluded from the good freedom": Thwarted expectations of independence in the Luapula Province of Zambia, 1964–6', *JAH*, 47:1 (2006), 43–56.

130. Cooper, 'Writing the History of Development', 15; see also the same author's 'Possibility and constraint: African independence in historical perspective', *JAH*, 49:2 (2008), 167–96; Young, 'The end of the post-colonial state', 31.

131. Hodge, 'British colonial expertise', 25; Bonneuil, 'Development as experiment', 258–60, 264; Jim Masselos, 'Decolonized space: the reconfiguring of national and public space in India', in Els Bogaerts and Remco Raben (eds), *Beyond Empire and Nation: The Decolonization of African and Asian societies, 1930s-1960s* (Leiden: KITLV Press, 2012), 189–211.

132. Andreas Eckert, 'Useful instruments of participation? Local government and cooperatives in Tanzania, 1940s to 1970s', *International Journal of African Historical Studies*, 40:1 (2007), 97–118.

133. Larmer, *Rethinking African Politics*, 6. For a critical analysis of 'development' and its long-term effects, see Arturo Escobar, *Encountering Development: The Making and Unmaking of the Third World*, 2nd edn (Princeton, NJ: Princeton University Press, 2012), esp. vii–xliv.

134. Stephen Ellis, 'Writing histories of contemporary Africa', *Journal of African History*, 43:1 (2002), 6–7.

135. For stimulating introductions to a vast and varied literature, see Jean Drèze and Amartya Sen, *An Uncertain Glory: India and its Contradictions* (London: Allen Lane, 2013); Amartya Sen, *The Argumentative Indian: Writings on Indian History, Culture and Identity* (London: Allen Lane, 2006); Judith M. Brown, *Nehru: A Political Life* (New Haven: Yale University Press, 2003); and Francine R. Frankel, *India's Political Economy: The Gradual Revolution, 1947-2004*, 2nd edn (New Delhi: Oxford University Press India, 2006).

Chapter 5

1. Marie-Paule Ha, 'Engendering French colonial history: the case of Indochina', *Historical Reflections*, 25:1 (1999), 110–12, 120, See also Ha, *French Women and the Empire: The Case of Indochina* (Oxford: Oxford University Press, 2014).

2. Eric Jennings, *La France libre fut africaine* (Paris: Perrin, 2014), troisième partie.

3. Wilder, *The French Imperial Nation-State*, 25.

4. The conjunctions between gender discrimination and racial prejudice in interwar France are explored by Jennifer Boittin, *Colonial Metropolis: The Urban Grounds of Anti-Imperialism and Feminism in Interwar Paris* (Lincoln, NE: University of Nebraska Press, 2010), especially chs 3 and 6.

5. Boittin, *Colonial Metropolis*, 126.

6. Alice L. Conklin, *A Mission to Civilize: The Republican Idea of Empire in France and West Africa, 1895-1930* (Stanford: Stanford University Press, 1997); Conklin, '"Democracy" rediscovered: civilization through association in French West Africa (1914-1930)', *Cahiers d'Etudes Africaines*, 145:37 (1997), 59–84; 'Colonialism and human rights, a contradiction in terms? The case of France and West Africa, 1895-1914', *American Historical Review*, 103:2 (1998), 419–42; and her 'A Force for Civilization. Republican Discourse and French Administration in West Africa, 1895-1930', in C. Becker, S. Mbaye, and I. Thioub (eds), *AOF: réalités et heritages. Sociétés ouest-africaines et ordre colonial, 1895-1960*, 2 vols (Dakar: DAS, 1997), I: 283–302. See also Gary Wilder, 'Framing Greater France between the wars', *Journal of Historical Sociology*, 14:2 (2001), 198–225; Wilder, 'The politics of failure: historicising Popular Front colonial policy in French West Africa', in Tony Chafer and Amanda Sackur (eds), *French Colonial Empire and the Popular Front: Hope and Disillusion* (London: Macmillan, 1999), 33–55; and his 'Panafricanism and the republican political sphere', in Sue Peabody and Tyler Stovall (eds) *The Color of Liberty: Histories of Race in France* (Durham, NC: Duke University Press, 2003), 237–58.

7. Frederick Cooper, *Colonialism in Question: Theory, Knowledge, History* (Berkeley: University of California Press, 2005), 174–7.

8. Mona Siegel, *The Moral Disarmament of France: Education, Pacifism, and Patriotism, 1914-1940* (Cambridge: Cambridge University Press, 2004), 178–81; Boittin, *Colonial Metropolis*, 173–8, 209–11. The legal implications of children born to mixed-race parents are explored by Emmanuelle Saada, *Empire's Children: Race, Filiation, and Citizenship in the French Colonies* (Chicago, IL: University of Chicago Press, 2012).

9. Nicolas Bancel, Pascal Blanchard, and Françoise Vergès, *La République coloniale. Essai sur une utopie* (Paris: Editions Autrement, 2003), especially chs 1 and 4.

10. Eric Savarese, *L'Ordre colonial et sa légitimation en France métropolitaine* (Paris: Harrmattan, 1998), 46–51, 212–27.

11. James E. Genova, *Colonial Ambivalence, Cultural Authenticity, and the Limits of Mimicry in French-Ruled West Africa, 1914-1956* (New York: Peter Lang, 2004), 94–9.

12. Wilder, *The French Imperial Nation-State*, part III.

13. Boittin, *Colonial Metropolis*, 78–101.

14. For incisive discussion of this associationism, see Alice Conklin, *A Mission to Civilize*; Genova, *Colonial Ambivalence*. For Labouret's contribution, see Wilder, *The French Imperial Nation-State*, 58–61.

15. Mahmood Mamdani, *Citizen and Subject: Contemporary Africa and the Legacy of Late Colonialism* (Princeton, NJ: Princeton University Press, 1996), 17–18; also cited in Genova, *Cultural Ambivalence*, 8.

16. See Hélène Blais, Florence Deprest and Pierre Singaravélou (eds), *Territoires impériaux: Une histoire spatiale du fait colonial* (Paris: Sorbonne, 2011).

17. Emmanuelle Sibeud, *Une science impériale pour l'Afrique? La construction des savoirs africanistes en France 1878-1930* (Paris: EHESS, 2002), 257–72; for broader analysis of French colonial ethnology, see: Alice Conklin, *In the Museum of Man: Race, Anthropology, and Empire in France, 1850-1950* (Ithaca, NY: Cornell University Press, 2013), especially chs 3–5.

18. Benoît de l'Estoile, 'Rationalizing colonial domination: anthropology and native policy in French-ruled Africa', in Benoît de l'Estoile, Federico Neiburg, and Lygia Sigaud (eds), *Empires, Nations, and Natives. Anthropology and State-Making* (Durham, NC: Duke University Press, 2005), 44–7.

19. Cooper, *Colonialism in Question*, 144.

20. Conklin, '"Democracy" rediscovered', 59–60.

21. Benjamin N. Lawrence, Emily Lynn Osborn, and Richard L. Roberts (eds), *Intermediaries, Interpreters, and Clerks: African Employees in the Making of Colonial Africa* (Madison, WI: University of Wisconsin Press, 2006), 3–34.

22. Martin Klein, 'African participation in colonial rule: the role of clerks, interpreters, and other intermediaries', in Lawrence, Osborn, and Roberts, *Intermediaries*, 273–8.

23. Cooper, 'The dialectics of decolonization', 409–11.

24. Regarding early French rule, see J. Kim Munholland, '"Collaboration strategy" and the French pacification of Tonkin, 1885-1897', *Historical Journal*, 24:3 (1981), 629–50.

25. See P. Norindr, *Phantasmatic Indochina: French Colonial Ideology in Architecture, Film and Literature* (Durham, NC: Duke University Press, 1996); Nicola Cooper, *France in Indochina: Colonial Encounters* (Oxford: Berg, 2001), 2–3.

26. Pierre Brocheux and Daniel Hémery, *Indochine la colonisation ambiguë 1858-1954* (Paris: Découverte, 2001), 84–6.

27. Eric T. Jennings. *Imperial Heights: Dalat and the Making and Undoing of French Indochina* (Berkeley: University of California Press, 2011).

28. Van Nguyen-Marshall, 'The moral economy of colonialism: subsistence and famine relief in French Indo-China, 1906-1917', *International History Review*, 27:2 (2005), 240–2, 257–8.

29. Herman Lebovics, *Imperialism and the Corruption of Democracies* (Durham, NC: Duke University Press, 2006), 64. Ironically, Lebovics' wider argument is that possession of empire did profound damage to the democratic integrity of the European colonial powers.

30. Martin Stuart-Fox, 'The French in Laos, 1887-1945', *MAS*, 29:1 (1995), 111–39.

31. Michael G. Vann, 'Of rats, rice, and race: the great Hanoi rat massacre, an episode in French colonial history', *French Colonial History*, 4 (2003), 191–203; Cooper, *France in Indochina*, ch. 8.

32. John F. Laffey, 'Imperialists divided: the views of Tonkin's *colons* before 1914', *Histoire Sociale/Social History*, 9 (May 1977), 92–113, quote at 109.

33. David Marr, *Vietnamese Anti-Colonialism, 1885-1925* (Berkeley: University of California Press, 1971); Peter Zinoman, 'Colonial prisons and anti-colonial resistance in French Indochina: the Thai Nguyen rebellion, 1917', *MAS*, 34:1 (2000), 57–98.

34. Stephen Ellis, 'The political elite of Imerina and the revolt of the Menalamba: the creation of a colonial myth in Madagascar, 1895-1898', *JAH*, 21 (1980), 221–8, 232–3.

35. Centre des Archives Diplomatiques, Nantes, Fonds Beyrouth, Cabinet Politique, vol. 466, tel. 250, Ponsot to Foreign Ministry, 14 January 1928; Philip S. Khoury, *Syria and the French Mandate: The Politics of Arab Nationalism, 1920-1945* (Princeton, NJ: Princeton University Press, 1987).

36. Elizabeth Thompson, *Colonial Citizens: Republican Rights, Paternal Privilege, and Gender in French Syria and Lebanon* (New York: Columbia University Press, 2000), part III.

37. Jennifer M. Dueck, *The Claims of Culture at Empire's End: Syria and Lebanon under French Rule* (Oxford: Oxford University Press, 2010).

38. Daniel Neep, *Occupying Syria under the French Mandate: Insurgency, Space and State Formation* (Cambridge: Cambridge University Press, 2012), chs 2 and 7.

39. Pascal Venier, 'A campaign of colonial propaganda: Gallieni, Lyautey and the defence of the military regime in Madagascar, May 1899 to July 1900', in Tony Chafer and Amanda Sackur (eds), *Promoting the Colonial Idea: Propaganda and Visions of Empire in France* (London: Palgrave Macmillan, 2002), 29–39.

40. Eric T. Jennings, *Vichy in the Tropics: Pétain's National Revolution in Madagascar, Guadeloupe, and Indochina, 1940-1944* (Stanford, CA: Stanford University Press, 2001), 24; Jean-Pierre Biondi, *Les anticolonialistes*, 93–4. Gustave Le Bon was appalled by the behaviour of the Paris Communards in 1871, and wrote a loaded analysis of collective behaviour in his *The Psychology of Crowds* published in 1895. Jules Harmand, a former Resident-General of Tonkin and the author of *Domination and Colonisation*, shared Le Bon's social Darwinist ideas.

41. Mary Dewhurst Lewis, 'Geographies of power: the Tunisian civic order, jurisdictional politics, and imperial rivalry in the Mediterranean, 1881-1935', *Journal of Modern History*, 80:4 (2008), 791–830.

42. Martin Thomas, *Violence and Colonial Order: Police, Workers, and Protest in the European Colonial Empires, 1918-1940* (Cambridge: Cambridge University Press, 2012), chs 1, 4–5.

43. Gary Wilder, 'Framing Greater France', 210.

44. Martin Thomas, 'Economic Conditions and the Limits to Mobilisation in the French Empire, 1936–1939', *Historical Journal*, 48:2 (2005), 471–98.

45. TNA, FO 371/20695, tel. 36, Saigon Consul to FO, 3 May 1937.

46. Jacques Marseille, *Empire colonial et capitalisme français: Histoire d'un divorce* (Paris: Albin Michel, 1984), 44–8.

47. Marseille, *Empire colonial et capitalisme français*, 370.

48. Patrick Braibant, 'L'administration coloniale et le profit commercial en Côte d'Ivoire pendant la crise de 1929', *Revue Française d'Histoire d'Outre-Mer*, 63:3–4 (1976), 555–7.

49. Claudette Regad-Pellagru, 'La conception de la politique française des grands travaux et l'évolution de l'Indochine de 1936 à 1947', in Charles-Robert Ageron (ed.), *Les Chemins de la décolonisation* (Paris: CNRS, 1986), 148–9. By 1939 annual increases to the Vietnamese territories' population topped 300,000.

50. Irene Nørlund, 'The French Empire, the colonial state in Vietnam and economic policy: 1885-1940', *Australian Economic History Review*, 31:1 (1991), 80–7.

51. Herman Lebovics, *True France: The Wars over Cultural Identity, 1900-1945* (Ithaca, NY: Cornell University Press, 1992), xii–xiv.

52. Elisa Camiscioli, *Reproducing the French Race: Immigration, Intimacy, and Embodiment in the Early Twentieth Century* (Durham, NC: Duke University Press, 2009), esp. 99–128.

53. Marilyn Lake and Henry Reynolds. *Drawing the Global Colour Line: White Men's Countries and the International Challenge of Racial Equality* (Cambridge: Cambridge University Press, 2008), 310–34.

54. Rabah Aissaoui, *Immigration and National Identity: North African Political Movements in Colonial and Postcolonial France* (London: I.B. Tauris, 2009), esp. chs 3–4.

55. Boittin, *Colonial Metropolis*, 173–8.

56. Clifford Rosenberg, *Policing Paris: The Origins of Modern Immigration Control between the Wars* (Ithaca, NY: Cornell University Press, 2006).

57. Neil Macmaster, 'The rue Fondary murders of 1923 and the origins of anti-Arab racism', in Jan Windebank and Renate Gunther (eds), *Violence and Conflict in the Politics and Society of Modern France* (Lampeter: Edwin Mellen Press, 1995), 149–60; Mary Dewhurst Lewis, *The Boundaries of the Republic: Migrant Rights and the Limits of Universalism in France, 1918-1940* (Stanford, CA: Stanford University Press, 2007), 196–211.

58. W. B. Cohen, 'The colonial policy of the Popular Front', *French Historical Studies*, 7:3 (1972), 368–93.

59. France Tostain, 'The Popular Front and the Blum-Viollette plan', in Chafer and Sackur, *French Colonial Empire*, 218–27.

60. Benjamin Stora, *Nationalistes Algériens et Révolutionnaires Français au temps du Front Populaire* (Paris: Harmattan, 1987), 30–5, 85–104.

61. Martin Thomas, *The French Empire between the Wars: Imperialism, Politics, and Society* (Manchester: Manchester University Press, 2005), 288–9.

62. Editors' introduction in Chafer and Sackur, *French Colonial Empire*, 1–29.

63. Genova, *Colonial Ambivalence*, 146–68.

64. Olivier Wieviorka, 'Replacement or renewal? The French political elite at the Liberation', and Martin Shipway, 'Whose liberation? Confronting the problem of the French Empire, 1944–47', both in Andrew Knapp (ed.), *The Uncertain Foundation: France at the Liberation, 1944-1947* (Basingstoke: Palgrave Macmillan, 2007), 75–86, 139–59.

65. Limor Yagil, *L'homme nouveau et la révolution nationale de Vichy (1940-1944)* (Paris: Septentrion, 1998).

66. Ruth Ginio, *French Colonialism Unmasked: The Vichy Years in French West Africa* (Lincoln, NE: University of Nebraska Press, 2006).

67. Ginio, *French Colonialism Unmasked*, part IV.

68. Martin Thomas, 'Resource war, civil war, rights war: factoring empire into French North Africa's Second World War', *War in History*, 18:2 (2011), 225–48.

69. For the impact of Free France's racially codified recruitment on local peoples, see Jennings, *La France libre*, 147–70.

70. Philip M. Williams, *Crisis and Compromise. Politics in the Fourth Republic*, 3rd edn (London: Longman, 1964), 20–2. Only one administration broke with this tripartite arrangement: Léon Blum's caretaker government of December 1946 contained Socialists alone.

71. A. N. Wilson, *African Decolonization* (London: Edward Arnold, 1994), 148.

72. This was certainly the case in the Indochina War. For example, see Jacques Dalloz, 'Alain Savary, un socialiste face à la guerre d'Indochine', *Vingtième Siècle*, January (1997), 42–54.

73. Philippe Buton, 'Le Parti communiste français et le stalinisme au lendemain de la Seconde Guerre Mondiale', *Review of Modern European History* 2:1 (2004), 67–70; Marc Lazar, 'The Cold War culture of the French and Italian communist parties', *Intelligence and National Security*, 18:2 (2003), 216–17.

74. TNA, FO 371/60048, Z7714/2830/17, Duff Cooper to Ernest Bevin, 26 August 1946.

75. Paul Clay Sorum, *Intellectuals and Decolonization in France* (Chapel Hill, NC: University of North Carolina Press, 1977), 31.

76. Quoted in Paul Isoart, 'L'élaboration de la constitution de l'Union française: les Assemblées constituantes et le problème colonial', in Ageron, *Les Chemins*, 19.

77. Charles-Robert Ageron, 'L'Opinion publique face aux problèmes de l'Union française', in *Les Chemins*, 37.

78. Laurentie's preferences are discussed in Martin Shipway, 'Thinking like and empire: Governor Henri Laurentie and postwar plans for the late colonial French "Empire-State"', in Martin Thomas (ed.), *The French Colonial Mind. I: Mental Maps of Empire and Colonial Encounters* (Lincoln, NE: University of Nebraska Press, 2011), 227–36.

79. James I. Lewis, 'The MRP and the genesis of the French Union, 1944-1948', *French History*, 12 (1998): 282–98, *passim*.

80. Odile Rudelle, 'Le vote du statut de l'Algérie', in Serge Berstein and Pierre Milza (eds), *L'Année 1947* (Paris: Presses de Sciences Po, 2000), 312–15.

81. Ministère des Affaires Etrangères (MAE), série Algérie, vol. 2, Depreux to Bidault, 19 August 1946; Direction d'Afrique-Levant au Cabinet du Ministre, 'Statut de l'Algérie', 3 June 1947. The principal reform enshrined in the Statute for Algeria was the creation of a 120-member Assembly with power of budgetary supervision, elected on a dual college system.

82. Henrik Spruyt, *Ending Empire: Contested Sovereignty and Territorial Partition* (Ithaca, NY: Cornell University Press, 2005), 4–8.

83. Lewis, 'The MRP and the genesis', 276.

84. TNA, FO 371/67688, Z4026/312/17, FO memorandum, 'The French Union', 21 April 1947.

85. Michel, 'L'Empire colonial dans les débats parlémentaires', in Berstein and Milza, *L'Année 1947*, 211–15.

86. Owen White, *Children of the French Empire: Miscegenation and Colonial Society in French West Africa 1895-1960* (Oxford: Oxford University Press, 1999), 147–8. For more long-term background to the '*métis problem*', see Ann Laura Stoler, 'Rethinking colonial categories: European communities and the boundaries of rule', *Comparative Studies in Society and History*, 31:1 (1989), 134–61; Jean Elizabeth Pederson, '"Special customs": paternity suits and citizenship in France and the colonies, 1870-1912', in Julia Clancy-Smith and Frances Gouda (eds), *Domesticating the Empire: Race, Gender, and Family Life in French and Dutch Colonialism* (Charlottesville, VA: University of Virginia Press, 1998), 55–7.

87. For various examples of this process in action, see Daniel Hémery, 'Du patriotisme au marxisme: l'immigration vietnamienne en France de 1926 à 1930', *Le Mouvement Social*, 90:1 (1975), 3–54; Mahfoud Kaddache, *Histoire du nationalisme algérien: tome I* (Algiers: ENL, 1993), 182; Francis Koerner, *Madagascar: Colonisation française et nationalisme malgache XXe siècle* (Paris: Harmattan, 1994), 189.

88. Gwendolyn Wright, 'Tradition in the service of modernity: architecture and urbanism in French colonial policy, 1900-1930', *Journal of Modern History*, 59 (June 1987), 315. For urban case studies, see Janet L. Lughod, *Rabat: Urban Apartheid in Morocco* (Princeton, NJ: Princeton

University Press, 1980); David Prochaska, *Making Algeria French: Colonialism in Bône, 1870-1920* (Cambridge: Cambridge University Press, 1990); Zeynep Celik, *Urban Forms and Colonial Confrontations: Algiers under French Rule* (Berkeley: University of California Press, 1997).

89. Andrew Hardy, 'The economics of French rule in Indochina: a biography of Paul Bernard (1892-1960)', *MAS*, 32:4 (1998), 833–4.

90. Marc Michel, 'L'Empire colonial dans les débats parlémentaires', in Berstein and Milza, *L'Année 1947*, 191, 200.

91. Martin Shipway, 'Reformism and the French "official mind": the 1944 Brazzaville Conference and the legacy of the Popular Front', in Chafer and Sackur, *French Colonial Empire*, 131.

92. The roots of this tension are discussed in Uday S. Mehta, 'Liberal strategies of Exclusion', in Cooper and Stoler, *Tensions of Empire*, 59–86.

93. Sorum, *Intellectuals*, 80–1.

Chapter 6

1. While AEF is still neglected, there are now several outstanding studies of AOF in French: J-R. de Benoist, *L'AOF de 1944 à 1960* (Dakar: Nouvelles Editions Africaines, 1982); Catherine Coquery-Vidrovitch and Odile Goerg (eds), *L'Afrique occidentale au temps des français. Colonisateurs et colonisés, c. 1860-1960* (Paris: La découverte, 1992); Charles Becker, Saliou Mbaye and Ibrahima Thioub (eds), *AOF: Réalités et héritages. Sociétés ouest-africaines et ordre colonial, 1895-1960* (Dakar: Direction des Archives du Sénégal, 1997). In English-language studies, the comparative neglect of French West Africa, partially rectified by John Hargreaves' subtle treatment in his *Decolonization in Africa*, has at last been corrected by an excellent detailed study: Tony Chafer, *The End of Empire in French West Africa, 1936-60. France's Successful Decolonization?* (Oxford: Berg, 2002).

2. Nwaubani, *The United States and the Decolonization of West Africa*, 16–17.

3. Nwaubani, *The United States and the Decolonization of West Africa*, 19–24.

4. Richard Joseph, *Radical Nationalism in Cameroun: Social Origins of the UPC Rebellion* (Oxford: Oxford University Press, 1977), 4; Achille Mbembe, *La naissance du maquis dans le Sud-Cameroun (1920-1960)* (Paris: Karthala, 1996).

5. Elizabeth Schmidt, 'Top down or bottom up? Nationalist mobilization reconsidered, with special reference to Guinea', *American Historical Review*, 110 (October 2005), 975–1014; *idem, Mobilizing the Masses: Gender, Ethnicity, and Class in the Nationalist Movement in Guinea, 1939-1958* (Portsmouth, NH: Heinemann, 2005), 145–92, *passim*.

6. Frederick Cooper, 'Alternatives to nationalism in French Africa, 1945-1960', in Jost Dülffer and Marc Frey (eds), *Elites and Decolonization in the Twentieth Century* (Basingstoke: Palgrave Macmillan, 2011), 110–24.

7. Shipway, *Decolonization and its Impact*, 130–1.

8. Cooper, *Colonialism in Question*, 29, 207–8.

9. Catherine Coquery-Vidrovitch, *Africa, Endurance and Change South of the Sahara* (Berkeley: University of California Press, 1988), chs 9 and 12.

10. Gregory Mann, 'Fetishizing religion: Allah Koura and French "Islamic policy" in late colonial French Soudan (Mali)', *JAH*, 44:2 (2003), 263–5, 280–1.

11. Robert Launay and Benjamin F. Soares, 'The formation of an "Islamic sphere" in French colonial West Africa', *Economy and Society*, 28 (1999), 497; also cited in Mann, 'Fetishizing Religion', 265.

12. Elizabeth Schmidt, 'Cold War in Guinea: The Rassemblement Démocratique Africain and the struggle over communism, 1950-1958', *Journal of African History*, 48:1 (2007), 99–103.

13. J. G. Vaillant, *Black, French and African: A Life of Léopold Sédar Senghor* (Cambridge, MA: Harvard University Press, 1990). It is noteworthy that Kwame N'Krumah was a vituperative critic of 'Negritude', dismissing it as elitist and not authentically African.

14. G. Wesley Johnson, 'William Ponty (1866-1915) and republican paternalism in French West Africa', in L. H. Gann and P. Duignan (eds), *African Proconsuls. European Governors in Africa* (New York: Free Press, 1978), 127–56.

15. Yves Person, 'French West Africa and decolonization', in Prosser Gifford and Wm. Roger Louis (eds), *The Transfer of Power in Africa: Decolonization, 1940-1960* (New Haven: Yale University Press, 1982), 141–2.

16. Holland, *European Decolonization*, 158.

17. Conklin, *A Mission to Civilize*, 23–37.

18. Timothy C. Weiskel, *French Colonial Rule and the Baule Peoples: Resistance and Collaboration, 1889-1911* (Oxford: Clarendon, 1980).

19. Municipal councils and a *conseil général* were established in Senegal between 1872 and 1879, see H. O. Idowu, 'The establishment of elective institutions in Senegal, 1869-1880', *JAH*, 9:2 (1968), 261–77. On 1 October 1916 male adult *originaires* (original inhabitants) of the four communes were granted French citizenship without any revocation of their customary rights as practising Muslims.

20. Catherine Coquery-Vidrovitch, 'Nationalité et citoyenneté en Afrique occidentale française: Originaires et citoyens dans le Sénégal colonial', *JAH*, 42:2 (2001), 285–305.

21. Regarding Diagne and Senegalese politics, see Stanford: Stanford University Press, 1971.

22. Aldrich, *Greater France*, 213–14.

23. Gregory Mann, 'What was the *indigénat*? The "empire of law" in French West Africa', *JAH*, 50 (2009), 334.

24. Mann, 'What was the *indigénat*?', 336.

25. Timothy C. Weiskel, 'Independence and the Longue Durée: The Ivory Coast "Miracle" Reconsidered', in *Decolonization and African Independence*, 358–63.

26. USNA, RG 59, Department of State decimal files, 851T.00, French West Africa, Political 1945-49, box 6328, US Consul, Brazzaville, 'Post War Prospects in French Equatorial Africa', 14 July 1945.

27. Elikia M'Bokolo, 'French colonial policy in Equatorial Africa in the 1940s and 1950s', in *The Transfer of Power in Africa*, 173.

28. See Richard Joseph, 'Radical nationalism in French Africa: The case of Cameroon', in Gifford and Louis, *Decolonization and African Independence*, 335–41, and his 'Ruben Um Nyobé and the "Kamerun" Rebellion', *African Affairs*, 73:293 (1974), 428–48.

29. USNA, RG 59, 851T.00, French Africa, Political 1945-9, box 6328, US Consulate Brazzaville memcon., 'Post-war prospects in French Equatorial Africa', 14 July 1945.

30. This and subsequent paragraphs draw heavily on Catherine Coquery-Vidrovitch, 'L'Impact des intérêts coloniaux: S.C.O.A. et C.F.A.O. dans l'Ouest Africain, 1910-1965', *JAH*, 16:4 (1975), 595–621.

31. Joseph, 'Settlers, strikers and *sans-travail*', 669.

32. John Kent, 'United States reactions to empire, colonialism, and Cold War in black Africa, 1949-57', *JICH*, 33:2 (2005), 198–209.

33. Catherine Hodeir, *Stratégies d'Empire. Le grand patronat colonial face à la décolonisation* (Paris: Belin, 2003), 222–3.

34. USNA, RG 59, 851T.00, French West Africa, Political 1945-49, box 6327, AMCONGEN, Dakar, 'Long range economic and social planning in French West Africa', 5 December 1945.

35. USNA, RG 59, 851T.00, French West Africa, Political 1950-4, box 5008, AMCONGEN, Dakar, 'Tentative proposals for development of Africa by ECA funds', 29 June 1950.

36. Dominique Barjot, 'Les Entreprises de travaux publics face à la décolonisation: une adaptation difficile, mais réussie? (1940-1956)', in Ageron, *Les Chemins*, 162–3.

37. J-C. Berthélemy, 'L'économie de l'Afrique occidentale française et du Togo, 1946-1960', *Revue Française de l'Histoire d'Outre-Mer*, 67:248 (1980), 301, also cited in Hargreaves, *Decolonization in Africa*, 139.

38. Catherine Coquery-Vidrovitch, 'L'impérialisme français en Afrique noire: Idéologie impériale et politique d'équipement, 1924-1975', *Relations internationales*, 7 (1976), 276–7.

39. Jean Suret-Canale, *Les Groupes d'études communistes en Afrique noire* (Paris: Harmattan, 1994).

40. Chafer, *End of Empire*, ch. 2. The essential qualification for subject voting rights was a French education or military service.

41. Martin Thomas, 'The colonial policies of the Mouvement Republicain Populaire, 1944-54: From reform to reaction', *English Historical Review*, 118:476 (2003), 380–411.

42. Led by Léon Viard, the *États généraux* was built around pre-existing Chambers of Commerce networks in Douala, Dakar, Conakry, and other major trading ports, see USNA, RG 59, 851T.00, French West Africa, Political 1945–9, box 6326, AMCONGEN, Dakar, to State, 3 November 1945.

43. Christian Bidegaray, 'Le tabou de l'indépendance dans les débats constituants sur les pays de l'outre-mer français: 1945-1958', in Ageron and Michel, *L'Afrique noire française*, 195.

44. Chafer, *End of Empire*, 64–5.

45. Chafer, *End of Empire*, 64–5, ch. 3; Rokhaya Fall, 'Le système d'enseignement en AOF', in Becker et al., *AOF*, 1078.

46. Alexander Keese, 'A culture of panic: "Communist" scapegoats and decolonization in French West Africa and French Polynesia (1945-1957)', *French Colonial History*, 9 (2008), 131–45.

47. Person, 'French West Africa and Decolonization', 155.

48. Chafer, *End of Empire*, 105–9.

49. Philippe Dewitte, 'La CGT et les syndicates d'Afrique occidentale française (1945-1957)', *Le Mouvement Social*, 117 (1981), 4–5, 10–11.

50. Philippe Dewitte, 'La CGT et les syndicates d'Afrique occidentale française (1945-1957)', *Le Mouvement Social*, 117 (1981), 98–9.

51. Gregory Mann, *Native Sons: West African Veterans and France in the Twentieth Century* (Durham, NC: Duke University Press, 2006), esp. 108–45; Jacqueline Woodfork, '"It is a crime to be a tirailleur in the army": The impact of Senegalese civilian status in the French colonial army during the Second World War', *Journal of Military History*, 77:1 (January 2013), 115–39.

52. Coquery-Vidrovitch, *Africa, Endurance and Change South of the Sahara*, 265–8.

53. Frederick Cooper, *Decolonization and African Society: The Labor Question in French and British Africa* (Cambridge: Cambridge University Press, 1996), 241–7. Idem, *Citizenship between Empire and Nation: Remaking France and French Africa* (Princeton, NJ: Princeton University Press, 2014).

54. Cooper, *Decolonization and African Society*, 278–86; Timothy Oberst, 'Transport workers, strikes and the imperial response: Africa and the post World War II conjuncture', *African Studies Review*, 31:1 (1988), 117–33; Jean Suret-Canale, 'L'indépendance de la Guinée', in Ageron et al., *L'Afrique noire française*, 131–2.

55. Frederick Cooper, 'The Senegalese general strike of 1946 and the labor question in post-war French Africa', *Canadian Journal of African Studies*, 24:2 (1990), 165–215, and idem, 'Our strike': Equality, anticolonial politics, and the 1947–48 railway strike in French West Africa', *JAH*, 37:1 (1996), 81–118.

56. Cooper, *Decolonization and African Society*, 241–4, 247.

57. Cooper, *Decolonization and African Society*, 282. Equivalent benefits for African workers in the private sector were not conceded until 1956.

58. A useful summary is Lansine Kaba, 'From colonialism to autocracy: Guinea under Sékou Touré, 1957-1984', in Gifford and Louis, *Decolonization and African Independence*, 225–44.

59. Cooper, 'The Dialectics of Decolonization', 425.

60. Elikia M'Bokolo, 'Forces sociales et idéologies dans la décolonisation de l'A.E.F', *JAH*, 22:3 (1981), 393–407.

61. Jacques Valette, 'L'Afrique équatoriale française: le cas du Congo (1958-1960)', and Bernard Lanne, 'L'indépendance du Tchad', in Ageron and Michel, *L'Afrique noire française*, 316, 448.

62. Florence Bernault-Boswell, 'Le rôle des milieux coloniaux dans la décolonisation du Gabon et du Congo-Brazzaville (1945-1964)', in Ageron and Michel, *L'Afrique noire française*, 288–9.

63. Richard A. Joseph, 'Settlers, strikers and *sans-travail*: The Douala riots of September 1945', *JAH*, 15:4 (1974), 669–87.

64. Joseph, 'Radical nationalism in French Africa: The case of Cameroon', 325–8; some of Delavignette's proposed reforms are reproduced in William B. Cohen (ed.), *Robert Delavignette on the French Empire. Selected Writings* (Chicago: University of Chicago Press, 1977), 100–7.

65. Joseph, 'Radical nationalism in French Africa', 341.

66. M'Bokolo, 'Forces sociales', 404–7.

67. For details, see Keese, 'A culture of panic'.

68. Person, 'French West Africa and decolonization', 151; Hargreaves, *Decolonization in Africa*, 141–2.

69. Chafer, *End of Empire*, ch. 3. René Pleven was leader of the UDSR.

70. Benjamin Stora, *Nationalistes Algériens et Révolutionnaires Français au temps du Front Populaire* (Paris: Éditions l'Harmattan, 1987); T.-A. Schweitzer, 'Le parti communiste français, le Comintern et l'Algérie dans les années 1930', *Le Mouvement Social*, 78 (1972), 115–36; Manuela Semidei, 'Les Socialistes français et le problème colonial entre les deux guerres (1919-1939)', *Revue Française de Science Politique*, 18:6 (1968), 1115–53.

71. These ambiguities are discussed in G. Wesley Johnson, 'Les élites au Sénégal pendant la période d'indépendance', in Ageron and Michel, *L'Afrique noire française*, 26–36.

72. Tony Chafer, 'Students and nationalism: The role of students in the nationalist movement in Afrique occidentale française (AOF), 1946-60', in Becker et al., *AOF*, 395–6, 402–3.

73. Thierno Bah, 'Les étudiants de l'Afrique noire et la marche à l'indépendance', in Ageron and Michel, *L'Afrique noire française*, 41–56.

74. USNA, RG 59, 751T.00, French West Africa, Political 1955–9, box 3389, AMCONGEN, Dakar, 'Survey of political situation in French West Africa', 30 November 1956.

75. Person, 'French West Africa', 161.

76. Cooper, *Decolonization and African Society*, 424–5.

77. Chafer, *End of Empire*, ch. 6.

78. USNA, RG 59, 751T.00, French West Africa, Political 1955–9, box 3389, AMCONGEN, Dakar, to State, 14 June 1956.

79. Frederick Cooper, 'Possibility and constraint: African independence in historical perspective', *JAH*, 49:1 (2008), 167–8, 175–6.

80. Catherine Atlan, 'Demain la balkanisation? Les députés africains et le vote de la Loi-cadre (1956)', in Becker, *AOF*, 358–75.

81. Crawford Young, 'The politics of balkanization: AOF in comparative perspective', in Becker, *AOF*, 227.

82. Claudine Cotte, 'Géopolitique de la colonisation', in Coquery-Vidrovitch and Goerg, *L'afrique occidentale au temps des français*, 99–100.

83. Albert Bourgi, 'Passé colonial et évolution des états d'Afrique noire francophone', in Catherine Coquery-Vidrovitch and Alain Forrest (eds), *Décolonisations et nouvelles dépendances* (Lille: Presses Universitaires de Lille, 1986), 112–16.

84. Chafer, *End of Empire*, ch. 6.

85. Paul Isoart, 'Le conseil exécutif de la Communauté', in Ageron et al., *L'Afrique noire française*, 214–25.

86. Elizabeth Schmidt, *Cold War and Decolonization in Guinea, 1946-1958* (Athens, OH: Ohio University Press, 2007), 125–79, *passim*.

87. Founded in March 1958, the PRA united two inter-party coalitions established in January of that year: Senghor's Convention Africain and the Mouvement Socialiste Africain.

88. Monique Lakroum, 'Sénégal-Soudan (Mali): deux états pour un empire', in Coquery-Vidrovitch and Goerg, *L'afrique occidentale au temps des français*, 188–9.

89. Finn Fuglestad, 'Djibo Bakary, the French, and the referendum of 1958 in Niger', *JAH*, 14:2 (1973), 313–30.

90. Person, 'French West Africa and decolonization', 169.

91. Valette, 'L'Afrique équatoriale française', 317–19; and Lanne, 'L'indépendance du Tchad', 446–7.

92. Florence Bernault-Boswell, 'Le rôle des milieux coloniaux dans la décolonisation du Gabon et du Congo-Brazzaville (1945-1964)', in Ageron and Michel, *L'Afrique noire française*, 291–3.

Chapter 7

1. For a sceptical, but balanced treatment of these conflicts, see Anthony Clayton, *The Wars of French Decolonization* (Harlow: Longman, 1994).

2. Robert Mortimer, 'Algeria, Vietnam and Afro-Asian solidarity', *The Maghreb Review*, 28:1 (2003), 60–6.

3. William Duiker, 'Ho Chi Minh and the strategy of people's war', in Mark Atwood Lawrence and Fredrik Logevall (eds), *The First Vietnam War. Colonial Conflict and Cold War Crisis* (Cambridge, MA: Harvard University Press, 2007); Gilbert Meynier, *Histoire intérieure du FLN 1954-1962* (Paris: Fayard, 2002), 137–56, 258–68; for Portuguese Africa: Patrick Chabal, *Amilcar Cabral. Revolutionary Leadership and People's War* (London: Hurst, 1983), 188–218.

4. Christopher E. Goscha, 'A "total war" of decolonization? Social mobilization and state-building in Communist Vietnam (1949–54)', *War & Society*, 31:2 (2012), 136–62; more generally: Fredrik Logevall, *Embers of War: The Fall of an Empire and the Making of America's Vietnam* (New York: Random House, 2012).

5. David Marr, 'Creating defense capacity in Vietnam, 1945-1947', in Lawrence and Logevall (eds), *The First Vietnam War*.

6. Gil Merom, *How Democracies Lose Small Wars. State, Society, and the Failures of France in Algeria, Israel in Lebanon, and the United States in Vietnam* (Cambridge: Cambridge University Press, 2003), 92–3.

7. James D. Le Sueur (ed.), *Mouloud Feraoun, Journal 1955-1962. Reflections on the French-Algerian War* (Lincoln, NA: University of Nebraska Press, 2000), 53.

8. Matthew Connelly, *A Diplomatic Revolution: Algeria's Fight for Independence and the Origins of the Post-Cold War Era* (Oxford: Oxford University Press, 2002).

9. These comments draw upon Patrick Chabal, 'People's war, state formation and revolution in Africa: A comparative analysis of Mozambique, Guinea-Bissau and Angola', *Journal of Commonwealth and Comparative Politics*, 21:3 (1983), 104–23.

10. Regarding Giap's role, see Mark Philip Bradley, *Imagining Vietnam and America. The Making of Postcolonial Vietnam, 1919-1950* (Chapel Hill: University of North Carolina Press, 2000), 42–3.

11. Christopher E. Goscha, *Vietnam: Un état né de la guerre* (Paris: Armand Colin, 2011), 161–4.

12. Christopher E. Goscha, 'Hanoi and Saigon at war: Social dynamics of the Vietminh's "underground city" (1945-54)', *War in History*, 20:2 (2013), 222–50.

13. Christopher E. Goscha, *Thailand and the South East Asian Networks of the Vietnamese Revolution, 1885-1954* (Richmond: Curzon Press, 1999), chs 4–5.

14. Bradley, *Imagining Vietnam*, 148–60.

15. William J. Duiker, *The Communist Road to Power in Vietnam*, 2nd edn (Boulder, CO: Westview Press, 1996), 134–6.

16. The Islamist label was particularly ill-suited to the FLN, see Monique Gadant, *Islam et Nationalisme en Algérie d'après El Moudjahid organe central du FLN de 1956 à 1962* (Paris: Harmattan, 1988), and Gilbert Meynier, *Histoire Intérieure du F.L.N. 1954-1962* (Paris: Fayard, 2002), especially chs 1–3.

17. Matthew Connelly, 'Taking off the Cold War lens: visions of North-South conflict during the Algerian war for independence', *American Historical Review*, 105:3 (2000), 750.

18. Alain Ruscio, 'Le monde politique français et la révolution viêtnamienne (août–décembre 1945)', in Ageron, *Les Chemins*, 209–14. For leftist opinion, see Ruscio, *Les Communistes français et la guerre d'Indochine, 1944-54*, new edn (Paris: Harmattan, 2004). As Foreign Minister, the MRP leader Georges Bidault denigrated the Vietminh as former collaborators incapable of running a government, see *Documents Diplomatiques Français* (*DDF*) (Paris: Imprimerie Nationale, 2000), *1945*, vol. II, no. 227, Bidault circular, 30 September 1945.

19. Alain Ruscio, 'French public opinion and the war in Indochina, 1945-1954', in M. Scriven and P. Wagstaff (eds), *War and Society in Twentieth Century France* (Oxford: Berg, 1992), 117–29.

20. Cooper, *France in Indochina*, 183–90.

21. A. J. Stockwell, 'Imperialism and nationalism in South East Asia', in Brown and Louis (eds), *OHBE IV: The Twentieth Century*, 479.

22. Jennings, *Vichy in the Tropics*, chs 6–7; Martin Thomas, *The French Empire at War, 1940-45* (Manchester: Manchester University Press, 1998), ch. 7.

23. Hue-Tam Ho Tai, *Radicalism and the Origins of the Vietnamese Revolution* (Cambridge, MA: Harvard University Press, 1992), 254–7; for those unfamiliar with events: Ralph B. Smith, 'The Japanese Period in Indochina and the coup of 9 March 1945', *Journal of South East Asian Studies*, 9:2 (1978), 268–301; Kiyoko Kurusu Nitz, 'Independence without nationalists? The Japanese and Vietnamese nationalism during the Japanese period, 1940-45', *Journal of South East Asian Studies*, 15:1 (1984), 108–33.

24. Gary R. Hess, 'Franklin Roosevelt and Indochina', *Journal of American History*, 59:2 (1972), 353–68; Christopher Thorne, 'Indochina and Anglo-American relations, 1942-1945', *Pacific Historical Review*, 45:1 (1976), 73–96.

25. Quoted in Bradley, *Imagining Vietnam*, 76.

26. It has been suggested that Roosevelt tempered his views in 1944–5: Paul Orders, '"Adjusting to a new period in world history": Franklin Roosevelt and European colonialism', in David Ryan and Victor Pungong (eds), *The United States and Decolonization: Power and Freedom* (London: Macmillan, 2000), 63–5. Regarding trusteeship planning, in the same volume, see Victor Pungong, 'The United States and the international trusteeship system', 85–101.

27. Mark Atwood Lawrence, *Assuming the Burden: Europe and the American Commitment to War in Vietnam* (Berkeley: University of California Press, 2005), 59–101.

28. For French perspectives on Roosevelt's anti-colonialism, see Edward Rice-Maximin, *Accommodation and Resistance. The French left, Indochina and the Cold War, 1944-1954* (Westport: Praeger, 1986).

29. Smith, 'The Japanese period', 268–301; David P. Chandler, 'The kingdom of Kampuchea, March-October 1945: Japanese-sponsored independence in World War II', *Journal of South East Asian Studies*, 17:1 (1986), 80–93.

30. Sugata Bose, 'Starvation amidst plenty: The making of a famine in Bengal, Honan and Tonkin, 1942-45', *MAS*, 24:4 (1990), 720, 726.

31. Greg Lockhart, *Nation in Arms: The Origins of the People's Army of Vietnam* (London: Allen and Unwin, 1989), 109–11.

32. DRV strategic and economic policies are examined in David G. Marr, *Vietnam, 1945* (Berkeley: University of California Press, 1997). See also Service Historique de l'Armée de Terre, *1945–1946: Le Retour de la France en Indochine*, and *Indochine 1947: Reglement politique et Solution Militaire*, (Vincennes: SHA, 1987).

33. Duiker, *The Communist Road*, 122–3. Sainteny was increasingly anxious about French underestimation of Vietminh organizational capacity, see Jean-Marie d'Hoop, 'Du coup de force japonais au départ du Général de Gaulle', in Gilbert Pilleul (ed.), *Le Général de Gaulle et l'Indochine, 1940-1946* (Paris: Plon, 1982), 142–3.

34. Général Paul Huard, 'La Rentrée politique de la France au Cambodge (octobre 1945 – janvier 1946)', in Ageron, *Les Chemins*, 215–29.

35. Lawrence, *Assuming the Burden*, 116–17, 144.

36. National Archives of Australia, CRS, series A1838/283, item 463/6/2/1, Office of the Special Commissioner in South East Asia, APLO memo. no. 18, 'Situation in Cambodia', 20 October 1946.

37. Duiker, *The Communist Road*, 127.

38. Martin Shipway, *The Road to War. France and Vietnam, 1944-47* (Oxford: Berghahn, 1996), 104–5.

39. Stein Tønnesson, *The Birth of Tragedy: Vietnam 1946* (Berkeley: University of California Press, 2008), ch. 2: 'The Chinese Trap'.

40. Philippe Devillers, *Paris-Saigon-Hanoi, Les archives de la guerre, 1944-1947* (Paris: Gallimard, 1988); Stein Tønnesson, *1946: Déclenchement de la guerre d'Indochine* (Paris: Editions L'Harmattan, 1987); Shipway, *Road to War*, chs 7–8; Lawrence, *Assuming the Burden*, ch. 4.

41. Duiker, *The Communist Road*, 125.

42. Jacques Valette, 'La Conférence de Fontainebleau (1946)', in Ageron, *Les Chemins*, 247–9.

43. Lawrence, *Assuming the Burden*, 150–4.

44. Hugues Tertrais, *La piastre et le fusil. Le coût de la guerre d'Indochine 1945-1954* (Paris: Comité pour l'histoire économique et financière, 2002), 34–9.

45. Tønnesson, *1946*, 83–115, *passim*.

46. Martin Thomas, 'Divisive decolonization: The Anglo-French withdrawal from Syria and Lebanon, 1944-46', *JICH*, 28:3 (2000), 81.

47. Shipway, *Road to War*, 240–7; Lockhart, *Nation in Arms*, 162.

48. Maurice Agulhon, *The French Republic, 1879-1992* (Oxford: Blackwell, 1993), 337.

49. Shipway, *Road to War*, 260–7; Duiker, *The Communist Road*, 130–1.

50. The argument that the outbreak of war was avoidable is a central thesis of Tønnesson, *The Birth of Tragedy*.

51. Jean-Pierre Rioux, *The Fourth Republic 1944-1958* (Cambridge: Cambridge University Press, 1987), 120.

52. Pierre Letamendia, *Le Mouvement Républicain Populaire. Histoire d'un grand parti français* (Paris: Beauchesne, 1995), 98–101.

53. Martin Thomas, 'French imperial reconstruction and the development of the Indochina War', in Lawrence and Logevall (eds), *The First Vietnam War*, 141–4.

54. Duiker, *The Communist Road*, 134.

55. Buton, 'Le Parti communiste français et le stalinisme', 65.

56. Michel, 'L'Empire colonial dans les débats parlémentaires', in Berstein and Milza (eds), *L'Année 1947*, 191–201.

57. P. Bodin, 'Le combattant français du corps expéditionnaire en Extrême Orient (1945-1954)', *Guerre Mondiales et Conflits Contemporains*, 168 (October 1992), 175–93.

58. For background, see R. E. M. Irving, *The First Indochina War* (London: Croom Helm, 1975), 49–68.

59. Rice-Maximin, *Accommodation and Resistance*, 65–7.

60. Lawrence, *Assuming the Burden*, especially chs 5 and 6.

61. Irwin M. Wall, *The United States and the Making of Postwar France, 1945-1954* (Cambridge: Cambridge University Press, 1991), 237–8.

62. Lawrence, *Assuming the Burden*, 269. When, in April 1950, Prime Minister Long dared to open a dialogue with the United States in a bid to strengthen his own position, the French authorities evicted him from office.

63. Chen Jian, 'China and the First Indochina War, 1950-54', *The China Quarterly*, 133 (1993), 85–93; Christopher Goscha, 'L'aide militaire chinoise au Viêt-minh (1949-1954)', *Revue Historique des Armées*, 3 (2000), 15–24; Qiang Zhai, *China and the Vietnam Wars, 1950-1975* (Chapel Hill: University of North Carolina Press, 2000), ch. 1.

64. Michael Creswell, *A Question of Balance. How France and the United States Created Cold War Europe* (Cambridge, MA: Harvard University Press, 2006), 29–30.

65. Lawrence, *Assuming the Burden*, 279–80.

66. Clayton, *The Wars of French Decolonization*, 53–5.

67. Clayton, *The Wars of French Decolonization*, 55. The best account of this cataclysmic event is Logevall, *Embers of War*, 238–59.

68. Bernard Fall, *Street Without Joy: The French Debacle in Indochina* (Mechanicsburg: Stackpole, 1994), 32–33; also cited in Creswell, *A Question of Balance*, 184n.34.

69. Jian, 'China and the First Indochina War', 92–5.

70. Pierre Mendès France, *Oeuvres Complètes, tome 2: Une Politique de l'économie 1943-1954* (Paris: Gallimard, 1985), 297–303.

71. Alain Ruscio, 'L'opinion publique et la guerre d'Indochine: Sondages et témoignages', *Vingtième Siècle*, 1 (1991), 35–46.

72. Sorum, *Intellectuals and Decolonization*; David Schalk, *War and the Ivory Tower. Algeria and Vietnam* (Oxford: Oxford University Press, 1991).

73. Jean-Pierre Rioux, 'Varus, Qu'as-tu fait de mes légions?', in Maurice Vaïsse (ed.), *L'Armée française dans la guerre d'Indochine* (Paris: Complexe, 2000), 21–31; Frédéric Turpin, *De Gaulle, les Gaullistes et l'Indochine* (Paris: Les indes Savantes, 2005), 571–2.

74. Logevall, *Embers of War*, ch. 11.

75. Anthony Clayton, *Three Marshals of France: Leadership after Trauma* (London: Brasseys, 1992); Alexander Zervoudakis, '"Nihil mirare, nihil contemptare, omnia intelligere": Franco-Vietnamese Intelligence in Indochina, 1950-1954', *Intelligence and National Security*, 13:1 (1998), 195–229.

76. USNA, State Department files, Policy Planning Staff records, RG 59/250/D/12/01, Box 15, Record of Washington discussions with general de Lattre de Tassigny, 7 September 1951.

77. AN, 363AP, René Mayer papers, box 28, Robert Schuman letter to Dean Acheson, 25 August 1951. Marc Michel, 'De Lattre et les débuts de l'américanisation de la guerre d'Indochine', *Revue Française d'Histoire d'Outre-Mer*, 77 (1985), 321–34.

78. USNA, State Department files, Policy Planning Staff records, RG 59/250/D/12/01, Box 18, PPS briefing paper for Secretary of State's conversation with M. Jean Letourneau, 16 June 1952.

79. François Guillemot, 'Be men!': fighting and dying for the state of Vietnam (1951–54)', *War & Society*, 31:2 (2012), 194–210.

80. Rioux, *The Fourth Republic*, 211.

81. George Herring, *America's Longest War. The United States and Vietnam 1950-1975* (New York: Knopf, 1986), 26.

82. Duiker, *Communist Road*, 148–9.

83. Jian, 'China and the First Indochina War', 97–9.

84. Lockhart, *Nation in Arms*, 254n.123.

85. USNA, State Department files, Policy Planning Staff records, RG 59/250/D/12/01, Box 15, PPS memo. for National Security Council, 'Further U.S. support for France and the Associated States of Indochina', 5 August 1953.

86. Logevall, *Embers of War*, 355.

87. Cooper, *France in Indochina*, 183–90.

88. Jian, 'China and the First Indochina War', 101–5.

89. For the Geneva conference and its aftermath, see James Cable, *The Geneva Conference of 1954 on Indochina* (London: Macmillan, 1986); Lawrence Kaplan, Denise Artaud, and Mark R. Rubin (eds), *Dien Bien Phu and the Crisis of Franco-American Relations, 1954–1955* (Wilmington, DL: SR books, 1990).

90. Phillip Hughes, 'Division and Discord: British Policy, Indochina and the Origins of the Vietnam War, 1954-56', *JICH*, 28:3 (2000), 94–7; Jian, 'China and the First Indochina War', 105–9; Kevin Ruane, 'Anthony Eden, British Diplomacy and the Origins of the Geneva Conference of 1954', *Historical Journal*, 37:1 (1994), 152–73.

91. USNA, Policy Planning Staff records, RG 59/250/D/12/01, Box 15, W. Park Armstrong note for John Foster Dulles, 'Probable Communist reactions to certain possible U.S. courses of action in Indochina', 22 December 1953.

92. For background, see Richard Immerman, 'Between the unattainable and the unacceptable: Eisenhower and Dien Bien Phu', in Richard A. Melanson and David Mayers (eds), *Reevaluating Eisenhower. American Foreign Policy in the Fifties* (Urbana, IL: University of Illinois Press, 1987), 121–30.

93. David L. Anderson, *Trapped by Success: The Eisenhower Administration and Vietnam, 1953-61* (New York: Columbia University Press, 1993), chs 4–6.

94. Bethany S. Keenan, '"Flattering the little sleeping rooster": The French Left, de Gaulle, and the Vietnam War in 1965', *Historical Reflections*, 37:1 (2011), 95–100.

95. Tertrais, *La piastre et le fusil*, 225–31.

96. Cited in Cooper, *France in Indochina*, 182.

Chapter 8

1. Benjamin Claude Brower, *A Desert Named Peace: The Violence of France's Empire in the Algerian Sahara, 1844-1902* (New York: Columbia University Press, 2009), 14–51.

2. Jennifer E. Sessions, *By Sword and Plow: France and the Conquest of Algeria* (Ithaca, NY: Cornell University Press, 2011), 67–96.

3. Sessions, *By Sword and Plow*, chs 5–6.

4. Kamel Kateb, *Européens, 'Indigènes' et Juifs en Algérie (1830-1962)* (Paris: Institut National d'Études Démographiques, 2001), 40–7, 80–8; Kjell Halvorsen, 'Colonial Transformation of Agrarian Society in Algeria', *Journal of Peace Research*, 15:4 (1978), 323–48.

5. Brower, *A Desert Named Peace*, 47, 104–10, 114–17; Peter von Sivers, 'Rural uprisings as political movements in colonial Algeria, 1851-1914', in Edmund Burke III and Ira M. Lapidus (eds), *Islam, Politics, and Social Movements* (Berkeley: University of California Press, 1988), 39–59; Fanny Colonna, 'Cultural Resistance and Religious Legitimacy in Colonial Algeria', in A. S. Ahmed and D. M. Hart, *Islam in Tribal Societies* (London: Routledge, 1984), 106–26.

6. William Gallois, *A History of Violence in the Early Algerian Colony* (Basingstoke: Palgrave Macmillan, 2013), chs 3–5.

7. John Ruedy, *Modern Algeria: The Origins and Development of a Nation* (Bloomington, IN: Indiana University Press, 1992), 57–68.

8. Bennoune, 'The introduction of nationalism into rural Algeria', 1–2.

9. John Ruedy provides a succinct and illuminating account of the devastating effects of early French colonization on Algerian society in his *Modern Algeria*, 44–79.

10. Bennoune, 'The introduction of nationalism into rural Algeria', 2. Mahfoud Bennoune estimates cholera deaths at 67,000, and the losses during the 1868 famine at between 300,000 and 500,000.

11. Charles-Robert Ageron, *Les Musulmans algériens et la France (1871-1919)*, vol. I (Paris: Presses Universitaires de France, 1968), 94; Bennoune, 'The introduction of nationalism into rural Algeria', 2.

12. Ruedy, *Modern Algeria*, 81.

13. Figures from Ruedy, *Modern Algeria*, 69, table 3.1.

14. Lizabeth Zack, 'Who fought the Algerian War? Political identity and conflict in French-ruled Algeria', *International Journal of Politics, Culture, and Society*, 16:1 (2002), 65.

15. Neil MacMaster, 'The roots of insurrection: the role of the Algerian village assembly (djemâa) in peasant resistance, 1863-1962', *Comparative Studies in Society and History*, 52:2 (2013), 429–32.

16. William Hoisington Jr., *Lyautey and the French Conquest of Morocco* (London: Macmillan, 1994), especially chs 3–5; Moshe Gershovich, *French Military Rule in Morocco: Colonialism and its Consequences* (London: Frank Cass, 2000).

17. Juliette Bessis, 'Le mouvement ouvrier tunisien: de ses origines à l'indépendance', *Le Mouvement Social* 89 (1974), 85–108.

18. Eqbal Ahmad and Stuart Schaar, 'M'hamed Ali: Tunisian labor organizer', in Edmund Burke, III (ed.), *Struggle and Survival in the Modern Middle East* (London: I. B. Tauris, 1993), 199–203.

19. M'Barka Hamed-Touati, *Immigration maghrébine et activités politiques en France de la première guerre mondiale à la veille du front populaire* (Tunis: Université de Tunis, 1994); Charles-Robert Ageron, 'L'Association des étudiants musulmans nord-africains en France durant l'entre-deux-guerres. Contribution à l'étude des nationalismes maghrébins', *Revue Française d'Histoire d'Outre-Mer*, 70:258 (1983), 25–56.

20. James McDougall, *History and the Culture of Nationalism in Algeria* (Cambridge: Cambridge University Press, 2006), especially chs 1, 4, and 5.

21. Martin Thomas, 'Colonial violence in Algeria and the distorted logic of state retribution: the Sétif uprising of 1945', *Journal of Military History*, 75:1 (2011), 535–6, 548–50.

22. Fahd Abdullah al-Semmari, 'The role of the ulama in the Algerian revolution: 1945-1954', *UCLA Journal of Middle Eastern Studies*, 2 (1986), 92.

23. Kamel Bouguessa, *Aux sources du nationalisme algérien: Les pionniers du populisme révolutionnaire en marche* (Algiers: Éditions Casbah, 2000).

24. Omar Carlier, 'Mouvements de jeunesse, passage des générations et créativité sociale: la radicalité inventive algérienne des années 1940-1950', in Nicolas Bancel, Daniel Denis, and Youssef Fates (eds), *De l'Indochine à l'Algérie: La jeunesse en mouvements des côtés du miroir colonial 1940-1962* (Paris: Découverte, 2003), 169–70.

25. Mortimer, 'Algeria, Vietnam and Afro-Asian solidarity', 61–2.

26. Matthew Connelly, *A Diplomatic Revolution: Algeria's Fight for Independence and the Origins of the Post-Cold War Era* (Oxford: Oxford University Press, 2002).

27. Jim House and Neil MacMaster, *Paris 1961: Algerians, State Terror, and Memory* (Oxford: Oxford University Press, 2006), ch. 1.

28. MAE, série Afrique-Levant, 1944–59, sous-série Algérie, vol. 6, Algiers Prefect, 'Note sur l'activité subversive du PPA-MTLD dans le Département d'Alger', n. d. 1950.

29. The most detailed analysis of the FLN is now Gilbert Meynier, *Histoire Intérieure du FLN, 1954-1962* (Paris: Fayard, 2002).

30. Celik, *Urban Forms*, chs 1–2.

31. Paul Rabinow, *French Modern: Norms and Forms of the Social Environment* (Chicago: University of Chicago Press, 1989), 2–4.

32. Paul Rabinow, *French Modern*, ch. 9.

33. Ali Yedes, 'Social dynamics in colonial Algeria: the question of *pieds-noirs* identity', in Stovall and van den Abbeele, *French Civilization and its Discontents*, 244.

34. Jim House, 'L'impossible contrôle d'une ville colonial? Casablanca, décembre 1952', *Genèses*, 1:86 (2012), 79–83.

35. The term 'urban apartheid' was coined by Janet Abu Lughod in her *Rabat: Urban Apartheid in Morocco* (Princeton, NJ: Princeton University Press, 1980).

36. Xavier Malverti 'Heurs et malheurs de l'architecture algéroise', in Jean-Jacques Jordi and Guy Pervillé (eds), *Alger 1940-1962: Une ville en guerres* (Paris: Autrement, 1999), 167.

37. Celik, *Urban Forms*, 44–8.

38. Celik, *Urban Forms*, 81–2.

39. Ryo Ikeda, 'French policy towards Tunisia and Morocco: the international dimensions of decolonization, 1950-1956', University of London PhD, 2006, pp. 26–8.

40. Ikeda, 'French policy towards Tunisia and Morocco', University of London PhD, 39.

41. Ikeda, 'French policy towards Tunisia and Morocco', University of London PhD, 42–4, 51–3.

42. Wm. Roger Louis, 'American anti-colonialism and the dissolution of the British Empire', *International Affairs*, 61 (1985), 395–420; Saul Kelly, *Cold War in the Desert. Britain, the United States and the Italian Colonies, 1945-52* (London: Macmillan, 2000), 132–45; Yahia H. Zoubir, 'U.S. and Soviet policies towards France's Struggle with anticolonial nationalism in North Africa', *Canadian Journal of History*, 30 (1995), 439–66.

43. Martin Thomas, 'Defending a lost cause? France and the United States vision of imperial rule in French North Africa, 1945-1956', *Diplomatic History*, 26:2 (2002), 218–36.

44. Ikeda, 'French policy', 82–7.

45. Ikeda, 'French policy', 112–14.

46. Ikeda, 'French policy', 116–22.

47. Martin Thomas, *The French North African Crisis: Colonial Breakdown and Anglo-French Relations, 1945-1962* (London: Macmillan, 2000), 51–2.

48. House, 'L'impossible contrôle d'une ville colonial?' 89–95. Residency officials initially admitted to thirty-six deaths, certainly a gross underestimate.

49. Ikeda, 'French policy', 91–100.

50. Adria Lawrence, 'Triggering nationalist violence: competition and conflict in uprisings against colonial rule', *International Security*, 35:2 (2010), 99–114.

51. Lawrence, *International Security*, 104–5.

52. Thomas, *French North African Crisis*, 53–4.

53. TNA, FO 371/102973, JM1013/14, Rabat quarterly report, 5 October 1953; USNA, RG 59, 771.00, box 3998, Rabat consulate report on Oudja trial, 28 December 1954.

54. Ikeda, 'French policy', 106–9.

55. François Bédarida and Jean-Pierre Rioux (eds), *Pierre Mendès France et le mendésisme: L'expérience gouvernementale et sa postérité (1954-1955)* (Paris: Fayard, 1985); René Girault (ed.), *Pierre Mendès France et le rôle de la France dans le monde* (Grenoble: presses Universitaires de Grenoble, 1991).

56. Ikeda, 'French Policy', 125–6.

57. Philip Williams, *Crisis and Compromise*, 46–7; *DDF*, 1955, vol. I, no. 71, Note de la Direction générale au Ministère des affaires marocaines et tunisiennes, 11 February 1955.

58. Anthony Clayton, 'Emergency in Morocco, 1950-56', in Robert Holland (ed.), *Emergencies and Disorder in the European Empires after 1945* (London: Frank Cass, 1994), 137–8.

59. Thomas, *French North African Crisis*, 61.

60. Ikeda, 'French Policy', 151–7; Thomas, *French North African Crisis*, 62–3.

61. *DDF*, 1955, vol. II, docs. 25, 26, 27, 75 and 76.

62. *DDF*, 1955, vol. II, doc. 145, 'Entretiens franco-marocains d'Aix-les-Bains, procès-verbaux', 22–28 August 1955.

63. *DDF*, 1955, vol. II, docs. 157, 177, 199; Henri Lerner, *Catroux* (Paris: Albin Michel, 1990), 325–6.

64. Ikeda, 'French Policy', 163–74 *passim*.

65. Bernard, *The Franco-Moroccan Conflict*, 300–7, 323–4.

66. *DDF*, 1955, vol. 11, doc. 343, Antoine Pinay to overseas ambassadors, 2 November 1955.

67. *DDF*, 1956, vol. I, docs. 159 and 202, Foreign Ministry notes, 10 and 26 March 1956.

68. Lawrence, 'Triggering nationalist violence', 111–13.

Chapter 9

1. Jean-Pierre Rioux, 'Les Français et la guerre des deux Républiques', in Mohammed Harbi and Benjamin Stora (eds), *La Guerre d'Algérie, 1954 2004: La fin de l'amnésie* (Paris: Robert Laffont, 2004), 17.

2. Neil MacMaster, 'The "silent native": *attentisme*, being compromised, and banal terror during the Algerian War of independence, 1954-62', in Thomas, *French Colonial Mind: Violence*, 283–303; on the divisiveness of escalation, see Martin Evans, *Algeria: France's Undeclared War* (Oxford: Oxford University Press, 2012).

3. Rioux, 'Les Français et la guerre des deux Républiques', 18–19.

4. Martin Alexander, 'Seeking France's "lost soldiers": reflections on the military crisis in Algeria', in Kenneth Mouré and M. S. Alexander (eds), *Crisis and Renewal in France, 1918-1962* (Oxford: Berghahn, 2002), 242–4.

5. The reluctance to concede the existence of war in Algeria continued long after 1962, see Benjamin Stora, *Le Gangrène et l'oubli: La mémoire de la guerre d'Algérie* (Paris: Découverte, 1991), 13–14, and Anne Donadey, '"Une Certaine Idée de la France": The Algeria syndrome and struggles over "French" identity', in Steven Ungar and Tom Conley (eds), *Identity Papers: Contested Nationhood in Twentieth Century France* (Minneapolis: University of Minnesota Press, 1996), 215–18.

6. Guy Pervillé, 'La guerre d'Algérie: combien de morts?' in Harbi and Stora, *La Guerre d'Algérie*, 476. One French historian has recently accepted these very high estimates: see Marc Ferro, *Le Livre noir du colonialisme* (Paris: Robert Laffont, 2003), 560.

7. Pervillé, 'La guerre d'Algérie: combien de morts?' 482.

8. Xavier Yacono, 'Les pertes algériennes de 1954 à 1962', *Revue de l'Occident Musulman et de la Méditerranée*, 34 (1983), 119–34; also cited in Pervillé, 'La guerre d'Algérie: combien de morts?' 480.

9. Rémi Kauffer, 'OAS: la guerre franco-française d'Algérie', in Harbi and Stora, *La guerre d'Algérie*, 470; Pervillé, 'La guerre d'Algérie: combien de morts?' 484–5.

10. Jean-Charles Jauffret, 'The origins of the Algerian War: the reaction of France and its army to the emergencies of 8 May 1945 and 1 November 1954', *JICH*, 21:3 (1993), 17–29; Charles-Robert Ageron, 'Les troubles du nord-constantinois en mai 1945: une tentative insurrectionelle?', *Vingtième Siècle*, 4 (October 1984), 23–38; Annie Rey-Goldseiguer, *Aux origines de la guerre*

d'Algérie 1940-1945: De Mers-el-Kébir aux massacres du nord-constantinois (Paris: Editions la Découverte, 2002), part III. The most detailed treatment is now Jean-Louis Planche, *Sétif, 1945: Histoire d'un massacre annoncé* (Paris: Perrin, 2006).

11. Charles-Robert Ageron, 'Le "drame des harkis": mémoire ou histoire?' *Vingtième Siècle*, 68 (October–December, 2000), 3–15.

12. The best account of the FLN-MNA conflict is now Linda Amiri, *La Bataille de France: La guerre d'Algérie en France* (Paris: Robert Laffont, 2004); see also Jacques Valette, *La guerre d'Algérie des Messalistes 1954-1962* (Paris: L'Harmattan, 2001).

13. Irwin M. Wall, *France, the United States and the Algerian War* (Berkeley: University of California Press, 2001), 2.

14. Martha Crenshaw Hutchinson, *Revolutionary Terrorism: The F.L.N. in Algeria, 1954-1962* (Stanford, CA: Hoover Institution Press, 1978).

15. The role of logic, or political calculation, in the cruelties of fratricidal conflict is explored in Stathis N. Kalyvas, *The Logic of Violence in Civil War* (Cambridge: Cambridge University Press, 2006).

16. Merom, *How Democracies Lose Small Wars*, part II.

17. A point compellingly made by James McDougall, 'Savage wars? Codes of violence in Algeria, 1830s-1990s', *Third World Quarterly*, 26:1 (2005), 117–31.

18. Daniel Lefeuvre, *Chère Algérie: Comptes et mécomptes de la tutelle coloniale, 1930-1962* (Paris: Société Française d'Histoire d'Outre-Mer, 1997), 64–6.

19. Ahmed Henni, 'La naissance d'une classe moyenne paysanne musulmane après la Première Guerre Mondiale', *Revue Française d'Histoire d'Outre-Mer*, 83:311 (1996), 54.

20. Jacques Simon (ed.), *Messali Hadj par les textes* (Paris: Editions Bouchène, 2000), doc. 38, 'Message à la conférence de Bandoeng', 19 March 1955.

21. MAE, série Afrique-Levant 1944–59, sous-série Algérie 1944–52, vol. 6, Algiers prefecture report, 'Note sur l'activité subversive du PPA-MTLD dans le Département d'Alger', n. d. 1950.

22. Jauffret, 'The Origins of the Algerian War', 26–7; Lefeuvre, *Chère Algérie*, 266–7.

23. Valette, *La guerre d'Algérie des Messalistes*, 23–6.

24. Emmanuel Blanchard, *La Police parisienne et les Algériens (1944-1962)* (Paris: Nouveau Monde, 2011), parts II–IV; Linda Amiri, 'La répression policière en France vue par les archives', in Harbi and Stora, *La guerre d'Algérie*, 408–16.

25. Ali Haroun, *La 7e Wilaya: La guerre du FLN en France 1954-1962* (Paris: Seuil, 1986), 251–87.

26. James McDougall, 'S'écrire un destin: l'Association des 'ulama dans la revolution algérienne', *Bulletin de l'IHTP*, 83 (premier semestre 2004), 43–7. McDougall also points to the abiding tensions between the AUMA and FLN leadership, typified by nagging suspicions of ALN involvement in the disappearance of 'ulama leader, Larbi Tebessi, on 8 April 1957.

27. Meynier, *Histoire intérieure du FLN*, 569–80.

28. Simon (ed.), *Messali Hadj par les textes*, doc. 58: 'Rapport politique de Messali Hadj à la Direction du MNA', 29 April 1958.

29. Valette, *La guerre d'Algérie des Messalistes*, deuxième partie.

30. Simon (ed.), *Messali Hadj par les textes*, doc. 53: 'Appel au peuple algérien', 1 September 1957.

31. Valette, *La guerre d'Algérie des Messalistes*, 135–49; Clayton, *Wars of French Decolonization*, 136, 155.

32. Amiri, *La Bataille de France*, 43–52.

33. Charles-Robert Ageron, 'L'Opinion française à travers les sondages', in Jean-Pierre Rioux (ed.), *La guerre d'Algérie et les Français* (Paris: Fayard, 1992), 26–7.

34. Emma Kuby, 'A war of words over an image of war: the Fox-Movietone scandal and the portrayal of French violence in Algeria, 1955-1956', *FPCS*, 30:1 (2012), 46–57.

35. Charles-Robert Ageron, 'L'insurrection du 20 août 1955 dans le nord Constantinois: de la résistance armée à la guerre au peuple', in Charles-Robert Ageron (ed.), *La guerre d'Algérie et les Algériens, 1954-1962* (Paris: Armand Colin, 1997), 27–50; Clayton, *The Wars*, 118–19.

36. Regarding these earlier measures, see *DDF*, 1955, vol. I, doc. 300, Antoine Pinay to Couve de Murville, 26 May 1955; TNA, FO 371/113788, Algiers consular note to FO African Dept., 8 July 1955.

37. Evans, *Algeria*, chs 6–7.

38. Philippe Bourdrel, *La dernière chance de l'Algérie française: Du gouvernement socialiste au retour de De Gaulle, 1956-1958* (Paris: Albin Michel, 1996); see also Gérard Bossuat, 'Guy Mollet: La puissance française autrement', *Relations Internationales*, 57 (1989), 25–48.

39. TNA, FO 371/125913, Consul R. Sarell (Algiers), 'Algeria, annual review for 1956', 14 January 1957.

40. SHA, 1H1379/D1, EMA-1, 'Plan d'urgence – 1e partie', 18 March 1956; Thomas, *French North African Crisis*, 103–6.

41. Sorum, *Intellectuals and Decolonization*, 107.

42. SHA, 1H1374/D3, 'Situation des effectifs des trois armées en Algérie, 1956'.

43. Cherifa Bouatta, 'Feminine Militancy: *Moudjahidates* during and after the Algerian War', in Valentine M. Moghadam (ed.), *Gender and National Identity: Women and Politics in Muslim Societies* (London: Zed Books, 1994), 19–21, 25–6.

44. Neil MacMaster, *Burning the Veil: The Algerian War and the 'Emancipation' of Algerian Women, 1954-62* (Manchester: Manchester University Press, 2009), chs 5–7; Natalya Vince, 'Transgressing boundaries: gender, race, religion, and "Françaises musulmanes" during the Algerian War of Independence', *French Historical Studies*, 33:3 (2010), 415–74.

45. ALN 'Directives sur la propagande et la contre-propagande au sujet de la femme', 2e semestre, 1958, in Harbi and Meynier, *Le FLN: Documents et histoire*, 609–12.

46. Catherine Lloyd, 'From taboo to transnational political issue: violence against women in Algeria', *Women's Studies International Forum*, 29 (2006), 454–7.

47. 'Directives de la wilaya 2 mintaqa 2 sur les "questions féminines" et le mariage', in Harbi and Meynier, *Le FLN: Documents et histoire*, 614–15.

48. MacMaster, *Burning the Veil*, ch. 9; Natalya Vince, *Our Fighting Sisters: Nation, Memory and Gender in Algeria, 1954-2012* (Manchester: Manchester University Press, 2014).

49. Marnia Lazreg, *Torture and the Twilight of Empire: From Algiers to Baghdad* (Princeton, NJ: Princeton University Press, 2008).

50. On the SAS, see Grégor Mathias, *Les Sections administratives spécialisées en Algérie: Entre idéal et réalité (1955-1962)* (Paris: L'Harmattan, 1998); Sylvian Bartet, 'Aspect de la pacification en Grande Kabylie (1955-1962). Les relations entre les sections administratives spécialisées et les populations', *Revue Française d'Histoire d'Outre-Mer*, 85:319 (1998), 3–32.

51. The consequences of army action are explored in Raphaëlle Branche, *La torture et l'armée pendant la Guerre d'Algérie: 1954-1962* (Paris: Gallimard, 2002); Fabian Klose, *Human Rights in the Shadow of Colonial Violence: The Wars of Independence in Kenya and Algeria* (Philadelphia: Pennsylvania University Press, 2013).

52. Sylvie Thénault, *Une drôle de justice: Les magistrats dans la guerre d'Algérie* (Paris: La Découverte, 2001), especially part II.

53. Martin Thomas, 'Policing Algeria's borders, 1956-1960: arms supplies, frontier defences and the Sakiet affair', *War and Society*, 13:1 (1995), 81–99.

54. Michel Cornaton, *Les Camps de regroupement de la guerre d'Algérie* (Paris: L'Harmattan, 1998); Keith Sutton, 'Army administration tensions over Algeria's *Centres de regroupement*, 1954-1962', *British Journal of Middle Eastern Studies*, 26:2 (1999), 243–70.

55. The fullest account of this process remains George Armstrong Kelly, *Lost Soldiers: The French Army and Empire in Crisis, 1947-1962* (Cambridge, MA: MIT Press, 1965).

56. For interplay between Gaullist foreign policy and Algeria, see Maurice Vaïsse, *La grandeur: Politique étrangère du Général de Gaulle, 1958-1969* (Paris: Fayard, 1998), 60–103; Michèle Cointet, *De Gaulle et l'Algérie française, 1958-1962* (Paris: Perrin, 1995).

57. James D. Le Sueur, *Uncivil War: Intellectuals and Identity Politics during the Decolonization of Algeria* (Philadelphia: Pennsylvania University Press, 2001), 23–7; Todd Shepard, *The Invention of Decolonization: the Algerian War and the Remaking of France* (Ithaca, NY: Cornell University Press, 2006), 47–54, 75–7; Stephen Tyre, 'From *Algérie française* to *France musulmane*: Jacques Soustelle and the myths and realities of 'integration', 1955-1962', *French History*, 20:3 (2006), 276–6.

58. Jean-François Guillaume, *Le mythes fondateurs de l'Algérie française* (Paris: Harmattan, 1992), 188–99; Patricia M. E. Lorcin, 'Rome and France in Africa: Recovering colonial Algeria's Latin past', *French Historical Studies*, 25:2 (2002), 295–329.

59. Yedes, 'Social dynamics in colonial Algeria', 243.

60. Jeannine Verdès-Leroux, *Les Français d'Algérie de 1830 à aujourd-hui* (Paris: Fayard, 2001), 180–1.

61. Neil MacMaster, 'Writing French Algeria', *French Cultural Studies*, 11:1 (2000), 149–50.

62. For one such case, see Jim House, 'L'impossible contrôle d'une ville coloniale: Casablanca, décembre 1952', *Genèses*, 1:86 (2012), 78–103.

63. Lefeuvre, *Chère Algérie*, 58–61.

64. The best recent accounts tracing the origins of this process are Brower, *A Desert Named Peace*; Sessions, *By Sword and Plow*.

65. Verdès-Leroux, *Les Français d'Algérie*, 11.

66. David Carroll, 'Camus's Algeria: birthrights, colonial injustice and the fiction of a French Algerian people', *Modern Language Notes*, 112 (1997), 529–31. The best treatment of Camus and the Algerian War is Le Sueur, *Uncivil War*, ch. 4.

67. Daniel Lefeuvre, 'Les réactions algériennes à la propagande économique et sociale française', in Ageron, *La guerre d'Algérie et les Algériens*, 237–8.

68. Cited in Verdès-Leroux, *Les Français d'Algérie*, 12–13.

69. Figures reproduced in Verdès-Leroux, *Les Français d'Algérie*, 270–4.

70. The most probing account of Algerian national identity and cultural authenticity, particularly in relation to key Islamic reformers, is now James McDougall, *History and the Culture of Nationalism in Algeria* (Cambridge University Press, 2006).

71. Si Abderrahmane Arab, 'The National Liberation War in the French language novel of Algeria', *Bulletin of the British Society for Middle Eastern Studies*, 17:1 (1990), 33–46.

72. Le Sueur, *Uncivil War*, 28–59, *passim*.

73. Jane E. Goodman and Paul A. Silverstein (eds), 'Introduction', in *Bourdieu in Algeria: Colonial Politics, Ethnographic Practices, Theoretical Developments* (Lincoln, NE: University of Nebraska Press, 2009), 10–22.

74. Carole Reynaud-Paligot, 'Les surréalistes et la guerre d'Algérie', *French Cultural Studies*, 13:1 (2002), 36–7.

75. Sorum, *Intellectuals and Decolonization*, 15–18, 238–40.

76. Danièle Joly, 'France's military involvement in Algeria: the PCF and the *Oppositionnels*', in M. Scriven and P. Wagstaff (eds), *War and Society in Twentieth Century France* (Oxford: Berg, 1992), 137–9.

77. Le Sueur, *Uncivil War*, 150–62.

78. William B. Cohen, 'The sudden memory of torture: the Algerian War in French discourse, 2000-2001', *French Politics, Culture and Society* 19:3 (2001), 82–3.

79. Sorum, *Intellectuals and Decolonization*, 114–21

80. This paragraph draws heavily from Judith Surkis, 'Ethics and violence: Simone de Beauvoir, Djamila Boupacha, and the Algerian War', *French Politics, Culture, and Society*, 28:2 (2010), 40–9.

81. For wider discussion about how the war was remembered, see Raphaëlle Branche and Jim House, 'Silences on state violence during the Algerian War of independence: France and Algeria, 1962-2007', in Efrat Ben Ze'ev, Ruth Ginio, and Jay Winter (eds), *Shadows of War: A Social History of Silence in the Twentieth Century* (Cambridge: Cambridge University Press, 2010).

82. British diplomatic observers sometimes read de Gaulle's Algeria policy this way. See TNA, FO 371/147328, Consul Trefor Evans, 'annual review, Algeria, 1959', 8 March 1960.

83. The FLN's approach is brilliantly explained in Connelly, *A Diplomatic Revolution*.

84. Betts, *France and Decolonization, 1900-1960*, 107–8.

85. Alexander, 'Seeking France's "lost soldiers"', 246–50, 260n.13; Clayton, *The Wars*, 161–72.

86. *DDF*, 1960, vol. II, doc. 7, 'Conclusions sur les entretiens de Melun', 5 July 960; Redha Malek, *L'Algérie à Evian : Histoire des négociations secrètes 1956-1962* (Paris: Éditions du Seuil, 1995), 62–6; Agulhon, *The French Republic*, 395–6.

87. For insights into OAS attitudes, see Alexander Harrison, *Challenging De Gaulle: The O.A.S. and the counterrevolution in Algeria, 1954-1962* (New York: Praeger, 1989).

88. The subtlest analysis of the war's impact on French society is now Todd Shepard, *The Invention of Decolonization: The Algerian War and the Remaking of France* (Ithaca, NY: Cornell University Press, 2006).

89. Surkis, 'Ethics and violence', 41.

90. Jim House, 'Memory and the creation of solidarity during the decolonization of Algeria', *Yale French Studies*, 118/119 (2010), 18–23.

91. House and MacMaster, *Paris 1961*, 88–99, 162–79. Through research of police and hospital records, the authors estimate 'well over' 120 police killings of Algerians in the Paris region in September–October 1961.

92. House and MacMaster, *Paris 1961*, 214–15.

93. Jim House and Neil MacMaster, '"Une journée portée disparue" The Paris massacre of 1961 and memory', in Mouré and Alexander, *Crisis and Renewal*, 267–90.

94. Jean-Paul Brunet, *Police contre F.L.N. Le drame d'octobre 1961* (Paris: Flammarion, 1999), 12.

95. Neil MacMaster, 'The role of European women and the question of mixed couples in the Algerian nationalist movement in France, circa 1918–1962', *French Historical Studies*, 34:2 (2011), 374–8.

96. Martin Evans, *The Memory of Resistance: French opposition to the Algerian War (1954-1962)* (Oxford: Berg, 1997), 36–7, 122–5, 205.

97. Le Sueur, *Uncivil War*, 205–13.

98. These included *Fils du pauvre* (1950); *Terre et le sang* (1953); and *Les Chemins qui montent* (1957).

99. De la Sueur (ed.), *Mouloud Feraoun: Journal*, xi–xxxi.

100. SHA, 1H2036/D1, no. 30/ART, Final artillery report, 30 March 1962.

101. Malek, *De l'Algérie à Evian*, annex IV.

102. Colette Zytnicki, 'L'administration face à l'arrivée des repatriés d'Algérie: l'exemple de la region Midi-Pyrenées (1962-1964)', *Annales du Midi*, 110:224 (1998), 501–21.

103. Agulhon, *The French Republic*, 403–5. The most senior leaders of the OAS, the former commanders in Algeria, Generals Maurice Challe, André Zeller, and Edmond Jouhaud, received prison sentences of between ten and fifteen years. Like most other OAS leaders, their sentences were later commuted.

104. Martin Evans, 'Rehabilitating the traumatized war veteran: the case of French conscripts from the Algerian War 1954à1962', in Martin Evans and Kenneth Lunn (eds), *War and Memory in the Twentieth Century* (Oxford: Berg, 1997), 73–85.

105. Christopher Flood and Hugo Frey, 'Defending the empire in retrospect: discourse of the extreme right', in Chafer and Sackur, *Promoting the Colonial Idea*, 94–210; Driss Maghraoui, 'French identity, Islam, and North Africans: colonial legacies, postcolonial realities', in Stovell and Abbeele, *French Civilization*, 223–4.

106. Michael Seidman, *The Imaginary Revolution: Parisian Students and Workers in 1968* (Oxford: Berghahn, 2004), 222, 250, 257–8; Alexander, 'Seeking France's "Lost Soldiers"', 258–9.

107. Todd Shepard, '"Something notably erotic": politics, "Arab men," and sexual revolution in postdecolonization France, 1962–1974', *Journal of Modern History*, 84:1 (2012), 80–115.

108. Mireille Rosello, 'North African women and the ideology of modernization', in Hargreaves and McKinney, *Post-Colonial Cultures in France*, 240–2.

109. Andrew Hussey, *The French Intifada: The Long War between France and its Arabs* (London: Granta, 2014); See also the essays in Hargreaves and McKinney cited above, particularly David Blatt, 'Immigrant politics in a republican nation', 40–51.

Chapter 10

1. This and subsequent paragraphs draw heavily on Marc Michel, 'Le Togo dans les relations internationales au lendemain de la guerre: prodrome de la décolonisation ou "petite mésentente cordiale"? (1945-1951)', in Ageron, *Chemins*, 95–107.

2. Hargreaves, *Decolonization in Africa*, 143.

3. John Kent, *The Internationalization of Colonialism: Britain, France and Black Africa, 1939-1956* (Oxford: Clarendon, 1992), ch. 7; Marc Michel, 'La coopération intercoloniale en Afrique noire, 1942-1950: un néo-colonialisme éclairé?', *Relations internationales*, 34 (1984), 155–71.

4. Solofo Randrianja, *Société et luttes anticoloniales à Madagascar (1896 à 1946)* (Paris: Karthala, 2001), chs 3–4.

5. Martin Shipway, 'Madagascar on the eve of insurrection, 1944-47: The Impasse of a Liberal Colonial Policy', *JICH*, 24:1 (1996), 77–86.

6. Koerner, *Madagascar: Colonisation française et nationalisme malgache*, 191–4, 307–12.

7. Martin Thomas, *The French Empire at War, 1940-45* (Manchester: Manchester University Press, 1998), 152–3; Jacques Tronchon, *L'insurrection malgache de 1947* (Paris: Karthala, 1986), 23–4.

8. G. Wesley Johnson, 'African political activity in French West Africa, 1900-1945', in Michael Crowder and J. Ajayi (eds), *History of West Africa* (Harlow: Longman, 1987), 542; also cited in Ginio, *French Colonialism Unmasked*, 5.

9. Lucile Rabearimanana, 'Les Malgaches et l'idée d'indépendance de 1945 à 1956', in Ageron, *Chemins*, 263; Shipway, 'Madagascar', 81–2.

10. The forebears of the MDRM are discussed in Solofo Randrianja, 'Aux origines du M.D.R.M. 1939-1946', in Francis Arazalier and Jean Suret-Canale (eds), *Madagascar 1947 La tragédie oubliée* (Paris: Temps des Cérises, 1999), 65–79.

11. Douglas Little, 'Cold War and colonialism in Africa: the United States, France, and the Madagascar Revolt of 1947', *Pacific Historical Review*, 59:4 (1990), 529, 535–8.

12. Rabearimanana, 'Les Malgaches et l'idée d'indépendance', 265; Raymond Delval, 'L'Histoire du PADESM (Parti des déshérités de Madagascar) ou quelques faits oubliés de l'histoire malgache', in Ageron, *Chemins*, 276–7.

13. Delval, 'L'Histoire du PADESM', 277–8.

14. Shipway, 'Madagascar', 91–4; Clayton, *The Wars*, 82n.8.

15. Shipway, 'Madagascar', 94.

16. Tronchon, *L'insurrection malgache*, 37–42.

17. Jacques Tronchon, 'La nuit la plus longue ... du 29 au 30 mars 1947', in Arazalier and Suret-Canale, *Madagascar 1947*, 118–26.

18. Rabearimanana, 'Les Malgaches et l'idée d'indépendance', 267; Clayton, *The Wars*, 83.

19. Tronchon, *L'insurrection malgache*, 74–9, also cited in Little, 'Cold War and Colonialism in Africa', 540.

20. Tronchon, *L'insurrection malgache*, 48–53.

21. Little, 'Cold War and colonialism in Africa', 542.

22. Jennifer Cole and Karen Middleton, 'Rethinking ancestors and colonial power in Madagascar', *Africa*, 71:1 (2001), 10–11.

23. Lucile Rabearimanana, 'Femmes Merina et vie politique à Madagascar durant la décolonisation (1945-1960)', in Chantal Chanson-Jabeur and Odile Goerg (eds), *"Mama Africa": Hommage à Catherine Coquery-Vidrovitch* (Paris: L'Harmattan, 2006), 320–7.

24. Tronchon, *L'insurrection malgache*, 82–100, reviews the MDRM position in early 1947.

25. Sorum, *Intellectuals and Decolonization*, 42, 57.

26. Rabearimanana, 'Les Malgaches et l'idée d'indépendance', 268–70.

27. Rabearimanana, 'Les Malgaches et l'idée d'indépendance', 271–4; Delval, 'L'Histoire du PADESM', 287.

28. Lucile Rabearimanana, 'Les Tananariviens face à la proclamation de l'indépendance de Madagascar', in Ageron and Michel (eds), *L'Afrique noire française*, 577–9.

29. Rabearimanana, 'Les Tananariviens', 582. Rainilaiarivony married Queen Ranavalona II and, after her death, married his step-daughter Queen Ranavalona III. He was exiled to Algiers by the conquering French army in 1895.

30. Robert Aldrich, *France and the South Pacific since 1940* (Honolulu: University of Hawaii Press, 1993), 33, 66.

31. Kim Munholland, *Rock of Contention: Free French and Americans at War in New Caledonia, 1940-1945* (Oxford: Berghahn, 2005).

32. Robert Aldrich, 'Le Lobby colonial de l'Océanie française', *Revue Française d'Histoire d'Outre-Mer*, 76 (1989), 411–24.

33. Georges Froment-Guieysse, 'La Polynesie Française et l'après-guerre', *L'Océanie Française*, 14:46 (November–December 1918), 73–7; Lacave La Plagne, 'L'avenir de la Nouvelle-Calédonie', *L'Océanie Française*, 17:56 (March–April 1921), 26–7.

34. Aldrich, *France and the South Pacific*, 59–60.

35. Robert Aldrich and John Connell, *France's Overseas Frontier: Départements et Territoires d'Outre-Mer* (Cambridge: Cambridge University Press, 1992).

36. Aldrich, *France and the South Pacific*, 69–70.

37. Aldrich, *France and the South Pacific*, 158–61.

38. Jean-Marc Regnault, 'Le mouvement nationaliste en Polynésie française de 1940 à nos jours,' in Thierry Michalon (ed.), *Entre assimilation et émancipation: L'Outre-Mer français dans l'impasse* (Rennes: Editions les Perséides, 2006), 181–93.

39. Aldrich, *France and the South Pacific*, 171–80.

40. Aldrich, *France and the South Pacific*, 180–90.

41. Aldrich, *France and the South Pacific*, ch. 7.

42. Frank Schwarzbeck, 'Guyane: A département like the others?' in Paul Sutton (ed.), *Dual Legacies in the Contemporary Caribbean: Continuing Aspects of British and French Dominion* (London: Frank Cass, 1986), 171–3. For comparison of the prison regimes in Guiana and New Caledonia,

see Stephen A. Toth, *Beyond Papillon: The French Overseas Penal Colonies, 1854-1952* (Lincoln, NE: University of Nebraska Press, 2006).

43. Laurent-Félix Lambert, 'Political illusions of an intervention in the linguistic domain in Martinique', *International Journal of the Sociology of Language*, 102 (1993), 135–6.

44. Michel S. Laguerre, *Urban Poverty in the Caribbean: French Martinique as a Social Laboratory* (London: Macmillan, 1990), 22.

45. Michael Sleeman, 'Sugar in Barbados and Martinique: A socio-economic comparison', in Sutton, *Dual Legacies*, 64–6, 79–80. It was the descendants of this planter class who formed what Sleeman terms the 'agro-business bourgeoisie' who turned away from sugar production *en masse* in the 1970s by which time the high price of Martinique sugar rendered it internationally uncompetitive.

46. Edith Beaudoux-Kovats and Jean Benoist, 'Les blancs créoles de la Martinique', in Jean Benoist (ed.), *L'Archipel inachevé: Culture et société aux Antilles françaises* (Montreal: Université de Montréal, 1972), 109–32.

47. Ellen M. Schnepel, 'The Creole movement in Guadeloupe', *International Journal of the Sociology of Language*, 102 (1993), 118–20.

48. Don R. Hoy, 'Changing agricultural land use on Guadeloupe, French West Indies', *Annals of the Association of American Geographers*, 52:4 (1962), 441–54.

49. Cited in Jennings, *Vichy in the Tropics*, 128.

50. William F. S. Miles, *Elections and Ethnicity in French Martinique: A Paradox in Paradise* (New York: Praeger, 1986), 6.

51. Hoy, 'Changing agricultural land use on Guadeloupe', 445–6.

52. Laurent Jalabert, 'La politique économique et sociale de la France dans les DOMs depuis 1945, ou l'histoire d'un mal-développement. L'exemple martiniquais', in Michalon, *Entre assimilation et émancipation*, 367–90.

53. Schwarzbeck, 'Guyane', 176–81.

54. Jean Crusol, 'An economic policy for Martinique', in Sutton, *Dual Legacies*, 189–91. Registered unemployment on Martinique remained above 20 per cent between the years 1961 and 1981.

55. John La Guerre, 'The social and political thought of Aimé Césaire and C.L.R. James: some comparisons', in Sutton, *Dual Legacies*, 208–21.

56. Schnepel, 'The Creole movement in Guadeloupe', 120–1.

57. Schnepel, 'The Creole movement in Guadeloupe', 122–5.

58. Miles, *Elections and Ethnicity*, chs 4 and 5.

59. Schnepel, 'The Creole movement in Guadeloupe', 125–31.

60. Miles, *Elections and Ethnicity*, 203–4.

Chapter 11

1. H. L. Wesseling, 'The giant that was a dwarf, or the strange history of Dutch imperialism', *JICH*, 16:3 (1988), 58–70, here 60. Remco Raben, 'A New Dutch Imperial History? Perambulations in a Prospective Field', *BMGN Low Countries Historical Review*, 128:1 (2013), 5–8.

2. Raben, 'A new imperial history?', 10.

3. Wesseling, 'The giant that was a dwarf', 64–5.

4. Raben, 'A new imperial history?', 10.

5. Hans Buddingh', *Geschiedenis van Suriname* (Utrecht, 1995), 209; E. H. Kossmann, *The Low Countries, 1780-1940* (Oxford: Clarendon, 1978), 163.

6. Amry Vandenbosch, 'The Dutch in the Far East', in B. Landheer (ed.), *The Netherlands* (Berkeley: University of California Press, 1943), 337.

7. Henri Grimal, *Decolonization: The British, French, Dutch and Belgian Empires 1919-1963* (London: Routledge, 1978), 75-6.

8. J. J. P. de Jong, *De Waaier van het Fortuin: De Nederlanders in Azië en de Indonesische Archipel* (Den Haag: SDU, 1998), 199–200, cites M. C. Ricklefs, *A History of Modern Indonesia since 1300* (Bloomington: Indiana University Press, 1981), 113. Petra Groen, 'Colonial warfare and military ethics in the Netherlands East Indies, 1816-1941', *Journal of Genocide Research*, 14:3 (2012), 277–96. The war cost an estimated 200,000 Javanese lives as well as 8,000 European and 7,000 indigenous soldiers.

9. Kossmann, *Low Countries*, 163–4; Vandenbosch, *Dutch East Indies*, 58; Grimal, *Decolonization*, 76.

10. Vandenbosch, *Dutch East Indies*, 59. Two hundred and thirty-six million was used to reduce the public debt, 115 million for tax reduction, 153 million to build railways in the Netherlands, and the remaining 146 million for other purposes, including defence. Edwin Horlings, 'Miracle cure for an economy in crisis? Colonial exploitation as a source of growth in the Netherlands, 1815-1870', in Bob Moore and Henk van Nierop(eds), *Colonial Empires Compared* (Aldershot: Ashgate, 2003), 155–6.

11. Vandenbosch, *Dutch East Indies*, 60.

12. See W. R. Baron van Hoëvell, *Parlementaire redevoering over koloniale belangen*, 4 vols (Zaltbommel, 1862–5), cited in Kossmann, *Low Countries*, 268n.2.

13. H. W. van den Doel, *Afscheid van Indië: De val van het Nederlandse imperium in Azië* (Amsterdam: Prometheus, 2000), 18; Kossmann, *Low Countries*, 269–70.

14. Wim van den Doel, 'The Dutch Empire: an essential part of world history', *BMGN The Low Countries History Review*, 125:2–3 (2010), 197.

15. Kossmann, *Low Countries*, 398.

16. Grimal, *Decolonization*, 76; Vandenbosch, *The Dutch East Indies*, 63.

17. Kossmann, *Low Countries*, 271, 388–99.

18. Kossmann, *Low Countries*, 398–9.

19. D. Coombs, *The Gold Coast, Britain and the Netherlands, 1850-1874* (Oxford: Oxford University Press, 1963); M. Kuitenbrouwer, *The Netherlands and the Rise of Modern Imperialism* (Oxford: Berg, 1991), 62–4. There was a good deal of domestic political opposition, both the secession of the African territories and the Siak Agreement on Sumatra. Indeed, the first version of the latter was voted down by the Second Chamber in July 1871.

20. Kossmann, *Low Countries*, 400–1; Kuitenbrouwer, *Modern Imperialism*, 342, 344.

21. Kuitenbrouwer, *Modern Imperialism*, 328–9, quote at 260.

22. Wesseling, 'The giant that was a dwarf', 62.

23. Wesseling, 'The giant that was a dwarf', 263–4. Military measures taken to counteract local resistance provoked a scandal in the Netherlands when there were reports of thousands of civilian deaths. The territories were given civilian government only in 1918. Van Heutsz returned in triumph to the Netherlands in 1904 and was rewarded with the governor generalship of the Netherlands-Indies.

24. Bernhard Dahm, *History of Indonesia in the Twentieth Century* (London: Pall Mall, 1971), 12–13.

25. Grimal, *Decolonization*, 81–2.

26. Ismail H. Göksoy, 'The policy of the Dutch government towards Islam in Indonesia', *The American Journal of Islamic Social Studies*, 19:1 (2002), 76.

27. Opponents of the policy argued that its supporters were intent on Christianizing the interior, and it was this that had led to Muslim resistance, see Vandenbosch, *The Dutch East Indies*, 66.

Notes

28. Vandenbosch, *The Dutch East Indies*, 65; Grimal, *Decolonization*, 79–80.

29. C. B. Wels, *Aloofness and Neutrality: Studies on Dutch Foreign Relations and Policy-making Institutions* (Utrecht: H&S, 1982), 61.

30. C. B. Wels, *Aloofness and Neutrality*, 62, notes that Tsar Nicholas II proposed the conference. Although it did not discuss many of the issues of importance to the Dutch, establishment of the permanent court for arbitration in The Hague led to the appointment of numerous Dutch jurists and to the second conference in 1907 on Dutch soil.

31. In this context, see Raben, 'A new Dutch imperial history?', 20, Martin Bossenbroek, *Holland op zijn breedst. Indië en Zuid-Afrika in de Nederlandse cultuur omstreeks 1900* (Amsterdam: Bakker, 1996) and Henk te Velde, *Gemeenschapzin en plichtsbesef: Liberalisme en nationalisme in Nederland, 1870-1918* ('s-Gravenhage: Sdu, 1992).

32. While it would be wrong to assume that political groupings in the Netherlands were entirely coherent in the late nineteenth century, the basic division between the secular liberals and the Roman Catholic and Protestant (Calvinist) confessional parties formed the basis for politics in the period. These three were later joined by a fourth zuil (pillar) built on the principles of social democracy.

33. Vandenbosch, *The Dutch East Indies*, 144–6.

34. For a wider discussion, see Gerrit J. Knaap, 'Islamic resistance in the Dutch colonial empire', in David Motadel (ed.), *Islam and the European Empires* (Oxford: Oxford University Press, 2014), 213–30 and Karel Steenbrink, *Dutch Colonialism and Indonesian Islam: Contacts and Conflicts, 1596-1950* (Amsterdam: Rodopi, 2006).

35. Dahm, *History of Indonesia*, 4; Vandenbosch, *The Dutch East Indies*, 316–18; Grimal, *Decolonization*, 85–7.

36. Kees van Dijk, *The Netherlands Indies and the Great War* (Leiden: KITLV, 2007), 622.

37. Grimal, *Decolonization*, 77–80. There were 269 states (2 in Java) controlled by indigenous rulers – comprising 2 million people out of a total population of 48 million.

38. Vandenbosch, *The Dutch East Indies*, 115.

39. Remco Raben, 'Hoe wordt men vrij? De lange dekolonisatie van Indonesië', in Els Bogaerts and Remco Raben (eds), *Van Indië tot Indonesië* (Amsterdam: Boom, 2007), 17–18.

40. Grimal, *Decolonization*, 80.

41. Vandenbosch, *The Dutch East Indies*, 320–1; Grimal, *Decolonization*, 88. These included a communist attack on the prison and telephone exchange in Batavia on 12 November 1926. The failure of the Dutch intelligence services was also a cause for concern. See, Marieke Bloembergen, 'Koloniale Staat, Politiestaat? Politieke Politie en het Rode Fantoom in Nederlands-Indië', *Leidschrift*, 21:2 (2006), 69–90.

42. van Dijk, *The Netherlands Indies and the Great War*, 627.

43. Takashi Shiraishi 'The Phantom World of Digoel', *Indonesia*, 61 (1996), 93–118.

44. Shiraishi 'The Phantom World', 96, 101.

45. Grimal, *Decolonization*, 88, notes 13,000 arrests and 813 deportees to Tanahmerah. Van den Doel, *Afscheid*, 31. The camp was 455 km upstream on the River Digoel in New Guinea and surrounded by impenetrable terrain and dangerous indigenous Papuan tribes.

46. Dahm, *History of Indonesia*, 51–60.

47. van Dijk, *The Netherlands Indies and the Great War*, 629–30.

48. Groen, 'Colonial warfare', 278.

49. Groen, 'Colonial warfare', 277.

50. Remco Raben, 'On genocide and mass violence in colonial Indonesia', *Journal of Genocide Research*, 14:3 (2012), 489. Groen, 'Colonial warfare', 294.

51. K. F. Kreutzberg and J. Erkelens, 'Beschouwingen over de Staatsrechtelijke Toekomst van Nederlandsch-Indië', *Bijdragen en Mededelingen betreffende de Geschiedenis der Nederlanden*, 89:1 (1974), 32–61.

52. Elizabeth B. Fitzpatrick, 'The public library as an instrument of colonialism: the case of the Netherlands East Indies', *Libraries and the Cultural Record*, 43:3 (2008), 270–85.

53. Vandenbosch, *The Dutch East Indies*, 322, 327. It was originally called *Perserikatan Nasional Indonesia* and espoused political independence as its main goal.

54. George McTurnan Kahin, *Nationalism and Revolution in Indonesia* (Ithaca, NY: Cornell University Press, 1952), 92–3; Van den Doel, *Afscheid*, 36–41; Grimal, *Decolonization*, 88.

55. Van den Doel, *Afscheid*, 41; Grimal, *Decolonization*, 89.

56. For more details of the mutiny and Dutch reaction, see J. C. H. Blom, *De Muiterij op De Zeven Provinciën* (Utrecht: HES, 1983).

57. Van den Doel, *Afscheid*, 42. The son of a millionaire, Thamrin was regarded as extremely dangerous, and the governor general would have been pleased to have him interned, but as de Jonge recorded in his memoirs, 'he never gave me the chance'. S. L. van der Wal (ed.), *Herinneringen van mr. B. C. de Jonge* (Groningen, 1968), 191.

58. Shiraishi 'The Phantom World', 101–2, 104. Although there were escape attempts, all those involved were ultimately recaptured by the Dutch or Australians, or fell victim to diseases or the local population.

59. Kahin, *Nationalism and Revolution*, 97–8.

60. Grimal, *Decolonization*, 89; Dahm, *History of Indonesia*, 73.

61. For an extensive analysis and documentation on nationalism in Indonesia before 1942 see, R. C. Kwantes, *De Ontwikkeling van de Nationalistische Beweging in Nederlandsche-Indië*, 4 vols (Groningen: Wolters-Noordhoff, 1975–82).

62. H. L. Wesseling, *Imperialism and Colonialism. Essays on the History of European Expansion* (Westport, CT: Greenwood, 1997), 127–8.

63. See R. C. Kwantes (ed.), *De Ontwikkeling van de Nationalistische Beweging in Nederlands-Indië, 1917–1942*, 4 Vols ('s-Gravenhage: Staatsuitgeverij, 1975–83).

64. Joost Coté, 'Missionary Albert Kruyt and colonial modernity in the Dutch East Indies', *Itinerario*, 34:3 (2010), 11–24, here 12.

65. Raben, 'Hoe wordt men vrij?', 21–3.

66. Buddingh', *Geschiedenis*, 199.

67. Cornelis C. Goslinga, *A Short History of the Netherlands Indies and Surinam* (The Hague: Nijhoff, 1979), 156–9. It was estimated that 75 per cent of the immigrants were Hindus, the remaining 25 per cent Muslims.

68. *Surinaamsch Verslag 1940 II Statistisch Jaaroverzicht van Suriname over het jaar 1939* ('s-Gravenhage: Rijksuitgeverij, 1947), 4. For later figures see Philip Hanson Hiss, *Netherlands America: The Dutch Territories in the West* (New York: Duell, Sloan and Pearce, 1943), 190.

69. Henk E. Chin and Hans Buddingh', *Surinam: Politics, Economics and Society* (London/New York: Pinter, 1987), 11. After the Government Order of 1936, the franchise was open to all those who paid more than Sfl.1,000 per annum in income tax. In addition, five of the fifteen representatives in the *Staten* were appointed by the Governor. See Goslinga, *Short History*, 168–9.

70. Buddingh', *Geschiedenis*, 260, 265–8; Bob Moore, 'Anglo-American security policy and its threats to Dutch colonial rule in the West Indies', *JICH*, 23 (1995), 455.

71. Goslinga, *Short History*, 141–3.

72. Chin and Buddingh', *Surinam*, 11.

73. Chin and Buddingh', *Surinam*, 12. The so-called Killinger coup was a plan formulated by Frans Killinger, a former German and Dutch Colonial soldier, to turn the colony into an independent presidential republic. The coup was thwarted but the resultant trial did serve to give the ideas involved a public airing.

74. Buddingh', *Geschiedenis*, 247–9. De Kom remained in the Netherlands and became active in the resistance during the German occupation. He died, aged forty-seven, in a concentration camp shortly before the liberation.

75. Goslinga, *Short History*, 165.

76. Buddingh', *Geschiedenis*, 250.

77. Ramsoedh, *Suriname 1933-1944*, 58.

78. This was based on his own experience of the policies being adopted by the colonial administration in the Dutch East Indies, and the backing of Colijn. See Hans Ramsoedh, 'Suriname en de Nederlandse Koloniale Politiek in het Interbellum', *Tijdschrift voor Geschiedenis*, 103:4 (1990), 602–14.

79. Buddingh', *Geschiedenis*, 253.

80. Moore, 'Dutch Colonial Rule', 456–8. Washington had effectively sanctioned the British occupation of Iceland a month previously and, although the Dutch Caribbean possessions were much closer to the American mainland, the Roosevelt administration seemed prepared to turn a blind eye as no transfer of sovereignty was envisaged.

81. Sir Hesketh Bell, *Foreign Colonial Administration in the Far East* (London: Arnold, 1928), 123–4, cited in Bob de Graaf, '*Kalm temidden van woedende golven*' Het ministerie van Koloniën en zijn taakomgeving 1912-1940 ('s-Gravenhage: Sdu, 1997), 293.

82. John Ingleson, 'Fear of the kampong, fear of unrest: urban unemployment and colonial policy in 1930s Java', *MAS*, 46:6 (2012), 1633–71, here 1651.

83. De Graaf, '*Kalm temidden*', 448–9.

84. De Graaf, '*Kalm temidden*', 293.

85. Jennifer Foray, 'A unified empire of equal parts: The Dutch Commonwealth schemes of the 1920s-1940s', *JICH*, 41:2 (2013), 261 notes that although the actual contribution to national income was around 14 per cent, many people thought it was much higher at 40–50 per cent.

86. C. G. S. Sandberg, 'Indië verloren, rampspoed geboren' ('s-Gravenhage, 1914).

Chapter 12

1. Indeed, the terms were never finalized as the Netherlands was overrun before the agreement was signed. See W. N. Medlicott, *The Economic Blockade*, 2nd edn (London/Nendeln, 1978), vol. I, 223; Bob Moore, 'British economic warfare and relations with the neutral Netherlands during the 'phoney war', *War and Society*, 13:2 (1995), 65–89.

2. Amry Vandenbosch, *The Dutch East Indies: Its Government, Problems and Politics* (Berkeley: University of California Press, 1941), 349.

3. '"Durch kamen sie doch" Het Nederlandse Defensiebeleid in de jaren dertig opnieuw beschouwd', in J. C. H. Blom, *Crisis, Bezettting en Herstel: Tien Studies over Nederland 1930-1950* (Rotterdam: Universitaire, 1989), 43.

4. Louis de Jong, *Het Koninkrijk der Nederlanden in de Tweede Wereldoorlog*, vol. 11a, II, ('s-Gravenhage: Staatsuitgeverij, 1984), 548–9.

5. There was some debate in Dutch circles about releasing them and asking for their help, but this was not carried out. Lambert Giebels, *Soekarno: Nederlandsch onderdaan. Een biografie, 1901-1950* (Amsterdam: Bakker, 1990), 250; De Jong, *Het Koninkrijk*, vol. 11a, II, 551.

6. De Jong, *Het Koninkrijk*, 11a, II, 613–14.

7. For a detailed chronology of the Japanese occupation and an extensive documentary collection on conditions in the Dutch East Indies, see I. J. Brugmans, H. J de Graaf, A. H. Joustra, and A. G. Vromans (eds), *Nederlandsch-Indië onder Japanse Bezetting 1942-1945* (Franeker: T.Wever, 1960).

8. William H. Frederick, *Visions and Heat: The Making of the Indonesian Revolution.* (Athens, OH: Ohio University Press, 1989), 87.

9. De Jong, *Het Koninkrijk*, 11a, II, 884.

10. De Jong, *Het Koninkrijk*, 11a, II, 830.

11. Elly Touwen-Bouwsma, 'De Japanse bezettingspolitiek ten aanzien van de Nederlanders en Indo Europeanen', in P. J. Drooglever (ed.) *Indisch Intermezzo: Geschiedenis van de Nederlanders in Indonesië* (Amsterdam: Bataafsche Leeuw, 1994), 61–79. M. C. Ricklefs, *A History of Modern Indonesia c1300 to the Present* (Basingstoke: Macmillan, 1981), 188, gives somewhat different internment figures of 65,000 Dutch military, 25,000 other allied servicemen, and 80,000 civilians.

12. The Dutch flag continued to fly in the capital of Dutch New Guinea, Meruake.

13. Frederick, *Visions and Heat*, 105.

14. Kahin, *Nationalism and Revolution*, 132. Ricklefs, *A History of Modern Indonesia*, 188–9 notes that some Europeans remained at liberty in the short term if their expertise was vital to keep industrial production going.

15. H. L. Zwitser, 'De Ooorlog tegen Japan en enkele aspecten van de Japanse Bezetting', in P. J. Drooglever (ed.) *Indisch Intermezzo: Geschiedenis van de Nederlanders in Indonesië* (Amsterdam: Bataafsche Leeuw, 1994), 55.

16. This did not prevent them from using the Dutch to train others and to use Chinese and Eurasians to fill gaps in the administration rather than Indonesians. Frederick, *Visions and Heat*, 99. Grimal, *Decolonization*, 185.

17. Zwitser, 'De Oorlog tegen Japan', 53–4.

18. Jan Pluvier, *Indonesië. Kolonialisme, onafhankelijkheid, neo-kolonialisme: Een politieke geschiedenis van 1940 tot heden* (Nijmegen: Socialistische Uitgeverij Nijmegen, 1978), 42. By 1945, the *Keibodan* had around 1.3 million members and the *Seinendan* 700,000; see Van den Doel, *Afscheid van Indië*, 66. H. Th. Bussemaker, *Bersiap! Opstand in het paradijs. De bersiap periods op java en Sumatra 1945-1946* (Zutphen: Walburg Pers, 2005), 30 gives slightly different figures. Frederick, *Visions and Heat*, 115–17.

19. Shigeru Sato, '"Economic soldiers" in Java: Indonesian laborers mobilized for agricultural projects', in Paul Kratoska (ed.) *Asian Labor in the Wartime Japanese Empire* (Singapore. Singapore University Press, 2006), 129.

20. Kahin, *Nationalism and Revolution*, 108. Frederick, *Visions and Heat*, 104. Pluvier, *Indonesië*, 43. The manpower contribution made by Indonesian *rōmusha* was huge. Pluvier estimates up to 500,000 unemployed workers and indigent farmers were used as labourers, of whom 300,000 were sent to other parts of South East Asia and 230,000 died as a result of their experiences. The Indonesian government gave a total of 4.1 million in 1951, but many of these were employed only for a short time and locally. L. de Jong, *The Collapse of a Colonial Society: The Dutch in Indonesia during the Second World War* (Leiden: KITLV, 2002), 243.

21. De Jong, *The Collapse*, 249.

22. The so-called *Sukarela Tentara Pembala Tanah Air* (Peta), Zwitser, 'De Oorlog tegen Japan', 55–6. Pluvier, *Indonesië*, 43.

23. Kahin, *Nationalism and Revolution*, 109.

24. Zwitser, 'De Oorlog tegen Japan', 57.

25. George Sanford Kanahele, 'The Japanese occupation of Indonesia: prelude to independence' (Ph.D. Cornell University, 1967), 17.

26. Raben, 'Hoe wordt men vrij?', 18.

27. De Jong, *The Collapse*, 267.

28. Ricklefs, *A History of Modern Indonesia*, 191, 206. Kahin, *Nationalism and Revolution*, 112. Sjarifoeddin undertook anti-Japanese resistance, but his movement was penetrated by the *Kempetai* and destroyed. Many of his fellow leaders were condemned and shot but his sentence was commuted to life imprisonment after the intervention of Sukarno and Hatta.

29. Pluvier, *Indonesië*, 38. Kanahele, 'The Japanese occupation of Indonesia', 14–18 argues that even Sukarno had been aware of Japanese imperialist designs and that their conquest on Indonesia 'would put [the country] back two or three centuries'.

30. Giebels, *Soekarno*, 289–95; Pluvier, *Indonesië*, 39–40. Kahin, *Nationalism and Revolution*, 106–7. The Japanese also made attempts to coordinate the Islamic clergy who, they felt, had more influence among the population at large.

31. Brugmans, *Nederlandsch-Indië*, 525–8; Ricklefs, *A History of Modern Indonesia*, 194.

32. Van den Doel, *Afscheid van Indië*, 66 gives the membership in August 1945 as 36,000 men but says that the force had only 17,000 rifles and 900 machine guns.

33. Grimal, *Decolonization*, 187–90; Pluvier, *Indonesië*, 49. Van den Doel, *Afscheid van Indië*, 67. De Jong, *The collapse*, 268. For the first time, the Japanese talked about independence and also referred to Indonesia as a political rather than as a geographical entity. Koiso had replaced Tōjō as Prime Minister in July 1944. Ricklefs, *A History of Modern Indonesia*, 195; May, *The Indonesian Tragedy*, 58. Theodore Friend, *The Blue-Eyed Enemy. Japan against the West in Java and Luzon, 1942-1945*, (Princeton, NJ: Princeton University Press, 1988), 107–8. Taufik Abdullah, 'Preface', ix and Aiko Kurasawa Inomata, '*Indonesia Merdeka Selekaslekasnya*: preparations for independence in the last days of Japanese occupation', 97–113, both in Taufik Abdullah (ed.) *The Heartbeat of Indonesian Revolution* (Jakarta: Gramedia Pustaka Utama, 1997).

34. Zwitser, 'De Oorlog tegen Japan', 58; Ricklefs, *A History of Modern Indonesia*, 192. Bussemaker, *Bersiap!*, 30 describes the Barisan as suicide troops and the Peloppor separately as shock troops or commandos.

35. Brugmans, *Nederlandsch-Indië*, 585.

36. Brugmans, *Nederlandsch-Indië*, 650.

37. Zwitser, 'De Oorlog tegen Japan', 58; Pluvier, *Indonesië*, 50.

38. C. Fasseur, 'A cheque drawn on a failing bank: the address delivered by Queen Wilhelmina on 6th/7th December 1942', *The Low Countries History Yearbook*, 15 (1982), 102–15, here at 104.

39. Fasseur, 'A cheque drawn on a failing bank', 106, cites S. L. van der Wal, *De Volksraad en de staatkundige ontwikkeling van Nederlandsche-Indië*. Een Bronnenpublicatie part. 2, 1927–42 (Groningen, 1965), 653.

40. Van den Doel, *Afscheid van Indië*, 58. Fasseur, 'A cheque drawn on a failing bank', 106–8.

41. Fasseur, 'A cheque drawn on a failing bank', 110–13.

42. J. van den Tempel, *Nederland in Londen: Ervaringen en Beschouwingen* (H. Haarlem: Tjeenk Willink, 1946), 90.

43. Van den Doel, *Afscheid van Indië*, 60; Fasseur, 'A cheque drawn on a failing bank', 114. Foray, 'A United Empire of Equal Parts', 273.

44. For a reflection on this see, P. J. A. Idenburg, 'Het Nederlandse Antwoord op het Indonesisch Nationalisme', in H. Baudet and I. J. Brugmans (eds), *Balans van Beleid: Terugblik op de laatste halve eeuw van Nederlansch-Indië* (Assen: van Gorcum, 1984), 121–51.

45. Van den Doel, *Afscheid van Indië*, 61. From this came the Netherlands Indies Civil Administration (NICA).

46. Coincidentally, this was on the same day, 15 August, that Emperor Hirohito announced his government's willingness to surrender unconditionally. Oey, *War and Diplomacy*, 19.

47. Peter Dennis, *Troubled Days of Peace: Mountbatten and South East Asia Command* (Manchester: Manchester University Press, 1987), 67.

48. Gary R. Hess, *The United States' Emergence as a Southeast Asian Power, 1945-1950* (New York: Columbia University Press, 1987), 55.

49. Gouda and Brocades Zijlberg, *American Visions*, 115.

50. For a more detailed discussion, see Idrus Nasir Djajadiningrat, *The Beginnings of the Indonesian-Dutch Negotiations and the Hoge Veluwe Talks* (Ithaca: Cornell University Press, 1958), 17–27.

51. Yong Mun Cheong, *H.J. van Mook and Indonesian Independence: A Study in his Role in Dutch-Indonesian Relations, 1945-1948* (The Hague: Nijhoff, 1982), 31.

52. Dennis, *Troubled Days*, 93. Van Mook had spent the previous two years in Brisbane preparing for the Dutch return to the Indies. His pre-eminent role came about because the Governor General A. W. L Tjarda van Starkenborgh Stachower had been in Japanese internment. Oey, *War and Diplomacy*, 22.

53. De Jong, *Het Koninkrijk* XII, 692. De Jong also argues that the United States was keen to avoid involvement in Indonesia because of potential problems with indigenous nationalists.

54. Oey, *War and Diplomacy*, 20–1; Van den Doel, *Afscheid van Indië*, 73; Dennis, *Troubled Days*, 69–70.

55. Dennis, *Troubled Days*, 73.

56. Kahin, 'Some recollections', 22.

57. Oey, *War and Diplomacy*, 22; Dennis, *Troubled Days*, 75.

58. Gouda and Brocades Zijlberg, *American Visions*, 115–18; Van den Doel, *Afscheid van Indië*, 79.

59. Dennis, *Troubled Days*, 77. Like Hubertus van Mook, van der Plas had been a member of the so-called 'Stuw' a group of progressive thinkers on colonial matters in the 1920s and 1930s Drooglever, 'The *Komite Nasional Indonesia Pusat*', 154.

60. This claim was made by Rear-Admiral Cyril Douglas-Pennant in a speech in Sydney in 1946. See Greg Poulgrain, *The Genesis of Konfrontasi: Malaya, Brunei, Indonesia, 1945-1965* (Bathurst, NSW: Crawford House, 1998), 35.

61. New Guinea was never fully occupied by the Japanese and areas of the interior remained under (nominal) Dutch control. It was invaded by the Americans in April 1944, although Japanese guerrilla resistance continued until September 1945.

62. Cheong, *H.J. van Mook*, 39.

63. Pluvier, *Indonesië*, 52. The day before the Japanese surrender Sukarno and Hatta had been in Saigon where they were told by the Commander-in-Chief of the Southern Territories that Tokyo was to announce the independence of Indonesia. Kahin, *Nationalism and Revolution*, 136–8. Van den Doel, *Afscheid van Indië*, 76–8. Abdullah, 'Preface', x.

64. Giebels, *Soekarno*, 356–61; Ricklefs, *A History of Modern Indonesia*, 201. Pluvier, *Indonesië*, 53.

65. Abdullah, 'Preface', x.

66. Kahin, *Nationalism and Revolution*, 139–41.

67. Kahin, *Nationalism and Revolution*, *Het Koninkrijk* XII, 693–4.

68. Kahin, *Nationalism and Revolution*, 706, 727. Unlike the Dutch, Eurasians, and Ambonese who became targets for extremists, the Chinese were initially left alone because this might assist Chinese nationalist support for the new regime.

69. Oey, *War and Diplomacy*, 24–5.

70. De Jong, *Het Koninkrijk* XII, 694. This advance party was led by Rear-Admiral William Patterson aboard the cruiser HMS *Cumberland*.

71. Cheong, *H. J. van Mook*, 34. Oey, *War and Diplomacy*, 26–7.

72. Dennis, *Troubled Days*, 86–8. Dennis argues that the appointment of Lt. General Sir Philip Christison to command this force was a deliberate ploy by Mountbatten to preserve his own reputation if the mission went wrong or became embroiled in a wider conflict.

73. At the same meeting, Lawson also made promises to the French about Vietnam which were subsequently sacrificed in the interests of prioritizing the return of prisoners and internees. See Peter Neville, *Britain in Vietnam: Prelude to Disaster 1945-1946* (London: Routledge, 2007), 96.

74. Djajadiningrat, *The Beginnings of the Dutch-Indonesian Negotiations*, 25–7.

75. Dennis, *Troubled Days*, 89–92.

76. Oey, *War and Diplomacy*, 28–9.

77. Verslag van de delegeerde bij het geallieerd opperbevel in Zuid-Oost Azië (van der Plas) van zijn besprekingen te Singapore met de geallieerde opperbevelhebber in Zuid-Oost Azië (Mountbatten), undated. *Officiële Beschieden Betreffende de Nederlands-Indonesische Betrekkingen 1945-1950*, (henceforward OB) I, 10 August–8 November 1945 ('s-Gravenhage: Nijhoff, 1971), no. 133, 226–35, at 229.

78. Oey, *War and Diplomacy*, 23.

79. P. J. Drooglever, 'The *Komite Nasional Indonesia Pusat* and internal politics in the Republic of Indonesia', in Abdullah (ed.) *The Heartbeat of Indonesian Revolution*, 153.

80. Frances Gouda with Thijs Brocades Zaalberg, *American Visions of the Netherlands East Indies/Indonesia* (Amsterdam: Amsterdam University Press, 2002), 128. De Jong, *Het Koninkrijk* XII, 695. J. J. P. de Jong, 'De bersiap-periode', in P. J. Drooglever (ed.) *Indisch Intermezzo: Geschiedenis van de Nederlanders in Indonesië* (Amsterdam: Bataafsche Leeuw, 1994), 85. Dennis, *Troubled Days*, 98, 118.

81. De Jong, 'De bersiap-période', 85.

82. Göksoy, 'The policy of the Dutch government', 77–80.

83. Professor Dr. J. H. A. Logemann, Minister for the Overseas Territories 1945–6 and leader of the Partij van de Arbeid in the Parliamentary Second Chamber.

84. De Jong, *Het Koninkrijk* XII, 695–6.

85. For a detailed account of the period see especially, Bussemaker, *Bersiap!* De Jong, 'De bersiap-période', 81. '*Siap*' means ready or prepared. Van den Doel, *Afscheid van Indië*, 89–93.

86. Ricklefs, *A History of Modern Indonesia*, 204–5.

87. De Jong, *Het Koninkrijk* XII, 719. The Ambonese were traditionally major contributors to the strength of the Dutch colonial army.

88. Frederick, *Visions and Heat*, 197–201.

89. Frederick, *Visions and Heat*, 242.

90. Cheong, *H. J. van Mook*, 45; De Jong, *Het Koninkrijk* XII, 720.

91. Van den Doel, *Afscheid van Indië*, 82. See also Frederick, *Visions and Heat*, 238–43.

92. Frederick, *Visions and Heat*, 293–4.

93. Oey, *War and Diplomacy*, 31.

94. Oey, *War and Diplomacy*, 32.

95. J. C. Bijkerk, *De Laatste Landvoogd: Van Mook en het einde van de Nederlandse invloed in Indië* (Alphen a/d Rijn: Sijthoff, 1982), 180–1.

96. Verslag van de 34ste gemengde bijeenkomst van de geallieerde opperbevelhebber in Zuid-Oost Azië (Mountbatten), 10 October 1945. OB, I, 10 August–8 November 1945, no. 164.

97. Bijkerk, *De Laatste Landvoogd*, 182. Dennis, *Troubled Days*, 109, notes that this wariness originated in the events after the collapse of ABDA in 1942 when the British were perceived to have acted in their own imperial interests in withdrawing their naval forces from the region in spite of Helfrich's desire – as senior commander – to stay and fight.

98. Djajadiningrat, *The Beginnings of the Dutch-Indonesian Negotiations*, 29–30; Bijkerk, *De Laatste Landvoogd*, 183.

99. De Jong, *Het Koninkrijk* XII, 719; Van den Doel, *Afscheid van Indië*, 83. This was the so-called 10th Battalion.

100. Oey, *War and Diplomacy*, 31–7; Van den Doel, *Afscheid van Indië*, 83, 90.

101. Dennis, *Troubled Days*, 120.

102. Van den Doel, *Afscheid van Indië*, 83, cites Dennis, *Troubled Days*, 107 and Doulton, *The fighting cock: Being the history of the 23rd Indian Division 1942-1947* (Aldershot, 1951), 239–41.

103. Kahin, *Nationalism and Revolution*, 143.

104. Oey, *War and Diplomacy*, 34, citing Christison to SACSEA, 4 October 1945.

105. De Jong, *Het Koninkrijk* XII, 728.

106. De Jong, *Het Koninkrijk* XII, 714–15.

107. Djajadiningrat, *The Beginnings of the Dutch-Indonesian Negotiations*, 31.

108. Bijkerk, *De Laatste Landvoogd*, 192–4.

109. Some 3,000 supposedly pro-Dutch men and boys had been arrested and imprisoned in Surabaya during October and were only saved from a mass slaughter by the intervention of a British tank and twelve Gurkha soldiers who took over the prison and then expedited the evacuation of the prisoners to the harbour. De Jong, *Het Koninkrijk* XII, 721–2.

110. Oey, *War and Diplomacy*, 45.

111. At the time, there was some debate about how exactly he had met his death. Djajadiningrat, *The Beginnings of the Dutch-Indonesian Negotiations*, 38 cites David Wehl, *The Birth of Indonesia*, 60–1 and Parliamentary Debates: Commons, 1945–6, vol. 419, 1213–15.

112. Giebels, *Soekarno*, 386–91; Dennis, *Troubled Days*, 124; De Jong, *Het Koninkrijk* XII, 709–10; Van den Doel, *Afscheid van Indië*, 102. For a more recent assessment based on newly released documents see, Richard McMillan, *The British Occupation of Indonesia 1945-1946. Britain, the Netherlands and the Indonesian Revolution* (London: Routledge, 2005), 46–52.

113. Minister van Overzeesgebiedsdelen (Logemann) to van Mook, 13 October 1945, *OB*, I, 10 August–8 November 1945, no. 183, 351.

114. Cheong, *H. J. van Mook*, 46. Bijkerk, *De Laatste Landvoogd*, 195. Van den Doel, *Afscheid van Indië*, 97. De Jong, *Het Koninkrijk* XII, 732. Djajadiningrat, *The Beginnings of the Dutch-Indonesian Negotiations*, 32; J. J. P. de Jong, 'Winds of Change. Van Mook, Dutch policy and the realities of November 1945', *Utrechtse Historische Cahiers*, VII 2/3 (1986), 163–82.

115. Van den Doel, *Afscheid van Indië*, 97–8. Prime Minister Schermerhorn warned that any replacement for van Mook was likely to be more intransigent and high-handed: De Jong, *Het Koninkrijk* XII, 733.

116. Oey, *War and Diplomacy*, 41; Bijkerk, *De Laatste Landvoogd*, 197.

117. De Jong, *Het Koninkrijk* XII, 720. The Japanese had often allowed Eurasian women and children to leave the camps (to go home), but the Europeans remained.

118. Ricklefs, *A History of Modern Indonesia*, 205; Van den Doel, *Afscheid van Indië*, 103–5. McMillan, *British Occupation*, 165–7.

119. De Jong, *Het Koninkrijk* XII, 698–9; Hess, *United States' Emergence*, 186–7.

120. As the Surabaya incident demonstrated, the Republican movement varied from area to area and lacked central control of the armed forces inside the country, see De Jong, *Het Koninkrijk* XII, 706–9.

121. De Jong, *Het Koninkrijk* XII, 725.

122. Oey, *War and Diplomacy*, 46, quotes SACSEA 295th Staff Meeting, 16 November 1945.

123. This grew out of the Komite Nasional Indonesia Pusat, an organization designed to limit the powers of Sukarno and the government, by making it more answerable. Djajadiningrat, *The*

Beginnings of the Dutch-Indonesian Negotiations, 33. Van den Doel, *Afscheid van Indië*, 117. At the same time, the internal social revolution continued, with the *pemudas* kidnapping, intimidating, or killing all those whose loyalty was in doubt. Ricklefs, *A History of Modern Indonesia*, 207. Cheong, *H. J. van Mook*, 49.

124. Van den Doel, *Afscheid van Indië*, 114–16. Drooglever, 'The *Komite Nasional Indonesia Pusat*', 154. Sjahrir had produced a brochure that made explicit but unnamed criticism of the nationalists who had sided with the Japanese during the occupation.

125. Rudolph Mrázek, *Sjahrir: Politics and Exile in Indonesia* (Ithaca, NY: Cornell University Press, 1994), 292–3.

126. Giebels, *Soekarno*, 394–8; Oey, *War and Diplomacy*, 47.

127. De Jong, *Het Koninkrijk* XII, 716–17. Sukarno was aware of the Dutch objections to him and was content to take a back seat if it produced progress.

128. Benedict R. O'G. Anderson, *Java in a Time of Revolution: Occupation and Resistance, 1944-1946* (Ithaca, NY: Cornell University Press, 1972), 296–9; Mrázek, *Sjahrir*, 301.

129. Cheong, *H.J. van Mook*, 52–3.

130. Oey, *War and Diplomacy*, 49. The lack of control over the Ambonese, Manadonese, and Eurasian Dutch troops could not be excused but the reason for their behaviour was attributed to the Indonesians' ill treatment of their wives and children while they had been prisoners of the Japanese.

131. Van den Doel, *Afscheid van Indië*, 106.

132. Cheong, *H.J. van Mook*, 61–2.

133. Broadcast on BBC Home Service, 28 November 1945; Oey, *War and Diplomacy*, 51.

134. Oey, *War and Diplomacy*, 51. Admiral Helfrich made similarly extreme remarks at a SACSEA meeting in December where he spoke of destroying the Republic by force and had to be reprimanded by Mountbatten and Alanbrooke.

135. Bijkerk, *De Laatste Landvoogd*, 207. Gerretson was a professor at the University of Utrecht and Meyer Ranneft was member of the Council of State. Gerbrandy's continuing opposition can be seen in P. S. Gerbrandy, *De Scheuring van Het Rijk: Het Drama van de Indonesische Crisis* (Kampen: Kok, 1951).

136. De Jong, *Het Koninkrijk* XII, 728, 741.

137. Kahin, *Nationalism and Revolution*, 145. See also J. A. de Moor, *Westerling's Oorlog: Indonesië 1945-1950; De geschiedenis van de commando's en parachutisten in Nederlands-Indië* (Amsterdam: Balans, 1999).

138. Cheong, *H.J. van Mook*, 58–60.

139. Djajadiningrat, *The Beginnings of the Dutch-Indonesian Negotiations*, 42–3.

140. De Jong, *Het Koninkrijk* XII, 705.

141. Djajadiningrat, *The Beginnings of the Dutch-Indonesian Negotiations*, 44–5.

142. J. J. P. de Jong, 'The Indonesian question: international intervention as an option? Aspects of British, Dutch and American policy, 1945-47', in Roosevelt Study Center, *The Decolonization of Indonesia: International Perspectives* (Middelburg: Roosevelt Study Center, 1988), 24–7. Drooglever, 'The *Komite Nasional Indonesia Pusat*', 158.

143. Oey, *War and Diplomacy*, 57.

144. Oey, *War and Diplomacy*, 54; Bijkerk, *De Laatste Landvoogd*, 217; De Jong, *Het Koninkrijk* XII, 740.

145. Van den Doel, *Afscheid van Indië*, 123–4. Helfrich was replaced by Rear-Admiral A. S. Pinke and van Oeyen by Major-General Spoor.

146. De Jong, *Het Koninkrijk* XII, 737. Mountbatten made it clear on 6 December that he would not allow Dutch troops in until their government agreed to negotiate with the Indonesian Republic.

147. Djajadiningrat, *The Beginnings of the Dutch-Indonesian Negotiations*, 47–8.

148. De Jong, *Het Koninkrijk* XII, 733–4, 762.

Chapter 13

1. This was the Persatuan Perdjuangan (United Front) Djajadiningrat, *The Beginnings of the Dutch-Indonesian Negotiations*, 53. Ricklefs, *A History of Modern Indonesia*, 211–12. Van den Doel, *Afscheid van Indië*, 125–7. On Tan Malaka's career see Harry A. Poeze, *Tan Malaka: Stijder voor Indonesië's Vrijheid. Levensloop van 1897-1945* ('s-Gravenhage: Nijhoff, 1976) and more recently, idem, *Verguisd en vergeten: Tan Malaka, de linkse beweging en de Indonesische revolutie, 1945-1949*, 3 vols (Leiden: KITLV, 2007).

2. It is interesting to note that the timescale for this had been given as twenty-five years in the Dutch text submitted to the Attlee government, De Jong, *Het Koninkrijk* XII, 740.

3. This he obtained after resigning on 28 February and being reappointed two days later when the opposition failed to form an alternative regime. Djajadiningrat, *The Beginnings of the Dutch-Indonesian Negotiations*, 52.

4. Anderson, *Java in a Time of Revolution*, 313–16. Mrázek, *Sjahrir*, 315, 318 argues that Sjahrir was weakened by this and was given back the Prime Minister's role by Sukarno and Hatta only to thwart Tan Malaka. This was reinforced when Sjahrir was kidnapped in July 1946 and released only through the intervention of Sukarno.

5. Oey, *War and Diplomacy*, 66.

6. Djajadiningrat, *The Beginnings of the Dutch-Indonesian Negotiations*, 55. De Jong, *Het Koninkrijk* XII, 771.

7. Oey, *War and Diplomacy*, 72.

8. One of the major debates was about the question of what status the Indonesian groups should have in any agreement – with the Dutch refusing to countenance the idea of a treaty: Cheong, *H.J. van Mook*, 78–9; Van den Doel, *Afscheid*, 130. Djajadiningrat, *The Beginnings of the Dutch-Indonesian Negotiations*, 61–106.

9. At the time, blame was also attached to the behaviour of Catholic Party leader C. P. M. Romme who, in the course of the first post-war elections, wrote an article for the leading daily newspaper *De Volkskrant* called 'The Week of Shame' where he ridiculed the 'so-called' Republic. Giebels, *Soekarno*, 414.

10. De Jong, *Het Koninkrijk* XII, 748.

11. De Jong, *Het Koninkrijk* XII, 753–4. Expecting to be greeted as liberators, like the British before them, the Dutch were surprised to find that their arrival was either ignored or resented by local populations.

12. Oey, *War and Diplomacy*, 78–9.

13. McMillan, *British Occupation*, 87–8.

14. Violent indiscipline may be partially explained by the *ad hoc* composition of the first Dutch units to arrive, see: Peter Romijn, 'Learning on "the job": Dutch war volunteers entering the Indonesian war of independence, 1945-46', in Bart Luttikhuis and A. Dirk Moses (eds), *Colonial Counterinsurgency and Mass Violence: The Dutch Empire in Indonesia* (Abingdon: Routledge, 2014), 91–107.

15. Romijn, *Colonial Counterinsurgency and Mass Violence*, 93–4. The formal handover actually took place on midnight of 13/14 July after which the evacuated territory would cease to be a part of SEAC. This led to a hastily convened conference at Malino (South Celebes) between van Mook and representatives from these territories. This was in fulfilment of the promises made in the Queen's radio broadcast of 7 December 1942. Van den Doel, *Afscheid*, 142; Cheong, *H.J. van Mook*, 86–8.

16. De Jong, *Het Koninkrijk* XII, 765. The report was adopted by the Second Chamber on 7 May 1946.

17. Van den Doel, *Afscheid*, 156–9. In spite of his stridency on Indian affairs, Romme had never visited the colonial empire, see Cheong, *H.J. van Mook*, 82–3.

18. Van den Doel, *Afscheid*, 143–4. Malino also did nothing to improve security in the outer islands and nationalist insurgency in South Celebes led to the deployment in December 1946 of the KNIL *Depot Speciale Troepen* under Lt Raymond Westerling. His forces used severe methods to fight 'terrorism' including summary executions. This first 'police action' is estimated to have cost 5,000 Indonesian lives.

19. Bijkerk, *De Laatste Landvoogd*, 234; De Jong, *Het Koninkrijk* XII, 769. Schermerhorn was the dominant personality of the three; De Boer and van Poll had little political influence.

20. Van den Doel, *Afscheid*, 162.

21. Kahin, *Nationalism and Revolution*, 196–8; Van den Doel, *Afscheid*, 169; Oey, *War and Diplomacy*, 111; De Jong, *Het Koninkrijk* XII, 774–8.

22. Mun Cheong Yong, *The Indonesian Revolution and the Singapore Connection, 1945–1949* (Leiden: KITLV, 2003), 145–6. Pinke was at the forefront of the campaign to prevent armaments and materiel reaching the Republic by intercepting and searching shipping.

23. Oey, *War and Diplomacy*, 113.

24. McMillan, *British Occupation*, 106, 168, takes the view that British policy was neither indifferent to Dutch aspirations, nor committed to a brutal restoration of colonial interests, nor an orderly and impartial temporary occupation, but rather a pragmatic approach to a situation in which the local commanders found themselves politically and militarily out of their depth.

25. M. D. Bogaarts (ed.), *Parlementaire Geschiedenis van Nederland na 1945: De Periode van het Kabinet-Beel*. Band D/1a Nederlands-Indië (Nijmegen: Gerard Noodt Instituut, 1995), 2475–91; Van den Doel, *Afscheid*, 174–5.

26. Giebels, *Soekarno*, 429.

27. Van den Doel, *Afscheid*, 171.

28. Bogaarts, *Parlementaire Geschiedenis*. Band D/1a Nederlands-Indië, 2509; Cheong, *H.J.van Mook*, 99.

29. De Jong, *Het Koninkrijk* XII, 782.

30. G. Puchinger, *Tilanus vertelde mij zijn leven* (Kampen: Kok, 1966), 251.

31. Bogaarts, *Parlementaire Geschiedenis*. Band D/1a Nederlands-Indië, 2523.

32. C. Smit (ed.), *Het dagboek van Schermerhorn*, I (Utrecht: Nederlands Historisch Genootschap, 1970), entry for 23 December 1946.

33. Puchinger, *Tilanus vertelde mij zijn leven*, 252. H. W. Tilanus as leader of the CHU also recalled that many voters wanted continuing protest actions and implied that the CHU would suffer at the polls, when in fact they increased their seats from eight to nine.

34. Van den Doel, *Afscheid*, 166–71; De Jong, *Het Koninkrijk* XII, 783.

35. This came about in part through the surprise adoption of a motion by Manai Sophian, a journalist and KNIP delegate, according to which the inclusion of the outer territories then held by the Dutch were to be a central goal for the future. Drooglever, 'The *Komite Nasional Indonesia Pusat*', 164. De Jong, *Het Koninkrijk* XII, 786.

36. Van den Doel, *Afscheid*, 170–1, 188; Oey, *War and Diplomacy*, 129.

37. Mavis Rose, *Indonesia Free: A Political Biography of Mohammad Hatta* (Singapore: Equinox, 2010), 219.

38. Drooglever, 'The *Komite Nasional Indonesia Pusat*', 165. See also Rudolf Mrázek, *Sjahrir: Politics and exile in Indonesia* (Ithaca, NY: Cornell University Press, 1994), 332–46.

39. Oey, *War and Diplomacy*, 132.

40. De Jong, *Het Koninkrijk* XII, 791–3. Gerbrandy had been advised by Professor F. C. Gerretson that a coup under these circumstances could not be legally justified.

41. De Jong, *Het Koninkrijk* XII, 779. Defectors were from an increasingly intransigent element within the Catholic group unsettled by press reports about the negotiations carried out by the Commission-General.

42. Oey, *War and Diplomacy*, 133–4.

43. Van den Doel, *Afscheid*, 214.

44. Van den Doel, *Afscheid*, 199–200; Cheong, *H.J.van Mook*, 129–30.

45. Hess, *United States' Emergence*, 210–13; Oey, *War and Diplomacy*, 139–40.

46. Van den Doel, *Afscheid*, 216.

47. Drooglever, 'The *Komite Nasional Indonesia Pusat*', 167–8.

48. Drooglever, 'The *Komite Nasional Indonesia Pusat*', 201, 217. The Dutch had 5,000 marines, 44,000 KNIL soldiers, and around 70,000 from the Netherlands. These troops from the Netherlands were largely conscripts whose terms of service had been altered to allow the state to send them to the Indies. Desertion rates were high and the first troop transports left Amsterdam harbour with only 85 per cent of their contingents.

49. Robert J. MacMahon, *Colonialism and Cold War: The United States and the Struggle for Indonesian Independence* (Ithaca, NY: Cornell University Press, 1981), 168, 171; Van den Doel, *Afscheid*, 201, estimates Indonesian military strength at 174,000 with another 167,000 in militias and paramilitary formations.

50. Ricklefs, *A History of Modern Indonesia*, 213; Oey, *War and Diplomacy*, 146.

51. J. A. Jonkman, *Nederland en Indonesië: Beide Vrij. Memoires* (Assen/Amsterdam, 1977), 118–19.

52. Van den Doel, *Afscheid*, 222–3, notes the resumption of boycotts of Dutch shipping in Australian ports and protests from the Australian government. For examination of the United Nations and Indonesia, see Alastair Taylor, *Indonesian Independence and the United Nations* (London: Stevens, 1960).

53. Roel Frakking, '"Who wants to cover everything, covers nothing": the organization of indigenous security forces in Indonesia, 1945–50', in Luttikhuis and Moses, *Colonial Counterinsurgency*, 113–20.

54. Oey, *War and Diplomacy*, 147.

55. Bijkerk, *De Laatste Landvoogd*, 269; Van den Doel, *Afscheid*, 224.

56. The resolution was passed on 1 August 1947; both sides agreed to it by 4 August 1947.

57. MacMahon, *Colonialism*, 173, cites memorandum from H. Freeman Matthews to Secretary of State George Marshall, 24 July 1947, USNA, RG59 856D.00/7-2447.

58. Gouda and Zaalberg, *American Visions*, 153, 162–71. US support was also based on protecting substantial American investment in the region, and bolstered by the reporting from its diplomats in the region.

59. Gouda and Zaalberg, *American Visions*, 174–83. See also, Kahin, *Nationalism and Revolution*, 217–26.

60. The Australian representative was R. C. Kirby, a lawyer who was undoubtedly pro-Republican. Conversely, the Belgian representative was Paul van Zeeland, a former Foreign Minister and Prime Minister of his country, whom van Mook described as 'unhelpful'. Cheong, *H.J. van Mook*, 167; Van den Doel, *Afscheid*, 239; Oey, *War and Diplomacy*, 155.

61. This massacre was the subject of a 1948 UN enquiry under the auspices of the Good Offices Committee. Although included in the list of Dutch war crimes published in 1969, the number of victims was still given as c150 until a television programme in 1995 cited

the figure of 433 given by the local mullah to the original enquiry. At this point, the Dutch government reversed its previous decision not to take action against the army major responsible. Hella Rottenberg, 'VN-stuk over Rawahgedeh komt na 47 jaar boven water', *De Volkskrant*, 16 August 1995. In 2011, the Dutch courts ruled the state responsible and awarded compensation to the survivors and the Dutch ambassador to Indonesia made a formal apology on the site of the massacres. 'De weduwen glunderen, zij hebben Nederland verslagen', *De Volkskrant*, 10 December 2011.

62. Rémy Limpach, 'Business as usual: Dutch mass violence in the Indonesian war of independence, 1945–49', in Luttikhuis and Moses, *Colonial Counterinsurgency*, 64–87.

63. Van den Doel, *Afscheid*, 229; MacMahon, *Colonialism*, 190; Van den Doel, *Afscheid*, 252.

64. Oey, *War and Diplomacy*, 158–9; Van den Doel, *Afscheid*, 249; Grimal, *Decolonization*, 199–200.

65. On the negotiations prior to the CGO meetings on USS *Renville*, see MacMahon, *Colonialism*, 193–6.

66. Van den Doel, *Afscheid*, 245–7.

67. MacMahon, *Colonialism,* 199–201.

68. This was bolstered by knowledge of the 'Fox contract', a detrimental treaty the republic signed with a US businessman: Cheong, *H.J. van Mook*, 171–2.

69. MacMahon, *Colonialism*, 200, notes that Graham, having been well disposed towards the Dutch at the outset, was becoming increasingly alienated by their continued intransigence.

70. Oey, *War and Diplomacy*, 163. The European Recovery Programme and economic aid for Indonesia's reconstruction were mentioned in this respect, but the precise nature of this threat was not clarified until after the Dutch assented to the proposals: Van den Doel, *Afscheid*, 255; MacMahon, *Colonialism*, 203.

71. MacMahon, *Colonialism*, 204–6; Van den Doel, *Afscheid*, 256.

72. Drooglever, 'The *Komite Nasional Indonesia Pusat*', 168.

73. Grimal, *Decolonization,* 201–2; Van den Doel, *Afscheid*, 258; MacMahon, *Colonialism*, 208–10.

74. He was welcomed by the Dutch as a favourable realist, having been Consul-General in Batavia from 1927 to 1930. However, a three-day visit to the interior convinced him of the overwhelming support for the Republic, much to Dutch disgust; see Van den Doel, *Afscheid*, 259–63.

75. MacMahon, *Colonialism*, 228–9, 242.

76. Drooglever, 'The *Komite Nasional Indonesia Pusat*', 171.

77. Van den Doel, *Afscheid*, 273. See also Gouda and Zaalberg, *American Visions*, 261–2 and Chris A. J. van Koppen (ed.), *Den Haag antwoordt niet: Herinneringen van Jhr H.L.F.K van Vredenburch* ('s-Gravenhage: Nijhoff, 1985).

78. Thomas K. Critchley was a noted economist serving in the Australian Department of External Affairs. MacMahon, *Colonialism*, 213; Cheong, *H.J. van Mook*, 178–9.

79. MacMahon, *Colonialism*, 224–5.

80. At the time, his departure was interpreted by the Indonesians as a US repudiation of his proposals. Kahin, *Nationalism and Revolution*, 250.

81. Van Vredenburch was replaced by T. Elink Schuurman, see Oey, *War and Diplomacy*, 182.

82. Bogaarts, *Parlementaire Geschiedenis* Band D/1b Nederlands-Indië, 3321–3452; Oey, *War and Diplomacy*, 183. Another complication was that any government required a two-thirds parliamentary majority to alter the constitution, see Taylor, *Indonesian Independence and the United Nations*, 287–8.

83. George McT Kahin, 'Some recollections from and reflections on the Indonesian Revolution', in Abdullah (ed.), *The Heartbeat of Indonesian Revolution*, 14. Musso's arrival and public speeches were greeted as a vindication of free speech – with many hoping that he would discredit himself in the process. Van den Doel, *Afscheid*, 274–9; MacMahon, *Colonialism*, 236–9.

84. This was H. Merle Cochran, a career diplomat and replacement for DuBois who had returned to the United States due to ill health. Van den Doel, *Afscheid*, 280.

85. D. U. Stikker, *Memoires* (Rotterdam/The Hague, 1966), 109–10, cited in Oey, *War and Diplomacy*, 189. Dr L. G. M. Jacquet, *Minister Stikker en de souvereiniteitsoverdracht aan Indonesië* ('s-Gravenhage: Nijhoff, 1982), 57–9.

86. Jacquet, *Minister Stikker en de souvereiniteitsoverdracht aan Indonesië*, 60. Stikker admitted after the meeting that the last chance of a peaceful settlement was lost.

87. Van den Doel, *Afscheid*, 279. Ricklefs, *A History of Modern Indonesia*, 216–17; MacMahon, *Colonialism*, 242–4; Cheong, *H.J. van Mook*, 182; Kahin, *Nationalism and Revolution*, 256–303.

88. Kahin, 'Some Recollections', 15–16; Jacquet, *Minister Stikker*, 63–79.

89. Bijkerk, *De Laatste Landvoogd*, 272–8. Van den Doel, *Afscheid*, 283. Although born and raised in Indonesia, van Mook never returned to his homeland, first becoming a professor of Political Science at UC Berkeley, and then director of UN's Public Administration Division. He retired to France in 1960 where he died five years later, aged seventy. The defence of his policy can be found in H. J. van Mook, *Indonesië, Nederland en de Wereld* (Amsterdam: Bezige Bij, 1949); see also Jacquet, *Minister Stikker*, 82–3. On Beel, see Ronald Gase, *Beel in Batavia: Van Contact tot Conflict. Verwikkelingen rond de Indonesische kwestie in 1948* (Amsterdam: Anthos, 1986).

90. Oey, *War and Diplomacy*, 193.

91. Jacquet, *Minister Stikker*, 98–104; Van den Doel, *Afscheid*, 284–7. The military had been preparing for the elimination of Republican power through a direct assault on Yogyakarta and the former Fort de Kock.

92. It could also be argued that the blockade had done much to foster support for the communists in this period. Kahin, 'Some Recollections', 11, 19.

93. Oey, *War and Diplomacy*, 200. See also Lovink Foreign Ministry Secretary-General, to Stikker, 17 December 1948 in S. van der Wal et al. (eds), *Officiële beschieden betreffende de Nederland-Indonesische betrekkingen*, OB, XVI, 1 December 1948 to 16 January 1949, No.132, 209. Cochran also warned Stikker in similar terms, Van den Doel, *Afscheid*, 284; MacMahon, *Colonialism*, 247.

94. Aide Mémoire attached to Ministerie van Buitenlandse Zaken to van Kleffens, 7 December 1948, OB XVI, 1 December 1948 to 12 Januari 1949, no. 31, 157; Jacquet, *Minister Stikker*, 126–8.

95. Jacquet, *Minister Stikker*, 127; MacMahon, *Colonialism*, 248.

96. Grimal, *Decolonization*, 205; Van den Doel, *Afscheid*, 284.

97. Ide Anak Agung Gde Agung, *'Renville' als keerpunt in de Nederlands-Indonesische onderhandelingen* (Alphen a/d Rijn: Sijthoff, 1980), 204 suggests that Beel deliberately delayed the ultimatum to Hatta in order to give him no time to respond; Jacquet, *Minister Stikker*, 143–53.

98. Lovink to Stikker, 17 December 1948, OB, XVI, no. 132, 209.

99. Even Stikker agreed with the move to a military solution, although he later argued that this was on pragmatic grounds to prevent a cabinet crisis. Van den Doel, *Afscheid*, 287–9 quotes Cochran to Secretary of State Marshall, 18 December 1948. The former foreign minister and ambassador to Washington, Eelco van Kleffens was the only voice that spoke out against this course of action, warning of the severe damage such an action would do to the Netherlands' international prestige and reputation in the United States. Van Klefffens had sent warnings to the Dutch politicians before this, for example, in a private letter to Stikker on 27 October 1948, see, Jacquet, *Minister Stikker*, 80–1, 119.

100. Only 150 of 10,000 civil servants were reportedly still at their posts, kept there by orders from the pro-Republican Sultan of Yogyakarta to ensure that hospitals, power, and water supplies were maintained. Kahin, 'Some Recollections', 23; Kahin, *Nationalism and Revolution*, 332–9.

101. Kahin, 'Some Recollections', 23–4.

Notes

102. Van den Doel, *Afscheid*, 291; Jacquet, *Minister Stikker*, 156; Grimal, *Decolonization*, 206–7.

103. Crown High Commissioner Beel to Minister for Overseas Territories Sassen, 19 December 1948, *OB*, XVI, no. 157, 236.

104. Pierre van der Eng, 'Marshall Aid as a Catalyst in the Decolonization of Indonesia, 1947-49', *Journal of Southeast Asian Studies*, 19:2 (1988), 341, 345–7; MacMahon, *Colonialism*, 292.

105. Oey, *War and Diplomacy*, 209, cites Lovett to Jessup, *Foreign Relations of the United States* (*FRUS*), VI, 1948 (Washington, DC, 1974), 618–19; Van den Doel, *Afscheid*, 294; Grimal, *Decolonization*, 208–9.

106. Mrázek, *Sjahrir*, 390; Oey, *War and Diplomacy*, 205, 209; Van den Doel, *Afscheid,* 301.

107. MacMahon, *Colonialism*, 252–3.

108. Ide Anak Agung Gde Agung, '*Renville*', 221–5; Jacquet, *Minister Stikker*, 171; MacMahon, *Colonialism*, 264–5 argues that the US position on these resolutions shows how Washington attempted to condemn Dutch actions in Indonesia while maintaining reasonable relations with The Hague.

109. Jessup to Secretary of State, *FRUS* (1949) VII, 162, 183.

110. MacMahon, *Colonialism*, 273.

111. Only France, the Soviet Union, and the Ukrainian SSR abstained from the vote: Oey, *War and Diplomacy*, 214; Van den Doel, *Afscheid*, 297; Jacquet, *Minister Stikker*, 190–3.

112. Oey, *War and Diplomacy*, 219.

113. Van der Eng, 'Marshall Aid', 348–9; Oey, *War and Diplomacy*, 218–20; MacMahon, *Colonialism*, 275–6. On the same day the Senate discussed the Brewster resolution condemning Dutch actions.

114. Van den Doel, *Afscheid*, 303–5; Oey, *War and Diplomacy*, 217. P. M. H. Groen, 'Dutch armed forces and the decolonization of Indonesia: the second Police Action (1948-1949) A Pandora's Box', *War and Society*, 4:1 (1886), 79–104.

115. Kahin, *Nationalism and Revolution*, 406.

116. Jacquet, *Minister Stikker*, 194–211.

117. Grimal, *Decolonization*, 209; Oey, *War and Diplomacy*, 221.

118. Jacquet, *Minister Stikker*, 245.

119. Van den Doel, *Afscheid*, 305–6. See also, for example, Aantekening van minister van buitenlandse zaken Stikker, 23 March 1949. *OB*, XVIII, no. 146.

120. This was the so-called van Roijen-Roem Agreement. Van den Doel, *Afscheid*, 307–8; Jacquet, *Minister Stikker*, 292–305.

121. Grimal, *Decolonization*, 210; Van den Doel, *Afscheid*, 309.

122. Jacquet, *Minister Stikker*, 212; Oey, *War and Diplomacy*, 234. Sassen had resigned in early February 1949. His hard line has been partly attributed to the fact that large numbers of the Dutch troops deployed in the Indies were from the Catholic south of the country – the heart of his political constituency. Taylor, *Indonesian Independence and the United Nations*, 289.

123. Baruch dispatch, *FRUS* (1949) VII, 444–5. The difficulty in the Netherlands was that the 'war' appeared won, with only small pockets on the maps not apparently controlled by Dutch forces. Thus, Dutch politicians and public alike had to be acquainted with the true state of affairs.

124. Van den Doel, *Afscheid*, 310; Oey, *War and Diplomacy*, 236.

125. Van den Doel, *Afscheid*, 312–13.

126. Puchinger, *Tilanus vertelde mij zijn leven*, 218. Tilanus' evaluation of Logemann makes interesting reading, describing him as a shrewd minister, but extremely left wing on the Indies, see ibid., 248.

127. J. J. A. van Doorn, *De Laatste Eeuw van Indië: Ontwikkeling en ondergang van een koloniaal project* (Amsterdam: Bert Bakker, 1994), 251–2.

128. Wesseling, *Imperialism and Colonialism*, 126–9.

129. Wesseling, *Imperialism and Colonialism*, 137 notes the Hueting scandal of January 1969 where in a television programme a psychologist revealed stories of atrocities committed by Dutch troops.

130. Wesseling, *Imperialism and Colonialism*, 133. Martin Bossenbroek, *De Meelstreep: Terugkeer en opvang na de Tweede Wereldoorlog* (Amsterdam: Bert Bakker, 2001). Elsbeth Locher-Scholten, 'After the "distant war", Dutch public memory of the Second World War in Asia', in Remco Raben (ed.), *Representing the Japanese Occupation of Indonesia* (Zwolle: Waanders/NIOD, 1999), 55–70.

131. Wesseling, *Imperialism and Colonialism*, 134–5. H. L. Wesseling, 'Nederland zonder Indië', *Hollands Maandblad*, 379/380 (1979), 3–14. For a detailed description of the South Moluccan question see, Richard Chauvel, 'Ambon: not a revolution but a counterrevolution', in Audrey R. Kahin (ed.), *Regional Dynamics of the Indonesian Revolution* (Honolulu: University of Hawaii Press, 1985), 237–64.

132. Locher-Scholten, 'After the "distant war"', 61–6. David Wertheim, 'Over and done with?', in Raben, *Representing the Japanese Occupation of Indonesia*, 200–1.

133. These include memorials in Amstelveen, Roermond, and 's-Hertogenbosch.

Chapter 14

1. Arend Lijphart, *The Trauma of Decolonization: The Dutch and West New Guinea* (New Haven, CT: Yale University Press, 1966), 12–14.

2. Smit, *Liquidatie*, 193.

3. Kees Lagerberg, *West Irian and Jakarta Imperialism* (London: Hurst, 1979) 21; Smit, *Liquidatie*, 197.

4. The most recent, and by far the most exhaustive, discussion on this comes from P. J. Drooglever, *Een daad van vrije keus: De Papoeas van westerlijk Nieuw Guinea en de grenzen van het zelfbeschikkingsrecht* (Amsterdam: Boom, 2005), subsequently published as *An Act of Free Choice: Decolonization and the Right to Self-determination in West Papua* (New York: Oxford University Press, 2009). However, his moral interpretation of events and underestimation of Indonesian nationalism has not gone unchallenged. See R. E. Elson, 'Marginality, morality and the nationalist impulse: Papua, the Netherlands and Indonesia: a review article', and Hans Meyer, '"Geschiedenis is nu eenmaal altijd politiek": De studie-Drooglever als symptom van de moeizame omgang van Nederland met het koloniaal verleden en de complexe relatie met Indonesië', *Bijdragen en mededelingen betreffende de geschiedenis der Nederlanden*, CXXI:1 (2007), 65–71, 72–90. See also P. J. Drooglever, 'Een paar bedekingen' in ibid., 91–104.

5. Lijphart, *The Trauma of Decolonization*, 286.

6. For a detailed discussion of the disputes, see van der Kroef, *The West New Guinea Dispute*, 3–8; Lijphart, *The Trauma of Decolonization*, 22–35.

7. Van der Kroef, *The West New Guinea Dispute*, 9; Lagerberg, *West Irian and Jakarta Imperialism*, 34–5.

8. Jan Pouwer, 'The Colonization, Decolonization and Recolonization of West New Guinea', *The Journal of Pacific History*, 34:2 (1999), 161.

9. Lagerberg, *West Irian and Jakarta Imperialism*, 21; van der Kroef, *The West New Guinea Dispute*, 11; Lijphart, *The Trauma of Decolonization*, 23–4.

10. Van der Kroef, *The West New Guinea Dispute*, 3, cites C. Smit, *De Indonesische Quaestie: De Wordinggeschiedenis der Souvereiniteitsoverdracht* (Leyden: Brill, 1952), 97–8 and Justus van der Kroef, 'Dutch Policy and the Linggadjati Agreement, 1946-1947', *The Historian*, 15 (1953), 163–87.

11. Van der Kroef, *The West New Guinea Dispute*, 14.

12. Hans Meijer, '"Het uitverkoren land": De lotgevallen van de Indo Europese kolonisten op Nieuw-Guinea (1949-1962)', *Tijdschrift voor Geschiedenis*, 112:3 (1999), 253–84. Lijphart, *The Trauma of Decolonization*, 90–8; van der Kroef, *The West New Guinea Dispute*, 15.

13. They were claimed to number some 15,000–20,000 SS volunteers and around 50,000 Dutch NSB members. Lijphart, *The Trauma of Decolonization*, 99, cites G. L. Tichelman and Jonkheer W. H. Alting van Geusau, *NSB-deportatie naar Oost en West* (Amsterdam: D.A.V.I.D., 1945), 16.

14. Vlasblom, *Papoea*, 187. He summed up the utter confusion of the event. 'Suddenly everything was on the beach, a piano, a chicken coop and a picture of the Pope.'

15. Van der Kroef, *The West New Guinea Dispute*, 12.

16. Lijphart, *The Trauma of Decolonization*, 83–5, 106.

17. Lijphart, *The Trauma of Decolonization*, 154.

18. B. Krijger, 'Nieuw-Guinea', *Tijdschrift voor Economische en Sociale Geografie* (February 1953), 44, cited in Lijphart, *The Trauma of Decolonization*, 155.

19. Ulbe Bosma, 'Nederlands Nieuw-Guinea en de Late *Empire Builders*', *Tijdschrift voor Sociale en Economische Geschiedenis*, 6:3 (2009), 4–5. See also R. Robinson, 'Non-European foundations of European imperialism: sketch for a theory of collaboration', in R. Owen and B. Sutcliffe (eds), *Studies in the Theory of Imperialism* (London: Longman, 1972), 117–42.

20. Bosma, 'Nederlands Nieuw-Guinea', 5.

21. Bosma, 'Nederlands Nieuw-Guinea', 156.

22. Van den Doel, *Afscheid van Indië*, 325; Lijphart, *The Trauma of Decolonization*, 105.

23. Lijphart, *The Trauma of Decolonization*, 107–10, 114. The relevant figures were 71 for and 29 against in the Second Chamber and 34 for and 15 against in the First Chamber.

24. Jaquet, *Minister Stikker*, 198; Lijphart, *The Trauma of Decolonization*, 121–3.

25. Chris van Esterik, *Nederlands laatste bastion in de Oost: ekonomie en politiek in de Nieuw-Guinea-kwestie* (Baarn: Anthos/In de Toren, 1982), 52–3; Smit, *Liquidatie*, 198.

26. De Geus, *De Nieuw-Guinea Kwestie*, 61–5; Van Esterik, *Nederlands laatste bastion in de Oost*, 57.

27. Lijphart, *The Trauma of Decolonization*, 125–6.

28. Smit, *Liquidatie*, 217.

29. Lijphart, *The Trauma of Decolonization*, 127.

30. Hiroyuki Umetsu, 'Australia's response to the West New Guinea dispute', *The Journal of Pacific History*, 39:1 (2004), 61, 69.

31. Umetsu, 'Australia's Response', 74–6. Lijphart, *The Trauma of Decolonization*, 64–5, 127.

32. van der Kroef, *The West New Guinea Dispute*, 6.

33. De Geus, *De Nieuw-Guinea Kwestie*, 67; Vlasblom, *Papoea*, 192.

34. Lijphart, *The Trauma of Decolonization*, 41–2; van der Kroef, *The West New Guinea Dispute*, 13 gives a much higher figure for 1950 of fl.23,355,896 and cites *Vademecum voor Nederlands-Nieuw Guinea 1956* (Den Helder, 1956).

35. Lijphart, *The Trauma of Decolonization*, 45, 49.

36. Lijphart, *The Trauma of Decolonization*, 44–5. The Company was 40 per cent owned by Royal Dutch Shell, 40 per cent by Standard Vacuum, and 20 per cent by Far Eastern Investments: Van der Kroef, *The West New Guinea Dispute*, 13.

37. See, Greg Poulgrain, 'Delaying the "discovery" of oil in West New Guinea', *The Journal of Pacific History*, 34:2 (1999), 205–18.

38. For the most part, energies were put into developing plantation crops for export such as copra, nutmeg, cocoa, coffee, and rubber. Pouwer, 'Colonization', 169–71.

39. Lijphart, *The Trauma of Decolonization*, 50–62.

40. Jhr.mr. J. L. R. Huydecoper van Nigtevecht, *Nieuw-Guinea: Het einde van een koloniale beleid* ('s-Gravenhage: SDU, 1990), 22.

41. Lijphart, *The Trauma of Decolonization*, 287. For a different view of the economic potential of New Guinea, see TAPOL, *West Papua: Obliteration of People* (London: TAPOL, 1983), 17.

42. Lijphart, *The Trauma of Decolonization*, 138, 142.

43. M. Klaassen, 'Zoeklicht op Nieuw-Guinea', *Marineblad*, 60 (1950), 518, cited in Lijphart, *The Trauma of Decolonization*, 157–8.

44. Lagerberg, *West Irian and Jakarta Imperialism*, 37. The importance of these early settlements should not be overstated. The first missionary posts were very small and largely unsuccessful. The 1855 settlement was made by German missionaries.

45. Lijphart, *The Trauma of Decolonization*, 152.

46. Smit, *Liquidatie*, 217.

47. Lijphart, *The Trauma of Decolonization*, 146–7.

48. S. Gerbrandy, *Indonesia* (London: Hutchinson, 1950), 178, 191, cited in Lijphart, *The Trauma of Decolonization*, 165–6.

49. Lijphart, *The Trauma of Decolonization*, 167–71.

50. De Geus, *De Nieuw-Guinea Kwestie*, 67; Lijphart, *The Trauma of Decolonization*, 172.

51. For a detailed discussion of the political position in the Netherlands in the early 1950s see Van Esterik, *Nederlands laatste bastion in de Oost*, 58–96.

52. van der Kroef, *The West New Guinea Dispute*, 19.

53. De Geus, *De Nieuw-Guinea Kwestie*, 68. Umetsu, 'Australia's response', 63.

54. van der Kroef, *The West New Guinea Dispute*, 23.

55. Smit, *Liquidatie*, 210.

56. C. B. Wels, *Aloofness and Neutrality: Studies on Dutch Foreign relations and Policy-Making Institutions* (Utrecht: HES, 1982), 137.

57. Smit, *Liquidatie*, 211–12; van der Kroef, *The West New Guinea Dispute*, 25–6; Lagerberg, *West Irian and Jakarta Imperialism*, 79; Vlasblom, *Papoea*, 266–7; De Geus, *De Nieuw-Guinea Kwestie*, 72–8.

58. Hiroyuki Umetsu, 'Australia's actions towards accepting Indonesian control of Netherlands New Guinea', *Journal of Pacific History*, 41:1 (2006), 32–3. Hiroyuki Umetsu, 'The impacts of Indonesia's civil war and the US-Soviet tug-of-war over Indonesia on Australia's diplomacy towards West New Guinea', *Journal of Pacific History*, 40:2 (2005), 174–6.

59. United Nations General Assembly, 12th Session, Plenary Meeting 724, 2, 9 November 1957.

60. Van den Doel, *Afscheid van Indië*, 328–9; Jan Pluvier, *Indonesië: kolonialisme, onafhankelijkheid, neo-kolonialisme: Een politieke geschiedenis van 1940 tot heden* (Nijmegen: Socialistiese Uitgeverij, 1978), 228. This continued as Indonesia attempted to remove her economy from links with the Netherlands. Thus in December 1958, legislation was passed moving the Indonesian tea and tobacco markets to Antwerp and Bremen. See also De Geus, *De Nieuw-Guinea Kwestie*, 88–94.

61. Dahm, *History of Indonesia*, 184; Christopher J. McMullen, *Mediation of the West New Guinea Dispute: A Case Study* (Washington, DC: Georgetown University, 1981), 2.

62. Smit, *Liquidatie*, 212.

63. Van den Doel, *Afscheid van Indië*, 329.

64. De Geus, *De Nieuw-Guinea Kwestie*, 78–81; van der Kroef, *The West New Guinea Dispute*, 22; Lijphart, *The Trauma of Decolonization*, 200–10.

65. Lijphart, *The Trauma of Decolonization*, 215.

66. By this stage it was also clear that the oil reserves were too small to be of any great importance. Vlasblom, *Papoea*, 278–82; Lijphart, *The Trauma of Decolonization*, 220.

67. Lijphart, *The Trauma of Decolonization*, 232.

68. See also the Catholic author F. J. F. M. Duynstee, *Nieuw-Guinea als schakel tussen Nederland en Indonesie* (Amsterdam: De Bezige Bij, 1961); Lijphart, *The Trauma of Decolonization*, 242–8. This change in press opinion was not mirrored by public opinion where commitment to sovereignty before self-determination was still very strong.

69. L. Palmier, *Indonesia and the Dutch* (London: Oxford University Press, 1962), 124; Smit, *Liquidatie*, 218.

70. Vlasblom, *Papoea*, 254–7.

71. Lijphart, *The Trauma of Decolonization*, 195.

72. Lijphart, *The Trauma of Decolonization*, 258–9, 262. Lijphart notes that the Catholic Party had actually become more conservative on the issue as a result of its merger with the smaller Catholic National Party.

73. Pluvier, *Indonesië*, 229; Vlasblom, *Papoea*, 271. The use of an aircraft carrier was also a quick way of getting aircraft to New Guinea as they did not have to be dismantled and came with their own airfield. Huydecoper van Nigtevecht, *Nieuw-Guinea*, 48.

74. Huydecoper van Nigtevecht, *Nieuw-Guinea*, 48; De Geus, *De Nieuw-Guinea Kwestie*, 122–6; Pluvier, *Indonesië*, 229. From then on, the British became the protectors of Dutch interests in Indonesia and Egypt carried out the same function for Indonesian interests in the Netherlands.

75. Vlasblom, *Papoea*, 271.

76. Umetsu, 'Australia's Actions', 33 gives a figure of $500 million or approximately eight times what the United States had provided over the same period since 1957.

77. Pluvier, *Indonesië*, 228–9; van der Kroef, *The West New Guinea Dispute*, 27–8. At the same time, they also made it clear to the Dutch that they would not provide any military support. De Geus, *De Nieuw-Guinea Kwestie*, 96, 102.

78. Lagerberg, *West Irian and Jakarta Imperialism*, 84; Smit, *Liquidatie*, 219–21.

79. John Saltford, *The United Nations and the Indonesian Takeover of West Papua, 1962-1969: The Anatomy of Betrayal* (London: Routledge, 2003), 6.

80. Van der Kroef, *The West New Guinea Dispute*, 30.

81. Huydecoper van Nigtevecht, *Nieuw-Guinea*, 50. Saltford, *The United Nations and the Indonesian Takeover*, 6, cites Audrey R. and George McT. Kahin, *Subversion as Foreign Policy: The Secret Eisenhower and Dulles Debacle in Indonesia* (New York: New Press, 1995), 17.

82. Van den Doel, *Afscheid van Indië*, 330. At the same time, Luns, as Minister without Portfolio, was ostensibly assured at a dinner in Washington that the United States would not tolerate an Indonesian military invasion of New Guinea.

83. De Geus, *De Nieuw-Guinea Kwestie*, 95.

84. McMullen, *Mediation*, 7; Pluvier, *Indonesië*, 230.

85. Huydecoper van Nigtevecht, *Nieuw-Guinea*, 57.

86. De Geus, *De Nieuw-Guinea Kwestie*, 134–7; Lagerberg, *West Irian and Jakarta Imperialism*, 63–4; Dahm, *History of Indonesia*, 208. David Webster, 'Self-determination abandoned: the road to the New York Agreement on West New Guinea, 1960-62', *Indonesia*, 95 (2013), 11. Pouwer, 'Colonization', 168.

87. Vlasblom, *Papoea*, 301.

88. Saltford, *The United Nations and the Indonesian Takeover*, 10–11.

89. These were the resolutions of the Brazzaville Group and of the Indian government. The defeat of these resolutions was blamed on the opposition of the Arab States who, although seeing the benefits of the resolutions, opposed them on principle because of the Netherlands' traditional support for Israel: Lagerberg, *West Irian and Jakarta Imperialism*, 81; Lijphart, *The Trauma of Decolonization*, 276; Dahm, *History of Indonesia*, 208; Smit, *Liquidatie*, 222.

90. Huydecoper van Nigtevecht, *Nieuw-Guinea*, 50–2. Webster, 'Self-determination abandoned', 14.

91. McMullen, *Mediation*, 9.

92. The so-called 'Trikora' statement. Van den Doel, *Afscheid van Indië*, 331; Saltford, *The United Nations and the Indonesian Takeover*, xviii; De Geus, *De Nieuw-Guinea Kwestie*, 154–5.

93. Dahm, *History of Indonesia*, 209; Pluvier, *Indonesië*, 232; Van den Doel, *Afscheid van Indië*, 331; De Geus, *De Nieuw-Guinea Kwestie*, 163–4; Vlasblom, *Papoea*, 313–14. The most serious incident was a battle between Indonesian MTBs and Dutch naval vessels on 15 January 1962. Lagerberg, *West Irian and Jakarta Imperialism*, 82.

94. McMullen, *Mediation*, 11; Vlasblom, *Papoea*, 312; De Geus, *De Nieuw-Guinea Kwestie*, 169–70; van den Doel, *Afscheid van Indië*, 331; De Geus, *De Nieuw-Guinea Kwestie*, 157–60.

95. Webster, 'Self-determination abandoned', 12.

96. Robert Komer to Walt Rostow, 30 November 1961 Foreign Relations of the United States 1961–3, vol. 13, 469–70 cited in Webster, 'Self-Determination Abandoned', 16.

97. McMullen, *Mediation*, 10, 12.

98. Smit, *Liquidatie*, 223. Although emanating from Bunker, the plan had been derived from conversations between Sir Garfield Barwick, the Australian Minister of Foreign Affairs, and the Dutch Ambassador, Dr de Beus. Lagerberg, *West Irian and Jakarta Imperialism*, 85; Saltford, *The United Nations and the Indonesian Takeover*, 11–13. For a detailed discussion surrounding the negotiation of the Bunker Plan, see Huydecoper van Nigtevecht, *Nieuw-Guinea*, 59–189.

99. Pluvier, *Indonesië*, 233.

100. Lagerberg, *West Irian and Jakarta Imperialism*, 88–9.

101. Dahm, *History of Indonesia*, 210, Smit, *Liquidatie*, 225. The agreement actually made no explicit reference to sovereignty but the Dutch merely indicated that in transferring authority to the UN administrator, they withdrew from the sovereignty of the territory. See also David Webster, 'Race Identity and Diplomacy in the Papua Decolonization Struggle, 1949-1962', in Philip E. Muehlenbeck (ed.), *Race, Ethnicity and the Cold War: A Global Perspective* (Nashville: Vanderbilt University Press, 2012), 96–7.

102. Van den Doel, *Afscheid van Indië*, 332; Pluvier, *Indonesië*, 233.

103. Van den Doel, *Afscheid van Indië*, 332.

104. See, Ronald Gase, *Misleiding of zelfbedrog: Een analyse van het Nederlandse Nieuw Guinea-beleid aan de hand van gesprekken met betrokken politici en diplomaten* (Baarn: In den Toren, 1984).

105. Lijphart, *The Trauma of Decolonization*, 288.

106. Van Esterik, *Nederlands laatste bastion in de Oost*, 196–9.

Chapter 15

1. For the most comprehensive history of Suriname, see Hans Buddingh', *Geschiedenis van Suriname* (Utrecht: Spectrum, 1995). On the later stages of the old colonial regime see three works by the following authors: Hans Ramsoedh: *Suriname 1933-1944: Koloniale Politiek en Beleid onder Gouverneur Kielstra* (Delft: Eburon, 1990); 'De geforceerde onafhankelijkheid', *OSO*, 12 (1993), 43–62; 'De dekolonisatie van Suriname: opgedrongen onafhankelijkheid?', *Spiegel Historiael*, 30 (1995), 382–6. Edward Dew, *The Difficult Flowering of Surinam: Ethnicity and Politics in a Plural Society* (The Hague: Nijhoff, 1978).

2. USNA, RG 59, Decimal Files, 1940 44, 856A.00/5, Carl Norden, Vice-Consul, Paramaribo, to State, 21 January 1941.

3. Moore, 'Anglo-American security policy', 456–62. For a more detailed study, see F. A. Baptiste, *War Cooperation and Conflict: The European Possessions in the Caribbean, 1939-1945* (New York: Greenwood Press, 1988).

4. Moore, 'Anglo-American Security Policy', 463. The arrival of sixty soldiers of the Dutch Regular Army to reinforce the garrison in Suriname led to all manner of problems when it was discovered by their counterparts in the Colonial Army that these men were on much higher rates of pay.

5. Algemeen Rijksarchief, The Hague (hereafter ARA) Ministerie van Kolonien (hereafter MvK) LA-Geheim/137, Brandkast II(8) Suriname, no. 5038GA, Alexander Loudon, Netherlands ambassador Washington, to E. H. van Kleffens, 16 September 1941; USNA, RG 59, Decimal Files, 1940–44, 856A.20/7, Norden to State, 4 September 1941; Buddingh', *Geschiedenis*, 274–5.

6. Hiss, *Netherlands America*, 197, In 1941, imports totalled Sfl.9,429,922 and exports Sfl.11,398,377. Liesbeth van der Horst, *Wereldoorlog in de West: Suriname, de Nederlandse Antillen en Aruba, 1940-1945* (Hilversum: Verloren, 2004), 27–36. See also O. M. de Munnick, *Het Rijke Ertsland: Suriname* (Hengelo: H.L. Smit, 1946).

7. Pieter Jan van Eyck, *Nederland en West Indië: De Betekenis van de Tweede Wereldoorlog voor het Nederlandse Koloniale Beleid ten opzichte van Suriname en de Nederlandse Antillen* (Doctoraalscriptie, K. U. Nijmegen, 1988), 149; Buddingh', *Geschiedenis*, 273; Hiss, *Netherlands America*, 171, 173; van der Horst, *Wereldoorlog in de West*, 27–36.

8. Hiss, *Netherlands America*, 174.

9. Gert Oostindië and Inge Klinkers, *Knellende Koninkrijksbanden: Het Nederlandse dekolonisatiebeleid in de Caraiben, 1940-2000*, 3 vols (Amsterdam: Amsterdam University Press, 2001), I, 71; van der Horst, *Wereldoorlog in de West*, 89–90.

10. USNA, RG 59, Decimal Files, 1945-1949, 856.00/4-1845, Lee R. Blohm, US Consul, Paramaribo, to State, 18 April 1945, and 856a.504/5-1045, Blohm to Secretary of State, 10 May 1945. Blohm noted that the economic demands of the people of Suriname should not be equated with a separatist movement.

11. Edwin Marshall, *Ontstaan en Ontwikkeling van het Surinaams Nationalisme: Natievorming als opgave* (Delft: Eburon, 2003), 45–62.

12. Oostindië and Klinkers, *Knellende Koninkrijksbanden*, I, 66–70; van der Horst, *Wereldoorlog in de West*, 81–94; Chin and Buddingh', *Surinam*, 14.

13. Oostindië and Klinkers, *Knellende Koninkrijksbanden*, I, 70.

14. Founded by the Creole elite in 1943, the *Unie Suriname* was ostensibly a cultural organization, but with political overtones. It sought to counter the governor's attempts to limit their advancement through the policy of *verindisching* (Indianization). Buddingh', *Geschiedenis*, 272; Marshall, *Ontstaan en Ontwikkeling*, 48.

15. Chin and Buddingh', *Surinam*, 15; Buddingh', *Geschiedenis*, 419.

16. Dew, *Difficult Flowering*, 59–64; Buddingh', *Geschiedenis*, 279; Peter Meel, 'Verbroederingspolitiek en nationalisme: het dekolonisatievraagstuk in de Surinaamse politiek', *Bijdragen en Mededelingen Betreffende de Geschiedenis der Nederlanden*, 109:4 (1994), 638–59 (641). See also Peter Meel, 'A reluctant embrace: Suriname's idle quest for independence', in Gary Brana-Shute (ed.), *Resistance and Rebellion in Suriname: Old and New* (Williamsburg, PA: College of William and Mary, 1990), 275–8.

17. Oostindië and Klinkers, *Knellende Koninkrijksbanden*, I, 79–81. The three commissions were De La Try Ellis (Curaçao), De Niet (Suriname) and van Helsdingen (Antilles). All three reports were published in 1946.

18. Oostindië and Klinkers, *Decolonising the Caribbean*, 74–5.

19. Ramsoedh, 'Geforceerde onafhankelijkheid', 45, notes that the delegation was poorly timed as the Schermerhorn-Drees Cabinet was a caretaker government. See also TNA, FO 371/60219/Z 9077, Sir Nevile Bland, The Hague, to Ernest Bevin, Foreign Secretary, 22 October 1946.

20. Dew, *Difficult Flowering*, 65–6.

21. Ramsoedh, 'Geforceerde onafhankelijkheid', 46, points out that the Dutch were also under some pressure from events elsewhere in Latin America. The Pan-American Conferences in Bogota (1948) and Havana (1949) both discussed the European colonies and, led by Venezuela, pressed for

these to be appended to existing Latin American states or given full independence. (Venezuelan designs on Curaçao and Aruba were well known.) However, the effects of this pressure were dissipated by US preoccupation with Cold War politics and its reluctance to offend its European defence partners. The overthrow of the radical Betancourt regime in Venezuela in 1948 also had an impact.

22. Oostindië and Klinkers, *Decolonising the Caribbean*, 77.

23. TNA, FO 371/73259/Z 3275, Lt. Cmdr. John Fitzhardinge Berkeley Gage (RNVR), to Ernest Bevin, 12 April 1948.

24. Ramsoedh, 'Geforceerde onafhankelijkheid', 46.

25. Oostindië and Klinkers, *Decolonising the Caribbean*, 80.

26. TNA, FO 371/101940/WN 1511/10, F. C. D. Sargeant, The Hague, to FO, 11 December 1952.

27. Dew, *Difficult Flowering*, 98; Ramsoedh, 'Geforceerde onafhankelijkheid', 47. This was never really considered seriously by the politicians involved at the time. See Lou Lichtveld, *Suriname's Nationale Aspiraties: Een aanleiding tot discussies over de grondslagen van een al-omvattend ontwikkelingsplan* (Amsterdam: Arbeiderspers, 1953), 9–19.

28. The Dutch had indicated at the 1951 session of the United Nations that they would no longer submit reports on their West Indian possessions on the grounds that these were only required for non-self-governing territories under Article 73e of the UN Charter. This attempt to make the Dutch West Indies seem more independent than they actually were and deflect international criticism led to 'acrimonious debate' and deferral of discussion until the 1952 session: TNA, FO 371/101940/WN 1511/3, Sir Nevile Butler, The Hague, to N. J. A. Cheetham, FO, 19 June 1952; FO 371/101940/WN 1511/6, Butler to Anthony Eden, 31 October 1952.

29. Ramsoedh, 'Geforceerde onafhankelijkheid', 47, cites Handelingen Eerste Kamer 1952–3, 11e vergadering, 13 januari 1953, 12e vergadering, 14 januari 1953.

30. ARA MvK 2.10.41 Inventaris, Inleiding, 15–16.

31. Ramsoedh, 'Geforceerde onafhankelijkheid', 48.

32. Oostindië and Klinkers, *Decolonising the Caribbean*, 85.

33. Known as *verbroedering* (fraternization), the NPS-VHP coalition owed something to the cross-ethnic alliance of Jeddi Jagan and Forbes Burnham in neighbouring British Guiana, but unlike the latter, which fragmented in 1954–5, Pengel and Lachmon made major sacrifices to keep the coalition in power. Dew, *Difficult Flowering*, 102; Meel, 'Verbroederingspolitiek en nationalisme', 642.

34. It should be borne in mind here that the effective political party leaders did not always hold the highest executive offices, but preferred to stay as politicians with seats in the Staten.

35. Ramsoedh, 'Geforceerde onafhankelijkheid', 50. He notes how authors have found it difficult to analyse the complex interaction of power politics and opportunism, coupled with an intricate patronage system and personal followings which did so much to characterize Surinamese politics in this era.

36. Marshall, *Ontstaan en Ontwikkeling*, 108–21.

37. Meel, 'Verbroederingspolitiek en nationalisme', 642–3.

38. Ramsoedh, 'Geforceerde onafhankelijkheid', 52, sees this not as a real change in Lachmon's thinking, but as a political manoeuvre to bolster Pengel's power among the Creole population.

39. ARA MvK 2.10.41/72, minute 20f, Nr.2720, Ministerraad Notulen, 24 March 1961.

40. ARA MvK 2.10.41/91, Drs. K. H. De Boer, Imperial Cabinet Secretary, to Korthals, 4 April 1961.

41. USNA, RG 59, Decimal Files, 1960–4, 756a.00/11-2262, Guest to State, 22 November 1962.

42. Ramsoedh, 'Geforceerde onafhankelijkheid', 52, argues that the VHP was heavily influenced by the racial tensions engendered in both Trinidad and Guyana by moves towards independence.

43. USNA, RG 59, Decimal Files, 1960–4, 756A.02/7-361, Guest to State, 3 July 1961.

44. ARA MvK 2.10.41/72, minute 2h, Ministerraad Notulen, 19 April 1963.

45. Ministerraad Notulen, 27 October 1961, minute 21b, Nr.2866, ARA MvK 2.10.41/72.

46. Meel, 'Verbroederingspolitiek en nationalisme', 638, 650, 654. Bruma had been active since before the 1950s, founding the organization Wie Eegie Sanie (Our Own Affairs) in 1950 and being widely thought of as a crypto-communist, especially during the height of the Cold War.

47. Marshall, *Ontstaan en Ontwikkeling*, 143–2, 153–61. This was the first Surinamese political party to have an ideological rather than a racial base. It claimed to be anti-colonialist and anti-communist.

48. Chin and Buddingh', *Surinam*, 28. Ramsoedh, 'Geforceerde onafhankelijkheid', 51.

49. Meel, 'Verbroederingspolitiek en nationalisme', 643.

50. Chin and Buddingh', *Surinam*, 28. The Dutch government had become increasingly unhappy about the growth (and cost) of the Suriname civil service. Pengel and the NPS had used preferment as a means to reward followers to keep their political alliances together. Handing one or more ministries to the VHP would further restrict their ability to exercise what they regarded as essential political patronage. Ramsoedh, 'Geforceerde onafhankelijkheid', 53, cites VHP worries about Pengel attempting to take over control of the internal security service. Meel, 'Verbroederingspolitiek en nationalisme', 649.

51. Ramsoedh, 'Geforceerde onafhankelijkheid', 59.

52. Oostindië and Klinkers, *Decolonising the Caribbean*, 97–101. At the same time, new information about Dutch military actions in Indonesia were the subject of press discussion and inevitably comparisons were made between the two events.

53. Meel, 'Verbroederingspolitiek en nationalisme', 658.

54. Buddingh', *Geschiedenis*, 295–6; Ramsoedh, 'Geforceerde onafhankelijkheid', 47. It had been the only party prepared to support the idea of self-determination during the crisis of 1952–3.

55. Meel, 'Verbroederingspolitiek en nationalisme', 650 makes the point that the coalition was aided by all the parties having been in opposition to the previous VHP regime.

56. Ramsoedh, 'Geforceerde onafhankelijkheid', 48, 55–7, 59; Buddingh', *Geschiedenis*, 289. Marshall, *Ontstaan en Ontwikkeling*, 165–6.

57. Meel, 'Verbroederingspolitiek en nationalisme', 653. The main difference between NPS and PNR became the timescale within which independence might be achieved. Meel also notes how Bruma and Pengel remained in conflict during the 1960s because they were competing for the same electorate but came together through joint trade union action against the Sedney Cabinet after 1969 (655–7).

58. Oostindië and Klinkers, *Knellende Koninkrijksbanden* II, 124–5; Chin and Buddingh', *Surinam*, 29; Oostindië and Klinkers, *Decolonising the Caribbean*, 103.

59. Dew, *Difficult Flowering*, 162.

60. Buddingh', *Geschiedenis*, 289.

61. Chin and Buddingh', *Surinam*, 32.

62. André Haakmat, *Herinneringen aan de toekomst van Suriname: Ervaringen en beschouwingen* (Amsterdam: Arbeiderspers, 1996), 46.

63. Oostindië and Klinkers, *Knellende Koninkrijksbanden* II, 126; Haakmat, *Herinneringen*, 48.

64. Buddingh', *Geschiedenis*, 297.

65. ARA MvK 2.10.41/97, Verslag van het Intern Beraad der Nederlandse Delegatie, 17 May 1975, 5–6; Verslag van het Bilateraal Overleg Suriname-Nederland, 21 May 1975.

66. ARA MvK 2.10.41/97, Regeringsoverleg, Nederland-Suriname, 17–19 March 1975; Buddingh', *Geschiedenis*, 298–9; Oostindië and Klinkers, *Decolonising the Caribbean*, 103. Thus, much of

the debate was on questions of nationality and immigration rights, see Oostindië and Klinkers, *Knellende Koninkrijksbanden* II, 130–1.

67. Buddingh', *Geschiedenis*, 298–301; ARA MvK 2.10.41/97, Bilateraal Overleg tussen Nederland en Suriname, 25–26 June 1975. In 1976, it was estimated that there were 130,000 Surinamese in the Netherlands, of whom approximately 50,000 had come in the period around independence. The crisis years of 1979–80 saw the arrival of another 25,000–30,000.

68. Buddingh', *Geschiedenis*, 301.

69. Large sections of the constitution were, in fact, drafted by civil servants in The Hague: Oostindië and Klinkers, *Decolonising the Caribbean*, 107–8.

70. VHP delegate Mungra, cited in Oostindië and Klinkers, *Decolonising the Caribbean*, 107. See also, Peter Meel, 'Dimensies van onafhankelijkheid', *Bijdragen en mededelingen betreffede de Geschiedenis der Nederlanden*, 117:2 (2002), 200–1.

71. Oostindië and Klinkers, *Decolonising the Caribbean*, 111.

72. Oostindië and Klinkers, *Decolonising the Caribbean*, 108–12.

73. Bob de Graaff, 'Kalm temidden van woedende golven': Het Ministerie van Koloniën en zijn taakomgeving, 1912-1940* (Leiden: SDU, 1997), 650–1.

74. It is worthy of note that recent histories of the Den Uyl Cabinet barely mention Suriname as an issue but concentrate on the domestic crises of the mid-1970s. See for example, Peter Bootsma and Willem Breedveld, *De Verbeelding aan de Macht: Het Kabinet den Uyl 1973-77* (Den Haag: SDU, 1999).

75. The most important works in this context are Dew, *Difficult Flowering*; id, 'Anti-consociationalism and independence in Surinam', *Boletín de Estudios Latinoamericanos y del Caribe*, 21 (1976), 3–15; idem, 'Apanjaht and revolution in Caribbean politics: the case of Suriname', in Scott B. MacDonald, Harold M. Sandstrom, and Paul B. Goodwin Jr. (eds), *The Caribbean after Grenada: Revolution. Conflict and Democracy* (New York: Greenwood Press, 1988); Albert J. Gastmann, *The Politics of Surinam and the Netherlands Antilles* (Puerto Rico, 1968); M. Bos, 'Surinam's road from self-government to sovereignty', *Netherlands Yearbook of International Law*, 7 (1976), 131–55. Arend Lijphart, *Democracy in Plural Societies: A Comparative Exploration* (London: Yale University Press, 1977); Henk E. Chin and Hans Buddingh', *Surinam: Politics Economics and Society* (London: Francis Pinter, 1987).

76. Oostindië and Klinkers, *Decolonising the Caribbean*, 119–20, 131–5. The original intention had been that Aruba would be granted full independence in ten years, but this was shelved in 1990. By then, even the Social Democrats had abandoned their ideological commitment to immediate decolonization.

77. Oostindië and Klinkers, *Decolonising the Caribbean*, 135, 141–2.

78. For a more detailed survey of Dutch policy towards the Antilles since 1975 see Oostindië and Klinkers, *Knellende Koninkrijksbanden*, III, 13–290.

79. See, for example, Miriam Sluis, 'Echte Curaçaoënaars verkopen eiland niet', *NRC Handelsblad*, 19 April 2007.

Chapter 16

1. Martin Ewans, 'Belgium and the colonial experience', *Journal of Contemporary European Studies*, 11:2 (2003), 167–80 (at 167); also cited in Guy Vanthemsche, *Belgium and the Congo, 1885-1980* (Cambridge: Cambridge University Press, 2012), 99.

2. Vanthemsche, *Belgium and the Congo*, 44–8.

3. M. Van Spaandonck, 'Belgium: a colonial power becomes a federal state', *Itinerario*, 20:2 (1996), 64–75.

4. Vanthemsche, *Belgium and the Congo*, 18–22.

5. Martin Ewans, *European Atrocity, African Catastrophe: Leopold II, the Congo Free State and its Aftermath* (London: Routledge/Curzon, 2002), 157–201, *passim*; Vanthemsche, *Belgium and the Congo*, 22–5.

6. Jonathan E. Robins, 'Slave cocoa and red rubber: E. D. Morel and the problem of ethical consumption', *Comparative Studies in Society and History*, 54:3 (2012), 596–9.

7. Kevin Grant, 'Christian critics of empire: missionaries, lantern lectures, and the Congo reform campaign in Britain'; Andrew Porter, 'Sir Roger Casement and the international humanitarian movement', both articles in *JICH*, 29:2 (2001), 27–58 and 59–74.

8. Matthew G. Stanard, *Selling the Congo: A History of European Pro-Empire Propaganda and the Making of Belgian Imperialism* (Lincoln, NE: University of Nebraska Press, 2012).

9. Matthew G. Stanard, 'Bilan du monde pour un monde plus déshumanisé: the Brussels World Fair and Belgian perceptions of the Congo', *European History Quarterly*, 32:2 (2005), 267–98; idem, 'Interwar pro-empire propaganda and european colonial culture: toward a comparative research agenda', *Journal of Contemporary History*, 44:1 (2009), 27–48.

10. Vincent Viaene, 'King Leopold's imperialism and the origins of the Belgian Colonial Party, 1860-1905', *Journal of Modern History*, 80:4 (2008), 761–80.

11. This is a central argument in Vanthemsche, *Belgium and the Congo*, 68–100, *passim*.

12. Jean Stengers, 'Precipitous decolonization: the case of the Belgian Congo', in Gifford and Louis, *The Transfer of Power*, 305–36.

13. Ewout Frankema, 'Colonial education and post-colonial governance in the Congo and Indonesia', in Ewout Frankema and Frans Buelens (eds), *Colonial Exploitation and Economic Development: The Belgian Congo and the Netherlands Indies Compared* (Abingdon: Routledge, 2013), 170–2.

14. David Maxwell, 'Photography and the religious encounter: ambiguity and aesthetics in missionary representations of the Luba of South East Belgian Congo', *Comparative Studies in Society and History*, 53:1 (2011), 49–66.

15. P. Bouvier, 'Le role des enseignements universitaire et supérieur dans le processus de la décolonisation congolaise', in *Congo, 1955-1960: Recueil d'études* (Brussels, 1992), 81–93; also cited in Vanthemsche, *Belgium*, 85–6.

16. On missions, education, and support for independence, see Marvin Markovitz, *Cross and Sword: The Political Role of Christian Missions in the Belgian Congo, 1908-1960* (Stanford, CA: Hoover Institution, 1973); Patrick M. Boyle, 'School wars: church, state, and the death of the Congo', *Journal of Modern African Studies*, 33:3 (1995), 451–68.

17. B. A. Yates, 'Educating Congolese abroad: an historical note on African elites', *International Journal of African Historical Studies*, 14:1 (1981), 34–64.

18. Holland, *European Decolonization*, 176–7.

19. Nancy Rose Hunt, 'Noise over camouflaged polygamy: colonial morality taxation, and woman-naming crisis in Belgian Africa', *JAH*, 32:3 (1991), 471–2.

20. Vincent Houbert and Julia Seibert, '(Un)freedom: colonial labour relations in Belgian Congo and the Netherlands Indies compared', in Frankema and Buelens, *Colonial Exploitation*, 182–5.

21. Mahmood Mamdani, *When Victims Become Killers: Colonialism, Nativism, and the Genocide in Rwanda* (Princeton, NJ: Princeton University Press, 2001), 12–16.

22. Mamdani, *When Victims Become Killers*, 25, 87–94.

23. Mamdani, *When Victims Become Killers*, 29, 99–101.

24. Mamdani, *When Victims Become Killers*, chs 2 and 3.

25. Hargreaves, *Decolonization in Africa*, 176.

26. Hargreaves, *Decolonization in Africa*, 178–9.

27. H. S. Wilson, *African Decolonization* (London: Edward Arnold, 1994), 173.

28. Holland, *European Decolonization*, 181–2.

29. David N. Gibbs, 'The United Nations, international peacekeeping and the question of "impartiality": revisiting the Congo operation of 1960', *Journal of Modern African Studies*, 38:3 (2000), 359–82.

30. Cited in Alan James, 'Britain, the Cold War, and the Congo Crisis, 1960-63', *JICH*, 28:3 (2000), 154. Kasavubu toured Leopoldville, his regional stronghold, in an open-topped car; by contrast, Lumumba's closed car was pelted with stones by Kasavubu's supporters.

31. For background to *Force Publique* origins, see L. H. Gann and P. Duigan, *The Rulers of Belgian Africa, 1884-1914* (Princeton, NJ: Princeton University Press, 1979), ch. 2.

32. Westad, *The Global Cold War*, 137.

33. Romain Takemtchouk, *Aux origines du séparatisme katangais* (Brussels: Académie royale des sciences d'outre-mer, 1988).

34. Regarding the mining sector, and *Union Minière* workers' conditions, see John Higginson, *A Working Class in the Making: Belgian Colonial Labour Policy and the African Mineworker, 1907-51* (Madison: University of Wisconsin Press, 1989).

35. Matthew Hughes, 'Fighting for white rule in Africa: the Central African Federation, Katanga, and the Congo Crisis, 1958-1965', *International History Review*, 25 (2003), 592–613.

36. Olivier Boehme, 'The involvement of the Belgian central bank in the Katanga secession, 1960-1963', *African Economic History*, 33 (2005), 1–13.

37. Jean Stengers, 'La reconnaissance *de jure* de l'indépendance katangaise', *Cahiers d'Histoire du Temps présent*, 11 (March 2003), 177–91; John Kent, *America, the UN and Decolonisation: Cold War Conflict in the Congo* (London: Routledge, 2010), 7–11.

38. Miles Larmer and Eric Kennes, 'Rethinking the Katangese secession', *JICH*, 42 (2014), 1–6.

39. Holland, *European Decolonization*, 180.

40. Alfred E. Eckes, *The United States and the Global Struggle for Minerals* (Austin, TX: University of Texas Press, 1979), 150–3.

41. Jonathan E. Helmreich, *United States Relations with Belgium and the Congo, 1940-1960* (Cranbury, NJ: Associated Universities Press, 1998), especially chs 2 and 5.

42. Westad, *The Global Cold War*, 138–9; and, more generally, Kent, *America, the UN and Decolonization*, chs 1–2.

43. Larmer and Kennes, 'Rethinking the Katangese secession', 8–10.

44. Miles Larmer, 'Of local identities and transnational conflict: the Katangese gendarmes and Central-Southern Africa's forty years war, 1960-99', in Nir Arielli and Bruce Collins (eds), *Transnational Soldiers: Foreign Military Enlistment in the Modern Era* (Basingstoke: Palgrave Macmillan, 2012), 160–80.

45. David N. Gibbs, *The Political Economy of Third World Intervention: Mines, Money, and U.S. Policy in the Congo Crisis* (Chicago: University of Chicago Press, 1991), 96–9.

46. For details see Ludo De Witte, *The Assassination of Lumumba* (London: Verso, 2002); Westad, *The Global Cold War*, 139–40.

47. Alan James, *Britain and the Congo Crisis, 1960-63* (London: Macmillan, 1996), 113.

48. *Foreign Relations of the United States* (FRUS), 1961-1963, vol. XX: Congo Crisis (Washington, DC: US Government Printing Office, 1994), doc. 7, 'Briefing paper prepared in the Department of State', n.d. 1961.

49. *FRUS*, 1961-1963, vol. XX, doc. 2, Special National Intelligence Estimate, 'Main elements in the Congo situation', 10 January 1961.

50. For a sympathetic, subtle view of UN objectives, see James, *Britain and the Congo Crisis*, 208–14.

51. Gibbs, *The Political Economy of Third World Intervention*, 126–34.

52. Gibbs, *The Political Economy of Third World Intervention*, 141–2. Tshombe's defeat was assured by 'Operation Grand Slam' in which UN forces seized full military control of Elisabethville at the end of December 1962.

53. Gibbs, *The Political Economy of Third World Intervention* 146–51.

54. Gibbs, *The Political Economy of Third World Intervention* 152–8.

55. Lawrence S. Kaplan, 'The United States, Belgium and the Congo Crisis of 1960', *Review of Politics*, 29:2 (1967), 239–56.

56. This foundation myth was at the core of colonial education of settler children, although it was steadily undermined in practice, see Antoinette Errante, 'White skin, many masks: colonial schooling, race, and national consciousness among white settler children in Mozambique, 1934-1974', *International Journal of African Historical Studies*, 36:1 (2003), 7–33.

57. Peter Karibe Mendy, 'Portugal's civilizing mission in colonial Guinea-Bissau: rhetoric and reality', *International Journal of African Historical Studies*, 36:1 (2003), 35.

58. Omar Ribeiro Thomaz, '"The good-hearted Portuguese people": anthropology of nation, anthropology of empire', in Benoît de l'Estoile, Federico Neiburg, and Lygia Sigaud, *Empires, Nations, and Natives* (Duke University Press, 2005), 58–60.

59. Alan K. Smith, 'The idea of Mozambique and its enemies, c, 1890-1930', *Journal of Southern African Studies*, 17:3 (1991), 517–24.

60. Thomas J. Noer, *Cold War and Black Liberation: The United States and White Rule in Africa, 1948-1968* (Columbia, Missouri: University of Missouri Press, 1985), 5.

61. Thomaz, '"The good-hearted Portuguese people"', 69.

62. Thomaz, '"The good-hearted Portuguese people"', 61–6.

63. Meera Sabaratnam, 'History repeating? Colonial, socialist and liberal statebuilding in Mozambique', in David Chandler and Timothy Sisk (eds), *The Routledge Handbook of International Statebuilding* (London: Routledge, 2013).

64. Miguel Bandeira Jerónimo and José Pedro Monteiro, 'Internationalism and the labours of the Portuguese colonial empire (1945-1974)', *Portuguese Studies*, 29:2 (2013), 142–63.

65. Norrie MacQueen, *The Decolonization of Portuguese Africa: Metropolitan Revolution and the Dissolution of Empire* (London: Longman, 1997), 205.

66. G. Clarence-Smith, *The third Portuguese empire, 1825-1975* (Manchester: Manchester University Press, 1985), 193.

67. Spruyt, *Ending Empire*, 195–7, 198–201.

68. Clarence-Smith, *The third Portuguese empire*, 213.

69. Bowen, *The State against the Peasantry*, 45.

70. Gerald J. Bender, *Angola under the Portuguese: The Myth and the Reality* (London: Heinemann, 1978), 127–31.

71. See, for example, Leroy Vail and Landeg White, *Capitalism and Colonialism in Mozambique* (Minneapolis: University of Minnesota press, 1980), chs 6–8; Gerald J. Bender, *Angola under the Portuguese: The Myth and the Reality* (London: Longman, 1978), especially ch. 6.

72. Paul Nugent, *Africa since Independence* (Basingstoke: Palgrave Macmillan, 2004), 263.

73. Mustafah Dhada, 'The liberation war in Guinea-Bissau reconsidered', *Journal of Military History*, 62:3 (1998), 574–6.

74. Norrie MacQueen, 'Portugal's first domino: 'Pluricontinentalism' and colonial war in Guiné-Bissau, 1963-1974', *Contemporary European History*, 8:2 (1999), 210–13.

75. 'Memorandum enviado ao govérno português pelo Partido Africano da Independência', (Memorandum stating the PAIGC's nationalist demands to the Portuguese Government), issued in

Conakry [French Guinea] by Amilcar Cabral and other PAIGC executive members, 1 December 1960, in Ronald Chilcote (ed.), *Emerging Nationalism in Portuguese Africa* (Stanford, CA: Hoover Institution Press, 1972), 367.

76. Mustafah Dhada, *Warriors at Work: How Guinea Was Really Set Free* (Boulder, CO: University Press of Colorado, 1993), 87–90, 97–115.

77. Fernando Andresen Guimarães, *The Origins of the Angolan Civil War: Foreign Intervention and Domestic Political Conflict, 1961-76* (Basingstoke: Palgrave Macmillan, 2001), 51–3.

78. Luís Nuno Rodrigues, 'The international dimension of Portuguese colonial crisis, 1961-1968', in Miguel Bandeira Jerónimo and António Costa Pinto (eds), *The Ends of European Colonial Empires: Cases and Comparisons* (Basingstoke: Palgrave Macmillan, 2015).

79. *FRUS*, 1964-1968, vol. XII Western Europe (Washington, DC: US Government Printing Office, 2001), doc. 149, NSC standing group, 'Record of Actions', n.d. February 1964; Nugent, *Africa since Independence*, 265.

80. *FRUS*, 1964-1968, vol. XII, doc. 151, Telegram from the Embassy in Portugal to Department of State, 18 April 1964.

81. Michael A. Samuels and Stephen M. Haykin, 'The Anderson Plan: an American attempt to seduce Portugal out of Africa', *Orbis*, 23:3 (1979), 661–9.

82. Chabal, *Amílcar Cabral*, 191.

83. Thomas H. Henriksen, 'People's war in Angola, Mozambique, and Guinea-Bissau', *Journal of Modern African Studies*, 14:3 (1976), 377–99.

84. These points are made in Chabal, *Amílcar Cabral*, 198.

85. Nugent, *Africa since Independence*, 262–6.

86. Chabal, *Amílcar Cabral*, 205.

87. Edward A. Alpers, 'Islam in the service of colonialism? Portuguese strategy during the armed liberation struggle in Mozambique', *Lusotopie* (1999), 171–83.

88. Linda M. Heywood, 'Towards an understanding of modern political ideology in Africa: the case of the Ovimbundu in Angola', *Journal of Modern African Studies*, 36:1 (1998), 149–51, 164–5.

89. Chabal, *Amílcar Cabral*, 206–7.

90. Bender, *Angola under the Portuguese*, 159–65.

91. Inge Brinkman, 'War, witches and traitors: cases from the MPLA's Eastern Front in Angola (1966-1975)', *JAH*, 44 (2003), 303–25. It bears emphasis that MPLA brutality was exceeded by that of UNITA.

92. Inge Brinkman, 'Ways of death: accounts of terror from Angolan refugees in Namibia', *Africa*, 70:1 (2000), 1–24.

93. Inge Brinkman, 'Routes and the war for independence in Northern Angola (1961-74)', *Canadian Journal of African Studies*, 40:2 (2006), 205–19.

94. Didier Péclard, 'Religion and politics in Angola: the church, the colonial state and the emergence of Angolan nationalism, 1940-1961', *Journal of Religion in Africa*, 28:2 (1998), 173–8.

95. Brinkman, 'War, witches and traitors', 311.

96. Linda Heywood, 'Unita and ethnic nationalism in Angola', *Journal of Modern African Studies*, 27:1 (1989), 50–4.

97. Bowen, *The State against the Peasantry*, 49–53.

98. NSC Memorandum from Samuel E. Belk to President Kennedy's special assistant, Ralph A. Dungan, Washington, DC, 9 January 1962; Research memorandum from Director of the Bureau of Intelligence and Research to Secretary of State, 5 November 1963, both *FRUS*, 1961–3, vol. XXI, 553–4, 579–80.

99. Piero Gleijeses, *Conflicting Missions: Havana, Washington and Africa, 1959-1976* (Chapel Hill: University of North Carolina Press, 2003); Witney W. Schneidman, *Engaging Africa: Washington and the Fall of Portugal's Colonial Empire* (Dallas, TX: University Press of America, 2004); Robert Scott Jaster, *The Defence of White Power: South African Foreign Policy Under Pressure* (London: Macmillan, 1988), Part III.

100. Westad, *The Global Cold War*, 212–24.

101. Douglas Wheeler, 'African elements in Portugal's armies in Africa (1961-1974)', *Armed Forces and Society*, 2:2 (1976), 233–50; Thomas H. Henriksen, 'Some notes on the national liberation wars in Angola, Mozambique and Guinea-Bissau', *Military Affairs*, 41:1 (1977), 30–7.

102. Norrie MacQueen and Pedro Aires Oliveira, '"Grocer meets butcher": Marcello Caetano's London visit of 1973 and the last days of Portugal's *Estado Novo*', *Cold War History*, 10:1 (2010), 31. The United States abstained on eleven occasions, the British on seven, and the French on four. Their remaining votes (five, nine, and twelve respectively) were critical of Portugal.

103. Isaacman, 'Peasants, work and the labor process', 815–56.

104. Clarence-Smith, *The Third Portuguese Empire*, 214–16.

105. MacQueen, 'Portugal's first domino', 213.

106. Spruyt, *Ending Empire*, 196.

107. Pedro Ramos Pinto, *Lisbon Rising: Urban Social Movements in the Portuguese Revolution, 1974-75* (Manchester: Manchester University Press, 2013), 105.

108. MacQueen, *Decolonization of Portuguese Africa*, 207.

109. Richard A. H. Robinson, 'The influence of overseas issues in Portugal's transition to democracy', in Stewart Lloyd-Jones and António Costa Pinto (eds), *The Last Empire: Thirty Years of Portuguese Decolonization* (Bristol: Intellect, 2003), 4–9.

110. Dhada, 'The Liberation War in Guinea-Bissau reconsidered', 584–9.

111. MacQueen, 'Portugal's first domino', 213–16.

112. Spruyt, *Ending Empire*, 199–200.

113. MacQueen, 'Portugal's first domino', 216–21.

114. Robinson, 'The influence of overseas issues', 5.

115. Robinson, 'The influence of overseas issues', 224–5.

116. Robinson, 'The influence of overseas issues', 226–9.

117. For interesting treatment of the internecine warfare in Angola and Mozambique, see MacQueen, *Decolonization of Portuguese Africa*, chs 5 and 6.

118. Heike Schmidt, *Colonialism and Violence in Zimbabwe: A History of Suffering* (Woodbridge: James Currey, 2013), 42–4, 142–5.

119. Margaret Hall, 'The Mozambican National Resistance Movement (Renamo): a study in the destruction of an African country', *Africa*, 60:1 (1990), 39–40.

120. Ramos Pinto, *Lisbon Rising*, 125–7.

121. Ramos Pinto, *Lisbon Rising*, 126.

122. António Costa Pinto, 'The transition to democracy and Portugal's decolonization', in Stewart Lloyd-Jones and António Costa Pinto (eds), *The Last Empire*, 19–20.

123. Norman MacQueen, 'Portugal and Africa: the politics of re-engagement', *Journal of Modern African Studies* 23:1 (1985), 33–5.

124. For detailed treatment of the civil war's outbreak, see Franz-Wilhelm Heimer, *The Decolonization Conflict in Angola 1974-1976* (Geneva: IUHEI, 1979).

125. For shrewd analysis of US and Soviet interventionist motives, see Westad, *The Global Cold War*, 224–7 and Thomas H. Henriksen, 'Angola, Mozambique and Soviet intervention: liberation and the quest for influence', in Warren Weinstein and Thomas H. Henriksen (eds), *Soviet and Chinese*

Aid to African Nations (New York: Praeger, 1980). Regarding China's intervention, see Steven F. Jackson, 'China's Third World foreign policy: the case of Angola and Mozambique, 1961-1993', *China Quarterly*, 142 (1995), 388–422.

126. Jaster, *The Defence of White Power*, 70–4.

127. Westad, *The Global Cold War*, 228–38.

128. MacQueen, 'Portugal and Africa', 38–51.

Conclusion

1. This leaves the vexed question of South Africa. For constitutional purists, the issue had been resolved with the granting of self-government to the new Union of South Africa in 1910. Others, however, see the achievement of majority rule in 1994 as marking the equivalent of colonial independence.

2. Joseph Hodge, 'Colonial experts, developmental and environmental doctrines, and the legacies of late British colonialism', in Christina Folke Ax, Niels Brimnes, Niklas Thode Jansen, and Karen Oslund (eds), *Cultivating the Colonies: Colonial, States and their Environmental Legacies* (Athens, OH: Ohio University Press, 2011), 300–19; Véronique Dimier, 'Recycling Empire: French Colonial Administrators at the Heart of European Development Policy', in Thomas, *The French Colonial Mind, I*, 251–74.

3. Brad Simpson, 'The United States and the curious history of self-determination', *Diplomatic History*, 36:4 (2012), 675–85.

4. Rob Nixon, *Slow Violence and the Environmentalism of the Poor* (Cambridge, MA: Harvard University Press, 2011).

5. Philip Murphy, '"An intricate and distasteful subject": British planning for the use of force against the European settlers of Central Africa, 1952-1965', *English Historical Review*, CXXI:492 (2006), 746–77.

6. Wm. Roger Louis, 'The dissolution of the British Empire', in Brown and Louis, *OHBE Vol. IV The Twentieth Century*, 329–55.

7. John Kent, *America, the UN and Decolonisation: Cold War Conflict in the Congo* (London: Routledge, 2010).

8. Jennifer E. Sessions, *By Sword and Plow: France and the Conquest of Algeria* (Ithaca, NY: Cornell University Press, 2011), part I.

9. Peter Mark, 'The evolution of 'Portuguese' identity: Luso-Africans on the Upper Guinea coast from the sixteenth to the early nineteenth century', *JAH*, 40 (1999), 173–91; C. R. Boxer, *Race Relations in the Portuguese Colonial Empire, 1415-1825* (Oxford: Clarendon, 1963), 2–3, 31–69.

10. The limits to this collaboration are explored in J. P. Daughton, *An Empire Divided: Religion, Republicanism, and the Making of French Colonialism, 1880-1914* (New York: Oxford University Press, 2008).

11. J. Thomas Lindblad, 'Economic aspects of the Dutch expansion in Indonesia, 1870-1914', *Modern Asian Studies*, 23:1 (1989), 1–23.

12. D. Killingray, 'Guardians of Empire', in D. Killingray and D. Omissi (eds), *Guardians of Empire: The Armed Forces of the Colonial Powers, 1700-1964* (Manchester: Manchester University Press, 1999), 1–24.

13. For details, see the essays in J. A. de Moor and H. L. Wesseling (eds), *Imperialism and War: Essays on Colonial Wars in Africa and Asia* (Leiden: Brill, 1989).

14. Wheeler, 'African elements in Portugal's armies in Africa', 233–9.

15. Robert Gerwarth and John Horne, 'Bolshevism as Fantasy: Fear of Revolution and Counter-Revolutionary Violence', in Robert Gerwarth and John Horne (eds), *War in Peace: Paramilitary Violence in Europe after the Great War, 1917-1923* (Oxford: Oxford University Press, 2012), 40–51.

16. A process examined in Martin Thomas, *Violence and Colonial Order: Police, Workers, and Protest in the European Empires, 1918-1940* (Cambridge: Cambridge University Press, 2012).

17. On Anglo-American economic rivalry in the interwar period, see P. J. Cain and A. G. Hopkins, *British Imperialism 1688-2000*, 2nd edn (Basingstoke: Macmillan, 2002), esp. 442–60.

18. Cain and Hopkins, *British Imperialism 1688-2000*, 218–31.

19. See, for example, Anne L. Foster, *Projections of Power: The United States and Europe in Colonial Southeast Asia, 1919-1941* (Durham, NC: Duke University Press, 2010); Rana Mitter, *China's War with Japan, 1937-1945: The Struggle for Survival* (London: Allen Lane, 2013).

20. Belgium, which also declared neutrality in October 1936, was sucked into war in 1939.

21. Pierre van der Eng, 'Marshall Aid as a catalyst in the decolonization of Indonesia, 1947-1949', *Journal of Southeast Asian Studies*, 19 (1988), 335–52; MacMahon, *Colonialism and Cold War*, 133–43; Westad, *The Global Cold War*, 113–19, *passim*.

22. Lawrence, *Assuming the Burden*; Andrew J. Rotter, 'The triangular route to Vietnam: the United States, Great Britain, and Southeast Asia, 1945-1950', *International History Review*, 6:3 (1984), 404–23.

23. See, e.g., A. J. Stockwell, 'The United States and Britain's decolonization of Malaya, 1942-57', in D. Ryan and V. Pungong (ed.), *The United States and Decolonization: Power and Freedom* (Basingstoke: Macmillan, 2000), 188–206.

24. Louis and Robinson, 'The imperialism of decolonization', 462–511.

25. For the 'maximalist' view of the Cold War's significance, see Ronald Hyam, 'Africa and the Labour government, 1945-1951', in Andrew Porter and Robert Holland (eds), *Theory and Practice in the History of European Expansion Overseas: Essays in Honour of Ronald Robinson* (London: Frank Cass, 1988), 148–72.

26. Louis, 'The dissolution of the British Empire', 354–5.

27. P. S. Gupta, 'Imperialism and the Labour government of 1945-51', in J. M. Winter (ed.), *The Working Class in Modern British History: Essays in Honour of Henry Pelling* (Cambridge: Cambridge University Press, 1983), 99–124; R. Hyam (ed.), *British Documents on the End of Empire: Series A, Volume 2. The Labour Government and the End of Empire 1945-1951* (London: The Stationery Office, 1991). On proposals for coordinated initiatives with other colonial powers, see John Kent, 'Bevin's imperialism and the idea of a Euro-Africa', in M. L. Dockrill and J. W. Young (eds), *British Foreign Policy, 1945-56* (London: Macmillan, 1989).

28. Robert Frank, "The French alternative: economic power through the Empire or through Europe?," in Ennio di Nolfo (ed.), *Power in Europe? II: Great Britain, France, Germany and Italy and the Origins of the EEC, 1952-1957* (Berlin: Walter de Gruyter, 1992), 165–6.

29. Hitchcock, 'Crisis and Modernization', in Alexander and Mouré, *Crisis and Renewal in France*, 222.

30. Marseille, *Empire colonial et capitalisme français*, 356–64.

31. Hodeir, *Stratégies d'Empire*, 196.

32. Lefeuvre, *Chère Algérie*, 53, 207–8.

33. Hugo Tertrais, 'Le poids financier de la guerre d'Indochine', in Maurice Vaïsse (ed.), *L'Armee française dans la guerre d'Indochine (1946-1954): adaptation ou inadaptation?* (Paris: Complexe 2000), 34, 47.

34. Richard Kuisel, *Seducing the French: The Dilemma of Americanization* (Berkeley: University of California Press, 1993), 103–30; Barnett Singer, *The Americanization of France: Searching for Happiness After the Algerian War* (New York: Rowman and Littlefield, 2013); Kristin Ross, *Fast Cars, Clean Bodies: Decolonization and the Reordering of French Culture* (Cambridge, MA: MIT Press, 1994), 6–9.

35. Ross, *Fast Cars, Clean Bodies*, 151–6.

36. Holland, *European Decolonization*, 208–9.

37. Barnett Singer, 'Lyautey: an interpretation of the man and French imperialism', *Journal of Contemporary History*, 26 (1991), 134.

38. Robert Aldrich, *Vestiges of the Colonial Empire in France: Monuments, Museums and Memories* (London: Palgrave Macmillan, 2005), 15–16.

39. Aldrich, *Vestiges of the Colonial Empire*, 333.

40. For insights into this process, see House and MacMaster, *Paris 1961*, part II.

41. Benjamin Stora, *La gangrene et l'oubli*; Martin Evans, 'Rehabilitating the traumatized war veteran: the case of French conscripts from the Algerian War, 1954-1962', in Martin Evans and Ken Lunn (eds), *War and Memory in the Twentieth Century* (Oxford: Berg, 1997), 73–88; Aldrich, *Vestiges of the Colonial Empire*, 134–5.

42. Richard J. Golsan, 'Memory's *bombes à retardement*: Maurice Papon, crimes against humanity and 17 October 1961', *Journal of European Studies*, 28:1 (1998), 153–72.

43. Aldrich, *Vestiges of the Colonial Empire*, 124–36, 150–2.

44. Aldrich, *Vestiges of the Colonial Empire*, 20, 34–5.

45. Frances Gouda, *Dutch Culture Overseas: Colonial Practice in the Netherlands Indies, 1900-1942* (Amsterdam: Amsterdam University Press, 1995), 242.

46. Ann Hironaka, *Neverending Wars: The International Community, Weak States, and the Perpetuation of Civil War* (Cambridge, MA: Harvard University Press, 2005); Patrick Chabal and Jean-Pascal Daloz, *Africa Works: Disorder as Political Instrument* (Oxford: James Currey, 1999).

47. Chabal, 'People's War', 113–19, quote at 113.

48. Robert H. Jackson, *Quasi-States: Sovereignty, International Relations and the Third World* (Cambridge: Cambridge University Press, 1993); Jeffrey Herbst, *States and Power in Africa: Comparative Lessons in Authority and Control* (Princeton, NJ: Princeton University Press, 2000).

49. These ideas are explored in Westad, *The Global Cold War*.

50. The connections in the Portuguese case are nicely described in Kenneth Maxwell, 'Portugal: "the revolution of the carnations", 1974-75', in Roberts and Garton Ash, *Civil Resistance and Power Politics*, 110–26.

51. Robert Gildea, James Mark, and Anette Warring (eds), *Europe's 1968: Voices of Revolt* (Oxford: Oxford University Press, 2013), 24–6, 260–70.

52. The suggestion that such a correlation exists is proposed by Benjamin E. Goldsmith and Baogang He, 'Letting go without a fight: decolonization, democracy and war, 1900-94', *Journal of Peace Research*, 45:5 (2008), 494–7, 602–5.

53. See, e.g., N. Owen, 'Decolonisation and postwar consensus', in Harriet Jones and Michael Kandiah (eds), *The Myth of Consensus: New Views on British History, 1945-64* (Basingstoke: Macmillan, 1996), 157–81. An older, but still very useful study is D. J. Goldsworthy, *Colonial Issues in British Politics 1945-1961: From 'Colonial Development' to 'Wind of Change'* (Oxford: Oxford University Press, 1971).

54. David Anderson, *Histories of the Hanged: Britain's Dirty War in Kenya and the End of Empire* (London: Weidenfeld and Nicholson, 2005); Caroline Elkins, *Britain's Gulag: The Brutal End of Empire in Kenya* (London: Pimlico, 2005). In this, as in other areas, perhaps, Britain's 'exceptionalism' appears less convincing than earlier, rose-tinted accounts have implied.

55. Mandy Banton, 'Destroy? "migrate"? conceal? British strategies for the disposal of sensitive records of colonial administrations at independence', *JICH*, 40:2 (2012), 323–37.

56. David M. Anderson, 'Mau Mau in the High Court and the 'lost' British Empire archives: colonial conspiracy or bureaucratic bungle?' *JICH*, 39:5 (2011), 699–716; idem, 'British abuse and torture in Kenya's counter-insurgency, 1952-1960', *Small Wars and Insurgencies*, 23:4/5 (2012), 700–19.

57. 'Kenya and Britain: Drawing a line under history', *The Economist*, 15–21 June 2013.

58. A. S. Thompson, *The Empire Strikes Back: The Impact of Imperialism on Britain from the Mid-Nineteenth Century* (Harlow: Longman, 2005) 8, 203–5, 223, 234; see also A. G. Hopkins, 'Accounting for the British Empire', *JICH*, 16:2 (1988), 245.

SELECT BIBLIOGRAPHY

Essay collections

Ageron, Charles-Robert (ed.), *Les Chemins de la décolonisation*, Paris: CNRS, 1986.

Anderson, David M. and David Killingray (eds), *Policing and Decolonization: Politics, Nationalism and the Police, 1917-1965*, Manchester: Manchester University Press, 1992.

Bancel, Nicolas, Daniel Denis and Youssef Fates (eds), *De l'Indochine à l'Algérie: La jeunesse en mouvements des côtés du miroir colonial 1940-1962*, Paris: Découverte, 2003.

Ben Ze'ev, Efrat, Ruth Ginio, and Jay Winter (eds), *Shadows of War: A Social History of Silence in the Twentieth Century*, Cambridge: Cambridge University Press, 2010, 119–20.

Bessel, Richard and Claudia B. Haake (eds), *Removing Peoples: Forced Removal in the Modern World*, New York: Oxford University Press, 2009.

Bickers, Robert (ed.), *Settlers and Expatriates: Britons over the Seas* (OHBE Companion Volume), Oxford: Oxford University Press, 2010.

Blais, Hélène, Florence Deprest, and Pierre Singaravélou (eds), *Territoires impériaux: Une histoire spatiale du fait colonial*, Paris: Sorbonne, 2011.

Boahen, A. Adu, *African Perspectives on Colonialism*, Baltimore: The Johns Hopkins University Press, 1987.

Bogaerts, Els and Remco Raben (eds), *Beyond Empire and Nation: The Decolonization of African and Asian societies, 1930s-1960s*, Leiden: KITLV Press, 2012.

Bridges, Roy (ed.), *Imperialism, Decolonization and Africa: Studies Presented to John Hargreaves*, London: Macmillan, 2000.

Brown, Judith M. and Wm. Roger Louis (eds), *The Oxford History of the British Empire (OHBE) Volume IV: The Twentieth Century*, Oxford: Oxford University Press, 1999.

Butler, L. J. and Sarah Stockwell (eds), *The Wind of Change: Harold Macmillan and British Decolonization*, Basingstoke: Palgrave Macmillan, 2013.

Chafer, Tony and Amanda Sackur (eds), *French Colonial Empire and the Popular Front: Hope and Disillusion*, London: Macmillan, 1999.

Clancy-Smith, Julia and Frances Gouda (eds), *Domesticating the Empire: Race, Gender, and Family Life in French and Dutch Colonialism*, Charlottesville: University of Virginia Press, 1998.

Constantine, Stephen and Marjory Harper (eds), *Migration and Empire* [Oxford History of the British Empire Companion Series], Oxford: Oxford University Press, 2010.

Cooper, Frederick and Ann Laura Stoler (eds), *Tensions of Empire: Colonial Cultures in a Bourgeois World*, Berkeley: University of California Press, 1997.

De l'Estoile, Benoît, Federico Neiburg, and Lygia Sigaud (eds), *Empires, Nations, and Natives: Anthropology and State-Making*, Durham, NC: University of North Carolina Press, 2005.

Dockrill, Michael and J. W. Young (eds), *British Foreign Policy, 1945-1956*, London: Macmillan, 1989.

Dülffer, Jost and Marc Frey (eds), *Elites and Decolonization in the Twentieth Century*, Basingstoke: Palgrave Macmillan, 2011.

Dumett, Raymond E. (ed.), *Gentlemanly Capitalism and British Imperialism: The New Debate on Empire*, Harlow: Longman, 1999.

Gerwarth, Robert and John Horne (eds), *War in Peace: Paramilitary Violence in Europe after the Great War, 1917-1923*, Oxford: Oxford University Press, 2012.

Gifford, Prosser and Wm. Roger Louis (eds), *The Transfer of Power in Africa: Decolonization, 1940-1960*, New Haven: Yale University Press, 1982.

Gifford, Prosser and Wm. Roger Louis (eds), *Decolonization and African Independence: The Transfers of Power, 1960-1980*, New Haven: Yale University Press, 1988.

Select Bibliography

Gildea, Robert, James Mark, and Anette Warring (eds), *Europe's 1968: Voices of Revolt*, Oxford: Oxford University Press, 2013.

Hodge, Joseph M., Gerald Hödl, and Martina Kopf (eds), *Developing Africa: Concepts and Practices in Twentieth-Century Colonialism*, Manchester: Manchester University Press, 2014.

Holland, Robert (ed.), *Emergencies and Disorder in the European Empires after 1945*, London: Frank Cass, 1994.

Howe, Stephen (ed.), *The New Imperial Histories Reader*, Abingdon: Routledge, 2009.

King, R. D. and R. Kilson (eds), *The Statecraft of British Imperialism: Essays in Honour of Wm. Roger Louis*, London: Frank Cass, 1999.

Lee, Christopher J. (ed.), *Making a World After Empire: The Bandung Moment and its Political Afterlives*, Athens: Ohio University Press, 2010.

Lloyd-Jones, Stewart and António Costa Pinto (eds), *The Last Empire: Thirty Years of Portuguese Decolonization*, Bristol: Intellect, 2003.

Lynn, Martin (ed.), *The British Empire in the 1950s: Retreat or Revival*, London: Palgrave Macmillan, 2006.

Motadel, David (ed.), *Islam and the European Empires*, Oxford: Oxford University Press, 2014.

Ovendale, Ritchie (ed.), *The Foreign Policy of the British Labour Governments 1945-1951*, Leicester: Leicester University Press, 1984.

Peabody, Sue and Tyler Stovall (eds), *The Color of Liberty: Histories of Race in France*, Durham, NC: University of North Carolina Press, 2003.

Roberts, Adam and Timothy Garton-Ash (eds), *Civil Resistance and Power Politics: The Experience of Non-Violent Action from Gandhi to the Present*, Oxford: Oxford University Press, 2011.

Ryan, David and Victor Pungong (eds), *The United States and Decolonization: Power and Freedom*, Basingstoke: Macmillan, 2000.

Stovall, Tyler and Georges van den Abbeele (eds), *French Civilization and its Discontents: Orientalism, Colonialism, Race*, Lanham: Lexington, 2003.

Suny, Ronald Grigor and Terry Martin (eds), *A State of Nations: Empire and Nation-Making in the Age of Lenin and Stalin*, Oxford: Oxford University Press, 2001.

Tiffin, Chris and Alan Lawson (eds), *De-Scribing Empire: Post-Colonialism and Textuality*, London: Routledge, 1994.

Thomas, Martin (ed.), *The French Colonial Mind. I: Mental Maps of Empire and Colonial Encounters* Lincoln, NE: University of Nebraska Press, 2011.

Thomas, Martin (ed.), *The French Colonial Mind. II: Violence, Military Encounters, and Colonialism* Lincoln, NE: University of Nebraska Press, 2011.

Thompson, Andrew S. (ed.), *Britain's Experience of Empire in the Twentieth Century* (OHBE Companion Volume), Oxford: Oxford University Press, 2011.

Young, John W. (ed.), *The Foreign Policy of Churchill's Peacetime Administration 1951-1955*, Leicester: Leicester University Press, 1988.

British Empire

Anderson, David M., 'Mau Mau in the High Court and the "lost" British Empire archives: colonial conspiracy or bureaucratic bungle?' *Journal of Imperial and Commonwealth History*, 39:5 (2011), 699–716.

Ashton, Stephen R. and Sarah E. Stockwell (eds), *Imperial Policy and Colonial Practice, 1925-1945: British Documents on the End of Empire Series A, Volume I*, London: HMSO, 1996.

Banton, Mandy, 'Destroy? "Migrate"? Conceal? British Strategies for the Disposal of Sensitive Records of Colonial Administrations at Independence', *Journal of Imperial and Commonwealth History*, 40:2 (2012), 323–37.

Burridge, T., *Clement Attlee: A Political Biography*, London: Jonathan Cape, 1985.

Cain, P. J. and A. G. Hopkins, *British Imperialism 1688–2000*, Basingstoke: Macmillan, 2002.

Cell, John W., *Hailey: A Study in British Imperialism*, Cambridge: Cambridge University Press, 1992.

Clarke, P. and C. Trebilcock (eds), *Understanding Decline: Perceptions and Realities of British Economic Performance*, Cambridge: Cambridge University Press, 1997.

Clayton, Anthony, *The British Empire as a Superpower, 1919-39*, London: Macmillan, 1986.

Constantine Stephen (ed.), *Emigrants and Empire: British Settlement in the Dominions Between the Wars*, Manchester: Manchester University Press, 1990.

Darwin, John, *Britain and Decolonisation: The Retreat from Empire in the Post-War World*, London: Macmillan, 1988.

Darwin, John, *The Empire Project: The Rise and Fall of the British World-System, 1830-1970*, Cambridge: Cambridge University Press, 2009.

Darwin, John, *Unfinished Empire: The Global Expansion of Britain*, London: Allen Lane, 2012.

Drummond, I. M., *Imperial Economic Policy 1917-1939 Studies in Expansion and Protection*, Toronto: University of Toronto Press, 1997.

Fedorowich, Kent and Carl Bridge, 'Mapping the British World', *JICH*, 31:2 (2003), 1–15.

Furedi, Frank, *Colonial Wars and the Politics of Third World Nationalism*, London: I.B. Tauris, 1994.

Grob-Fitzgibbon, Benjamin, *Imperial Endgame: Britain's Dirty Wars and the End of Empire*, Basingstoke: Palgrave Macmillan, 2011.

Harper, Tim and Christopher Bayly, *Forgotten Wars: The End of Britain's Asian Empire*, Harmondsworth: Penguin, 2008.

Hinds, A., *Britain's Sterling Colonial Policy and Decolonization, 1939-1958*, Westport, CN: Greenwood Press, 2001.

Hodge, Joseph M., *Triumph of the Expert: Agrarian Doctrines of Development and the Legacies of British Colonialism*, Athens: Ohio University Press, 2007.

Holland, Robert F., *The Pursuit of Greatness: Britain and the World Role, 1900-1970*, London: Fontana, 1991.

Holland, Robert F., *Britain and the Revolt in Cyprus 1954-1959*, Oxford: Clarendon Press, 1998.

Hyam, Ronald (ed.), *British Documents on the End of Empire Series A, Volume 2: The Labour Government and the End of Empire 1945-1951*, London: HMSO, 1992.

Hyam, Ronald (ed.), *Britain's Declining Empire: The Road to Decolonization, 1918-1968*, Cambridge: Cambridge University Press, 2007.

Jackson, Ashley, *The British Empire and the Second World War*, London: Hambledon, 2006.

Jeffery, Keith, *The British Army and the Crisis of Empire, 1918-22*, Manchester: Manchester University Press, 1984.

Kennedy, Greg and Keith Neilson (eds), *Far-Flung Lines: Studies in Imperial Defence in Honour of Donald Mackenzie Schurman*, London: Frank Cass, 1997.

Lake, Marilyn and Henry Reynolds, *Drawing the Global Colour Line: White Men's Countries and the International Challenge of Racial Equality*, Cambridge: Cambridge University Press, 2008.

Lee, J. M. and M. Petter, *The Colonial Office, War, and Development Policy: Organisation and the Planning of A Metropolitan Initiative*, London: Maurice Temple Smith, 1982.

Levine, Philippa, *The British Empire: Sunrise to Sunset*, Harlow: Longman, 2007.

Louis, Wm. Roger and Ronald Robinson, 'The Imperialism of Decolonization', *JICH*, 22:3 (1994), 462–511.

Mackenzie, John M. (ed.), *Imperialism and Popular Culture*, Manchester: Manchester University Press, 1986.

McIntyre, W. David, *Background to the ANZUS Pact: Policy-Making, Strategy and Diplomacy, 1945-55*, London: Macmillan, 1995.

McIntyre, W. David, *British Decolonization, 1946-1997*, London: Macmillan, 1998.

Omissi, David E., *Air Power and Colonial Control: The Royal Air Force 1919-1939*, Manchester: Manchester University Press, 1990.

Ovendale, Ritchie, *The English-Speaking Alliance: Britain, the United States, the Dominions and the Cold War, 1945-1951*, London: Allen & Unwin, 1985.

Reynolds, David, *Britannia Overruled: British Policy and World Power in the Twentieth Century*, Harlow: Longman, 1991.

Sanger, C., *Malcolm MacDonald: Bringing an End to Empire*, Liverpool: Liverpool University Press, 1995.

Schenk, Catherine R., *The Decline of Sterling: Managing the Retreat of an International Currency, 1945-1992*, Cambridge: Cambridge University Press, 2013.

Select Bibliography

Schofield, Camilla, *Enoch Powell and the Making of Postcolonial Britain*, Cambridge: Cambridge University Press, 2013.

Stockwell, A. J., 'British Decolonisation: The Record and the Records', *Contemporary European History*, 15:4 (2006), 573–83.

Thomas, Martin, *Violence and Colonial Order: Police, Workers, and Protest in the European Colonial Empires, 1918-1940*, Cambridge: Cambridge University Press, 2012.

Thompson, Andrew S., *The Empire Strikes Back: The Impact of Imperialism on Britain from the Mid-Nineteenth Century*, Harlow: Longman, 2005.

White, Nicholas J., *Decolonisation: The British Experience since 1945*, 2nd edn, Abingdon: Routledge, 2014.

Indian subcontinent

Ahmed, A. S., *Jinnah, Pakistan and Islamic Identity: The Search for Saladin*, London: Routledge, 1997.

Ashton, S. R. and D. Killingray (eds), *The West Indies British Documents on the End of Empire Series B, Volume 6*, London: The Stationery Office, 1999.

Blyth, Robert J., *The Empire of the Raj: India, Eastern Africa and the Middle East, 1858-1947*, London: Palgrave Macmillan, 2003.

Jalal, A., *The Sole Spokesman: Jinnah, the Muslim League and the Demand for Pakistan*, Cambridge: Cambridge University Press, 1997.

Mansergh, Nicholas and P. Moon (eds), *Constitutional Relations between Britain and India: The Transfer of Power, 1942-47 Volumes IX-X*, London: Foreign and Commonwealth Office, 1980–1.

Misra, M., *Business, Race and Politics in British India, c.1860-1960*, Oxford: Oxford University Press, 1999.

Moore, R. J., *Escape from Empire: The Attlee Government and the Indian Problem*, Oxford: Clarendon Press, 1983.

Murphy, Philip, *Alan Lennox-Boyd: A Biography*, London: I.B. Tauris, 1999.

Nanda, B. R., *In Search of Gandhi: Essays and Reflections*, Oxford: Oxford University Press, 2002.

Omissi, David E., *The Sepoy and the Raj: The Indian Army, 1860-1940*, London: Macmillan, 1994.

De Silva, K. M. (ed.), *British Documents on the End of Empire, Series B, Volume 2: Sri Lanka Part I*, London: HMSO, 1997.

Talbot, Ian and S. Thandi (eds), *People on the Move: Punjabi Colonial, and Post-Colonial Migration*, Karachi: Oxford University Press, 2004.

Tomlinson, Brian R., *The Political Economy of the Raj, 1914-47: The Economics of Decolonization in India*, London: Macmillan, 1979.

Wolpert, S., *Shameful Flight: The Last Years of the British Empire in India*, Oxford: Oxford University Press, 2006.

Anglophone Africa

Anderson, David M., *Histories of the Hanged: Britain's Dirty War in Kenya and the End of the Empire*, London: Weidenfeld and Nicolson, 2005.

Anderson, David M., 'British abuse and torture in Kenya's counter-insurgency, 1952–1960', *Small Wars and Insurgencies*, 23:4/5 (2012), 700–19.

Baker, C., *State of Emergency: Crisis in Central Africa, Nyasaland 1959-1960*, London: I.B. Tauris, 1997.

Bennett, Huw, *Fighting the Mau Mau: The British Army and Counter-Insurgency in the Kenya Emergency*, Cambridge: Cambridge University Press, 2013.

Berman, Bruce, *Control and Crisis in Colonial Kenya: The Dialectic of Domination*, London: James Currey, 1990.

Butler, L. J., *Copper Empire: Mining and the Colonial State in Northern Rhodesia, c.1930-1964*, Basingstoke: Palgrave Macmillan, 2007.

Chanock, M., *Unconsummated Union: Britain, Rhodesia and South Africa, 1900-1945*, Manchester: Manchester University Press, 1977.

Cooper, Frederick, *Africa since 1940: The Past of the Present*, Cambridge: Cambridge University Press, 2002.

Darwin, John, 'The Central African Emergency, 1959', *JICH*, 21:3 (1993), 217–34.

Elkins, Caroline, *Britain's Gulag: The Brutal End of Empire in Kenya*, London: Jonathan Cape, 2005.

Flint, John E., 'Planned decolonization and its failure in British Africa', *African Affairs*, 82:328 (1983), 389–411.

Hyam, Ronald and Peter Henshaw, *The Lion and the Springbok: Britain and South Africa since the Boer War*, Cambridge: Cambridge University Press, 2003.

Kanogo, T., *Squatters and the Roots of Mau Mau 1905-63*, London: James Currey, 1987.

Killingray, David and Richard Rathbone (eds), *Africa and the Second World War*, London: Macmillan, 1986.

Kyle, Keith, *The Politics of the Independence of Kenya*, London: Macmillan, 1999.

Lewis, Joanna, *Empire State-Building: War and Welfare in Kenya 1925-52*, Oxford: James Currey, 2000.

Lynn, Martin (ed.), *British Documents on the End of Empire Series B, Volume 7: Nigeria*, London: The Stationery Office, 2001.

Murphy, Philip, *Party Politics and Decolonization: The Conservative Party and British Colonial Policy in Tropical Africa 1951-1964*, Oxford: Clarendon Press, 1995.

Murphy, Philip (ed.), *British Documents on the End of Empire Series B, Volume 9: Central Africa*, London: The Stationery Office, 2005.

Murphy, Philip (ed.), *Central Africa: Part I Closer association 1945-1958 British Documents on the End of Empire*, London: The Stationery Office, 2005.

Murphy, Philip, '"An intricate and distasteful subject": British planning for the use of force against the European settlers of Central Africa, 1952-1965', *English Historical Review*, CXXI:492 (2006), 746–77.

Ovendale, Ritchie, 'Macmillan and the Wind of Change in Africa, 1957-60', *Historical Journal*, 38:2 (1995), 455–77.

Pearce, R. D., *The Turning Point in Africa: British Colonial Policy 1938-1948*, London: Frank Cass, 1982.

Percox, D., *Britain, Kenya and the Cold War: Imperial Defence, Colonial Security and Decolonisation*, London: I.B. Tauris, 2004.

Rathbone, Richard, *Nkrumah and the Chiefs: The Politics of Chieftancy in Ghana 1951-60*, Oxford: James Currey, 2000.

Stockwell, Sarah, *The Business of Decolonization: British Business Strategies in the Gold Coast*, Oxford: Clarendon Press, 2000.

Throup, David W., *Economic and Social Origins of Mau Mau 1945-53*, London: James Currey, 1987.

Middle East

Ashton, Nigel J., *Eisenhower, Macmillan and the Problem of Nasser: Anglo-American Relations and Arab Nationalism, 1955-59*, London: Macmillan, 1996.

Cohen, M. J., *Palestine and the Great Powers, 1945-1948*, Princeton, NJ: Princeton University Press, 1982.

Cohen, M. J. and M. Kolinsky (eds), *Britain and the Middle East in the 1930s: Security Problems, 1935-39*, London: Macmillan, 1992.

Darwin, John, *Britain, Egypt and the Middle East: Imperial Policy in the Aftermath of War 1918-1922*, London: Macmillan, 1981.

Daly, M. W., *Imperial Sudan: The Anglo-Egyptian Condominium, 1934-56*, Cambridge: Cambridge University Press, 1991.

Farouk-Sluglett, M. and P. Sluglett, *Iraq Since 1958: From Revolution to Dictatorship*, London: KPI, 1987.

Fernea, R. A. and Wm. Roger Louis (eds), *The Iraqi Revolution of 1958: The Old Social Classes Revisited*, London: I.B. Tauris, 1991.

Fieldhouse, David K., *Western Imperialism in the Middle East 1914-1958*, Oxford: Oxford University Press, 2006.

Gershoni, Israel and James P. Jankowski, *Egypt, Islam, and the Arabs: The Search for Egyptian Nationhood, 1900-1930*, Oxford: Oxford University Press, 1986.

Gershoni, Israel and James P. Jankowski, *Redefining the Egyptian Nation, 1930-1945*, Cambridge: Cambridge University Press, 1995.

Kelly, Saul, *Cold War in the Desert: Britain, the United States and the Italian Colonies, 1945-52*, London: Macmillan, 2000.

Kent, John (ed.), *British Documents on the End of Empire Series B, Volume 4: Egypt and the Defence of the Middle East*, London: HMSO, 1998.

Kingston, P. W. T., *Britain and the Politics of Modernization in the Middle East, 1945-1958*, Cambridge: Cambridge University Press, 1996.

Kyle, Keith, *Suez: Britain's End of Empire in the Middle East*, London: I.B. Tauris, 2003.

Louis, Wm. Roger, *Imperialism at By: The United States and the Decolonization of the British Empire, 1941-1945*, Oxford: Oxford University Press, 1978.

Louis, Wm. Roger, *The British Empire in the Middle East 1945-1951: Arab Nationalism, The United States, and Postwar Imperialism*, Oxford: Clarendon Press, 1984.

Louis, Wm. Roger and Roger Owen (eds), *Suez 1956: The Crisis and its Consequences*, Oxford: Clarendon Press, 1989.

Mawby, Spencer, *British Policy in Aden and the Protectorates 1955-67: Last Outpost of a Middle East Empire*, London: Routledge, 2005.

Ovendale, Ritchie, *Britain, the United States and the Transfer of Power in the Middle East, 1945-1962*, Leicester: Leicester University Press, 1996.

Porath, Yoshua, *The Palestinian Arab Movement Volume Two: 1929-1939 From Riots to Rebellion*, London: Frank Cass, 1977.

Sharkey, Heather J., *Living with Colonialism: Nationalism and Culture in the Anglo-Egyptian Sudan*, Berkeley: University of California Press, 2003.

Smith, Simon C., *Britain's Revival and Fall in the Gulf: Kuwait, Bahrain, Qatar, and the Trucial States, 1950-71*, London: Routledge Curzon, 2004.

Smith, Simon C. (ed.), *Reassessing Suez 1956: New Perspectives on the Crisis and Its Aftermath*, Farnham: Ashgate, 2008.

Thomas, Martin, *Empires of Intelligence: Security Services and Colonial Control after 1914*, Berkeley: University of California Press, 2007.

East/South East Asia

Ashton, S. R. and Wm. Roger Louis (eds), *British Documents on the End of Empire Series A, Volume 5: East of Suez and the Commonwealth*, London: Stationery Office, 2004.

Bayly, Christopher and Tim Harper, *Forgotten Armies: The Fall of British Asia 1941-1945*, London: Allen Lane, 2004.

Bayly, Christopher and Tim Harper, *Forgotten Wars: The End of Britain's Asian Empire*, London: Allen Lane, 2007.

Best, Antony, *British Intelligence and the Japanese Challenge in Asia, 1914-1941*, London: Palgrave Macmillan, 2002.

Carruthers, Susan L., *Winning Hearts and Minds: British Governments, the Media and Colonial Counter-Insurgency 1944-1960*, Leicester: Leicester University Press, 1995.

Darby, Philip, *British Defence Policy East of Suez, 1947-1968*, Oxford: Oxford University Press, 1973.

Dockrill, Saki, *Britain's Retreat from East of Suez: The Choice between Europe and the World?*, London: Palgrave Macmillan, 2002.

Hack, Karl, *Defence and Decolonisation in Southeast Asia: Britain, Malaya and Singapore 1941-68*, Richmond: Curzon, 2000.

Harper, Tim N., *The End of Empire and the Making of Malaya*, Cambridge: Cambridge University Press, 1999.

Jones, Matthew, *Conflict and Confrontation in South East Asia, 1961-1965: Britain, the United States and the Creation of Malaysia*, Cambridge: Cambridge University Press, 2001.

Lowe, Peter, *Contending With Nationalism and Communism: British Policy Towards Southeast Asia, 1945-65*, Basingstoke: Palgrave Macmillan, 2009.

Ramakrishna, Kumar, *Emergency Propaganda: The Winning of Malayan Hearts and Minds, 1948-1958*, Richmond: Curzon, 2001.

Smith, Simon C., *British Relations with the Malay Rulers from Decentralization to Malayan Independence 1930-1957*, Kuala Lumpur: Oxford University Press, 1995.

Stockwell, A. J. (ed.), *British Documents on the End of Empire Series B, Volume 3: Malaya*, London: HMSO, 1995.

Stockwell, A. J. (ed.), *British Documents on the End of Empire Series B, Volume 8: Malaysia*, London: The Stationery Office, 2004.

Tarling, Nicholas (ed.), *The Cambridge History of Southeast Asia: Volume Two: The Nineteenth and Twentieth Centuries*, Cambridge: Cambridge University Press, 1996.

French Empire

Aissaoui, Rabah, *Immigration and National Identity: North African Political Movements in Colonial and Postcolonial France*, London: I.B. Tauris, 2009.

Aldrich, Robert, *France and the South Pacific since 1940*, Honolulu: University of Hawaii Press, 1993.

Aldrich, Robert, *Vestiges of the Colonial Empire in France: Monuments, Museums and Memories*, London: Palgrave Macmillan, 2005.

Aldrich, Robert and John Connell, *France's Overseas Frontier: Départements et Territoires d'Outre-Mer*, Cambridge: Cambridge University Press, 1992.

Benoist, Jean (ed.), *L'Archipel inachevé: Culture et société aux Antilles françaises*, Montreal: Université de Montréal, 1972.

Betts, Raymond, *France and Decolonisation, 1900-1960*, Basingstoke: Macmillan, 1991.

Boittin, Jennifer, *Colonial Metropolis: The Urban Grounds of Anti-Imperialism and Feminism in Interwar Paris*, Lincoln, NE: University of Nebraska Press, 2010.

Camiscioli, Elisa, *Reproducing the French Race. Immigration, Intimacy, and Embodiment in the Early Twentieth Century*, Durham, NC: Duke University Press, 2009.

Clayton, Anthony, *The Wars of French Decolonization*, Harlow: Longman, 1994.

Conklin, Alice L., *In the Museum of Man: Race, Anthropology, and Empire in France, 1850-1950*, Ithaca, NY: Cornell University Press, 2013.

Cooper, Frederick, *Colonialism in Question: Theory, Knowledge, History*, Berkeley: University of California Press, 2005.

Daughton, J. P., *An Empire Divided: Religion, Republicanism, and the Making of French Colonialism, 1880-1914*, New York: Oxford University Press, 2008.

Dueck, Jennifer M., *The Claims of Culture at Empire's End: Syria and Lebanon under French Rule*, Oxford: Oxford University Press, 2010.

Hodeir, Catherine, *Stratégies d'Empire: Le grand patronat colonial face à la décolonisation*, Paris: Belin, 2003.

Hussey, Andrew, *The French Intifada: The Long War between France and its Arabs*, London: Granta, 2014.

Knapp, Andrew (ed.), *The Uncertain Foundation: France at the Liberation, 1944-1947*, Basingstoke: Palgrave Macmillan, 2007.

Laguerre, Michel S., *Urban Poverty in the Caribbean: French Martinique as a Social Laboratory*, London: Macmillan, 1990.

Lawrence, Adria, *Imperial Rule and the Politics of Nationalism: Anti-Colonial Protest in the French Empire*, Cambridge: Cambridge University Press, 2013.

Lebovics, Herman, *Imperialism and the Corruption of Democracies*, Durham, NC: Duke University Press, 2006.

Lewis, Mary Dewhurst, *The Boundaries of the Republic: Migrant Rights and the Limits of Universalism in France, 1918-1940*, Stanford, CA: Stanford University Press, 2007.

Marseille, Jacques, *Empire colonial et capitalisme français: Histoire d'un divorce*, Paris: Albin Michel, 1984.

Miles, William F. S., *Elections and Ethnicity in French Martinique: A Paradox in Paradise*, New York: Praeger, 1986.

Neep, Daniel, *Occupying Syria under the French Mandate: Insurgency, Space and State Formation*, Cambridge: Cambridge University Press, 2012.

Rosenberg, Clifford, *Policing Paris: The Origins of Modern Immigration Control between the Wars*, Ithaca, NY: Cornell University Press, 2006.

Ross, Kristin, *Fast Cars, Clean Bodies: Decolonization and the Reordering of French Culture*, Cambridge, MA: MIT Press, 1994.

Saada, Emmanuelle, *Empire's Children: Race, Filiation, and Citizenship in the French Colonies*, Chicago, IL: University of Chicago Press, 2012.

Savarese, Eric, *L'Ordre colonial et sa légitimation en France métropolitaine*, Paris: Harmattan, 1998.

Sorum, Paul Clay, *Intellectuals and Decolonization in France*, Chapel Hill: University of North Carolina Press, 1977.

Thomas, Martin, *The French Empire at War, 1940-45*, Manchester: Manchester University Press, 1998.

Thomas, Martin, *The French Empire between the Wars: Imperialism, Politics, and Society*, Manchester: Manchester University Press, 2005.

Thomas, Martin, 'Resource war, civil war, rights war: factoring empire into French North Africa's Second World War', *War in History*, 18:2 (2011), 225–48.

Thomas, Martin, *Fight or Flight: Britain, France and their Roads from Empire*, Oxford: Oxford University Press, 2014.

Thompson, Elizabeth, *Colonial Citizens: Republican Rights, Paternal Privilege, and Gender in French Syria and Lebanon*, New York: Columbia University Press, 2000.

Toth, Stephen A., *Beyond Papillon: The French Overseas Penal Colonies, 1854-1952*, Lincoln, NE: University of Nebraska Press, 2006.

Wilder, Gary, *The French Imperial Nation-State: Negritude and Colonial Humanism between the Two World Wars*, Chicago: University of Chicago Press, 2005.

Francophone Africa and Madagascar

Ageron, Charles-Robert and Marc Michel (eds), *L'Afrique noire française: l'heure des Indépendances*, Paris: CNRS, 1992.

Arazalier, Francis and Jean Suret-Canale (eds), *Madagascar 1947 La tragédie oubliée*, Paris: Temps des Cérises, 1999.

Benoist, J. R. de, *L'AOF de 1944 à 1960*, Dakar: Nouvelles Editions Africaines, 1982.

Bourgi, Robert, *Le Général de Gaulle et l'Afrique noire*, Paris: LGDJ, 1980.

Chafer, Tony, *The End of Empire in French West Africa, 1936-60: France's Successful Decolonization?* Oxford: Berg, 2002.

Chipman, John, *French Power in Africa*, Oxford: Blackwell, 1989.

Clark, John F. and David E. Gardinier (eds), *Political Reform in Francophone Africa*, Boulder CO: Westview, 1997.

Conklin, Alice L., *A Mission to Civilize: The Republican Idea of Empire in France and West Africa, 1895-1930*, Stanford: Stanford University Press, 1997.

Cooper, Frederick, 'The Senegalese General Strike of 1946 and the Labor Question in Post-War French Africa', *Canadian Journal of African Studies*, 24:2 (1990), 165–215.

Cooper, Frederick, *Decolonization and African Society: The Labor Question in French and British Africa*, Cambridge: Cambridge University Press, 1996.

Cooper, Frederick, '"Our Strike": Equality, Anticolonial Politics, and the 1947–48 Railway Strike in French West Africa', *Journal of African History*, 37:1 (1996), 81–118.

Cooper, Frederick, 'Possibility and constraint: African independence in historical perspective', *Journal of African History*, 49:1 (2008), 167–96.

Cooper, Frederick, *Citizenship between Empire and Nation: Remaking France and French Africa, 1945–1960*, Princeton, NJ: Princeton University Press, 2014.

Coquery-Vidrovitch, Catherine, 'L'Impact des intérêts coloniaux: S.C.O.A. et C.F.A.O. dans l'Ouest Africain, 1910-1965', *Journal of African History*, 16:4 (1975), 595–621.

Coquery-Vidrovitch, Catherine and Odile Goerg (eds), *L'Afrique occidentale au temps des français: Colonisateurs et colonisés, c. 1860-1960*, Paris: La découverte, 1992.

Genova, James E., *Colonial Ambivalence, Cultural Authenticity, and the Limits of Mimicry in French-Ruled West Africa, 1914-1956*, New York: Peter Lang, 2004.

Ginio, Ruth, *French Colonialism Unmasked: The Vichy Years in French West Africa*, Lincoln, NE: University of Nebraska Press, 2006.

Gershovich, Moshe, *French Military Rule in Morocco: Colonialism and its Consequences*, London: Frank Cass, 2000.

House, Jim, 'L'impossible contrôle d'une ville coloniale: Casablanca, décembre 1952', *Genèses*, 1:86 (2012), 78–103.

Joseph, Richard, *Radical Nationalism in Cameroun: Social Origins of the UPC Rebellion*, Oxford: Oxford University Press, 1977.

Keese, Alexander, 'A culture of panic: "Communist" scapegoats and decolonization in French West Africa and French Polynesia (1945–1957)', *French Colonial History*, 9 (2008), 131–45.

Lewis, Mary Dewhurst, 'Geographies of Power: The Tunisian Civic Order, Jurisdictional Politics, and Imperial Rivalry in the Mediterranean, 1881-1935', *Journal of Modern History*, 80:4 (2008), 791–830.

Lughod, Janet L., *Rabat: Urban Apartheid in Morocco*, Princeton, NJ: Princeton University Press, 1980.

Mann, Gregory, *Native Sons: West African Veterans and France in the Twentieth Century*, Durham, NC: Duke University Press, 2006.

Mann, Gregory, 'What was the *indigénat*? The 'empire of law' in French West Africa', *Journal of African History*, 50 (2009), 331–53.

Mbembe, Achille, *La naissance du maquis dans le Sud-Cameroun (1920-1960)*, Paris: Karthala, 1996.

M'Bokolo, Elikia, 'Forces sociales et idéologies dans la décolonisation de l'A.E.F.', *Journal of African History*, 22:3 (1981), 393–407.

Nwaubani, Ebere, *The United States and Decolonization in West Africa, 1950-1960*, Rochester: University of Rochester Press, 2001.

Randrianja, Solofo, *Société et luttes anticoloniales à Madagascar (1896 à 1946)*, Paris: Karthala, 2001.

Schmidt, Elizabeth, *Mobilizing the Masses: Gender, Ethnicity, and Class in the Nationalist Movement in Guinea, 1939-1958*, Portsmouth, NH: Heinemann, 2005.

Schmidt, Elizabeth, *Cold War and Decolonization in Guinea, 1946-1958*, Athens, OH: Ohio University Press, 2007.

Schmidt, Elizabeth, 'Top down or bottom up? Nationalist mobilization reconsidered, with special reference to Guinea', *American Historical Review*, 110 (October 2005), 975–1014.

Tronchon, Jacques, *L'insurrection malgache de 1947*, Paris: Karthala, 1986.

Woodfork, Jacqueline, '"It is a Crime to be a Tirailleur in the Army": The Impact of Senegalese Civilian Status in the French Colonial Army during the Second World War', *The Journal of Military History*, 77:1 (January 2013), 115–39.

French Indochina

Anderson, David L., *Trapped by Success: The Eisenhower Administration and Vietnam, 1953-61*, New York: Columbia University Press, 1993.

Bradley, Mark Philip, *Imagining Vietnam and America: The Making of Postcolonial Vietnam, 1919-1950*, Chapel Hill: University of North Carolina Press, 2000.

Cooper, Nicola, *France in Indochina: Colonial Encounters*, Oxford: Berg, 2001.

Devillers, Philippe, *Paris-Saigon-Hanoi, Les archives de la guerre, 1944-1947*, Paris: Gallimard, 1988.

Duiker, William J., *The Communist Road to Power in Vietnam*, 2nd edn, Boulder, CO: Westview, 1996.

Goscha, Christopher E., *Vietnam: Un État né de la guerre 1945-1954*, Paris: Armand Colin, 2011.

Goscha, Christopher E., 'A "total war" of decolonization? Social mobilization and state-building in Communist Vietnam (1949–54)', *War & Society*, 31:2 (2012), 136–62.

Guillemot, François, 'Be men!': fighting and dying for the state of Vietnam (1951–54)', *War & Society*, 31:2 (2012), 184–210.

Ha, Marie-Paule, *French Women and the Empire: The Case of Indochina*, Oxford: Oxford University Press, 2014.

Jennings, Eric T., *Vichy in the Tropics: Pétain's National Revolution in Madagascar, Guadeloupe, and Indochina, 1940-1944*, Stanford, CA: Stanford University Press, 2001.

Jennings, Eric T., *Imperial Heights: Dalat and the Making and Undoing of French Indochina*, Berkeley: University of California Press, 2011.

Jian, Chen, 'China and the First Indochina War, 1950-54', *The China Quarterly*, 133 (1993), 85–93.

Kaplan, Lawrence, Denise Artaud, and Mark R. Rubin (eds), *Dien Bien Phu and the Crisis of Franco-American Relations, 1954-1955*, Wilmington, DL: SR books, 1990.

Lawrence, Mark Atwood, *Assuming the Burden: Europe and the American Commitment to War in Vietnam*, Berkeley: University of California Press, 2005.

Lawrence, Mark Atwood and Fredrik Logevall (eds), *The First Vietnam War: Colonial Conflict and Cold War Crisis*, Cambridge, MA: Harvard University Press, 2007.

Logevall, Fredrik, *Embers of War: The Fall of an Empire and the Making of America's Vietnam*, New York: Random House, 2012.

Marr, David G., *Vietnam 1945: The Quest for Power*, Berkeley: University of California Press, 1997.

Rice-Maximin, Edward, *Accommodation and resistance: The French left, Indochina and the Cold War, 1944-1954*, Westport: Praeger, 1986.

Ruscio, Alain, *Les Communistes français et la guerre d'Indochine, 1944-54*, Paris: Harmattan, 2004.

Shipway, Martin, *The Road to War: France and Vietnam, 1944-1947*, Oxford: Berghahn, 1996.

Tertrais, Hugues, *La piastre et le fusil: Le coût de la guerre d'Indochine 1945-1954*, Paris: CHEF, 2002.

Tønnesson, Stein, *1946: Déclenchement de la guerre d'Indochine*, Paris: Harmattan, 1987.

Wall, Irwin M., *The United States and the Making of Postwar France, 1945-1954*, Cambridge: Cambridge University Press, 1991.

Zhai, Qiang, *China and the Vietnam Wars, 1950-1975*, Chapel Hill: University of North Carolina Press, 2000.

Algeria/Algerian War

Ageron, Charles-Robert (ed.), *La guerre d'Algérie et les Algériens, 1954-1962*, Paris: Armand Colin, 1997.

Amiri, Linda, *La Bataille de France: La guerre d'Algérie en France*, Paris: Robert Laffont, 2004.

Blanchard, Emmanuel, *La Police parisienne et les Algériens (1944-1962)*, Paris: Nouveau Monde, 2011.

Branche, Raphaëlle, *La torture et l'armée pendant la Guerre d'Algérie: 1954-1962*, Paris: Gallimard, 2002.

Branche, Raphaëlle and Sylvie Thénault (eds), *La France en guerre 1954-1962: Expériences métropolitaines de la guerre d'indépendance algérienne*, Paris: Autrement, 2008.

Brower, Benjamin Claude, *A Desert Named Peace: The Violence of France's Empire in the Algerian Sahara, 1844-1902*, New York: Columbia University Press, 2009.

Çelik, Zeynep, *Urban Forms and Colonial Confrontations: Algiers under French Rule*, Berkeley: University of California Press, 1997.

Cole, Joshua, 'Massacres and their historians: recent histories of state violence in France and Algeria in the twentieth century', *French Politics, Culture, and Society*, 28:1 (2010), 106–26.

Connelly, Matthew, 'Taking off the Cold War Lens: Visions of North-South Conflict during the Algerian War for Independence', *American Historical Review*, 105:3 (2000), 739–69.

Connelly, Matthew, *A Diplomatic Revolution: Algeria's Fight for Independence and the Origins of the Post-Cold War Era*, Oxford: Oxford University Press, 2002.

Evans, Martin, *The Memory of Resistance: French opposition to the Algerian War (1954-1962)*, Oxford: Berg, 1997.

Evans, Martin, *Algeria: France's Undeclared War*, Oxford: Oxford University Press, 2012.

Gadant, Monique, *Islam et Nationalisme en Algérie d'après El Moudjahid organe central du FLN de 1956 à 1962*, Paris: Harmattan, 1988.

Gallois, William, *A History of Violence in the Early Algerian Colony*, Basingstoke: Palgrave Macmillan, 2013.

Goodman, Jane E. and Paul A. Silverstein (eds), *Bourdieu in Algeria: Colonial Politics, Ethnographic Practices, Theoretical Developments*, Lincoln, NE: University of Nebraska Press, 2009.

Harbi, Mohammed and Benjamin Stora (eds), *La Guerre d'Algérie, 1954-2004: La fin de l'amnésie*, Paris: Robert Laffont, 2004.

Harrison, Alexander, *Challenging De Gaulle: The O.A.S. and the counterrevolution in Algeria, 1954-1962*, New York: Praeger, 1989.

House, Jim and Neil MacMaster, *Paris 1961: Algerians, State Terror, and Memory*, Oxford University Press, 2006.

Kaddache, Mahfoud, *Histoire du nationalisme algérien*, 2 vols, Algiers: ENL, 1993.

Klose, Fabian, 'The colonial testing ground. The International Committee of the Red Cross and the Violent End of Empire', *Humanity*, 2:1 (2011), 107–26.

Klose, Fabian, *Human Rights in the Shadows of Colonial Violence: The Wars of Independence in Kenya and Algeria*, Philadelphia: Pennsylvania University Press, 2013.

Kuby, Emma, 'A war of words over an image of war: The Fox-Movietone scandal and the portrayal of French violence in Algeria, 1955-1956', *FPCS*, 30:1 (2012), 46–57.

Lazreg, Marnia Lazreg, *Torture and the Twilight of Empire: From Algiers to Baghdad*, Princeton, NJ: Princeton University Press, 2008.

Lefeuvre, Daniel, *Chère Algérie: Comptes et mécomptes de la tutelle coloniale, 1930-1962*, Paris: SFHOM, 1997.

Le Sueur, James D., *Uncivil War: Intellectuals and Identity Politics during the Decolonization of Algeria*, Philadelphia: Pennsylvania University Press, 2001.

MacMaster, Neil, *Burning the Veil: The Algerian War and the 'Emancipation' of Algerian Women, 1954-62*, Manchester: Manchester University Press, 2009.

McDougall, James, 'Savage wars? Codes of violence in Algeria, 1830s-1990s', *Third World Quarterly*, 26:1 (2005), 117–31.

Merom, Gil, *How Democracies Lose Small Wars: State, Society, and the Failures of France in Algeria, Israel in Lebanon, and the United States in Vietnam*, Cambridge: Cambridge University Press, 2003.

Meynier, Gilbert, *Histoire intérieure du FLN 1954-1962*, Paris: Fayard, 2002.

Rioux, Jean-Pierre (ed.), *La guerre d'Algérie et les Français*, Paris: Fayard, 1992.

Ruedy, John, *Modern Algeria. The Origins and Development of a Nation*, Bloomington, IN: Indiana University Press, 1992.

Schalk, David, *War and the Ivory Tower: Algeria and Vietnam*, Oxford: Oxford University Press, 1991.

Sessions, Jennifer E., *By Sword and Plow: France and the Conquest of Algeria*, Ithaca, NY: Cornell University Press, 2011.

Shepard, Todd, *The Invention of Decolonization: The Algerian War and the Remaking of France*, Ithaca, NY: Cornell University Press, 2006.

Shepard, Todd, '"Something notably erotic": politics, "Arab men," and sexual revolution in postdecolonization France, 1962–1974', *Journal of Modern History*, 84:1 (2012), 80–115.

Stora, Benjamin, *Le Gangrène et l'oubli: La mémoire de la guerre d'Algérie*, Paris: Découverte, 1991.

Surkis, Judith, 'Ethics and violence: Simone de Beauvoir, Djamila Boupacha, and the Algerian War', *French Politics, Culture, and Society*, 28:2 (2010), 38–55.

Thénault, Sylvie, *Une drôle de justice: Les magistrats dans la guerre d'Algérie*, Paris: Découverte, 2001.

Thomas, Martin, *The French North African Crisis: Colonial Breakdown and Anglo-French Relations, 1945-1962*, London: Macmillan, 2000.

Thomas, Martin, 'Colonial violence in Algeria and the distorted logic of state retribution: The Sétif uprising of 1945', *Journal of Military History*, 75:1 (2011), 523–56.

Select Bibliography

Valette, Jacques, *La guerre d'Algérie des Messalistes 1954-1962*, Paris: Harmattan, 2001.
Vince, Natalya, 'Transgressing boundaries: gender, race, religion, and *"Françaises musulmanes"* during the Algerian War of Independence', *French Historical Studies*, 33:3 (2010), 445–74.
Vince, Natalya, *Our Fighting Sisters: Nation, Memory and Gender in Algeria, 1954-2012*, Manchester: Manchester University Press, 2014.
Wall, Irwin M., *France, the United States and the Algerian War*, Berkeley: University of California Press, 2001.
Zeilig, Leo, *Frantz Fanon: The Militant Philosopher of Third World Liberation*, London: I.B. Tauris, 2014.
Zoubir, Yahia H., 'U.S. and Soviet Policies towards France's Struggle with Anticolonial Nationalism in North Africa', *Canadian Journal of History*, 30 (1995), 439–66.

Dutch Empire: New Guinea

Esterik, Chris van, *Nederlands laatste bastion in de Oost:ekonomie en politiek in de Nieuw-Guinea-kwestie*, Baarn: Anthos/In de Toren, 1982.
Geus, P. B. R. de, *De Nieuw-Guinea Kwestie: Aspecten van buitenlands beleid en militaire macht*, Leiden: Nijhoff, 1984.
Lijphart, Arend, *The Trauma of Decolonization: The Dutch and West New Guinea*, New Haven, CT: Yale University Press, 1966.
Saltford, John, *The United Nations and the Indonesian Takeover of West Papua, 1962-1969: The Anatomy of Betrayal*, London: Routledge Curzon, 2003.
Smit, C. *De Liquidatie van een Imperium: Nederland en Indonesië 1945-1962*, Amsterdam: Arbeiderspers, 1962.
Vlasblom, Dirk, *Papoea: Een Geschiedenis*, Amsterdam: Mets en Schilt, 2004.

Dutch Empire: Suriname

Baptiste, F. A., *War Cooperation and Conflict: The European Possessions in the Caribbean, 1939-1945*, New York: Greenwood Press, 1988.
Buddingh', Hans, *Geschiedenis van Suriname*, Utrecht, 1995.
Chin, Henk E. and Hans Buddingh', *Surinam: Politics Economics and Society*, London, 1987.
Dew, Edward, *The Difficult Flowering of Surinam; Ethnicity and Politics in a Plural Society*, The Hague, 1978.
Goselinga, Cornelis, *A Short History of the Netherlands Indies and Surinam*, The Hague, 1979.
Lijphart, Arend, *The Trauma of Decolonization: The Dutch and West New Guinea*, London: Continuum International Publishing, 1966.
Oostindië, Gert and Inge Klinkers, *Knellende Koninkrijksbanden: Het Nederlandse dekolonisatiebeleid in de Caraiben, 1940-2000*, 3 vols, Amsterdam: Amsterdam University Press, 2001 [Abridged English translation: *Decolonizing the Caribbean: Dutch Policies in Comparative Perspective*, also published by Amsterdam University Press.]
Ramsoedh, Hans, *Suriname 1933-1944: Koloniale Politiek en Beleid onder Gouverneur Kielstra*, Delft: Eburon, 1990.

Dutch Empire: Indonesia

Baudet, H. and I. J. Brugmans, *Balans van Beleid: Tergugblik op de laatste halve eeuw van Nederlansch-Indië*, Assen: van Gorcum, 1984.
Bosma, Ulbe and Remco Raben, *De Oude Indische Wereld, 1500-1920*, Amsterdam: Bakker, 2003.
Dahm, Bernhard, *History of Indonesia in the Twentieth Century*, London: Pall Mall, 1971.

Dennis, Peter, *Troubled Days of Peace: Mountbatten and South East Asia Command*, Manchester: Manchester University Press, 1987.

Doel, H. W. v.d., *Afschied van Indië: De val van het Nederlandse Imperium*, Amsterdam: Promethius, 2000.

Drooglever, P. J. (ed.), *Indisch Intermezzo: Geschiedenis van de Nederlanders in Indonesië*, Amsterdam: Bataafsche Leeuw, 1994.

Fasseur, Cees, 'A cheque drawn on a failing bank: the address delivered by Queen Wilhelmina on 6th/7th December 1942', *The Low Countries History Yearbook*, 15 (1982), 102–15.

Gouda, Frances, *Dutch Culture Overseas: Colonial Practice in the Netherlands Indies 1900-1942*, Amsterdam: Amsterdam University Press, 1995.

Graaff, Bob de, *Kalm temidden van woedende golven: Het ministerie van Koloniën en zijn taakomgeving 1912-1940*, 's-Garvenhage: SDU, 1997.

Jong, Louis de, *The Collapse of a Colonial Society: The Dutch in Indonesia during the Second World War*, Leiden: KITLV, 2002.

Luttikhuis, Bart and A. Dirk Moses (eds), *Colonial Counterinsurgency and Mass Violence: The Dutch Empire in Indonesia*, Abingdon: Routledge, 2014.

MacMahon, Robert J., *Colonialism and Cold War: The United States and the Struggle for Indonesian Independence*, Ithaca, NY: Cornell University Press, 1981.

Smit, C., *De Liquidatie van een Imperium: Nederland en Indonesië 1945-1962*, Amsterdam: Arbeiderpers, 1962.

Spruyt, Henrik, *Ending Empire: Contested Sovereignty and Territorial Partition*, Ithaca, NY: Cornell University Press, 2005.

Staatuitgeverij, *Officiële Beschieden Betreffende de Nederlands-Indonesische Betrekkingen 1945-1950, I, 10 Aug.-8 Nov. 1945*, 's-Gravenhage: Nijhoff, 1971.

Belgian Africa

De Witte, Ludo, *The Assassination of Lumumba*, London: Verso, 2002.

Gibbs, David N., *The Political Economy of Third World Intervention: Mines, Money, and U.S. Policy in the Congo Crisis*, Chicago: University of Chicago Press, 1991.

Higginson, John A., *Working Class in the Making: Belgian Colonial Labour Policy and the African Mineworker, 1907-51*, Madison: University of Wisconsin Press, 1989.

James, Alan, *Britain and the Congo Crisis, 1960-63*, London: Macmillan, 1996.

Kent, John, *America, the UN and Decolonisation: Cold War Conflict in the Congo*, London: Routledge, 2010.

Mamdani, Mahmood, *When Victims Become Killers: Colonialism, Nativism, and the Genocide in Rwanda*, Princeton, NJ: Princeton University Press, 2001.

Markovitz, Marvin, *Cross and Sword: The Political Role of Christian Missions in the Belgian Congo, 1908-1960*, Stanford, CA: Hoover Institution, 1973.

Stanard, Matthew G., 'Interwar Pro-Empire Propaganda and European Colonial Culture: Toward a Comparative Research Agenda', *Journal of Contemporary History*, 44:1 (2009), 27–48.

Stanard, Matthew G., *Selling the Congo: A History of European Pro-Empire Propaganda and the Making of Belgian Imperialism*, Lincoln, NE: University of Nebraska Press, 2012.

Takemtchouk, Romain, *Aux origines du séparatisme katangais*, Brussels: Académie royale des sciences d'outre-mer, 1988.

Van Spaandonck, M., 'Belgium: A colonial power becomes a federal state', *Itinerario*, 20:2 (1996), 64–75.

Vanthemsche, Guy, *Belgium and the Congo, 1885-1980*, Cambridge: Cambridge University Press, 2012.

Viaene, Vincent, 'King Leopold's Imperialism and the Origins of the Belgian Colonial Party, 1860-1905', *Journal of Modern History*, 80:4 (2008), 741–90.

Westad, Orde Arne, *The Global Cold War: Third World Interventions and the Making of Our Times*, Cambridge: Cambridge University Press, 2005 [also excellent on Portuguese Africa.]

Young, Crawford, *The Politics of the Congo: Decolonization and Independence*, Princeton, NJ: Princeton University Press, 1965.

Select Bibliography

Portuguese Africa

Bender, Gerald J., *Angola under the Portuguese: The Myth and the Reality*, London: Heinemann, 1978.

Bethencourt, Francisco and Adrian Pearce (eds), *Racism and Ethnic Relations in the Portuguese-Speaking World*, New York: Oxford University Press, 2012.

Bowen, M., *The State against the Peasantry: Rural Struggles in Colonial and Postcolonial Mozambique*, Charlottesville: University of Virginia Press, 2000.

Brinkman, Inge, 'Routes and the war for independence in Northern Angola (1961-74)', *Canadian Journal of African Studies*, 40:2 (2006), 205–34.

Chabal, Patrick, *Amilcar Cabral: Revolutionary Leadership and People's War*, London: Hurst, 1983.

Chabal, Patrick, 'People's War, State Formation and Revolution in Africa: A Comparative Analysis of Mozambique, Guinea-Bissau and Angola', *Journal of Commonwealth and Comparative Politics*, 21:3 (1983), 104–23.

Chabal, Patrick, *A History of Postcolonial Lusophone Africa*, Bloomington: Indiana University Press, 2002.

Chilcote, Ronald (ed.), *Emerging Nationalism in Portuguese Africa*, Stanford, CA: Hoover Institution Press, 1972.

Clarence-Smith, G., *The third Portuguese empire, 1825-1975*, Manchester: Manchester University Press, 1985.

Dhada, Mustafah, *Warriors at Work: How Guinea Was Really Set Free*, Boulder, CO: University Press of Colorado, 1993.

Dhada, Mustafah, 'The Liberation War in Guinea-Bissau Reconsidered', *Journal of Military History*, 62:3 (1998), 571–93.

Gleijeses, Piero, *Conflicting Missions: Havana, Washington and Africa, 1959-1976*, Chapel Hill: University of North Carolina Press, 2003.

Guimarães, Fernando Andresen, *The Origins of the Angolan Civil War: Foreign Intervention and Domestic Political Conflict, 1961-76*, Basingstoke: Palgrave Macmillan, 2001.

Henriksen, Thomas H., 'People's War in Angola, Mozambique, and Guinea-Bissau', *Journal of Modern African Studies*, 14:3 (1976), 377–99.

Henriksen, Thomas H., 'Some notes on the National Liberation Wars in Angola, Mozambique and Guinea-Bissau', *Military Affairs*, 41:1 (1977), 30–7.

Heywood, Linda, 'Unita and ethnic nationalism in Angola', *Journal of Modern African Studies*, 27:1 (1989), 47–66.

Isaacman, Alan, 'Peasants, Work and the Labor Process: Forced Cotton Cultivation in Colonial Mozambique, 1938-1961', *Journal of Social History*, 25:4 (1992), 815–56.

Jerónimo, Miguel Bandeira and José Pedro Monteiro, 'Internationalism and the labours of the Portuguese colonial empire (1945-1974)', *Portuguese Studies*, 29:2 (2013), 142–63.

MacQueen, Norrie, *The Decolonization of Portuguese Africa: Metropolitan Revolution and the Dissolution of Empire*, London: Longman, 1997.

MacQueen, Norrie, 'Portugal's first Domino: "Pluricontinentalism" and Colonial War in Guiné-Bissau, 1963-1974', *Contemporary European History*, 8:2 (1999), 209–30.

MacQueen, Norrie and Pedro Aires Oliveira, '"Grocer meets butcher": Marcello Caetano's London visit of 1973 and the last days of Portugal's *Estado Novo*', *Cold War History*, 10:1 (2010), 29–50.

Schneidman, Witney W., *Engaging Africa: Washington and the Fall of Portugal's Colonial Empire*, Dallas, TX: University Press of America, 2004.

Vail, Leroy and Landeg White, *Capitalism and Colonialism in Mozambique*, Minneapolis: University of Minnesota press, 1980.

Wheeler, Douglas, 'African elements in Portugal's armies in Africa (1961-1974)', *Armed Forces and Society*, 2:2 (1976), 233–50.

INDEX

Abadan   52, 88
ABAKO cultural association: Belgian Congo   312
Abbas, Ferhat   131
ABC (American-British-Canadian) talks (1941)   25
'Abd al-Qadir, Emir   178
ABDA command: Dutch East Indies   245
Aceh (Dutch East Indies)   233
Acheson, Dean   100
Aden   68, 83, 87, 89, 103, 104
Adoula, Cyrille   317
Africa
    British and   35, 58–60
    France and   135
Africa Official Committee: Britain   90–1
African Survey (1938): Britain   36
Africans, racialization of: France   117
Ageron, Charles-Robert   127
Agrarian Law (1870): Java   231
agriculture   54, 67, 77
Ahidjo, Ahmadu   150
Ahmad Bey *see* ibn Mohammed, Ahmad
aid
    Britain   103
    France   124
air power: Britain (1918–45)   22
Ait Ahmed, Hocine   182
Aix-les-Bains accords (1955): France   191
Algeria   8, 113, 122, 124, 127, 128, 131, 134, 158, 170,
    193–209, 312, 340
Algerian war of independence   193–209
Algiers   196, 205, 206
    battle of   203, 204, 209
Alleg, Henri   203
Allenby Declaration (1922): Egypt   33
Along Bay convention (1947): French
    Indochina   169, 170
Alvor Agreement (1975): Angola   330
Ambonese refugees: Netherlands   283
American South-West Pacific Area (SWPA)   248
Amritsar massacre (1919): India   28
Anderson, George W.   322
Anderson Plan (1965): Portuguese Africa   323
Anglo-Egyptian Treaty (1936)   33, 51
Anglo-Irish Treaty (1921)   21
Anglo-Japanese Alliance (1902)   24
Anglo-Jordanian Treaty (1957)   87
Angola   8, 307, 318, 320, 321, 322, 323, 327,
    330, 336
Antananarivo (Madagascar) *see* Tananarive
anthropology   119

anti-colonialism
    France   171
    West Africa   136
Anti-Revolutionary Party (ARP): Netherlands   265, 282
Antilles   11, 218, 296, 297, 298, 302–3
Antirevolutionary Party: Dutch East Indies   233
Anzus Pact (1951)   37, 45
apartheid: South Africa   45, 62–3, 85, 92, 100
Apithy, Sourou Migan   145, 152
Arab-Israeli war (1948)   52
Arab League   89
Arabs: Palestine   34
Arden-Clarke, Sir Charles   60, 61, 75, 211
Argenlieu, Admiral Georges Thierry d'   165, 166,
    167, 344
Armée de Libération Nationale (ALN): Algeria   159,
    194, 197, 198
Arron, Henck   299
Aruba (Dutch West Indies)   238, 239, 240, 242, 294,
    302, 303
Ashanti region: Gold Coast   75
Asian defence bloc   74
Asians
    East and Central Africa   76
    Kenya   96
assimilationism
    French Equatorial Africa   152
    Senegal   148
Associated States: French Indochina   173
associated territories: France   131, 132
associationism: French colonies   118, 119, 121
Aswan High Dam Project (Egypt)   69
Atlantic Charter (1941): Dutch East Indies   247
Atlantic Charter and British West Africa plan (1943)   40
atrocities: Algerian war of independence   203
    see also torture
Attlee, Clement   43, 46, 50
Audin, Maurice   203, 342
Australia   45
    and defence   65
    imperial ambitions of   21
    and New Guinea   283
    Second World War   26, 37
Azikiwe, Nnamdi   40

Baal, Jan van   288
Baganda elite: Uganda   93
Baghdad Pact (1955)   69, 83, 88, 89
Bakary, Djibo   156
Bakongo people: Angola   325

Balfour Declaration (1917) 32
Bali 231, 259
Bamako Congress (1946): French Union 145
Banda, Dr Hastings 97, 98, 100
Bandung meeting (1955): Indonesia 195
Bank of England 53, 82
Bao Daï 163, 168, 169, 170, 173, 174, 177
Barthes, René 147
Basutoland 68
Batavia (Indonesia) 230, 245, 247
battle of Algiers *see* Algiers, battle of
BBC (British Broadcasting Corporation) 22
Beauvoir, Simone de 204
Béchard, Paul 148
Bechuanaland 63
Beel, L. J. M. 263, 266, 271, 272, 274
Beel plan: Indonesia 274
Belgian Congo 9, 156, 307, 310
Belgium 12
Bellounis, Si Mohammed 196, 197
Ben Arafa, Sidi Moulay Mohammed 189, 191
Ben Bella, Ahmed 194, 206
Ben Youssef, Salah 190
Bengal famine (1943) 31
Berlin conference (1954) 174
Betsimisaraka people: Madagascar 214
Betts, Raymond 7
Bevin, Ernest 44, 50, 52
Bidault, Georges 130, 131, 145, 167, 189,
    209, 344
bidonvilles (shanty towns): French colonies 123, 182,
    183, 200
black-majority rule
    Central African Federation 91, 98
    East Africa 92–3
Bledisloe Commission (1939): Rhodesias 40
Blum, Léon 125, 167
Blum-Viollette Plan: France 125
Blundell, Michael 94
Boedi Oetomo: Java 234
Bonaire 238, 302, 303
Borneo 231, 245, 259, 265
    see also North Borneo
Bose, Subhas Chandra 31
Bourdet, Claude 203
Bourguiba, Habib 187, 190
Brazzaville conference (1944) 128, 137, 151
Breton, André 207
Bretton Woods Agreement (1944) 43
Brévié, Jules 123
Briggs Plan: Malaya 58, 73
Britain 10–11
    and African territories 58–60
    and aid 72
    and colonies 339
    and consumerism 340
    and decolonization 343
    and defence 64, 68, 72

and Dutch East Indies 248, 249, 254–61, 267
and Dutch West Indies 242
and 'East of Suez' policy 83, 86, 89, 102–4
and economy 43–4, 54, 64, 85, 103
emigration from 22
and Falkland Islands 106
and France 74, 210–11
and Gibraltar 106
and Hong Kong 106
immigration to 65
and Indonesia 262–3, 273
and Madagascar 210–11
and Malaya 338
and Netherlands 244
and trade 85
British Army 22, 37
    Far East 103, 104
    Middle East 50, 89
British Commonwealth 10, 15, 42, 43, 65–6, 91, 334
British Empire
    defence 21–2, 24, 63, 64
    and India 25, 27–31
    and Middle East 31–5
    post-First World War 21–4
    and Second World War 25–7, 37–42
    and 'trusteeship' 35–7
British Guiana 38, 70
British Nationality Act (1948) 46
British navy (1918–45) 22
Brockway, Fenner 70
Brook, Sir Norman 88
Bruma, Eddy 297, 300
Brunei 74, 103
Bugeaud, General Thomas Robert 179
Bunker Plan (1962): New Guinea 291
bureaucracy
    French colonies 134
    Indochina 125
    New Guinea 281
Burkina Faso *see* Upper Volta
Burma 26, 27, 44, 49, 50
Burundi *see* Rwanda-Burundi
Butler, R. A. 99, 101

Cabral, Amilcár 322, 323, 329
Cabral, Luis 329
Caetano, Marcello 320, 329
Cambodia 120, 163, 164, 170, 175, 176
Cameroon *see* French Cameroon
camps de regroupement: Algeria 198
Camus, Albert 200
Canada
    and British Commonwealth 45
    and Suez crisis 82
Cao Bang (Vietnam) 171
Carpentier, General Georges 171
Carthage Declaration (1954) 190
Castries, Colonel Christian de 177

Catholic National Party: Netherlands 282, 285
Catholic People's Party (KVP): Netherlands 289
Celebes 231, 245, 259
censorship: Madagascar 215
Central African Federation 62, 63, 71, 72, 86, 90–1, 96–100
Central African Republic 156
Césaire, Aimé 131, 220
Ceylon 39, 49, 56
Chabal, Patrick 323
Chad 142, 149, 156, 157
Challe, General Maurice 205, 206
Chamberlain, Neville 23, 24
Chanak crisis (1922) 21
Charter of the Kingdom of the Netherlands (1954) 296
Chauvet, Paul 149
Chen Geng, General 171
chiefs, African 26
China
    and Indochina 161–2, 170
    and Portuguese Africa 325, 330
Chinese
    Malaya 41, 56, 73
    Singapore 26
Chinese Civil War 160, 169
Chinese communists: Malaya, Second World War 27
Chinese labourers: Dutch West Indies 239
Chirac, Jacques 342
Christian Democrat Party: France 130, 131
Christian Historical Union (CHU): Netherlands 265, 282, 288
Christianity 57, 70
Christison, Lieutenant General Philip 251, 252, 254, 255, 256, 258, 259, 261
Churchill, Sir Winston 41, 64, 65
cities: French colonies 134
citizenship
    French colonies 122, 127, 140
    French Union 133
    Malaya 56, 57
civil service
    Britain see 'Overseas Civil Service': Britain
    New Guinea 287
Cochin-China 123, 159, 163, 164, 165
Cochran plan (1948): Indonesia 271, 272
cocoa production: Gold Coast 75
coffee cultivation: Java 231
Cohen, Sir Andrew 59, 62, 80, 92, 211
cold war 3, 16, 43, 55, 57
Colijn, Hendrik 236, 237, 241
'collaboration' 10
Colombo Plan 54, 74
Colonial Act (1930): Portugal 319
Colonial Estates: Dutch West Indies 240
Colonial Office: Britain 25, 32, 35, 36, 38, 39, 40, 41, 42, 49, 52, 54, 58, 59, 67, 72, 74, 91, 94
Colonial Policy Committee: Britain 86

Colonial Service: Britain 73
colonial withdrawal: Britain 3
colonization: New Guinea 280, 284
COMININDO: Indochina 167
commerce: French Africa 143
Commonwealth see British Commonwealth
Commonwealth Immigration Act (1962) 46
Commonwealth Relations Office: Gold Coast 76
Commonwealth Strategic Reserve 65
Communauté of French African states 137, 154–7
'Communes': Senegal 140, 144
communism 53
    Africa 92
        Algeria 196
        Belgian Congo 339
        French West Africa 144, 145
        see also Marxism
    France 168, 171, 203
    Indonesia 270, 277
    Java 234
    Madagascar 213
    Malaya 27, 57
    Portugal 330
    Vietnam 169
Comoros islands 156, 216
concentration camps: Algeria see camps deregroupement: Algeria
Confédération du Travail (CGT): French West Africa 146
Congo see Belgian Congo
Congo Brazzaville see Middle Congo
Conklin, Alice 8
conscripts: Algeria 197, 198
conservation 54, 97
    Kenya 77
Constantine Plan (1959): Maghreb 185, 200
Constituent Assembly: French West Africa 142
consumerism: Britain and France 340
Convention People's Party (CPP): Gold Coast 61, 75
Cooper, Frederick 6
Coppet, Marcel de 212, 213
Coste-Floret, Paul 167
Cot, Pierre 130
Côte d'Ivoire see Ivory Coast
Coussey Committee: Gold Coast 61
Creoles
    French Antilles 218, 220
    Suriname 295, 301
Cripps, Sir Richard Stafford 30
Crown Colonies 41
Cuba
    and Angola 327
    and Belgian Congo 318
    and Portuguese Africa 325–6
cultural exclusion: France 124
culture
    French Empire 9, 120, 137
    Dutch East Indies 230

Index

Cunha, Joaquim da Silva 329
Curaçao 238, 239, 240, 242, 294, 295, 298, 302, 303
currency: Vietnam 166
Curzon, George Nathaniel, Lord 32
customary labour: French West Africa 147
customary law: French Union 133
Cyprus 64, 68, 71, 72, 81, 83, 87, 89–90

Dahomey 138, 145, 146
Darwin, John 19, 43, 80
de Gaulle, General Charles 128, 149, 154, 155, 176
Debré, Michel 154
decolonization 1–12, 178–92, 333–45
    Africa 90–9
        East and Central Africa 76–81
        Gold Coast 75–6
        South Africa 68
        Britain 64–83, 334, 339
        France 334, 341
        Malaya 73–4
        Middle East 68–9
        Netherlands 335
        Portugal 334–5, 343
defence: British Empire 21–2, 24, 63, 64
Defferre, Gaston see Gaston Defferre law (1956)
Dekker, Eduard Douwes 231
Delafosse, Maurice 118–19
Delavignette, Robert 150, 153, 195, 211
democracy
    East and Central Africa 77
    French colonies 135
    French Union 132
    India 28
    Suriname 241
Dening, Maberly E. 256
départements d'outre-mer (DOMs): France 155, 217
dependent territories: France 128
Depression: and French decolonization 123
detention camps: Kenya 97
detribalization: French colonies 119
development
    British colonies 38–9, 54, 66–7
    French Africa 143
    Maghreb 122
Deventer, C.Th. van 233
Devlin enquiry (1959) 92
Devlin Report (1959) 97, 98
devolution 72
    Gold Coast 62, 75
Devonshire Formula (1923) 94
Dia, Mamadou 153
Diallo, Yacine 145
diarchy see dyarchy
Diego Garcia 116
Dien Bien Phu fortress (Vietnam) 161
Djibouti 156, 218
dominions: British Empire 15, 19, 21, 22, 23, 24, 37
Dong Khe (Vietnam) 171
Douglas-Home, Sir Alec 76, 90, 96

Doumer, Paul 120
Drees, Willem 262, 273
duBois, Coert 270
Dulles, John Foster 82, 175, 289
Duras, Marguerite 207
Dutch, the see Netherlands
Dutch army 244, 248, 265
    Indonesia 264, 265, 266
    see also KNIL (Dutch colonial army)
Dutch East India Company (VOC) see United Dutch
    East India Company (VOC)
Dutch East Indies 230–8
Dutch government in exile 247
Dutch intelligence service 249
Dutch Reformed Church 285, 287
Dutch West India Company (WIC) 230
Dutch West Indies 238–42
Duverger, Maurice 203
dyarchy: India 28, 29

East Africa 40, 71, 80, 92
East African Governors' Conference (Second World
    War) 25
East African Royal Commission (1953) 79
East Indian Auditing Act (1864) 231
East Indian Government Act (1854) 230
East Indies see Dutch East Indies
East Indonesia 265
'East of Suez' policy: Britain 83, 86, 89, 102–4
Eastern Group Supply Council (Second World War) 25
Ecochard, Michel 182
École Coloniale (Paris) 119
Economic Cooperation Administration (ECA):
    Indonesia 272
economic migration: French West Africa 138
economies 415
    Dutch West Indies 240
    French Africa 142–4
    New Guinea 280
    Portuguese Africa 323, 324
Eden, Sir Anthony 34, 64, 69, 72, 82, 175
education
    Belgian Congo 310
    Dutch East Indies 232, 245
    French Equatorial Africa 149
    French West Africa 146
    Indonesia 236
    EEC see European Economic Community
Egypt 3
    Britain and 32–3, 50, 68–9
    Israeli invasion of (1956) 82
    and United Arab Republic 87
Eisenhower Doctrine (1957) 87
Eisenhower, President Dwight D. 82, 84
el-Glaoui, T'hami, pacha of Marrakech 187, 189, 191
el-Kettani, Abdelhaï 189
elections
    Cambodia 164
    Dutch East Indies 235

Dutch West Indies 240
French Pacific territories 217
French Union 132
French West Africa 144–5
Gold Coast 61, 75, 76
India 29–30
Kenya 79
Madagascar 213
Malaya 73
Netherlands 263
Rhodesias 99
Suriname 240, 297–9
Tunisia 188
Uganda 93
elites 5, 58
Belgian Congo 311
French colonies 119, 134
French Cameroon 142
Indochina 121
Ivory Coast 140
Madagascar 212
Uganda 93
emigration 22, 23, 45
see also economic migration; immigration
Empire Settlement Act (1922): Britain 23
employment
Belgian Congo 311
French Antilles 220
Portuguese Africa 319–20
Erskine, General Sir George 78
Esterik, Chris van 292
États Généraux de la Colonisation Française 145, 150
ethical policy: Dutch East Indies 233
ethnic minorities: Indonesia 251
Eurasians: New Guinea 280, 287
European Defence Community (formerly Pleven Plan):
Vietnam 170, 174, 190
European Economic Community (EEC) 84, 101,
286, 298
European Free Trade Area (EFTA) 66
Evian accords (1962) 208
évolués
French Africa 118, 149
Rwanda 311
Ewe people (Madagascar) 210
ex-servicemen
Algeria 208
French West Africa 147
Madagascar 213
Netherlands 285
'exceptionalism' 11
exports: Madagascar 212

Fabians 20
Falkland Islands 106
famines
Algeria 179
Bengal 31
Vietnam 163

Fanon, Frantz 7, 207
Farge, Yves 130
farming industry
Britain 23
Ivory Coast 140
Kenya 77, 79, 95
Vietnam 124
Faure, Edgar 153, 190
Federal Review Conference (1960) 98
Federation of Malaya 57
Federation of Rhodesia and Nyasaland see Central
African Federation
federations 131, 140
Africa 62, 80
Central African Federation 63, 96–100
French Africa 155
Gold Coast 75
British colonies 67, 68, 72
Indochina 120
Indonesia 264
Malaysia 57
South Arabian Federation 83
West Indies 41
Netherlands Antilles Federation 303
Feraoun, Mouloud 159, 207
FIDESTOM: French Pacific territories 217
'flag independence' 3
FLN: Algeria see Front de Libération Nationale (FLN)
FNLA party: Angola 322
Fouchet, Christian 190
Fourth Republic: France 126, 128, 131, 143
France 9, 11
and Britain 74, 211
colonial legacy 342
colonies
Africa 118, 339
Indochina 120, 338
Madagascar 121
Middle East 121
North Africa 122
Algeria 178–82, 207
Morocco 181
Tunisia 181
Pacific territories 216–18
Togo 210–11
West Indian territories 218–21
and culture 340
and decolonization 101, 341
and Dutch West Indies 242
and economy 122–3
and Vietnam 170, 171, 173
Republican imperialism 117
and Syria 32
and United States 340
France, Pierre Mendès 153, 171, 174, 189, 195
Franco-African Study Groups (CEFA) 144
Franco-Prussian War (1870–1) 179
Franco-Vietnamese conference (1946) 165
Free France: Second World War 127, 219

FRELIMO party (Mozambique)   323, 324, 325, 329, 330, 343
French Antilles   118, 131, 140, 218
    see also Guadeloupe; Martinique
French army
    Algeria   193, 198
    Vietnam   167
French Cameroon   131, 136, 142, 144, 150, 156
French Communist Party   130, 145, 156
French Congo   150
French Equatorial Africa (AEF)   142, 149, 311
French Guiana see Guyanne
French Indochina   158–77
French Oceania (EFO)   216
French Polynesia   218
French Socialist Party (SFIO): French West Africa   146
French Somaliland   131, 132
French Sudan   138, 145, 155
French Togo   138, 210–11
French Union   114, 128, 129–35, 145, 211, 213, 214, 341
French West Africa (AOF)   115, 120, 125, 127
Front de Libération Nationale (FLN): Algeria   159, 182, 196
Front Nationale: France   209

Gabon   142, 156
Gabungan Politik Indonesia (GAPI)   237
Gallieni, General Joseph   121, 211
Gandhi, Mohandas K.   28
Gaston Defferre law (1956): French West Africa   148, 153, 154, 215
Gaullism   126, 154, 155, 167
Geneva conference (1954)   174–6
genocide: Rwanda   307, 312
Gerbrandy, Pieter   247, 259, 265
Germany, and New Guinea   280–1
Ghana   84
    see also Gold Coast
Gibraltar   106
Gizenga, Antoine   316, 317
'Global Strategy Paper' (1952)   64
Goa   328, 329
Gold Coast   26, 38, 60–2, 70, 96, 210
Gouda, Frances   343
Government of India Act (1919)   28
Government of India Act (1935)   29, 47
Graham, Frank Porter   269
Grandval, Gilbert   191
Groupe d'Organisation Nationale de la Guadeloupe (GONG)   220
Guadeloupe   123, 132, 218, 219
guerrilla warfare
    Guiné-Bissau   321
    Indonesia   283
Guèye, Lamine   133, 144, 145
Guillaume, General Augustin   188, 189
Guiné-Bissau   307, 318, 321, 322, 324

Guinea   136, 138, 143, 148, 151, 154
Guyanne (French Guiana)   130, 218, 221, 341

Hague Conventions (1899)   233
Hailey, Lord   36, 39
Haiphong (Vietnam)   161, 165
Hammarskjöld, Dag   316, 317
Hardy, Georges   119
Hatta, Mohammed   236, 237, 245, 246, 250, 257, 269, 273
Havana Conference (1940)   294
Helfrich, Admiral   249, 255, 258
High Commission Territories: Britain   63
Hindus
    India   47
    Suriname   298, 299
Ho Chi Minh   160, 163, 167, 213
Hoang Van Hoan   170
Hoëvell, W. R., Baron van   230
Hola   78, 90, 94
Hong Kong   46, 106, 248
Hopkinson, Henry   72
Houphouët-Boigny, Félix   140, 142, 144, 145, 151, 154, 156
Hussein, King of Jordan   87
Hutus: Rwanda   311

ibn Mohammed, Ahmad (Ahmad Bey)   178
immigration
    Algeria   180
    Britain   65, 100
    Central Africa   80
    Dutch West Indies   239
    France   196, 209
    Jews   51
    Netherlands   278
    New Guinea   280
    Palestine   33–4, 51
Imperial Conference (1923): Britain   21
Imperial Conference (1926): Britain   22
Imperial Economic Conference (1932): Ottawa   23
imperialism see Republican imperialism
'imported states'   5
independence
    Algeria   208
    Belgian Congo   313
    Dutch East Indies   249–50
    Dutch West Indies   298–9
        Suriname   297, 299–300
    French Africa   148, 156
    Madagascar   215
    Malaya   74
    Nigeria   62
    Portuguese Africa   323
Indépendants d'Outre-Mer (IOMs)   146
India   19, 38–9
    Britain and   21, 46–7, 48
    and British Commonwealth   45
    British withdrawal from   44
    defence   32

nationalism 27–31
partition 47
production, Second World War 25
see also Goa
Indian army 29
Indian immigrants
Dutch West Indies 239
Suriname 241
Indian National Army (INA) 31
Indian National Congress 74
Indians: Malaya 41
'indirect rule': Africa 35, 36, 55
Indochina 114, 120, 123, 125, 133, 337
see also French Indochina; Vietnam
Indochina Communist Party (ICP) 160, 161
Indochina War 158–66
Indonesia 11, 103
British military occupation 254–61
communism 277
Dutch return 262–6
effects of Japanese rule 248–54
first 'police action' 267–71
and New Guinea 290
as Republic 274–6
second 'police action' 271–5
effects of Second World War 293–5
see also East Indonesia
industrialization: India 29
inflation 25, 57, 60, 294
Inskip, Sir Thomas 24
intellectuals: Algeria 201, 203
intelligence 45, 61, 65
Inter-Indonesian Conference (1949) 275
International Monetary Fund 82, 317
internment camps: Dutch East Indies 235, 236
see also camps de regroupement: Algeria
Iran 51, 69
Iraq 50, 68
and Arab Federation 87
Britain and 32, 88
Ireland 21, 22, 37
Islam: French African states 137
Israel: invasion of Egypt (1956) 82
Istiqlal (Constitution) Party: Maghreb 181, 186, 187, 188
Ivory Coast 136, 138, 140, 142

Jamaica 36, 38, 41, 89
James, C. L. R. 20
Janssens, General (Belgian Congo) 313
Japan
and Britain 22
and Dutch East Indies 245–6, 276
and Indochina 163
Second World War 27, 249
Java 261, 262, 263, 264, 280, 286
'Jeanson network': Paris 207
Jeffries, Sir Charles 70
Jews: immigration to Palestine 34
Jinnah, Mohammed Ali 30, 47

Jonkmann, J. A. 264, 266
Jordan 68, 69, 83, 87
Joseph, Richard 136
Juin, General Alphonse 187
July, Pierre 190

Kamba 26, 80
Kampuchea *see* Cambodia
Kanak Liberation Party: New Caledonia 218
Kasavubu, Joseph 313, 316
Katanga (Belgian Congo) 314, 316, 317
Katholieke Volkspartij (KVP): Netherlands 264
Kennedy, President John F. 289, 290
Kennedy, Robert 290
Kenya 38, 39, 40, 71, 93
independence 86, 95
political unrest in 77
Kenyan African Democratic Union (KADU) 95
Kenyan African National Union (KANU) 95
Kenyatta, Jomo 58, 79, 94
Kernkamp, W. J. A. 296
Khama, Seretse 63
Kielstra, Johannes C. 241, 295
Kikuyu community: Kenya 77
Kimbangu, Simon 312
King David Hotel 51
Kleffens, Eelco van 244
KNIL (Dutch colonial army) 244, 245, 256
Kom, Anton de 241
Komite Nasional Indonesia Pusat 261
Korean War 44
Krijger, B. J. 281
Kuyper, Abraham 233
Kuwait 88, 89, 104

labour 53, 57, 65, 77, 78
Labour government (Britain) 35, 46, 51, 52
Labouret, Henri 119
Lachmon, Jagernath 297, 299, 301
Lamine, Sidi 187
Lancaster House agreement (1979) 106
Lancaster House Conference (1960) 94
land reform 50, 176
land use
French Antilles 219
Portuguese Africa 327
language 11
Dutch East Indies 245
Laos 120, 121, 163, 170
Latour, General Pierre Boyer de 190, 191
Latrille, André 142
Lattre de Tassigny, General Jean de 160, 173
Laurentie, Henri 128, 130, 213
law and order: colonies 336
Law, Andrew Bonar 21
Lawson, J. J. 252
League for the Independence of Vietnam 158
Lebanon 88, 121
Leclerc, General Philippe 164

Leeward Islands   238
Legentilhomme, Paul   212
Lennox-Boyd, Alan   69, 73, 76, 77, 90, 91, 92, 94
lettrés: French Africa see évolués
Levant High Commission   121
Liberals
    Dutch East Indies   231, 233
    Netherlands   282, 286
Libya   33, 34, 52, 68
Lijphart, Arend   284, 291
Linggadjati agreement: Indonesia   279, 295
Logemann, J. H. A.   250, 259, 277
Lumumba, Patrice   307, 310
Luns, Josef   290, 291
Luns Plan (1961): New Guinea   289
Lyautey, Marshal Louis-Herbert   121, 181, 341
Lyttelton, Oliver   67, 69, 75

MacArthur, General Douglas   249
M'Bokolo, Elikia   149
MacDonald, Malcolm   39, 58
Machel, Samora   325
Macleod, Iain   90, 91, 93, 94
Macmillan, Harold   40, 67, 76, 83, 84, 88, 90, 91, 92
Macpherson, Sir John   75
MacQueen, Norrie   320, 327
Madagascar   114, 121, 122, 125, 127, 132, 145, 191,
    210, 211–16, 344
magazines: France   203
Maghreb   152
    see also Algeria; Morocco; Tunisia
Makarios, Archbishop   70, 89
Malacca   73
Malawi see Nyasaland
Malay Chinese Association   73
Malaya   41, 53, 54, 56–8
    independence   74, 86
    Second World War   26
    post-Second World War   54, 73–5
Malayan Indian Congress   73
Malayan Union   41–2, 56
Malaysia   103–4
Mali federation   155, 156
Malvern, Sir Godfrey Huggins, Lord   80
mandates
    British Empire   21
    French Empire   121
Mangoenkoesoemo, Tjipto   244
'Manifesto of the 121': Algeria   207
Mao Zedong   169
Marshall Aid   44
    Dutch East Indies   272–3
    French West Africa   144
Martinaud-Deplat, Leon   189
Martinique   123, 130, 218, 219, 220
Marxism
    Angola   324, 343
    Mozambique   324, 325, 343
    Vietnam   160

Masai Development Plan (MDP): Tanganyika   55
Massu, General Jacques   203
Mau Mau: Kenya   77–8, 94, 345
Maudling, Reginald   95
Mauriac, François   203
Mauritania   138, 143
Mayer, René   131
media: Algerian war of independence   205
memorials: France   342
Menon, Krishna   45
Menzies, Robert   65, 289
Merina elite: Madagascar   212
Messali Hadj, Ahmed   195, 196
middle classes see Creoles; évolués
Middle Congo   142, 156
Middle East   31–5
    Britain and   31–5, 68–9
    see also Egypt; Iran; Iraq; Israel; Palestine; Suez;
        Suez Canal
mining
    Belgian Congo   313
    French Africa   143
missionaries
    Netherlands   285
    New Guinea   287
Mitterrand, François   151, 221
mixed race citizens: French Union   134
    see also Creoles
mobilization   55, 96
Mobutu, Colonel Joseph-Désiré   316, 317, 318
modernization   1, 4, 5, 10, 108, 109
Mohammed V, Sultan of Morocco   186, 187, 189,
    191, 192, 344
Mollet, Guy   197
Moluccas   245, 283
Monckton Commission (1960)   98–9
Mondlane, Eduardo   325
Monnoni, Professor O.   135
Monroe doctrine   242
Montagu Declaration (1917)   27
Montego Bay Conference (1940)   90
Mook, Hubertus J. van   247, 249, 250, 251, 252, 255,
    258, 259, 261, 262
Morlière, General Louis   166
Morocco   121, 122, 127, 131, 134, 153, 179
Mossadegh, Dr Mohammad   52
Mountbatten, Lord Louis   47, 248, 249, 250, 251, 261
Moutet, Marius   166
Movement for Colonial Freedom: Britain   90
Moyne Commission (1940)   41
Mozambique   307, 318, 320, 321, 324, 327, 330
MPLA party: Angola   330, 331, 343
Mpolo, Maurice   316
multiracialism
    Africa   76, 84, 96
    British Commonwealth   44, 100
    Malaya   57, 74
Mus, Paul   168
Muslim Brotherhood: Egypt   33

Muslim League   30, 46
Muslims
    Comoros islands   216
    India   30, 46, 48
    Levant   121
    Mozambique   324
    North Africa   124
        Algeria   178, 194, 200
Musso (Indonesian Communist leader)   270, 271

Namibia   8
Nasser, Gamal Abdel   68, 69, 81–2, 86
nationalism   46, 49, 53
    Africa   59, 94, 97
        Algeria   159, 181, 196, 200
        Angola   323
        French Africa   151, 152
    Arab   50, 88
    British colonies   21
    Ceylon   49
    Dutch East Indies   234, 252, 276, 282
    Egypt   33
    French Antilles   219
    Gold Coast   75
    India   27–31
    Indochina   121
    Indonesia   237, 268
    Iran   52
    Iraq   50
    Java   252
    Levant   121
    Madagascar   211
    Maghreb   181
    Malaya   56
    Morocco   185
    Portuguese Africa   320
    Suriname   297
    Tanganyika   78
    Tunisia   185
    Vietnam   123, 159
    West Africa   136
Nationalization   69, 88
Nattes, Ernest de   219
Navarre, General Henri   173, 174
Negritude movement: French Africa   118, 220
Nehru, Jawaharlal   81, 82
Neo Destour Party: Maghreb   181, 186, 187, 188
Netherlands   11
    Charter of the Kingdom of the Netherlands
        (1954)   296
    and decolonization   341, 342
    and economy   278
    and immigration   278
    and Indonesia   244–61, 339
    and New Guinea   279–82, 339
    post-Second World War   248
    and West Indies   230–8
        Antilles   302–3
        Suriname   293–303

Netherlands Antilles Federation   303
Netherlands Indies Civil Administration (NICA)   248
Netherlands-Indonesian Union   295
Neto, Agostinho   324
New Caledonia   216, 218, 294
New Guinea   245, 250, 253, 275, 279–92
New Hebrides   216
New Kenya Group (NKG)   94, 95
New Zealand   21, 25, 37, 65
newspapers
    France   203
    Netherlands   288
Nguyen Phan Long   170
Nguyen Van Xuan, General   169
Niger   138, 143, 156
Nigeria   38, 62, 72, 75, 86
Nkrumah, Kwame   58, 61, 75, 76, 81
North Borneo   41, 74, 103
Northern Rhodesia   35, 54, 62, 96, 97, 98, 99
Nyasaland   40, 62, 71, 80, 90
Nyerere, Julius   92, 93

OAS: Algeria see Organisation de l'Armée Secrète
Obote, Milton   93
oil
    Dutch East Indies   245
    Dutch West Indies   239–40, 242
    Middle East   51, 88
    New Guinea   283–4
Okita, Joseph   316
Olympio, Sylvanius   211
Organic Charter of the Portuguese Empire (1933)   319
Organisation de l'Armée Secrète (OAS): Algeria   194,
    205, 206, 208
Organisation Spéciale (OS): Algeria   182, 196
'Overseas Civil Service': Britain   73
overseas departments: France   103, 114, 130
overseas territories: France   114, 127, 131
Ovimbumdo people: Angola   325
Oyen, General van   261

Padmore, George, 20
PAIGC party: Guiné-Bissau   324, 327, 328, 335
Pakistan   30, 44, 45, 47, 49, 65
Palestine: Britain and   32, 34, 43, 44
pan-African conference (1943)   37
pan-African congress, fifth (1945)   58
pan-Africanism   91
Papon, Maurice   182, 206, 342
Papua see New Guinea
paramilitary organizations: Dutch East Indies, Second
        World War   245
'Paris massacre' (1961)   207
Parti Colonial (French Oceania Committee)   217
Partij van de Arbeid (PvDA): Netherlands   264, 268,
    286, 288, 291
peasants
    Algeria   179, 195
    Java   230

Index

Tunisia 190
Vietnam 174
Péchoux, Laurent 146
pemudas see terrorism: Indonesia
Pengel, Johan Adolf (Jopie) 297, 298
People's Security Army (TKR): Indonesia 251
Périllier, General Louis 186
Pinke, Admiral 264
plantations: Dutch West Indies 238–9
Plas, Charles Olke van der 249, 252, 256, 258, 259
Pleven Plan: Vietnam 170
police: Gold Coast 75
political parties 299
    Algeria 194, 196
    French Africa 137, 144–6
    Indonesia 236
    Madagascar 212, 214
    Martinique 220
    Portuguese Africa 323
    Suriname 297, 298, 301
political prisoners: Madagascar 215
political violence 5, 7
    Algeria 178, 200
    Madagascar 214
    see also torture
Ponsot, Henri 121
Ponty, William 138
Popular Front coalition: France 125
Portugal
    army 328, 336
    and decolonization 343
    and Goa 328
    Organic Charter of the Portuguese Empire
      (1933) 319
Portuguese Africa 9, 12, 309–31
Portuguese Guinea *see* Guiné-Bissau
post-colonialism 7–8
Potsdam conference (1945) 248
Pouvanaa a Oopa 218
Powell, Enoch 94
Pré, Roland 150
press
    Belgian Congo 311
    and New Guinea 288
    see also magazines; newspapers
prisoners: Curaçao 303
prisoners of war 251, 255
    Java 249
    see also RAPWI units
propaganda
    Britain, Second World War 27
    Vietnam 160
Prost, Henri 183
PUTERA (Centre of People's Power): Dutch East
    Indies 246

Rabemananjara, Jacques 213
race: Guiné-Bissau 324

'race sentiment': British Dominions 22
    see also white supremacy
race theory: Rwanda 311
racial discrimination: Tunisia 181
racial hierarchies: French Union 132
racial politics: French colonies 121
racial segregation: Maghreb 183
racial stereotyping
    Britain 56
    France 117, 175
'racialization': Vichy regime 127
radio *see* wireless broadcasting
Rahman, Tunku Abdul 74, 103
railways: French Africa 140, 144
Ramadier, Jean 156
Ramadier, Paul 167
RAPWI units: prisoners of war (Dutch East
    Indies) 251, 255, 256
Raseta, Dr Joseph 212, 213
Rassemblement Démocratique Africain (RDA) 145, 148
*Rassemblement Démocratique des Peuples Tahitien*s
    (RDPT) 218
Rassemblement du Peuple Français (RPF) 150, 167
Ravoahangy-Adrianavalona, Dr Joseph 212
Red River Delta (Vietnam) 171
referenda
    French Africa 155
    Madagascar 216
    Vietnam 165
reforms
    French colonies 125, 134
      French Equatorial Africa 152
      French West Africa 140
      Madagascar 212
      Tunisia 186
    Java 230, 231
    Portuguese Africa 327
refugees *see* Ambonese refugees: Netherlands
religion: French African states 137
    see also Islam
RENAMO movement: Mozambique 330
Renville agreements: Dutch East Indies 279
Republican imperialism: France 117
republicanism: Indonesia 272
resistance movements: Dutch East Indies,
    Second World War 207
retraditionalization: France 119
Réunion 130, 131, 132, 140, 156, 217
Rhodesia 8, 71, 80, 96, 97, 325
    see also Northern Rhodesia; Southern Rhodesia
Rhodesian Front 105
Roijen, J. Herman van 274, 289
Roman Catholic Church: Netherlands 285
Romme, C. P. M. 263, 289
Roosevelt, President Franklin D. 161, 176, 248
Round Table Agreement (1950): New Guinea 285
Rous, Jean 203
rubber planters: Dutch East Indies 235

rubber production: Malaya   75
Russia *see* Soviet Union
Rwanda-Burundi   310

Saba (Dutch West Indies)   238, 302, 303
Sabah *see* North Borneo
Sahel   138
Sainteny, Jean   164, 165
St Eustatius (Dutch West Indies)   238, 303
St Maarten (Dutch West Indies)   238, 302
Salazar, António de Oliveira   9, 307, 318–19, 323, 327
Salisbury, Lord   70, 89
Saller, Raphael   151
Santos, Marcelino dos   325
Sarawak   41, 74, 103
Sarekat Islam: Java   234, 235
Sarraut, Albert   122, 133
Sartre, Jean-Paul   203, 207
Sassen, E. M. J. A. van   271, 274
Saudi Arabia   52, 89
Sauvy, Alfred   3
Savary, Alain   190
Savimbi, Jonas   325
SAWO: Suriname   241
Schermerhorn, Willem   261, 264, 265
Schultz, Arnaldo   321
Schuman, Robert   186
Schumann, Maurice   131
'Second Colonial Occupation'   54
Second World War   337
    British Empire   25–7, 37–42
    India   25
    Suriname   293–5
Sedney, Jules   298
Senanayake, D. S.   39, 49
Senatus-Consulte code: Algeria   179
Senegal   136, 138, 140, 143, 144, 146, 147, 148, 152
Senghor, Léopold Sédar   137, 144, 145, 148, 152, 329
Servan-Schreiber, Jean-Jacques   203
settlers
    British African territories   62, 76–81, 92
    French colonies   132
        French Cameroon   142
        French Equatorial Africa   150, 157
        French Pacific territories   217
        French West Africa   140, 145
        Madagascar   213
        North Africa   123
            Algeria   179, 182, 191
            Morocco   188, 190, 191
        Vietnam   170, 171
    New Guinea   280
    Portuguese Africa   327
sharecroppers: Guadeloupe   219
Sharpeville Massacre (1960)   85
Sihanouk, Prince   163
Simon, Paul-Henri   203
Singapore   24, 26, 27, 31, 41, 73, 74, 86, 103

Sissoko, Fily Dabo   145, 148
Six Day War (1967)   104
6 March accords (1946): Vietnam   165
Sjahrir, Soetan   236, 237, 246, 258, 262, 268
Sjarifuddin, Amir   267, 269, 271
slave labour: French Antilles   218
slaves: Dutch West Indies   238
Smith, Ian   105
Smuts, General Jan   37
Soares, Mário   330
social class: French Antilles   218–19
    see also elites
socialists: and French colonies   129, 130, 133, 145, 146
social welfare   55, 58
Somalia see French Somaliland
Soulbury Commission (1948)   39, 49
South Africa   21, 22, 37, 45, 62–3
    and British Commonwealth   45, 85, 91
    imperial ambitions of   21
    and Portuguese Africa   325
South Arabian Federation   83
South East Asia
    Second World War   26, 41
        post-Second World War   54
South East Asia Command (SEAC)   248, 250, 251, 257, 264
South Kasai (Belgian Congo)   316, 317
South Moluccans: Netherlands   278
South Vietnam   176
Southern Rhodesia   37, 40, 62, 80, 91, 96, 98, 99
Soviet Union
    and British Empire   43
    and Indochina   163
    and Middle East   69, 88
    and New Guinea   289
    and Portuguese Africa   325, 326
    and United Nations   91
    and West Africa   155
Spínola, General António de   327, 328, 329, 330
Spoor, Major General   268, 274
Spruyt, Hendrick   321, 328
squatters: Kenya   77
Sri Lanka *see* Ceylon
Stack, Sir Lee   33
Stanley, Oliver   38, 40
state marketing: British Empire, Second World War   25
Statute of Westminster (1931)   22
stereotyping *see* racial stereotyping
Sterling: devaluation of   43, 104
Sterling Area   25, 44, 50, 54, 56, 57, 63
Stikker, Dirk   271, 273, 275, 282
strikes
    Dutch East Indies   235
    Dutch West Indies   298
    France   168
    French West Africa   120, 147–8

students
  Algeria   201
  French Equatorial Africa   152
  Netherlands   299
Sudan: Britain and   33, 68
Suez   68–9, 81–3
Suez Canal   22, 32, 34, 35, 51, 68, 81
sugar production: Guadeloupe   219
Sukarno, Ahmed   236, 237, 245, 246, 251, 252, 259,
    262, 263, 265
sultans: Malaya   42, 74
Sumatra   233, 234, 235, 236, 249
Sunda Islands (Indonesia)   259
Surabaya (Java)   236, 251
Suriname   11, 238, 239, 293, 294, 300, 334
Swaziland   68
Swynnerton Plan: Kenya   79, 93
Syria   32, 69, 87, 121

Tahiti   216, 218
Tan Malaka, Ibrahim D.   273
Tananarive (Madagascar)   212, 213
Tanganyika   54, 78, 92
Tanganyikan African National Union (TANU)   92–3
Tanzania see Tanganyika
taxation
  British Empire, Second World War   25
  Java   231
Templer, General Sir Gerald   71
Terauchi, Field Marshall Count   251
territoires d'outre-mer (TOMs): France   217
Territorial Assemblies: French Equatorial Africa   154,
    155
terrorism
  Algeria   194
  Dutch East Indies   253, 272
  Morocco   191
  Netherlands   278
  Palestine   51
Thamrin, Mohammed Husni   237
Third Republic: France   117
Third World: origin of   6
Tilanus, H. W.   277
Tillion, Germaine   201
Tobago   90
Togoland see French Togo
Tomáz, Admiral Américo   329
Tombalbayé   157
Tonkin (Indochina)   123, 166
torture
  Algerian war of independence   203
  Indonesia   257, 273
  Madagascar   214
Touré, Ahmed Sékou   156, 329
towns
  French Africa   147
  French West Africa   138
  North Africa   182, 189

trade   333
  Britain   20, 66
  see also commerce
trade unions   53
  Africa   6, 96
  British colonies   42
  French colonies   125
    French Equatorial Africa   150
    French West Africa   146–9
    Morocco   188
    Tunisia   181, 186
Trades Union Congress: Britain   42
'transfer of power'   6
Transjordan   50
Treaty of Fez (1912): abolition of   187, 191
Treaty of London (1814)   229
Trinidad   36, 89
Truman Doctrine (1947)   267
Truman, President Harry S.   51, 275
trusteeship: British colonies   35–7
Tshombe, Moïse   314, 315, 317
Tsiranana, Philibert   215, 216
TUC see Trades Union Congress: Britain
Tunisia   8, 113, 122, 131, 153, 181, 185–92
Turkey: Britain and   69, 72
Turnbull, Sir Richard   93
Tutsi people: Rwanda   311, 312
Twa people: Rwanda   311

Ubangi-Chari see Central African Republic
Uganda   71, 80, 93
'ulama associations: Algeria   181
UN Special Committee on Palestine (UNSCOP)   52
unemployment
  Algeria   195
  Suriname   241
Unilateral Declaration of Independence   105
Union Calédonienne (UC)   218
Union Démocratique et social de la Résistance
    (UDSR)   152
Union générale des travailleurs d'Afrique noire
    (UGTAN)   148
Union Populaire de la Guadeloupe (UPLG)   220
UNITA party: Angola   324, 325, 327
United Dutch East India Company (VOC)   229
United Gold Coast Convention (UGCC)   60
United Hindu Party (VHP): Suriname   295
United Malays National Organization (UMNO)   56
United National Independence Party (UNIP): Northern
    Rhodesia   98
United Nations (UN)   49, 52, 53, 58, 81
  and Belgian Congo   316
  and Indonesia   268, 272
  and Maghreb   187
  and Suriname   296
United Nations Trusteeship Council   210
United States
  and Angola   330

and Belgian Congo 313, 317
and British colonies 37, 82
and Dutch East Indies 248, 268, 282
and France 340
and French Pacific territories 216
and French West Africa 143
and Indonesia 273
and Middle East 87
and New Guinea 289
and North Africa 185, 187
and Portuguese Africa 323
and Second World War 25
and Suez crisis 81–3
and Suriname 293, 297
and Vietnam 169, 338
Upper Volta 138, 146
urbanization *see* towns
Urundi *see* Rwanda-Burundi
USSR *see* Soviet Union
Uyl, Joop van 299, 300

Valluy, General Jean 166, 167
van Mook line: Indonesia 268, 270
Venezuela 238, 240, 242
Vichy regime: France 114, 126
Victoria Falls conference (1951) 62
Vidal-Naquet, Pierre 207
Vietminh 158, 159, 214, 338
Vietnam 102, 113, 114, 214, 290
Vietnamese National Army 167
Vietnamese Workers Party (VWP) 173
vineyards: Algeria 195
violence *see* political violence
Viollette, Maurice 125
Vo Nguyen Giap 160, 163, 167
Voizard, General Pierre 188
Volksraad (People's Council): Dutch East Indies 234, 235, 237
Vorrink, Koos 280
Vredenburch, H. F. L. K. van 270

Wafd movement (Egypt) 33
wage labour: French colonies 119

Walker, Patrick Gordon 104
'war crimes': Indonesia 278
Warnier Law (1873): Algeria 180
Washington Naval Conference (1921–2) 22
Watson Commission: Gold Coast 60
Wavell, Archibald Percival, 1st Earl 46
Welensky, Sir Roy 80, 96, 97, 98
welfare state: Britain 340
Welter, Charles 244, 247, 285, 294
West Africa 11, 25, 35, 62, 63, 91, 92, 125
West African War Council (Second World War) 25
West Indian Federation 72, 90
West Indies: independence 89–90
see also Dutch West Indies; Jamaica; Trinidad
Westad, Odd Arne 3
Western Sudan 138
white supremacy 91, 276
see also apartheid
Whitehead, Sir Edgar 99
whites *see* settlers
Widjojoatmodjo, Abdulkadir 252
Willem I, King 230
Wilson, Harold 84, 102, 103, 104
wireless broadcasting: British Dominions 22
women
Algerian war of independence 198
Belgian Congo 311
France 117
Ivory Coast 146
Kenya 77–8

Yemen 89, 104
Yogyakarta (Indonesia) 258, 270, 271
Youlou, Abbé Fulbert 157
Young, Crawford 5

Zambia *see* Northern Rhodesia
Zhou Enlai 175
Zimbabwe 106
see also Southern Rhodesia
Zimbabwe African National Union (ZANU) 105, 106
Zimbabwe African People's Union (ZAPU) 105, 106
Zionism 32